MAN
THE MEASURE

~~~~~~~~~~~~~~~~~~~~~~

A New Approach to History

ERICH KAHLER

New York
GEORGE BRAZILLER, INC.
1956

Copyright ● 1943, by Pantheon Books, Inc.

1956, by Erich Kahler

Designed by Stefan Salter

Printed in United States of America

Photolithographed by
The Murray Printing Company

And he said unto them, The sabbath was made for man,
and not man for the sabbath ...

MARK 2, 27

Però, se il mondo presente disvia
In voi è la cagione, in voi si cheggia;
Ed io te ne sarò or vera spia.

DANTE, PURGATORIO XVI

Je combattrai pour la primauté de l'Homme sur l'individu—
comme de l'universel sur le particulier.
Je combattrai pour l'Homme. Contre ses ennemis.
Mais aussi contre moi-même.

ANTOINE DE SAINT EXUPÉRY

PUBLISHER'S NOTE

Man the Measure was first published in 1943. It was the author's first work in English and won for him remarkable critical acclaim. Appearing in the midst of the war years, it did not reach the wider public and was overlooked by many, despite the fact that it may be one of the most significant discussions of history in our time.

The intended revision of this book for its 4th edition could not be undertaken at this moment due to other projects on which the author is engaged. This revision would have meant no alteration of the structure and substance of the book but only additions and corrections of detail such as might appear desirable in consideration of new historical material.

The author takes "his new approach to history" up to the atomic age. The present-day world scene with its radical changes was already foreseen by him some years ago, and the insight and philosophy of this book may be of even greater import in the light of our contemporary world.

March, 1956

PREFACE

The concepts embodied in this book summarize thoughts and studies of more than two decades. They are presented here as an elaboration of lecture courses held at the New School for Social Research in New York in 1941 and 1942.

It is a pleasure for me to acknowledge the help of friends without whom the book would never have reached its present shape.

I can hardly express what it owes to Miss Eleanor Wolff who gave it all the disinterested and passionate intellectual enthusiasm of which she is capable. This book, especially in the parts dealing with the difficult problems of our time, bears the traces of her inspiration, her ardent interest and her critical intransigence.

I am profoundly grateful to Miss Carol North Valhope and Dr. Ernst Morwitz who revised the manuscript with the greatest care and understanding. Many important improvements are due to their friendship and aid.

I also feel prompted to mention with warmest thanks the help of Miss Isabella Athey who read the proofs and contributed valuable hints and suggestions, of Mr. Bernard V. Bothmer who assisted me in checking references, and of Dr. Hans Nachod who prepared the Index. I am further indebted for good advice and information to Professors Roger Sessions and Julian Bonfante of Princeton University. It would be impossible adequately to appreciate the broadminded support of my publishers.

The possibly overambitious undertaking which this book represents is based on the work of so many scholars that an approximate account of the literature concerned would have excessively swelled the size of the volume. The bibliography, therefore, could not be anything but a very incomplete selection of references.

E. K.

September, 1943.

TABLE OF CONTENTS

INTRODUCTION

THE BASIC PROBLEM OF OUR TIME

THIS BOOK IS AN ATTEMPT to write history as the biography of man and from it to gain a view of the future of man. To call this emphasis on man "a new approach to history" may require an explanation. After all, history is generally thought of as the history of mankind, and what have historians ever been concerned with but conditions and events relating to man? Then how can man constitute a new principle of historical survey?

The answer is this: Just because history has always, as a matter of course, been the history of human beings and their experiences, man as such has never been consciously considered a special subject for historical survey; anthropologists have traced man's physical development, but historians have written of men, not of man. To be sure, throughout Christian civilization it was basically understood that all men form a huge family, that is, mankind, and history has been assumed to be the story of the development of this human family. Mankind, however, the body of all members of this human family, is not identical with man, or human nature, which is to be the subject of this book.

The great crisis that began in the nineteenth, and came to a head in the twentieth century, has undermined the concept of mankind as a coherent body, together with the concept of history as the consistent evolution of mankind. Both the coherence of mankind and the consistency, indeed the fact, of historical evolution have been challenged, and so for the first time they have become the focus of conscious attention. This challenge confronts us with the fundamental question on which the destiny of our civilization hinges: Is there a human quality common to men and distinguishing man from the animal? Does history give evidence of the evolution of this human quality? It is the necessity to find an answer to these questions that makes man, for the first time, the specific and explicit subject of history.

The idea of the coherence of humanity and the idea of the consistency of history were linked together from the outset, they are linked together today; whether we consider the old Christian concept, mankind, or our present concept of a human quality, both imply a history in the sense of consistent evolution. Mankind as an intrinsic community had to have a common destiny, and if there is a common and specific human quality, it must have had an evolution. Unless there is a continuous whole, either of mankind or of human nature, there is no such thing as human history, just as there could be no individual biography without the continuous identity of personality. History implies a continuity of something more than time; only if history can be seen as a one and consistent human evolution, only then has it a meaning. Otherwise it would be nothing but an incoherent mass of rising and falling powers, growing and dying peoples and individuals. Eternity has no history, and neither has chaos.

Both ideas, then, the unity of humanity and the unity of history, stand and fall together; both originate in the Christian world religion. Before the emergence of world religion, there were only histories of isolated tribes, and even these histories were not history in the sense of consistent development. Events were pictured against a background of eternal rest, of eternal divine order, which man could desert or pervert, but in which development would have been synonymous with blasphemy. The inner movement of human events, in so far as it was considered at all, was seen as a rising, falling, wavelike or circular motion within changeless eternity, as a regular recurrence of the same processes. All ancient cultures, including the Greek, were governed by this idea of the cyclic nature of human happenings and thus they were essentially unhistorical. What we call history begins with the Jewish-Christian concept of man as the image of God, the creator of the universe. This concept involves the idea of the common origin of all men from the same ancestor, and of a common God-given destiny of all men. The history of man was seen as his progress from fall to salvation. The subject-matter of history, however, was not exactly man as a secular entity, but the spiritual welfare of the human soul, the purification of the soul and its approach to God.

Beginning with the Renaissance, when man freed himself of the tutelage of religion, the idea of human evolution was transferred to profane ideology. Man's joy in the unfettered development of his intellectual and technical faculties gave rise to belief in the limitless, straight-line progress of mankind, in the boundless power of human reason. Salvation came to mean a self-salvation of man through growing enlightenment. Through increasing enlightenment, or through an improvement of material conditions, men were supposed to become better and happier. Thus, in this epoch too, the subject-matter of history was not man, it was human reason, or the economic condition of man.

The rapid developments of the nineteenth century, however, proved that men became neither better nor happier. Problems increased, and the naive optimism of the first centuries of secularized life began to change into profound pessimism. The sufferings and crises men had prepared for themselves through their proudest conquests made all human development appear a failure. And since the idea of human development, that is, the very idea of history, is inseparably bound up with the idea of the unity and community of mankind, the doubt of the one shook the belief in the other. Those modern thinkers who denied development in mankind, who split human history up into isolated cultures rising senselessly and fading away into nothingness, those thinkers, Nietzsche and Spengler, were the same who attacked the fundamental values of our civilization: love and brotherhood among men.

At the same time that the disappointments of the period were undermining belief in the unity of history, historical investigation was snowing it under with an immense and ever-increasing mass of facts. History had broken up into histories of the various pursuits of man that had, in the course of human development, become elaborate and autonomous fields: politics, economics, sociology, law, language, literature, art, science, technology. These fields proceeded to claim attention for their endless contents and concepts to such a degree that their common human origin and inner connection were almost ignored. The fact that they were functions of man, subordinate to man, was lost sight of. History, accordingly, consisted either of a series of developments of peoples or of developments in those specialized fields. What goes under the name of world history today is a combination of these two points of view, but not the history of man and his development as such. As a matter of fact, the breakdown of the unity of history is so complete that modern historians do not dare to assume that there is such a thing as history, or a consistent human evolution. They manifest the deepest distrust toward any claim of meaning in history and regard any interpretation of history as unfounded speculation. In reality, there is no presentation of facts without interpretation. The choice of facts in itself constitutes an interpretation, whether it is determined consciously or subconsciously, whether the material is deliberately chosen to back up an argument or whether it appears to impose its own arrangement.

Out of the ruins of the concepts of mankind and history a new literature arose that may be designated as moral anthropology. It deals with the question: What is man and what is his function?— a question behind which lies another: Is there a human quality, or are men, assuming themselves to be but a more highly developed form of beast, to develop beastliness to ever-higher forms? Are men bound together by the ties assumed by Christianity, or by a common human nature, or are both to be denied or ignored, and men, believing themselves tied by no bonds but those of their making, to break those and their civilization with them? Is the devil to take the hindmost, and the foremost too?

This is the question at the heart of the present catastrophe. It is the true issue about which war is being waged on all levels: military, political, economic and intellectual. There is no other question that is so urgent and frightening, no other question that so intimately affects every person even though he be unaware of it in the come-and-go of daily life. It is not a question posed by scholars and intellectuals for scholars and intellectuals only, it is a question on which the life and death of mankind hinge. And when we look to the past of mankind for the answer to this question, we are looking to the future of man.

WHAT IS HUMAN?

SEEN IN THE LIGHT of this fundamental question—What is man and what is his function?—history is not concerned with a sequence of struggles for power, not with the sum of developments of peoples or developments in special fields, but with the development of a specific organism, the human being, of a specific quality, the quality of being human.

To begin with, we must ask: Is there a clear *distinction between man and animal,* has man any special characteristic? If a characteristic that makes man human does exist, it did not come into being suddenly, but, like all that has to do with living matter, in the course of a long development.

Now there is one respect in which anyone will admit man differs from the animal. The development of a species of animal goes no further than the development of its physical type, of its anatomical, physiological, biological features. But man, after having completed his development as a biological species, goes on changing and even developing—for the change from the Neanderthal man to Dante and Shakespeare can hardly be considered to be other than some kind of development. Man, then, develops in two zones, the biological, which he shares with the animal, and a new zone that is exclusively human. To look for a specifically human quality is therefore identical with looking for what it is that develops in this new zone—the zone of history.

If we find what we are looking for, if the facts of history can be interpreted as the development of a specific human quality, then history, in turn, takes on coherence and meaning. And if this is so, if history shows man to have a common human nature, then the norms of unity that developed in the course of human history are not mere lofty ideals but rooted in fact; they are not arbitrarily imposed abstractions, beyond human reality and averse to human nature, but are inherent in the very existence of a shared human quality and therefore have an organic validity originating in the basic constitution of man.

Heretofore the question—What is man?—has been approached from three angles: the theological, the rationalistic (or idealistic) and the biological (or naturalistic).

The first, the *theological* theory, sees the human being from the point of view of his divine origin. Man is the creature of God and made in His image; he is part earthly, part spiritual. Herein lies his sinfulness and, at the same time, his God-given potentiality to achieve salvation by will and grace. Human history is the history of man's preparation for salvation. Thus, for this theory, the existence of a distinguishing quality in man, as well as the consistency of human history, is beyond doubt. But both are interpreted from without, from the premise of the existence of God vouched for by revelation.

The validity of the Christian theory of man was uncontested throughout the Middle Ages and has since been upheld in various versions by Catholic and Protestant thinkers, in the last decade most brilliantly by the Catholic, Theodor Haecker, in his book, "Was ist der Mensch?" (What is Man?) and by the Protestant, Reinhold Niebuhr, in "The Nature and Destiny of Man".

The second, the *rationalistic* theory, originated in the Greek and Roman view of man and was revived in a new form from the Renaissance on. This theory sees reason as man's specific feature, whether "speculative", that is, purely theoretical and disinterested reason as maintained by Alfred Whitehead, or "pragmatic" reason (involved in or directed toward practical aims) as, for instance, John Dewey contends, or the "spirit" of the German idealistic philosophy which makes spirit and reason equivalent. According to the rationalistic theory, reason is the pride and virtue of man. It is identical with the right and the good, and, consequently, human history appears either as a straight or as a dialectic progress toward a set goal—the reign and the perfection of reason. In this theory, in fact, reason has assumed the absolute and providential quality of God.

The third, the *biological* or *naturalistic* theory, sees the human being from the angle of his natural origin, that is to say, as a stage in the gradual evolution of organic nature. In this view the human being as a form of organic nature has no essential feature except his advanced anatomical and physiological complexity. Intellect, reason, is merely a manifestation of this greater complexity; it implies a difference of degree, but not of kind, between man and animal.

There are two interpretations of this biological theory: the mechanistic and the vitalistic. According to the first, organic evolution proceeds like a self-motivated machine, according to the second, it is brought about by a vital impulse (élan vital). While these two variants of the biological theory share the view that reason does not constitute an essential difference between man and animal, they differ widely in the valuation of reason. The mechanistic version concedes it to be an advance, but entirely disregards the changes it has effected in the world structure in the course, indeed in the fact, of history. The vitalistic interpretation, on the contrary, considers rational evolution not as an advance, but as an aberration, and the rational faculty of man as the source of all evil, a falling-away from the harmony of nature, a weakening of instincts and vital impulses. This view was first expressed by Jean-Jacques Rousseau as a protest against the overvaluation of reason; it came into its own in the concepts of Nietzsche and Bergson, who exalted the vital impulses and called reason in question. Their reversal of previous values was carried to extremes by Spengler, to whom man is the beast of prey in its most perfect form. To these thinkers, human history must inevitably appear meaningless.

Does any one of these theories offer a satisfactory answer to our question: What is human? The theological view, though it sees an essential difference between man and animal, interprets this difference from a point beyond man's existence, indeed, beyond the known world. It deduces the distinguishing feature of the human being from a decision of God, which, in itself, is an assumption of human faith. Those, however, to whom faith does not suffice must seek within our known world for further evidence of the human quality.

The rationalistic view furnishes at least a substantial answer to our problem by identifying the essential quality of the human being with man's rational faculty. Yet recent research shows that the roots of the rational faculty of man can be found in animals. The experiments of modern biologists and psychologists, Wolfgang Koehler's experiments with apes, for instance, have demonstrated that animals are capable of drawing simple conclusions and not only of using instruments, but of discovering the use of such instruments independently. The mental capacity of certain mammals corresponds to that of a three-year-old child. So reason is only a more highly developed form of dispositions already present in the animal and cannot be considered the exclusively human faculty it is held to be by the rationalistic view.

The third, the naturalistic theory, which denies any essential difference between man and animal, in its mechanistic aspect totally disregards fundamental facts that it would be unable to explain in a satisfactory way. It ignores the values developed in antiquity and Christianity, self-restraint, the domination of desires and impulses, love, charity and humanity. It does not consider the achievements of human contemplation, of man's efforts to mirror the world and himself in art and philosophical speculation, to re-shape, to re-create himself through the power of his intellect. And where vitalistic thinkers have taken these things into account, they have—Bergson excepted—regarded them as a perversion of natural instincts, as an insidious distortion of the will-to-power by which the weak succeeded in dominating the strong.

But even if we suppose that the major part of human history were a dead end, were perversion and degeneration, then this very perversion and degeneration would constitute a special feature of the human being, one that has no parallel in animals. Art and speculation do indeed spring from a want, from suffering. They represent a refinement of impulses, a sublimation that implies a more delicate physical constitution, a weakening of the robust appetites of life. According to the premise chosen, one may evaluate these processes either as the generation of a new form of life or as a degeneration of the old. In any case, the fact that the increasing vulnerability of the organic constitution resulted in a new form of dominating the outer world, a new sphere of life that is distinctly human—this fact cannot be explained away by the invalidation of intellectual life implied in the naturalistic theory. Thus even this negative interpretation of a specifically human quality presupposes an essential difference between man and animal. In denying this difference, the naturalistic theory contradicts itself.

The exclusively human feature we are seeking is to be found not in any partial functioning of the human constitution, but rather in a general quality of man that is the pivot of all the various achievements and manifestations of his civilization, a quality that cannot be localized anatomically or physiologically, but that emerges gradually from the complex totality of the human organism. This is *man's faculty of going beyond himself,* of transcending the limits of his own physical being. This quality, which was first stressed by Max Scheler and Reinhold Niebuhr, does not coincide with reason, for it manifests itself not only intellectually but emotionally. It is this faculty, for instance, that makes man capable of true love based on choice and affecting his whole existence, of love regardless of recompense.

Man's faculty of overstepping his own being is identical with what is understood by the term *"spirit".* The functions of this faculty are twofold. In the first place, it enables and induces man to discern, and to detach himself from, an outward, contrasting being which is recognized in its own distinct orbit. Or, to be more exact— for the order is rather the reverse—spirit is at first the faculty of detaching and discerning a definite non-self from a definite self. It is the ability to objectivate and to subjectivate.

This act of discerning and detaching, of objectivation and subjectivation (or self-objectivation), is the prerequisite for the second

move, for the actual transcending of the limits of the self, for entering into a conscious, super-corporeal relationship with the non-self.
In acknowledging a non-self as a distinct entity, man puts himself
into the place of the other being, he becomes capable of vicarious
feelings and thus transcends his own limits. Limits cannot be
transcended before they are recognized.

Thus spirit is not only the faculty of discerning and detaching,
but, at the same time, of establishing a relation between a self and
a non-self, the faculty of overstepping the limits of the self. It is
discerning and uniting in one. It is the very essence of a being concerned with more than itself. A person leads a spiritual life in so
far as he rises above his personal, "practical" interests, as he is able
to detach himself from his own and conceived self and to grow
more and more objective, to integrate himself in a higher, com-
prehending objective.

Let us take an example. To a lion, a deer is only prey; it serves
no purpose but to provide food and satisfy appetite. To a man, a
deer may be prey, but it is also a deer, a being with an independent
existence. Man can imagine himself in the place of an animal, he
does so every time he studies its special conditions, requirements
and ways of life. To be sure, his purpose is often to make the animal an even more useful prey; he protects and breeds it in order to
provide more or better food for himself, to have it work for him,
or even for the mere pleasure of hunting it. He is even capable of
such a paradoxical attitude as to love the animals he kills. Even
when man's purpose is the same as the animal's, his method is
different. In so far as man uses the animal as a prey, he does not
differ from the animal. But in so far as he protects, breeds, studies
and loves the animal, he recognizes it as having an orbit of its own,
he establishes an orbit separate from his self, an orbit that he can
enter deliberately, and thus brings about a new and conscious relationship. This attitude is distinctly human and is made possible
only by the faculty of discerning and transcending, the faculty of
spirit.

Man's transcending, his overstepping of self, is more easily recognized when not only his methods but his purpose differ from the

animal's, as in his disinterested pursuit of art, philosophy and science. Where man's methods differ from the animal's, his faculty of spirit may be recognized as a fact. Where his purpose differs, spirit has come to be accepted as a value to such a degree that its being and remaining a fact is often forgotten or denied. We want to emphasize here that, although spirit as value must and will be treated in its proper place in this book, the term spirit as we use it is not meant to carry any value overtones with it.

Spirit emerges from the totality of the human organism. Its gradual evolution becomes manifest only by the results it produces, by the sequence of growing objectivations that make the way mankind travels a mirrored and known way—human history. Spirit is at first a new force, a new impetus in man. By its increasing activity, it develops into a perfected faculty of the human being. Finally its accumulation of objectivations comes to constitute an entire sphere of life, comprising various fields such as religion, art, philosophy and science. It is in the course of this development that spirit, just because it is man's faculty of rising beyond his corporal self, becomes a value, a good worth striving after. Indeed, by setting it up as a value, man implicitly recognizes spirit to be his distinguishing quality. It must, however, be kept in mind that, as we saw before and as we shall see later, spirit as a fact can also work in a sense contrary to itself and to its meaning as a value, not toward the human, but toward the inhuman.

Accordingly, spirit does not mean something outside or above man, in either the popular or the theological sense; it is not to be confused with spirits, holy or unholy. It is especially not to be confused with reason, though reason has been developed and perfected by spirit and was part of the spiritual evolution.

Since spirit evolves from the human organism as a whole, since it is a vital impetus, it comprises and moves the human organism as a whole. It comprises emotional as well as intellectual life; it forms and affects human impulses and the whole vital attitude of the human being. Reason, on the other hand, is a faculty and function of the intellect only. It is the intellectual act of associating and connecting experiences, of assembling them into a chain of cause and effect, that is, of drawing conclusions. Out of this follows another act: abstracting generalities from repeated single conclusions and so making conclusions reliable and available for general use. "This stone cuts because it has an edge" is an example of the simplest kind of conclusion. "All stones that have an edge cut", the step from "many" to "all", is the great short cut, the step from repetition to generalization. This act of generalization is a second and higher form of conclusion. It leads to a third, still more complex and general conclusion, the purely abstract concept of cause and effect as such. And this concept is the prerequisite of all the elaborate short cuts, the elimination, description and creation of repetition that constitute logic, science and technics. Out of the practical applications of this assembling of conclusions, generalizations and abstractions come all our methods of procedure, institutions and instruments of life; indeed, the assembly-line is materialized reason, the materialized chain of cause and effect. This whole scheme of the rational structure is, of course, not to be taken as a description of the actual evolution of reason, which happened in an entirely different way.

The structure is one which emotional life can only disrupt. Reason cannot include emotional life; on the contrary, it imposes itself on it, in the final analysis, it opposes it. While spirit is an educator of emotional life, shaping and sublimating it, reason appears as a dictator who does not take emotions into account at all. Of course, reason too is influenced and determined by emotional life, as psychoanalysis has shown in regard to individual psychic processes. But this very evidence brings out the fact that this influence is illegitimate and contradictory to the essential principle and claim of reason.

Spirit—man's faculty of discerning and transcending—manifests itself in three ways, each essentially and exclusively human: the first is what we shall call *existence,* the second is *history,* and the third is that special demeanor and psychic attitude which is rightly termed *humanity.* To speak of a feature of the human being as humanity may appear to be a tautology. But it is not a tautology, because the species man, and so, mankind, unfortunately cannot be identified with the behavior we call humanity. This behavior is an exclusively human feature, but it is not a general feature of mankind.

Existence, the primary and general form in which spirit manifests itself, is the basic procedure of discerning and transcending, of objectivation and subjectivation (or self-objectivation), by conceiving a non-self, or a self, as an exact, finite entity. To exist means more than merely to be. The word existence derives from the Latin "ex-sistere", "ex-stare", and means to be out-standing, out-staying, out-lasting. It means being in a prominent, distinct and lasting way. The animal lives unaware of itself; it simply *is*. It has only immediate, corporal being, a being in the instant, from moment to moment. Man lives in awareness of himself, of a constantly conceived, constantly felt whole of personal life, distinct from both the world around him and his own corporal being, his being in the instant. So he lives outside as well as inside himself, outside as well as inside the instant. His awareness of himself is a form of discerning, his living outside himself and the instant is a form of transcending. Together they enable him to alter instants and merge them into a continuity, a conscious life, in which he forms a lasting unit, a personality, a character; in a word, they enable him not only to be but to exist.

From the same root as existence grows *history*. Detaching, as we shall show later, first a past and then a future from the instant in which he lives physically, man discerns the dimension of time from his own corporal present. So he comes gradually to distinguish his temporal self, his individual lifetime, first from the life of his stock and then from the life of the whole of humanity, comes, that is, to conceive first of genealogy and then of history. He becomes capable of drawing conclusions from the past to the formation of the future, of planning, transforming not only his own life but the life of coming generations. And the concept of history, that is, the unity of mankind in the dimension of time, induces man to adapt his life to ideal, universally human goals.

Humanity, a specific attitude of man toward his fellow man and his fellow creature, is also based on man's faculty of discerning and transcending, on his faculty of conceiving another human being as a distinct and independent existence and, at the same time, of putting himself in the place of that other being. This leads to the sublimation of erotic impulses; it leads to love in the full sense of the word, to true friendship, in other words, to all kinds of spiritually established, disinterested relationships. Eventually it leads to an attitude of regard for fellow men and fellow creatures, to respect for the rights and for the dignity of the human being. And it leads to the concept and the postulate of a unity of mankind in space, of an actual human community.

The important thing to remember is that the whole development from the animal to the highest of human goals is simply a development of the primary faculty of discerning and transcending, those acts of spirit which make man human. Spirit as a value derives from spirit as a fact, an impulse.

WHAT IS EVOLUTION?

WHEN WE SET OUT to consider history as human evolution, new problems immediately arise. Throughout the modern era, belief in historical *evolution* has been synonymous with a belief in *progress,* in the ever-increasing perfection and happiness of man. When, in our century, people began to realize that man was far from growing better and happier, that, on the contrary, barbarism and anarchy were springing up among apparently civilized peoples, they abandoned in their disillusionment the idea of human evolution too.

The instance of individual life shows clearly that evolution is not identical with moral improvement or greater happiness. An adult is not necessarily better and hardly happier than a child. His rational faculty has developed, but this rational faculty does not imply moral improvement or increased well-being. Yet it cannot be denied that a certain evolution takes place in the growing-up of an individual. In the sphere of national life, also, plain people whose intellectual faculties are not developed to any high degree often show more kindness and happiness than people of great intellectual development. So we must separate the problem of evolution from the problem of progress.

The problem of progress in itself is very intricate. The progress of the individual does not coincide with that of the masses. Historical evidence shows that the perfection and the well-being of the individual is restricted by the rising standard of the average. This phenomenon may even cause a complete reversal: the lowering, the leveling-down of the standard of the leading individuals.

We must also differentiate natural kindness from conscious and conscientious moral behavior. Then, too, simple happiness under primitive, natural conditions may decline when rationally organized welfare in a highly civilized society is attempted. The moral and social status may break down completely when the former decays before the latter has been achieved. We are now in such a period. In times like these, decent behavior is no simple matter, for it is no longer merely a moral, but also a mental, task. It requires a highly developed intellectual faculty, the ability to grasp the very complex social situation of a closely interrelated nation and world, a task so difficult that people abandon it and relapse into the moral and social anarchy of today. Since this anarchy is as much an intellectual as a moral question it is not necessarily evidence against a general progress of mankind. If man should succeed in mastering his world intellectually then the process we are going through just now may turn out to have been "reculer pour mieux sauter". The whole problem of human progress is a moral one, with which we cannot deal until we have done what we can to understand the condition of our world through investigating human evolution. Although morality and organized welfare form an integral part of human evolution, their development is not simply identical with it, and a specifically moral point of view would only serve to blur our subject.

Apart from the theories that affirm or deny evolution according as they assume mankind to progress or decline, there is the *cyclic theory,* which holds that life in general, and human life in particular, does not proceed along straight lines, be it upward or down-ward, but rather in a circular movement as eternal recurrence of the same processes.

The cyclic theory is, in fact, the only basic argument against the idea of evolution as such. Still, it cannot invalidate this idea. As we said before, the difference between the Neanderthal or Aurignac type of man and Dante or Shakespeare is the first and simplest evidence of human evolution. On the other hand, the cyclic theory cannot be altogether rejected. It contains a certain amount of truth in so far as it corrects and modifies earlier concepts of evolution as a straight, upward movement, a steady advance without relapse or interruption. From our survey of human history, the realization will crystallize that there is no evolutionary process without power-ful set-backs and reverses that apparently imperil the whole move-ment but actually drive it forward all the more. Every action arouses a reaction, it even requires this reaction to provide a fresh impulse to further actions. Thus reversals are the strongest, though the cruelest, carriers of every evolutionary and revolutionary proc-ess. And, in the long run, a progressive movement is sometimes more effectively aided by reactionaries than by promoters.

The idea of a cyclic motion of history, then, does not wholly con-tradict the idea of evolution. Evolution is a most complex process that includes both a progressing and a reversing element; it is neither straight nor circular, but proceeds in a revolving movement, at once expanding and advancing, like a spiral.

We have defined the human quality as man's overstepping of the limits of his own being, and have stated that it consists of two main acts, the establishment of these limits by detaching and discerning a non-self from a self, and the establishment of a new and con-scious relationship with the clearly conceived non-self by transcend-ing self toward the non-self.

History as the evolution of the human quality, then, is the *suc-cessive development of these two acts or faculties of man.* In its early periods, human history is mainly the formation of the faculty of detaching and discerning. The later part of human history is the genesis and perfection of the quality of transcending.

Accordingly, the subject of human history is man's relation to the world that surrounds him. This world consists of a broader, non-human sphere, the universe, and a narrower, human sphere, the human community. In the process of his evolution, man first, by a series of objectivations, detaches and discerns these two spheres from his own gradually conceived existence, and later establishes his new, transcending relation to them. The differentiation of man's relation to the universe develops the human mind. The differentiation of man's relation to the human community develops the human individual.

Both processes of differentiation are a kind of focusing, a narrowing-down, in the one case, of a separate human mind or soul, as distinct from the universe, and in the other, of a separate individual, as distinct from the human community. By discerning and conceiving the objects and beings of the outer world as separate, distinct existences, man implicitly discovers his own existence and soul. And by distinguishing, first his fellow kinsmen, and then his fellow men, from his own, gradually conceived personality, he evolves as an individual. But no sooner has this narrowing-down taken place, than a broadening-out on a different plane automatically begins. Man develops techniques of thought that make his perceptions more and more a part of him, and so in a process of transcending, he begins to integrate a wider and wider area of the objective world in the human mind and in the human world. And the human individual no sooner comes into existence than the conflicts and the loneliness engendered by the separation of one man from another of themselves create a need to close the widening gap and, in the end, to establish a new and consciously organized society. So the mind, in the course of transcending, takes in more and more of the universe, and the individual shares, and includes in his more and more coordinated and cooperating existence, an ever-larger part of the human community.

For a full understanding of the crucial relation between the individual and the community, it is necessary to define terms. The contrary of individual, or rather the complementary term to "in-

dividual", is "community" or "common". The term "individual"
has only one meaning; it is unambiguous. There are, to be sure,
many steps between a mere outward appearance and a thorough,
intrinsic realization of individuality, which does not come about
until late in history; but the difference is only one of degree, not of
kind. No such unambiguity exists, however, as to the term "community". There are many kinds of communities, and there are
many respects in which men may form a community. A family or a
primitive tribe is a community, so is a factory or a labor union; the
factors that make each a community are essentially different.

The members of a family or of a tribe are bound into a community by consanguinity, by common physical features, behavior
and mental cast, by common traditions, customs, habits, rituals, by
a common way of life, an unconscious way of life handed down as
a heritage from generation to generation. Members of a labor union
or factory workers, on the other hand, are held together by a common will, by common tasks, conscious common purposes aiming
at a future. A tribe and a family are entities in themselves, they
govern their members intrinsically by the undefined rule of common features, habits and attitudes that these members are unable
to alter at will. The members of a family or tribe derive from the
existence of their community, which forms them. The community
of a factory or a labor union, on the contrary, derives from the
existence of the members, who form it. Such a community is built
up, it is brought into being by the work or the free will, by the
aggregation and cooperation of individuals. It derives from the
future, not from the past.

The first kind of community, the pre-individual community, is
adequately characterized by the term "species", and the second
kind, the post-individual community, is best expressed by the term
"collective". Modern sociologists frequently apply the term "collective" to all kinds of communities, a use which is likely to lead
to confusion. This term is properly applicable only to the post-
individual community, since collecting means the gathering and
putting-together of different and previously existent individual entities. Thus collectivity presupposes individuals who may collect.

Neither does the term "collective", as we use it here, necessarily and exclusively designate a socialist or communist unit. It is intended to indicate any post-individual community, any community based on the common aims or purposes of pre-existent individuals.

In the light of this basic distinction, human history appears as an evolution leading from the pre-individual community to the post-individual community, through the development and completion of the individual.

The first period, from the condition of primitive man to the end of antiquity, comprises the process of man's detachment and discernment of an outer world from an inner world. This implies the disintegration of the primeval, corporal community and of the primeval conformity of man with the universe, and, correspondingly, the formation of the human individual and the human soul. The second period, from the end of antiquity to the Renaissance, includes the completion and emancipation of the human individual, his final deliverance from a superhuman rule and the setting free of the human intellect. The third period, the modern era, means the process of man's transcendence toward a clearly conceived, objective world of nature and toward a conscious, organized human community. The theme of this age is the struggle for man's reintegration in a clearly conceived universe and the struggle for a collective order.

Up to now, the huge body of historical facts has been presented according to two principles of arrangement: the development of peoples and cultures and the development of fields of human activity. To regard history as history of the human quality requires a new principle of arrangement and hence a new selection of facts. From the very outset, our undertaking could meet with the objection that the longitudinal section we make through the material of facts may not be representative of the development of man.

This objection is especially weighty in regard to *cultures*. For the unity of history can be questioned not only with reference to the consistency of human evolution, but also with reference to the variety of human cultures. Can we regard the development of man as a single, broad stream, or has it several equally important streams, none of which can be considered fully representative?

The new "universal history", as Spengler and Arnold J. Toynbee conceived it, assumes a multiplicity of cultures, each in its own orbit and none actually to be taken as a paradigm, all having in common only general features of rise and fall, "laws of history" on the line of "laws of nature". The assumption of a plurality of human centers is, of course, indisputable. There are different branches of human evolution, different human orbits, fairly independent of one another and each of them showing specific developments. The question is whether these various orbits differ fundamentally in their human characteristics, and, if they do, whether they are really equivalent with regard to human evolution or whether one of them can be considered representative.

First of all there is that great stream of evolution that is to be the subject of our survey. We have just traced its course. It starts from the ancient Near East, from Egypt, Mesopotamia and the Iranian Plateau where manifold stocks converged and intermingled. It proceeds along the Mediterranean, crosses over to Southern Europe, to Greece and Rome, gradually expands over the whole of Europe, including Russia, and eventually extends to the Western Hemisphere.

And there are other, distinctly separate, human centers. There are different centers of primitive stocks which, as a matter of fact, have remained prehistoric, since their evolution was stunted in its beginnings. There were richly developed cultures of half-primitive peoples, Negro kingdoms in Africa, the Aztec and Maya kingdoms of the American Indians, the Malay tribes in the East Indies. Last but not least, there are the two great peoples of the Far East, the Chinese and the Indians, whose culture and human attitude touch the heights of human achievement. These two peoples, that represent huge and highly differentiated cultural spheres of their own— indeed worlds of their own—are, in fact, the only ones to challenge the course of Western civilization as the leading and representative trend of human evolution. They have a history covering three millennia of migrations, invasions, conquests, dynastic and social upheavals, of thoughts and concepts and arts that reach the utmost peak of subtlety and perfection.

These cultures, however, developed within the stage of human evolution where life is determined by the rule of religion, by religious ritual, precept and tradition. This means that life actually rests upon a steady and immobile foundation, and that no currents or changes appreciably alter the ways of human existence, which are conservative and governed by the magic power of an eternal world order. India is, in fact, a matrix of the cyclic theory of life, the idea of eternal recurrence. And if we observe an evolution in Indian thought, it is rather an inversion of European evolution, it leads altogether away from earthly, temporal life. Motionlessness so absolute that it attains nothingness is its most sublime, its most valued, concept.

In both these countries, up to recent times, deep reluctance and distrust prevailed against any change in general, and particularly against the introduction of new methods and tools, which were supposed to pervert and demoralize man. This attitude may be illustrated by a story of Chuang Tzu, a Chinese thinker who lived about 300 B.C.

When Tzu Kung went South to the Ch'u State on his way to the Chin State, he passed through Han-yin. There he saw an old man engaged in making a ditch to connect his vegetable garden with a well. He had a pitcher in his hand, with which he was bringing up water and pouring it into the ditch —great labor with very little result.

"If you had a machine here," cried Tzu Kung, "in a day you could irrigate a hundred times your present area. The labor required is trifling as compared with the work done. Would you not like to have one?"

"What is it?" asked the gardener.

"It is a contrivance made of wood," replied Tzu Kung, "heavy behind and light in front. It draws up water as you do with hands, but in a constantly overflowing stream. It is called a wellsweep."

Thereupon the gardener flushed up and said: "I have heard from my teacher that those who have cunning implements are cunning in their dealings, and those who are cunning in their dealings have cunning in their hearts, and those who have cunning in their hearts cannot be pure and incorrupt, and those who are not pure and incorrupt are restless in spirit, and those who are restless in spirit are not fit vehicles for Tao [this is, very vaguely characterized, the principle of harmony]. It is not that I do not know of these things. But I should be ashamed to use them."

The same argument was repeated about 1900 A.D. by a modern Chinese scholar, Ku Hung Ming, who calls the mind of modern European civilization a "fox mind", and who assails the Europeans violently for compelling his people to accept modern trade methods and to construct railways.

When Western economic and political imperialism was looking for raw materials and colonial markets, it forced modern European civilization upon the populations of the Near and Far East. This intervention was followed by the most violent revolts, such as the Chinese Tai-ping rebellion from 1850 to 1864 and the uprising of the Boxers in 1900. And to this very day, all the industrial exploitation and selfish reorganization on the part of the Western nations have not succeeded in thoroughly Europeanizing these countries. They are helplessly dragged along by this overwhelming European civilization which, in the end, they will have to adopt in order to match its assaults.

These great cultures of the East may have attained the heights they did just because they had a chance to reach fruition within an unchanging stage of development; the point for us, however, is that they had no evolution beyond that stage which the Western world, for better or worse, has long ago left behind. It may be said that those peoples are nobler than the average people of the Western world of today, but, as we have pointed out, moral perfection and evolution are not identical. There are two decisive arguments in favor of the assumption that the broad current of Western evolution has been, up to now, the representative human evolution: first, that Western evolution has passed through the same stages as that of the East, and secondly, that it went on to further stages and developed the forms, methods and ways of life that are about to swallow all other remaining forms of culture and that are bound to become the determining factors of all future developments. Thus we may consider this Western trend as representative of human evolution as a whole, and we may, therefore, confine ourselves to the survey of this representative trend.

As for the development of *special fields of human activity*—with few exceptions, such as the development of music, which would have led us too far—they are included in our survey, not altogether as autonomous, parallel developments, but rather with a view to their changing relation to the development of the human quality. The autonomy of special departments of human activity is a disastrous phenomenon of modern times, and to extend the dividing lines backward into former ages is a falsifying interpretation of history. These fields developed as functions of man; their history is the history of their changing significance for man.

The author has attempted to re-interpret history, not by discussing it, but by re-telling it, by allowing interpretations to arise spontaneously from the arrangement of facts; he has tried to write history, not to write about history. So, if he has sometimes treated as though for the first time of events and developments fairly familiar to the reader, he begs his indulgence.

THE FORMATION OF THE
HUMAN INDIVIDUAL

PARTICIPATION

PRIMITIVE MAN

A HISTORY OF THE HUMAN QUALITY of man must begin with an investigation of his primary condition; and, to a certain extent, this condition still prevails among the so-called primitive peoples of our contemporary world. While it is true that all stages of human evolution have persisted through the ages and are still present today, this statement must be qualified by several important restrictions. The peoples that are now living in the uncivilized areas of America, Africa, Australia and the East Indies cannot be termed primitive in the strict sense of the word. The conditions of their existence are not exactly those of the early stages of humanity, for the touch of Time is laid upon all things. Even the most stable conditions are subject to change. Climate and environment, inbreeding or intermingling with neighbors, may cause decay and degeneration, further development or the falling into disuse of established customs. No human habitations are so hermetically sealed away from the rest of the world that indirect influences or rumors of far-away happenings do not seep through. Thus we can be fairly certain that the state of primitive peoples today is not wholly identical with that of early man, and so the term primitive as applied to such peoples may be inaccurate. But in the general picture they present to us, through the medium of ethnological reports, we can recognize the basic forms of the attitudes and of the mentality of primeval man. We are the more confirmed in this assumption by the fact that the picture constitutes an evolutionary link between the mental behavior of the highly developed mammals and the first stages of historical mankind, since it combines traces of the former with elements of the latter. Thus the primitive peoples of today give the impression of dead ends branching off from human evolution. They follow their own isolated development which can hardly be called evolution, for it is halted in its beginnings, nipped in the bud. They follow their own small, isolated and limited rise and decline. And still, when all is said and done, they do furnish an outline of a certain preliminary phase of human evolution.

There has been a good deal of discussion as to why these primitive peoples have never attained higher stages of development. The answer is twofold: for one thing they may have been stopped by their limited potentialities; for another, it is certain that development, or at least the kind of development that is shown by the progression of humanity, cannot be evolved by an individual people, by a limited population, nor can it occur in groups living in seclusion from free intercourse with other groups. In tracing the steps of human development through the history of Europe, it becomes clear that tremendous efforts were necessary to effect this development, and that constant reinforcement, the repeated impact of fresh human forces was needed to bring about the civilization we live in—however poor that may still be. Such a development could be achieved only by a sequence of connected and intermingled peoples and civilizations, by the successive cooperation of various stocks, by a historical relay, a handing on of the torch. Historical evidence proves beyond doubt that the exact opposite of what the so-called race theory pretends is true: any decisive advance in human evolution has been accomplished not by breeds that are pure either mentally or physically, not by any cultural inbreeding, but by an intermixture, by the mutual impregnation of different stocks and cultures.

The understanding of primitive mentality requires a flexible imagination. Ethnologists and anthropologists have long been hampered by their method of approach; they have collected quantities of valuable data on their expeditions, but were unable to give a comprehensive picture of the primitive state of mind because their inquiries and explorations, their stating of problems and commenting on results, were all colored by their habits of thinking and by the traditional categories of our era applied to an entirely different order of mentality. They were either puzzled by an apparently incoherent response to their questions, or they translated what they heard into their own logical terms and thereby violated the original meaning. It is only in the last decades that a group of French sociologists, most conspicuously represented by Emile Durkheim and Lucien Lévy-Bruhl, have arrived at an objective approach and thorough understanding of the primitive state of mind. The chief find of these scholars is that in trying to understand the primitive mentality we must discard the whole apparatus of modern intellectual concepts, we must renounce our premise of logical coherence and put ourselves in the place of primitive man. The features of primitive life are all-too-easily distorted by pressing them into our rational molds. In order to understand these peoples, we must think in their terms, we must familiarize ourselves with their way of dealing with problems and of viewing the world. With this approach, it becomes obvious that there is indeed coherence in the thinking of primitive peoples, but that this coherence is utterly different from ours; it is a pre-logical, emotional coherence.

What does this mean? For illustrative purposes, let us consider the *mental life of animals*. If you ever had a dog and took the trouble to watch his behavior on walks or in your room, you will certainly have observed that he regarded every moving object, a rolling stone, a wave, a book falling from the desk, as a living force. The dog does not simply dodge the object as you would, he barks at it, attacks it, bites it or retreats from it, as though it were an enemy or some uncanny power acting of its own volition. Even when an object does not move but is merely unusual, bizarre in shape or odd in its proportions, the dog behaves in the same way. For him there is no difference between inanimate objects and living bodies. If only they obtrude themselves by a motion or by some peculiar characteristic, both are equally animate.

A dog is a domestic animal, a creature almost human, living

under artificial, planned and fairly safe conditions. He does not lead an independent, wandering life in the wilderness, in an ever-changing environment. He does not have to hunt his food or to be aware of constant dangers that threaten his very life. He has grown accustomed to stable and familiar surroundings and has acquired a feeling of security. He can always turn to his master for reliable protection.

But if you have ever watched a deer or any other wild creature in its native habitat, you have probably noticed that it lives in a state of perpetual vigilance, that it is beset with fears not only of animal foes but of elemental powers as well. A sudden wind, a rustling tree, a distant rumble cause terror and flight. Its senses are sharpened to a degree which in man would be called hysterical. It registers the most minute sensations, the most distant events. It always seems to be in mystical touch with a multitude of potential hovering powers. It must always be on the alert among unknown dangers that may materialize at any moment. Its vulnerability consists not only in being exposed to actual peril, but in the lack of consciousness and of a systematic memory mechanism. For, of course, an animal does have a certain kind of memory that is part of its instincts and of its sense reactions. But since it lacks consciousness, it cannot properly register experiences, it cannot re-call them at will or abstract from them general conclusions as to how to meet recurring experiences of a similar and yet different kind. None of us is completely aware of the amount of protection that consciousness affords. A life without consciousness is naked and meagre. It is wholly exposed and always at the mercy of the unknown and the unexpected. It is a life in the present with no past and no future. But this present is quite different from our present that is lapped in memory and anticipation, that is only a ripple in a vast sea of conscious, half-conscious, subconscious experi-ences, plans and ideas. Our present is a minute transition from past to future, a continuous flux in the broad current of a known intentional life. But the present of the animal is an overwhelming, all-comprising present, cupped in darkness, a present where there is no consciousness of either birth or death. It is a present so stable, so immobile that it is all but identical with permanence, with eternity.

This is the premise for the understanding of the *primitive soul*. There is, of course, a great difference between animals and primitive man who is already illumined by the first flashes of consciousness, by certain ideas or the shadows of ideas. Yet there are astounding similarities between animal attitudes and the attitudes of primitive man. Knut Rasmussen gives a very revealing report of an interview he had with an Eskimo Shaman, that is, a wizard, a medicine man. Lévy-Bruhl, who has a profound knowledge of the huge extant ethnological and anthropological material, calls this report a unique document since this is the only instance where primitive man, by a happy chance, has succeeded in clarifying and expressing a basic feature of his mental attitude. Rasmussen was half Eskimo himself. He was thoroughly acquainted with the language and customs of his people and had gained the complete confidence of the Eskimo men. The Eskimo Shaman said:

". . . we explain nothing, we believe nothing . . .

"We fear the weather spirit of earth, that we must fight against, to wrest our food from land and sea . . .

"We fear dearth and hunger in the cold snow huts.

"We fear Takánakapsâluk, the great woman down at the bottom of the sea that rules over all the beasts of the sea.

"We fear the sickness that we meet with daily all around us . . . We fear the evil spirits of life, those of the air, of the sea and the earth, that can help wicked shamans to harm their fellow men.

"We fear the souls of dead human beings and of the animals we have killed.

"Therefore it is that our fathers have inherited from their fathers all the old rules of life which are based on the experience and wisdom of generations. We do not know how, we cannot say why, but we keep those rules in order that we may live untroubled. And so ignorant are we in spite of all our shamans, that we fear everything unfamiliar. We fear what we see about us, and we fear all the invisible things that are likewise about us, all that we have heard of in our forefathers' stories and myths. Therefore we have our customs, which are not the same as those of the white men, the white men who live in another land and have need of other ways."

In analyzing this account, you will find that the life of primitive man, like that of an animal, is a life of alertness and fear, a life that is essentially on the defensive. In his fear and defensiveness, primitive man is unable to make a distinction between the material and the immaterial, the visible and the invisible world, an animate or an inanimate object. What matter to him are only the present or potentially present sensations and effects he continually encounters. He perceives sensations as acting forces, as spirits or as animated bodies. He does not differentiate inner and outer life, dream, hallucination or imagination born of fear and reality. Such distinctions would imply logical operations of a complex order; they would imply the systematization of experiences, the ability to abstract general conclusions from experiences—in other words, all those functions of reason that primitive man has not yet developed.

Since to him the world consists of a legion of immediate sensations and emotions embodied in the forces of nature, his life, much as the life of an animal, is based on the present and is consumed by a sovereign present that is synonymous with eternity. Primitive man is surrounded by a system of forces existing always and everywhere. They are both personal and impersonal—call them spirits, demons or souls. They are in close communication; they pass into one another. Here and there they suddenly emerge from the dark, they become manifest and dip back into darkness again. A secret, constant interchange of these mystical forces goes on in the primitive world, and it is difficult to discern whether it is a question of many single interchangeable forces or of one all-pervading force or soul or life principle that materializes in various forms and in various places.

What Lévy-Bruhl calls "a mist of unity" embraces the whole world, material and immaterial, visible and invisible, imagined and real—a unity which is not in any way clearly conceived or conceivable, but only felt and lived and therefore purely emotional and mystical; and this whole world consists of embodied emotions and sensations. So we may well call primitive man a metaphysician. But since to him the metaphysical and the physical form one indistinct and indistinguishable entity, he is a sensual or emotional metaphysician in contrast to our concept of the metaphysical thinker who separates the physical from the abstract and is aware of a metaphysical principle as set against secondary physical phenomena.

This emotional coherence which unites the primitive world has been summed up by Lévy-Bruhl as the *"law of participation"*. In the primitive world, everything and everybody participates with everything and everybody. Such participation functions as a continuous cycle. One form slips into another and still retains the same substance. Man can be or become an animal, plant, mineral and vice versa, in order to carry out some deed or effect. In every experience related to himself, primitive man suspects that such a participation or transformation has taken place. If a stone falls and bruises him, it is because an enemy sorcerer has slipped into it, or the stone people may have been offended by a kinsman and taken revenge. These stone people or plant people are the same in kind as human beings, and sometimes assume human form. To give an instance: W. E. Armstrong reports of the people of Rossel Island in New Guinea: "The stone . . . is, of course, a good deal more than it appears to the eye—it would seem to have a sort of dual existence . . . for it has an existence in Temewe (a subterranean or submarine abode), where it is human in form—in fact there seems to be a vague idea that that which really is the stone may be at the same time a stone on Rossel (Island) and a man, or perhaps it would be better to say spirit . . . in Temewe." In his report on the Maori people of Tahiti Island, Elsdon Best says: "When the Maori entered a forest he felt that he was among his own kindred, for had not trees and man a common origin, both being the offspring of Tane. Hence he was among his own folk as it were, and that forest possessed a tapu life principle even as man does. Thus, when the Maori wished to fell a tree wherefrom to fashion a canoe or house timbers . . . he was compelled to perform a placatory rite ere he could slay one of the offspring of Tane. He saw in the majestic trees living creatures of an elder branch of the great family . . . he heard the voices of unseen beings in the rustling of branches, in whispering winds, in the sound of rushing waters . . ." Before cutting down a tree, the natives of Kiwai Island in New Guinea, as we learn from G. Landt-mann, ask the spirit to leave the tree and to go to live somewhere else. To the Caribs of British Guiana, animals live and act just like human beings. "In the morning the animals go to their work, like the Indians do. The tiger and the snake and all other animals go out hunting, having to look after their family like the Indian has . . ." "To the Malays," according to a report of W. Skeat, "the tigers are human beings who assume, for purposes of their own, the tiger's shape and who have, moreover, in various parts of the penin-sula . . . settlements of their own . . . There is an elephant city just as there is a city of the tigers . . . and it is the same for the rhinoceros, crocodile, wild deer, wild hog, etc."

Traces of this participation and interchange of forms among primitives are also contained in the early legends and sagas of ad-vanced cultures, in the metamorphoses of Greek, Celtic and Ger-manic heroes and gods, and even in the fairytales we liked best in our own childhood, which, to a certain degree, reflects that of man-kind as a whole. In his extensive studies on child psychology, the Swiss psychologist, Jean Piaget, has demonstrated a similar mental state for the child up to about seven or eight years: "The child is a realist, since he supposes thought to be inseparable from its object, names from the things named, and dreams to be external. His realism consists in a spontaneous and immediate tendency to con-fuse the sign and the thing signified, the internal and external, and the psychical and the physical."

The sphere of primitive life where participation is most pro-nounced, where it is, in fact, very close to simultaneousness and identity, is the *relation between the individual and the community,* be it family, clan or tribe. Here we are confronted with a funda-mental phenomenon of primitive life, a phenomenon which is a starting point of human history. Primitive man has no distinct feel-ing of individuality, no realization of an individual self. Nor has he as yet a definite knowledge of the limits of individual life, of birth and of death. The span of his individual existence lacks clearly defined boundaries. Like a child, he is not able to speak of himself as "I". He confuses "I" and "we". What Lévy-Bruhl calls an "organic or physiological solidarity" prevails between the individual and his community, between ancestor and offspring, that is, between the living and the dead. The individual has no life of his own, no life at all beyond the pale of his species. The species, not the individual, is the primary, the fundamental, the almighty unit and standard, the crux of every value and every event—this is what modern man finds so difficult to conceive. The individual has merely a secondary, derivative existence, and if we may speak of individuality at all, it is only "relative individuality", a shade, a slight differentiation within the compact entity of the species. The individual is a mere specimen of the species. Among the Maori, says Elsdon Best, "a native so thoroughly identifies himself with his tribe that . . . in mentioning a fight that occurred possibly ten generations ago, he will say: 'I defeated the enemy there,' mentioning the name of the tribe. In like manner he will carelessly indicate ten thousand acres of land with a wave of his hand, and remark: 'This is my land.' He would never suspect that any person would take it that he was the sole owner of such land, nor would any one but a European make such an error. When Europeans arrived on these shores many troubles arose owing to the inability of the Maori to understand individual possession of land, and land selling."

When we speak of the "members of a family", we are using a metaphor, but, as an anthropologist remarks in analyzing the language of the Melanesian people, in the case of primitive man "the solidarity of relatives among themselves is denoted in the same way as that of the various parts of an individual. The individual is to the family what a limb—head, arm, leg—is to the living body."

In hurting or offending a human being, in killing an animal or cutting down a tree—since animals and trees are conceived of as human—the native does not strike at the individual but at the whole species, of which the individual in question is only a transitory form. It is the species that will perform the task of vengeance and this vengeance will fall not on the individual perpetrator of the offence but on any of his kinsmen, on his species as a whole. The species is responsible for every individual, and every individual is responsible for the species. There is no distinction between individual and common guilt. This is the basic explanation for the ancient custom of "vendetta" or blood-vengeance that we find even today, among some European peoples.

This is also the reason why marriage was the affair of the whole clan, why the wife was chosen, captured or bought by the clan and belonged to it as such. The appropriation of a wife did not rest exclusively with the individual man to whom she was assigned. The other men of the clan retained a potential or even virtual right to her. Among many primitive clans there are no special words for "father". The translation for the term "father" would be "old man". Children know only their mother, and that, like animals, only up to a certain age. Later even this special relationship is forgotten and entirely supplanted by the feeling of membership in a certain clan. Within such a group there are only "men" and "women". Some peoples have no designation for "husband"; they only speak of men in general.

At a more advanced stage of development, a vestige of this condition persists among many primitive peoples in the right of a brother to his brother's wife. Brothers are considered as one, a man's wives are at least the "potential" wives of his brother and, as a result of this custom, conflicts and even tragedies occurred at transitional stages of this development, when a wife grew attached to an individual man and resented the older brother-right over her. Such a brother-right institution is mentioned in the Bible as an old custom of the Jews, the Levirate, the right and even the duty of a brother to marry his brother's widow.

Another peculiar institution of primitive peoples may be understood as an expression of such pre-individual relations between the sexes: exogamy or "marrying out", which John Ferguson McLennan, the first explorer to find it, describes as "a common rule with savage and barbarous peoples never to marry a woman of their own tribal sub-division or group but always to marry a woman of a sub-division or group different from their own."

Since primitive peoples have scarcely any feeling for individuality, they have no individual property. "Primitives cannot understand that land may be an individual and inalienable property. That which may be granted to individuals, and pass from one to another, is the use of the soil and the appropriation of its fruits . . . but nothing more . . . The land, as a matter of fact, belongs—and this, in the fullest sense of the word—to the social group in its entirety, that is, to the living and dead collectively." Even all tools, household goods, weapons and other articles of use, belong to the clan. Whatever an individual may acquire or receive from a foreign visitor, he immediately distributes among the members of his clan. B. Spencer, in his report on the native tribes of Northern Australia, says: "Give a man a shirt in return for work . . . and the chances are that you will find a friend of his . . . wearing it next day."

This phenomenon has often been called "primitive communism". But this is a misnomer based on a misconception. Communism is a collectivist theory and a collective social movement. And collectivism presupposes developed individuals who collect. It presupposes a clearly conceived, deliberate intention on the part of these individuals to set up a collective. But nothing of this kind is to be found in a primitive community. The species, the tribe, the clan, the family, is an entity of its own, an original, all-powerful entity from which individuals have not as yet separated. It is this original, sovereign entity which commands its members, members, as we have seen, in the sense of "limbs". Though primitive participation and modern communism show a superficial resemblance of traits and effects, they are diametrically opposed in their trends of development. While primitive participation springs from the community and tends toward the development of the individual, modern communism begins with the individual and leads toward the development of the collective. In primitive participation the species or the tribe precedes the individuals; in modern communism the individuals precede the collective. Thus we must consider the primitive tribe as an independent entity which has a mystical effect upon the whole emotional existence of its members. The tribe produces its individuals but is not derived from them. The modern collective is built up by rationally conceived outward aims that individuals have in common.

This primeval stage of man is the point of departure for human evolution, and its preliminary step consists in man's first acts of detaching and discerning a self from a non-self. His primitive participation with his universe and with his community begins to disintegrate as soon as he becomes aware of the *passage of time*. The participation with natural forces, animals and plants, the organic solidarity and almost identity of the clan members with one another and with their all-powerful clan, existed in that overwhelming present which is the frame of primitive life and of the primitive mind, a present which is identical with motionless duration, with eternity. To this island of an almighty present surrounded by darkness the utterly exposed life of the animal is forever confined. But man was soon led to break away from his confinement. He acquired the ability to extend his experience into another dimension, into the realm of Time. And the form in which time first manifested itself to the human mind was the past. Indeed, the first development of any true consciousness was the building up of a consciousness of the past. For the concept of the past signifies the detachment of an objectivated sphere of existence from the life in a vast present. The past gradually emerges from the omnipresent. It steals between Eternity and Now, and eventually takes over the power which was first exerted on man by the perennial present with its cycle of participating forces.

For a long time, however, this past was fixed in eternity. It was an estuary of eternity opening into the present, and it derived its strength from the dominance of eternity, or to be more exact, from a system of perennial powers. This system of perennial powers, of deities, constituted itself as an independent sphere ruling a merely present, a merely human world. It represents an objectivation of the eternal element in the primitive omnipresence of natural forces. And this process of objectivation is identical with the rise of religion. Concomitant with this first emphasizing and organizing of man's relation to the universe is a differentiation within the primitive community that initiates the development of human personality.

These processes of differentiation originated in two focal points of primitive life: in the special participation between the living and the dead, and in the specific forms of intercourse in which all participation occurred between primitive man and the various forces that constantly surrounded and haunted him.

To the primitive mind, men are not necessarily bound to die through natural causes in the natural course of events, just as no change, no event whatsoever, comes about of necessity or through what we call "natural causes", that is objective, automatic processes. All events are due to accidents, or rather, to the deeds of evil spirits.

As a matter of fact, men do not die at all in our sense of the word. They do not cease to be what they are, they merely move away—go somewhere else where they continue to live in one form or another, as human beings or as animals or plants. At any rate, the dead persist as what they were. They eat and drink, and their sustenance must be supplied by the living. They suffer cold and must be clad. They require fuel, they need all the utensils they employed in actual life, their oil, their hides, their weapons, their kettles and pans. And again it is the living who must provide them. These customs reach far into the history of civilization. The Egyptians buried household goods together with their dead; the Chinese still burn paper money for their dead so that these may buy what they want. In such concepts we also find one important origin of the sacrifice or offering. Another important origin is the self-surrender of a human being as a penance for the crime of the tribe, as the propitiation of demons, an act that is designed to turn away or to transfer a misfortune aimed at the tribe. Later, man was replaced by the animal, "the scapegoat", or by a consecrated image. But from these earliest human sacrifices a line of development leads to the most exalted sacrificial death in the history of mankind, to the crucifixion of Christ.

Primitive man has no more realization of natural birth than of death. Men are not propagated by a union of the sexes but by what we would call immaculate conception, by a sort of incubus. A spirit

enters into a girl or woman who happens to be passing by, and the
child she brings forth is at first hardly considered as a human being. It is a kind of sacred and, as it were, hybrid being, half human,
half spirit. And it is supposed to be in close contact with the world
of spirits whence it comes. Many initiations, rites and ceremonies
are required to attach it gradually to earth, to make it a member of
the present community. Thus birth is only another connection with
the sphere of the dead, with the spirits of the clan. This is the source
of the belief in metempsychosis, or transmigration of the soul,
which runs through the great religions and metaphysical theories of
the world.

   The dead are the spirits of the species. They leave and they return. They themselves are reincarnated; through them the species
is reincarnated again and again. For instance, when a native kills
a tiger, he has, in a certain sense of the word, driven away the species tiger, he has banished it to the realm of spirits, and the next
tiger he meets with is not another tiger, a different tiger, but Tiger;
the species tiger has simply reappeared. So the dead are really living,
and as they have a more constant, an apparently less vulnerable life,
they are even living par excellence. They know more than the people who are actually alive, and have uncontrolled power. For this
they are reverenced and feared. More and more they become the
very essence of the species. They become the true owners of the soil
and are given the best and the first of its fruits. Since they themselves
are the essence of the species, of the clan, they partake only of the
essence of the foodstuffs and leave the gross remainder to the offer-
ers, who, by eating it, communicate in some way with the essential
spirit of the species. Thus a first sublimation of the offering is
brought about, and all the venerated and feared dead become *ancestors*. A personified essence of the species, a divine emissary, takes
shape as a First Ancestor, a personal "archetype", a legendary "Elder Brother", who represents both the origin and the substance of
the species. Or, too, he may be regarded as the maker, the first creator of the species. He is considered bigger and better than other
members of the species. He lives elsewhere in a remote place and

can be perceived only under extraordinary conditions, in dreams, in visions or in ecstatic union. All his kinsmen draw their life and force from him.

This first ancestor need not always be a human being. He may be an animal or a plant, a rock or a star. He may or may not temporarily assume human form. Even his descendants may be not merely human beings, but leopards, aras, or crocodiles. This phenomenon is known as "totemism". (The name "totem" is of Chippeway Indian origin. Its original meaning is tribe, but ethnologically it is used to denote any ancestral or spiritually related non-human being or object which is considered as a patron by a primitive people.) According to J. G. Frazer, the paramount investigator of totemism, its origin lies in a primitive explanation that ancestral mothers "were impregnated by the entrance into their wombs of spirit animals or spirit fruits", and that the descendants, accordingly, "are nothing but the particular animal or plant which effected a lodgment in their mother and in due time was born into the world with a superficial and deceptive resemblance to a human being."

Residues of this chimerical and dual character of primitive representations are still manifest in the art, legends and poems of the great peoples of antiquity, where we encounter creatures half-animal and half-human in sphinxes, satyrs, tritons and centaurs, to mention only a few. Such hybrids appear as fixations or incarnations of the form-fluctuations in the primitive mind. The last remnants of these persist in our civilization as heraldic symbols and as mascots.

There was, then, in the earliest stages, no clear distinction, no gap between primitive man and these creative and life-giving forces. A state of perfect participation existed. The life-giving forces were present always and everywhere. Still, in our explanation of totemism, we have the first nucleus of an ancestral myth, of an account of origins. But to shift the ancestral spirit, the totemistic essence of life to a distinct and different sphere of existence, to make a clear cut between eternity, the past and the present—for this a further development was necessary, a process of objectivation which transformed participation into religion. This process was identical with the development of actual *worship and cult*.

A sharp distinction must be made between participation and religion. Religion begins when a human being in his present life on earth, faces a being that has existed in a past and that will exist in eternity. The word "God" originally signifies "the being worshipped", "the one to whom sacrifice is offered". And there is evidence that true worship began only when participation had paled.

"In pure totemism", says Frazer, ". . . the totem is never a god and is never worshipped. A man no more worships his totem . . . than he worships his father and mother, his brother and his sister . . . No doubt totemism may under favorable circumstances develop into a worship of animals or plants, of the sun or the moon, of the sea or the rivers . . . but such worship is never found amongst the lowest savages who have totemism in its purest form." Worship is a specific form of intercourse between human beings and divine powers, whether they be ancestors, totems or sublimations in the forms of deities. It is an advanced form of relationship and implies an objectivation if not a real sublimity of those powers.

The form of intercourse in the earliest stage, the stage of participation, was magic. Since primitive man was utterly exposed among a multitude of ever-present spirits, and suspected the work of some spirit in every happening, his life was replete with magical acts. Whatever man embarked upon was accompanied or rather enveloped by many magical procedures. There are two main courses of magical procedure: one offensive and the other defensive. The offensive course is an attempt to seize the spiritual forces, to take possession of them by some sort of communication, identification, imitation, for instance by eating the patron or hostile totem—this is the original significance of cannibalism and head-hunting—or by wrapping oneself in its hides, by wearing its feathers, imitating its gestures or habits and merging with it in mystical union, music, dance or ascetic practices. This kind of magic, in so far as it was imitation, may be considered as the "nursing mother of art", to use an expression of Frazer's. Primitive naturalism, as we find it in the famous rock drawings of African and prehistoric peoples, has probably its origin in the magical attempt to appropriate animal forces by seizing upon their exact form.

The second course of magic, the defensive, prevails in the later and more advanced stages of development, and is characterized by exorcism, invocation and pleading, by numerous rites of atonement and propitiation. Both forms are, of course, still effective in the cults of world religions, but it is the latter, the defensive, the gentler method of dealing with the spiritual forces, from which cult and worship derived.

This began with the institution of restricted magical spheres where spiritual forces dwell and work, spheres that are comparable to electrical fields, fields vibrant with power. Ethnologically these spheres are termed "taboo", an untranslatable Polynesian word combining a propitious with a malicious significance. It means sacred as well as uncanny. Objects and beings that are taboo are considered sacred. They cannot be killed or eaten, hurt or offended, without the utmost danger. They must be approached or touched with various procedures of caution and reverence. The taboo is the nucleus of the concept sacred or holy. For example, the Hebrew word for holy, "kadosh", originally meant detached, remote, isolated. In fixing and objectivating the taboo of human ancestors, totems or places where spirits dwelt, in conjuring these spirits into holy images, in combining both forms of magic, union and propitiation, through special ceremonies of sacrifice and pleading, worship and religion gradually developed.

In the process of being handed down from generation to generation, rites and ceremonies became rigid. They were observed with anxious accuracy, they grew into a complex system, they became fixed ritual. Since they could not be changed, they petrified, and, as we saw in the confession of the Eskimo Shaman to Rasmussen, the fears of primitive creatures became embodied in the strict observance of the rituals, in resistance to changes. They developed a consciousness of past generations, of tradition, of a distinct past.

Myths arose as a first form of history, and the division of time into three spheres became clearer: eternity, the dwelling-place of the originator, the essence of life; the past, in which former generations have learned how to deal with the deity and have transmitted myths of primal happenings (cosmogony); the present, the sphere of those now living. Eternity and the past, as the spheres of life-origin, maintained their domination over the present for a long time. In New Guinea, people remember a time when the dead and the living were not separated from one another but lived together peacefully. Here we observe the shaping of the concept of a Golden Age that prevailed at the beginning of time.

In this process of detachment of an eternal sphere from the Here and Now, heaven played an important part. It was formerly represented as not very high, as a tight cover, a hood resting on earth at the horizon. Many myths relate that at first heaven touched the earth and that one day it was sundered and lifted high up. It became the natural, the most sublime dwelling-place for the gods.

Thus man's intercourse with deity reached a stage where, for the first time, he was confronted with the principle of his origin, where, from the level of the present, he faced his beginnings in time. Mentally he detached himself from his beginnings and, at the same time, reconnected himself with them. He felt himself face to face both with the deity and with the beginning of all things.

This is what we call *religion*. Religion, in its pure sense, is still characterized by the physical bond felt in the stage of participation. The deity is still the essence of the species, the source of life of the specific tribe. But the fact that man faces the deity constitutes an essentially new relationship which goes beyond this physical bond.

Rites and ceremonies also become subjects of wisdom and knowledge. They call for experts who know. Such experts, such inspired mediators, existed previously. Even in the early stages of humanity there were wizards, sorcerers, medicine men who were supposed to know how to deal with spiritual forces, who were thought to be in closer contact with these powers and at times, indeed, to be themselves transformed into such powers and spirits. They were consulted in every difficult case. But as the traditional rituals developed more and more, the wisdom of those wizards was systematized and canonized and with it their position. It was the wizard who was to perform or to direct the great ceremonies in man's life. The wizard became a priest, the regular representative of the highest power, and as such he himself became vested with that highest power.

The *priest* is the first form of chieftain, the first form of king. He becomes the core, the essence of the present community. In this capacity he is the actual owner of land and distributor of goods, a vicarious owner, of course, a representative or administrator of property that belongs to the true essence of the tribe: the ancestors, the totem, the god. And, as a sacred chief who is connected with the essential powers, the priest himself becomes taboo. The sacred king is the first step in the shaping of individuality, individuality still in a relative sense, since he is only the deputy incarnate of the substance of the tribe. In a later phase, the sacred king was represented as a direct offspring of the divine power, as a son of god. And on this assumption sacred dynasties have been founded.

By gradual objectivation, sublimation and symbolization, by removing the enduring powers of the species from the present into a mythical past and a distinct and distant sphere of eternity, by conjuring them into images and confining them to abodes under or over the earth or to sacred temples, man came to visualize these powers as gods. The development of magical intercourse with spirits resulted in a system of worship, ritual and ceremonies, of sacrifice and communion, adoration and pleading, from which prayer evolved. The ordinary human being has not the inner strength or wisdom to establish direct connection with his god. He requires a mediator, the sacred priest who originated in the wizard, and sometimes the mediator himself was, or became, a god.

Along with this whole process, an extension, subdivision and emphasizing of the world of superhuman, divine powers was developing. Men not only worshipped the originators of their own tribe but the spirits of other tribes who had to be dealt with as relatives, friends or potential enemies. This extension reflects social de-

velopments, fusions and subdivisions of tribes, wars and subjugation of enemy tribes, whose gods were gradually recognized and
included in the original cult of the tribes.

Within a tribe, age and occupational groups were differentiated
and each was under the protection of a special patron spirit. Often
the gods of conquered populations or inferior domestic spirits persisted as a lower class of popular demons, beneath the heavenly
world of ruling deities and degraded by them. They sometimes developed into attendants of the ruling gods, into divine messengers,
i.e. angels. Gods were supposed to descend to earth and to engender
half-gods, heroes, conquering kings and founders of cities.

Thus the step from participation to religion meant an evolution
of human imagination from the indistinct emotional and sensational pandemonium of a vague life principle to the distinctly conceived pantheon of polytheism, an evolution from the "mist of
unity" to the clearness of multiplicity. At the same time it meant a
first detachment and discernment of a non-self from a self in the
three spheres of existence, history and humanity.

In the objectivation of the source of life of the species as deity,
man not only began to conceive of his own being on a higher plane
of existence, but in the various particular totem deities, all the various objects and beings of the outer world—animals, plants, rocks,
stars, the sea and the earth—emerged as distinctly conceived, separate, finite existences.

In dividing the confused, omnipresent demonic forces into those
of a distant eternity and a distinct past deriving from this eternity,
past and present took shape. All present life, however, remained
under the absolute domination of the divine order that was handed
down through the sacred past. It was governed by a comprehensive
ritual that offered powerful resistance to any fundamental change.

In instituting the priest, the sacred chieftain, the king, as the
earthly deputy, as the incarnation of the deity, the individual was
acknowledged for the first time. And in the constant presence of
conquered, subdued populations within the community, the problem of the human being as a stranger, a being alien and yet related

in that it was human in the face of a non-human world, began to make itself felt and to call for administrative distinctions in organization.

This was the condition of man when he entered upon the stage of history.

RELIGION

IN THE FOLLOWING CHAPTERS, we shall trace the steps leading from the concept of tribal deities as the essence of a particular tribe to the concept of a universal god. And this evolution implies important changes in the fields of history and human relationships—the realization of a common destiny of mankind and of a mutual bond among men, a mutual obligation of men toward one another that grows into what we call ethics and morality. In other words, we shall observe the gradual transition of man from the stage of tribal religion to the stage of world religion, a process which fundamentally alters the character of man's relation to the deity. This development was carried out by the great peoples of the Near East, the Egyptians, Babylonians, Assyrians, Persians and Jews.

Man's relation to the powers of the universe appears in three forms, as participation, religion and world religion.

Participation is a purely physical bond: through his emotions, his sensations and through magic, man merges with his ancestral and totemistic demons. In religion, man for the first time faces his life-giving principle in the deity per se, detached from its human descendants. Man differentiates and disconnects himself from his life-giving principle and, at the same time, reconnects himself with it mentally. In worshipping the deity, he considers himself face to face with the deity. Accordingly, religion, in its pure sense, still contains the physical bond of participation. The deity is still the source of life, the essence of the specific tribe. But the fact that man by his worshipping faces and envisages the deity constitutes an essentially new relationship which goes beyond the physical, biological bond.

This new, essentially spiritual relationship is the point of departure for the development of the world religions.

The concept of world religion is the profession of a universal god as creator, lord and savior, who is no longer a biologically related ancestor. The emphasis shifts more and more from the character of the creator to the character of the actual ruler, leader and future savior. Consequently, the physical bond between man and the deity is abolished altogether. The spiritual connection, a connection sprung of faith and of confidence, constitutes the sole basis of man's allegiance to God. World religion, therefore, is not religion in its original sense, it is a creed, a spiritual profession of faith.

Participation is a physical, emotional relation to the originating power. Religion is a dual, physical and mental relationship. World religion, or profession of faith, is a purely spiritual relationship. Thus the development we shall see presently is a process of gradual spiritualization of the deity and of man's relation to the deity. At the same time, man becomes temporal, personal and human, since a universal God no longer appeals to a particular tribe but to a single human personality as such.

A spiritual god relying on the essentially spiritual relationship of faith and profession presupposes the foil of an essentially temporal and physical life. The higher the divine eternal power mounts, the more spiritual it becomes, the more it separates from an earthly, temporal existence, and the more does earthly, temporal existence become known as such, become aware of itself and emancipated.

This process of the spiritualization of the deity and of the development of the temporal world was continued by the Greeks. With them the spiritual universal God developed into a spiritual substance of the universe, and the juxtaposition of an eternal, spiritual substance and an earthly, varied and changing present brought up the problem of the various sources of human knowledge and so begot philosophical speculation.

And finally we shall see a parallel development within the world of man, the development of the first urban communities and of city life in the Greek polis, the unfolding of the individual in the course of this development, the spread of the Roman polis to world dominion and the development of a contrast between the earthly universality of the Roman Empire and the rootless individuals that are created through the intermingling of these peoples in the empire. The earthly universality of this world empire affords the secular frame and stage for the spiritual universality of Christianity.

ORIENTAL KINGDOMS

THE FIRST HISTORICAL STAGE of mankind is represented and characterized by the great kingdoms of the ancient Orient, Egypt, Babylon, Assyria and Persia. These first great kingdoms as well as the smaller kingdoms which rose and fell in the early millennia before Christ, for instance, the kingdoms of the Minoans, the Mittani, the Hittites, the Hurrians, the Phrygians, the Lydians—all these kingdoms had one fundamental feature in common, they were all theocracies. They were ruled and owned by gods or by kings and dynasties that were supposed to be either descendants or deputies of gods, "tenant farmers" of gods, as the Sumerians put it.

These kingdoms were agglomerations or fusions of tribes which settled along and between the great rivers and seas of North Africa and the Near East. It is no mere coincidence that human history started on its great progression from that region around the Eastern and Southeastern shores of the Mediterranean that may be compared to a grandiose amphitheater. From inner Africa, from Arabia, from the heart of Asia, the Iranian Plateau, the Caucasus and the Black Sea, a variety of tribal stocks came together at this focus. There was friction, competition, interrelation and intermingling of peoples drawn to the Mediterranean as filings to a magnet.

Frequent wars were caused by a struggle for expansion and for favorable dwelling-places. And those tribes that were numerically the strongest and that were most vital—which often meant more barbarous—overran the smaller tribes and established cultures. In this way, their sacred rulers gained enslaved populations for manual labor, and this enabled them to erect their mighty temples, pyramids and palaces—gigantic, indestructible monuments.

Eventually, by such incorporation of different stocks, these peoples succeeded in building up the first empires in history. One may, in fact, call the Egyptian, the Babylonian and the Persian kingdoms the first world powers, not only internally, with regard to the extent of their territories and the vast unfolding of their administrations, but also externally, in that they were the first to establish what we should call international relations on a large scale and international cultural standards. Alliances were formed, sporadic diplomatic intercourse was fostered. And along the great rivers and across the linking Mediterranean Sea, a slow, cumbersome trade with foreign powers was beginning to flourish and with it an exchange of cultural achievements and influence.

But with all their achievements, these ancient kingdoms never went beyond the primeval, tribal stage of humanity. The essence of the tribe was, and remained throughout, the predominant if not sole concern of communal life. Yet the primary state of the so-called primitive communism, of the leveled and undivided power and property of the whole tribal body, had been overcome. The essence of the tribe was already concentrated and crystallized in fixed and powerful deities and divine rulers.

Originally, kings were mainly priests, but later, owing to the frequency of tribal conflicts and the task of military organization and leadership, they became primarily warriors. And though they remained the divine or at least sacred chiefs, who still performed essential cult ceremonies, a special class of priests and their subordinates arose to perform cultic functions, and sometimes rivalry and antagonism broke out between kings and priests.

The population was a mere ramification of the central core. And life went on dominated by rituals and regulations grown rigid through the practice of generations, and watched over by a hierarchy already intent on the increase of personal power. Even the great new achievements of these peoples, the invention and development of writing, for instance, the Egyptian hieroglyph and the Sumerian cuneiform writing, at first helped all the more in the preservation of the past, in the codification of the ancient rites and customs. The present was rigorously chained to the past.

The so-called cities of these kingdoms were huge temples built like fortresses and palaces, surrounded by monumental tombs and habitations of a large priesthood, of court officials and sacred bureaucracies. The priesthoods and bureaucracies were mainly concerned with the worship of the gods and the service of the god-kings. Everything else was secondary and accessory. The land was fundamentally and originally the property of the gods and the god-kings. It belonged to the essence of the tribe or was derived from it. The soil was cultivated by workers who, as remnants of conquered tribes, were serfs bound to the soil and owned by the god-kings or the sacred officials. Later on, especially in Babylon and Persia, the soldiers were rewarded with small farms and settled as farmers. All officials were maintained and equipped by the court, and services were paid and rewarded by hereditary land-assignments. Land was also let out against duties in kind. Economy was based on payment in kind. The precious metals, however, were highly valued as jewelry and treasure. Hence they were granted as a mark of special favor to privileged officials and used as gifts for foreign princes and later for the pay of foreign mercenaries. Because they were rare and indestructible—not subject to oxidation—the precious metals gradually came into use as standards of price measurement. Babylon was the first country to have a clumsy tender in the form of metal bars. These metal bars were circulated by individual merchants. Merchants who were known to be reliable in the matter of weighing put their stamp upon the bars. This was the origin or rather the precursor of the coin. It was not until the seventh century B.C. that coins were made in Lydia as the official form of exchange favored by the political ruler and used primarily in dealing with foreign countries.

Thus, through land-assignments and gifts, private property was evolving, especially among the great officials and the governors of the provinces, the Satraps, whose households were shaped on the pattern of the hieratical court of the god-kings.

The administration became more and more complex. The power of the governors increased, and accordingly there were rebellions, changes of rulers and dynasties. This always meant a new capital and, as every city had a main worship of its own, it also meant the rule of a new central god, a new head god from whom all power and earthly authority was derived.

Jurisdiction was generally in the hands of the priests. Later on, in Mesopotamia, it became an office of the elders of a clan or a settlement, but it was still conducted on ritual, hieratical lines.

All these Oriental peoples were entirely dominated by divine powers that were supposed to rule not only through their own intrinsic might, but through a sacred dynasty begotten by them and through priests and administrators whom they authorized and consecrated. A constant cloud of eternal power hung over human life, and every move, every institution had some bearing upon cult. People's lives, therefore, did not as yet develop as an intercourse of free individuals, acting independently upon their own impulses. Man's center of gravity was not yet in his own individual heart and mind, in his present aims and actions and in his relation toward others. Whatever was undertaken, was, in a way, related and referred to the essence of the tribe, to the eternal gods and their earthly administrator, the sacred king.

Trade, to be sure, and even credit operations were developed to a certain extent. But the very documents from which we know that there was such a commercial life show how complicated, clumsy and involved this traffic was. Every little transaction was closed by a ceremonious treaty written on clay tablets and deposited in the temples. This commerce, therefore, cannot have been very great.

It is not surprising that in the numerous preserved documents of these peoples there is no individual note, no characteristic account of events or persons. The so-called autobiographies of Egyptian officials are pompous self-glorifications, intended to be carved into the walls of tombs. They tell of services performed for gods and for divine kings, and of rewards and marks of favor granted by these kings. All descriptions, whether they deal with social revolutions, such as the invasion of Egypt by the Semitic Hyksos tribes, or with the mood of a person weary of life, are written in a hieratic, stereotype style, and human relationships are usually conveyed by the deeds and the complicated relationships between gods. They are virtually viewed from the plane of the gods.

Only the sacred kings themselves have a shimmer or suggestion of human personality. But even they do not give the atmosphere of real human personality, not even the more clearly defined figures of the great Persian conquerors, Cyrus, Cambyses and Darius. There is no flavor of human feeling and thinking about them, as we sense it, for instance, in King Saul or King David, in the Jewish prophets or the Homeric heroes. Although they show shades of differentiation, there is a certain general standard, a tribal standard that pervades them all.

Yet, there are important differences, fundamental differences between the cultural features of these first tribal kingdoms as whole entities. And the essence of these differences may be grasped in their religion which is the very center of their life. The cultures of these days merely reflect the structure of their religion.

Egypt, Babylon and Persia succeeded one another in building up a powerful empire, comprising and uniting various tribal stocks. But none of them succeeded in comprising the whole contemporary civilized world in a world empire. None of them succeeded in making its own form of civilization the all-comprising civilization of the world, although for some millennia the size of these empires was successively increased.

Egypt's Old Kingdom (from about 3000 to about 2270 B.C.) for a time extended over part of Nubia, that is, the country between Egypt and the Sudan today, and Palestine. Its later kingdoms, the Middle and the New Kingdom, even included Phoenicia and Syria for a certain period, and reached the upper Euphrates. The Babylonian kingdom of Hammurabi (about 1950 B.C.) extended over all of Mesopotamia. For part of the seventh century B.C., the Assyrian empire covered the whole area from Mesopotamia and Northern Syria to Egypt. In addition to that entire area, the Persian empire, in bout 500 B.C., included Iran to the borders of India, the Arabian Sea in the South and the Oxus River in the North, as well as Asia Minor.

There was still Greece, however, which the Persian kings were not able to conquer, and this historical fact was of crucial importance for the development of civilization. And it was a Greek, Alexander the Great, who made the first, if futile, attempt to found a world empire.

The sequence of these Oriental kingdoms shows an ever-increasing accumulation of worldly power. At the same time, their religion is characterized by the gradual emerging of clearly conceived divine powers from animal totems, and along with it, the growing concept of a distinctly human and earthly being. The three types of religion—the Egyptian, the Babylonian and the Persian—represent three evolutionary rungs toward a spiritualization of the divine powers. Simultaneously, they reflect a waxing sense of the human and the temporal, an increasing flexibility and versatility in the life of man. As a matter of fact, the evolutionary process manifested in the sequence of these religions appears as a gradual descent of man's attitude from eternity to the Here and Now.

The *religion of Egypt* clearly shows the state of emergence from a primitive mentality. It may be characterized as an ancestral religion, a worship of the dead and of animal totems, in transition to a higher form of religion, the cult of astral deities.

In this confusing variety of animal, human and astral forms, in which the concepts of gods divided and fused again, corresponding to the changes of dynasties and capitals, one can still observe a residue of that primitive "mist of unity", of that all-pervading, life-giving force which is projected now and again in different shapes. Gods were part animal, part human, part astral deities. They had heads of hawks, wolves, rams, bulls, cats, crocodiles on human bodies. And there were the most ancient cults of animals proper, the cult of the sacred ram in Mendes, the cult of the Apis bull in Memphis.

We also recognize traces of primitive beliefs in that human mortality has not as yet been actually realized, a fact which manifested itself in a most elaborate cult of the dead. The dead were supposed to survive in another part of the world, which for the ordinary people lay under the earth, or rather, on the other side of the earth, the dark side, where the sun sets in the West to light it during the night. The residence of the noble and powerful was heaven, where they joined the sublime deities.

A revival of the dead was regarded as possible when they recovered their life-giving substance, called the Ka, which is represented as a shadow of the human form walking invisibly behind the human being. In order to preserve the body intact, so that this life-giving substance might recognize it, the dead were embalmed and mummified, their tombs were equipped with all the paraphernalia of living. This custom appears as a presentiment of the significance of the earthly life of the individual.

Later, instead of real objects, the dead were given only painted or sculptured images. This fostered the development of art which, from a hieratical "frontal" shape that rendered only the flat, rigid, profiled contours of bodies, became more vivid and plastic.

The *Babylonian religion,* at its peak, is already detached from the primitive stage. Its gods are represented in plainly human form. They are distinctly separate from animal totems and demons. On the images, they merely stand on animals or are accompanied by animal emblems. They are bound and organized into a closed system; they form an elaborate cosmic pantheon. And, notwithstanding their variety as different natural forces and local deities, they represent an organic union which preserves the feeling of cosmic unity, of an all-pervading and creative power.

These gods are conceived as the spirits of the elements of the universe. At the top stands the divine trinity, Anu, the Sky, Enlil (later Bel), the Earth, and Ea, the Sea, followed by Sin, the Moon, Samar, the Sun, Ishtar, the Great Mother and Tamuz or Saturn, the Vegetation and Cycle of Cosmic Life. These seven powers again form a broader unity symbolizing the positions of the planets and the lesser constellations. That is why the tales of gods are essentially based on the relation and motion of heavenly bodies. Within wide limits, mythology and astronomy coincide.

The planets were considered interpreters and heralds of the di-

vine will. Their motion and position revealed the events in the sky
and hence those that must take place on earth, the reflection of the
sky. There is both parallelism and coherence between a celestial
world of the gods and a terrestrial world of earthly beings, between
space and time, that is to say, between the eternal cosmic formation
and the eternal and ever-repeated cosmic cycle, between the course
of the stars and the seasons of the year. Because of this, the calendar
was a sacred institution. There is even a secret and sacred interrelation between the cosmic body of the universe and the human or
animal body.

A complex system of astrology, vaticination, interpretation of
physical omens and magical medicine was founded on the presumption of such interrelation. The divine powers begin to have a new
connection with the experiences of earthly, of human life. Among
the Babylonians, moreover, we find a clear realization of man's
mortality. The world of the dead is surrounded by seven circular
walls. It is called "the land without return" and lies at the core of
the earth. While, in Egypt, the dwelling-place of the dead was
looked upon as a sphere of higher being, the Babylonian and Assyrian civilization regarded it as a degraded, shadowy existence.
And although it was assumed that there were different planes of
survival according to merit earned on earth and the manner of
grave-tending, still, by and large, the death cult had a subordinate
role.

There was also a concept of the emergence of the organized world
from the dark, and this division was recorded as a mythical process
or rather a struggle of the deified heroes against the flood and the
monsters of a prehistoric chaos. Later, the whole cosmic union was
incorporated in a plainly tribal god, such as Marduk and Assur,
whose name was already identified with the name of the tribe itself,
its capital and its empire.

A further advance toward an animated, humanized world manifests itself in the *Persian religion,* which, in its final shape, was
evolved by a single personality, the prophet Zarathustra or Zoroaster, who was born about 660 B.C. This religion shows three im-

portant new features: a sober, earthly, not to say materialistic, character, a dynamic nature, a tendency toward abstraction.

It is evidently a religion of agriculture in which the values and mentality of peasants prevail. It is the first religion that is not intended as a privileged sphere of a mediating priesthood or hierarchy. On the contrary, it obviously came into being through Zarathustra's opposition to ancient rites and their guardians, the priest class of the Magi. So this religion in its original shape, as represented by the original preachings of Zarathustra, the Gathas, means a broadening of the religious basis, an expanding contact between the deity and the people, an inclusion of the poor and simple in the circle of the gods. Of course, this is true only for the original meaning of the teachings of Zarathustra. Soon it was obscured by an elaborate, formal, official cult in which the Magi restored their power.

In this religion, the trinity, or the unity of seven powers of the Babylonians, is contracted into a duality or rather a sheer opposition, an antagonism of two main cosmic powers: the god of light and clarity, who at the same time represents the sound and wholesome, Ahura Mazda, and the spirit of the dark, the evil and unwholesome, Angra Mainu (Ahriman). These two deities, which are akin to principles, reflect the opposition of the settled, rooted and determined life of the peasant to the restless, uncertain life of the nomads. The antagonism of the two deities was not conceived as an eternal or ever-repeated struggle, or as a struggle which occurred once in the past, but—and this is an extremely important new feature—as a single, definite happening which goes on in the universe as well as in human souls, and will end in the ultimate triumph of the Light and the Good.

There will be a final day of judgment when men will have to give an account of their deeds. Those who helped the spirit of the Light and the Good in his struggle will be resurrected and rewarded in a "paradise", a word of Persian origin that signifies "enclosing wall"; the beautiful gardens and richly cultivated estates of the Persian satraps were called "paradises". This account given on the last day was supposed to be an account in the literal sense of the word, a commercial balance of the amounts of good and evil thoughts and works. And, characteristically, the reward consisted in a healthy and beautiful body, an inexhaustible cow and never-fading pastures. So the Good is identical with the Sound, the Wholesome and the Useful. Zarathustra himself has the attribute of a bringer of profit. Hence the ritual regulations have, roughly speaking, a moral character, a bearing on the behavior of man to his fellow men. Ethics, however, is still a kind of hygiene and a source of practical advice for the farmer. The care of domestic animals, especially of the cow, plays a predominant part in it. Its main objectives are precepts for purification, precepts for a clean and sound natural life.

Both gods, the good, and the evil who is the prototype for the biblical Satan, have many attendant spirits or demons that have been degraded to a lower sphere. The new feature of these demons is that many of them are personifications of abstract qualities and attitudes, for instance, "the best justice", "the sacred devotion", "obedience", "truth", "lie", "hope", and so on. And in their dual quality of absolute and real beings, existences on the one hand, and thoughts and attributes of the human soul on the other, the angels of the good god, the fravashis, are also precursors of the Platonic Ideas. It was thought that they had descended from heaven into the human soul in order to support the God of Light in his struggle against the evil spirit and to help man in his struggle for the Good.

The concepts of these three religions and their deities reflect man's increasing awareness of himself. Particularly in the Persian religion, a new feature appears: a presentiment of human destiny as a whole, a presentiment of a progression of mankind. For the first time a common *future* of mankind as a whole begins to play a part in human concepts. Here let us note that in all languages the future tense is the last to develop. Indo-European was originally "time-less", that is, time was expressed neither in the verb nor in any other grammatical category. There was, therefore, no present, no past, no future. The same is true of the Semitic and the Finno-Ugrian, the languages of the Sudan, of New Guinea and others. They usually have "aspects" instead of tenses, such as Russian has today. Several other languages or families of languages have nothing comparable to our verb, that is to say, they are lacking in an expression for motion, for the dynamics of life.

In the documents of the Egyptian and the Babylonian religions we already find evidence that man gave an account of his actions to the deities. In the Egyptian "Books of the Dead", whose purpose it was to furnish the deceased with incantations, prayers and key words to help him reach the kingdom of Osiris, to join the gods in heaven—in this very old Egyptian book, confessions are given as follows:

"Homage to thee, O Great God, thou Lord of Maati (the goddesses of physical and moral law, and the personification of the conscience). I have come to thee, O my Lord, and I have brought myself hither that I may behold thy beauties. I know thee. I know thy name. I know the names of the Forty-two gods (the gods of the forty-two nomes, or counties into which Egypt was divided), who live with thee in this Hall of Truth, who keep ward over sinners, and who feed upon their blood on the day when the lives of men are taken into account in the presence of Un-Nefer (i.e. the Good Being or Osiris) . . . Verily I have come unto thee, I have brought truth unto thee . . . I have not done evil to men. I have not oppressed . . . my family. I have not done wrong instead of right. I have not been a friend of worthless men . . . I have not tried to make myself over-righteous. I have not put forward my name for exalted positions. I have not entreated servants evilly. I have not defrauded the man who was in trouble. I have not done what is hateful (or taboo) to the gods . . . I have not permitted any man to go hungry. I have made none to weep. I have not committed murder . . . I have not robbed the temples of their offerings. I have not stolen the cakes of the gods . . . I have not committed fornication. I have not committed acts of impurity in the holy places . . . I have not encroached upon the fields (of my neighbors). I have not added to the weights of the scales . . . I have not driven away the cattle that were upon their pastures. I have not snared the feathered fowl in the preserves of the gods . . . I have not stopped water at the time (when it should flow). I have not breached a canal of running water. I have not extinguished a fire when it should burn. I have not violated the times (of offering) chosen meat-offerings . . . I have not repulsed the god in his manifestations. I am pure. I am pure. I am pure. I am pure."

There are similar lists of sins in Babylonian documents of conjuring, born of the fear of a divine power and intended to atone and to reconcile the gods.

These prayers are appeals of individual men arising from their personal anxiety. Such accounting is a single, ever-repeated happening within a stable and fixed world order. It is not connected with any general progression of mankind, with any common purification and salvation. It is utterly different from that Persian concept of the continuous struggle of the two principles to which men are subject, and of a universal last judgment. This Persian concept of the world as a definite progression is new. It foreshadows future developments and influences the Jewish and Christian concepts, although there are fundamental differences. There is as yet no concept of humanity as such in all these early Oriental religions, not even in the Persian. The standard of mankind is identical with the standard of the particular tribe and its creed. And when the documents of these religions speak of men and contemplate the destiny of men, they actually mean only Egyptians, or Babylonians, or Persians, adherents of the Parsi creed. There is, indeed, the suzerainty of a tribal god over other peoples and over their gods, and consequently the naive extension of his power and his commands over alien territory. The tribal god can, then, have significance beyond the pale of the tribe, but he is not consciously conceived as universal, he has no direct human appeal.

As the precepts of these religions do not refer to the human being as such, they are not essentially ethical, as the Egyptian document given above clearly shows. They are tribal rules, in part hieratical, in part practical and administrative, concerning either the service of the gods and the sacred kings or the strictly tribal community and common life. Religious ethics coincide with regulations of tribal administration.

The two peoples that succeeded in transcending their own particularity, that initiated the concept of humanity proper and its complement, the concept of human individuality—for one corresponds to the other, one calls for the other—these two peoples, that thereby founded our civilization, were the Jews and the Greeks.

The *Jewish people* is a peculiar, a really unique phenomenon, for it combines two apparently contradictory elements, a strict particularity and an outspoken trend toward universality. In its social structure, as well as in its history, it is a transition from particularity to universality. And this is not a mere mixture, it is an intrinsic union of the two features and trends. Oddly enough, paradoxically, one supports the other, one fosters and foments the other.

The Jews began as a distinct tribe, a particular tribe, and in a way they even preserved themselves as a tribe throughout human history. They clung to their own particular religion and even to their most minute atavistic tribal ritual with the utmost rigor and stubbornness. But the content of this religion is in itself universal, a universal appeal and a universal mission. They would not have preserved themselves as a particular people without their religion, but this very religion made them interpret themselves, interpret their lasting survival as a particular people, only as a means of propagating humanity, a universal Kingdom of God, identical with a realm of peace and harmony on earth, a realm of brotherly, united mankind, of perfected humanity. The particular tribal impulse, the biological impulse, was needed for carrying out an appeal to humanity, a drive toward humanity. Judaism is still a pure, genuine religion, but it transcends religion toward world religion by the universality and spirituality of its God. The Jewish people is still a tribe, but through its missionary character it transcends the tribe and strives toward humanity.

All this was established from the very beginning in the special character of the Jewish God, the special character of his relation to the tribe and the special character of his commands. The concept of the Jewish God comprehends and involves the whole history of the Jewish people. This is the only history we know that begins with an exile, with homelessness and oppression. There are many peoples whose history begins with migrations and invasions, there is none which, like that of the Jews, begins with an exodus and a wandering toward an imagined land. The first pilgrimage of the Jewish tribes from Egypt to the Promised Land, this physical pilgrimage, appears as a symbol of that long spiritual pilgrimage of the Jewish people through human history that was to come later. The concept of the Jewish God was formed during this wandering, which probably took place in the thirteenth century before Christ.

Accordingly this Jewish God is a nomad God, a wandering God, not a local god attached to a particular place. He is, moreover, an essentially tribal god whose outstanding feature is his relation to the tribe. He incorporates and comprehends all the cosmic forces, he actually integrates the cosmic forces in his overwhelming personality. The deities of the settled Oriental kingdoms were half totemistic, half cosmic forces, none of which entirely integrated an inherent multiplicity of clan particularities and cosmic complexities. None of them attained such predominance of human character, human personality as to overcome completely the elemental source.

The fact that this Jewish God is the first to be human and personal, that he has grown beyond the forces of nature, explains his remoteness, his detachment from all natural genealogical systems. He has neither a father nor a mother nor kinsfolk, he has no spouse, he is without sexuality. He did not originate. Hence there is no mythology connected with him. He has not engendered offspring that rank with him; he has only created them. All this makes him unique and lends him the first true sublimity. The Jewish God is a guiding God, not one who is merely there, self-sufficient, remote and immobile, like the other Oriental deities. He is intensely concerned with the particular destiny of his people, he has special plans, special intentions and purposes with regard to his people. He incites it and drives it forward, he leads it toward a history, toward a future, toward special aims. He does not reside in a stable past, a stable eternity, he wanders through time also, he is an essentially dynamic, historic God, in fact a revolutionary God, who is ahead of his people, not simply behind and above it in the ancestral way.

These fundamental qualities of the Jewish God have other far-reaching implications: As a nomad God who does not reside in any particular place, he shall not be fixed or conjured in any place or image, he shall not be grasped anywhere, he shall not be embodied or conceived in any earthly form. He is the everlasting, present everywhere and always, but present spiritually, not in the primitive sense of omnipresence, confused with elemental forces and endowed with physical shapes. He is an essentially spiritual and invisible being, separated from and contrasted to the natural and human world of which he is the creator and ruler. Thus he is imageless and nameless—God Proper. His only representations are the human beings whom he created in his image. His name Yahveh, probably means creator: "He causes to be". This name was not to be pronounced. It had to be circumscribed. God was not to be grasped in a word just as he was not to be confined in an image. To look upon him or to name him—in a word, to conjure him in any way—was fatal. At first, to be sure, there were traces of the old forms of elemental appearance and magic intercourse, of the stage of participation. Mount Sinai is a clear instance of taboo. And all we call miracles are remnants of primeval magic intercourse. But, more and more, magic in itself became a taboo, as evident in the prohibition of image and name; more and more the Jewish God was considered averse to, condemning, these primitive forms of intercourse.

As a spiritual and invisible, as a nameless and everlasting, as an all-comprising God, he is the essentially one and undivided, the one and only God. He is the most exclusive, the zealous and jealous, the one who does not tolerate any god besides himself, while all other Oriental deities only claimed to be mightier than others and did not exclude the existence of other foreign gods.

Close adherence to the Persian religion, for instance, did not prevent King Darius from presenting offerings to Egyptian gods as an act of courtesy. Relations between ancient Oriental deities were much the same as relations between modern governments. Often diplomatic greetings were interchanged. Otherwise a phenomenon, such as the Hellenistic syncretism, a fusion and intermingling of cults, would not have been possible. The Jewish religion never allowed such recognition and such intermingling. This exclusiveness was never understood and was considered extremely arrogant by the other ancient peoples. It was the cause of the first form of Anti-Judaism in Hellenistic times.

Consequently the Jewish God, with his claim to uniqueness and all-inclusion, with his invisibility and spirituality, was implicitly a universal God, the first universal God in history. His province comprehended all human beings as images of himself: it was mankind as a whole. To him, the children of Israel were not identical with mankind proper, as the Egyptians, the Babylonians, the Persians were to their deities. The Jews did not represent the whole of humanity, they were only God's preferred, God's chosen people among other peoples to be won over to him. And they were his chosen people only with regard to a special task, a mission that he entrusted to them. As a result of the universal aims of the Jewish God, Jewish religion is the first missionary religion, the first religion to strive for proselytes. This is very different from the concepts of previous peoples. The idea of the chosen people is in fact a limitation, and it has been interpreted as an arrogant prerogative. Looking backward, it does seem like arrogance, but one must consider its origins.

This also makes for an entirely new relation between the Jewish God and his people, a relation that marks a new epoch of human evolution in many respects. First of all, it was an actually human relationship, a relationship of perpetual communication on both sides, a dialogue, a dialectic, dramatic relationship of perpetual question and answer, of violent rebellion on the part of man, and wrath and threats on the part of God; but also of passionate attachment and of true love on both sides. And it was more than that! After the emergence of worship and religion from primitive participation, as a first form of objectivation, a first setting apart, detaching and envisaging the essence of the tribe, the Jewish people took the second step toward objectivation in that its relation to God was put on a lawful basis. It was represented as an explicit covenant which made man into a free partner of God. The Sinaitic Covenant, in the final analysis, founded the freedom of man and the free decision of the human being. Then too, it confirms the primary universality of God. For it implies that God is originally the God of all people and of all peoples, and that the special relation between him and the Jewish people was established through a formal agreement and the giving and assuming of a mission. The other peoples—so it was said —ignored the call of God. Only Abraham "believed in the Lord" (Gen. 15, 6). Here, for the first time, faith becomes a basic element in the relationship between man and God.

God no longer makes known his will incidentally, irrationally, arbitrarily, he made it known once and for all in an explicit spiritual revelation which has the character of a binding law. That there was such a revelation was considered as a special and very imposing particularity and privilege of the Jewish tribe among all the peoples of antiquity, and won many proselytes for Judaism.

The content of the Jewish law and the character of its commands are also new. It took over sections of the famous Babylonian code of the King Hammurabi, but it reflects the special concepts of the Jewish God and his aims that are the aims of the Jewish people. It connects a tribal ritual, governing every aspect of human life, with the first truly moral code in history. This means: with commands concerning man's behavior toward his fellow men, not fellow kinsmen! Not only more clearly but more categorically than any other previous law, it ordained justice, harmony, charity, regard for the poor. It was the first law on earth to ordain, "love thy neighbor as thyself" (Leviticus 19, 18), to ordain social adjustment, prohibition of an interest charge, a day of rest for man and beast and a season of rest for nature. It was the first to show a regard for the alien, to set down a command like this: "The stranger that dwelleth with you shall be unto you as one born among you and thou shalt love him as thyself; for ye were strangers in the land of Egypt" (Lev. 19, 34). This command is one of the oldest. It is similarly expressed in the twenty-third chapter of Exodus, belonging to the so-called Book of the Covenant, which dates from the ninth century B.C., and the contents of which, judged by the archaisms, trace back to an even much earlier period.

In Jewish law one must differentiate apodictic and casuistic law. Apodictic law, to which the ten commandments belong, appears for the first time and has no parallel elsewhere. Its spirit and form are fundamentally different from the Egyptian negative confessions and from similar Babylonian documents to which it has often been compared. The casuistic law, as the Book of the Covenant demonstrates, has much in common with other codices of the Near East, the Codex of the Babylonian King Hammurabi (about 1950 B.C.), the Hittite law (about 1400 B.C.), the Assyrian law (twelfth century). But a careful comparison of the laws in the Codex Hammurabi with the corresponding headings in the laws of Israel also points to a decisive difference in the attitude, especially with regard to the evaluation of the human being and of individual life, whether it be that of free men or of slaves. In connection with this, the later development of Jewish law, and its interpretation through the prophets, must also be taken into consideration.

The aim of all these commands—a realm of true brotherhood among human beings, a united humanity—this Israel was to accomplish and propagate among the peoples. This was to be the mission of Israel: to become the mediator, the "light to the Gentiles", as Isaiah subsequently proclaimed. What that meant is expressed in Deuteronomy 28, (seventh century before Christ): "And the Lord shall scatter thee among all people, from the one end of the earth even unto the other . . . and thou shalt become an astonishment, a proverb, and a byword, among all nations whither the Lord shall lead thee . . . And among these nations shalt thou find no ease, neither shall the sole of thy foot have rest: but the Lord shall give thee there a trembling heart, and failing of eyes, and sorrow of the mind . . . And thou shalt not prosper in thy ways: and thou shalt be only oppressed and spoiled evermore, and no man shall save thee . . . so that thou shalt be mad for the sight of thine eyes which thou shalt see."

The particular relationship between the Jewish people and their God had a decisive bearing on the social and political structure of this people. For the Jewish tribe and the Jewish states were in the main a pure theocracy, a theocracy in the literal sense of the word. God himself, the spiritual God, was the actual ruler, the direct ruler of the country. There was no human descent from God. No leader or king of Israel and Judah ever pretended to be a descendant of God, as the Egyptian kings. None of them even pretended to be a sacred administrator or "tenant farmer" of God, as the Babylonian kings. None of them pretended to belong by birth to a different order from that of his compatriots. And all of them were made responsible before the divine law and were most severely punished for their failures. We have the testimony of one of the Jewish judges, Gideon, who expressly refused to become king of Israel, when he was invited to take up the rule over the people after he had delivered the country from the Midianites: "I will not rule over you," he said, "neither shall my son rule over you: the Lord shall rule over you." (Judges 8, 23). This principle was to play an important part in the controversy between the Pharisees and Jesus Christ.

A hereditary aristocracy of priests, a clan of priests, arose, as among other Oriental peoples. The Levites were a caste corresponding to the Amon priests in Thebes, the Chaldeans in Babylon and the Persian Magi. Among the Jews, however, another, unofficial line of religious tradition developed, of personal, individually inspired and authorized mediators between God and the people, the prophets who, with ever-increasing power, controlled and matched the power of the hereditary priests. Through the activity of the prophets, the special prerogative of mediation of the priests was eventually abolished and the priests were reduced to mere scholarly superiority, on the strength of a particular knowledge of the Law and a special ability to interpret it. But the prophets decreed that every man was to have a direct and personally independent relation to God and had to answer for his deeds himself and alone.

This whole development made for an essentially individualistic and republican constitution. And, as a matter of fact, the stories in the Bible are full of individual characters, of individual human life. The Bible and the Homeric Epics are the first books where the human being appears in his full stature.

After the Jews had settled in the Holy Land, they set up an independent state of their own, just as the other neighboring peoples. In this period of the independent Jewish states, the tribal particularity prevailed. The Everlasting was a tribal God among other tribal gods, and his insistence on his commands, even on his moral commands, and his attitude of spirituality, were mainly intended to preserve the physical body, the breed and the purity of Israel.

Yet the Jewish states were small and powerless. They never achieved world domination. The Jews have always been a numerically small people. They could never have maintained their tiny homeland in the face of the mighty kingdoms that overran it. Their territorial destruction would have been inevitable, even if their religion had not, from the very outset, had so spiritual a basis and had been so inimical to the power of the state. The political failure seems to have been conceived as an integral part of the Jewish destiny. In Deuteronomy 7, 7-8, it is said: "The Lord did not set his love upon you nor choose you, because ye were more in number than any people; for ye were the fewest of all people: But because the Lord loved you." And in Hosea 1, 7: "But I will have mercy upon the house of Judah, and will save them by the Lord their God, and will not save them by bow, nor by sword, nor by battle . . ."

By virtue of that spiritual basis and of that religious constitution, however, the Jews raised themselves, for all their weakness, above the powers by which they were subdued. And the ominous date of 586 B.C., the conquest of Jerusalem by the Babylonians, was in fact the historical birthday of true Judaism. The Babylonian destruction of the Jewish kingdom brought about an extraordinary thing: a people not only outlived the destruction of its state, but, during an exile of fifty years, built up its essential being on a higher level and began its real life. In the Palestinian homeland, only the most elect spirits had grasped the purified monotheistic concept of a world-creator who could not be represented in any image. In the exile, the uprooted masses were pervaded by it. The priests became scribes who elaborated the priestly code and prepared the Torah as the constitution of Judaism. The prophetic mediation reached its zenith in Ezekiel and Deutero-Isaiah. The prophets freed religion from the official forms of worship and drove it deeper into the soul of the individual man with his private sense of personal moral responsibility. They brought into the foreground the universal and messianic quality of Jewish religion, which led to the Essenes and to Christianity. So in this period, in the sixth century before Christ, not only true Judaism was founded, but implicit in it, all the elements of what may be called true Christianism.

THE GREEK POLIS

THE GRADUAL EVOLUTION of the human mind, manifesting itself in the religious concepts of the Egyptians, the Babylonians, the Persians and the Jews, must be considered as successive steps in the process of humanization, personalization and spiritualization of the deity, and at the same time, humanization, personalization and temporalization of the human being. The same slow, humanizing process which transformed the god into a more and more spiritual being developed man himself into a more and more temporal, worldly being, increasingly attached to this real and present earth.

As the divine powers became more and more humanized, a closer spiritual contact was established between the deities and the human being, such as the Babylonian interrelation between the cosmic cycle and the functioning of the human body; the Persian cooperation of man in the struggle of the two divine principles, Light and Dark, and the dual character of the mediators, the fravashis, who were represented as angels on the one hand and as human qualities, attributes or thoughts on the other; and finally that most intimate, even passionate relationship between the Jewish God and his people, this perpetual dialogue of love and wrath, of rebellion and devotion. In the course of this development, the God became more and more personal in a human sense, more and more a personal, actual, deliberate ruler and leader of the world. He began to reflect man's growing awareness of himself, and simultaneously, as a ruler and molder of the world, the God began to comprehend and represent the whole of the universe within himself, in his spiritual unity. The spiritual, personal unity of God began to fuse with the universe itself.

But in contrast to this growing spiritual element, the other ele-

ment, the temporal, earthly element in man, in his actual surroundings and among his fellow creatures, the life on earth and in the
present, the Here and Now, began to stand out in bold relief. Man
grew sharply aware of the urge of the flesh, of his emotional and
sensual quality, his quality as a mortal and single and rebellious
human being. Such objectivation and subjectivation progressed at
the same time.

In the sphere of history, the torpid stability of the divine order
was quickened into dynamic motion. In the Persian and Jewish
religious concepts, the perennial cycle of the Babylonian cosmic
processes became one great historical process, a destiny, a moving
life, a sacred history of the world. For the first time a future, a
common future of mankind, began to play an important part in
human imagination. Especially in the Jewish biblical concept of
the destiny of man, a projection of the past into the future took
place. According to this concept, man was driven from paradise,
from his golden age of natural innocence and peace, from a life in
harmony with the universe and with all creatures, as a consequence
of his curiosity, his impertinence, his individual detachment from
the eternal world order. And he is bent upon recovering this blessed
condition through deliberate, laborious striving for all the things
he has lost by his self-isolation. As a matter of fact, the biblical story
of the fall and the redemption of man gives the first, still purely
religious vision of the true history of man. There is a parallel in
the Greek legend of the Titans struggling with the gods, and of
Prometheus who was punished for having stolen the divine creative fire. All these legends betray the growing consciousness of
human existence as such.

In the sphere of humanity, of man's relation to his community,
a moral order among human beings, an order concerning the behavior of men toward one another, became apparent, and the concept of humanity and of the human individual emerged. To sum
up: spiritualization of the deity and temporalization of man was
developed and felt.

The social structure of the ancient Oriental peoples was still what we would call a *tribe*. A tribe is a social community which is founded entirely on a specific religion of its own and is held together actually by nothing but its religion. The whole life principle, the whole substance of such a community, is expressed by its religion and all human relations and institutions exist only in cultic forms and concepts. Of course, there are beginnings of a social differentiation and social administration, of a consciously organized community, a state. And as the social structure of the tribe is only the reflection of its religious constitution, it shows the same duality as religion itself. The bond between the members of the community and their sacred ruler and his hierarchies is pre-eminently a physical, emotional, ancestral bond, but at the same time a bond that is mentally conceived and destined to serve the purpose of organization. But the earthly home and the land, the state, individual power and possession, human intercourse—all this has its ultimate meaning only with reference to that divine essence of the species; it is in some way related to the essence of the species; it exists only as derived from and authorized by that divine essence. Therefore, to the Oriental peoples, the earthly dwelling-place per se had as yet no vital significance. It was important only in that it was the residence of a deity. This is indicated by the names. Babylon means Bab-ilu, the gate of god. The original name of Nineveh, the Assyrian city, was Nina from Innina, the ancient name of the goddess Ishtar. The Assyrian city, Assur, bore the very name of the tribal god of the Assyrians. Many Egyptian cities also were called after the gods who resided there.

The social system of these peoples reflected this condition. In its earthly function, the essence of the species is concentrated in a sacred head of the community which is the source of all power and ownership. An integral autocracy of a sacred king established itself with all the pomp and show of a great court, an elaborate hierarchy and officialdom, which, as a matter of fact, comprised the overwhelming majority of the free population. Law was sacred law, ordained and observed in all respects with regard to the cult of the deities. Private possession, which had developed from rewards for administrative and military services, consisted mainly of land, with its resources and duties in kind, and slave labor. Some trade had already developed, but since communication was slow, it could not assume large proportions, and—this is of paramount importance —trade did not give a man high standing! The economy of all these countries was based on agriculture.

This general condition of the ancient Oriental peoples must be borne in mind for a thorough understanding of the fundamental change that occurred when leadership in human evolution passed to the Mediterranean and over to Europe.

The Greek and Roman peoples were in close and even in blood relation to the Oriental peoples, and their initial position in a primeval age was much the same as that of the Oriental peoples. In their origins we find the same features as in primitive society, the same totemistic and animistic beginnings, remnants of which extend even to their late periods. In growing up they went through the same phases of development. But they went through these phases much more quickly, as though the journey lay along a road already opened and paved. And they did not stop at these phases; they went further with undiminished forces. The known histories of Egypt and Babylon cover about two and a half millennia. Greek history, which includes far more fundamental and far-reaching events, indeed the most crucial turn in the story of mankind, comprises less than one millennium.

Between the Oriental peoples and the Greeks there is a people that represents in some respects an intermediary link: the *Phoenicians*. They were a Semitic tribe that belonged, with the Israelites, the Arabs, the Amorites, Edomites, Moabites, Arameans and others, to the western branch of the Semites. The eastern branch consisted mainly of the Babylonians and the Assyrians. Among the western Semites, there was distinct opposition between two kinds, two types of deities: the true gods, and the local gods. The true gods were the tribal gods, the god-leaders called "malk". The Israelites used Molekh or Moloch as a derogatory perversion of the Phoenician "malk". These gods were not attached to any particular earthly place, but represented the essence of the tribe, working within it and embodying its intentions. The most eminent example is the Jewish God who developed into something new, something more advanced and sublime. The other type of deities, the local gods, were the survivals of the primeval demons, the "baals", i.e. "lords", which were embodied in sacred places and images. The "malks" were related to the tribe. The "baals" were elemental phenomena in a certain place or in a force of nature.

Almost everywhere the primeval demons survived for a long time under the dominance of the actual gods, and there were different kinds of relations between the gods and the demons. In Egypt, the demons themselves were raised to cosmic deities. In Persia, the demons were degraded to a lower group of demi-gods, attendants of the divine principles. The Jewish God, finally, aimed at the complete annihilation of the local demons, the "baals", and the activity of the priests and prophets at last succeeded in extinguishing their cults among the people. The "baals" are the idols of the Bible, and the most violent fury of God and his true adherents was directed against them.

In Phoenicia a fusion between the tribal gods and the local demons took place. The god of Tyre was Melquart, which means "leader of the city", and thus the earthly place, the dwelling-place, assumed a new significance. This phenomenon foreshadows the Greek development where the same thing happened in a more pronounced manner.

There are still other features pointing to the Greeks. The Phoenicians had already engaged in sea trade on a large scale. From about the eleventh century B.C., they dominated the commerce of the whole Mediterranean and of the caravan roads and rivers of Mesopotamia. They dealt in timber (oak and cedar from their extensive forests around Gebal, Byblos, and on the Lebanon), in wine, fruits, leather, slaves and even manufactured goods of their own, purple, perfumes, glassware, jewels and textiles. Prior to them, there had been other peoples who dominated the seas and engaged in maritime trade, the Pelasgians, the original inhabitants of Greece, from the fourteenth to the thirteenth century B.C., the Rhodesians (Achaeans) from the twelfth to the eleventh century B.C. and above all the Cretans (Minoans) from 2000 to about 1250 B.C. But, as far

as we know, it was first among the Phoenicians that people became rich and politically powerful through trade, a fact which had
an important bearing on their social structure.

It is the Phoenicians who demonstrate the first rough shaping
of the classic city-state, the polis. We do not know very much about
their social conditions, but we do know that they were organized
in many small independent city-states that occasionally united
against aggressors under the leadership of the most outstanding
among them, and this leadership often extended into a lasting
hegemony. These city-states were ruled by sacred kings, but what
made them into real city-states was the new factor that the rich
merchant families became a mighty aristocracy which gradually
limited the power of the kings, and for the first time formed an
assembly of aldermen who won an authority nearly equal to that
of the king. In Tyre they gained the right to pass resolutions in the
absence of the king. In Sidon they even enforced decisions against
his will. In a later period, the regime of the king of Tyre was transformed into a republican government of two judges, suffetes, who
were elected from the preeminent families.

The cities of the great Oriental kingdoms were not as yet real
cities. They were mere residences of gods and sacred kings, and
the intercourse of people was concerned mainly with the cult and
court service to which all occupations referred in some way. Accordingly, the inhabitants of these large settlements were not at
all what we call citizens. What constitutes a city and citizens is
some sort of free relationship between equal, fairly independent
people. And the first development of such a relationship was promoted by the predominance of trade and hence the formation of
an oligarchic rule.

The Phoenicians spread their colonies around the Mediterranean;
the most important of these was Carthage, "New City", a Tyrian
colony in North Africa in the region of the Tunis of today. This
city-state, which very soon became an oligarchic republic ruled by
two judges, was a great port and trading center from the eighth to
the second century B.C. It waged wars of conquest in Africa, Sicily
and Sardinia, and gained control of the Western Mediterranean,

until it was destroyed by the Romans in 146 B.C. It was of those powers that reach a certain transitory importance as antagonists of the
protagonists of human history—powers that seem predestined to
serve only as inciting rivals in the struggle for epochal predominance.

The civilization of the Phoenicians did not progress beyond the
very beginnings of the city-state. The perfection of the sacred city-
state, the polis, was achieved by the two great peoples of the classic
world, the Greeks and the Romans. And this perfection of the
polis means a great deal more; first of all it means the establishment of an actual city, and then that of a real state. It means the
initiation of democracy, the first form of self-government of a free
people aware of itself. It leads to the self-knowledge of the human
being; this implies the concept of the human individual and, along
with it, of a unified humanity.

With the transition from Asia to Europe, human history, in the
true meaning of the word, had begun, history, that is to say, the
evolution, the moving growth of human existence as a whole. And
indeed the history of the two classic peoples, the Greeks and the
Romans, shows us history in a classical sense, the archetype of
human history. These histories, starting from tribal origins and
ending in full-fledged world empires, are an abstract of human
evolution as a whole.

But not only this. In many other respects Greek and Roman history is classical, that means it is a standard for us. Our language,
grammar and logic, the whole stock of terms, the whole inventory
of our political structures, indeed the whole organization of our
constitutions and administrations, is derived from a Greek and
Roman pattern. To be sure, our institutions, our ways of living and
thinking have changed utterly since antiquity, and one must be
wary of a popular trend in the modern writing of history that tends
to equalize and level all epochs, all the various ages and stages of
history, by teaching that human nature has always been the same.
Such views, of course, have a great appeal, as they make things easy
to grasp. History becomes comfortably accessible to anyone when

everything in olden times can be compared to something very usual
and familiar to us today. Yet, unfortunately, this is not true, it is
misleading and prevents a real understanding of history, for history
means fundamental change.

Greek and Roman life centers in the sacred city-state, the *polis*.
A polis is, first of all, a fully developed city, a community of people,
a place solidly established on earth, where people live together and
where they deal with one another on an equal footing, where they
consult in common upon affairs of common interest, and compete
and trade freely with one another for power and wealth. A polis,
however, is not a mere city, not what we call a city, an incorporated
part of a larger and superior unit, a subordinate part of a state or
nation. A polis is not only a city but at the same time a comprehensive political and religious unit; it implies religious and political
sovereignty. This fact is indicated by the very words "politics" and
"policy", deriving from polis. The polis had its specific cult, its specific deity, that is, the founder of the place or the ancestor of the
founding dynasty or nobility. And no matter how far the political
power of the city extends, and should it include the whole contemporary world, it still remains a city, and its free subjects—in so far
as they enjoy full rights—are citizens in the strict and literal sense
of the word, members of the city.

The city is the standard unit, and city life is the standard way
of living. Life as a citizen, as a "cives", is identical with civilization. City life is essential for full political rights, for equal membership in the community and for any social or political position.
Every man is a citizen only in so far as he is actually present in the
city and takes an active part in its various functions and activities,
its cultic ceremonies and feasts, deliberations, decisions, legislation
and military service. Until very late, in the last stages of the Roman
Empire, there is no form of life such as we call private life. Within
the polis, a private life, as the clearly negative sense of the Latin
word "privatus" indicates, is a deprived existence, an existence
divested of all rights and privileges of the community. The Greek
word for private is even stronger in its negative character: it is
"idiotes", meaning a man who is concerned wholly with himself

and, accordingly, a base man, unskilled and uneducated, an utter ignoramus. One may gather the tenor of this word "idiotes", from the meaning in our word idiot, which derives from it. A man who retired from public life, who lacked interest in public affairs, such a man became utterly impossible, indeed inconceivable. His position was that of an exile in our times, that of a person without citizenship, and he was as outlawed as an exile.

Thus democracy in the polis has an utterly different character from that of modern democracy, the democracy of the British and the American commonwealths. Democracy in the polis is essentially active democracy, while modern democracy is mainly defensive democracy. Ancient democracy still implies the primeval belonging to the bulk of a pre-individual community that is just in the state of splitting up from a whole into its integral parts, the individuals. Modern democracy signifies protection of primary and private individuals from the demands of an increasingly collective order. It means protection of the individual and his economic activities from the state. Democracy in the polis signifies the privilege of a common building-up of the state, a common acting on behalf of the state, the privilege of being a vital part of the state. It is not the privilege of being as free as possible from interference of the state. It is the privilege of political duty rather than of political right.

Thus, from the tribe whence it sprang, the polis preserved the quality of a sacred entity that dominates all the members of the community. Like the tribe, the polis represents a species prevailing over its specimens. A fundamental change, however, took place and developed more and more in the course of Greek and Roman history. In the tribe, the core of the species was still comprehended, or, as it were, confined, in the god, his temple and his image, or in the sacred king, his residence and his hierarchy. In the polis, it rooted itself deeply and definitely in an earthly dwelling-place proper, and expanded and unfolded into a growing community of gradually developing individuals.

The Greeks as well as the Romans started from a strictly tribal condition. In their cults there are distinct traces of a totemistic and animistic background. From the so-called Mycenaean period, about 1600 to 1200 B.C., a fragment of a wall painting showing demons with donkey heads has been preserved. Similar images have been identified on many amulets. Cow idols of clay have been excavated in Mycenae. And in the Homeric epics the goddess Hera is often called "cow-eyed" (boopis), an epithet which is a residue of the ancient cult of the cow. In like manner, the goddess Athene is called "owl-eyed", and the owl has remained her symbol. In Arcadia, Zeus retained the name of "Wolf-Zeus". There are also the various hybrid forms, half animal, half human, in Greek sagas and on Greek art monuments, the many metamorphoses of Greek gods into animals, all betraying totemism. In Rome, the legend of Romulus and Remus, who were supposed to have been suckled by a she-wolf, informs us of an ancient worship of the wolf.

The root of the Greek word for temple, "naos" or "neos", probably goes back to the significance of the trunk of a tree, which indicates that the first temple was a hollow tree. As evidence shows, in Greece the tree was not the god, but the dwelling-place of the god. Yet, although afterwards the most magnificent temples were erected wherever Greeks settled, it is very significant that for the Greeks the temple is the shelter of the god and of his cult rather than his actual dwelling-place. It was always the sacred place itself, the specific spot on earth, that was regarded as the favorite residence of the god. When the temple was destroyed, the place as such was not profaned, a new temple had to be built on exactly the same spot. The earthly place had been endowed with a holiness that had often existed in pre-Greek and pre-Roman times, and persisted in the face of later conquests. And this eventually means the sanctification of the city as such, as it actually took place in the deification of Rome.

The tribal background of the Greeks and the Romans was preserved throughout their history in that their religion exerted a lasting power over the whole life of these peoples. Of course, religion underwent fundamental changes in the course of their history, but up to the very last days of the Roman Empire it made itself felt in all happenings as a vital and powerful factor of an importance and gravity that modern men are no longer able to imagine.

When we think of *Greek religion* it is mainly the Homeric conception of the Olympic gods that we have in mind. Yet this was not the only form of Greek religion. There are three branches, three spheres and currents of Greek religion, persisting side by side, conflicting with one another, interweaving and influencing one another.

The Homeric or Olympic religion is the most genuine Greek religion. It is the sublimation of ancient cults originating in the Greek mainland, in Thessaly, in the region of Mount Olympus, that snowy, inaccessible summit which was raised into a heavenly sphere where the gods live. With the migration of the Thessalian tribes to the Aegean Islands and the shores of Asia Minor, a move to which the struggle for Troy in the "Iliad" refers, these cults and their myths were transformed by Homer and the tradition of minstrels into what we know as the Olympic religion, and what was accepted as the sublime, common worship of all the Greek peoples at the beginning of their historic age, in about 700 B.C. The lively imagination of the Greeks worked for centuries on the characters of these Olympic gods, and enriched and enlivened them with innumerable myths. The various tribes and regions and cities fused their old local deities with Olympic gods, they transformed one into another and in this way localized the sublime gods and connected them with their respective homelands. Thus Pallas Athene, sprung from the head of Zeus, became the virgin goddess of Athens. The Olympic religion is an essentially aristocratic religion, originating in the times of primeval kingdoms and fostered by the early princes. It represents the more stable and conservative element in the Hellenic world.

There is another current of Greek religion, a darker and more emotional one that had a greater appeal for the people. This is the religion of the mysteries which originally came from Phrygia in Asia Minor and the wild regions of the Black Sea and the Propontis. This religion consists in the cults of chthonic deities, that is to say, deities of the depths of the earth and the sea and of the powers of vegetation and regeneration, the cults of Demeter, Hephaistus, Dionysus, all of whom in earlier times did not belong to the heavenly world of Olympus, but joined it late and with inferior ranking.

The most widespread of these cults was the Eleusinian worship of Demeter, Ge-meter, the great mother of the earth, and her daughter Cora (Kore) or Persephone, who was said to have been abducted by Hades, the great demon of the Nether World, as she was picking flowers with her playmates.

A counterpart to the Eleusinian cult of mother and daughter was the cult of father and son in the mysteries of the island of Samothrace, incorporated by the Cabiri, demons of the sea, whose worship in some places was connected with the cult of Hephaistus, god of the volcanic fire and the forge.

Another counterpart was the Orphic cult founded by the mythical Thracian minstrel Orpheus, who tried to recover his wife, the nymph Euridice, from Hades, through the power of his singing. Historically, this cult was transmitted by a sect of rhapsodists and thinkers who called themselves Orphics, and disseminated over the Greek mainland at a relatively late period. They worshipped Dionysus (Dios Nysos), son of Zeus, also called Jakchos, Bakchos (Bacchus), which in the Thracian language means the clamorous, a god of vegetation, especially of the culture of vines and the vintage.

While the worship of the Olympic gods was an open and official cult performed in the old ceremonial of offering and imploring, the worship of the chthonic gods was a wild and dramatic performance in which the worshippers themselves took an active part. Magical acts of initiation and participation with the deity, a residue from primitive rituals, eventually developed into a new worldly celebration of human destiny. The rituals were called mysteries— the word is derived from "myein", to close, especially to close the eyes—which indicated that the service was secret, an inmost merging, a union with the deity. It took place at night and was accessible only to the initiate. This may be partially due to the fact that these were originally cults of subdued peoples who had to meet in the dark and with extreme caution.

But the mysteries have one astonishingly new aspect (probably due to the same cause) that is absolutely unique among the religious movements before Christianity: they were accessible to any human being regardless of rank and breed and social standing; they were accessible even to slaves. In the mysteries, all human beings were equal. The only limitation was that the initiate must be free from blood-guilt.

The service of the mysteries began with an initiation and culminated in ecstasy, in rapture and madness, in a "sacred marriage" with the deity from which the human being was supposed to emerge reborn like the god himself, like Persephone who emerged from the dark, like Dionysus Zagreus, who was said to have been lacerated by the Titans and revived by Zeus. The climax of the Eleusinian initiation was the touching of an image of the maternal womb. At the Samothracian initiation it was the touching of a phallic image. And all of this meant rebirth and potential immortality.

The origins of the mysteries go back to the pre-religious era of participation, when the boundaries between life and death were not as yet fixed and the concept of mortality was still in the developmental stage. But the mysteries attain to a form of religious celebration that far surpasses the level of stable and conservative Olympic religion. They are a dynamic dramatization of the religious procedure. A new form of identification of man with the deity is in the making, not a primeval, confused, perpetual participation, but a single fusion with the deity by the transforming purification of an existence that is clearly felt to be human and mortal. The mysteries presuppose the knowledge and the experience of mortality as the normal destiny of mankind. The Greek dead were received in Hades, a joyless shadowy land comparable to the "land without return" of the Babylonians and the "scheol" of the Jews. Immortality, as it is achieved in the mysteries, is a privilege, is something to be sought after, to be gained by merit, by special deeds and ways of life. The dying and reborn god carries the initiated and purified human being with him into rebirth and rejuvenation. Accordingly, the former deities of vegetation and regeneration gradually became gods of the soul, saviors of the soul ("soters"). And it was these cults that fomented the Greek speculation on immortality of the soul, on resurrection and metempsychosis, on a life after death, be it in Hades, the world of shadows, or in Elysium, the revival of a Golden Age indifferent to Olympic religion.

Later, when the mysteries were officially recognized, they developed into great popular feasts which were celebrated by sacred banquets, rural processions, torch dances where ecstatic women took the part of enthusiastic maenads ("maenad" has the same root as "mania"), the raging female companions of Dionysus. The Greek word "ecstasis" means "to be beside oneself"; "enthusiasmos" means "to be in God". One of these maenads, the wife of the head-priest, had to consummate the marriage with a human substitute of the god.

From these presentations of divine and human destinies, from the mockeries and burlesques that accompanied the pageants of Dionysus, the god of the vintage who was thronged about by a crowd of satyrs, Pans and nymphs, sprang the drama, tragedy, and comedy, "kom-odia", pageant-song. Drama means acting, in the double meaning of the English word: to carry out a deed and to play a part. In the mysteries, there was a blending of both. The mysteries constituted a mystical drama, and the drama, in turn, was at first a true mystery in which the audience, represented by the chorus, participated. The audience lived the drama and through it underwent an inner transformation.

The drama originated in a lyrical chorus, the dithyramb, that described the sufferings of the dying and resurrected god and the sympathetic suffering of man. In this, the chorus came to regard itself as the retinue of Dionysus and thus fell into the role of satyrs, the natural following of the god. The leader of the chorus related the events and gradually embodied the suffering god and thus represented the theme on which the participating audience, the chorus, offered its comments. This choral leader was the first actor who, in the course of time, with the help of various masks, indicated the plot. Later the circle of themes widened to include the destinies of other suffering heroes. And so the celebration of the suffering god or demi-god gradually turned into a celebration of suffering man overcome by a tragic fate dealt out by the gods. It grew into a presentation of human suffering inherent in the lot of mortals, in earthly limitations and the weakness of man.

Through the form introduced by the tragedy, the old myths became at once human and spiritual. The main emphasis shifts from a mere presentation of events to psychic premises, to an analysis of motives. And thereby the basic cause of human suffering is exposed: the helplessness of even a noble individual to avoid becoming guilty when the gods, that represent the essence of the tribe, will it. This inescapable suffering makes the Greeks aware of their individuality, for this suffering is nothing but the struggle of incipient freedom of will with the sacred powers—above and before the individual—who seek to impose limitations. The recurring theme of the great Greek tragedians, Aeschylus, Sophocles, Euripides, is ancestral sin, willed by the gods and visited upon the children, the lasting curse, which, through the atavistic urge to blood-vengeance, drives the descendants deeper and deeper into blood-guilt. The compulsion to blood-vengeance, the "ius talionis", becomes synonymous with destiny. Man is caught between the inescapable tribal duties and the dawning awareness of free, individual morality. And with this the great theme of Greek man is given; it was carried further by Greek philosophy—the struggle for assertion of human individuality, the justification of the human being, unique and complex, before the eternal and changeless order of the gods. The disentanglement and, at the same time, expiation in Greek tragedy was called katharsis. This again means purification.

From the Orphics and their speculations, still another, indeed a revolutionizing movement evolved, the third Greek religion, the pantheistic search for a metaphysically divine, creative substance of the universe. This means an objectivation of the universe, not in the form of a personal universal god, as in Judaism, but as a spiritual entity. And this religious speculation developed into the

great Greek philosophy, the foundation of all philosophic speculation, now and hereafter, and the first emancipation of the human
mind from the overwhelming power of religion itself. All these
elements later passed over into Christianity.

Greek religion, as a whole, can only be understood from the
background of the Oriental religions. But it is a tremendous advance toward humanization and temporalization. The Olympic
Pantheon may remind us of the Babylonian Pantheon with its
divine personifications of cosmic forces headed by a heavenly king.
But what an immeasurable difference! The Greek Pantheon is no
longer a system, it is a world like ours. The hieratical inflexibility
of the Oriental gods has melted away; all has become human,
flexible and diversified. These gods manifest themselves to men
not only in human shape, but as human beings, with characteristic
feelings, thoughts, plans and ways, with complex individual lives
adorned by colorful and even libertine adventures. There is continuous intercourse with the world of man, through easy descend-
ing and ascending, through metamorphoses and epiphanies. They
all behave like a big family, marrying and begetting youthful
beings, fighting and annoying one another with jealousies and
intrigues. Nothing human, except mortality itself, is alien to them.
This is perfect anthropomorphism.

In the opposition of the Olympic cult to the mysteries, we are
struck by the same fundamental antagonism between the light and
the dark powers, between heaven and earth, that we found in
the Babylonian trinity and more distinctly in the Persian religion.
With the Greeks, this is no longer an opposition of mere elemental
powers, or even of moral tendencies, but an expression of the difference between aristocratic and popular, or between the two
layers within the human soul, the sublime and the instinctive.

Even in the Persian religion, cosmic stability breaks into dynamic movement, there is a struggle between the light and the
dark, which, at the end of time, results in the triumph of the light
and, for the righteous, in an eternal life of bliss. The cooperation
of the human being, however, remained rather vague and lacked

that dramatic urge to salvation that was implied in the Greek mysteries. It also lacked the extension of the human partnership beyond tribal limits.

And finally Greek religion itself underwent a process of fundamental evolution and transformation, denoting a profound mental development of the Greek people and of the human being as such. From the stable world of the Olympic Pantheon which prevailed in the early periods, it moved on to the prevalence of the dynamic, popular mysteries until, at last, under the broadening influence of the metaphysical schools, enlightened speculation had led people to the worship of one all-pervading spiritual divinity, to the very borders of Christianity.

The first milestone in this imposing process was set when the Eleusinian Mysteries became an official cult of Athens, and when in Delphi the worship of the Olympic Apollo fused with the cult of Dionysus. The second, when in Socrates and Plato all the known religious currents merged in the birth of rational thought and the Pantheon of gods was changed into a Pantheon of divine ideas.

Changes in religion and philosophy were only one aspect of the general evolution toward the forming of the human mind and the human individual. Another was the *social development,* the unfolding of the polis itself. The social condition of the Greek peoples as it is described in the Homeric epics (that reflect the so-called Minoan and Mycenaean age) was probably much the same when, in about 700 B.C., the Greeks settled on their peninsula, as well as on the Aegean Islands and along the shore of Asia Minor, as a fairly homogeneous people, united by a common language and tradition. This stage, similar to that of the Phoenicians, had left behind the so-called "primitive communism" without preponderance of anyone in the tribe. Sacred kings had arisen, and even more than that, a sacred aristocracy of privileged families that apparently had won authority in the course of campaigns and had succeeded in holding larger shares of the spoil and the land than the others. They already formed a special council of nobles or elders, a "gerousia", which was distinguished from the general

assembly of the common warriors, and had reached such power as
to limit that of the king. As a matter of fact, from the very beginning
the king appears only first among equals; this is indicated by the
significance of the Greek term for king, "basileus", which originally means prince, man of noble descent. The term may also be
used in the comparative and superlative, "basileuteros", "basileu-
tatos", the nobler, the noblest. In Athens, the king was very soon
limited to priestly functions when another chief, the chief of warfare, the "polemarchos", was installed, and shortly afterwards he
was altogether replaced by a supreme official, the "archon".

Thus, in the very beginning, the Greeks slurred over the stage
of Oriental sacred despotism. Correspondingly, the cities in which
they had gathered for protection, as a result of a process called
"synoikismos" (a concentrating of smaller settlements), were no
longer mere temples and fortresses as the Oriental god-residences
had been. Just as there had been consultation from the beginning,
there was also a special site for assembling and deliberating, a site
below the temple and the palace, the "agora", assembly-place.
When trade began to play an important role in certain cities, a
market-place was detached from the place of assembly. Thus, from
the first, these were real cities, and not the temple and the palace,
but the "agora" was the center of the community where people met
and chatted all day, as they still do in the open squares of Italy and
Spain.

The original organization of the people was plainly tribal. It
was an organization founded on blood-brotherhood which was
represented by the particular gods of the community. What we
call the Greek people was a group of tribes. The tribe was divided
into four clans ("phylai"), each clan into fraternities ("phratriai"),
and each fraternity into families in the broader sense of the word.
Around this nucleus of the people, external clans were gathered
consisting of the descendants of former populations that had been
conquered and subdued. Since these people on the Greek mainland
were of no different stock from that of the ruling clans, they were
often considered as members of the community, though not as
citizens with full rights and privileges. They were joined by mem-

bers of the ruling clans who had been deprived of their land in consequence of some misfortune.

We are told that the increase in population resulted in an unequal distribution of the land and the subdivision of many farms. Usually a father's property was divided among his sons. Hence, if there were several sons, the share of each was smaller than the paternal property. In antiquity, land under cultivation deteriorated rapidly, because whatever was removed from the soil was not restored. Without proper fertilization the land grew exhausted, and the fields were often allowed to lie fallow every other year. Thus only half of the land was cultivated each year. In Greece, by the seventh century B.C., those who depended on small farms could ordinarily scarcely get through the year on the year's crop. A bad season meant ruin and despair. The time had passed when the rich landowner would give his own surplus to his neighbors in need. The rich were exporting their surplus, or at any rate marketing it. Consequently the rich now put a charge on such loans. The poor man's farm was his security and, beyond this, his person and his family. In this way small landowners dropped to the ranks of the alien population and lost their full citizenship. They became either tenants, or hired laborers and servants, artisans ("demiourgoi", workers of the people), or even serfs, losing their freedom altogether and belonging to the lowest stratum of the population, the slaves.

For the setting up of the army, this tribal organization provided three classes according to nobility and wealth, that is, the means for a more or less costly equipment: the horsemen ("hippeis") consisted of the clan members; the heavy-armed footsoldiers ("hoplites") comprised the small farmers and freemen; the light-armed auxiliaries ("thetes") were made up of hired workers and artisans. From this, originally military, classification all later constitution of the Greek cities derived.

In the solidly settled, unfolding polis, the old tribal organization along the lines of descent and sacred tradition became more and more obsolete, and a classification according to a present and more and more individual evaluation of people became effective. In the development of the Athenian constitution, there is a distinct trend from the prevalence of clan-brotherhood and ancestral prestige toward the importance of locality and individuality, a shifting from the authority of the past to the power of the present.

The starting point was the development of a new wealth. In the early period, the nobles were also the rich, since wealth consisted mainly of landed property. But as a result of overpopulation and displacement of the small farmers, the great movement of colonization sprang into being and lasted to the middle of the sixth century. New emporia were spreading over the shores and islands of the Mediterranean. The displaced people were looking for other means to prosperity. Maritime trade began to flourish as well as the making of pottery, arms, metalware and other manufactured goods that were exchanged for a considerable import of raw materials and Oriental products.

The following constitutional reforms reflect the growing importance of movable, individual wealth, commercial and financial wealth, and eventually of personality regardless of wealth. All these transitions are steps in the development of individuality. The classification of Solon in 594, which is a military classification and simultaneously a corresponding distribution of political rights, is still based on agricultural wealth, no longer, however, on the stable amount of owned acres, but on the income in produce of grain, measured in "medimnai", a dry measure of corn. The reform of Cleisthenes in 508 replaced this valuation in kind by a taxation in money which detached political power and political influence completely from landed property, the original mark of nobility, and made it available to rich traders and manufacturers. Moreover, in order to crush the power of the nobles, Cleisthenes abolished the ancient tribal clans altogether and divided the people into local districts named for sacred heroes of the country.

Solon enacted the famous abolishment of debts, the "seisachtheia" (throwing off of burdens), which freed the poor farmers from their burden. An important step toward democracy was the admission to citizenship of the formerly barred class of poor freemen, granting them the right to vote in the general assembly and to participate in the election of officials and in jurisdiction. Citizenship, though, had still other gradations, and only citizens of the higher classes were eligible to office. Cleisthenes even extended citizenship to foreigners who had resided in the city for a prescribed time. He created ostracism, an institution that favored demagogy by enabling people to vote ten years' expulsion for any official considered detrimental or disturbing to the community. (The term ostracism derives from the "ostraka", the sherd of clay on which the name of the condemned statesman had to be scratched.)

Eventually, under the leadership of Pericles in 457, integral democracy, the first true democracy in history, was instituted by extending full citizenship and full and equal rights to all free people in the polis. It was a democracy so utter and so perfect as has hardly ever been attained again—except for the institution of slavery, the abolition of which was never even attempted in antiquity.

Athenian democracy is by no means comparable to the general consultation of clan members in a primitive age. For with primitive humanity it was not the actual, present people who ruled, not an assembly of self-determined individual citizens of the community, it was the clan or the tribe itself that ruled its members through its innumerable ancestral rites and sacred regulations. Nor is Athenian democracy comparable to modern democracy, not only because of its active character, but also because the relatively small size of the community did not as yet necessitate any system of representation. It allowed a thorough, most direct democracy, an immediate popular control of events. The totality of the free citizens formed the basic assembly which met four times a month and made all decisions. Officials were elected by lot for one year only. They were responsible to the assembly at the end of their term, and they could be dismissed at any moment. All jurisdiction devolved upon a jury. Administration was divided into different departments controlling one another, and the competence of the officials in general was limited. Eventually, the power of the traditional upper council, to which all former officials belonged, was abolished on behalf of the authority of the people itself.

Athenian democracy marked a victory of the local community over the tribal blood-brotherhood, of the power of the present over the forces of the past, of the autonomous personality over the bonds of heredity. It meant an immense widening of the human horizon, an opening of the human world at large. It meant an inciting and exciting competition of all human forces and faculties, but also of boundless passions and ambitions. It created the "agon", the sacred contest between free and beautiful bodies and minds, a contest of which the modern, record-hunting sports, the so-called "Olympic Games" of our days, are but a mean caricature. It meant an enfranchised view of the lithe, living body, a free art released from hieratical attitudes yet with newly discovered nature under the command of a divine, spiritual harmony. It meant the liberation of human speculation on the nature of the universe, on the welfare of the human soul and on the best political order. Here human reflection was born, as the symbolic inscription on the temple of Delphi shows: "gnothi seauton", know thyself.

It meant a new concept of the supreme value, the supreme quality of man, "arete", a term which is very badly and inadequately rendered by our term virtue. This supreme quality of man was first conceived as a traditional, god-given, tribal efficiency, resembling the standard value of all early cultures. It gradually changed its meaning into excellence of the moral, mental and physical character, an excellence which may be acquired by individual effort. The gods were thoroughly humanized; human life aimed at a divine harmony of all forces and qualities; the ideal was a combination, a union of goodness and beauty, it was beauty-goodness, "kalokagathia", and wisdom, too, was implied in it. This harmony of qualities in itself means the prevalence of the aesthetic value: It is very significant that to the Greeks the same term, "kosmos", meant simultaneously universe, order, harmony, embellishment, adornment. The words cosmic and cosmetic both come from the same root.

The ideal Greek was the all-around man, a type like Alcibiades whom the people loved more than any other: beautiful and courageous, noble and charming, wanton and capricious, mocking and brilliant, the dandy, the soldier, the statesman and the philosopher in one; a man who excelled in great battles, who would shock and intrigue public opinion by his innumerable love-affairs, who would carry his wife home in his arms from the agora, where she wanted to divorce him, and who could sit down with his friend and master, Socrates, for an eager discussion of life's ultimate problems. Without democracy, there would have been no such sublime controversies as those between the various philosophical schools, no Socratic dialogues and symposia. Neither would there have been such unscrupulous rhetoric demagogues, no word-juggling such as the Sophists initiated, no such unrestricted struggle for political power as appeared in Greek history for the first time.

To summarize: ancient democracy was the awakening of the human individual from the domination of the species, while modern democracy is the emerging of the collective from emancipated individuals. The trends of both are diametrically opposed. And this is no contradiction to the statement that ancient democracy is active, not defensive democracy. As ancient democracy was meant as an active participation of all citizens in the government, it unleashed all ambition and lust for power and drove it into the political field. Modern democracy means the warding-off of state interference from the unlimited development of economic enterprise, a development that finally leads to collectivism.

The struggle for political power among the Greeks constantly endangered and finally destroyed democracy. It even prevented the establishment of any lasting empire. For this struggle for power raged not only within the city-state, but also between the many Greek city-states. A number of them were always competing for domination, hegemony, leadership over the vaguely conceived but never realized Greek community.

Besides Athens, there were Sparta, Thebes, Corinth and others, all controlling leagues of adherent cities, city-states, colonies and entire regions. There was constant bargaining and breaking-up of alliances and federations among them. There was constant defaulting in keeping commitments, there were constant offences and betrayals, calls for aid and new entanglements. And the rivalries of individuals within the cities mingled with their external struggles, complicated them. Any ambitious politician who was ostracized from home presently joined the adversary of his city, to gain power from the outside.

One great antagonism dominated all the quarrels throughout Greek history, the antagonism between conservative Sparta—which always retained its ancient oligarchic constitution headed by two kings, as well as its famous military discipline, and which favored conservative regimes everywhere—and progressive Athens which led in democracy and excelled in commercial and maritime power. Only in the glorious defeat of the Persian invasion (490–479 B.C.) were they solidly united. But after this mortal danger was past, the struggle for hegemony never died down among the Greek cities until the deadly crippling of one another in the Peloponnesian Wars (431–404 B.C.), when they did not shrink from appealing to the common Persian enemy for help in their internal quarrels. The Persian Empire was weakened too. It was no longer a real menace to Greek existence. The internal strife of the Greek cities, however, had made it impossible to liberate the Aegean Islands and the Greek cities in Asia Minor from Persian influence and supremacy. The fundamental task of completely crushing this sworn enemy had never been accomplished.

To achieve this, a new power was called upon, the *Macedonians,* a tribe related to the Dorians. Like Sparta, the Macedonians had preserved their primeval, aristocratic kingdom as well as their rustic and military constitution. But, unlike Sparta, they had not yet wasted their strength in hegemonic struggles. Because of their rather primitive condition, the Greeks considered them half barbarian. Yet Philip II (359–336 B.C.), the first prominent king of the ruling dynasty, was thoroughly imbued with Greek culture, with Greek ambitions and aspirations which he made popular among his nobles and his people. In the middle of the fourth

century he occasionally came in conflict with Athenian policy in
neighboring Thrace, and he took the opportunity to meddle in
Greek affairs. In the end, he overran the terrified cities, set up a
new Hellenic League at Corinth under his hegemony and was
waging war with Persia when he was assassinated. And here began
the world empire of his successor, Alexander, the first world
empire in history.

Alexander (born 356, reigned 336–323 B.C.) was the son of the
sober and efficient Philip and the passionate and ambitious Olym-
pias, who was said to have joined the dancing Maenads in the
Dionysian orgies. He liked to derive his descent from Heracles
and Achilles. But it is perhaps more important that he was a disciple of Aristotle.

Alexander, with his well-trained army, swept the whole Orient
to the Indian borders in his fabulous campaign. He crushed the
Persians forever, conquered Phoenicia, Palestine and Egypt where
he founded Alexandria, the Hellenistic metropolis. But this first
world empire did not last. Alexander did not live long enough to
consolidate it. He died in Babylon at the age of thirty-three, immediately after the superficial completion of his conquest. Since he
opened the Orient for Hellenic civilization and since, from then
on, Hellenic thought and Hellenic customs poured confusedly
into the conquered territory, his conquest may well be called a first
world empire. For the Oriental kingdoms had never achieved an
even external unification of the whole cultural area of their time,
they had never achieved the undisputed rule of one culture dominant over the known world. Alexander inaugurated this, but
neither he nor those who came after him could administer this
rule through a perfected, elaborate political order. It remained
for the Romans to prepare such an order in the course of centuries.

Alexander abandoned his Greek background and complied with
the tribal customs of the populations he had conquered. He indulged in Oriental, deified autocracy, made himself Zeus Amon,
a half Hellenic, half Egyptian deity, and by this, estranged himself
from his Greek followers. Immediately after his death, his empire

collapsed in the strife of his rival diadochs. His greatest political achievement was the setting-up of a model, the prototype of a world empire in itself that became the dream of every conqueror thereafter, not only of insignificant rulers like Pyrrhus of Epirus or Mithridates of Pontus, but also of the great Roman commanders, of Scipio Africanus, Sulla, Pompey, Caesar, Anthony and Augustus. With Alexander's image before their eyes, these Roman conquerors succeeded in building up the true and perfected world empire.

THE EXPANSION OF ROME INTO A
WORLD EMPIRE

THE CITY OF ROME embarked on its career when the great days of Greece had already passed, and the lateness of this beginning was of the utmost importance. In Alexander's time, at the end of the fourth century B.C., Heraclides Ponticus, a disciple of Aristotle, referred to Rome as "a Hellenistic city situated somewhere near the Great Sea". Rome at this juncture was still concerned with establishing her predominance over her own peninsula.

Roman history in its early stages, or, to be more exact, the evolution of the *Roman Republic,* shows a great similarity to the evolution of the *Greek city-states*. Like the Greeks, the Romans are a mixture of Indo-Germanic and Asiatic elements. Like the Greeks, they started from tribal origins, gathering in a gradual concentration of small settlements on the seven hills of Rome, erecting a temple and a fortified palace first on the Palatine Hill (hence the palatium, the palace), and later on the Capitol Hill, the Capitol. In the valley between these hills lay the assembly- and market-place, the forum, where the "comitia" gathered, the council of the male members of the founding families, the fathers (the "patres" or "patricii", patricians), a council which from the early times limited the power of the sacred kings. A special council of the oldest, the heads of the noble families, later split off from this general assembly of all free people of the founding clans. This was the Roman Senate. As in Greece, the king soon became an elected official or was replaced by elected officials—how this evolution occurred in legendary times is not quite clear. Apparently the king, who exercised the functions of a priest, was replaced by two military leaders, the tribunes (the term derives from "tribus", the tribes which they originally commanded). Later they were called "praetors" ("praeitores"), that is, the head men, the men who walked ahead of the people, a term corresponding to the German "Herzog". Eventually this office was transformed into the consulate, represented by two consuls elected annually. Subsequently, various magisterial offices were connected with the title of tribune. The tribunes of the people are best known. They represented the originally alien "tribus" of the plebeians, who were the lower stratum of the people, small peasants, tradesmen and craftsmen who gradually acquired full citizenship. One of the most influential positions fell to the "censor", whose duty it was to take the census, to evaluate taxable property and to investigate breaches of custom or of morals. The title, "praetor", was finally given to the highest justices.

Upon the consuls the power of command, the "imperium", was conferred by the "comitia" of the patricians for the term of their office. Thus the "imperium", the empire, was at first a supreme function, a power of command. For the campaigns, for warfare, it was conferred temporarily and with unlimited authority upon a supreme army chief, the "imperator". From the "imperator", who was solely a military chief, we must distinguish the "dictator", who was elected for a term of six months at the most, as the supreme commander of the whole state in times of danger and emergency. The dictator replaced the consuls whenever quick decisions had to be made and the utmost concentration of authority was necessary.

In Rome, as in Greece, the nucleus of the landowning population was originally divided into tribal clans, the "tribus" (hence the term tribe), which were founded on blood-brotherhood. A military classification of the people was the basis for the administrative organization, and this organization developed from a taxation in terms of acres and agricultural income into a taxation in terms of money. It, too, proceeded from the clan standard to the standard of local districts.

As in Greece, different grades of citizenship, of "civitas", were evolving. ("Civitas" corresponds to the Greek "politeia" and means citizenship in the double sense of membership in a community and the community itself.) And the "plebs", the plebeians, a group that consisted of the remainders of conquered populations and degraded citizens, only gradually, through rebellions and secessions, obtained admission to equal rights. Later, along with the growth of the Roman Empire, the citizenship went on expanding to foreign peoples until it included the entire population of the Roman civilized world.

Thus Roman history shows the same trend as the history of the Greek cities: a trend toward the local, the democratic, the individual. We observe the same shifting from the authority of the ancestral past to the power of the present community. But here the differences set in; the step from the Greek cities to Rome accentuates this very trend and this shifting. Roman evolution carried this movement much farther. Rome was, as it were, a latecomer in ancient history, and politically this was of the greatest advantage to her. It saved her the strain of creating the cultural and intellectual prerequisites for her civilization. From the very beginnings of her history, Rome was subject to strong and near Greek influences. From the Greek cities in Sicily and Southern Italy, and via the Etruscans in the North—a people, probably of Asiatic origin, that was in close and early connection with Asia Minor and Greece—Hellenic deities, temples and images were introduced into Rome. They were followed by a continuous stream of legends, poetry, historiography, philosophical and political doctrines and speculations, of the whole artistic and intellectual equipment that Greek enlightenment had produced. Even the constitutional reforms of Solon probably contributed to the shaping of Roman political institutions.

Thus the intellectual life of the first, strictly republican period of Roman history was not very original or significant. This history was concerned with worldly affairs and proceeded along practical, political lines. It seems that all forces of the Roman polis were exploited for political action, for the solid establishment and steady expansion of political power.

Roman religion appears pale and abstract against the colorful prolixity of the Hellenic cults. The most genuine Latin god seems to be Mars, or Quirinus, who characteristically was a rural deity before he became a god of war. And though afterwards a pantheon, adapted from the Greek Pantheon, dominated Roman worship, the true religious life seems to have centered in a multitude of lower deities of a domestic and agricultural order. These deities were so numerous, and so specialized according to every act and situation of earthly life, that they appear to be mere allegorical abstractions of the various items of daily life itself.

There was two-faced Janus, the god of the gate, hence of all beginnings; there was Vesta, the goddess of the hearth and its fire, and so of household and cookery; there was Terminus, the god of boundaries. But there were also special deities for every phase of land cultivation, for the first and the second ploughing, for furrowing, sowing, harrowing, and so for every important period, attitude, occupation in personal, communal and political life. There was a goddess of nourishing the child in the maternal womb; there were others to help in every stage of delivery; and still others to be invoked when the child cried for the first time, when he lay in his cradle, when he was nursed, weaned and so forth. There was a goddess who strengthened the child's bones, a god who taught him to walk, another who taught him to talk; and so it went on for the whole course of human life. Religion descends to daily living. It shapes a parallel for every minute, profane aspect of it, until, at last, in the late Roman days, the city itself and man himself, the "dea Roma" and the emperor who represented the city-empire, were deified.

As to the *political and social evolution* itself, the fundamental difference between the Greek cities and Rome is that in Greece there were many cities competing with one another, achieving hegemony as the utmost form of domination, and achieving only limited and unsuccessful hegemonies. In the case of Rome, there was only one city that rapidly gained such superiority over its neighbors and potential competitors in the Italic peninsula, and reached such a strong and consolidated form of community that its preponderance could never again be contested.

To be sure, the existence of Rome was threatened for a long time and she was often in dangerous situations. Her early enemies, the Italian populations, missed no opportunity to revolt against Roman supremacy again and again, even long after their subjugation. The Samnites, for instance, revolted as late as 82 B.C., after all Italic populations had been granted Roman citizenship; they had to be destroyed by Sulla. Yet after the earliest campaigns against the Latins, the Etruscans, the Aequi and Volsci, the Gauls and the Samnites, that is, since the third century B.C., no serious competitor was left on the Italic peninsula.

As for the causes of this phenomenon, as far as they can be rationally explained, they may be found in the extremely favorable geographical situation of Rome in the center of a compact peninsula, on the mouth of a river and well protected by the sea and by mountains. Against the clear, concise shape of Italy, the contours of Greece appear ragged with innumerable bays and creeks and surrounding islands, and this geographical diversity and cleavage of Greece, the fact of her natural division into many separated regions, brought about a variety and multiplicity of independent communities favoring rivalry and preventing the definite supremacy of any one of them.

Furthermore, Rome appears as a synthesis of Sparta and Athens, for she combined rustic military discipline with sea power and trade. On the one hand, she built up the first true metropolis in history, with crowded, metropolitan city life, with all the ways and the means of struggle for wealth and power, to a much greater and more intense degree than Athens. And yet, on the other hand, she rested on the soil with much more firmness and poise. Her institutions were much more solid, elaborate, systematized, worked out more soberly and categorically. Though trade later played an important part in Rome, the social and economic foundation of this community was always mainly agricultural. The bonds of the soil remained much stronger than in Athens. The huge conquests, the incorporated provinces furnished quantities of land and natural resources. They called for a vast administration and created an extensive hierarchy of officials. And the transition from clan nobility to wealth nobility was brought about not so much, as in Greece, by the growing importance of trade, but rather by riches acquired through offices and the lease of offices.

The patrician senators were joined by a nobility of officials and ex-officials. The later aristocracy of the so-called "equites", the knights, consisted of rich merchants and money-lenders, as well as of "publicani", leaseholders of public revenues, public estates and taxes or public works. Besides, everyone who made money presently became a landed proprietor and enhanced his position by large estates surrounding sumptuous villas. Only in his capacity as a landowner was he admitted to the nobility. Senators were not allowed to engage in trade. The landed proprietors cultivated their estates through administrators and slaves. They themselves lived in the city and used their villas only as summer residences.

Thus, Roman constitution, which developed into a complex system of assemblies, offices and authorities, preserved a rather aristocratic character. Though democracy was legally instituted, the power of the senate and of the great landowners always remained preponderant. And all rebellions, all efforts of radical politicians and popular leaders did not succeed in fundamentally changing this situation. A huge proletarian population gathered in the city, poor freemen, "clients", enfranchised slaves—not to speak of the slaves themselves—who were wooed by the rival politicians giving them "panem et circenses", bread and shows, who fomented the civil wars and were the ever-vacillating and fluctuating support of ambitious leaders.

In conquering the various Italic tribes, in expanding further and further her domination over the peninsula, Rome collided with Carthage or, as the Romans said, the Punics ("poeni", i.e. the

Phoenicians) who then controlled the western Mediterranean and Sicily. It was a development parallel to the Greek, when Athens, in extending her influence to the Ionian cities in Asia Minor, had come in conflict with the power of Persia. And what the Persian Wars had become to Greece, the Punic Wars became to Rome: the turning point in her historical development. To Rome, "Hannibal ante portas" was the same ordeal as Xerxes at Thermopylae to the Greeks. In both cases, the outcome of this terrible situation could not have been foreseen at the moment, and still the outcome was bound to be the one we know if human history was to proceed on its way. While the Greeks, however, had never been able to rid themselves of their sworn enemy until the very last and indeed agonizing stage of their political existence, the Romans, in the course of these wars, succeeded in doing away with Carthage once and for all. This already shows the different range, the immense future, of their political power.

Another instructive parallel appears in the two internal crises of these two peoples. As the Greeks were divided into several city-states and city leagues, their civil war, the Peloponnesian War, was in part an external war, a deadly struggle for hegemony which was finally won by an outsider and a newcomer, the Macedonians. This civil war of the Greek cities exhausted their political strength; it was the beginning of the end of Greek history. The Roman civil wars, though interspersed with dangerous external wars against the first Germanic invaders, against Mithridates, King of Pontus, against the Celts, Samnites and Pirates, these civil wars, lasting a whole century, from 133 to 31 B.C., did not in any way destroy the power of the city, but, on the contrary, spurred the vehement ambitions of the competing leaders who alternated in saving the state from foreign assaults. Thus the Roman civil wars resulted in the conquests of vast new provinces. They initiated the second period of Roman history, the empire which extended from the British Isles and Spain to Egypt and Mesopotamia.

The senate and the people were not imperialistic from the outset. At first, by defending and strengthening their position, they were induced, indeed forced, to conquer. They had to defend themselves against the might of the Etruscans in the North, later, against the Celtic Gauls who invaded Italy in the sixth century, and against the Southern Italic tribes that were dislodged by Sicily and the expanding power of Carthage. It was only natural that the Romans began to enjoy their growing power. The conquests prodded the ambitions of the people and especially of the military leaders. The knights, the new wealth nobility of entrepreneurs in public works and taxes, became interested in the increase of their resources. Generals and governors of the newly conquered provinces rose to power.

In the course of this development, the imperator, the appointed military official of the republic, developed into the imperator in the later sense of the word, the *emperor,* the highest commander who became the ruler of the state. Early in the first century B.C., in response to a felt need for a standing army in the new provinces overseas, the old citizen army of the Roman republic had become a professional army of mercenaries. These received expert training and were led by generals who were adventurers as well as politicians. As a result of the conquests and the rivalry in leadership, this professional army, which was strongly attached to personal leaders, developed into a more and more potent factor in public affairs, until eventually appointments were no longer made by assemblies of the people and the senate, but by the army, and especially by its most important nucleus closest to the generals, by the Praetorian Guards. From early times, the military leaders, first called Praetors, had a special troop, an élite troop, as a body-guard. Caesar's famous Tenth Legion was such a guard. And these Praetorian Guards later assumed an increasingly important role in the army and the state and eventually selected the emperors.

This whole development first became apparent in the civil war between Marius, the leader of the popular party, and Sulla, the leader of the aristocratic patricians—both very successful generals. Marius defeated the Germanic Cimbri who had invaded Italy, in the Battle of Vercellae, 101 B.C. Sulla, after having defeated Mithridates, King of Pontus in Asia, and the rebellious Samnites as well as his Roman opponents in Southern Italy, in 82 B.C., had himself appointed dictator "for the purpose of restoring the state", that meant restoring the power of the aristocratic party, the old senatorial system. His dictatorship was the first to be unlimited in time. Still, it derived its authority from the senate and, after having completed his reforms, Sulla voluntarily retired from his post (79 B.C.).

But when Julius Caesar, in crossing the Rubicon (49 B.C.), decided to lead his army against the Roman senate that had ordered him to resign his command over his provinces and his troops, he effected a revolutionary turn in the history of mankind. He founded a new kind of rulership based on personality alone, corresponding and well-adapted to the first political unification of a conquered world.

In this, to be sure, he was not without forerunners. In Greece, this new kind of rulership had already come into being when, in times of emergency and social unrest, an ambitious leader had seized the opportunity to set up a personal regime which was not even formally sanctioned by any sacred traditional authority of the polis, which did not derive from any traditional office or appointment by the community. Those men, who were not considered legitimate rulers as compared with the sacred hereditary kings or appointed officials, were called tyrants. They were not necessarily what we call a tyrant, they were frequently good, deserving and even popular rulers, as they diminished the power of the nobles, encouraged trade and favored intellectual and artistic life. But the people did not continue to support them, though they tried to overcome the traditional misgivings against this type of merely personal rulership by tracing their descent to the heroic founder of the city. They had a personal body-guard of mercenaries in constant friction with the army. It was they who invented the secret service, as they employed a troop of spies responsible to them personally.

Caesar's innovation, however, consisted in that his rebellious personal regime, founded solely on present military power and illegitimate popular support, developed into a lasting monarchy of profound influence upon European history. Roman constitution had furnished the prerequisites for such power in the various offices already mentioned. Caesar now fortified his strength by consolidating and concentrating all these offices and by forcing the senate to extend the limits of these offices illegally in conferring them upon him. First, there was the office of the dictator, with a duration of six months at most and including military as well as judiciary power. Caesar was the first to have himself appointed perpetual dictator ("dictator perpetuus"). Secondly, there was the office of imperator, the commander-in-chief of the warring troops. Caesar was made imperator in the new and higher form of life-long sovereign whose office could be transmitted to his heirs. Thus he became imperator in the new sense of emperor. The word "imperium", the power of command, was associated with all ruling offices, and it also expressed the geographical area where this power of command was effective and legally valid. The "imperium" of a governor, for instance, was confined to the area of his province. It was void when the governor crossed the boundary of his province. Hence the geographical term signifying the sphere of dominion, the empire, evolved. Thirdly, Caesar was made consul for ten years, instead of the usual two, and vested with the power of a tribune ("tribunicia potestas") though, as a patrician, he could not become a tribune, which was a plebeian office. His tribunician power included "sacrosanctitas", sacred immunity, a privilege of the plebeian tribunes to protect them against the nobles.

Eventually, all these traditional terms of authority, deriving from republican offices, were overshadowed by his personal name, Caesar, in Greek, "Kaisar", which, without parallel in history, became a general designation for monarchs ruling over different stocks and countries. Caesar's career was prematurely cut short by his assassination, and his ultimate aims are not known. After his death, the transformation of the republic into an autocratic monarchy, the integral empire, or the Dominate, went on steadily but slowly. It would not have been successful if the succeeding emperors of the Julian family, Octavianus Augustus and Tiberius, had not been very cautious not to push the personal regime to extremes. Octavianus (31 B.C.–14 A.D.), in his civil war with Anthony, even upheld the republican tradition ostentatiously in the face of Anthony's

attempt to establish Oriental despotism over Rome. He emerged
as the savior of the republic which he shrewdly restored, only to
allow himself to be exalted all the more as Augustus, "the sublime"
or "the most venerable". He enjoyed unlimited power through
a cleverly balanced combination of "imperia" derived from the
various offices he caused to be conferred upon him. Moreover, the
senate bestowed the title of imperator upon him as a personal first
name. He, however, preferred to call himself "princeps", the first
among citizens, the first among equals.

It needed a long development for the Roman imperium to expand over the known world. The republican offices became obsolete and unimportant, and new personal offices, which were derived from the personal administration of the emperors, took their
place. Some of these are significant as links to the development
of the feudal structure of the medieval Holy Roman Empire and,
subsequently, to that of European countries.

The transformation of the Roman Republic into the *Roman
Empire* was the ultimate confirmation of that humanizing, indi-
vidualizing, personalizing, secularizing trend of Greek and Roman
history. A single individual, with nothing but his own individual
power, had succeeded in establishing a lasting rulership. And this
rulership differed not only from all sacred, traditional kingdoms,
representing the essence of the species, but also from the rulership
of the Macedonian Alexander. Of course, a formal investiture of
the imperial power to every new emperor was instituted through
the so-called "lex regia", in order to connect the new dignity with
tradition. And as religion still exerted a vital power over human
minds, the Roman emperors let themselves be deified and worshipped in order to strengthen their position. This deification was
at first impersonal, that is to say, a deification of the emperor as
such, or a deification of the institution of emperor. It became more
and more personal, a deification of the single, individual personality of the emperor. Like Alexander, who still had to identify himself with Zeus Amon, the first Roman emperors connected their
cult with the cult of particular deities. But in the end, the emperors

dropped this connection and made themselves gods in their own right. Finally, they were worshipped as individuals.

This thorough individualization went on not only in the highest stratum of this huge empire, but throughout its numerous and diverse populations. It was a natural consequence of the unifying, leveling and civilizing effects of the world empire. In 212 A.D., the Emperor Caracalla extended Roman citizenship to all free inhabitants of the empire. As equal Roman citizens, all these manifold tribesmen of the old and weary peoples of the East, as well as those of the newly conquered and only partly civilized barbarian peoples of the West, were weaned from their ancestral customs and their particular tribal bonds. They intermarried, intermingled, and mixed their cults and myths and customs. They were leveled by this intermixture, they were thrown into one huge melting pot.

The immense Roman civitas, however, was too large and dilute to compensate the lost tribal communities of these peoples and to afford a strong inner bond among citizens from Greece and Mesopotamia to Gaul and the Iberian peninsula, even though they were all proud to belong to this world-wide, standard citizenship which meant world domination and world civilization. They fell between two stools: the too narrow tribal bond which they had outgrown and left behind, and the too immense Roman city-empire with which they were connected only by administrations and institutions. Thus they became lost individuals, private individuals.

In this late Roman empire, private life, in our sense of the word, evolved for the first time, not only in the provinces and colonies, but in Rome itself. People were tired of the perpetual civil wars, of the succession of personal and more and more arbitrary, more and more ruthless, mad or barbarous rulers who were raised and overthrown by the troops. They retired and ceased taking an interest in public life. They led private lives.

This development of private life is also reflected in the evolution of Roman law, which is one of the fundamental achievements of Rome. It is the first systematized and elaborate worldly law in history, indeed, the foundation of European jurisprudence. Roman law, however, is not a perfected system, though it produced the first actual jurisprudence. It evolved step by step on strictly practical lines, from decisions on cases of the day. But the tremendous development of the Roman Polis and the Roman Empire, and the ever-larger range of problems, led automatically to general views and speculations and to a more systematized legislation. This is a general feature of all Roman developments, which always started from practical and empirical aims and purposes, and gradually reached monumental forms and dimensions. Roman art, for instance, or better, the genuine line of Roman art, grew out of equally practical purposes. Its special feature is the introduction of engineering into architecture. But the grandiose tasks of this civilization created those classical, poised forms of arches, bridges, aqueducts, arenas and buildings erected primarily for practical purposes, that became art through the stern, straightforward pursuing of ample and monumental plans.

Roman law, as every law of ancient tribal peoples, had at first been sacred law ("jus sacrum"), which was known and administered by the priests, the "pontifices". From this sacred law branched worldly, public law ("jus publicum"), concerned with the constitution of the gradually developing localized, temporalized present community, the "res publica". And a third branch was concerned with the relations of individuals to one another under the new worldly conditions. This branch was called "jus privatum", or private law. Of course, the influence of the old sacred customs and traditions extended to these more profane branches, and the term private must here be understood in only a relative sense. It may be remembered that private, with reference to the polis, means deprived, and implies a certain inferiority.

This early Roman law was restricted law, valid and applicable to genuine Roman citizens of Roman descent only, and it retained the rigidity of old tribal laws. With the extension of the city, the civitas, with its expanding domination over foreign countries and populations, the manifold laws and customs of the foreign peoples had to be recognized in some way. And thus a new branch, the "jus gentium", the law of the foreign peoples, evolved, and assumed an ever-increasing importance as it influenced Roman law to a high degree. The comparison of customs created a more liberal and individualistic interpretation and, thus, a detachment from the old traditional forms.

The law of the later republic was administered by praetors who had become special officers of jurisdiction. There were domestic, "urban", praetors, and praetors for foreigners. The urban praetors took over the "formulae", the praetorian decisions, from the peregrine praetor, the praetor for foreigners. The "formulae" were general definitions of civil wrongs which were not covered by specific laws and for which restitution was to be made. And gradually this "peregrine law", this law of the foreign populations ("gentes"), penetrated and transformed the genuine Roman law into a more and more liberal, individualistic instrument. The leading philosophy of the Roman Empire, Stoicism, a doctrine that mirrored man's weariness of political life, proclaimed innate, natural rights of every individual, a natural law valid for all human beings, regardless of stock and rank and social condition. It had a great influence on the development of the later Roman law.

In brief: the evolution of a world empire and the evolution of a purely worldly individual are but two sides of the same process. It had been initiated by Alexander; Caesar and his successors founded it. And the perfected empire became the earthly frame where a supplementary process in the spiritual sphere took shape, a corresponding juxtaposition of the individual and the universal—Christianity.

WORLD RELIGION

STEP BY STEP WE HAVE followed the way of man from religion to world religion. Religion, that is, the cult and worship of a tribal source of life, of a divine progenitor, was the first form of detaching and distinguishing a non-self from a self, the first objectivation and subjectivation. At this stage, the non-self, the divine source of life, was still in partial physical connection with the self, although cult and worship were already initiating a spiritual connection between man and god. The development from religion to world religion meant a gradual preponderance of this spiritual connection, a progressive spiritualization of a more universal god, and the increasing worldliness and individualization of man. And the result, that we shall consider in the following, consisted in a second objectivation, the concept of a purely spiritual, universal god or of a purely spiritual substance and soul of the world, and in a second subjectivation, the concept of the individual human soul that through moral responsibility and personal faith attains a spiritual relationship to the universal god.

A similar process took place in the sphere of the community, the development from the rulership of a divine king, in whom the entire life of the tribe centered, to the community life of a true city. The sacred aristocracy of founding families expanded to a democracy of individuals, who, to be sure, were still bound by the tribe. And the concept of a local community, the polis, corresponds to the genesis of individuals with equal rights. The expansion of the city-state to include foreign lands and peoples continues this dual movement. The result is the inclusion of the known world, or, as the ancients put it, of the whole inhabited world, the "oikumene", under one city rule, and, by implication, the evolution of the individual severed from his particular tribal bonds by the too large, too weak, and too dilute empire-citizenship, the evolution of the lonely, private individual.

This movement was carried out in two stages, the Greek and the Roman. The Greek polis only created the internal prerequisites, the fundamental elements of an order which enabled a human community to arrive at the concept of a true world empire. It created the nucleus of the first real self-determined and self-governing community of individuals, the first true city. It created the fundamental forms, offices and authorities of such a self-government, which were the prerequisites for the great and solid administration indispensable for a lasting world empire. Finally, it created the first true civilization in the literal sense of the word, which derives from city, "civitas", citizenship, and means the standard of true city life.

This Greek civilization was still limited. It was confined to the particular city and the radius of its supremacy, its hegemony. And the Greek cities, having spent all their force in this achievement, were not strong enough to press onward to the goal of a solidly established and organized world civilization. The worldly, political power necessary for such a feat was lacking. The fundamental achievements of the Greek polis were all due to a fierce competition between many communities of nearly equal size and strength, none of which reached a lasting, uncontested predominance over its fellow communities. Thus not even the premises for an extensive rule over foreign populations were fulfilled. In the Greek world, there was always a discrepancy between the adherence to a particular city community and its special mode of life, its specific city civilization and city patriotism and, on the other hand, the vague feeling of belonging to a wider community, the Ionian, for example, or the Greek in general as contrasted with the rest of the barbarian world. Eventually, a confederation like the great Attic Naval League, under the hegemony of Athens, developed citizenship in a broader sense. But this did not lead very far, for there were perpetual fluctuations as to the membership in this confederation, a continual round of joining and deserting it, so that a lasting order could never be established.

Neither was Alexander's unsuccessful attempt at a first world empire favorable for consolidating and for upholding an imperial rule of such vast scope. It was only the city of Rome which, after having perfected and stabilized its political methods and institutions, gained the power to complete this lasting and firmly founded world empire. Even this Roman World Empire was at first nothing more than a Roman Empire, the domination of the "inhabited earth" by one specific city, the expansion of this city over the earth. To make it into a world, what we mean by the human world in the sense of a union of men, a supplementary concept was essential, the spiritual concept of humanity.

The foundation for this was already laid in the Hellenistic civilization which had spread over the Oriental populations and the whole Mediterranean. It was the first undisputed reign of a unifying, supertribal civilization made up of heterogeneous elements. It was still a very confused civilization, a melting pot of many different customs, thoughts, myths, cults and rites which surged back and forth under a thin layer of the current world style of living. Hellenistic civilization was unified through the communication between peoples, communication which resulted in a comparison of their ways of life, in mutual fecundation and combination of them all. In the course of this development, Greek culture itself was as much modified by the Orientals as it, in turn, influenced them.

This complex intermingling would never have become unity without the guiding idea of a unity of mankind proper working persistently up toward the surface and gaining control over this immense diversity. Only after a century-long struggle, only through a difficult, complicated process of spiritual synthesis and compromise of the various living forces, did this idea of human unity, did this Christian idea of humanity prevail. And even then it was but an idea! It was arched over the European peoples like the vault of an impalpable sky, under which the perpetual struggle of the maddest human passions went on and on.

The advent of Christianity was the spiritual complement to the political expansion of the Roman Empire. The triumph of Christianity would not have been possible without this world empire which provided the stage for its development. And the Roman Empire, on its part, would have remained fragmentary and futile without this additional force. On the other hand, however, this spiritual force contributed greatly to the dissolution of the political power of the Roman Empire as such.

Now what is it that Christianity attained? What is the essential element and achievement of Christianity? We may well say that in Christianity man reaches the stage of humanity. For the first time, mankind is identified with humanity. Mankind, the mere outward mass, the aggregate of all human specimens, which up to this point had persisted in its physically, biologically bound tribal particularity, became aware of its existence as a whole, and that means aware of its human quality. Man realizes the existence of mankind as a whole and of the human being as such.

Humanity, therefore, is the clear conception of mankind as a whole and of human nature as a quality inherent in all human beings alike and in human beings alone. This idea of humanity, which is the essential achievement and substance of Christianity, presupposes the concept of one universal god as the creator and ruler of the universe and of equal human beings who are all images of this God.

Thus in Christianity the long process of the fundamental objectivation and subjectivation, of the fundamental detachment of the non-self from the self, came to a conclusion. The universe and the human character emerged into consciousness. A gap yawned between the complexities of this earthly life and the unattainable common goals.

The three elements which we recognized as the essential features of the human quality, existence, history and humanity, are born with Christianity—existence, crystallizing in the concept of the universe, of mankind as a whole and the human being as such;

history, the idea of human unity in time, arising in the concept of a common destiny of mankind, beginning with the fall of man and ending with the Day of Judgment, a history symbolized, lived and anticipated in the personal life of the Redeemer himself in whom God became flesh in order to save mankind; humanity, the idea of human unity in space, implying equality of all human beings and mutual regard and love of human beings for one another. These three elements emerging with Christianity are the three essential manifestations of the human quality.

This human quality is characterized as man's capacity of going beyond himself, of transcending the limits of his own physical being, which means the unfolding of what we call the human spirit. The functioning of the human quality consists of two acts, the differentiation, discernment and detachment of a non-self from a self, and the conscious step across the boundary of the self, the rise toward the non-self. The spiritual effort, so far, was mainly concerned with recognizing the non-self to which the self is to rise. In this first period of human evolution, the attempt at transcending was only rudimentary.

But in Christianity, this attempt to go beyond physical existence begins to play a predominant role for the first time. A person leads a spiritual life in so far as he is capable of overcoming his personal, physical life and well-being, in so far as he is able to devote himself to human and universal aims. This is exactly what Christianity calls for.

Now for the first time, the uniting force of the fully developed spirit prevails over its quality of differentiating and discerning. The existence of a universe, the clear concept of a whole, consistent and coherent world—expressed in the word universe and first represented in a universal god—the concept of a common destiny of mankind, the unity and continuity of mankind in time, finally, the concept of united humanity, of a unified community of equal human beings, in space—all these essentially Christian ideas involve unity, emphasize unity, call for unity. (The word catholic, incidentally, has the same meaning as universal. It derives from the Greek "kat holon", which means aiming at the whole, at the one.)

And the human spirit reveals itself as the uniting element par excellence.

From the beginning up to this present day, the Christian call for spiritual unity met with constant, fierce opposition of the physical, sensual diversity and the selfish and self-sufficient particularity of peoples and individuals. The essence of what may be called heathen or pagan, not only from the Christian but from the human point of view, the ever-recurrent trend of paganism, expresses itself in renewed revolts of particularism and egotism against the demand for human unity and solidarity. This fundamental antagonism is at work in the formation of Christianism itself.

Spirit emerges from religion, from religious developments. The universe first appears as a universal god; history first appears as sacred history; humanity first appears in divine commands, in a god-given law. Thus spirit is first a divine order, and man's realization of this divine order manifests itself first as his bad conscience, for he sees himself as a particular, sensual, earthly being and, therefore, as a sinful being, whose life is not justified in the face of universal, perennial and spiritual existence. Consciousness appears first as a bad conscience in all the various movements which converged to the genesis of Christianism.

Christianism as it is represented by the Christian churches, and as it has acted upon and shaped European history, is historically a confluence of three sources: Judaism, the history and destiny of the Jewish people; Greek philosophy, the essentially religious movement of Greek speculation; and the Hellenistic Mysteries, including not only the explicitly Greek Mysteries but also the assimilation of various Oriental cults—Egyptian, Babylonian, Persian, Phoenician, Phrygian—to the Greek mysteries under different forms and names. A vast religious movement pervaded the whole Hellenistic world in these times, quickening and mobilizing all the ancient Oriental cults, assuming the common form of mysteries, of the participation of the human soul in the transformation of a divine destiny. The ancient Oriental religions come together in a colorful apotheosis before they merge into the world religions of Christianity and Islam.

Greek philosophy prepared the Hellenistic world for Christianity by creating the mental susceptibility to a unifying religion, a world religion, an acceptance of a one and all-embracing God and his moral commands, that is, commands concerning human relations as such. Judaism brought about the Christian movement itself—original, early Christianity. The Christian movement was an autochthonous Jewish movement until its decisive transformation by Paul, when, at Antioch, he inaugurated the union between the Jewish Christians and the heathen. Through its shift from the Jewish center in Palestine to the open world of Hellenistic heathenism, the Christian movement became something essentially different. In this period, the Hellenistic ideologies, the Hellenistic mysteries, began to exert their powerful influence upon the original Christian idea. The result was a complete change from genuine Christianity, as it was conceived by Jesus himself, to the dogmatic, institutional and cultic Christianism of the church.

We may distinguish three main phases in the genesis of Christianity: an introductory, preparatory phase led by Greek philosophy; a phase that constituted the internal evolution of Christianity within Judaism; and the external development that transformed Christianity into a world and a huge, hieratical institution.

GREEK PHILOSOPHY

GREEK PHILOSOPHY IS NOT what we call philosophy today. Although it became fundamental for the philosophic speculation of all times, and represents enlightenment of a kind, its point of view is still essentially religious. Compared with the Oriental kingdoms, the classic polis rendered the life of man more diverse, untrammeled and human, and emancipated and enlightened the human individual. But this does not mean that the Greeks and the Romans had actually outgrown their tribal religious bonds. This was never the case. On the contrary, every institution of Greek and Roman life preserved a sacramental, a cultic bearing; it had a shimmer of the divine, of the eternal.

Religion itself became freer, more flexible and animated, but man did not yet free himself from the power of religion. Or, to put it in another way, religion began to move along with human life, to pulsate through human life, but human life did not move away from religion. And when modern scholars speak of Greek enlightenment, we must beware of interpreting this term in its modern meaning, of comparing it, for instance, to the enlightenment of the eighteenth century which was directed against the authority of religion altogether.

Enlightenment is a relative term, and we may distinguish many phases and steps of it. In a way, religion itself, the worship of a clearly conceived deity, crystallizing from confused, primitive participation in magic forces, was a first kind of enlightenment, in that it meant an objectivation of the essence, the life principle of the tribe. The concept of the Greek Pantheon was another phase of enlightenment, for human nature with all its motives and impulses projected itself into the Olympic world. A third phase was Jewish religion, with its one and only spiritual God, its innovations of the revelation, the covenant and the instituted law. And still another was the marvelous rise of Greek speculation which culminated in the first human introspection, in man's viewing and facing himself for the first time. The teaching of Heraclitus to "search into oneself", the inscription on the Delphic temple, "gnothi sauton", know thyself, express in a brief formula a turning point in human evolution. It is as lapidary a symbol of what the Greeks contributed to humanity as the formulation of the Jewish idea, love thy neighbor as thyself. The human capacity for reflection was developed in Greek speculation and this, in turn, proceeded from religious problems.

The new experience of nature, of natural diversity and variation, to which this lively and curious people awoke, and which already animated the Olympic Pantheon, conflicted with the old idea and the deep-rooted need of an eternal order that still exerted an overwhelming power over the human mind. All of pre-Socratic speculation, the so-called natural philosophy of the Greeks, was essentially concerned with the conciliation of this discrepancy between the eternal and changeless being, which was the underlying truth of all existence, and the manifest change and variety and multiplicity of life, which was taken only as an outward appearance and delusion of the senses, indeed as guilt on the part of the mortal creature, that had to be justified and atoned for. The individual, particular and temporal were considered culpable, an apostasy of the physical being, and the search for a comprehensive cosmic substance and for a justifying principle connecting sensual variety and intrinsic unity, apparent change and true eternity, this search was not only a longing for true knowledge but also for reconciliation and salvation. It was stimulated by that bad conscience with which the consciousness of a spiritual order always begins.

The discrepancy between apparent phenomena, which represent a delusion of the senses, and an intrinsic truth, which can only be grasped with the mind, led to a further differentiation between the two faculties of human perception. It led to the discovery of reason as a definite, specific faculty of human understanding. And in this way, speculation eventually turned from the contemplation of outward nature, of the cosmos, to an examination of the faculty of knowledge itself, and of the seat of knowledge, the human soul. Since the lasting substance, the eternal truth of all existence, could be grasped only with the mind and not with the senses, the predominance of the spirit over the senses, of reason over emotions and sensations, of the soul over the body, was established.

The epoch-making transformation of the cosmic problem into a problem of the human soul occurred in that period of political intensity when Athenian democracy was at its peak, when the agora resounded with the competing demagoguery of professional orators and ambitious politicians who confused and twisted terms and meanings in their word-juggling efforts to carry off the populace.

These unscrupulous people, the Sophists, evolved complete scepticism, which for the time being superficially dominated public opinion, and may be compared to the intellectual agitation that prevailed in the enlightenment of the eighteenth century. But in their very midst, an opposing force of much wider and deeper range was already at work, a man who combined the charm and brilliance of those eloquent demagogues with a mind of sovereign clearness, calm and perspicacity, and a profound sense of human responsibility—a man who was no less seductive than his opponents, but who used his seductive art to guide the Athenian youth to the search for eternal truth and goodness. This man was Socrates. His teachings were the point of departure not only for the new method of dialectic analysis and what he called "the art of giving birth to truth", but for a new philosophical trend of an essentially religious character.

In the theory of his disciple, Plato, the outward cosmos was transplanted into the soul and transformed into a province of the soul. The old, naive pantheon was replaced by an intrinsic pantheon of ideas, which were represented as absolute, divine entities of their own and at the same time as prototypes of human thoughts. We recall the Persian angels, the fravashis, who, forming the attendance of Ahura Mazda, the god of light, were also represented as independent, cosmic beings and at the same time as abstract terms of the human mind. The concept of the Platonic Ideas is very similar, but much more elaborate.

Platonic Ideas, for instance the Idea of the Good, of the Beautiful, the Brave, are not at all what we understand today as scientific or logical terms. They are divine images; idea, "eidos", means image. And they are supposed to have an independent, absolute, eternal existence apart from our grasp of them, just as deities may exist apart from human worship. The Platonic cosmos of ideas is no theoretical system, it is a living world in which all the antinomies of life are untouched and in which consistent thought is not driven to the point of enforcing logical coherence upon a living organism. All this made for the religious character of Plato's speculation. The Platonic world is even fundamentally dualistic, it is pervaded in all its different spheres, from the cosmic down to the personal, by the fundamental opposition of soul and body, of spirit and the senses. The soul and the spirit represent the very truth, substance and righteousness of existence, whereas the body and the senses are only reflections or shadows. The psychic, the spiritual and the good are one.

But in the concept of the divine ideas, some sort of reconciliation or harmonizing has, after all, been effected between the eternal and the temporal, between unity and diversity. And the realm of ideas is pervaded by an all-comprising soul of the world. It is headed by a divine creator and originator of the world, a "demiourgos", a unifying, spiritual god. And there is another very important feature of the Platonic theory which bears an essentially religious character. Knowledge, according to it, is not a search for new wisdom, it is no mere search at all, it is reminiscence, recollection of a far-off, eternal existence. It is an almost mystical, spiritual union or reunion with the original and enduring prototypes of existence.

The work of Socrates and Plato was nothing less than the establishment and equipment of the inner world of man, and it has determined Christian civilization unto this very day. The prevalence of one spirit over the various senses, of the recollecting soul over dispersed, physical emotions and sensations, of sovereign goodness over blind and narrow appetites—this has become the guiding principle throughout the centuries.

What Aristotle added was another, a final attempt to allay the old Greek concern about the justification of temporal change in the face of eternity. He attempted to justify growth and decay and the varying conditions of earthly life by rendering dynamic the principle of the soul and spirit. To him the spiritual world was not, as Plato saw it, an immobile heaven where ideas hung like remote stars, and the moves and perceptions of earthly creatures were but dim, mirror images and shadows of eternal beings. To him, the eternal spirit descends into matter, impregnates the earthly stuff, and the result is a synthesis of the lasting and the changing in the inspired process of evolution. Aristotle interpreted the spiritual soul as a formative principle pervading and indeed effecting evolution. The idea is conceived as inherent predestination, leading yearning man on his earthly path toward spiritual realization and perfection. Thus the idea becomes the propelling force of the individual being, and this inherent, eternal, spiritual part of man's existence prods him to his perfection. It leads man to his spiritualization, it leads him toward God, who is pure spirit.

The way to spiritualization and to perfection, the essential approach to God, is knowledge. It is the understanding of the interrelation of beings, of the interrelation of ideas which are the very substance of the various beings. Thus, advance in knowledge is true advance in existence, is the approach to spirit, approach to God. Knowledge, indeed, is a magical act, and it is easy to see how such a concept endowed methodical thinking with peculiar significance. Thinking in the right way meant living and acting in the right way, it meant advancing and rising in life.

It is from this angle that one must envisage the foundation of logic by Aristotle, the search for an infallible method of thinking, of acquiring knowledge, of grasping ideas and their connection. To achieve a true logical understanding meant coming closer to God. This first and fundamental scientific methodology still had a religious, an almost magic meaning, which was carried further and enhanced by neo-Platonic and early Christian thinking.

The concepts of Plato as well as those of Aristotle were still essentially and exclusively Greek ideologies, though they transcend the Greek plane in their significance and their effects. In the main, they reflect the idea of the Greek polis in its purest form. They were conceived for Greeks, and for Greeks only. Whenever there was talk of unity as opposed to variety or diversity, the unity of a Hellenic world was meant.

The utopia of Plato's Republic was a model Greek polis, and it was even an essentially aristocratic, almost theocratic one. This famous utopia, which was to be governed by sages and philosophers, was intended as the pedagogic preparation for creating the perfect Hellenic man and the perfect Hellenic way of life, a life of sublime cultivation—a cultic form of life. It was, in fact, intended as a realm of god, that is, a realm of the Supreme Idea on earth, a "Civitas Dei".

Not only was the institution of slavery preserved and considered essential, not only was this ideal polis supposed to be exclusive with regard to barbarians, in the old Hellenic manner, but the deep-rooted contempt of the ancient peoples for any kind of manual labor, for artisans, workers and even traders, was strongly emphasized in Plato's social order. The perfect life is held to be a life of sublime leisure and contemplation, devoted to the cult of the Idea. Any expansion of the polis, even the expansion of trade in excess of the absolutely necessary means of support, is considered detrimental to the community, a corrupting influence on the harmony, the beauty, the perfection of the polis. The political ideas of Aristotle did not deviate from this pattern to any significant degree.

What this main stream of Greek philosophy had accomplished in preparation for Christian civilization was chiefly the enthronement of the spirit as the legitimate ruler of human existence, be it spirit as a pure and abstract power, as Plato conceived it, or spirit as the inherent principle of form, unity, harmony, as Aristotle held. With this achievement, Greek philosophy expressed the trend of Greek life as a whole. In the creation and cultivation of the well balanced man, the strong, the beautiful, the good and the wise man in one, in whom all faculties, the mental as well as the physical, are equally and harmoniously developed, in the practice of this balance, which was called "askesis", exercise, we find the root of Christian discipline and self-restraint, of asceticism proper.

The feeling for human history, the other attribute of Christian civilization, was not yet clearly developed in Greek philosophy and in the life of the ancients as a whole. Human history had just begun with these peoples. Though they made and lived history, though they even created a standard historiography, a model record of political events like the "Commentaries" and "Annals" of Thucydides, Caesar, Tacitus—not to mention minor authors—though there was much speculation on cosmogony and evolution, an essentially historical consciousness, a realization of change and progress in human life as a whole did not yet exist. Even Aristotle's theory of evolution was mainly concerned with the recurrent evolution of beings, or of the organic world, but not with a progression of the human race. The general scheme of human events was that of perpetual recurrence, of a circle rather than a line of advance. And the general orientation was directed rather toward a better past than a better future, toward an ancestral Golden Age that was to be brought back. Thus the Greeks as well as the Romans were still essentially a-historic.

The third attribute of Christian civilization, humanity proper, was foreshadowed by another current of Greek philosophy which also started from Socrates, from this central and all-important figure in Greek history. It was a more popular current and of less genuinely Greek character. The position of Socrates in Greek history is in some respects similar to that of Jesus in Jewish history, though it became effective, according to the character of the two peoples, on a somewhat different and more limited plane. Socrates, too, was a man whose deepest concern was the salvation of the human soul, the perception and the realization of the essential, the right and the salutary. He was the great rebel, the great seducer and charmer whose task it was to re-interpret, to transform, to resubstantiate traditional values. He was neither a theoretical scholar nor an aristocratic sage. He liked to go about among the people, questioning everyone about the things that made up his daily life, teaching by discussion, by admonition and, before all, by providing a living example. Hence, on the one hand, the extraordinary influence, indeed the magnetism he exerted over people, especially over the Athenian youth, and on the other, the suspicion and the deep misgivings he aroused in the officials of the city. He died as a martyr, accused of "asebeia", blasphemy, impiety and disobedience to the divine commands. He inspired the most different human types: aristocratic Plato, the glamorous Alcibiades, Xenophon, the historian, military leader, economist and novelist, and also a group of popular philosophers, the Cynics, who carried on his way of teaching by discussion, exhortation and exemplary conduct. They were called Cynics, that is, dog-philosophers or simply dogs, because all of them belonged to the lowest class of the people—some of them were servants of foreign extraction and even born slaves—and because they clung to what they considered the only adequate and consistent mode of life for a true sage, a life without worldly goods, free from attachment to disturbing and dispersing pleasures, remote from all passions, appetites and desires that might dim the clear perception of truth and righteousness. They were seen wandering about in ragged cloaks and with un-trimmed beards, with knapsacks and sticks that were their only belongings. And they were heard preaching and exhorting people with colorful sermons, popular jokes, dialogues and parables, much as the mendicant friars and preachers of later Christian times. They invented the type of preaching called "diatribe", pastime. To them, there were no longer any distinctions between upper and lower classes, freemen and slaves, Greeks and barbarians. To them, human beings were all alike. Their country was the world, their god was an all-comprising, spiritual creator and supporter of the cosmos, who was to be revered not by offerings but by a holy life. The task of the true philosopher was considered as strenuous as that of the patron of philosophers, Heracles, who had cleaned the Augean stable to which Greek civilization was compared. Hu-man society, with its striving for power, wealth and pleasure, was thought to have utterly corrupted human beings. Man would have to turn back to Nature, to a simple and pure life. A thorough transformation of man was in order, a general re-evaluation. "Re-cast the coin" was the motto of the Cynic teachings.

From the small nucleus of these popular teachers and their preachings sprang a greater, more elaborate and much more famous philosophical movement which spread over the whole Hellenistic area from the Orient to Rome and Italy. It penetrated the Roman nobility and intelligentsia, and among its adherents there was even a Roman emperor, Marcus Aurelius. This great movement, the Stoic philosophy, was no longer genuinely Greek at all. Its main initiators came from the Mediterranean islands or from Oriental countries, and were of mixed or clearly Oriental descent. It gave expression to that widespread political weariness of the over-expanded Roman Empire and its overstrained civilizations, and it reflected the growing dissolution of the Roman "civitas" into an indistinct world-citizenship and a multitude of private individuals.

The Stoic ideal of indifference and insensibility toward the pleasures and sorrows of life, the attitude of sublime aloofness and tolerance and of a life according to divine nature, not only prepared the atmosphere for Christianity but already contained an element of Christianity. Yet in the main, it was a passive attitude, an attitude of noble resignation and apathy. It represented an end, not a beginning. It lacked the vital impulse that was needed to enforce the command óf humanity. This command would never have gained actual power over human minds without the vital impact which was to come from a new elemental force, from the particular missionary character and history of the Jewish people, that had been striving toward humanity for many centuries as though it aimed at this very moment in which it was needed.

Stoic tolerance, as well as the other Greek trends that indeed touched the very borders of Christianity, sprang from intellectual, philosophical movements. The Jewish trend toward humanity was a living impulse of a whole people, the substance and peculiar life principle of a particular tribe. This paradoxical connection of tribal particularity and universal humanity eventually brought about Christianity. Christianity could never have been effected by a mere intellectual theory, not even by one as widespread and influential as Stoicism. Christianity had to be lived, suffered, demonstrated by a living example. It had to be forced into life by the inherent, emotional and indeed biological urge of a tribal character, by the authoritative religious command of a particular people.

GENESIS OF CHRISTIANITY FROM JUDAISM

THE BOOK WHICH WE CALL the Bible—from the Greek "biblos", the book—is the first consistent history of the world. Parts of it are older than the first Greek attempts toward a universal historiography, the histories of Hekataios, Charon, and Herodotus, and give more than profuse descriptions of mere events and customs, since here, for the first time, we find a report of intrinsic human evolution.

The Bible begins with the mythical creation of the world, but, from Abraham on, it proceeds on historical grounds to the foundation of Christianity, and leads us through the subsequent stages of mankind to the most spiritual concept humanity has ever reached. Recent investigations and findings prove that the historical data in the Bible are reliable to an amazing degree.

In the stories of the Patriarchs, we have an excellent picture of primeval tribal conditions. The unfolding of tribes and of tribal subdivisions which later became tribes is told—according to the primeval identification of the individual with his tribe—as a family chronicle. Reading the names of the Patriarchs, Ham, Shem and Japheth; Abraham, the descendant of Shem; Moab and Ammon, the children of Abraham's nephew Lot; Isaac, Ismael and Midian, the sons of Abraham; Jacob or Israel, and Edom, the sons of Isaac, we must realize that these personalities represent tribes and clans and peoples, and that their genealogy, their story, is in reality the history of the emergence, the development, the relations, the conflicts and fusions of whole tribes. Thus the three brothers, Ham, Shem and Japheth, refer to a mythical, primary partition of vaguely conceived racial stocks, proceeding from a common origin of mankind. Abraham, which means "father of a multitude", "the father of the peoples", a descendant of Shem, is the outstanding ancestor and the chief of the Semitic family of the "Ibrim" or Hebrew populations, and his descendants, Ismael and Midian, Moab and Ammon, Edom and Israel, are six tribes, the Ismaelites (Arabs), Midianites, Moabites, Ammonites, Edomites, Israelites, that, later in biblical history, figure as fully developed peoples. They are all Hebrews. The twelve sons of Jacob represent the twelve clans of the children of Israel.

The nomad clans of the children of Israel appear to have swept into Egypt with the migration of large Semitic tribes, the Hyksos, who invaded Egypt in the course of the seventeenth century B.C. From the Joseph legend, which reflects this immigration, one may assume that the tribes of Israel did not enter Egypt at once but gradually, over a long period, and that all the Israelites probably did not go to Egypt. A part of them had already settled among the Canaanites. When the Egyptians restored their proper kingdom, the tribes of Israel were enslaved and forced to perform slave labor. And with the exodus from Egypt, about 1220 B.C., the actual history of the people of Israel begins, since only then, during this wandering, a first union of the separate tribes was effected. The tribes of Israel became the people of Israel. And this union is symbolized in the concept of the uniting tribal God of Israel, his revelation, his Sinaitic covenant and his instituted law. The founding leader in this whole process, Moses, is no longer the personification of a tribe, he is a single individual, a true personality. The recurring doubts of his historical authenticity or of his membership in the tribes of Israel are pure hypotheses without any factual proof.

The Jewish God, then, was a nomad God, a wandering God, not to be fixed or conjured in any place or image; he was an invisible, intangible and spiritual God, omnipresent and all-comprising; and these qualities implied the corollary of his claim to being the only God, the Universal Creator and Ruler of the world, of human beings, beyond all tribal limits. Accordingly, the Bible is the first history that expresses distinct consciousness of a common origin of mankind as a whole, and that relates the partition of mankind in detail. The Jewish God was, moreover, a dynamic and revolutionary God, leading and driving his people toward a definite future, toward the fulfilment of a special and ever-growing task.

This concept of the Jewish God, with all its human and moral implications, was not perfected all at once. It took shape during the wandering through the desert, but it required many bitter and sad experiences and the work of many reformers to complete the picture. The history of this perfecting process is the history of Christianity. This tragic history—for as the history of a particular people it was tragic indeed—consists of a series of arguments, now for *union,* now for *disunion.* And this union, established again and again on a more and more spiritual plane, was the result of more and more pressing peril and distress.

The first union was brought about by the exodus from Egypt and the wandering through the desert. When the tribes of Israel entered Canaan, they were a group of tribes united only for the purpose of defense and conquest of the country. This union dissolved when the tribes dispersed, settling down among and between the Canaanite populations, that for a long time remained a constant menace to the newcomers. In the period immediately following the settlement, the tribes of Israel were absorbed by the conflicts with the Canaanites, who were also Hebrew, until gradually the populations intermingled. In the second period, they had to cope with the attacks of neighboring tribes, the Moabites, Ammonites, Edomites, all of whom were of Hebrew extraction and belonged to the offspring or the family of Abraham.

In these times, each tribe was headed by an elder whose title, judge ("shofet"), carried with it a function similar to that of the Phoenician suffetes. In the case of imminent danger, or in actual campaigns, it sometimes happened that a popular hero who marshalled and led the people against the enemy was made "shofet". Men who had the reputation of having special gifts from God, or of being especially wise and just, were also appointed to this office. Such leaders and sages were famed beyond the limits of their tribe. And they were the first who temporarily united several tribes in order to meet the frequent assaults that necessitated the federation of tribes under a common command.

The stories of Jephtah and Gideon show how a new union of the tribes of Israel and a common leadership was developing. It was achieved when the country was threatened by an attack of the mighty Philistines (about 1050 B.C.), a non-Semitic people of bold pirates, from the southern shores of Palestine near Egypt. The Philistines were probably of Cretan descent, originating from an Aegean garrison established on the shores of Southern Canaan by the Pharaoh of Egypt. Hence the combination "Cherethites and Pelethites", Cretans and Philistines, mentioned in II Samuel (Chapter 8, 18), as mercenaries in David's army. At this time the united kingdom of Israel arose and lasted for one century, covering the reigns of Saul, David and Solomon (1030–930 B.C.). It was the only period in which the Jewish people was allowed to maintain a normal, independent state with a limited worldly power similar to other kingdoms.

After Solomon's death, a new disruption occurred as a conse-

quence of tribal rivalries. The united kingdom divided into two
kingdoms: the Northern Kingdom of Israel or Ephraim (as the
tribe of Ephraim was predominant in it) with the capital, Samaria,
and the Southern Kingdom of Judah with the capital, Jerusalem.
The following period of the two kingdoms, which was filled with
political troubles and wars between the two countries, was already
overshadowed by the approaching expansion of the overwhelming
Assyrian power which not even a united Israel would have been
able to escape. Neither appeasement nor resistance, both of which
were tried, had availed. From 740 B.C. on, the country became
a bone of contention, and the series of conquests and subjugations
merely reflected the changes and successions of Oriental empires,
the Assyrian, the Neo-Babylonian, the Persian, the Hellenistic and
the Roman. Over and over the people rebelled, and in the Hellenistic period, when the military power of the Seleucid king was
not all too strong, the Jews even succeeded in restoring their independence for a short time until, ultimately, it was destroyed by
the Romans.

While all other small tribes, however, vanished in the overflow
of these successive huge empires, the Jews outlived all dominations,
and by spiritual concentration and unification raised themselves
above the peoples that had subdued them. This rise was a kind of
spiritual compensation for all the earthly distress they had suffered.
Step by step they were goaded on by their misfortune and won
over to their supertribal concept of God and Humanity, and these
concepts bear the traces of all the sufferings and ordeals they had
to overcome.

The dialectic fluctuation between disruption and union was represented in Jewish history by a dialectic struggle between the leading nomad God and the local deities, the "baals", of the settled
agricultural populations with which the Jews came in contact after
the conquest of Canaan. Especially when the tribes of Israel entered
upon friendly relations with the people of Canaan and neighboring
populations, such as the Phoenicians, they were quite naturally
induced to comply with their cults, even to assimilate their own

worship to these native cults. When an Israelite sat down to a meal with a Canaanite, when he bargained with him or took his daughter to wife, when he learned agricultural work from him, he had to take part in the various cultic rites connected with all these performances. And to this very day, certain remainders of such rites are preserved in Jewish ritual, in the great Jewish feasts, for instance, which subsequently became Christian feasts when they were connected with the main events in the life and passion of Jesus Christ. Easter and Whitsuntide were originally such purely agricultural feasts.

Yet the original concept of the nomad God was so powerful that it did not merge or fuse with the local "baals". On the contrary, the nomad God gradually succeeded in annihilating them and becoming the sole and universal God. This was possible only because of the unique constitution of Israel which was a true and direct theocracy. From the very outset, God was considered the immediate ruler of the people. All its leaders, whether judges or kings, were mere temporary, temporal leaders, thought to be appointed and removed by God. Since they were neither descendants nor substitutes of God, they had no unlimited authority. They were accountable to God for their deeds, and there was always a higher authority to control them and to hold them responsible. This authority was represented by mediators between God and the people, mediators who were more powerful than the kings, who were always consulted and dreaded by them, who made and destroyed kings. There were, moreover, two kinds of mediators who controlled each other: *the priests and the prophets*. Both of these forces worked for the universal God and the particular people, and in times of danger they often worked together, but in a different way and with different premises.

The priests were the conservative, even reactionary, traditional, aristocratic element. They worked "in corpore", as a hereditary clan or caste or profession authorized by divine appointment of the whole group, not by an individual, personal vocation. They were always inclined to restrict and restrain, and they stood mainly for the preservation of the tribe and its integrity and particularity, for the meticulous observance of the ancient tribal commands, rituals and cultic forms. They were the ones who generally preferred the fixed cults, the palpable cultic forms, the normal temple service, who settled down easily and became attached to a sacred locality and, therefore, in the early periods, even adapted the Yahveh worship to the cultic forms of the Canaanites. They were, as a whole, the regular officers of God.

The prophets were the extreme opposite, the progressive, stirring, democratic element, drawing their authority from personal, individual inspiration, from immediate and intrinsic contact with God. Accordingly they were the ones who over and again revolutionized, personalized and spiritualized the concept of God, the relation to God and the ways of serving him. They were the vanguard of God, opposing the old cultic offerings and seeking to replace them by an intrinsic piety, by personal responsibility and life according to moral rather than only ritual commands. They were the ones who represented the elements of true Judaism and Christianity, universality, humanity, spirituality, and a common destiny of mankind; who worked out the concept of an ideal future, a Messianic kingdom of peace and brotherhood on earth, a Messianic day of fulfilment and the concept of the Messiah, a sacred king of this kingdom of God, destined to assume the future leadership in this blessed kingdom. Messiah means "the anointed", and the literal Greek translation is "Christos", Christ. Anointment was a method of the ancient peoples of keeping the body clean, and it has become a symbolic act of sacred purification, of sanctification. Thus the king and the high priests were anointed when they assumed their rulership, and the leader and sacred king of the kingdom of God on earth was called simply the Anointed.

The priests were the rearguard of God. They were always a step behind the prophets. In the early periods, when the prophets strove for the union of the tribes of Israel (the prophet Samuel created the Kingdom of Israel by choosing and anointing Saul), the priests clung to their local sanctuaries. And later, when the prophets proclaimed the universal scope of the Jewish God and the Jewish mission, when they emphasized the moral and broad human aims of the Law, the main concern of the priests was the preservation of the Jewish people as such, in its physical and mental particularity. This preservation was the principal achievement of the priests and it was a necessary counterbalance to the activity of the prophets. It helped keep the people together, it was the vital basis for the universal mission.

The line of *priests* leads from Aaron and the Levites to Esrah, the great tribal reformer, who, after the return from the Baylonian exile to Palestine, restored the purity of the tribal body and the worship of the intangible God by his regulations against mixed marriages and the foreign cults which, at the time when Palestine was abandoned and alien elements settled among the remaining Israelites, had spread profusely over the country and threatened to disintegrate the Jewish people. In the Babylonian Exile (586–538) during which Judaism was solidly established and perfected in all its features, the character of the priests had changed from a ritual caste into a spiritual profession. The old cultic service of offerings became obsolete as a result of the teaching of the prophets, and from this time on, the priests concentrated on the ritual observance of the Law. The priests became scribes, scholars of the Torah, with the task of preserving, codifying and interpreting the Law and the oral tradition, that is, the corpus of interpretations and additions made by holy men. Esrah himself was such a scribe.

In accordance with this development, the focus of the spiritual life of the people shifted from the Temple to the Synagogue (the Greek for assembly) which was an entirely different institution: an organized body of priestly scribes who, in these Hellenistic times when the great temptation presented by the Hellenistic civilization threatened to estrange the Jews from Judaism, defended the Torah and upheld the tribal tradition and the strict observance of the tribal ritual, such as circumcision, dietary laws, keeping the sabbath.

The period from Esrah to the third century B.C. is called the period of the "Men of the Great Synagogue". And in the first great persecutions of Judaism proper that were not an assault on the

Jewish country and the Jewish people but an official suppression of the Jewish religion, which first occurred under the reign of the Hellenistic king, Antiochus Epiphanes, in the second century B.C., the priests were the pre-eminent martyrs. Priests led the great revolt of the Maccabees (167–140) and established a new, independent Jewish state under their hereditary rule, lasting from 140 to 63 B.C., when Jerusalem was conquered by Pompey.

In the mean time, a new aristocracy of priests had formed. They traced their descent to King David's High Priest, Zadoc, and were called the Sadducees after him. They insisted upon the most literal interpretation of the Law and recognized as binding only the written word as it was preserved in the sacred books of the Torah. They were opposed by the more liberal party of the scribes, the Pharisees (this means the detached, the secluded), who wished to include the oral tradition in the sacred regulations. The influence of the Pharisees gradually prevailed, and they were the intransigent defenders of the Jewish Law when Jesus appeared.

The line of the Jewish *prophets* begins with Moses and ends with Jesus. The prophets are a unique feature of Judaism by the very fact that they are an institution, an ever-recurrent phenomenon and a salient factor in Jewish history. All ancient peoples had priests who played an important part in their history. All ancient peoples also had soothsaying and augury, functions deriving from the primitive wizards and sorcerers and for the most part given over to the priests. The Babylonian Chaldeans, the Persian Magi, combined both functions. So did Pythia, the Priestess of Delphi, and the Roman augurs. The Jewish prophets, however, were not only a distinct institution, different from the priests and opposed to them. They developed a new, intrinsic, spiritual form of oracle which did not wait for questions and consultations, but took the offensive, appealed to the people as well as to the rulers, supervised the whole community, scolded and cursed it, prodded it on and, in the final analysis, shaped its destiny. The only comparable phenomenon is the Persian Zarathustra, but he was a single individual.

Israel also had a lower class of prophets corresponding to the seers and sorcerers of other peoples, and they even formed a distinct professional class of soothsayers who prophesied for payment, in various situations of personal life. They were the "false prophets" whom the true prophets utterly despised and with whom they did not wish to be confused. Not all of them were necessarily false prophets, but they could be summoned to do the petty, daily work of predicting, advising, curing and working miracles, and they did it for money. They were the medicine men, the physicians of the people, and since their work was not based on solid knowledge but on inspiration and imagination, which are not always at beck and call, they could not be very reliable.

The true prophets changed the character of prophecy. They spoke only when they felt the call, when they were aroused by profound and inspired knowledge, they spoke freely and spontaneously, they spoke to the whole people and to the kings upon matters of common and main concern. Not only were they not rewarded for their prophecies, they were often imprisoned and in mortal danger.

Of course, the true and false prophets had a common origin. Prophecy was a common element, it hovered in the air around the people of Israel. It was born in the desert, in boundless, glittering space, in burning wind, in visions and fata morganas and in the untrammeled roving life. In fact, all the various prophetic movements of Jewish history and many of the great prophets themselves clung to the old desert way of life, the nomad way of life. There was, for instance, the religious movement of the Rechabites, a sect violently opposed to Canaanite culture and cults, opposed to agriculture and viticulture. They refused to conform to settled agricultural life, to cut their hair, to drink wine and to become inebriate with anything less than the sober and intrinsic ecstasy provided by the spirit of God. They wandered through Palestine in their old Bedouin garb. A similar movement was that of the Nazarites, also bound to abstain from grapes and wine and from the cutting of hair. Samson probably belonged to this group, and his story reflects their convictions.

The prophets themselves, schools, swarms of prophets, such as Saul encountered after he had been anointed by Samuel, the prophets moved about with "a psaltery, and a tabret and a pipe and a harp", like dancing, enraptured dervishes. And it is told that when Saul met them he was seized by their rapture, "the Spirit of God came upon him and he prophesied among them". This was when the people asked, "Is Saul also among the Prophets?" This story, as it is related in I Samuel (Chapter 10), gives a good picture of the character and the power of these movements. Many of the early prophets, Ahijah, Elijah, Amos, also retained desert habits and the appearance of Bedouins, and since they were often impelled to make unfavorable prophecies to the people and to the rulers, they were even forced into an unstable and wandering life and to flight into the wilderness.

The faithfulness to the old desert ways of life and to the nomad attitude is an expression of fanatic adherence to the nomad God with all his implications, of a firm, uncompromising opposition to the settled local cults of the Canaanites and to formal and official cults in general. The prophets kept the nomad God alive as the impalpable and spiritual God, and in their relentless opposition to the stabilized, comfortable, self-sufficient and ostentatious ways of life and forms of worship, they gradually elaborated and sublimated the concept of this nomad God. Their function of spiritualizing God and of making him universal was in open or latent conflict with that of the priests, the guardians of tribal integrity and particularity. There were prophets, such as Jeremiah and perhaps Amos, who were descended from the aristocracy of priests and still opposed its principles. The prophets were supported and confirmed in their achievements by the tragic destinies of the Jewish people, which they regarded as recurrent punishments of God. As a matter of fact, the ordeals of the Jewish people had something to do with the dialectic, ambivalent character of Judaism, with that paradoxical union of a particular earthly existence and a universal spiritual trend.

Among the great prophets of the early periods, who have significance only for Jewish history, is Samuel, who initiated the union of the tribes of Israel and created the Kingdom of Israel. And to Elija, the greatest of them, living in the ninth century B.C., the final purification of Jewish religion must be attributed, the established knowledge of the integral spirituality of Yahveh. This is expressed in his name: Eli Yahu, my God Yahveh. Elija was filled with the conviction that Yahveh existed independently of his people, that Yahveh would triumph even over his own people and over the Kingdom of Israel as a changeless, sovereign principle.

The super-tribal scope of the prophetic movement, which may have begun earlier, cannot be documented before the great catastrophes, the invasions by Assyria and Babylonia, took place or were at least in the offing. In connection with these events, the great reversal from the terrestrial to the spiritual, from the tribal and particular to the universal and human, occurred. At the same time there is another innovation. The prophecies are no longer preached and proclaimed but written down by the prophets in order to subject to proof the accuracy of the amazing predictions that were not believed at the time of the saying.

The *fundamentals of Judaism and Christianity* developed in the two centuries between about 760 and 530 B.C., that is, the period of the Assyrian and Babylonian conquests and the Babylonian Exile, the lifetime of the prophets Amos, Hosea, Micah, Isaiah, Jeremiah, Ezekiel and Deutero-Isaiah.

The decisive turn from the God of Justice or even the God of Vengeance, the old tribal blood-vengeance (eye for eye, tooth for tooth) to the God of Love and Charity, is connected with the most touching figure among the great prophets, with Hosea. With unprecedented daring, he projects his personal destiny, his personal experience into the destiny of his people, into the relation of God to his people. One can gather this from remarks scattered through his book, which is the tragic story of his life. He had a wife whom he loved and who deceived him. She had lovers and he put her away, but he could not cease from loving her. She was "beloved of her friend, yet an adulteress". And when she said, "I will go and return to my husband, for then it was better with me than now", he took her back. This story, as he puts it, is intertwined with his bitter complaint of Israel's whoredom, and God who takes her back. The moving result of this identification of himself with God is the concept of a suffering, merciful and loving God. Hosea's experience is a landmark in the development of Christianity. It is one of the few instances in which the destiny of an individual gave a decisive turn to the history of mankind. Here God speaks to Israel in the tone of Hosea's words to his wife: "When Israel was a child, then I loved him, and called my son out of Egypt . . . I taught Ephraim also to go, taking them by their arms; but they knew not that I healed them. I drew them with cords of a man, with bands of love . . . He shall not return into the land of Egypt, but the Assyrian shall be his king, because they refused to return [to me] . . . How shall I give thee up, Ephraim? how shall I deliver thee, Israel? . . . Mine heart is turned within me, my repentings are kindled together. I will not execute the fierceness of mine anger, I will not return to destroy Ephraim: for I am God, and not man . . ." (Hos. 11). "Therefore, behold, I will allure her, and bring her into the wilderness, and speak comfortably unto her. And I will give her her vineyards from thence, and the valley of Achor for a door of hope: and she shall sing there, as in the days of her youth, and as in the day when she came up out of the land of Egypt . . . I will take away the names of Baalim [these are the lovers] out of her mouth, and they shall no more be remembered by their name." And the effects are far-reaching, they reach to the institution of a kingdom of love and of peace: ". . . in that day will I make a covenant for them [the children of Israel and Judah] with the beasts of the field, and with the fowls of heaven, and with the creeping things of the ground: and I will break the bow and the sword and the battle out of the earth, and will make them to lie down safely. And I will betroth thee unto me for ever; yea, I will betroth thee unto me in righteousness, and in judgement, and in lovingkindness, and in mercies." (Hos. 2). This was written about 750 B.C.

Another innovation goes back to Micah, a contemporary of Hosea, a peasant prophet: the idea of a legal issue between man and God as between two independent partners who are equals before one unconditional law. This was of unique and astounding significance in antiquity and clarifies the particular Judaic relation of man to God. It was only possible on the basis of a revealed law to which God is bound as well as man, and on the basis of a covenant between man and God. These verses taken from Micah (Chapter 6) anticipate the magnificent dialogue of Job with God: "Hear ye, O mountains, the Lord's controversy . . . for the Lord hath a controversy with his people, and he will plead with Israel. O my people, what have I done unto thee? and wherein have I wearied thee? testify against me. For I brought thee up out of the land of Egypt, and redeemed thee out of the house of servants . . ." And against this are quoted the reciprocal acts that God demands from man: "Will the Lord be pleased with thousands of rams, or with ten thousands of rivers of oil? . . . He hath shewed thee, O man, what is good; and what doth the Lord require of thee, but to do justly, and to love mercy, and to walk humbly with thy God?" And again it is justice and mercy that is demanded, and here for the first time, in 740 B.C., the prophet, in the name of God, does not address the children of Israel, not his people, but simply man.

In Amos and Isaiah, about the middle of the eighth century, and in the undated psalms (I Sam. 2 and Ps. 113) there are the first utterances of a revolutionary and social character—the condemnation of the rich, praise and glorification of the poor. The result of the work of unnamed prophets appears in the social laws of Deuteronomy, at the beginning of the seventh century B.C., that designate the good of all, without exceptions, as the good of the community. The strong is responsible for the weak, the rich for the poor. There are strict prohibitions against every form of economic oppression, usury, unlimited exploitation of slave labor, deductions from or delay in the payment of daily wages. Landed proprietors are obliged to donate a part of the annual harvest to the poor. Every seven years all debts must be cancelled. Discharged slaves shall not leave with empty hands, but "thou shalt furnish him liberally out of thy flock, and out of thy floor and out of thy winepress." Fugitive slaves were not to be returned to their masters. (Deut. 15, 16, 23, 24, and other chapters.)

The following passages will show the development of the concept of mission, martyrdom and Christian humility. In Amos (Chapter 9), around 760 B.C., the equality of all men before God is emphasized: "Are ye not as children of the Ethiopians unto me, O children of Israel? saith the Lord. Have not I brought up Israel out of the land of Egypt? and the Philistines from Caphtor, and the Syrians from Kir?" On the other hand, it is said in Deuteronomy: "The Lord did not set his love upon you nor choose you, because ye were more in number than any people; for ye were the fewest of all people: But because the Lord loved you, and because he would keep the oath which He had sworn unto your fathers. . . ." Again in Amos (Chapter 3), God says to Israel: "You only have I known of all the families of the earth: therefore I will punish you for all your iniquities." And finally in Isaiah (Chapter 49): "It is a light thing that thou shouldest be my servant to raise up the tribes of Jacob, and to restore the preserved of Israel: I will also give thee for a light to the Gentiles, that thou mayest be my salvation unto the end of the earth . . . That thou mayest say to the prisoners, Go forth; to them that are in darkness, Shew yourselves . . . They shall not hunger nor thirst; neither shall the heat nor sun smite them: for he that hath mercy on them shall lead them." And Israel, the servant of God, says of himself (Is. 50): "I gave my back to the smiters, and my cheeks to them that plucked off the hair: I hid not my face from shame and spitting." And finally the heathen will say of Israel (Is. 53): "He is despised and rejected of men; a man of sorrows, and acquainted with grief: and we hid as it were our faces from him; he was despised and we esteemed him not. Surely he has borne our griefs, and carried our sorrows: yet we did esteem him stricken, smitten of God and afflicted. But he was wounded for our transgressions, he was bruised for our iniquities; the chastisement of our peace was upon him; and with his stripes we are healed."

This group of selected quotations makes clear the outline and coherence of the Christian Messianic idea: Originally all peoples were equal before God. The children of Israel were chosen by God for a special task, through a covenant he made with their fathers, and "an oath he swore unto these fathers." The proof of this choice can be seen in the fact that God "punishes the children of Israel for all their iniquities." The meaning of this choice and the special task of the children of Israel is "that they are given for a light to the Gentiles"—a task which implies that Israel "bears the griefs of the Gentiles and carries their sorrows," and that "the Gentiles esteem him stricken, smitten of God and afflicted." But, as it is said, "the chastisement of their peace is upon him and with his stripes the Gentiles will be healed." Thus this whole concept, developed in the sixth century B.C., was evolved on an exclusively Jewish basis and within the scope of Jewish history. And yet it is the quintessence of the Christian Messianic idea.

It remained to transfer this idea from the people of Israel to a single personality and from a vague time to come to a definite and near future. Even that was already prepared in this period, and shaped more and more distinctly in the following centuries under the growing pressure of subsequent travail and suffering. From Isaiah on, the idea of a Messiah, of an appointed and anointed leader into a Kingdom of God on earth, was in the making. At first, he was to be descended from King David's family and this is why, later, a genealogy of Jesus was constructed, connecting him with David. From a Savior of the Jews, the Messiah gradually grew into a Savior of the world. For he was the leader and the exponent of the Jewish people, that, as a people, was considered the future Savior of the Gentiles.

Some scholars claim that the idea of a Messiah originated in Egypt or Babylon. This is an excellent instance of the professional jealousies of Egyptologists and Assyriologists, who tend to ascribe all great achievements to the peoples they specialize in. We actually do possess an Egyptian text of the seventeenth century B.C. that describes a revolutionizing of conditions, probably through the invasion of the Hyksos, and then expresses the hope for the coming of a just sovereign, "a shepherd of men", of whom it is said that "there is no evil in his heart" and that if his herd goes astray, "he spends the whole day in bringing them back." A Babylonian document contains a similar prophecy. To interpret these primitive and purely tribal prophecies of a good ruler as early versions of the idea of a universal Messiah, is a failure to distinguish between the letter and the spirit of history. What was previously said about the fundamental difference between the Law of Israel and the body of laws of the Near East holds true here. Of course, one can establish the historical maxim that nothing is evolved suddenly and without long preparation. Every phenomenon is prefaced by an endless series of initiating events. Innovation, however, consists in the fact that an idea that was originally incidental, rudimentary, unimportant, and based on entirely different premises, that this idea, when the time and conditions are ripe for it, develops into its full significance as the focus of a whole people or even a whole period of mankind.

The concept of a Day of Judgment took shape in Amos and was elaborated more extensively by the prophets of the following generations. The gap between the present and the indistinct future of the expected Day of Judgment, the advent of the Kingdom of God, was slowly filled by the historical experiences of the Jewish people. For the Jewish people itself experienced and suffered world history and, by this means, was brought to create the concept of world history. It outsuffered and outlived the great empires of the Assyrians, the Babylonians, the Persians and the Macedonians, and thus the consciousness of history was hammered into it. The other Oriental peoples vanished and merged in the flood. The Greeks developed independent of the events in the Orient, with which they were only distantly connected. But the Jews went through all the fundamental changes, and they alone possessed a standard to measure these changes in their own everlasting God and their Messianic idea.

The vision of the prophet Daniel, which is related in the Book of Daniel, written in the Hellenistic era, is the first to include in its Messianic prophecy the enumeration of the four great Oriental empires, the Assyrian, the Babylonian, the Persian and the Macedonian, and to teach that after the downfall of the fourth, the advent of the eternal empire, the blessed Kingdom of God, is expected at a near and fixed date. It will be heralded by the Messiah, who is called the Son of Man and will overthrow the four beasts representing the empires of the heathen. The righteous of Israel will rise up from the dead and will become the core around which the righteous of all the peoples of the world will gather. God will be the ruler of this realm of peace, of this regained paradise on earth.

The details of this vision were greatly amplified by the imagination of the people and the ideas of many personalities, which are preserved in a group of books called Apocalypses (revelations). Under the impact of the Hellenistic and Roman upheavals, the impatience and the agitation of the people grew, and a feverish expectation, a visionary, prophetic state of mind seized upon the masses. Everybody, even the priestly Pharisees, waited for the near end and the advent of the Savior. And so did the Essenes, the "Pious", a sect of anarchists, if we may call them so, who rejected the worldly state altogether, who considered the state, the worldly power and might, as the origin of all sin, who vowed to abstain from all political and worldly life and thus also from war and armed resistance. They established communities in remote places far from cities. They were organized on purely religious lines in a hierarchy of holiness, and they worked out a rule and discipline of utmost severity and almost ascetic conduct of life. The initiates were tested during three years of probation and had to undergo rites of purification, such as plunging in water, the origin of baptism. There is the possibility of a connection with the Hellenistic Mysteries that had similar rites, and with the trends of Neo-Pythagoreanism. The Essenes believed in the utmost cleanliness of spiritual and physical life. They were absolutely truthful, humanitarian and altruistic. They did not marry, since feminine charm and the care for children made men unfree and selfish. They had property in common and repudiated trade. All these features characterize them as the first religious order, the first monks.

This was the world background when the last great prophet, *Jesus,* appeared. Theoretically and practically the way had been paved for the elements of his teachings. And even his sacrificial life and death were not new. It was the life and the passion of all prophets, among whom at least Elija and Jeremiah probably died as martyrs at the hands of their own people. All the aspects of the life and teachings of Jesus are the result of a long development of Jewish history, of the Jewish world in which Jesus arose. The new feature was that the time was ripe, mankind was ripe. For the first time all world motifs merged in one man, in a sovereign wisdom, in a sovereign heart. None of the great prophets before Jesus had his luminous serenity and his marvelous equilibrium between the strife for the sake of God and the love of man. All of his predecessors had been passionately involved in their struggles, their sufferings and their zeal; none of them had his complete, exalted detachment. Jesus combines unconditional idealism with a knowledge and care of man, and only he found contemporaries in all lands ready to accept his deeds and teachings and to follow them. What made Jesus the great leader of mankind was the crowning union of all these trends and qualities in a single man, was the conjunction of his saintly and sublime personality with the historical moment of his appearance. For "the time" was indeed "fulfilled". Everywhere in the ancient world one sensed an end and a new beginning. Jesus was the sum of sufferings of many past generations, the epic of a whole people in one simple, beautiful personal story, lived at a turning point in the history of man, and so he became the redeeming symbol of even all human suffering to come. His personal story became the symbol and nucleus of human history.

At the time it took place, the Passion of Jesus was still but an event in the history of the Jews, and one that was noted only in Palestine. The enmity between Jesus and the Pharisees was the climax of the old conflict between the prophets and priests. Both parties were the extreme exponents of the two ancient traditions and interpretations of the human relation to God, the priestly and the prophetic. The Pharisees were not at all the narrow-minded hypocrites they appeared in the later Christian version; the tradition of the prophets had stamped itself upon them too. And Jesus, on the other hand, was not as detached from the Jewish Law as the later versions have it.

The conflict centered on the validity of the Jewish Law; but it had nothing to do with the contents or with the spirit of the Law. It had nothing to do with the precepts for man's behavior toward his fellow man. On these points, both parties agreed completely. What the conflict was actually about was the maintenance of the ancient constitution of Israel, the integral theocracy of Israel— God being represented by the impersonal Law. And the question was whether man, whether a person, be he ever so inspired, should decide on what is right or wrong, or whether this should be determined by the impersonal, divine, spiritual Law; consequently, whether a human being could decide for himself, as well as for his followers about the Law itself, about what part of it is essential and what unessential. Jesus gave the strongest expression to the old prophetic tendency to let the free individual, inspired by his personal piety, make his own decision on the meaning, and the obligation entailed, of the Law. The Pharisees believed that they must hold fast to the ideal impersonal authority of the Law, preferring to pronounce every part of it as binding, to emphasizing the essential as against the unessential, the ethical, widely human principles as against the exactions of the tribal ritual.

The difference arose from questions like the one which is related in Mark 3, 1–6: Is it allowed to break the Sabbath rule in order to help your fellow man? The Pharisees adhered to the precepts of the Law that this be allowed only in the case of most dire need, of mortal danger. They held that whatever could be delayed should be left undone on the Sabbath. Jesus interpreted the Law in a more liberal way, contending that any help of an essential order could be given whenever it was necessary, regardless of the Sabbath. The Pharisees, on the other hand, knew that the Torah in its entirety was the sole support of the Jewish people; to abandon the ritual, under existing conditions, would mean the destruction not only of the Jewish people (soon afterwards [70 A.D.] Jerusalem was destroyed by Titus) but of Judaism and its superhuman idea. In his expectation of an end of the world that was close at hand and an advent of the Kingdom of God, Jesus, like the Essenes, considered every preservation of the old community futile. He wanted the individual to be prepared for the great reversal. The Pharisees, on their part, in so far as they also expected the Day of Judgment, stood all the more for the utmost obedience to the Law.

At any rate, Jesus himself observed the decree of the ritual, however freely he might interpret some points in it. In Matthew 5, 17–18, he warns: "Think not that I am come to destroy the Law ... I am not come to destroy, but to fulfil. For verily I say unto you, Till heaven and earth pass, one jot or one tittle shall in no wise pass from the Law, till all be fulfilled." And he himself was far from causing the fundamental rift between works and faith, between impersonal law and personal grace, which ultimately split Judaism from Christianism.

DOGMA AND CHURCH

IN ORDER TO UNDERSTAND the further developments, we must first consider the *situation in Judaea* at the time Jesus appeared. The central region of Judaea was ruled by a Roman procurator, while at the peripheries remnants persisted of a Judaized Edomite dynasty which was patronized and controlled by the Romans. Both regimes were hated by the people, the Roman administration as well as the corrupt rule of the Antipater and Herod, which suffered constant upheavals through family scandals. Both regimes were oppressive and arbitrary, favoring the rich and the obsequious at the expense of the patriots and the poor. There were always disorders, revolts and persecutions.

The repeated ordeals of the Jewish people, together with the stirring predictions and warnings of the prophets, had brought about the feverish expectation of a near end of the present world: it was assumed that the advent of a liberating Messiah would establish the Kingdom of God on earth.

Among the Jewish parties, the old priestly aristocracy of the Sadducees was inclined to comply with the regime. The Pharisees were relentlessly opposed to it, and tried to save the integrity of Judaism and the Jewish people by watching over the Torah and its strict observance as the stronghold of the Jewish people, until the day of the Messiah. This Messiah—so they thought—would appear first as the political liberator of the Jewish theocracy which later would become the nucleus of the universal Kingdom of God.

The prophet movement, represented chiefly by the Essenes, remained altogether aloof from all political affairs. They no longer cared about the Jewish state or the Jewish people. This was out of date, since they expected the imminent reversal to be fundamental and universal, and the Messiah to become the immediate savior of the world, without any particularly Jewish mediation. Thus the preparation for the Kingdom of God had to be individual, not tribal, the individual soul face to face with the universal God and personally responsible to him.

When Jesus was twenty to twenty-five years old, a prophet, who was in some way connected with the Essenes, was preaching. He emerged from the region where the Essenes dwelt, in the Judaean desert on the Dead Sea. He was a hermit, a man from the desert and wearing desert garb, "clothed with camel's hair and with a girdle of skin about his loins", a man who reminded the people of the prophet Elija. He wandered about, preaching along the borders of the Jordan and in Galilee, telling the people to do penance, "for the Kingdom of God is at hand." He was an extreme Nazarite, preaching abstinence from wine and women. Many followers gathered around him and he baptized them by plunging them into water in the manner of the Essenes. Hence he was called Johanan or John the Baptist. He asked people to give their belongings to the needy, he exhorted the publicans not to press the people, he told the soldiers to "do violence to no man." He said to the Pharisees, "Think not to say within yourselves: We have Abraham to our father [this means, we are safe, belonging to the preferred people]: for I say unto you that God is able of these stones to raise up children of Abraham." He attacked the tetrarch Herod on moral grounds, and he was imprisoned and executed as an insurgent, suspected of causing riots among the people.

Among those whom he baptized was *Jesus*. Jesus came from Galilee where the population consisted of poor and relatively ignorant people, fishermen, craftsmen and peasants, who were particularly susceptible to the prophetic and Messianic teachings and who had already participated in a number of political and religious uprisings. Perhaps under the influence of John the Baptist, Jesus was roused to prophecy and rapture and he preached on the same topics as John the Baptist, in the tradition of the Psalms and the Prophets, to whom he referred. He preached against the aristocracy of the priestly scribes, against the official religion and its literal observance. He taught the simple, humble piety of the heart and its good works. He spoke against the rich and the mighty as Amos and Isaiah and Jeremiah had done. Politically, this has never been harmless! He proclaimed the good message, the evangel ("eu-angelion"), the gospel, that is the God-spell, that the blessed kingdom is near. He was no more nor less than a prophet when he wandered about teaching in Galilee; in Nazareth, his birthplace, where the people did not believe him, he was not even that. He gathered poor fishermen and workers around him and some of these followed him when he went to Jerusalem. These original followers were the ones who later were called the apostles—in Greek, the "messengers".

He grew more radical in the tense atmosphere of Jerusalem, in friction with the center of the Pharisees, facing the direct impact of the terrorizing Roman administration and under the impression of the misery of the poor people. The controversies with his adversaries and the responsive enthusiasm of his followers drove him on into the role of the Messiah. Even on his way to Jerusalem, through Jericho, his popular following and support must have been considerable, according to Luke (18, 19), and he did not explicitly decline the enthusiastic acclamations greeting him as the Messiah. But the feeling that it was actually he himself who might be called upon to fulfil the Messianic task, must have grown upon him when he realized that there was no one to care for the poor and the oppressed, no one to protect them, to defend their cause and to give them comfort.

Nothing but this instinctive feeling that God intended him as the leader into the blessed kingdom, distinguished him from the earlier prophets, and this feeling dawned in his soul—as far as we can tell from the sources—in the midst of the social and political unrest among the people and at the climax of Messianic expectation.

He did not lay claim to a supernatural origin. He did not consider himself endowed with superhuman powers, as he was not able to heal people who did not believe in him (Mark 6, 5). He did not attribute to himself superhuman knowledge, for he could not tell when the Messianic realm would be established (Mark 13, 32). When he spoke of God as of his Father, he only used a phrase which was familiar and current among his contemporaries, as it is also used in the Lord's Prayer. And when he called himself a son of God, he merely referred to the old Jewish idea of men, and the peaceful and righteous men in particular, made in the image of God and children of God.

Neither did Jesus foresee or seek his martyr's death, though he was, of course, aware of the peril and the sufferings his activity involved, just as all prophets knew of the hardships and the dangers of their mission. He took every precaution against an attempt upon his life, but when he was seized by the authorities he did not resist, as he held useless every form of resistance to political power. Like the Essenes, he considered his sphere of action to be on a more fundamental and intrinsic plane.

In his death on the cross, when he cried the ancient words of the twenty-second Psalm, "My God, my God, why hast Thou forsaken me?", this was not an expression of shaken belief but of disillusionment in himself as the Messiah. But the people and especially his disciples had called him Messiah, the Anointed, the King of the Blessed Kingdom, and this roused the resentment and the fear of the Pharisees, from a religious angle, as well as that of the Roman officials, from the political point of view. The Roman procurator who sentenced Jesus to death was one of the most suspicious, one of the worst Judaea had ever had. He had already antagonized the people by having his troops march through Jerusalem wearing a picture of the Roman emperor as a god, and he executed the elders of Samaria when they arranged a popular pilgrimage in which he suspected the preparation of a political revolt. No wonder he resented Jesus being called King of the Jews, a title that he took literally, that is politically. And certainly the inscription on the cross had this meaning, although it was written in derision.

The salient feature of the development to follow was the assumption of the *disciples of Jesus* that he was the expected Messiah. Although immediately after his crucifixion they were deeply disillusioned and fled back to Galilee, frightened and discouraged, yet soon afterward they were seized with elation of which we only know the result, not the origin. We may merely guess that in his solitude, Peter, remembering his reverenced teacher, had an ecstatic vision not unlike the one that later came to Paul. Accordingly, the conviction must have grown within him that Jesus had been the Messiah, and that he was the first to have risen from his tomb and now sat at the side of God, as Daniel had prophesied when he said, "one like the son of man came with the clouds of heaven, and came to the Ancient of days [this is God] and they brought him near before him. And there was given him dominion, and glory, and a kingdom, that all people, nations, and languages, should serve him: his dominion is an everlasting dominion, which shall not pass away, and his kingdom that which shall not be destroyed." (Dan. 7, 13–14). And now Peter and his fellow disciples, to whom he communicated his faith, resumed the preaching and teaching of Jesus and returned to Jerusalem with their new message.

Yet their preaching was different from that of Jesus in that their message centered on the new vision and conviction of the Messianic character and the resurrection of Jesus. The stress had shifted from the moral content of the prophetic preachings, from the teaching concerning human behavior, to the person of the Savior himself, his resurrection and enthroning and his coming return to earth. The disciples referred to the previously quoted predictions of

Deutero-Isaiah, to the Psalms and to Daniel. Gradually, the events of Jesus' life assumed a new meaning in the light of his new position. His teachings were amplified and re-interpreted; a parallel was drawn between the Sermon on the Mount and Moses on Mount Sinai; and the Messianic character of Jesus was discovered retroactively in the whole course of his life. He was said to have been consecrated as the Messiah at the very moment John baptized him. The spirit of God was said to have descended upon him in the shape of a dove. The dove figures in an old legend of the Rabbis and it also is the bird that carries the olive branch to Noah's ark after the flood, as a message of peace and atonement. The descent of the Spirit of God was said to have been accompanied by a voice from heaven repeating the words of the second Psalm, "Thou art my Son; this day have I begotten thee."

The disciples, then, brought the new message that the Messiah had arrived and that he was a suffering Messiah, as predicted by Isaiah in his prophecy of Israel as the servant of God. The disciples, however, were still pious Jews, who observed the precepts of the Jewish Law and the Jewish rituals, as Jesus himself had done. Especially Jesus' brother, Jacobus (James), was an orthodox Jew; he even called the community of the apostles "the zealous of the Law". Like the Essenes, they carried on baptism, love-feasts and community of property.

The decisive turn toward the actual establishment of world religion was brought about by *Paul*. He effected this by fundamentally reversing original Christianity, by going beyond the bounds of Judaism, geographically, ethnically and intrinsically. We can understand the origin of this reversal only through the personality of Paul himself, his own origin and life, and his inner conflicts.

Paul, or Saul, which was his original Jewish name, was born and bred not in Judaea but in Tarsus in Asia Minor, in a Hellenistic city, where he came in close touch with Greek philosophy, especially of the Stoic School, and with the Hellenistic Mysteries, since Tarsus was an important center of the cult of Mithra, a

Persian god who became fused with Phrygian deities. Paul, however, was reared as an orthodox, law-abiding Jew, as a strict Pharisee. From allusions in his later period we may conclude that as a boy he must have suffered severely under the divergence of these two governing influences of his youth, that he must have felt torn between the sensual temptation of the Hellenistic world and the imperative commands of the Jewish Law. He threw himself all the more fanatically into Pharisaic activities and became a zealous Pharisee, conspicuous in persecuting the Christian movement. He was the chief witness to denounce one of the first Christian martyrs, Stephanus, and the Pharisees trusted him so completely as an eager partisan and anti-Christian, "breathing out threatenings and slaughter against the disciples of the Lord" (Acts 9, 1), that, at his own request, they sent him on a mission to Damascus where some of the scattered followers of Jesus had fled and where he was to hunt them out and put an end to the movement.

On this journey through the desert, the great reversal occurred, first as a fundamental change in Paul's own state of mind. It seems to have been a nervous reaction caused by an inner uncertainty rooted in his childhood, in the effect of Hellenistic impressions which he was forced to regard as illicit and forbidden. Undermined by this uncertainty, by repentance, by doubts as to the rightfulness of his persecution of the Christian movement, under the pressure of an imminent decision, the whole system of his Pharisaic convictions seems to have crumbled. He had a vision of the Messiah in heaven, ringed with splendor and calling him, "Saul, Saul, why persecutest thou me? . . . It is hard for thee to kick against the pricks." (Acts 9, 4-5). This clearly shows his previous mental struggle. The force of this struggle, his repentance for his former actions and stand, turned into a deep resentment against the Jewish Law, and from that moment on, he directed his high-strung, exaggerated eagerness and zeal against Judaism as a whole, as if it were his former self.

Thus his vision carried him much farther than Peter's had carried the disciples of Jesus. It carried him away completely, it detached him from Judaism. How it worked and where it led is clearly indicated by a later statement of Paul in the first Epistle to the Corinthians: "And last of all," he says, "Christ was seen of me also, as of one born out of due time. For I am the least of the apostles, that am not meet to be called an apostle, because I persecuted the church of God. But by the grace of God I am what I am: and his grace which was bestowed upon me was not in vain; but I laboured more abundantly than they all: yet not I, but the grace of God which was with me." (I. Cor. 15, 8–10). Here his psychological processes explain the ideological result as it is reflected in his teachings—his repentance, his resentment against his past, his jealousy of the disciples, the immediate and legitimate apostles whom he never could equal since they were sanctioned by the personal knowledge of Jesus and the close community with him. Thus he must of necessity overemphasize his missionary work, his "labouring more abundantly than they all". And he had to put stress on the grace of God which effected his conversion. For it was a conversion, and he himself was a convert, not a direct follower, won over by personal love and immediate contact.

The result of this psychological situation and of the tremendous persistent activity of Paul was what may be called his theological system, the foundation of the dogma and the church. Of course, it was not created all at once, but in a long process of gradual transformation and assimilation to the customs and ideas of the heathen. It was a fusion of the Messianic idea with the ideas and cults of the heathen, that is, with Greek philosophy and with the Hellenistic Mysteries. And this meant a complete shift, a moving of the center of gravity from the impersonal idea to the person of the Savior, from the moral content of the Law and the teachings of the prophets, including the teachings of the Prophet Jesus himself, to the passion and redemption of the Messiah. This meant, on the part of God, a shift from law to grace; on the part of man, from works to faith. It was, to express it in two words, a shift from Christianity to Christology.

The first result of Paul's change of heart was the abolishment of the Jewish Law. It is stated in the Epistle to the Romans: "For Christ is the end of the law for righteousness to every one that believeth." (Rom. 10, 4). The sacrificial death of Christ signified the end of the Law and of the old covenant between God and the Jewish people. Men were released from the commitment of this covenant and from all of its implications, because the Messiah had arrived, had died for all men and had been resurrected for all men, making all of them new and reborn to potential immortality, in so far as they believed in him. Man was transformed by the spirit of the Messiah.

This was, on the one hand, a reflection of Paul's personal experience, of his conversion by the appearance and inspiration of Christ. On the other hand, it was an effect of the *Hellenistic Mysteries* that celebrated the destinies of deities of vegetation and generation and thus contained implicitly magic acts of rejuvenation and rebirth of the human participants. Through the Hellenistic rites, human beings merged with the deities and emerged again with them, reborn to potential immortality. In the Hellenistic period, all the rigid, ancient Oriental cults became fluid and quickened. Everywhere the particular themes, the legends of divine transformations, and with them the gods of vegetation and generation, came into the foreground, everywhere the cults became mysteries, appealing to the desired participation of men, to the merging of men with divine destinies. They became orgies, that is sacred acts, from the Greek "ergon", work or deed. A general exchange of features, a mutual assimilation of cults occurred.

The Egyptian Osiris, the Babylonian god of vegetation and lord of the nether world, Tamuz, the Phoenician and Canaanite Adonis (Baal of Byblos), also a god of vegetation, the Phrygian Attis, who was said to have been born of a virgin—all these deities were supposed to undergo transformations in various ways, by dismemberment, merging with the depths, salvation, revival, resurrection. The Persian god of light, Mithra, in the religion of Zoroaster an inferior spirit among the attendants of Ahura Mazda, rose to predominance, and he too was connected with a story of resurrection. The soldiers of Pompey, fighting in the Near East, introduced this cult to Rome on their return, and there, in the later empire, it gathered crowds of adherents. It was the most powerful

of the Oriental cults in the capital, and Rome became the center
of this worship. One of its sanctuaries was situated in the very spot
where the Cathedral of St. Peter stands today, and this is not surprising, since new gods always liked to settle in places where their
defeated predecessors were worshipped, either because the sanctity
of the place was supported by this fact or because a certain sacred-
ness was inherent in certain places since prehistoric times. The
cult of Mithra fused with the rites of the Phrygian Attis whose high
priest was called "papas", pope, and "pater patrum", the father
of fathers, and wore the Phrygian cap, the Mithra and the Tiara
which the Christian popes took over and wear to this very day.
Even the throne of St. Peter still shows emblems of Mithra. Many
features of the Catholic cult were borrowed from this combined
worship of Mithra and Attis, and both eventually showed such
similarity that it was said, "ipse pileatus Christianus est"—"the
wearer of the Phrygian cap is a Christian himself". The taking of
the Holy Communion, bread and wine, originated in the rituals
of the Mithra cult, where it represented the mystical communication of the vital power of the deity to his followers. The adherents
of Mithra appeared at their ceremonies with animal masks, attributes of their god, and by this means signified that they had
donned their god. And it is to this pagan cult that Paul refers in
the Epistle to the Galatians, when he intimates that the baptized
have "put on Christ" (Gal. 3, 27).

Paul went so far in his resentment against Judaism as to reverse
the idea of the chosen people; the institution of the new covenant
meant that the heathen were now the preferred and the Jews the
temporarily rejected because of their blind fidelity to the Law.
The heathen were the true heirs and the Jews would be the last
to be redeemed.The radical rejection of the Jewish Law, with all
its implications, was the first postulate of Paul's doctrine. The
second, which originated in the Hellenistic Mysteries also and in
the Jewish eschatological speculations that were in turn influenced
by these, was that Christ was the Son of God from the outset, a
being that existed before there was even an earth, one who assumed
the form of man only to carry out the salvation of mankind, to

conquer and abolish death, and to become the restorer and redeemer of men.

And the final upshot of Paul's theory was that the new covenant between man and God was founded, as far as man was concerned, not on good works but on faith, as far as God was concerned, not on an impersonal law but on personal grace. This was the necessary prerequisite for unifying the people of all the different tribes in one creed that was not their own hereditary, innate religion. It meant a revolution in religion itself and the foundation of a world religion. It meant the abolishment of religion in its essential character, the transformation of religion into creed, into profession of belief. True religion was not founded on mere belief. It was not something one could accept and profess voluntarily and abandon voluntarily. It was a vital, biological bond, rooted in the very existence of man. It was identical with the ancestral, the tribal bond, it connected the human being with the essence of the tribe and he could free himself of it no more than of his ancestral generations, of his ethnic character. The new, Christian God was an outward God, one who came to men, appealed to them in their quality of human beings only, and with whom men were connected by a bond of confidence, of belief only. This was, as European history proves, a much looser, a partial bond, that affects only a part of human existence, and that released human beings more and more into their profane, worldly, secularized lives. To be sure, the assimilation of the Christian cult to the pagan cults maintained the power of faith over men for a considerable time, and the organization of the Catholic Church was a unique means to this end. Still, from then on, this maintenance was left to human individuals and organizations, and thus it slowly dwindled and lost its grip on the peoples.

The magical and mystical customs of the heathen, the rites of the Hellenistic Mysteries, were the stuff of which the power of the church was built. They provided faith with solid supports. Paul believed that the Christian community was in mystical union with Christ, that it represented the mystical body of Christ on earth

("Corpus mysticum Christi"). It was to be the continuation and
extension of the concept of the celestial man that Christ was the
first to incorporate. And the connection between the community
and Christ was established through definite mystical acts, *sacramental acts,* through baptism and Holy Communion. Both of these
acts originated in Jewish customs, but Paul completely changed
their meaning and character by connecting them with rites of the
mysteries.

Baptism was a custom of the Essenes and hence it was used by
John the Baptist. It was a rite of purification and sanctification. Paul
gave it the meaning of similar rites in the mysteries, a magical and
mystical meaning of sinking into death and emerging into life,
being reborn, not only symbolically but actually, in a magical way.
The baptized returns to the womb, symbolized by water, and
emerges into the air of earth, where he begins to breathe anew. He
has "put on Christ", he lives in Christ and Christ lives in him.

Holy Communion originated in the Jewish Easter Meal, the
Passah Meal, originally an agricultural feast which was later connected with the celebration of the Exodus from Egypt. Jesus observed it from the traditional angle, but his disciples carried on the
rite in memory of the Last Supper in order to honor him and to
maintain the communion of Jesus with his followers. It became the
so-called "Love Feast" of the early community. Paul transformed
it into a sacramental act, into the "Holy Communion" with Christ.
He gave it the meaning it had for the adepts of Mithra who performed the partaking of bread and wine as a magical partaking of
God, an incarnation of God. Bread and wine became the body and
blood of Christ. Later, in the Catholic Church, Holy Communion
assumed a still more complex character. It represents not only the
actual descent of God into the human body, but the magical re-
enacting, indeed the recurrence, of the sacrifice of Christ. And this
is the subject of Holy Mass.

To Paul, the bread and wine of Communion were a true taboo.
To partake of them in the wrong spirit would result in physical
death, to partake of them with a pure heart would be a means of
gaining eternal life, would be an antidote to death. As a sacramen-

tal act, Communion was detached from the common meal and the Love Feast, it became a strictly cultic performance.

In conformity with the hopes of the Jewish people, Paul believed that the Kingdom of God was close at hand. With the disciples of Jesus, he believed in the advent of Christ, in his descent from heaven. He even believed that Christ was to be only a temporary leader into the Blessed Kingdom, which God himself would rule over eventually. In this respect, he retained the old Jewish theocracy. He was, however, in great anxiety as to whether he would live to see the return of Christ. He liked to suppose that the true believers would be granted individual resurrection and individual salvation before the establishment of the Kingdom of God. This is the starting point of the concept of a Beyond, a spiritual Beyond, which later developed into a stable, ultimate sphere of salvation, the only possible remaining sphere of salvation, since the advent of the Blessed Kingdom on earth had failed to materialize.

The theological system of Paul developed in the course of his missionary work among the heathen and in his growing conflicts with his opponents, the Jewish disciples of Jesus, who strictly followed the precepts of Jesus himself, and who, therefore, did not renounce the Jewish Law. They did not agree to the table fellowship with the heathen that Paul established in Antioch. Here the name Christian appeared for the first time as a designation for the new community. This conflict eventually resulted in schism.

It was, of course, a crucial decision that had to be made. Judaism was the first missionary religion, the first religion to strive for proselytes. A considerable number of Jews were scattered through the countries of the Mediterranean as a result of the consecutive conquests of Palestine, and since the Hellenistic world was receptive to Jewish culture, the Jews had a great opportunity for making proselytes. But, on the other hand, the precepts of the tribal ritual, circumcision, dietary laws, Sabbath rest, were almost insuperable obstacles to proselytizing. For the heathen, especially the Greeks who were sympathetic to the idea of Judaism, to its spiritual God, its revelation, its moral teachings, were not inclined to accept the ritual also. Thus the Jewish communities in the Hellenistic world attracted groups of sympathizers, fellow travelers, so-called God-worshippers ("sebomenoi"), who did not become Jews because of the difficulty of the ritual, but who still worshipped the Jewish God.

Paul knew that there was no possibility of spreading the idea of the Christian community among the heathen unless it were severed from Jewish Law. He therefore had to choose between the Jews and the heathen, and he chose the heathen, not only because of his resentment against the Jews, but because this was the only opportunity for making Christianity a world religion and for spreading his faith among the peoples.

He went on a long missionary voyage through Asia Minor and Greece and finally came to Rome. Everywhere the Jewish communities, or rather the pagan sympathizers around the Jewish communities, the pagan "worshippers" of the Jewish God, were the most susceptible to the new faith. They became the core of the new Christian communities. The traces of the life of Paul, as those of Peter's, disappear in Rome. It is supposed that both died there as martyrs (about 64 A.D.).

As soon as Paul's combination of Judaism and Hellenistic Mysteries spread through the Hellenistic world, and Christian communities sprang up everywhere, the third element of Christianism joined and mingled with this synthesis: *Greek philosophy.*

In the third century B.C., a Greek translation of the Old Testament had been completed for the Hellenistic Jews in Alexandria, who no longer knew their mother tongue, but spoke and understood only Greek. At the time of Jesus, a scholarly Hellenistic Jew, Philo of Alexandria (about 25 B.C. to about 50 A.D.), worked out a blend of Judaism and Greek philosophy, especially Platonic and Stoic philosophy, and so initiated subsequent Christian theology. He fused the Jewish spiritual God with the Platonic and Stoic Supreme Idea or all-pervading spiritual force and soul, which dominates the corporeal world. His momentous innovation was that between the spiritual divine Idea and the corporeal and sensual world he inserted an intermediary link, the Logos, which was understood in the double meaning of the Greek, as word and reason. Word and reason are one in the Greek term. And in this intermediary link he had found the connecting factor between the eternal, spiritual God, who is identical with the Supreme Idea, and the corporeal world. The Logos was, on the one hand, the word of the revelation which carried the spirit of God to human beings, the word of God which created the world and gave substance to the divine spirit. The Logos was, on the other hand, the first son of God, the oldest angel, the genuine image of God, and as such the true mediator between God and man, the advocate of man before God.

From this intermediary link which Philo introduced, a mass of various intermediary substances, emanations, hypostases, stages, unfolded in the systems of Neo-Platonism and Gnosticism. And after the spread of Pauline Christianism, this philosophic trend fused with it, fused with the established synthesis of Judaism and Hellenistic Mysteries so that all three elements were united. The result was the most powerful Gnostic movement: philosophic mystery and a mystic and magic philosophy. Gnosticism animated philosophic speculation; it made it into a religious movement of life. To the Gnostics, knowledge became a magical, mystical process, a performance like the mysteries, a gradual approach, an ascent to God in many stages and initiations. Through ecstatic and ascetic exercises man raised himself toward the spiritual God, who in turn leaned down to man through his revelation—a scheme already traced in the philosophy of Aristotle.

The author of the Gospel of St. John (probably second century), who was well acquainted with the Gnostic systems, finally identified Christ with the Logos. Thus Christ became only the temporary incarnation of a divine and spiritual substance, and his personal life was no less than a continuous revelation of God. The authors of the earlier gospels had already established that Christ had been born by immaculate conception from the spirit of God. Jesus himself was deified more and more.

The Gnostic movement was the most dangerous competitor of Christianism proper, as it threatened to thin the actual personality and the personal life and passion of the Redeemer to a web of abstract speculation. After a long struggle it was declared heresy. The Roman Emperor Constantine, who, partly for political reasons, complied with Christianism and started the development which made it the official religion of the empire, decided to settle the quarrels once and for all. He summoned the first oecumenical synod (thereby creating this institution), and at this Synod (325 A.D.) the definite form of the Christian faith was stipulated and at the same time made into a binding law of the empire. The dogma, i.e. the creed that became compulsory, was established. The divinity of Christ, his immaculate conception and the Holy Trinity were included: God the Father, Christ and the Holy Ghost or the Logos, are three stages or forms of a single, divine substance.

Still another feature of later Christianism distinguishes it sharply from early Christianity and is significant for the transformation that original Christianity suffered by its fusion with pagan elements. This is the *worship of saints* and the *cult of relics*. This worship originated in the reverence for prominent martyrs for the Christian faith, and was, from the outset, connected with the cult of relics. It began in the second century A.D. The first traces of it, dating from about 150, were discovered in Smyrna, where the Roman governor had the corpse of the martyr Polycarp burned in order to prevent his adoration, and the Christians are said to have recovered his bones from the ashes, hiding them in a secret place where they gathered to celebrate the rebirth of the martyr to eternal life. Such celebrations increased and became more and more usual when people sought the mediation of the sanctified martyrs who were supposed to have been raised to God. Miraculous powers were attributed to their mortal remains.

With the reign of Constantine, when large sections of the population joined the Christian community, the cult of local martyrs who were supposed to protect and to patronize their local communities, began to develop into a new form of pagan worship of local deities. Indeed, it fused with the cult of old local heroes and deities, and it was even deliberately used by the church as a means to supplant and transform the local cults to which the heathen continued to cling. So the simple revering of martyrs became an elaborate adoration of saints, and the Christian heaven grew thronged with a multitude of sanctified mediating spirits, vested with supernatural powers. These worked miracles and patronized not only localities, cities and villages, but also special professions and conditions of life, in the manner of the ancient deities. Children were called after special saints in order to be put under their patronage; from this the custom of the name-day, the saint's festival, derived. In the course of this process, an exchange of saints and their cults among neighboring and even distant communities took place. A spreading of the cults followed, and eventually these more and more numerous half-deities, who were on a par with angels, were incorporated in the system of the Catholic faith. In a little place near Alexandria, in Egypt, for instance, the cult of the old Egyptian goddess Isis still flourished at the beginning of the fifth century. This cult attracted heathens and Christians alike because of the oracles and miraculous healings the Egyptian goddess was believed to accomplish. The Christian authorities proceeded to erect a church close to the temple of the goddess and transferred the relics of two newly discovered martyrs to this church, and through their relics, these saints forthwith competed in miraculous works and healings with the pagan deity and, in this way, succeeded in winning the population over to the Christian faith. Another method of luring the heathen into Christianism was the invention of legends of saints. The legends are the myths of Christianity.

Later on, as the persecutions ceased and there were no new martyrs, particularly pious and zealous men, missionaries, heroes of asceticism and the propagation of the faith, were officially raised to the status of saints, and it goes without saying that all apostles and fathers of the church were worshipped as saints. In the course of time, Mary, the mother of Jesus, attained a peculiar significance and position. According to the theory of Jesus' immaculate conception, Mary from the earliest days of Christianism was pictured as a chaste ascetic, living a life remote from the world and entirely devoted to God. At the beginning of the fourth century, she is called "Mother of God", the sinless saint, and as such, her cult rises and fuses with the worship of ancient mother deities. But this cult did not reach its extraordinary importance and exalted meaning until the late Middle Ages, when, among the Germanic and Romanic populations in Northern and Western Europe, it almost surpassed the worship of God the Father and even of Jesus Christ himself. It was then that the picture of Mary assumed the essentially feminine and motherly features of mercy and kindness, tenderness and solicitude, which prevailed over all other qualities. In this epoch she became "Our Blessed Lady", "Notre Dame" and "Madonna". The reason for this was that the church had evolved a new, stern law, the orthodox dogma, in which, through ecclesiastical authority, Jesus had been made the supreme judge. The human being, in his feeling of inescapable sinfulness, in his attempt to evade the severe rule of Christ, appealed to the clemency of the Blessed Lady and Mother for mediation and protection. In order to reassure themselves, people praised and exalted the power of her clemency. The adoration of the "Queen of Heaven" was expressed in countless songs of minstrels and poets, and in innumerable pictures of monks and lay artists, and together with the cults of the saints, became a powerful motive in the development of European art.

The Jewish God, as an invisible and essentially spiritual God, was not to be conjured in images since he was not to be grasped by the senses. It was strictly forbidden to picture him in a human or in any palpable form. With the Jews, image was identical with idol, and this radically distinguished their worship from all other ancient cults. That is why the Jews had no art of any importance. In the earlier periods of Christianism, image worship was a grave issue in the struggle between pagan and genuine Christian trends. In the end, the pagan influence prevailed here also. But the great reform movements at the turn of our modern world—Savonarola in Florence, the Anabaptists and the Reformation in Germany, Holland, England and Scotland—all went back to original Christianity, to the Bible text and even to the Old Testament, and, accordingly, all were iconoclastic.

Let us finally consider the *development of the church*. The first

Christian communities were of an informal character, in which all members were equal, and there were no offices, but only services voluntarily performed. In the post-apostolic communities, organization began with a group of elders, presbyters, eminent men who were the survivors of the founding generation and handed down the tradition. They were the representatives of the community in matters of common concern. This institution may go back to the elders of the Jewish Synagogues or to the senates of Roman provincial cities. When affairs grew more complex and serious responsibilities were involved, the community selected from among these presbyters special officials called "episkopoi", bishops, literally, overseers, supervisors (in Latin, pastores, shepherds), who were assisted in minor matters, such as caring for the poor, by deacons, that is, servants or assistants. These bishops and deacons, together with the presbyters, formed a body which was called "kleros", clergy, the men of rank, the élite. But these men were not yet limited in number, and, in addition to them, any inspired and prophetic personality could teach and gain influence in the community. In the course of the second century, internal troubles, the peril to the communities and, last but not least, the theological controversies and heresies strengthened the position of the officials, who demanded lifelong authority and referred to the example of the ancient priestly hierarchy and to military discipline. The bishop gradually achieved a monarchical function in which all the rights of teaching and supervising were concentrated. At the end of the second century, the fictitious assumption sprang up that the bishops were the successors of the apostles, the transmitters of the genuine, true, apostolic tradition and that they alone were endowed with the knowledge of the divine truth. No irregular, informal, personal appeal, no prophetic inspiration, was further recognized. As the sacred successors of the Apostles, tracing back their authority through this succession to the immediate contact with Jesus Christ himself, the bishops assumed the exclusive power of binding and loosing, that means of exercising and executing the church discipline, of punishment and of absolution from sins. The bishop became the supreme judge in the place of Christ. He was endowed with the so-called "power of the key", the key to the salvation of the soul.

In the middle of the third century, this position of the bishop was established as a sacred dogma. The bishops and the presbyters were recognized as priests, as substitutes for Christ and as the sole legitimate mediators between the layman and God. They had the privilege of performing Holy Communion, of bringing Christ down to the people and raising man up to Christ. They had the exclusive power to grant or deny the grace of God. This power became all the more effective as the hope of a near advent of the Kingdom of God on earth faded, and men had to comfort themselves with the hope of an individual salvation in the Beyond.

This state of mind and this state of affairs was confirmed and consolidated at the end of the fourth century by the theory of Augustine (354–430), an African convert whose hot-tempered sensuality changed to an ardent fanaticism and asceticism which made him one of the initiators of the Christian monastic orders. Being a convert, he again emphasized the omnipotence of the grace of God to which he attributed his conversion. He even went so far as to claim that human behavior was utterly unimportant in the light of this all-powerful grace of God. Grace, moreover, according to him, is an impersonal, objective force that Jesus Christ himself cannot dominate. He proclaimed the doctrine of original sin, the inevitable sin of all human beings and the predestined salvation or condemnation of individuals by the inscrutable grace of God. The bestowal of this grace becomes manifest to men through the fact that they are protected by the church. The church is the only infallible vessel of the Divine Spirit, it is, in itself, the earthly manifestation of the Kingdom of God, the "Civitas Dei". This theory greatly fortified the position of the church.

The feeling of sinfulness that made the layman dependent upon the church, was increased by the institution of confession that preceded absolution, Holy Communion and the bestowal of grace. In early Christian times, the view had prevailed that baptism cleansed man of his heathen sins and made him as one reborn. But soon it could not be denied that sin occurred within Christendom also, and accordingly, moral requirements were lowered; various degrees of sanctity, corresponding to the various abilities of man, were established. But as the feeling of inevitable sin became stronger, regular absolution grew necessary. Penances were interpreted as a voluntary anticipation and lessening of the punishments of Hell. Among these penances prescribed for the washing away of sin, self-humiliation in public became more and more common. As monastic life became more general, the monks, who had to measure up to the highest rung of sanctity, extended the idea of sin from actual misdeeds to evil thoughts and instincts in man. And in addition to the public confession of guilt that the brothers had to make every evening, special cases resorted to secret confession, which spread from the monastery to the lay world. Here the priests seized upon this new custom and made it a powerful tool of the might of the church over man.

The Roman bishop, as the ruler of the largest community and of the metropolis of the world, became predominant among all other bishops. This predominance was supported by the fact that two Apostles, Peter and Paul, had taught in Rome and that from these the Roman bishop could derive a line of traditional authority. But the Roman bishops went still further in strengthening their position. They connected Peter's sojourn in Rome with a saying of Jesus that had been inserted in the Gospel of Matthew (16, 18-19). The original name of Peter had been Simon and he was given the name of Petros, rock. Jesus was supposed to have said to Peter: "Thou art Peter and upon this rock I will build my church ... And I will give unto thee the keys of the kingdom of heaven: and whatsoever thou shalt bind on earth shall be bound in heaven: and whatsoever thou shalt loose on earth shall be loosed in heaven." On this passage the church based the authorization of its power over the destiny of souls, and the Roman bishop in particular, his rule over the church. Hence the See of the Roman bishop was called the See of Peter. Subsequently, the Roman papacy secured further privileges through falsifications. The most important of these was the so-called "donation of Constantine", according to which—so it was claimed—the Emperor Constantine, in gratitude for his baptism and for being healed of leprosy, granted to Pope Sylvester I "the dominion over Rome and over all the provinces of Italy, or the regions of the Occident" and also pre-eminence over all other bishoprics. This document that was probably manufactured by the papal secretary in the eighth century for the purpose of facilitating negotiations with the ruler of the Franks, was proven false as early as 1440 by the humanistic scholar, Laurentius Valla.

When the Roman Empire was divided and the emperor set up his residence in Byzantium, it looked as if the position of the Roman bishop would be diminished in importance. Actually, it became still more important. For this event was the cause of his independence, it laid the foundation for the temporal empire of the church.

Thus the great movement which began with the opposition of the prophets to the priests, and which led up to the spiritual triumph of deliverance brought by Jesus, finally fell into the hands of the priests. The priests had conquered.

SEPARATION OF THE SPIRITUAL
AND THE SECULAR

UNIVERSALITY AND INDIVIDUALITY

AFTER CHRISTIANITY had been securely established, human history came to a turning point. The stress shifted to a new scene of action, it began moving northward to the European mainland, and the whole direction of events, the whole trend of evolution prepared to change.

What stage had mankind reached at this point? First of all, a material, geographical unification of the "inhabited world", in the Greek and Roman sense of the word, a unification of the oecumenical world under one rule, had been achieved. This "inhabited world" was not identical with the actual inhabited world. A huge section of mankind, of which the peoples of the Mediterranean had no definite knowledge, was excluded from it, and even great cultures and civilizations, such as the Chinese and the Indian, were not taken into account. These peoples were building up their own cultures apart from Europe and the Near East, and were at this time in very distant, indirect and vague connection with other parts of the earth. They were to join the European world only at a much later date. The mere use of the term oecumenical for the scope of the Roman Empire, the identification of the "inhabited world" with the Roman Empire, shows the almost complete unawareness of those remote cultures. But the cultural sphere of the European world was united in the Roman Empire and not only superficially. It gradually gained a certain degree of homogeneousness through the extension of Roman civilization, of Roman city life and citizenship, over the whole area from Egypt and Mesopotamia to Britain and the Danube, from Spain and North Africa to the Black Sea. Everywhere there were Roman roads and buildings, Roman municipalities and institutions. Everywhere people had been taught to set up true cities, to live true city life.

The Roman Empire has often been compared to the British Empire, or vice versa, as both of them had a similar way of dealing with the foreign peoples under their domination. Thus the Roman administration was not as a rule despotic. It generally left the customs of the various populations untouched and let them go their own way; it merely put up its institutions in their midst in order to show them the conveniences of these institutions, and so, gradually, induced them to enjoy and emulate the new advanced forms and the concomitant comforts and pleasures. The Roman administration usually succeeded in making these populations eager and proud to belong to the oecumenical civilization of the world-dominating metropolis. In so doing, Rome was greatly helped by the fact that Roman civilization was intellectually identical with Hellenistic civilization, which for centuries had favored the intermingling of cults and customs. In the Mediterranean world there was only one exception to this rule—Judaism and Judaea, that stubbornly resisted this intermingling and that neither tolerated nor accepted the official cult of the divine city and the deified emperor as a tribute to the ruling civilization. It was the only people and the only religion that caused perpetual trouble and difficulties to the government; and the Romans were not able to incorporate it in their regime. They had to conquer Judaea again and again until they themselves were conquered by Christianity, which carried on the Roman struggle against Judaism for different reasons and on a different plane.

Under Caracalla (212 A.D.), the empire extended Roman citizenship to all free people that lived within its bounds. Thus, subjects who had been connected with Rome collectively, as whole provinces, through their respective provincial governments, their proconsuls and procurators, now achieved a direct relationship to the great city. They were allowed to rise to the highest ranks and to

hold the highest offices, even the supreme office of the emperor himself. This gradually changed the character and the constitution of
the city and empire of Rome. The extension of citizenship was accompanied by the gradual *transformation of the old city-state,* with
its nucleus of Roman nobility, its peripheral populations and its
sacred officials and authorities, into a centralized and leveled bureaucratic state with new imperial offices and functions supplanting
the old. Under the influence of the peregrine law, the original restricted law of the polis, which privileged the citizens of Roman
descent and retained the rigidity of the ancient tribal laws, was
transformed into the common law of the empire.

This process was first, and was first intended to be, a democratization. The anarchical raising of emperors by the armies during
the third century had already constituted a social revolution. It
was the revenge the barbarian and peasant population, which then
formed the bulk of the armies, took upon the rich and cultured
city bourgeoisie. Among the emperors who afterwards laid the
foundations for the new order of the state were men of non-Italic
descent, and some of their successors, who completed this new order, even rose from the lowest strata of the population, from peasant
origins. Diocletian is said to have been an enfranchised slave. The
trend which guided the reform was influenced by the Stoic ideal of
tolerance, as Marcus Aurelius expressed it, "the concept of a state
with one law for all, and founded on freedom of speech, of a government that sets the freedom of those governed before all." The
process resulted in a thorough bureaucratization, indeed, in a kind
of totalitarianism. All the equal citizens were equally compelled
and harassed by the centralized government of an absolute monarchy. Under the rulership of Diocletian, the sacred emperor became "dominus", lord, and was surrounded by a large, ostentatious
retinue and a meticulous court ceremonial, the famous Byzantine
ceremonial. Diocletian put an end to military anarchy and usurpation by separating the civil from the military command. He had
to reorganize the disrupted economic system brought about by an
inflation of the currency. He had to provide the means for the costly
administration of the court and the large mercenary armies which

protected the empire against the perpetual invasions of barbarian peoples who, driven by restlessness within and unrest without, wanted to change their location. Hence, a huge increase in taxes became necessary. The government had to resort to a system of forced levies in kind, and of compulsory state service, from which nobody was exempt and which gradually exhausted and ruined the population.

The Roman Empire, originating in a city-state, taught its peoples city life and civilization. They became accustomed to thinking and acting in urban terms. The state was identical with the dominating city. The country, the land, was only its extension, it had no life and meaning of its own and existed only for the purpose of feeding and supporting the city. The Roman government regarded the provinces merely as the territory surrounding cities. It ruled the land and exploited the resources of the land through the cities. But as all consistent pursuit of a principle finally leads to its reversal, so the extreme urbanization of the Roman city-state paradoxically resulted in the disruption of the cities and of city life.

The provincial cities were organized on the pattern of the metropolitan city-state, of the "metro-polis", the Greek for mother-city. They had their provincial senates consisting of rich landowners who originally lived in the city and, like the Roman senators, had their estates, their villas cultivated by slaves or free tenants ("coloni") under the direction of an administrator. These provincial bodies were called "municipia", municipalities, literally, "taking charge of services or disbursements (munera)", a meaning which indicates the custom of providing duties in kind or in money for the metropolis, the armies and the state. They had to deliver to the state part of their revenues, and the amount of these deliveries was fixed every year according to the requirements. Only the aristocracy of the Roman senators were exempt from all duties.

Under the new, centralizing order of Diocletian and Constantine, these provincial municipalities and their members and officials, the "decuriones", were held responsible for the deliveries of their ever-increased duties and taxes. The term "decuriones", originally a military designation of commanders of a "decuria", a division of ten horsemen, was later transferred to arrangements of the political administration, and was used for the leaders of sub-groups of the senate and other governmental bodies. In the provinces, it comes to mean simply the senators of municipalities. The taxes became so heavy that all tried to escape in every possible way, to desert the cities, to flee to the country and to become soldiers, monks or peasants, if escape upward into the ranks of the Roman senators could not be effected. The result was that the citizens were forcibly prevented from leaving their city. Every trip, every sale or lease of property, every bequest was made subject to the approval of the provincial governor. Only donations were free—and this became the preferred means of escape. A member of the municipality gave away his estates as a donation to some powerful patron, a senator, an official or a bishop, who were all in favored positions, and he took it back as a loan, a tenure. As this agreement was private and not protected by law, it was made on the basis of confidence. Neither the receiver of the donation nor the receiver of the tenure paid any fees. The former got the actual property and the latter all the rights of possession, including the right to make alterations on the property, but he got it as an act of benevolence on the part of his patron, he had no legal claim to it whatsoever. Such an agreement was called a *"precarium"*, as it was effected only by "preces", that is by request, by petition. And its grant was indeed rather precarious, as this word which derives from it, indicates. In fact, it put the receiver of the tenure at the mercy of the benefactor, who had to be courted and given service in return for the continuance of the tenure.

The position of the lower strata of the population was no better. The craftsmen and artisans of the cities were organized in hereditary guilds, that is to say, the groups that had originally formed for cultic purposes—since every craft had its patron deity—were transformed into compulsory unions in order to control and secure service, and thus the individuals were tied to their jobs. In the rural districts—since taxes were fixed according to the number of laborers as well as of acres—the condition of the slaves was theoretically improved, as they could no longer be bought and sold at the will of their owners. They became serfs, bound to the soil rather than to their owners. On the other hand, the free tenants sank to a much worse position, as the power of their landlord over them was considerably increased. Besides paying rent, they had to work for their landlords during a certain period. And since the landlord was responsible for their taxes, they also became bound to the soil. The landlord, moreover, exerted jurisdictional and police powers over them. Thus their position was practically the same as that of the serfs, and they began to fuse with the serfs into a single caste.

The condition of the free, small landowners was hardly more favorable, since they faced the same troubles from the tax collectors. They no longer had the ambition to improve their land, to extend their property, since they did not want to become members of the city municipalities, a rise in rank that meant only added burdens. The consequences of this sad state of affairs were blighting; the cities were deserted and their life was paralyzed. Even the great senators of the metropolis preferred to spend most of their time on their estates, where they lived quietly among many friends, clients and servants, undisturbed by dangerous court intrigues and rapidly changing political currents in which they no longer took an active part. Political influence had been delegated to the court and the army.

The functioning of the state and the official relations between the state and the people were reduced to the greatest possible exploitation of the citizens. The empire gradually lost its grip on the population. It could not prevent the people from escaping the official arrangements and seeking new kinds of arrangements which were all of a strictly private character and based only on relations between individuals. Besides the donation of property against tenure, another kind of private arrangement was the surrender of one's person to a powerful patron (again a metropolitan senator, an official or a bishop) for protection against administrative pressure, state services, taxes and so forth, an agreement which corresponded exactly to the donation of property. It, too, was based on loyalty, on "fides", fidelity, it, too, was private and unprotected, unacknowledged by the law. It exchanged protection on the part of the patron for personal attendance and services on the part of the client. This agreement was called the *"clientele"* (from the Latin "cluere", to hear, to listen to advice, to obey), and it was used as a means of escape by individuals of all ranks and classes of the free population. These new private and personal dependencies became the structural elements of the medieval world, of the social order designated as the feudal system.

The Roman Empire in its last expansion created a new attitude in the human being. It evolved the private individual estranged from the community and defending himself against the exactions of that community. Roman citizenship and Hellenistic civilization detached people from their particular tribal bond, but the huge dilute Roman "civitas", which in those times was identical with the universe, was no substitute at all for the tribal bond. It had indeed taught people many things; it had laid the foundation for the tradition of nations to come, but in itself it was too huge, too general to be grasped, and its main effect was to oppress and overburden its citizens.

The Hellenistic philosophy, especially the Stoic philosophy, was the theoretical counterpart of this practical attitude of abstention from public and political life. It advocated an intellectual and moral stand of tolerant resignation, of retirement and of meditation. It confronted man with the universe. Christianity created a corresponding attitude; the human being had to face his universal God and Redeemer of mankind. These three attitudes are the expression of the one feature essential to the epoch: *individuality facing universality* and facing it directly without any intermediary community, experiencing it as a contrast, as an outward phenomenon with which there is no intrinsic connection.

The fundamental innovation of this whole epoch is that the individual stands forth, the lonely private individual, with all his ancestral, tribal bonds broken off, the earthly individual standing on his own feet, under the vast sky of universality. And this is the turning point of human history. From now on, from the beginning of the Christian era, the individual is the point of departure for all coming events, and the new developments are directed toward building up worldly communities of individuals, toward the formation of collectives in the true sense of the word.

These new developments were very gradual, and it required centuries, during which apparently nothing at all happened, for these underground processes of history to run their secret course until they burst into the open and were acknowledged as human evolution.

The position of the individual had been created in the Roman Empire, but it was still a long way to his shaping and completion, a way leading from the decline of the Roman Empire to the European Renaissance. At first, this development went on under the surface. Even had it been recognized, it could not have been acknowledged, since the last apparently stable, eternal order still dominated the world.

This period of preparation, when a universal order still seemed to sway the world and when, under cover of this universal order, a turmoil of confused and complex developments was brewing, goes by the name of the Middle Ages, and the universal order was provided by the Catholic Church. This spiritual, universal order, which from the beginnings of Christianity unfolded to an immense vault protecting and breeding new processes, this protecting stability was born of sheer necessity. The church was plunged into a struggle for temporal power.

World religion is not a natural, vital bond, not an unquestioned bond such as the ancient, tribal religions. It is based on faith, and it must constantly strive to win, to maintain and to strengthen that faith. It was born from mission and conversion, and it has to carry on mission, persuasion and conversion in order to maintain its power over human beings. In meeting the multifold requirements of the human soul, of the lonely, exposed and confused individual, who is severed from his ancient ties and not as yet able to walk the ways of earth alone, in filling his needs, the Catholic Church grew and expanded and became a true "Catholic" Church, that is, a universal church ("Catholic" is the ecclesiastical correlative to the Roman and Hellenistic "Oikumene"). It became a "Catholic"

Church not only externally in that it covered and claimed the earth, but also intrinsically, in that it included all the ways and means of appeal to the human mind, wooing and threat, spiritual and sensual approach. It has become a world in itself. Its delegates are present in all movements. It plays its one broad theme in every key and on all the strings.

Through this immense latitude of its activity and appeal, the church was able to continue on a more profound level what the Roman Empire and Hellenistic speculation had begun. It achieved its great work of European civilization, human equalization and education, and it carried it to the saturation point. In order to imbue the human soul with even a small part of the teachings of Christ, it required the fusion with magic cults and mysteries, the politics of popes and the growing indulgence to the layman; perhaps—though this is a painful thought—it even required the massacres of heretics and Jews, the terror of the crusades and the Inquisition, and the atrocities of the conquests of Mexico and Peru, to sweep along and to spread these teachings. The powerful and pompous hierarchy made possible the existence and the exemplariness of true Christians, of humble saints and of devoted monks, and it is because the Catholic Church asserted and maintained itself that our civilization, such as it is, is a Christian civilization based on the idea of the unity of mankind.

The early church allowed the heathen the support of their familiar magic cults and mysteries, replacing the worship of local deities by the worship of its martyrs and saints, and so led these converts toward the imminent reversal of the world by the Messiah and toward a common resurrection in the Kingdom of God on earth. This was the time of the martyrs, of early Christian fanaticism and heroism. Later, when the Kingdom of God did not materialize, the dwindling hope for a common resurrection was replaced by the promise of individual resurrection and salvation in the hereafter, and the road to this led through the "power of the key" of an already organized church. And after Augustine, the powerful church itself became the antechamber on earth of the Kingdom of God, the well-established spiritual Kingdom of God on earth. Even before this, it had become the official religion of the empire with the emperor as its chief.

The inner torpor and disruption of the Roman Empire were furthered from without by the ever-increasing assaults and invasions of barbarian populations from the North, which were thrust forward by the great movement of migrations from the Far East. This dangerous situation made it necessary for Diocletian to share his power with other emperors of equal rank, to leave the imperial residence in Rome and to set up capitals closer to the frontiers, in Milan and in Asia Minor. Constantine, who for the time being had reunited the empire under his rule, transferred the residence to Byzantium (Constantinople) and ultimately the empire divided into two sections, a Western Latin section and an Eastern Greek section which became the Byzantine Empire, lasting up to the Turkish conquest of Constantinople in 1453.

The Western Latin section, however, was soon flooded by Germanic invasions to which it was much more exposed. The weakened regime of the Western Empire ended in the fifth century. And the Roman bishops, the popes, who had gradually built up their supremacy over the church, who, moreover, had been considerably enriched by the emperors and had become the wealthiest in the church—amid the turmoil of the barbarian conquests, these popes remained the only stronghold of the imperial tradition. With the network of their church organization, they became the transmitters of the Roman tradition to the North and the West. The organization and administration of the church was in close analogy to that of the Roman World Empire. Canon Law continued the tradition of Roman Law. The spiritual empire of the church, extending over the whole area of the Roman provinces to Britain and Gaul and the Danube, endured when these provinces were lost in the dissolution of the Western Empire. The popes retained their spiritual power and carried on the Roman work of civilization among the Germanic tribes, until their rivals, the German emperors, the rulers of a temporal Holy Roman Empire, which was in the making, began to compete with them and to revolt against their spiritual rule.

So the ancient Roman Empire also split into a spiritual section, represented by the papacy and the church, and a temporal section represented by the Germanic Empire. This partition reflects a new dualism, originating in the Platonic dualism, of the Christian dogma itself: the dualism of body and spirit. World religion became a definite, limited portion of human existence, a spiritual sphere of its own, but beneath it the evolution toward secularization had begun and at a given moment, in the Renaissance, broke through as an independent current of thought.

This dualism became much more obvious and led to much more radical consequences among the *barbarian peoples of the North* than among the heathen of the ancient Mediterranean world. Christianization and civilization of those Northern tribes presented many more difficulties than did that of the Oriental peoples. These had gone through more or less preparatory stages of civilization and Christianization. They had developed and perfected religious systems, pantheons, trinities and distinct deities, temples and images, sacred kingdoms and hierarchies, bureaucracies and great residences which had been the substratum for the development of the Greek and Roman city. They went through centuries of Hellenistic and Roman regime, and their cults and mysteries were part of the Christian world religion. Thus they easily and willingly adopted the customs and conveniences of Roman and Christian civilization, in which they found many familiar features.

It was entirely different with the barbarian tribes of the North. The Celtic tribes were the vanguard of the migrating populations that successively invaded the European continent. They were also the most advanced in culture. They pushed forward to the extreme West, into Gaul, the British Isles and Italy, in the early period of the Roman Republic, and were gradually penetrated by Roman rule. The Germanic peoples, on the other hand, were barbarians pure and simple when they came in contact with highly civilized Rome and Christianity. They were still in the first developmental stages of humanity, worshipping half-totemistic demons, natural forces without definite shape, and caught in the chaos of primeval participation and changing of forms. They had not developed any clear concepts, any images of deities, settled sanctuaries, temples or a definite priesthood. Socially and politically, these tribes were half nomadic, always ready to change their dwelling-places, never attached to the soil for any length of time and, accordingly, acquainted only with primitive, superficial methods of agriculture. For the most part they were unfamiliar with the idea of personal property. Only the use of the soil was meted out—not always equally, since successful war leaders already enjoyed special privileges. Among some of these tribes, a predominance of certain noble families deriving from such leaders, and even the rule of a hereditary chieftain or king, had been established. These chieftains, however, were merely first among equals, as is indicated by the term "Koenig" (king), which means simply "a man of good birth", and "Fuerst", which is identical with "first". They were elected by the tribal community, but the candidates had to belong to noble families. The Germanic tribes had no fixed centers, neither castles nor extensive settlements. They lived in scattered villages or even on isolated farmsteads. When they learned to know Roman cities they exhibited horror, as of something uncanny; they looked upon them as "burial places", according to the report of a baffled Roman historian, and they destroyed them wherever they could. Even after they had established close relations with Romans and had become Christians, the Merovingian kings of the Franks never became accustomed to city life or to any form of settled life. They moved from one farm on their estates to another, eating up their produce.

There was an immense gap between the primitive condition of these Germanic tribes and the refined Roman civilization they were called upon to inherit, particularly the sublimated, Christian world religion which they had to accept as part and parcel of this heritage. There were neither similarities nor reminiscences connecting them with these advanced cultural systems and concepts, which the Germans took a long time to understand and to assimilate—German civilization and Christianization, at least in the region beyond the Danube, which was never touched by Roman influence, always remained somewhat superficial. The inheritance of the Roman Empire which their kings were proud and eager to take over, as well as the Christian religion which they were called upon to protect and to propagate, was something entirely foreign to them. It caused a premature break of their tribal bonds, which had not yet developed to a point that would have prepared them for their new duties. The whole future of the German people, its whole fateful history, must be understood from this unfortunate beginning, from the too stringent demands on the part of their destiny.

The abrupt break of tribal bonds made of these tribesmen lost, desolate individuals, incapable of grasping the too high ideals of Christianity and of the empire. They clung to their saint missionaries and clergymen in a personal and private relationship based on personal confidence only. As to their political situation, one institution of the Germanic tribes became extremely important, an institution which was well adapted to the conditions that had developed as a result of the disintegration of the Roman Empire, and, in a way, corresponded to the private and personal dependencies that are known under the names of "precarium" and "clientele". Apart from the tribal kingdom or leadership which was authorized by the common consent of the tribe, it was a Germanic custom that a single, private warrior could summon personal followers in order to start a campaign on his own initiative. The bond between such a private leader and his personal follower, the *"Gefolgschaft"*, was a purely personal, mutual agreement, valid only for the duration of this special campaign. Such an agreement pledged the leader the full support of his follower, loyalty and faithfulness unto death, and, in return, promised the follower full instruction in the profession of arms, protection, community of goods and an adequate share of the booty. This relation, again, was based merely on personal confidence, on fidelity, on trust, and such followers were called trustees ("trustes"). The leaders sometimes gathered a considerable following. They competed with other leaders and made alliances of their own, regardless of the tribe or clan. Clovis, the Merovingian chief, who achieved the conquest of Gaul and who became the founder of the Frankish Monarchy, the nucleus of the Holy Roman Empire, was not a real, authorized king. He was just such a private leader who had gathered a group of followers for his campaign and who, after the conquest, rewarded their services with grants of land. The bulk of the Frankish tribes had been left behind in their homes along the Rhine.

This unique institution of the Germanic tribes became an essential element of the medieval feudal system, when it fused with the corresponding "precarium" and clientele system which had developed with the dissolution of city life in the disintegrating Roman Empire. Thus the feudal, medieval empire started from and consisted of mutual obligations between private individuals, obligations based on personal trust and confidence alone. The Holy Roman Empire was never a state, but only a complex system of such mutual bonds, an immense, confused hierarchy of vassals and feudal lords who, in turn, were vassals of higher lords, and so forth, up to the emperor. Because of this lack of all solidly established state institutions the juxtaposition of individuality and universality, of body and spirit, of worldliness and religion, reached its limit in the medieval empire.

The relation between *the Frankish king and the Roman Pope* was also in the nature of a personal bond of mutual support, patronage and promotion. In analogy to the general relations between the Germanic invaders and the Roman Empire, this bond developed into a peculiar, ambivalent and indeed paradoxical coordination and subordination.

The Germanic tribes were driven westward and southward in great masses, in consequence of the great migrations which probably started at the borders of the Chinese Empire in the first centuries A.D., when the emperors of the later Han Dynasty expelled the Mongolian Huns (Hsiung-nu) who had been a thorn in the side of civilized China. The Huns swept through the Sarmatian Steppes (the Russia of today), probably dragged the Slavs along with them and pushed the Sarmatians and the Germanic tribes westward and southward. Some of these Germanic tribes, such as the Goths, the Burgundians, the Lombards and the Vandals, in-

vaded the Roman Empire as entire tribes, and after setting up unsuccessful, tumultuous kingdoms, were overrun by others or slowly
merged with the settled populations. Their kings were respectfully
timid and reverential toward the institutions and authorities of the
defeated and frequently ravaged Roman Empire. Sigismund, the
Burgundian king, accepted the title of "patricius" (patrician) from
the Eastern Roman emperor and wrote to this emperor, who was
then powerless: "My people shall be yours and I had rather serve
you than rule them . . . All my ancestors have always valued more
highly what an emperor gave them than what they inherited from
their fathers." And Ataulf, the Visigothic chieftain, confessed,
according to the report of a contemporary historian, that "he had at
first wished to wipe out the name of Rome and to make all of Rome
into a Gothic Empire. Ataulf should have become what Caesar
Augustus had been. But he discovered that the Goths as untamed
barbarians would not subject themselves to laws and that to abolish laws would mean that the state ceased being a state. Because
of this, Ataulf preferred to seek fame in re-establishing and height-
ening the power of Rome with the help of Gothic strength and to
go down to posterity as the one who gave Rome her rebirth, since
it was impossible to replace her. This is why he refrained from
waging war; this is why he aimed at preserving peace."

These documents show how helplessly the new barbarian conquerors were facing the task of taking over the complex administration of a civilized state. They had been leaders of half-nomad
tribes, and now, all-too-suddenly, they became rulers of far-flung,
highly cultivated regions, of elaborate institutions and of all the
apparatus of a bureaucracy sanctified by the glory of the universal
empire. They had their vigorous troops and nothing else, no experience of how to handle an established state. They recoiled from
the devastations of their people and wanted the aid of the Roman
officials and especially of the Christian bishops who, particularly
in the provinces, were the only stable element in chaotic times and
who, in those days, represented the intelligentsia of the empire.

The core of the coming medieval empire was the Gallic province,
the France of today, that for a long time had been infiltrated by

Frankish groups pouring in through the weakening defenses of the old empire, occasionally siding with the Romans against other invaders, such as the Huns. These Frankish groups were joined by more and more of their tribesmen and thus gradually gained ground in this province. In 486, the powerful Frankish leader, Clovis, defeated the last Roman governor, Syagrius, in the battle of Soissons, and took over the practically autonomous rule of this Roman governor, thus also taking possession of the large estates of the Roman fisc in this province. The Western Roman Empire had been destroyed ten years earlier, when its last emperor, with the ominous name of Romulus Augustulus, had been deposed by the powerful Herulian chieftain Odovacar (Odoacer). The Merovingian Clovis, acting as the lawful successor of the imperial Roman government in this province, still bowed to the Byzantine emperor, accepted the title of Roman Consul from him and became a Christian, just as the other Germanic chiefs. From this new position, as the successor of the Roman emperor, he and his descendants subjected the Frankish tribes across the borders and added their land to the Gallic land. Out of their new fiscal estates they rewarded their personal followers and distributed land among them.

But the Merovingian family was soon ruined by continuous, ruthless struggles about the shares in the inheritance. Ambitious and ferocious wives played an important part in this disruption by fomenting quarrels with furious energy. A new family rose to power from the office of mayor of the royal household (majordomo), an office originating in the administration of the great senatorial estates. Step by step the Carolingian administrators conquered the Frankish kingdom from their chiefs. They too accepted Roman titles, and behaved as zealous Christians and active defenders and propagators of the faith in repelling the Islamic Arabs, the conquerors of Spain. These Carolingian monarchs and the Roman Popes were united by the bond of mutual protection and promotion, which had been foreshadowed in the general relation between the barbarian Germanic chiefs and the Roman and Christian authorities.

The Western Roman Empire had ceased to exist. The pope had

no material means to protect Italy and his Roman possessions, the inherited estates and properties of the Church. He was still formally dependent upon the Byzantine emperor who was head of the Church in the old Roman and Oriental manner. But the emperor was powerless to vouch for the safety of the pope, who at this time, moreover, was engaged in dogmatic conflict with him on the so-called iconoclastic question. In order to combat the influence of the monks on the people and the growing wealth of the Eastern monasteries that were exempt from taxation, the Byzantine emperor prohibited the worship of images and the performing of miracles. In so doing, he set himself against a great part of his own clergy and especially against the Roman Pope and the Western Church, a clash which resulted in lasting enmity between the two parties. Thus the pope looked elsewhere for aid and protection, and the trend of events directed him toward the rising Frankish monarchs who, on their part, had political reasons for wishing to strengthen this bond. Charles Martel (the hammer), the founder of the Carolingian dynasty, nominally the majordomo of the Carolingian household but virtually the ruler of the country, was courted by the pope who asked his assistance against the threatening Lombards. The pope gave him the title of "subregulus", subkinglet, and Prince of the Franks. His son, Pepin, helped the pope against the Lombards, and in return the pope encouraged Pepin to have himself crowned king. He anointed him (754) and formally deposed the last Merovingian. And more than this, he made Pepin a Roman patricius (patrician), a title and function which should have been conferred by the Byzantine emperor and which implied the imperial governorship of Italy and the right and duty to protect the Roman Church. In doing so by usurped right, the pope, who exerted authority over the influential Gallic clergy, took the first step toward emancipating himself from Byzantine rule, and he obtained even more than he had set out to get! For Pepin, by virtue of his new office, bestowed upon the pope all the land he had conquered from the Lombards which, according to law, should have gone to the Byzantine emperor.

This bond of mutual support was strengthened by the successors on both sides, and finally resulted in the memorable event which mapped out the broad contours of the medieval world. Pope Leo III, a man of shrewd and very questionable character, who was threatened by a powerful opposition among his own clergy, appealed to the son of Pepin, Charles, the later Charlemagne, for arbitration and help, and when the Frankish ruler appeared in Rome in order to investigate and to settle the quarrels personally, he took him by surprise and made him Augustus at the Holy Mass on Christmas Eve, 800 A.D. By this accomplished fact, he not only raised the Carolingian to the supreme worldly position with the intention of placing him under inescapable obligations, but he saved and emancipated himself completely from the Byzantine rule and made himself the sovereign head of Western Christendom. So that it was on the very same day that the Frankish king was made emperor and the bishop of Rome actually became a pope. The two successions of the Roman Empire, the spiritual and the temporal, the papacy and the Holy Roman Empire, were founded. As a matter of fact, it was the popes who promoted the Frankish chieftains to a dominant position in the temporal world. They intended to keep their barbarian protectors in permanent spiritual submission, so that they themselves might become the real rulers of a new, ecclesiastical empire, of a "civitas dei" on earth, of a Christian polis. Yet, in reality, they exalted and strengthened their deadly rivals. Later, the same thing happened inversely, when the emperors purged and revived the corrupt papacy, and so fostered the great popes who became their most dangerous competitors.

These two great institutions into which the succession of the one Roman Empire divided—the papacy and the Holy Roman Empire—were forever intrinsically bound up with each other. They alternately advanced and destroyed each other. They rose together and they fell together. The great struggle for supremacy that developed between them made the popes strive more and more for worldly power in order to compete with the emperors in their own field, and, on the other hand, induced the emperors to make their increasing attempts to conquer the spiritual power from the popes and to incorporate the spiritual authority in their imperial rule. The result was their mutual and common debasement.

Yet the foundation of the papacy and the Holy Roman Empire had another, still more momentous implication. It meant the ultimate separation and juxtaposition of spirit and body, of the earthly, political and the celestial, religious sphere. It was the beginning of the secularization of mankind.

RISE OF THE HOLY ROMAN EMPIRE

In comparing the disintegrated Roman Empire with the Germanic tribes that were prematurely interrupted in their tribal development, it becomes obvious that, although both developed from different origins, they were converging to the same point, the point where a new evolution begins.

They had three features in common; first, the abolishment of city life. On the one hand, the centralized, bureaucratic Roman state had effected the dissolution of city life. On the other hand, the barbarians lacked all the premises for city life.

They had further in common the invalidation and destruction of the ancient, tribal and official dependencies and the formation of new, individual and private dependencies. The Roman "precarium" and clientele corresponded to the Germanic "Gefolgschaft". All of these were based on personal confidence only. The Celtic tribes had a similar institution, with the difference that here the relationship was not wholly private but incorporated in the tribal system, and that the bond between the leader and the follower was not temporary but permanent, for as long as life lasted. The Celtic follower was called vassal, which means page or squire. As the Celts were thoroughly Romanized after centuries of Roman rule, their custom of vassalage was the first to fuse with the Roman clientele. And as the Holy Roman Empire came into being in originally Celtic Gaul, it was the Celtic term vassal that became current in designating the feudal follower.

As for the relationship between the Frankish king and the pope, it also evolved from a mutual, personal bond of the same quality, a bond of mutual protection and support. Only, in this case, it was never made clear who was the patron and who the follower, since the spiritual power was utterly different from the temporal, and both were maintained in equilibrium for a long time. The question of supremacy, however, became the subject of constant dispute between the emperor and the pope, and each attempted to appropriate both powers for himself. As the weight of mundane affairs was greater, the result was the emancipation and secularization of the empire and the world.

The third common feature of the epoch, originating from the Hellenistic intermingling, the Roman universal empire and the Christian world religion, on the one hand, and the Germanic breaking-up of the tribal bonds and merging with the empire and Christianism, on the other, was the creation of the lonely, private individual, face to face with an overwhelming universe. Thus the individual became the starting point of medieval development, and his correlation and juxtaposition to the terrestrial, as well as the celestial universe, contributed to the fundamental partition of the spiritual and the material, the religious and the earthly world, and also led to secularization, to the humanistic world of the Renaissance.

These three features of the transitional epoch, the dispersal of city life into the rural territory, the invalidation of tribal and official dependencies and formation of new private and personal dependencies and the creation of the isolated individual, became the basic elements for the social order of the Middle Ages: *Feudalism.*

The Merovingian chief took over the Roman province of Gaul and the estates of the Roman fisc, in his capacity of private war leader. He began as a private landed proprietor severed from his own tribal bonds, all the more since he soon became a Christian. He was quite unfamiliar with the remains of Roman civilization and ruled only over his private estates without interfering with the rest of the country, that was in a state of utter confusion. The cities were deserted and partly destroyed. In the country, the Roman and Romanized Gallic proprietors stayed on, living on their estates as before, exercising authority over their slaves, tenants and clients. They, as well as the influential bishops and the clergy, were courted by the Frankish leader who wanted to win them over and to learn from them. He drew them into his company and attached them to his person in a relation which was a mixture of Roman clientele, Gallic vassalage and Germanic following.

The court of the Merovingian chieftain resembled the private country estate of an upstart who, though brutal and boorish, capricious and uncontrolled, still wanted to appear a good companion and a benevolent patron to the Gallo-Roman grandees, and to imitate their ways and manners. This is how contemporary Roman authors describe these chieftains. It would be useless and impossible to make a distinction between private and public affairs in this first so-called Frankish Kingdom. There was only private property, a private body-guard, a private attendance, and yet, from this private property and this private attendance, the Holy Roman Empire unfolds in a development unique in world history. As the Merovingian chieftain was called King of the Franks, "rex", by the Romans, his estates were called "regnum", the original meaning of which is not kingdom but "land of the king". Only gradually did this land of the king become an actual kingdom. The officialdom of the Frankish kingdom and the later empire grew out of the private administration of these estates, and the feudal lords of the Holy Roman Empire evolved from the personal attendance, the great clientele of the Frankish leader.

Let us first consider the development of the officialdom. Out of his estates, his "land of the king", the Frankish leader distributed land among the Frankish followers with whom he had undertaken the campaign and with whom he afterwards conquered the neighboring territory of his own tribe. In the course of campaigns against the Frankish and other Germanic tribes, as well as against the Arabs in the South, the Frankish leaders had adopted the Roman military organization, as they generally adopted Roman institutions. Two types of command became the most important offices of the medieval empire: count and duke. The counts, "comites", were commanders of a unit of approximately the size of a modern regiment. When the troops settled down on their allotted lands, these counts retained their position as leaders of their groups and became the staff of the civil administration. And when, as a result of the conquests, the "land of the king" and the number of settlers grew, and the campaigning followers became farmers, attached to the soil and preferring their agricultural pursuits to warfare, the counts, as administrators of the king's dominion and as mediators between the people and the king, became extraordinarily powerful. They decided on the exemptions from war service and collected fees to be paid for such exemptions. Following the example of the Roman landowners, they assumed jurisdiction over their people. Jurisdiction had formerly been in the hands of the chieftain, or of a substitute for the chieftain, who had been elected by the people. They finally represented their people in the assemblies, which the peasants, on their widely scattered farms, could no longer attend in person. When rulers changed, the counts simply put their people collectively on an oath of loyalty, which replaced the old personal agreement between leader and follower. Thus the people gradually lost their freedom in various ways, and the counts as administrators came to combine the powers of both the people and the king.

The higher office of the dukes was a fusion of the position of a Germanic tribal chieftain with the Roman "dux", the supreme military commander of a province as created by Diocletian, when he separated civil and military provincial administration. The appointment of dukes as officials of the Frankish kings developed after the conquest of other Germanic tribes, such as the Bavarians, the Saxons, the Thuringians, the Swabians, in order to provide a loyal, trustworthy substitute for the position of the old tribal chieftains, who had to be removed because they were centers of constant rebellions.

As for the personal attendance, the great clientele of the Frankish leaders, the Frankish chieftains were eager to oblige and to attract the great Gallo-Roman land proprietors as well as the bishops, as followers and clients. They held out promises of large land-assignments which they took from their "land of the king". When the Merovingian heirs quarreled over their inheritance, they outdid one another in the race for adherents and powerful followers by means of such land-assignments. And now it was these great proprietors who were regarded as the followers of the king, not the original Frankish people who had become just subjects.

But not only land was at stake in joining the clientele of the king. When the matter of choosing an official came up, a count, for instance, the king naturally chose one of his personal followers, one of his great clients. In this way, the clients of the king possessed not only extensive property in terms of land but also the authority of officials. They used their wealth to increase their authority and they used their authority to increase their wealth.

When the Carolingians assumed their rule, which also originated in a private office of the household of the king, the office of major-domo, they faced the problem of many mighty lords, equipped with rich lands as well as with power over the people. When they needed troops, they could not rely on the general levy of their people, for this levy no longer functioned. They depended on the people the lords would raise, they depended on the personal followers of their personal followers. They were forced to acknowledge the situation, and this they did by reviving the old Germanic custom of followership ("Gefolgschaft") and combining it with Gallic vassalage. Lord and vassal were attached to each other by a mutual, solemn pledge, which inaugurated a lifelong personal bond granting the lord the support of his vassal and granting the vassal the investment with his land for all the days of his life. And when, eventually, the vassals of the king extended this institution by concluding the same agreement with the smaller lords whom they had brought into their sphere of influence, the feudal system was completed.

The feudal system was never a legal institution. It always remained a matter of custom. Since it was not legally secured and protected and there was no effective higher authority to enforce the observance of this mutual agreement, it rested entirely on trust and faithfulness; hence the dominant significance of faithfulness, of fidelity, in the medieval world. There were still remnants of officialdom left—there was the office of the count and that of the duke—but the holders of the offices and the great feudal lords were often the same person, though sometimes they were counts and lords in different districts. They belonged to the same social group and they strengthened their power by intermarrying. They were the knights who fought as armored horsemen after the Sarmatians and the Arabs had introduced the use of stirrups and spurs, which brought about new military tactics and made heavy cavalry the decisive factor in battle. This involved costly equipment, which only the rich could afford. In the competition between officialdom and feudality, officialdom was necessarily doomed to failure, as the scales were tipped in favor of the feudal system. Officialdom, at last, became a fief in itself, a claim among many other like claims that required personal power in order to become effective. And gradually fiefs became hereditary. With this, the power of the lords was made safe and firmly entrenched in their fiefs.

The feudal system originated in Gaul, and with the extension of the Frankish kingdom to the East, over the territories of other Germanic tribes, it spread over the whole growing empire. But there is a great difference between the way it worked in Gaul and the way it worked in the Germanic mainland, and this difference is implied in the fundamental difference between the two regions and the premises of their development.

The power of the Carolingian family rapidly waned. Like the Merovingians, the new dynasty became involved in quarrels concerning the inheritance, but this time these quarrels had a more than personal or dynastic significance, and the territorial division in which they resulted foreshadowed the natural divergence in the character of the two nations to come, the French and the German. In 843, by the Treaty of Verdun, the three grandsons of Charlemagne divided the Carolingian Empire among one another, into three dominions: a Western kingdom, mainly Romanic in tradition, custom and prevailing language, covering approxi-

mately the area of modern France; an Eastern kingdom, essentially
Teutonic in ethnography, geography and language; and an indistinct, somewhat amorphous kingdom in between these two,
extending from the Dutch and Frisian shores down through Italy
to Rome. This kingdom was assigned to the eldest of the three
brothers, Lothair, who inherited the imperial crown. The northeastern part, later called Lotharingia (Lorraine), was to become the
site of a very creative and mixed culture, where, and about which,
the fateful struggle between France and Germany was to go on
for many centuries, up to our own times.

After this division, the Gallic and the Teutonic kingdoms
separated once and for all. They separated not only geographically
and politically but also intrinsically. They developed in essentially
different directions and took on an almost opposite character. In
the West, a new dynasty arose from an indistinct origin, urban
according to legend. Not only did it originate in the very center
of the Gallic country, the Duchy of *Francia,* but it came from,
or was connected with, the city of Paris, a municipality which had
been prominent even in Roman times and had maintained its
position through the storms of invasions and upheavals during
the long transitional period. This region and this city seemed predestined by location and tradition to become the core of the country.
The first known ancestor of the new dynasty, Robert the Strong,
was of humble origin, as legend has it, the son of a butcher. For
ten years he fought against the Northmen (Normans), and died
in this campaign. His son, Odo, a count of Paris, successfully re-
pelled an attack on the city and was elected King of the West-
Franks by one faction of the magnates in opposition to the weakly
Carolingian heir who had failed to ward off the Northmen and
so had lost his grip on the country. A descendant of Odo, Hugh
the Great, is described as a mighty feudal lord who at the same
time held the official position of a "Duke of the French". He still
refused the crown, preferring to rule indirectly through the young
Carolingian heir, as the first great Carolingians had done as
majordomos of the Merovingians. But his son, Hugh Capet, was
made king by the powerful lords and bishops of his region and was

recognized by the then ruling emperor and Eastern Frankish ruler, Otto III (987). For a long time, this French kingdom of the Capets, who were to rule from then on for eight hundred years to come, was still formally dependent on, and incorporated in, the Holy Roman Empire, since this was taken to include the whole reach of Western Christianity. Actually, it became an independent and entirely separate kingdom with a development of its own.

In the urban center of the central region of this country, on the "Ile de France", the "island" bounded by five rivers, the French nation began to take shape; the first true nation of the world was born, a nation in the sense of a distinct, social form. Italy was at that time an agglomeration of disconnected cities and regions. Britain was to undergo many changes, intermixtures, fluctuations of stocks, regimes and cultural trends, before beginning its life as a homogeneous nation; in the eleventh century, Britain was still a mere colony of French Normandy, as it was ruled by the chief of the Normans. The Eastern and Northern peoples had hardly overcome the tribal stage. Germany was not even a geographical term as yet, far less a nationality, which it has not even achieved to this very day.

Usually the term *"nation"* is very carelessly employed. It is applied to ancient peoples as well, to the Egyptians, the Persians, the Greeks, the Jews. This is incorrect and inexact, as a nation has a definite social structure of its own, with special features and premises that were non-existent before the founding of the French nation. All the ancient peoples were either tribes and tribal states or sacred city-states. This means that, in all essentials, they were based on religion, and, accordingly, their particular religion; their characteristics were rooted in religion and first expressed in terms and forms of religion. This is evident in the tribes, and it is equally true of the sacred city-states of the Greeks and the Romans, where the beginnings of an earthly community were still determined by religious bonds. Even the Catholic creed, in its first stages, could be regarded as the religious basis and expression of the universal Roman Empire.

But in the Northern area of Europe, the Christian world religion had become a separate, purely spiritual part of human existence, concerning humanity as a whole and appealing to humanity in general, to the human being as such, and therefore not inherent in, not identical with, the particularities of the new folk structures in now divided Europe. These new folk structures were developing as temporal communities. While the ancient religions, the genuine religions, fostered or at least preserved the particularities of their peoples, the Christian world religion, in its trend and principles, was necessarily opposed to particularity. Wherever the Church did help and influence the formation of a new particularity, this was illicit. It was a compromise, a compliance with human impulses and political necessities. A nation is, therefore, a folk structure which forms after the creation and under the dominance of a world religion but independent of religious concerns, however strong the spiritual influence of the world religion may be in regard to its formation. Religion is no longer the core of the folk structure. A nation is a temporal community, based on physical geography, folk character, on homogeneous living, on institutions and cultural forms that evolve from the combination of specific popular stocks with the specific conditions of a country. The sum of the profane customs and achievements of such a community gradually develops a body of instinctive memories, a *tradition,* and this tradition becomes religious in its profound significance. It is in itself the profane religion of a nation replacing the ancient particular religion, it is a religion for the every-day of mundane existence.

France is the first country to develop such a tradition, such a homogeneous way of life, such true nationality. The process of shaping the French nationality, a model of clearness, proceeded from the Ile de France and its main city, Paris, as a central core, and expanded to the politically and culturally close-knit territory of the France of today. This was made possible by the thorough Romanization of the country, its saturation with Roman customs and institutions, and with the mode of Roman central and imperial administration. The urban tradition of Rome, her standard of city life and civilization, survived the destruction of that civilization in that region; it was carried on by the customs and ways of living of the Gallo-Roman magnates and upheld especially by the bishops whose office compelled them to reside in the city even when that city was almost deserted. The ecclesiastical life of the flat country was represented and taken care of by the monasteries. The clerics and, above all, the bishops, played an important part in the formation of the French kingdom and the establishment and the strengthening of the Capet dynasty.

Another cause of the splendid national development of France, a fortunate circumstance of inestimable importance, was the continuity of the Capet dynasty. For three hundred and forty years, that is, for the decisive period of national formation, the direct succession of inheritance from father to son was not interrupted. The Capet kings, moreover, did not follow the Frankish-Germanic custom of splitting up the inheritance equally among their descendants. They followed a rule, developed by Roman law, which favored the first son in order to avoid division of property, and this rule was also adopted by the great feudal lords of the country. Furthermore, the Capet kings took the precaution of having their sons made kings in their own lifetime, until gradually the old Germanic custom of the election of the king grew obsolete, and until the dynasty and its natural succession had become a national tradition. But the most significant factor in the development of the French monarchy, and for those times that meant of the French national unity and homogeneousness, was the special turn the feudal system took in this country. And again it was the Roman character of the country, the habit of imperial, centralized rule and administration persisting through change, that had a decisive effect on the kind of feudality developed by the French.

In France, the feudal system was established throughout and thoroughly. It covered almost the whole country. This means that there were practically no exceptions of importance, no remains of free land property, "allodial" property, no independent landed proprietors left. ("Allodial" property, an "alod", meant a free inheritance, property entirely one's own, "all-od", "od" being the old Frankish word for property. It was the opposite of "fe-od", "feud", the land granted by a superior for use, deriving from Old German "fehu", "feoh", "fee", cattle, i.e. mobile property, payment—hence feudality.) The very few petty enclaves of such free property were insignificant exceptions and the laughing-stock of the people. On the other hand, the authority of the royal offices, the dukes and the counts for instance, which, of course, fused with the feudal lordships, was not entirely wiped out in this region, also as an after-effect of the Roman tradition. The feudal lords could use their official positions to enforce recognition of their feudal lordship, to enforce military service among their followers and the remaining free landed proprietors by virtue of their official authority. This, in turn, helped to spread and to perfect the feudal system all over the country. There was an axiom in France at this time: "Nulle terre sans seigneur" (No land without a feudal lord).

This concentration of large, important regions in the hands of powerful feudal lords effected a great simplification and regularization of the country. In the first period, this imperilled the power of the king, but later it proved of great advantage, as the kings had to deal only with a relatively small number of lords, whom they overcame gradually and separately by various means. Some territories the kings obtained through marriage and inheritance, some by seizing forfeited fiefs—the German lords never allowed their rulers to do this. Other territories they acquired by permitting the lower vassals to appeal to their royal authority and complain against the lords for an actual or alleged breach of faith. They often purposely incited these vassals to complaints, in order to have a pretext for proceeding against a mighty lord and for confiscating the fief. They used the same method for the cities with which they entered into special relations of patronage, arbitration and granting of subsidies which they exchanged for important prerogatives, and thus they overreached and undermined the authority of the respective feudal lords of the cities.

The French kings were also the first to take into their service as private counsellors learned persons, scholars of the Roman law, the so-called "legists", who were petty clerics or monks, for the most part, but who also included burghers. These legists helped prepare the gradual restitution of the old Roman law and, in particular, the concept that for the region of Gaul the authority and concentration of power of the French king should equal that of the Roman emperor. The weapon of Roman law was to break down the institution of feudality. From the group of these legally trained advisors a new class of nobility developed, the "noblesse de robe". Accordingly, the legists were particularly attached and devoted to the monarchs and the monarchy as such; they called themselves "milites regis", the soldiers of the king. They were the prototypes and the forerunners of the great ministers of the later French kingdom, the Cardinal d'Amboise, Richelieu, Mazarin and others.

In their struggle for the complete control of the country, for outmanoeuvring the lords and centralizing their own power, the kings also created that supreme court of appeal which began as a jurisdictional and developed into a political institution—the parliament. It became a paramount instrument for the unification of the law and so, of the nation.

The most important result of the influence of Roman civilization on France, however, was the formation of a dominant city, a capital, a city that was not merely the residence of the king but that became the focal center for the whole nation of which the Capetian monarchs were the symbol. Paris emerged as the great center of the intellectual, cultural and social life of France. From the end of the eleventh century on, the great scholars of the medieval world gathered there, and it was on this stage that all the controversies of Scholastic philosophy were enacted. At the end of the twelfth century, a so-called "guild of masters" developed into one of the first universities of the Christian continent. The dialect spoken on the Ile de France became the foundation of the French language. The intellectual and social magnetism of the capital contributed greatly to the ultimate taming and subduing of the feudal lords, to transforming them from independent lords into courtiers. The "curia regis" was, at first, only an occasional meeting of the magnates summoned by the king. Through the inclusion of the legists, it developed into a permanent government body and gradually expanded into an elaborate royal court, the first appearance of a leading social group in the Christian world.

From Rome, the French capital took over the institution of the dominant city, the traditional standard of city life. In France, too, only the resident of the capital, only a member of court society, had social standing. He had to attend court if he wanted to obtain a position. Yet there is one distinct difference between Rome and Paris. Rome was identical with its dominion, it was the country, the empire itself. The republics of the Italian Renaissance that developed according to the Roman pattern were still city-republics. The country districts were identified with the ruling city to the extent of bearing the name of the city—Venice, Florence or Milan. Paris, however, was only the center, the symbol of the country, it was only the capital of France. The territory had a part in it, it was represented in it, included in it, it added weight to the position of the leading city. And this was the lasting effect of feudalism.

The developments in the *Eastern Frankish Kingdom,* which gradually merged with the Holy Roman Empire, are in sharp contrast to the favorable evolution of France. First of all, the territory was no longer connected with the place from which the Frankish kingdom sprang. It was detached from its origin, that is, from France. It consisted of peripheral territories of different Germanic tribes which had been gradually subjected and added to the Frankish kingdom. The greater part of the Eastern kingdom had never been touched by Roman rule and Roman civilization. There were no cities and no definite frontiers. No centers formed, and there was no fixed capital. Aside from the fact that the Germanic chieftains were not accustomed and not inclined to city life, the place of residence would have changed in any case, since the dynasties themselves changed frequently. Hardly one of these dynasties reached more than three or four direct successions, and even these were constantly challenged and contested. No Teutonic king or emperor ever succeeded in overcoming the custom of election of the king by the lords. None of them was capable of founding a successful dynasty. The kingdom was ruled by leaders of various Germanic tribes, the Franks, the Bavarians, the Saxons, the Swabians. And often they were not even genuine leaders but official dukes, of alien origin, who had replaced the native chieftains. Hence none of them could win a steady support from the people of his region. All of them depended on the good will of the lords who usually had more authority than the kings. This lasting dependence on the great lords, a dependence which not even the boldest and most energetic among the Teutonic emperors could ever overcome, was the main source of all the mischief, the troubles and the confusion which make up German history throughout the centuries. The first consequence was that every decision of common concern—the raising of troops, measures of defense and protection against invaders (the Slavs, the Magyars and later the Turks), elections, reforms—all had to be wrung from the lords, had to be bought from the lords for concessions, rights, lands and even money. The famous election of the Hapsburg, Charles V, amounted to a downright auction.

The German emperors were constantly en route, hastening breathlessly from one point to another, suppressing revolts, breaking up conspiracies, bargaining and playing one side off against the other. Not only the vast lands, which the first rulers had inherited or seized for the empire, not only this vast territorial property of the Crown was gradually sold out as donations and as fiefs that became hereditary, but all offices, prerogatives, claims, jurisdictional rights of the Crown were given away as fiefs or in some other form. In the course of time, by change in ownership, by division through inheritance, by bargaining and usurpation, lands, fiefs, offices and rights were torn asunder, split and splintered and thrown together in indescribable anarchy.

In German territories, the feudal system was never carried through as in France. In between the feudal estates, indeed in their very midst, were independent freeholds, the owners of which boasted that they were nobody's vassals, that they were committed to nobody and to nothing. They considered themselves the equals of the emperor and they did not even rise to salute him when he happened to pass by. But this did not prevent such freeholders from splitting their property into smaller fiefs. Sometimes a lord was a feudal lord in one district, a freeholder in another district and a count in a third; a territory had one lord as a feudal chief, another as a landed proprietor, a third as an official authority—not to mention a multitude of petty titles and privileges and the innumerable jurisdictional rights. Power that had been built up on personal relationships lost its subjective character and could be bartered for goods, services or privileges.

The German emperors were not only concerned with the extremely complicated task of ruling this country, they had inherited the duty to control the Roman Empire, and this was a claim of much wider, indeed, of universal range. It meant keeping a close watch on all sides, a constant meddling in the affairs of Italy and the Mediterranean, defense and expansion in the East and the North in fighting the Slavs, the Magyars, the Northmen, and curbing the French rival in the West. It meant keeping up the supreme claim of being the protector and defender of the Christian faith, of ruling and dominating the whole Christian world, in partnership or rather in competition with the other, the spiritual ruler of Christianity, the pope. This competition and this indissoluble entanglement became more and more the dominant, the all-absorbing motive for the emperors.

Charlemagne, and after him the Saxon, Otto the Great, were still powerful enough at home to impress the popes and to keep them in check. These early emperors, Otto I, Otto III, and the Salian Frank, Henry III, strengthened, purged and reformed the papacy, when they introduced the new mystic and monastic movements into the Roman hierarchy and the papacy itself. In doing so they hoped to build up for themselves a support and safeguard which would provide them with a divine authorization in fighting the presumption and the rebellion of their feudal lords at home. But, in reality, they were raising and strengthening their most dangerous rivals, popes like Gregory VII, Innocent III, and Gregory IX. More and more the emperors were throwing themselves into the fascinating, universal adventure, into the ancient, everrecurrent dream of world domination, partly inspired by the task itself, partly desiring escape from their hopeless German situation and seeking to establish and secure their domestic authority from the outside. This led them into the crusades, this estranged them from their German homeland to such a degree that the last emperor of the medieval line, the Stauffer Frederick II, chose Sicily for his headquarters.

This brilliant emperor, who was consumed by his ambition for the supreme position a man may reach on earth, this emperor, in competing for that position with his only rival, the pope, was carried away by his struggle so far as to claim for himself, the lay emperor, not only the terrestrial, but also the celestial, the spiritual power. He took it upon himself to sanctify, indeed to deify the imperial position in the old Cæsarian way, in pretending to a Messianic role. But as this was a Christian and no longer a pagan era, he effected the contrary; he was regarded and cursed as the Antichrist. It was he who initiated the great turn from the medieval Holy Roman Empire to the humanistic tyranny of the Renaissance. His governors in the Italian cities, his "vicars-general" and "podestàs", were the first Renaissance princes. The attempt at Messianic resurrection turned into the profane and secular movement of the Renaissance.

DISINTEGRATION OF THE HOLY
ROMAN EMPIRE

AFTER THE FAILURE OF THE last medieval emperor and first Renaissance tyrant, the Stauffer Frederick II, (1250), the character of both empire and papacy underwent a fundamental change. They began to lose their universality and to become mere parties among other parties, among new political and religious forces that outstripped them and deprived them of their undisputed position as spiritual and terrestrial poles of the world. They had wakened and fostered the forces which eventually destroyed their power. Aside from the undermining and discrediting of each other's authority that they themselves engaged in, other far-reaching developments were brewing to destroy them and the current order of the world. All these developments were parts of one dominant trend and converged in one direction: the secularization of man and his world.

Three political and social, and three intellectual processes became active simultaneously and initiated the new era. The former originated in the inner disintegration of the Holy Roman Empire and of the feudal system, the dissolution of the feudal hierarchy to a class of practically independent landowners. From the collapse of Christian unity emerged the manifold, secularized sovereign powers whose struggle constitutes the political history of the modern era.

Of special pioneer importance in this development was the rise of the Italian city-republics. As they were in the focus of the great struggle between the popes and the emperors, these city-republics were the first to realize the weaknesses of both, and took an active and prominent part in their disruption. They had, moreover, risen through trade. They were centers of world trade in the later Middle Ages, and for the first time brought economic and financial influence to bear on world affairs. Last but not least, the memories, the traditions and the relics of ancient pagan Rome were alive among them. Under the impact of their political and economic experiences, a new paganism arose, stripped of its ancient religious implications and preserving only ethnic and aesthetic values. The Italian city-republics were the first to develop a disillusioned, secular and individualistic mind.

A third process more important for the great reversal, though less conspicuous, was the emergence of a bourgeois spirit, the first bourgeois spirit in the world. This came with the evolution of the medieval German town. The spirit of the German town is not only the matrix of the Reformation, it is also the starting point of the dominating trend of the modern era, the trend toward collectivity, it is the nucleus of the modern state, and the origin of true capitalism. It is one of the decisive factors that shaped the modern, secularized relation of man to nature and effected the objectivation of nature, the concept of nature as a complex of material, elemental forces, severed from man and reason and subject to man's exploration and exploitation.

These political and social developments were accompanied and furthered by currents of thought that—after a long latent period—burst into the open toward the end of the Middle Ages. An underground religious movement slowly gained in strength through the entire period of the Middle Ages. Its aim was the liberation of Christian man from the domination and mediation of the ecclesiastical hierarchy, and the re-establishment of direct contact of the Christian individual with God. This movement started from ancient, pagan undercurrents. It made its way outside and inside the church through heretic sects and monastic and mystic trends. It was spurred on by spiritual as well as by emotional impulses and resulted in the Reformation and the splitting of universal Christianity. Though it sprang from religious motives, from a deep religious need in people's minds, a need for religious purification and regeneration, still, in the end, it led to secularization, owing to the fundamental change of the conditions and circumstances of mankind. Since profane and purely earthly developments had been initiated by the split between the spiritual and the temporal world, men were bound to become more and more entangled in wholly secular activities, endeavors and goals. They became aware of a separate and independent functioning of the profane nature and mind, and every trend of life inevitably led to secularization. Thus the Protestant Reformation, intent upon religious aims, struck the decisive blow at religion through those very aims and helped to dissipate, to paralyze and to secularize religion itself.

A second mental process, that had also grown through medieval centuries, matured at the same time; through the consistent development of Scholastic philosophy, the reason of man broke the shackles of Christian dogma and Christian authority and became autonomous. This opened the way for secular learning. And finally, the secularization of human life evolved from the Italian revival of Greek and Latin art, poetry and science; man became the hub of a world that was wholly of this earth.

The *disintegration of the Holy Roman Empire* became apparent
in the splitting-off of the French nation and the French kingdom
from the empire. England, though not so advanced in her national
formation, was still too far from the grip of the German emperors
to be subject to their influence. These German emperors were not
even capable of helping the remains of the Christian Visigoth
kingdoms in Spain in their struggle against the Moslem rule. They
had to leave Spain to its own national development, which was
completed at the end of the fifteenth century. But as early as 1135,
King Alfonso VII of Castile had himself crowned emperor as a
challenge of equality to the German emperors.

Italy was the main scene of action in the struggle for world
domination, where the emperors defended their claim to supremacy
against the popes and the Italian cities, which were developing
into mighty city-republics. Except for their conquests of the Sla-
vonian and Magyar (Hungarian) peoples in the East, and Burgundy in the West, except for the largely unsuccessful crusades,
the emperors never got farther than Italy and Sicily in their attempts
to make effective their universal rule. And only the three great
Stauffer emperors, Frederick I (Barbarossa), Henry VI and Frederick II, each actually controlled the whole of Italy for a few years.
But when they were forced to turn back and fight their feudal
antagonists in Germany, revolts broke out in Italy and they had
to begin fighting all over again. World domination seemed possible
only when Henry VI, after having conquered Italy, planned to
proceed against the Byzantine Empire and even France and England. But this was a brief dream as he died soon after, when he
was only thirty-two years old.

So, as far as the external position of the emperors was concerned,
their claim to universality never did materialize. It was upheld
mainly by the ancient, inherited glory of the Roman Empire which
still retained a magic, popular appeal, and by rare military successes that gave an illusion of power. How weak and hollow this
power had become, just when it was most resplendent in the last
Stauffer emperors, is proved by the internal developments of
Germany.

In contrast to France, the feudal system had never become established throughout Germany. There was no feudal hierarchy reaching from top to bottom, from the king through the ranks of the great lords and down to the lower vassals. Feudal and, at the same time, official power was not concentrated in the hands of a few lords whom the king could gradually subdue, win over and make part of the court. This means that power was not held together and administered by human will, human capacity and human personality only. It was not a matter of mere human influence, it was not entirely included and expressed in human relations.

Because of the emperors' dependence on the lords, not only the property but also the offices of the Crown had been bestowed as fiefs or donations in times of emergency. And this division and trading-in of inherited estates had detached them from their real owners and converted them into saleable merchandise. Consequently, the same territory could be subject to different authorities: to somebody who had the right to govern the county, that meant maintaining peace and exercising executive power; to one or more persons who had the right of jurisdiction which was independent of the county; to a third who had the feudal lordship, that is, the claim to the services of vassals; to a fourth who possessed the land and accordingly claimed the duties and taxes on land, the services and allegiance of tenants, bondsmen and villains of various kinds. If the landed proprietor happened to be an abbot or a bishop— clerics were formally prohibited by Canon Law from meddling in worldly disputes—the administration of the property was transferred to a lay substitute, an "advocate", a bailiff, and this important office, too, had become impersonal and saleable.

In their imperial dreams and ventures, the exuberant and extravagant Stauffer emperors wasted and exhausted not only the lands of the Crown and their own rights and authority, but also men—the blood of the German nobility. In the course of these ventures the old type of medieval knight vanished. In the mean time, a fundamental change was going on at home in masterless Germany, a turning of the tide, a social and mental transformation of far-reaching consequences not only upon the social structure

and the character of the German people, but through this, upon
European and human evolution. The transformation did not take
place under the direction and according to the aims of rulers, as
in France, where the Capet kings consistently influenced and
shrewdly induced developments until they succeeded in getting
them into their own hands. The German developments were uncontrolled and undirected. They occurred like a process of Nature,
beyond the reaches of human will. The various changes did not
converge, they did not culminate in one point. They resulted in
the establishment of several groups or classes of the population
that did not form according to an intrinsic national tradition but
according to the different kind of property held, the different
occupations and professions and ways of life of people. None of
these classes led or set a human standard, since political, intellectual
and economic leadership broke apart.

First of all, a class of political rulers, of *territorial rulers,* was
forming, a new type of territorial sovereign who had nothing in
common with the old feudal nobility. This class included those
former lords who had been able to preserve considerable property
of various kinds through the period of general anarchy, and a
group of newly rich who rose from inferior positions as administrators ("ministeriales") of feudal estates. They even were and remained bondsmen, but nevertheless acquired great influence when
their lords were absent on campaigns and unable to take care of
their property, or when the lords vested them with suitable equipment and appointments in order to have an imposing attendance.
It is characteristic of the development in Germany that some of
these new territorial dynasties were formally freed from this bonds-
manship long after they had come into power.

These new rulers increased their power by steadily and systematically collecting the various claims and rights concerning a
territory: the feudal, the jurisdictional, and the official power, the
land property and so forth. They gathered all these titles by bargain
or usurpation until they had complete control of the land. And
such tasks required new qualities. A different human type from

that of the feudal lords and emperors now prevailed. It was no longer the violence, aggression and impulsiveness of the medieval knight which enabled a man to gain control of a territory, it was caution, thrift, calculation and sober self-control. Not only the new territorial dynasts show these traits, as for instance the Hohenzollern and the Wurttemberg, who entered upon their career during this period, but also the families that after the collapse of the Stauffers and the chaotic period of the Interregnum initiated the new empire in 1273, the Hapsburgs and the Luxemburgs.

This new empire which evolved from utter anarchy was entirely different from the old; the emperor's position was no longer supreme. He had no substantial authority. He no longer had the support of imperial property. He had to build up a private territorial power of his own, a family power with which to compete with the other territorial dynasties existing at the time of his accession to the throne. He was henceforth a party among other parties, one territorial power among other rival territorial powers. All the succeeding emperors could do to uphold a certain superiority of position was to strive for a role of legal arbitration by increasing the importance of their private dominions. Frequently, these were even foreign dominions, situated beyond the boundaries of German territory; the Hapsburgs maintained their unrivalled position by acquiring the crowns of Bohemia, Hungary, Burgundy and Spain, among others. The Hapsburgs, who achieved a reign of six hundred years, interrupted only twice by the rule of the Luxemburgs (from 1308–1313 and again from 1347–1437) were particularly fitted for the role of predominance in this era, for building up a private dynastic power, as they were essentially a family, neither confined to merely personal aims or ambitions of individual rulers, nor deeply involved in the concerns of the countries they ruled. They lived, they thought, they acted, as a family. On the one hand, there was hardly one of them who enjoyed his power, who permitted himself to take a risk and hasten the measured pace of dynastic development at the expense of the continuity of family regime. They were constantly aware of the generations to come, they felt an obligation toward these generations, and they ruled as if it were

an obligation, a burden, which wearied them but would not let
them go. And there was perfect collaboration and a secret understanding among the members and the branches of this large
family, a steady mutual promoting and furthering, unmarred by
any serious conflicts throughout the centuries. On the other hand,
this family which ruled so many countries and peoples never thoroughly identified itself with any of these countries and nationalities.
They remained detached, aloof from the nations, above the nations,
and they utterly disliked national movements as something threatening their very existence. And it was, in fact, the rise of nationalism
that eventually ruined them.

The first Hapsburg emperor, Rudolf, initiated his rule by conquering a dominion for his sons. This was Austria, the only country
to which they became deeply attached, as its population, a mixture
of various stocks, in fact, an international people, was brought
together, indeed, created by the Hapsburgs themselves. It was an
extension and a mirror of the character and habits of the family.
The successors of Rudolf, especially the emperors Maximilian I
and Charles V, expanded this private dominion by marriages and
diplomatic negotiations rather than by wars, which were distaste-
ful to them and in which they were never very successful. They
preferred the peaceful and personal methods of marrying, bargaining, wooing and bribing. In this way they acquired Bohemia and
Hungary, on the one hand, and on the other, Burgundy, the
Netherlands and Spain, which at that time already included the
first American colonies. The contemporary saying, that the sun
did not set on the Hapsburg dominions, was correct.

Thus the Hapsburg emperors dropped the old universal claim
of the Holy Roman Empire and replaced it by a new private universality, by their own international, supernational regime. The
contest with the popes was over, as the papacy itself was weakened
and threatened from without and within by the growth of the
Italian city-republics and the rise of secular humanism and religious
reform. The papacy had lost its universal supremacy and it also
became a party among other parties. And as a party, as the representative of a mere religious ideology and policy, it was allied with

the party of the empire that became identical with the Hapsburg family and its interests. The front shifted from the struggle between the spiritual and the terrestrial power to a conflict on an entirely secular plane. The new antagonists, the sworn enemies of the Hapsburg monarchs, were the two worldly powers that represented the two growing trends of the modern world—nationalism and collectivism—and that uncompromisingly threatened their private internationalism. These were, from without the empire, the national power of France, the Capet kings and later the Revolution and Napoleon, and from within the empire, the gradually rising Protestant and collectivistic, militaristic and rationalistic power of Prussia and the Hohenzollern.

The new territorial dominions which emerged from medieval anarchy, and of which the Hapsburg power was one among others —though gradually the largest one—these territorial dominions, and not the empire, were the true German parallels and counterparts of the French and English kingdoms. The crucial difference was that they were not nations, they were not even compact, unbroken, homogeneous regions, complete in themselves, especially with respect to the populations. They were bare lands, bare territories haphazardly combined by dynastic events, regardless of the population involved. They were private estates that gradually became states. They consisted mostly of isolated pieces of territory, scattered all over the country and even all over the empire and held together only by the dynastic rule. There were a great many of them and of various sizes, and only a few comprised areas of any considerable extent. These few became the actual territorial principalities, which elected and controlled, or at least hampered, the emperors and brought a strong influence to bear on the Diet. They constituted a form of trust against the emperor and against the other classes of the population, closing their ranks against any newcomer from below.

Only one element, one class of the population, equalled them— the *cities,* which in Germany developed quite independently from political and territorial developments. A pernicious antagonism, indeed a rift, sprang up between country and city, between political power and intellectual and economic forces, and the fateful consequences of this unique destiny cannot be overrated. It deprived the territorial powers and their rulers of a social background in their formative period. It separated them from the scene of civilization and thus prevented the growth of an intrinsic tradition. And it deprived the cities and the rising bourgeoisie of political background, of political experience and of the possibility to develop taste and aptitude for politics. It deprived them of an adequate sphere of influence that would have opened and broadened their minds for the great currents of world ideas, and would have brought them into contact with the governing fashions and manners of European society. The German cities, though achieving territorial sovereignty, never attained any considerable land dominion, as the Italian cities, for instance, which would have made political powers of them. They had not the slightest ambition to become real dominions and political powers. The basic misfortune was that Germany lacked a main city, a residential capital which, from the outset, would have unified political, social and intellectual life. Politics and feudal intercourse would then have become urban; intellectual and economic activities would have centered in politics. And in this way, a core of comprehensive, national tradition would have formed. This destiny, this lack of a leading city, prevented Germany from becoming a nation.

Everywhere in Europe the new intellectual life emerged from the cities, after the early intellectual monopoly of the clergy and the monasteries had been broken. So this rift between city and country, between pure-bred burghers and a savage nobility, determined German intellectual evolution in a particularly disastrous way. In France, Italy, Spain and Britain, the nobility was imbued with intellectual currents. Noblemen were among the great thinkers and poets. The courts of monarchs and princes were centers of the arts and sciences—in France of the eighteenth century the new philosophy of enlightenment originated and flourished in the conversations of the leading "salons". During the first periods of secular world history, the Western and Southern courts led in intellectual as well as in social life. This intellectual life was an integral part of the new, courtly civilization, and a link between the different ranks and classes of society. So the intelligentsia had a wide social and political background and an adequate sense of national and public affairs. Ideology and reality were well balanced and connected in the mind. And the ruling class was taught by tradition to appreciate and properly estimate the value and dignity of cultural matters.

In Germany, education and mental life were originally the almost exclusive concern of cities, which were shut off from politics and the life of the princes. The noblemen, on the other hand, were boors, hostile to intellectual life. It was only to gain prestige that the German princes founded the first universities by imitating institutions of the Southern and Western countries. While the Universities of Paris, Bologna and Oxford were founded in the twelfth century, the first German university, the University of Prague, was founded two hundred years later, in 1348.

As a result, the bourgeois spirit of the German cities took the lead in intellectual life, a spirit fluctuating between narrow-minded provinciality and Utopian universality and abstractness, and divorced from social and political actualities. This is the cause for that lack of political perception, of a sense for measured reality, which has characterized the German intelligentsia ever since.

Between the territorial rulers and the cities, two rural classes arose, the knights and the peasants. In the hey-day of the Middle Ages, the term *"knight"* was a title of honor and glory, uniting all members of the feudal system, from the humblest vassals to the king. But later, a class barrier was reared between the fortunate lords, who succeeded in building up a territorial power, and the poor noblemen, who lost the bulk of their property while campaigning. Only these poor noblemen who had their rude castles without sufficient land to support them, and therefore had to give military service wherever it was required, were now classified as knights. Thus this term came to designate military service and the military profession. Beginning with the fourteenth century, the new fighting methods of the Swiss infantry, who fought everywhere as mercenaries, especially in Italy, fundamentally changed the ways of warfare. Confronted with the new line of battle formation of this new infantry, and with the firearms and war machinery that came into use subsequently, the knights became ineffectual. Their methods proved antiquated and useless, and military careers were closed to them thereafter. But they stubbornly refused city life and city callings, or services of any other kind, since they considered these unsuitable to their rank. They preferred to sulk in their moldering castles, herded together and poor, and finally they became robber barons, despoiling traveling merchants and harassing peasants. It was a time of complete anarchy, when no law at all could be made effective, when no authority was left to enforce it, as the numerous split jurisdictional powers had become objects of bargain, and nobody had the strength or the power to establish order. It was the time of the "right of the stronger", of the secret Vehmic courts, similar to the Ku Klux Klan, that condemned and executed people for purposes of private vengeance. The knights were, in fact, a huge proletariat of noblemen, which, in the fifteenth century, gathered in confederacies and attempted unsuccessful and useless uprisings. Eventually, when the territorial dominions were sufficiently consolidated for peace to be maintained, they were destroyed or forced into the territorial service.

The *peasants* were still more miserable. The term "peasant" came to be used generally for everyone doing farm work, since the differences between small freeholders, tenants and bondsmen of various kinds, had been gradually wiped out by a common serfdom of all these people. The peasants too, in their desperation, banded together and attempted local revolts, often incited and led by knights or connected with religious movements. But they had no effective organization or methods of warfare and were easily crushed by the princes.

In comparing the Italian city-republic, the French capital and the German city, it appears as a special characteristic of the last, that it was an independent entity of its own, and subject only to the emperor, like the highest feudal lords, but in an entirely different capacity and relationship. They were not incorporated in any superior political community, nor did they form political units of their own.

The Italian towns—Venice, Genoa, Milan, Florence, for instance —which were originally Roman provincial cities and emporia, centers of trade, carried on and renewed the Roman heritage even after they had mingled with the invading Germanic populations. When the crusades widened the horizon of the European peoples and reopened the Orient for a broad influx of ideas and goods, these cities, by virtue of their excellent location, became the first great centers of European trade. They grew rich and influential, and, following the Roman tradition, developed into powerful city-republics. Although their chief interest was trade, they still sought political power and used all their wealth toward obtaining it. Like the Greek and Roman city-states, the Italian cities were identical with their dominions, and vice versa. But, in some respects, they differed from the ancient city-states.

In the first place, they lacked the sacred character of the polis, they were temporal communities that had arisen under the dominance of the Christian world religion. In developing regional characteristics, traditions and ambitions, and, accordingly, a sense of regional homogeneousness, they represented an intermediary stage between the polis and the nation. One might call them *city-nations*.

A second difference is that they had risen through trade. Their power had been founded on trade—feudality had no essential part in it. This, combined with their profane character, made for a secular trend. In fact, what we call Humanism and the Renaissance, was not a mere revival of pagan origins; the revival was accidental, an intellectual by-product, as it were. The trend toward complete emancipation from religious bonds, toward the establishment of the worldly individual, was implied in their commercial development, in their absorption in so worldly an occupation, which stood in ill repute with the Christian dogma and was considered the most despicable of callings. The charging of interest, in particular, was utterly condemned by the official church as a consequence of the Jewish prohibition of interest. This, of course, did not prevent the Roman hierarchy from patronizing trade and introducing credit operations by their own agents. Such proceedings and the behavior of the popes and the Roman clergy, which the Italian citizens were in a position to observe closely, the struggle with the emperors in which the Italian cities played an important part, and the example of the German, especially the Stauffer emperors, constituted a rounded education in cynicism and in a disregard of religious and moral obligations. Thus the Italian city-republics completed the emancipation and secularization of the individual and of human life as a whole. Yet, with all their notorious lust for power, with all their criminal personal ambition, the citizens of these republics were still intrinsically bound by a common tradition which still, as we said, represents a profane religion. They were deeply concerned with the glory of their city, that they exalted and adorned with a unique cultural and intellectual display. A man like Cosimo Medici was neither a private banker, nor was he a mere autocrat, he was considered a "pater patriae", a father of the fatherland.

The second type of the European city was the *residential capital,* the leading city of a nation which exists in its own right, and which is no longer simply identical with the leading city but only represented by and included in it. Such a city is also the pattern for all the provincial cities of that nation. Paris, the classical example, demonstrates how a nation forms through the focusing of feudal dominions in one social and cultural center, and how a nation so formed retains the capital as its living core, although the national scope exceeds this central city. The representation of feudal dominions in the nobility of the court adds to the quality of the city and contributes to the court the special tone of the various rural districts. This was lacking in the Italian city-republics.

In contrast to these types of cities that are the source of their national communities, the *German cities* developed after the founding of the kingdom and the empire. They were not the origin but the result of this founding. Not before the thirteenth century was the development of the German cities completed. The Germanic tribes had always been averse to cities, and when the Eastern

Frankish kingdom was founded, there were no cities except for the ruins or empty sites of Roman cities on the Rhine and south of the Danube. On these sites of Roman cities the bishops had their residence, for this was their traditional duty. On the ruins of Roman walls new walls were built. The population consisted almost entirely of clerics and of those who served the administration of the bishops. The Anglican monk, Boniface, who was called the "Apostle of the Germans", was forced to break the rule of the city residence of bishops when he carried the Christian faith to the newly conquered tribes that had never been in contact with the Romans. He founded new bishoprics in Bavaria, Hessia and Thuringia. There, usually on elevations, the bishops erected their churches and fortified mansions as well as the habitations of their clerics, and below, at the foot of the hill, were the farmhouses and farmlands included in their property. These bishoprics with their church services, their synods and ecclesiastical tribunals, with their many gatherings and feasts, became centers for traveling merchants. Especially along the great rivers and the old Roman trade roads, a limited commercial traffic, a kind of caravan trade, was still active. It was maintained by Syrians and Jews, and later by the Germanic Frisians who had a special leaning toward trade. From the South they brought weapons, spices, silks and jewels, and from the North, furs and woolens (the Frisians raised sheep), and exchanged their wares for wine and corn. First, the traders were only attracted by special occasions; they came and went. Gradually, they settled, they built houses and farmsteads, and from their new homes they went on their trading trips. The result was that people, particularly the landed proprietors, awoke to the pleasure of buying, and to the desire of selling, bargaining and making profits. Neighboring proprietors or administrators began to trade among themselves as a hobby. They became accustomed to it and continued, especially as this sporadic form of trading was compatible with their standard of life as landed proprietors. The original merchants, who were free and even privileged people, and these trading proprietors formed the nucleus of the new trade centers from which the German cities evolved.

The establishment of these trade centers had far-reaching consequences. It brought with it the making of a new body of law. The Germanic tribal law, current among the rural population, was very primitive and involved. It was, in fact, nothing but a series of regulations governing blood-vengeance. The rule of these primitive tribes was not a systematic order of communal life, but the primeval harmony and peace of a community not yet disturbed by the continuous friction of individuals. Breach of law was therefore a breach of peace, an offense committed between families and clans, and peace had to be restored to the family or the clan with very complex, ritual procedure. Furthermore, there was no provision for the new conditions prevailing in a trade center, for the type of individual quarrels and insults that normally occur in the course of trading. A new law was required.

The Frankish king and his place of residence was protected by an intensified peace, called the "peace of the king", a kind of taboo. It meant that every offense to the king and his attendance, every offense committed in his place of residence, was to be punished immediately and with particular severity. As the churches stood under the patronage of the king, the bishops, as lords of their trading centers, obtained the grant of the "peace of the king" for these new trading centers. The insignia of the king, Cross, sword and glove, were put up in the market-place as a symbol of the continuous presence of the king. And from then on, the trade centers were exempt from the law of the territories surrounding them. While the territorial laws became more and more complex and chaotic, the law of the market-place developed according to definite requirements and regardless of the various ordinances and customs of the rest of the country. It grew more and more regular, homogeneous and effective.

This exemption of the market-place had implications of fundamental importance; for the duration of his stay, it freed everyone from all debt and servitude to which he was subject. Everyone was equal and free within the pale of the trading centers, and he had only to abide by the laws governing them. It was the law of trade, the law of equal partners, that reigned here.

This new freedom exerted great magnetism on the country folk. Peasants and craftsmen who brought their goods to market remained and settled. And the centers grew. A church was built, a market square, market halls, city halls arose, walls and fortifications were reared to protect the settlements. And so the city came into being. There was no outside tradition that contributed to the founding of these cities. This is indicated by the very name, which has no connection with the Roman "civitas", as the English word "city", the French "cité", the Italian "città" and the Spanish "ciudad". It does not recall the Roman "villa", as the French "ville" does. The German "Stadt", originally "Kaufstatt", simply means "place", market-place. The German cities took nothing from the outside, nothing from the past. Nothing influenced them, nothing hampered them, nothing prevented them from following their own immediate needs and trends, which were purely economic.

Yet there was still the bishop, the lord of the city, who was, and who increasingly became, a foreign element in such a community. There were merchants who were still partly landed proprietors and noblemen clinging to their rank. But now the great purge began, the gradual elimination of all elements that were not wholly urban and economic-minded, not wholly bourgeois.

The first onrush in this process eliminated the bishop who had become a mighty feudal lord, supervising the city through his administrators and bailiffs, and collecting increasing taxes for himself and for the empire. The citizens formed a council that wrested one right after another from the bishop. It won the right to levy taxes by itself and for itself, for armaments, for the fortifications of the city, for communal offices and buildings. It won the power of police, and jurisdictional autonomy. During the anarchy of the thirteenth century, the cities that had plenty of money acquired all the various rights and titles needed for complete territorial autonomy. The bishops left the cities or were expelled by force, and with them went all their administrators, all the landed proprietors and knights who lived within the pale of the cities, all persons who did not comply with the city standard, and that meant with the merchant standard.

This process was accompanied internally by a systematization of the city law, by an organization of the city administration and the establishment of departmental authorities and offices. But the council and the administration of the city was still in the hands of a few, rich and distinguished merchant families. It was an assembly of patricians, a kind of senate. Although these families were of merchant origin and set apart from the others only by their wealth, they were still inclined to land ownership and to expansion beyond the city walls, and considered themselves aristocrats because, in their eyes, trade was superior to the handicrafts. The last step which completed the bourgeois character, the "petty bourgeois" character of the German cities, was the conquest of the city by the craftsmen in the course of the fourteenth century. Only in Germany did the craftsmen gain uncontested predominance in many cities and a decisive influence in all of them. Only in Germany did they shape the whole character of the city population.

There were guilds all over Europe. But the course of their development and their significance differed. In the Romanic countries, the rise of the craftsmen met with opposition that hindered or changed its original meaning. In the cities of Italy and Southern France, the Roman city tradition, the incorporation of the nobility in the community and the persisting prevalence of their standard values, were strong enough to check the advance of the guild spirit. In the towns of Northern France, where the crafts were rapidly increasing in importance, the kingdom took over the autonomous development of the cities at the decisive moment. In the English cities also, the mild ambitions of the craftsmen were wet-blanketed by the aristocratic city governments that were influenced by the nobles and the king. In both France and England, the guilds were nationalized from the fourteenth century on, that is to say, they became subject to the rules and regulations of the monarchy. It was only in the German inland towns that, due to the barbarism of the nobles hostile to cities and civilization, due to the powerlessness of the central government, the rise of the crafts was not effectively opposed, and reached actual predominance. The spirit of the craftsmen, of the petty bourgeois, took over the leadership and education of the people in Germany and put its stamp on all the other classes.

The development of the German cities is an unprecedented phenomenon, for it shows the rise of a community from purely economic premises and along economic lines, a community beginning with a gathering of free individuals concerned with trade, and following only the directions and requirements of its economic concerns. But the predominance of the craftsmen brought about a still more important phenomenon, the first form of a true collective. As a matter of fact, it produced the first prototype of the German state.

When the wealthy *merchants* rose to power, they still behaved as aristocrats within the city. They began to hold aloof from the craftsmen, with whom, up to this point, they had intermingled and made common cause. They monopolized the profitable offices among their group, they still clung to land property and to what they considered the mark and distinction of their rank, to what has been the distinction of all nobility since ancient times—idleness! By this they meant abstention from all work likely to "blacken one's finger nails" and the pursuit of the honorable, stately and leisurely occupations of holding office in the city government and of carrying on trade. Trade at this time, in thirteenth century Germany, did not include industry and banking, but meant only trade in goods, such as had brought prosperity to the cities and peoples of the Mediterranean, especially the great maritime city-republics of Italy. In Germany, too, it was largely the Northern seaports, the Hansa towns, that carried on commerce in this sense, while the interior served mainly as a thoroughfare. Here it was only an extension of the far more abundant and ample Italian trade, and it was soon surpassed in its significance by other kinds of economic activity, which brought about the flowering of the German inland towns: handicraft, industry and banking. In so far as trade in goods—spices, silks, jewels, but mainly cloth—was an economic activity in the period of the patrician German merchant councils, it was, on the one hand, practised in an irregular and leisurely manner, and, on the other, it was connected with fighting and adventure, as the roads were poor and led across lawless and unprotected regions where there was constant danger of holdups by robber barons and thieves. And so commerce was a knightly and seignorial concern. The craftsmen finally revolted against the arrogant attitude of the merchants and their careless, arbitrary and selfish administration of the city.

In gaining control of the cities, the German *craftsmen* were helped by the comparative weakness of their adversaries; the German merchants lacked political background and power. They lacked the large means of the Italian merchants, who had accumulated vast riches and developed into great families with strong castles in the cities and huge estates and villas in the country, who maintained body-guards to fight their family feuds for them, and who, if victorious, ruled the city-state. Aside from the different background of the German merchants, the slow, meagre, cumbersome inland trade of Germany could never yield such fortunes.

The German merchants in every city already formed a professional group, a professional union, called "guild", which enabled them to rid themselves of the lords of the city, to achieve the possession, the independence and autonomy of the city. These guilds were loose social units, clubs as it were, originating in round-table associations of an informal, convivial character. The membership in such a guild was a mark of distinction and a source of advantage and pleasure, so, although it was not compulsory, it was voluntarily sought. Commerce, especially in its first evolutionary stage, is essentially an individual occupation. After the autonomy of the city had been won, the only motive to association was the protection of the transports which could be effectively accomplished only in common. This, in fact, was the origin of the Hansa, which literally means "convoying squad". The other incentive to trading associations, the combining of capital, had not as yet become necessary. There was hardly any competition, but an unlimited demand for goods—and goods were scarce. No systematic procedure was needed, no rational speculation, accounting and economy. What the German merchants wrested from the city lords was individual freedom and the opportunity of free and equal partnership in trading.

The craftsmen, on the other hand, were particularly strong in the German cities. They also formed guilds, but these guilds were different. First of all, there was not one but a number of guilds in every town, as they were based on specific forms of craft. The merchants in their external struggle against the lords had conquered the very site, the soil, the dominion of the city. In the final analysis, they had conquered it with money. The conquest of power by the craftsmen was an internal conflict within the autonomous city. It was a struggle centering in the system of administration, not a struggle for autonomy. The craftsmen, moreover, had no money with which to buy influence. They had to use different means. And these means were the strictest and closest collective organization, materially as well as morally. They had to prove that they were indispensable and to use this pressure just as the labor unions do today. Accordingly, they had to resort to disciplined solidarity, to disciplinary force of various kinds. They had to make membership and the observance of the guild rules compulsory for everybody who wanted to carry on his calling, for the effectiveness of the pressure they exercised depended upon the exclusiveness and comprehensiveness of their professional organization, and membership was not attractive in itself as in the case of the merchant guilds. They had to protect themselves with firm regulations against wild competitors, "disturbers and bunglers", as they called them, just as the labor unions proceed against scabs. Since, moreover, they fought the government of the merchants because of its careless and selfish class administration which they wished to improve upon with efforts toward the welfare of the community, since their struggle was enacted in small communities, (20,000 to 25,000 people at most), where all kept a close watch on one another and on every happening, these craft guilds had to strengthen their outward discipline with an inner, moral discipline.

They exerted entire control over the quality, the "honor", of the work of their members in order to impress the population and to inspire confidence. They protected the consumer as well as the producer. The most detailed regulations provided for equality in the position and working conditions of all members; raw materials and tools had to be bought either by a delegate purchaser of the guild, who distributed them equally among the masters, or at least they had to be bought publicly, on the open market, under the supervision of overseers and quality testers. Secret purchase and secret sale were severely punished. The sources of supply and the amount of sales were fixed. In many cases, the products had to be tested by the guild before they were admitted to the market. Prices were fixed and limited to secure a comfortable living for the master and a moderate expense for the consumer. The use of special tools was prohibited, the number of journeymen limited. Conspicuous advertising was not allowed; each master had but one window for the display of his products and he had to be master in the production of the goods he sold.

Thus the craft guild is a true collective, in the strictest sense of the word. It is an organization, an organized community of individuals intended for a common purpose. And in its small and closely controlled sphere it achieved a degree of solidarity far beyond that of the modern labor union, of which it is the prototype.

At the end of the thirteenth century, the craft guilds were strong enough in themselves to take concerted action against the council of the merchants. They enforced an account of the budget, financial control and participation in the government. The increasing conflicts led to open revolts and eventually, in the fourteenth century, to the conquest of the administration by the craft guilds of many cities. As a result, the craft guilds exerted a decisive influence on the city population. The ultimate purge was being administered to the German inland cities. The merchants were either expelled, as the lords and the landed proprietors before them, or they had to give up their aristocratic "idleness" by joining a craft guild or by adapting their merchant guild to the regulations of the craft guilds. And now, under the rule or the predominance of the craft guilds, whole cities were transformed into collectives, into organized working communities of individuals.

The first true form of public life arose in these cities, for in the Holy Roman Empire there had been no public life, only a chaotic multitude of private relationships. These cities, then, were the real nuclei of the German state. They developed the offices, administrative departments and authorities which later became the patterns of territorial state administrations. The law of the trade centers was the first public law in Germany. A first public, publicly controlled financial administration evolved, with common fiscal burdens, individual income taxes and indirect "excises", with public loans and credit operations, and a military administration with a draft for all. For the first time public welfare and health, buildings and schools, were under official supervision and management.

But the most important innovation of the craft-controlled German city was the establishment of a new public morality, indeed, the foundation of all bourgeois morality, which emerged from the discipline and the professional ethics of the craft guilds. It was the first morality which did not spring from a particular tradition, be it tribal, national or Catholic, the first morality which did not develop from the emulation of a mythical or ecclesiastical or traditional élite, the first morality which did not set up the aristocratic standard of heroes or saints but rather that of an average— the collective standard of a good, useful citizen. The ideal exponent of this morality is the citizen who fits into the common order, who adapts himself to the collective requirements. This morality is the result of a community built up by individuals who contribute their essentially economic labors to the support of the collective. All the values of bourgeois morality—diligence, studiousness, zeal, efficiency, economy, sobriety, orderliness, decency, peaceableness (not as an active striving for peace but in the meaning of docility and tractability)—this whole canon and code of bourgeois values unfolded from the city of the craft guilds in sharp contrast to the feudal values.

All the various ranks and castes of the Middle Ages based their behavior on Christian values and drew the authorization of their standards from these. But every class, according to its specific attitude and way of life, laid emphasis on certain qualities among these

Christian values. The knights chose the more aristocratic and ecclesiastical virtues in the Catholic code: self-restraint, ascetic perseverance, protection of the weak and the helpless, the women and the children, the maintenance of peace and the defense and spreading of Christianity. This concept permitted, and even sanctioned, the unlimited display not only of all the virtues but also of all the savageries of warfare, which, of course, were in contradiction to the genuine Christian teachings. But the craftsmen, with their popular movement, emphasized the values of early Christianity which had been deliberately neglected by the ruling clergy with its stress on cultic ritual and on "holy works" and services on behalf of the church. These genuine Christian values had been upheld and revived by the monks, and above all by the mendicant friars who preached in the cities and were in close touch with the lower classes of the population. These popular preachers initiated the German mystic movement which was the forerunner of the Reformation. The mystic movement both answered and expressed a profound need of the people in the cities, who hated the ruling bishops and the arrogant, rich, aristocratic clergy, who began to repudiate the ecclesiastical mediation between God and Man and to seek a new immediate contact with God.

The early German mystics attacked the knightly ideals of the nobles and of the militant church. They stressed the early Christian values and adapted them to the bourgeois spirit prevailing in the craft cities. These values lost the dramatic, apocalyptic and cosmic scope they had had when the advent of the Kingdom of God seemed imminent, and "the last" were expected to become "the first". They were leveled down to every-day use and the pride in craftsmanship of a working community. It was recalled that Jesus himself had been the son of a craftsman. In early Christianity the workers and craftsmen had been the preferred, mainly because they were poor and unhappy and untouched by worldly temptations, and hence more responsive and prepared for the teaching of the expected reversal. Now the same people were glorified simply for the sake of their work and the general influence it represented. Love and charity were deprived of their extraordinary, heroic merit. They were gradually reduced to a standardized service to the community. From this blend of the genuine Christian values with the common sense and the new bourgeois spirit developed by the evolution of the German city, the middle-class morality of our modern world was born.

Three important currents of influence emanated from the German city. One led directly to the Reformation, which was a result of the popular revolution against the rule of the church and its key position between man and God, a result of that mystic movement that tried to reaffirm the early Christian values within the narrow bounds of an organized worldly community. The Reformation divided into a number of branches: the Eastern, Lutheran branch provided the intrinsic foundation and religious authorization of the German state, which originated in Prussia and gradually developed into the second German Reich of Bismarck, and eventually into the third Reich of the National Socialists. The Western, Calvinistic branch had a decisive bearing on the shaping of the British Commonwealth and of the United States, and through them, on all of Western democracy.

A second current of influence proceeding from the German city led to the development of a type of entrepreneur who combined the adventurous, individualistic mind of the merchant with the technological, collective working spirit of the craftsman. In other words, the first modern industrialist, and more than that, the first form of true capitalism, evolved from the specific conditions of the medieval German inland city.

And, finally, the particular social and psychological circumstances of the German inland city were a decisive factor in the development of the modern relation of man to nature. The rift between city and country encouraged the representation of nature as a chaotic, elemental wilderness of soulless forces, opposed to man and his rational civilization, and due to become an object of his exploration, exploitation and recreation.

These three currents are only different manifestations of one main trend that dominates the modern world: the trend toward a rationally organized human community, toward a collective world order, the trend to attempt the mastery of nature through the human spirit, to establish a new, conscious harmony of the human mind with the universe.

THE FORMATION OF THE HUMAN
COLLECTIVE

AUTONOMY OF THE SECULAR
WORLD

AT THE BEGINNING of the second part of this book, a brief summary of the phases in the evolution of man into man is necessary for a better understanding of the more complex developments to come.

In attempting to define the essential characteristic of the human being, as contrasted with the animal, we found that this characteristic is man's general faculty to transcend the limits of his own being. This human faculty is identical with what we mean by the term "spirit". The procedure of transcending the limits of one's own being, this psychic procedure, consists of two acts: the establishing of these limits by detaching and discerning a non-self from a self, an alien, outward existence from one's own clearly conceived existence, that is, an act of objectivation and subjectivation; and the establishing of a new, conscious relationship between one's own existence and the clearly conceived non-self, the objectivated, outward existence, by a feat of deliberate vicariousness.

The evolution of the quality of being human is the successive genesis of these two acts and faculties in man. In its early periods, the main concern of human history is the formation of the faculty of detachment and discernment. The later part of human history, which we are about to consider, deals with the genesis and completion of the faculty to transcend.

The subject of human history, therefore, is man's relation to the world surrounding him. And this surrounding world comprises two spheres: a wide circle, consisting in the non-human world, i.e. the universe, and a narrow circle, consisting in the human world, i.e. the human community. These two spheres are the foils of man in the process of his evolution. First he discerns and detaches them from his own existence, of which he is increasingly aware, and later, in transcending them, he establishes a new relationship with them.

The unfolding of man's relation to the universe develops the human mind. The unfolding of man's relation to the human community develops the human individual. In the first relation, man gradually distinguishes and conceives the objects and beings of the outer world as separate and distinct existences and, in contrast to these outward existences, he discovers his own human existence and soul. And in the subsequent process of transcending, these outward objects and beings gradually become incorporated in the human mind and so in the human world. The world of the human mind expands over greater and greater domains of the objective world with the help of man's capacity to form concepts and to transform reality. In the second relation, the relation to the human community, man begins by distinguishing first his fellow kinsman and then his fellow man from his own gradually perceived personality. This is how the individual evolves. The completion of the individual coincides with his inevitable efforts toward a new, deliberately organized community.

So the process of human evolution begins with a physical connection with the universe that is prior to all awareness and concept. Through the forming of the human mind and the human soul, it proceeds to the conscious striving for a spiritual conformity with a universe distinctly visualized and comprehended. Human evolution is, at the same time, a development from a pre-individual community held together only by physical ties, a community identical with what we understand by the term "species", via the formation of the human individual, toward the striving for a consciously built and organized, post-individual community, a collective order.

In considering the earlier periods of human evolution, we observed the gradual detachment and discernment of a non-self from a self: the detachment of everything that is cosmic, plant and animal from a distinctly conceived human being, and the detachment and discernment of the fellow kinsman and later the fellow man, as distinct and different personalities, from an ego which grew more and more conscious of itself, more and more self-reliant with regard to its cosmic and human community, and consequently more and more isolated and lonely, that means, more and more individual.

This gradual detachment and discernment occurred through a series of subsequent objectivations, the first of which was identical with the emergence of religion from participation. This took place when the dead of a clan, the ancestors and the demons of animal, plant and cosmic forces—all of which represented life principles, creators, ancestors of clans—began to be conceived as a category of beings different and remote from living people. They became the eternal core of their tribe, they were worshipped, conjured into images, taboos and sanctuaries, they developed centers of cults, offerings, rituals and prayers, in a word, they became deities. Along with this, time fell into periods that were distinguished from one another; eternity separated from the past, and the past from the present. So it was in the form of deities that man first detached and discerned the clearly objectivated forces and beings in his world as distinct, outward existences. For the first time he faced these forces as independent and, in a way, opposite beings. This clear conception of the deity implied a spiritual bond side by side with the physical bond that still persisted, as the deity was the ancestor, the life-giving essence of a particular tribe. Thus genuine religion is partly a spiritual and partly a physical bond.

A parallel process took place in the relation of man to his human community, which was conceived as a definite and present sphere. Here the mediator between man and deity, the priest, was singled out as the earthly substitute for the deity, proprietor of the soil and distributor of goods. He became the chieftain and sacred king, descended from, or appointed by, the deity. And as such, he was the first to assume the shape of a single and definite personality.

The second great objectivation occurred when man's relation to the cosmic forces developed from religion to world religion. It was the objectivation of the universe as a whole, as an all-comprising and therefore purely spiritual power, detached from man and all earthly, material things, and so necessitating a spiritual approach. This conception of a consistent and coherent world, as it is expressed by the very word "universe" and as it is first represented in a universal God, involved a corresponding realization and conception of a united humanity, a community of equal, brotherly human beings, of human beings as such, subject to a universal God, and the concept of a common destiny of mankind, a unity and continuity of human history and evolution.

The completing of this second great objectivation was the contribution to the history of man by the three great peoples of antiquity: the Jews, the Greeks and the Romans. Judaism created the concept of the universal, spiritual God and of the human being made in the image of God, regardless of tribal origin and tribal particularity. This concept involved the creation of the standard values of our civilization: universal peace and justice, regard and love for one's fellow men. The Greeks created the temporal community of free and equal citizens in the sacred city-state; they created democracy. They also created the self-objectivation of the human being, the concept of the human soul, of the inner life of man, as a distinct sphere, subject to human reflection and speculation. And the Romans were responsible for the expansion of the city-state into a true world empire, the framework of a united humanity in which world religion could develop and spread. The outcome of the combined achievements of these three peoples, was Christianity; that implies a spiritual relation of man to his universal God, a relation divested of any physical bond to a particular tribal ancestor, a relation in which the human individual, as a personality, faces his spiritual, universal God, a profession of a creed based on faith alone.

At the same time, the Roman world empire, by its mingling of many populations severed from their particular tribal roots, by its late concentration into a centralized, bureaucratic state machinery under the emperors Diocletian and Constantine, had developed its citizens into rootless, isolated, private individuals, facing the earthly universality of the world-wide empire.

The second great objectivation, that of the spiritual universe, eventually brought about actual opposition of the spiritual to the earthly, material sphere. After the disintegration of the Roman Empire, the administration of the Christian world religion, the Catholic Church, took over the heritage of Rome. And since the church, which considered itself the "City of God" on earth, had no worldly power at its disposal, its rule was bound to be a spiritual rule, a purely spiritual world empire. Lacking the strength to build up a worldly power of its own, as it had first intended to do, the church needed worldly support, which it sought and found in the Germanic chieftains. Between the Frankish rulers and the Roman bishops a bond of mutual support and protection was formed, by which the Frankish rulers were made emperors and the Roman bishops, popes. In this way, the Roman Empire, which had been both spiritual and terrestrial—since the Roman emperor had been regarded as the head of the Christian Church—this one Roman Empire divided into a spiritual empire, the papacy, and a terrestrial empire, the Holy Roman Empire. And so, once and for all, the spiritual rule was divorced from the terrestrial, secular rule —a crucial development, which contained the germ of the secularization of the world of man. The break reflected the dualism intrinsic in the rift between the spirit and the body, that carried with it the corollary of the demotion of the body to a lower and only transitory plane of human existence. According to such a principle, the Christian religion could no longer permeate and legitimately foster temporal developments, as the pagan religions had done. Affairs that were of this earth were left to their own direction. In the struggle between the popes and the emperors, both the papacy and the Holy Roman Empire crumbled. The spiritual rule of a united, world religion melted into thin air, and the result was the secular and profane world of the Renaissance, consisting of many individual territorial powers that initiated the political struggles and the international anarchy of the modern world. A multitude of emancipated, self-reliant individuals faced

the task of ruling themselves, of building up a deliberately organized community, a collective order. And Man, in his relation
to the universe, made a third and last objectivation, within the
secular world and on the level of this secularized world. The second
part of this survey must start from this most important objectivation, which shaped the world of today.

MAN AND NATURE

THE FINAL OBJECTIVATION consisted in the detachment and discernment of nature from man. In all previous systems of human life,
man was included in the universe, he was intrinsically connected
with the forces of nature. He was part of the cycle of natural forces
which were considered animate as man himself. In the primeval
system of participation, man was on the level of animals, plants,
rocks and stars. He could even assume their appearance, and they,
his. In the subsequent religious systems, man was in close connection and communication with a pantheon of deities, which represented not only the essence of his particular tribe but also the
elementary powers of nature, and these powers, in the form of
deities, influenced, imbued and even dominated human life and
tribal modes of life. The universal God of Judaism was the epi-
tome of all the elemental powers, and also their creator. In the
strong, overwhelming personality of this universal God, human
character had already begun to supersede the inherent, elemental
qualities. Spirit, the essentially human quality, began to prevail.
In Greek speculation, especially at the turn of human thought that
came with Socrates, Plato and Aristotle, the sovereignty of spirit
over the senses, the sovereignty of the newly discovered world of
the human soul and of human reason over the world of the body
and the deceptive sensual semblance, came into being. Man became
the center, the standard of the universe. The Greek universe, however, was still one consistent, coherent, all-comprising system, it
was still represented as a united cosmos, ruled and animated by a
focal soul. It was only in Christianism, in the doctrine of the

established Catholic Church, that the dualism of spirit and body developed into a fundamental rift, that the life of the body was forced into a lower sphere and regarded as sinful and transitory, as only a prelude to a wholly spiritual life in the beyond. Earthly, natural life sank to a lower level.

But even here, in the Catholic doctrine, in spite of this fundamental rift, both spheres still belonged to one system. They were connected with each other through a common origin in divine creation, and the spiritual rule was still a divine, all-comprising rule. But in the secularized rule of the Renaissance, when this all-comprising divine rule paled, when the spiritual rule of God was replaced by the rule of human reason, both spheres broke definitely asunder. There is a saying—and this saying is essentially correct—that in this period which begins at the end of the thirteenth century nature was discovered. And it has been a matter of much discussion why this discovery of nature, with all its implications and consequences—such as empirical studies, experimental research and the deluge of technical inventions that set in at that time and go on to this very day—why all this arose precisely in this period. Why did the great ancient cultures, especially the Greek and the Roman, with their high development of the intellect and of political, social and commercial life, never focus their attention on nature as an object of human exploration and exploitation? Why did they not achieve a technical civilization, such as that of the modern world?

There is an earlier theory that they were not capable of this because of their evolutionary immaturity. There is a later theory that they had all the intellectual and cultural prerequisites for exploring nature in the modern experimental way and for the development of modern technical and industrial civilization, and simply did not want it, as their attention was fixed on other aims. Their state of mind, their cultural trend differed from ours. This second theory contains more truth than the first, for it is evident that the intellectual faculties of the Greeks and the Romans, as well as their cultural level, more than sufficed for the undertaking and the achievement of technical perfection. The mechanical inventions of Archimedes, Ctesibius and others—especially war machinery and mechanical toys—and the engineering, road building and architecture of Rome, show a very high standard of technical ability. The Byzantine mathematician and architect, Anthemius, a favorite of the Emperor Justinian, was even completely aware of the technical application of steam pressure. He could easily have invented the steam engine, but he used his knowledge only to organize an artificial earthquake as a jest to frighten his friends. So different was the trend of those times from ours. This second theory, however, does not explain satisfactorily in what the difference of the ancient state of mind actually consisted.

It seems that there is only one answer to this problem: the prerequisite for the tremendous technical and industrial progress of our era is the modern concept of nature, and what prevented the ancient peoples from forming this concept, was religion, and the power it exerted over their minds throughout all ages and stages of their development. Religion is the one great antagonist of technology and economy. Religion presents the world as a consistent and coherent universe including both man and natural forces, connecting and uniting them intrinsically through a common divine origin and a common divine order. And religion ties man down to rituals and customs, and thus deters him from giving his uninhibited and undivided attention to worldly purposes, from a concentrated perseverance in his worldly aims. So it was the crumbling of the idea of a sanctified universe and the withering of the power of religion over man, it was, in brief, the process of secularization that divorced man from nature and freed his reason for mastering, exploring and exploiting the forces of the profane and material world. It was not merely the dwindling of Christian unity and of supernatural rule over human minds, it was not a mere slackening of religious fervor that brought about secularization. But the active forces, the very impulses of new religious movements themselves—the monastic, mystic and protestant movements—directed and indeed thrust man into his secular work and toward completely secularized, social and economic goals.

As man becomes emancipated from religious bonds, from the

bonds of innate, irrational beliefs and customs, as he spends all his thoughts, forces and activities on earthly goals as such, his whole attitude changes. He no longer lives by the past, according to the pattern of a sacred origin, but rather by a future, by the aims toward which he is striving. And so he is more and more compelled to use his rational faculty, to develop his reason.

Reason is the intellectual faculty of drawing conclusions from experiences and perceived facts, in order to make them available for future application. Not only science, but all our tools, indeed all of technology, is the evidence and the concrete manifestation of our rational processes.

Emancipated, secularized man necessarily becomes increasingly rational. He identifies himself with his rational quality, and the stuff on which he exerts his pure reason is secularized, profane nature which, correspondingly, is regarded as pure matter. Nature first becomes the object of man's rational domination and gradually the object of his study and research, of his exploration and exploitation, and not only outward nature in the shape of animal, plant and cosmic forces but also physical and psychical human nature.

In the first period, when man was enraptured with his newly discovered rational power, which he believed to be unlimited, he used his power in a violent and autocratic way. In the Renaissance and the Baroque, especially in the case of the Romanic nations, the Italians and the French, human reason was to dominate nature, to impose its law ruthlessly. Later, under the prevalence of the Anglo-Saxon and Germanic peoples, man began to realize that he might exploit nature more successfully by taking into account her own course. The difference in approach is illustrated by two types of gardens; in the Italian and French Renaissance and Rococo gardens, nature was subdued and forced into artificial regularity, transformed, in fact, into a playground for society, but in the English landscape gardens, natural forms were preserved, enjoyed in all their irregularity and abundance and made available for objective understanding and recreation of a more profound variety.

The different forms of man's relation to nature are reflected in the intellectual attitudes of the modern era; the autocratic attitude expresses itself in complete rationalism, the compliant attitude leads to materialism and romanticism. Rationalism subjects the whole world to the exclusive rule of human reason; God becomes reason and reason becomes God. Materialism projects rational procedure into a mechanical functioning of natural processes. The automatic, mechanical causality of nature, the "laws of nature" which are investigated and studied, are, in fact, derived from this procedure of human reason. Romanticism, finally, is the result of man's emulation of nature, since it sounds and exalts nature in its very irrationality, in its profound, chaotic vitality. From these various intellectual attitudes of the modern mind—to be discussed more extensively in the following—modern science and art, modern politics, technology and economy evolved.

From this point on, then, man is keyed to the subjection of nature, to her exploitation for his own purposes. But nature is divided from and opposed to man, as a soulless and infinite mass of blind, elemental forces and processes. She lures man, who seeks to dominate her, more and more from his own domains and into labyrinthine vistas and depths. His powers are strained to the utmost. As an individual, he is not equal to the demands put upon him. He is forced to cooperate with others in the exploration as well as in the exploitation of nature.

Cooperation in the exploration of nature leads to modern science, that is, to collective knowledge. The principle of scientific knowledge is to create a body of exact concepts and methods, logically explained and connected, that is equally accessible to all and at all times and that constitutes a generally valid criterion of the truth and usability of explored facts. By means of this rational body of concepts, individual findings can be examined and methodically collected and arranged with reference to their reliability, their validity and their future application. Universal laws can be abstracted, and thus a collective system of knowledge beyond the scope of the individual is developed, a system that can be passed on from generation to generation, that can be expanded, a framework into which all further investigations and results can be fitted.

This collective, systematic body of knowledge is the premise for the methodical application of knowledge to dominate and to exploit nature.

The application of collective knowledge produces collective implements and apparatus, mechanical implements, machines (from the Greek "mechane", an invented tool). These mechanical implements do not merely make possible a common, standardized use, independent of individual conditions, they demand a common, cooperative work and use. And so the development of modern technology and industry begins.

The principle of collective exploration and exploitation of nature has a further consequence. Given that nature is a vast complex entity beyond the grasp of individual man, not only the cooperation of collective work in accordance with certain goals and purposes becomes requisite. Specific aims and concepts of work develop a more and more strict division of labor into special categories and special groups, and the more these increase and expand, the more they lose their connection with the whole and become autonomous. The means become the end.

In the period of pure rationalism, when nature was considered subject to the reason of man, there were still individual metaphysical systems, that is to say, the thinking and searching of a single person could still embrace the whole sphere of cosmic order. Knowing and searching was still synonymous with philosophical interpretation. The more nature was stressed as matter, the more the "laws of nature"—the laws of autonomous nature—were investigated with the help of the collective rational apparatus, the more nature was divided up into separate fields to which human effort was subordinated. Philosophy, that is, the personal comprehensive interpretation of the universe, was forced back into a border region where its preoccupation was only with preliminaries, with the potentialities and methods of human knowledge.

The same process occurred in the sphere of the human community, in dealing with the new secular problems of which there was legion. In the religious form of life, all domains of the life and work of man were subject to divine control. Now that this complete, homogeneous way of life disappeared, all these domains that had been intimately connected fell apart and became independent functions; research separated from speculation and poetry, art from craft; economy, politics and law became autonomous. Religion itself was limited to one separate, well-bounded, atrophied sphere of man's interest. The great process of detachment and discernment, the last great objectivation, that of nature, went on and on and resulted in the autonomy of all those domains that had formerly been parts of a whole.

Consequently man himself, no longer determined by a divine origin but by the goals of his worldly work, no longer turned to the past but to the future, became more and more identified with his work, with his function; he himself became his function. This means that life-emphasis shifted from being to doing, from personal, inner existence to continued effort toward a goal, to the objective goal itself. It means that man became a functional part in a combination set above and beyond the individual. It means that he transcended his existence—at first involuntarily, then more and more deliberately—toward a collective, a cause, intellectual work or general human awareness of the universe. The industrial capitalist who exhausts his life for ever-increasing production, the servant of the totalitarian state who spends himself for the abstract collective, the social revolutionary who sacrifices himself for an ideal community, the artist and the scientist whose life is devoted to the labors of the intellect—they all have one thing in common, the transcending of a personal self to an objective non-self. The disintegration of the secular world and of human life tended toward the conscious organization of life and the world, but the immediate effect was that the community of man, that the personality of man, was rent apart and driven into growing anarchy. In this grand confusion, individuals, and even peoples, grew weaker and weaker, since a grasp, even a purely theoretical grasp of the whole far exceeded their powers. In the mean time, the domains of the species, man, were constantly expanding.

In the following chapters, this process of becoming autonomous and collective, and the process of transcending, will be considered in detail. The initiating factors were the movements toward independence in the various domains of human life, and first among them was that which secularized religion and made it a separate domain of human life.

REFORMATION

A NEW ERA BEGINS with the secularization of the world of man, a process originating in the disintegration of Christian unity and completed in the period known as the Renaissance which covers at least three centuries but was actually under way for a much longer time. Many people are accustomed to think of the Middle Ages as a period of stagnation, as a stand-still, and the term "Dark Ages" has even come into use as a synonym for the medieval era. This is incorrect and must be revised. In examining the currents leading up to the Renaissance, we arrive back at source-streams flowing uninterruptedly through earlier centuries. In considering these various sources, we shall begin with two, one emotional and one intellectual, both leading to secularization. The first is the emancipation of piety by means of the reformation of Christian faith, an emancipation *of* religion resulting in a gradual emancipation *from* religion. The second is the emancipation of reason through the transformation of theology into philosophy. The former is the development of the Protestant movement, the latter that of Scholastic speculation.

The Catholic Church established itself as a Kingdom of God on earth, as the mediating body and the mediating stage between man and God. It assumed the so-called "power of the key" to the grace of God and to the access to heaven, the exclusive power of "binding and loosing", that is, punishment for or absolution from sins. The threat of hell and the promise of heaven rested with the priest, and in the Middle Ages this threat and this promise were unquestioned reality, around which the creative imagination of many generations and traditions circled. Anathema and interdict were terrible and effective weapons in the hands of the popes and were feared even by the most rebellious rulers, if only for the horror they aroused in the people. The church had instituted a system of Christian dogma. It had prescribed what was to be believed and how people were to behave. And with its profound knowledge of human nature, in order to adapt Christian rule to every gradation of human capacity, the church shrewdly differentiated various grades of sanctity and pious life. Had the church insisted upon exacting the same degree of piety from all—as some intransigent Church Fathers had urged—it would have lost most of its adherents and, at the same time, the means to exert the power of absolution upon men, the power which was the foundation of its universal strength. Thus, under the universal rule of the Catholic Church, Christianity outside and inside the church comprised various grades of religious behavior: the intrinsic, sincere devotion of ascetic saints, the superficial ritualism of the powerful church officials, and the lax, unconcerned way of living of the masses who observed the ceremonial services and the "holy works" the church imposed upon them. The weaker, the more sinful people were, the more they depended on the church, the more they were compelled to woo the church in their anxiety to save their souls. In the early medieval centuries, the sacraments, the magical and mystical ceremonies were the only part of Christianism which the barbarian populations were able to grasp at all. Not before the eleventh century, at the beginning of the crusades, did the more intrinsic implications of Christianity begin to penetrate the minds of the masses.

Under the surface of the authoritative rule of the church, heretic movements still went on continuously—among the intelligentsia, that is, the learned clerics who dwelt earnestly upon their faith, and among the plain people who were stirred by an emotional want of direct communication with God. There was, in fact, no period in which the church had not to defend itself against such underground movements.

The emotional and the intellectual currents were connected. They helped and influenced each other, and all were fed at pre-Christian, pagan springs. We can distinguish three trends: first, a rationalistic trend that goes through Scholastic philosophy. Here the elements of Platonic and Aristotelian philosophy, especially Aristotle's logic, worked on in the minds of the clerical scholars. The Christian doctrine had taken over the main problems of Greek speculation; it had assimilated and incorporated them in its dogma and in the teachings of the Church Fathers. These very problems, however, handed down in the translations of and commentaries on Greek writings, presented themselves also in their original pagan form. The similarities of the Christian and pagan problems, and the sharp contrast in the manner of treatment in the Christian and in the original Greek tradition, developed a strange antagonism between dogma and speculation, faith and knowledge, authority and reason. And the outcome of the conflict was the emancipation and autonomy of reason which led to modern philosophy and science.

The second trend was that of intellectual mysticism. It goes back to neo-Platonic systems of Greek philosophy that were brought into harmony with Christian teachings through Apocryphal writings and, in this form, were handed down to the Middle Ages. These systems, that were philosophical mystery and mystical, magical philosophy in one, had a great influence on the formation of the Christian dogma. According to them, God manifests himself through a hierarchy of beings half human, half divine, and through emanations. Man becomes one with God by ascending to God through ecstatic and ascetic exercises, through and beyond the steps of knowledge and existence. These teachings were subsequently modified in accordance with the Christian doctrine. "We recognize God"—so Dionysius Areopagita says—"by ascending from the order of all that is, an order determined by Him and containing, as it were, images . . . of divine prototypes, to that which is supreme over all. We ascend, as far as we are able, by the true way that . . . rises above everything and so leads to the cause of everything. The most divine recognition of God is accomplished through ignorance, in that union beyond the reaches of the mind, where the mind relinquishing everything that is, surrenders itself and merges with an ecstasy of light . . ." These teachings have already a tendency to change personal divinity, in the pantheistic manner, to a vague being inherent in all earthly creatures. In the twelfth century, they brought about the mystic movement of the Victorines, canons of the abbey of St. Victor in Paris. The Scotchman, Richard of St. Victor (died 1173) claimed the existence of a secret soul substance reaching beyond the separate powers of the soul, in which the union with God occurs. From here the mystic movement extended beyond the monasteries to the lay world, and, especially in Germany, combined with a third, emotional, popular movement directed to the immediate union with God.

This movement kept the piety of the people alive throughout the Middle Ages and carried on the prophetic trend of old, in opposition to the ruling hierarchy of the priests. It, too, was connected with pre-Christian, pagan origins. Its beginnings are a direct continuation of ancient, Oriental cults and mysteries, especially Persian, Mithraistic teachings blended with Christian elements. It cropped up in the Bulgarian sect of the Bogomiles (this means "friends of God") who were the Bolsheviks of the eleventh century and carried their much dreaded influence to Italy and the South of France, where their beliefs were shared by the Albigenses, a sect originating in the French city of Albi, which had become so strong and powerful in the twelfth century that it took a veritable crusade to annihilate them. Their dogma was founded on the opposition of the God of Light, and of the invisible spiritual beings, to the prince of the visible, earthly beings, whose mischievous son, Luciferus, had lured the celestials to the abject world of earth. Salvation was accomplished by Jesus Christ, an angel of the God of Light. Men may gain salvation through a pure, ascetic life and gradually ascend to a higher level of perfection and sanctity through spiritual initiations, unions with the Savior, and even metempsychosis. The Albigenses were vehemently opposed to the authority of the pope and the "power of the key" of the Catholic Church.

There was another popular movement connected with the above-mentioned heretic sects, the Waldensian movement, founded about

1200 by Peter Valdes or Waldo, a French merchant from Lyons, who felt inspired to a prophetic calling after the death of a close friend, when he began to read the Gospels. He practised and preached a life of poverty, chastity, charity and penitence, following the example of Jesus Christ and the first Christian community. He tried to bring people into direct contact with Jesus and the apostolic life, by translating parts of the Gospels into the vernacular and reading them to his assemblies. This was an extraordinary procedure, as, in those times, not even all clerics but only the scholars among them were familiar with the text of the Scriptures.

At the same time, in the twelfth century, the monk Joachim de Floris prophesied an age of the spirit and of free promulgation of the Scriptures. There was also the movement of the Augustine friar, Arnold of Brescia, who, during the great struggle between the Stauffer emperors and the popes, preached against the corruption and worldly ambitions of the Roman hierarchy. As early as the twelfth century, he tried to revive the ancient Roman republic and instigated a democratic revolt against the pope. His adherents, the Arnoldines, later united with the Waldensians.

An underground resentment, then, was constantly working against the rule and the abuses of the church and more and more the people strove for a direct contact with God. Wherever they gathered strength, the church labored to crush the heretic sects by anathema, persecution, expulsion and death at the stake, and enlisted the aid of lords and princes. But in addition to the use of force, the church resorted to still other means to combat the danger. It tried to meet the growing dissatisfaction and the increasing need for a regeneration of religion by utilizing the popular element among the clerics, the monks, especially the mendicant friars, all of whose orders had originated in loyal opposition to the official hierarchy, in attempts to purify the life of the clergy.

In general, the monks represented the ascetic, holy element in the Christian community. They stood for abstention from all worldly ambitions and aims, for a life of seclusion, penitence and contemplation, and the zealous preparation for eternal salvation.

All the establishments and re-establishments of monastic rule, all consecutive reforms—the foundation of the Benedictine order in Italy by Benedict of Nursia in the sixth century, its reform in France by Benedict of Aniane about 800, the reform of Cluny a hundred years later, of Citeaux in 1100, and the founding of the various mendicant orders around 1200—all these reforms aimed at a recovery of genuine Christianity that lapsed time and again and compromised with temporal life. In the very character of these reforms, however, a growing tendency toward worldly goals becomes more and more apparent.

As in antiquity, and in the Orient, early monastic life was concerned only with the individual's preparation for eternal life and salvation by means of meditation, prayer and penance. Meditation included the study of the traditional teachings and writings of the Church Fathers and other venerated and sanctioned authorities. The monks were not supposed to have anything to do with worldly affairs, or to engage in worldly occupations, which were thought to distract attention from the celestial goal. Contemplative life was valued far above active life, no matter how full of goodness the latter might be. The great innovation that was introduced by the monks of Citeaux and their Cistercian order, founded in the twelfth century, consisted in their deliberate engaging in worldly activities of common usefulness, especially in land cultivation and farming. It seems that every intellectual revolution that strives to influence outward living begins by furthering of the peasants, in order to justify the movement by its interest in that age-old occupation indispensable to life. The monks became active, they turned from inner life to outer life. Hard labor was now considered an appropriate means to keep man away from temptations. In this epoch, only the monk led a life according to a schedule, according to a division of time. The striking of the hour calling him to his prayers, his spiritual exercises and his work, existed for him alone, and this sort of life involving a plan was the first form of an organized and rational life, as the sociologist Max Weber has established.

The mendicant friars finally had to move freely among the

people in order to fulfil their tasks of teaching, preaching and nursing. This monastic change from contemplative to active life reflects the general trend in Western and Northern Europe toward worldly and active existence guided by Reason. The church utilized the mendicant friars in its attempt to ward off the threat of popular discontent. All these orders, originally engendered by a spirit of opposition to the hierarchy, the Augustinians, the Dominicans, the Franciscans and others, were gradually won over by the popes and became the most efficient and important agents of the church. The Dominicans, for example, developed into the foremost executers of the Inquisition. They were called "domini canes", the bloodhounds of the Lord. The popes, moreover, used the well-known, perennial antagonism of the mendicant friars to the official clergy, and their penitent and ascetic demeanor, to win the confidence of the petty bourgeois. Many of these friars actually took sides with the people and their mystic tendencies toward a direct union with God. Most of the German mystics who prepared the way for the Reformation were Dominicans or Franciscans, and Luther himself was an Augustine friar. These mendicant friars were frequently the sons of petty bourgeois, whose views they shared. And particularly in the German cities, there was a mutual penetration going on between the mentality of the craft guilds and that of the friars.

In contrast with the old religious orders that resided in the country in large, beautifully situated monasteries surrounded by broad estates, the mendicant friars settled in the cities where they furthered the craftsmen and wandered about preaching and demonstrating their Christian poverty and chastity. These unpretentious clerics were in natural agreement not only with the bourgeois population as a whole against the bishops and the feudal lords but, in the city, with the craftsmen, whose work was blessed according to the teachings of Jesus Christ, against the rich merchants whose trade tallied ill with the Christian doctrine.

The official Catholic Church, the hierarchy, had fostered a scale of values in which the heroic ideal prevailed, first the ideal of the martyr saint who suffered for his faith, and later the ideal of the militant knight who fought for the faith. Both of these ideals were now dethroned and replaced by a specifically bourgeois interpretation of Christian values. In the German cities, among the craftsmen and those who spoke for them, the mendicant friars, these values were, for the first time, adapted to the use of a steady, settled working community, a handicraft community. From the thirteenth century on, the popular preachers in these cities, the German mystics, undermined and refuted the knightly ideals of the militant church. At the beginning of the fourteenth century, for instance, the Dominican, Johannes Tauler, taught that the shoemaker's work, if well done, is a higher calling than even that of the priest.

This has very important implications. For the glorification of plain, honest handicraft was now being combined with the popular longing for an immediate contact with God. And the teachings of the mendicant friars united the intellectual mystic trend with the mood of the people. In Germany, the mystical union with God assumed a character different from all previous mysteries and mystic movements, an abstract, purely intellectual and thoroughly bourgeois character. In every simple, humble man, it was said, Christ may arise and perform an even greater work than by His life and passion, and this arising of Christ in man himself, this union of man with God, was not to be brought about by extraordinary suffering, "by sleeplessness and fasting, by the wearing of unusual and uncomfortable clothing, and the doing of great and holy works. . . . You shall not strive after great and sublime performances," says Tauler, "look humbly into yourself, into the depths of your soul, commune with yourself in the spirit and in nature, and do not seek for a hidden or occult God." The Dominican, Eckhart, the most eminent of the German mystics, who played a role at least as important as Luther's in forming the German language, advises people to behold God not in ecstasies and visions and inspirations, but "at the hearth and in the stall." Since, therefore, Christ may arise in the soul of anyone without any special act of magic unification, since God is accessible everywhere in daily life and its activities, the Christian virtue becomes identical with the public morality of the craft community. It becomes identical with man's being a good, useful, accommodating citizen and member of the community, doing his honest work in the place where God has set him, and not asking for any conspicuous accomplishments or vocations. It is obvious that these teachings are simultaneously bourgeois and pagan. They clearly illustrate the trend toward secularization. No wonder that Eckhart was accused of heretical pantheism. He died pending the action that the church had brought against him, in 1327, two hundred years before the Reformation.

Yet here already is the verge of Protestant reform. The doctrine of Luther is anticipated in these teachings of the German mystic friars. What was needed for the actual schism was merely an external stimulus. Such a stimulus was provided by the behavior of the papacy, its ruthless striving for worldly power and its unscrupulous use of the "power of the key" for extorting money, and, on the other hand, by the gradual weakening of its political and moral position as a result of its temporal aspirations.

The Holy Roman Empire and the papacy rose together and fell together. The Empire was split up into a multitude of territorial powers in the thirteenth century. This development had been greatly hastened by the last violent struggle between the Stauffer emperors and their rivals, the popes. In 1245, Frederick II, the last Stauffer, was formally deposed by Pope Innocent IV, and it was very significant that this act of deposition took place in France during the Council of Lyons. In order to get rid of the Stauffer family, these "spoliators of the Church", this "dragon's brood", as the pope called them, he cast himself upon the mercy of France, the mightiest of the rising territorial powers. Unable himself to expel the Stauffers from Southern Italy, he delivered Sicily to Charles of Anjou, the brother of the French king, Louis IX (Saint Louis), a prince who turned out to be even worse than the Stauffers. The result of this policy was the humiliation of Pope Boniface VIII by the French king, Philippe le Bel, when the pope wished to emphasize his supreme authority by mediating between France and England, the capture of the pope in Anagni in 1303, and the so-called "Babylonian captivity" of the papacy in Avignon for a period of over seventy years (1305–1378). The result was that the papacy submitted to the domination of the French monarchs, who made it into an instrument of French national policy by appointing Frenchmen as popes and to high clerical offices. There was a series of schisms, one of which lasted for forty years, when there were two and sometimes three popes, each of whom was recognized in different parts of Europe—"the papal trinity", as it was mockingly called. Territorial and national churches were established, strengthened and controlled by territorial rulers. The final result was the awful moral decline of the papacy in its attempt to recover territorial power and to tighten its grip on its dwindling dominions. For this competition with the territorial powers the popes needed more and more money, and they extorted it from the people by the famous letters of indulgence. These had originally been intended as a means of financing the crusades and as a taxation of those persons who did not participate in them. But the institution remained and flourished, long after the crusades were over, and was used for the sole purpose of obtaining money for the pope and his hierarchy.

The popes, at their pompous courts in Rome, did not behave at all differently from the other Renaissance princes. There was no crime, no abuse, no libertinage which was not a matter of course with the brilliant but ruthless popes of this epoch. Innocent VIII has been called the "Father of Rome" because he produced so many children. This same pope founded a "bank of temporal indulgence", where absolution from murder and manslaughter was sold at accordingly high prices. And Pope Leo X, the son of Lorenzo Medici, was credited with saying: "This story of Jesus has helped us a lot."

In all nations there were reactions against the various encroachments of the Roman hierarchy. In France, in 1438, the national movement under Charles VII, which completed the expulsion of the British from France, also laid the foundation of the so-called "Gallicanism", the nationalization of the French Church, its autonomy and emancipation from Roman influence, an act which put an end to the pope's unlimited demands on the population. In England, the revolt against the concessions which Pope Innocent III had wrung from King John (Lackland), gave rise to what is considered the foundation of English democracy, the Magna Charta (1215). At the end of the fourteenth century, John Wyclif, a clergyman and dean of Balliol College in Oxford, who had been employed by the king in negotiations with the pope, was driven so far in his irritation and indignation against the Roman clergy as almost to achieve a fundamental reform. He attacked the central positions of the Catholic Church, not only its worldly power and property but also its "power of the key", its whole sacramental mediation between man and God. He referred to Augustine's theory of predestination, which later became the basic dogma of Calvinism. He advocated a spiritual, evangelical, national church without temporal power, under the supremacy of the king. The community of this church was to consist of all those predestined to salvation. The church was to be based solely on the Bible, which he translated into English. Though he gained a large number of adherents, even among the English nobility, he did not succeed in his reform. The English clergy, in agreement with the king and the upper classes, was too strong, and his followers, the "poor priests" or Lollards (from the Latin "lollium", the weeds, as they were called by the pope), were suppressed and persecuted and soon reduced to an insignificant sect. Under the influence of Wyclif, the Czech scholar and priest, Jan Hus, aroused his people to a similar movement, also joined with aspirations toward national independence. But the Luxemburg King of Bohemia dreaded his growing influence on the masses and, with a treacherous safe-conduct, sent him to the Council of Constance, where he was condemned and burned in 1415.

It is no mere chance that the Protestant reform was accomplished in Germany; in this country, a fundamental predisposition of the independent German cities coincided with the lack of a national body and a national concentration of political power to check the abuses of the hierarchy and also the radical procedure of the reformers. Luther did not make national resentment his point of departure, though undoubtedly his activities were spurred by a strong and real anti-Roman impulse. His problem was theological and religious, and he avoided political implications. This attitude was the result of the rift between intellectual and political leadership in Germany.

The psychic process which gradually goaded Luther to the accomplishment of his reform was a long and difficult inner struggle, which had some similarity to that of Paul when he separated from the Pharisees. In Luther's case, also, a sudden shock, interpreted as a call of God, was the immediate impulse to his religious career, to becoming a monk. He was almost struck by lightning. And he also had to fight desperately against the temptations of the flesh which made him despair of the efficacy and merits of holy works and exercises. Like Augustine, he became convinced of the original sin of man, he came to consider faith and grace as the only means to salvation. These elements, the impact of the clerical abuses, the established public morality of the German craft guild city, and the interpretation of this morality by the mystic friars, worked together toward the ideology of the Protestant reform. First of all, the sacramental mediation of the church, the "power of the key", the "power of binding and loosing", was abolished. The direct contact between man and God was re-established. Every layman had to answer for himself, had to see to his own salvation. And with the mediation of the church, the mediating magical acts and ceremonial procedures, the effectiveness of works and holy services as means to salvation were discredited. What brings salvation is, on the part of man, faith, and on the part of God, grace—a faith that cannot be replaced by any special performance; a grace that cannot be secured through any human mediation. Ascetic exercises are of no avail, but since all men are sinful from the outset, as "our Lord Jesus Christ says, 'do penance', so", according to a saying of Luther, "he wants the whole of life of all the faithful, to be one long penance."

Thus asceticism, which up to then had been an extraordinary heroic mode of life of an élite of saints, now, in a moderate, bourgeois way, became every man's duty. Asceticism was released into the temporal world; it was secularized. It consisted in a life over-shadowed by the consciousness of original sin, a life restricted in all its pleasures and aspirations by this permanent, depressing con-ciousness. Asceticism, moreover, came to mean man's doing his daily work wherever God has placed him, without striving be-yond his reach and rank, without seeking any special excellence and preference. Everybody has to devote himself to his special call-ing, in the double meaning of occupation and divine call. And promotion may occur only in the course of regular work, the regu-lar every-day procedure as it is imposed on people by God through his appointed state authorities, who must be respected and fol-lowed, whoever and whatever they are, and in whatever they may ask of you. Accordingly, everybody in his daily work is an official of his community and, as such, by implication, an official of God. The clergyman is no more and no less than others. In so far as he attends to his calling, he may have precedence. Beyond this, he is a normal citizen like everyone else. And as he is divested of any innate pre-eminence, he no longer has the sole privilege of partak-ing both the bread and the wine of Holy Communion, as was the case with the Catholic priest. Every man now had the same right and duty.

In this whole doctrine, we may easily detect traces of the craft guild organization and morality. And we can foresee the conse-quences, namely, the inevitable secularization not only of asceti-cism, but of all that was left of religion. The importance of church services and all obvious holy works was minimized, and man re-ferred entirely to justification through inmost belief. But this in-most faith was to be demonstrated by profane works, by a worldly calling and middle-class morality. Along with the ritual, the serv-ices were deprived of all vital significance, and the religious im-pulse was directed to service to the state, to service in a bourgeois community. There was no longer a church service in the true sense of the word, and temporal activities were sovereign over life. Religion grew to be a mere part, a remote region, of the individual soul. It had no longer an immediate outlet in the frame of man's active life, and so it necessarily became atrophied.

REASON AND SCIENCE

THE INTELLECTUAL MOVEMENT of Scholastic speculation undermined the Christian dogma and resulted in the liberation of reason
and in the founding of modern philosophy and science. It is impossible to understand this very complex process without reconsidering
the background: *Greek speculation.*

The Greeks were the first to take the step from religion to philosophy. They discovered, or rather created, the world of the human
soul, the inner life of man, as a sphere of its own. They turned
the outward cosmos of deities and natural forces, which had dominated man, into an inner, humanized cosmos. The cosmos was
transformed according to ideas; ideas were projected into the cosmos. This made for the twofold character of the Platonic ideas,
which were absolute, cosmic entities of their own, on the one
hand, and human ideas, on the other. In dealing with the preliminaries of Christianity, we considered the different stages of
this process which are represented by the work of the three great
thinkers, Socrates, Plato and Aristotle. The first factor to set this
development in motion was the Greek awareness of the contrast
between divine eternity and human change. Man realized the
diversity and individualization of his kind in the face of that eternal order which still exerted its old religious power over him. There
was no other way out of this painful situation than to assume that
change and diversity were a mere delusion of the senses, and that
the intrinsic truth, which was eternity and a permanent basic substance and principle of the universe, could be grasped only by a
correspondingly intrinsic sense which proved to be the faculty of
reason. In this way, man was led to explore his own mind, to unfold the inner world of his thoughts and ideas.

So the Greeks had already discovered reason. In the logic of
Aristotle they even discovered the laws of thinking. And, more
than that: Aristotle found a way of reconciling the eternal spiritual principle with apparent sensual diversity. To him, the eternal
spirit descends into matter and permeates earthly matter, and as

a result, the permanent and the transient are blended. He sees the soul as the principle that pervades and indeed effects evolution, as an inherent predestination, guiding yearning man on the ways of earth toward spiritual perfection. Thus, the idea becomes the driving force for the individual. This implies that the acknowledgment of sensually perceived facts and experiences, that empirical knowledge, is to a certain extent authorized and made legitimate. And, as a matter of fact, the Greeks, especially in the later periods, made a good beginning in empirical research. Apart from their great achievements in mathematics, which is a purely speculative discipline, they attained to a high degree of knowledge in medicine, zoology, botany, mineralogy, astronomy and theoretical geography, among other subjects. Aristarchus and Heracleides Ponticus introduced the heliocentric system of the universe, the so-called Copernican system. Dicaearchus and Eratosthenes knew that the earth was spherical. Aristotle dissected animals and collected information on animal life and animal behavior from shepherds, fishermen and hunters. Galenus even used vivisection for his medical research. All these endeavors, however, remained isolated, personal attempts and did not develop into a systematic body of science. A consistent method of inquiry and procedure was entirely lacking, and consequently, also an established, coherent system of empirical knowledge which could continue to expand on the basis of its own principle. This was due to the intrinsically religious and cosmic view of the world which prevailed in this epoch. It must be stressed that Greek speculation remained a religious movement throughout, that is to say, it presupposed an eternal basic substance or life principle of the world, which pervades and embraces all the different grades and forms of beings and forces. Greek research centered on the working of this fundamental substance or life principle, and so all experimental or empirical studies were merely accessory and superficial. To Aristotle, who began to draw conclusions from empirical facts, this method of induction was only a complement of the method of deduction, that is, of conclusion from an established, purely speculative principle. And the great medical thinker of antiquity, Hippocrates, who is accepted as the

founder of medicine, is credited with the significant maxim that
the nature of the body cannot be understood without the knowledge of the whole. True science was to develop from an entirely
different stand when man faced nature objectivated and divorced
from him and suitable as a subject for investigation.

In the latest stages of Greek philosophy, in the neo-Platonic
systems—that might just as well be called neo-Aristotelian systems,
since they contain as many Aristotelian as Platonic elements and
represent a synthesis and an apotheosis of the whole of Greek
thinking—in these systems, the religious character of Greek speculation again became manifest. And in this form it passed over into
the Christian doctrine.

The process of the emancipation of reason, which, by implication, is the process of building up science, had to pass through the
narrow defile of *Christian theology,* because it was only under the
pressure of the rigid Catholic dogma that the inherited elements of
pagan thinking began to ferment and to break free, not merely
from the domination of Catholic theology but from their own religious implications as well. In Greek speculation, the god, the divine spirit of the world, had never manifested himself through
revelation, so that a free interpretation remained possible. The
Catholic dogma was bound to the inescapable data of an established
revelation, and still it could not ignore the existence of a highly
developed, pagan speculation prior to and even part of it. The working of these controversial elements in the body of this dogma gradually revealed the fundamental incompatibility of faith and reason,
of dogmatic assumptions and empirical experiences, and, by this
sharp juxtaposition, reason and science were set free.

Christian theology was initiated by the Hellenistic Jew, Philo
of Alexandria, who worked out a synthesis of Judaism and Platonic
and Stoic philosophy by fusing the Jewish spiritual God with the
Stoic and Platonic supreme idea and soul of the world, and by
inserting between the spiritual and divine idea and the corporeal
and sensual world a chief intermediary being, the Logos, which was
understood in the double meaning of the Greek term, as word and

reason. In the subsequent movement of Neo-Platonism, and the early Christian movement of Gnosticism, which fused Greek philosophy with the teachings of the mysteries, the intermediary beings or emanations multiplied and represented an elaborate system of stages of human perfection and knowledge, and of an approach to God. Gnosis, that is, knowledge, became a magic and mystic process. In the course of this train of ideas, Jesus Christ was identified with the Logos, his personal life and passion were interpreted as a continuous revelation. These concepts were not only the source of intellectual mysticism but of all the thought sequences of the Middle Ages.

In this era of the so-called *Patristic philosophy,* that is, the speculation of the Church Fathers, the relation of Greek thinking to Christian faith became a dangerous problem. The influence of Greek speculation on the first Church Fathers, especially the Greek and Hellenistic, was very strong. Some of them were born as pagans and became converts. Justinus, Clement of Alexandria and Origen were still intent upon a synthesis of both beliefs. They assumed that the so-called natural, that is, pagan knowledge was in fundamental harmony with revealed, that is, Christian knowledge. To them, natural knowledge was a preliminary phase of revealed knowledge. Philosophy educates pagans, who have only an incomplete Logos, to the realization of Christ who is the complete and perfect Logos. Philosophy is the "paidagogos eis Christon", the educator to Christ. And, accordingly, reason leads to the acceptance of faith.

The struggle against Gnosticism, which in the end was declared a heresy, gave rise to an opposite stand. Its advocates were the Roman, Tertullian, who was not a philosopher, but a jurist, and the head of the anti-Gnostic thinkers, Irenaeus. These Church Fathers initiated one of the dominant attitudes of Christian theology: the radical rejection of philosophy. These men saw an irreconcilable antagonism between Christianity and philosophy. "For philosophy", says Tertullian, "feeds the wisdom of the world. She is the rash interpreter of divine nature and of the arrangements of God. She puts weapons into the hand of heresy itself . . . The same subjects are treated by heretics and philosophers. The same reflections

occur. Whence does Evil come? Why does it exist? . . . Whence
Man? . . . Whence God? . . . Poor Aristotle! You taught her dialectics, the art of building up and tearing down, dialectics, so mischievous in locution, so far-fetched in conclusions, so harsh in
proofs, so labored in claims, a burden to itself, dealing with all and,
in the final analysis, with nothing . . . What has Athens to do with
Jerusalem, the Academy with the Church! Let them try to produce Stoic, Platonic and dialectic Christianity! After knowing
Jesus Christ, we need no investigation, after the tidings of the Gospels, we need no searching." And he proceeded to the most fanatical
and extreme formula of faith: "The Son of God died—this is credi-
ble just because it is folly. He has been buried and resurrected
—this is certain because it is impossible."

Thus, from the very outset, the problem was formulated, and
two diametrically opposed attitudes toward it were defined and
upheld to the end of the Middle Ages. But since, at the time of the
Church Fathers, these contradictory opinions were both religious in
themselves, they did not effect a clear delimitation of profane
knowledge. This difficult and elaborate process of separation was
to take place within Christian theology itself, and only so was the
autonomy of reason to be achieved.

The next important move, which reached down to the very
heart of medieval controversies, was effected by Augustine. He was
a convert and was led to Christianism in the way indicated by
Justinus and his followers; he was trained and prepared for the
Christian faith by neo-Platonic, pagan philosophy. But he reversed
the formula of Justinus and Clement of Alexandria in asserting
that knowledge and understanding are not the preliminaries but
the results, the rewards, of faith. "Unless you believe," he taught,
"you shall not understand." This theory made him a precursor of
one of the outstanding exponents of Scholastic philosophy, Anselm
of Canterbury. Yet he came to this theory by the very Platonic
assumption that the findings of reason, the logical and mathematical conclusions, were "eternal truths", originating in the one supreme truth which is God—as sunbeams originate in the sun. These
eternal truths have nothing to do and are in no way connected with

the empirical world, so that the understanding of these truths cannot be the prerequisite for but only the result of faith. In the fully developed Scholastic speculation, the situation was quite different, as logic, or as it was then called, dialectics, intruded into Christian theology from without and from an entirely opposite angle. But to this end, it had first to be submerged and forgotten.

The *break between Patristic and Scholastic thinking* was caused by two important factors: the interruption of any kind of steady, consistent intellectual effort, caused by the decay of the Roman Empire, the barbarian invasions, perpetual change of rulers, the unrest and anarchy that followed; and the shifting of the scene of decisive developments to the slowly rising countries of the European continent. The scene of Patristic speculation had been the ancient Mediterranean area of Hellenistic and Roman civilization. Scholastic speculation developed in France, the British Isles and Germany. There is a gap between the two epochs, the disruption of the Roman Empire and the consolidation of the new powers—the Holy Roman Empire, the French monarchy and the papacy—bridged by a very incomplete and crumbling tradition. From the sixth century on, learning and cultural life were almost at a standstill in the ancient sections of the Roman world. Schools and the intellectual standards of the clergy deteriorated, and to the extent intellectual life was sustained at all, it did not produce new creative concepts, but only more and more mechanical, literal repetitions and compilations of the writings and teachings of established authorities. More often the compilators did not even understand what they were copying and handing down. And the encyclopedic works which first transmitted the remnants of previous knowledge to the rising European countries were crude and confused documents, unscholarly collections of mere debris.

There was a great difference between the intellectual level in the home regions of ancient civilization and that of the Northern provinces and their Gallo-Roman and Germanic populations. In Italy, Spain and Africa, some sort of lay knowledge, concerned with the remains of pagan literature, still persisted beyond the pale of the church. But the intellectuals had lost all direct contact with the documents of Greek speculation, which had been the foundation of Roman learning. And even with the classical Roman literature they were acquainted only through the channels of distorting commentaries and interpretations. A good example for the variety of intellectual activity prevailing in these Mediterranean regions at the time is the encyclopedic manual of an African scholar, Martianus Capella, who lived at the beginning of the fifth century. He was considered an authority on ancient literature, and his work was widely used as a general reference book comprising the whole of contemporary knowledge of the so-called seven "artes liberales", the seven liberal disciplines: grammar, dialectics (what we call logic), rhetoric, geometry, arithmetic, astronomy and music. His encyclopedia, a compilation of earlier Roman compendia, has the curious title "On the Wedding of Philology to Mercury", and its entire content is cast in the form of an allegorical romance between Mercury, the god of trade and meditation, the messenger, who in neo-Platonic systems impersonated the Logos of the world, with philology, that is, the encyclopedic, all-embracing discipline. Mercury wishes to marry and upon the advice of Apollo chooses the most erudite maiden, philology, who was thus raised to Olympus. But before assuming the position of a goddess, she had to rid herself of her burden of books, which she spews forth. The remaining disciplines pick up what they need. At the wedding, they appear as bridesmaids and deliver lectures on their respective subjects, and each of these lectures fills an entire volume. From this form in which knowledge is presented, the character of this knowledge itself may be gauged. It is a mixture of allegorical and sometimes lascivious stories, interspersed with confused and indiscriminate data.

It is significant that Italy preserved intellectual lay activity and a faint tradition of pagan knowledge throughout the Middle Ages, an important factor in the rise of the Renaissance spirit in this region. Italy, on the other hand, was not the main scene of theological speculation, in spite of and perhaps even because of the fact that the papacy resided there. Scholastic speculation developed

chiefly in the Northern and Western countries, in the virgin minds
of young barbarian peoples, since here all knowledge, including
ancient pre-Christian speculation, was transmitted and provided
by the church alone. And it was within the Christian doctrine that
the discrepancies between pagan and orthodox elements developed
the rift which resulted in the emancipation of reason and science.

The erudition of the ecclesiastical scholars was no more substantial than that of the laymen. It lacked acquaintance with the original documents, the writings of the Greek thinkers as well as the
Holy Scriptures. The knowledge of these scholars was also a
hodge-podge of odds and ends, especially from teachings of the
Church Fathers, whose orthodox interpretations were accepted and
copied in a literal, really school-boy manner. There was no original,
creative thinking, only mechanical memorizing from those naive
encyclopedias which were a feature of the epoch, and from the
so-called "catenae"—chains—excerpts from the commentaries of
the church authorities following the Holy Scriptures. The seven
liberal disciplines were studied to the extent they were considered
useful to the Christian doctrine and to the interpretation of this doctrine. As far as the beginnings of medieval learning are concerned,
the name of *Scholasticism* is wholly justified. It was a learning
relying on established authorities and merely discussing and interpreting these authoritative views. This sterile type of learning,
however, is not only characteristic of the Middle Ages. A similar
Protestant Scholasticism appeared in the sixteenth and seventeenth
centuries, and recurrent trends of modern philosophy, following
in the tracks of Kant, Hegel, Marx and others, deserve to be put
in the same category. On the other hand, when medieval philosophy reached its peak, it produced thinkers of true originality and
unmatched boldness—in this epoch any liberal opinion, any deviation from the orthodox, carried with it the risk of moral and even
physical suffering As a matter of fact, the term Scholasticism derives from the so-called "scholasters", or "scholastici", the head-
masters of the schools which, from the ninth century on, developed
around the cathedrals of French cities. These "scholasters" were
the first teachers of medieval speculative theology.

The speculative movement in medieval theology was aroused by the *remnants of Greek philosophy* which gradually came to light. And it was the essential difference between the theories of the two main Greek thinkers, Plato and Aristotle, it was the implications of these different principles as applied to the problems of the Christian doctrine, that fomented the crucial struggle between faith and knowledge, between authority and reason. It was, in particular, the manner in which Aristotle's work reappeared in medieval knowledge that determined his powerful influence on medieval thought and, by implication, the triumph of reason and science.

There is a distinct difference between the views held by Plato and Aristotle. Plato's was an essentially dualistic theory. To him, the divine ideas, the universals, the general qualities, the genera, were the only real beings, that, like the deities, had an absolute, independent existence. God himself was the supreme idea. *The* man, *the* animal, *the* beautiful, *the* good, *the* brave, and so on, represented realities, the archetypes of life of which the individuals, the earthly forms of those general qualities, as they appeared in daily life, were mere shadows and faint replicas. Men, conceiving those general qualities, merely recall their own original existence, which they will recover only after death, when the immortal soul leaves the body and joins the world of essential beings, the spiritual world of ideas. In this concept, the spiritual and the physical world, the world of general ideas and the world of individual bodies, obviously form two different spheres, and the world of ideas is the true and essential, and has absolute existence, independent of the realm of bodies.

Aristotle connected the two spheres by seeing the spiritual soul and the intrinsic idea as the formative principle of the body, and, at the same time, as an "entelechy", an innate, ideal goal of the individual that effects evolution. The individuals, then, participate in the essential reality of ideas. This participation becomes effective when man comprehends the ideas and their connections, when he gathers and abstracts the ideas from their multifold, individual manifestation, in short, when he thinks logically. This procedure implied the legitimacy of empirical observation, and of inductive conclusion from observed facts to abstract generalities.

Thus, to Plato, ideas were realities in themselves, to Aristotle, they were likewise realities, but inherent in individual beings, and, by the process of logical thinking, they were even, in a way, created by individual reason. They were concepts and terms of human reason. This difference was carried to extremes by Scholastic philosophy. It was interpreted far beyond its original meaning, it was developed into a diametrical opposition. It furnished the main theme for the famous Scholastic controversy between the Realists and the Nominalists.

The Realists were those orthodox thinkers who asserted the absolute and exclusive reality of the universals. The Nominalists were the progressive thinkers who, in simplifying and misinterpreting Aristotle, contended that the universals were mere concepts of human thinking, mere "voces", voices, or "nomina", names, terms of human understanding, destitute of any reality. This was no mere theoretical dispute. It was aroused by dogmatic quarrels concerning such problems as the Trinity and Transubstantiation, and it had serious implications.

In comparing the Platonic and the Aristotelian systems, it is easy to understand that originally it was the Platonic teachings that were more akin and fitted to the Christian doctrine. As a matter of fact, these teachings, especially in their interpretation by Philo of Alexandria and the neo-Platonic school, contributed greatly to the formation of the Christian doctrine and were incorporated in it. So, from the outset, Christian theology contained Platonic elements, and in so far as any pagan thinker was recognized and esteemed by the church authorities, it was Plato. But Aristotle they rejected, since they instinctively felt that his teachings encouraged reasoning and empirical inquiry. Still it was *Aristotle* who eventually gained a predominant influence on Scholastic speculation. The reason for this paradoxical development lies in what seems to be mere chance, but what, viewed from the broad aspect of human evolution, assumes the character of true predestination. The original writings of

Plato were almost entirely lost in the early period of Scholastic speculation. Only the most obscure and difficult of his dialogues, "Timaios", was known, and this deals with the cosmic theory of Plato and is hardly understandable without the preliminaries provided by the other dialogues, which did not reappear before the twelfth century. On the other hand, circumstances were much more favorable in the case of Aristotle's work. Nothing of his much dreaded and repudiated metaphysical system had survived, but what was preserved, and much better preserved than anything else of ancient literature, was his Logic, and this could be taken and has been taken for a mere methodological guide to thinking, regardless of the thought content, that is, without any philosophical implications. At that time logic, or as it was called, dialectics, had nothing to do with philosophy, and the fragments of Aristotle's Logic went by the name of "Organon", that is, "instrument" of thinking. One of the seven liberal disciplines, which in this epoch formed the substratum of all teaching and learning, was dialectics, and dialectics meant the Logic of Aristotle. So the most important and dangerous part of Aristotle's system slipped into Christian theology inconspicuously, by the back door, as it were. In this isolated form, as a purely technical instrument, it was much more dynamic than it could possibly have been in connection with the metaphysical system from which it sprang. It began to ferment in Christian theology when it was applied to the vulnerable and problematical issues of the Christian dogma.

The authors who handed down Aristotle's Logic in a Latin translation had also transmitted and added commentaries and explanations of the text, as was the custom in these times. In their commentaries, they set down the questions that Aristotle's teachings had raised for them: whether the universals, the general qualities that may be predicated of individual beings, whether these general ideas are realities or mere abstractions of the human mind; whether they have a corporeal existence, even though unperceived by human senses; whether they have a separate existence, if any, or whether they exist only in connection with corporeal and individual beings. These problems, annexed to the Logic of Aristotle, and stated so plainly, not only became the main problems of Scholastic philosophy but contain the germ of all modern epistemology and theory of knowledge. Their implications reach into the very heart of the speculation of David Hume and Immanuel Kant.

Theological speculation began in the consolidated Frankish monarchy of Charlemagne, who promoted learning and enlightenment—one might even speak of an early rationalistic movement, that died down again under his successors. Among the clerical scholars of the Carolingian era, in the eighth century, there was a trend against magic and superstition of every kind, against ordeals, belief in witches and even against the adoration of images. Dialectic studies began to flourish and controversies concerning dogma came up.

An abbot of Tours, in France, named Fredegisus, attempted to substantiate the biblical story of creation by the dialectic method. As it is inconceivable, he argued, that one can create something out of nothing—as God was supposed to have done in creating the world—this nothingness must have real existence. It must be something, accordingly, it must *be*. This train of reasoning was still very clumsy and naive, for it was based on the confusing of logical and grammatical connections and also on confusing the logical term of nothingness with the sensual phenomenon of the dark. Fredegisus reflected: When I say that nought is nothing, I still use the word "is", I predicate of it a *being* nothing, accordingly a *being*. And *being* is naively identified with a substantial, a material being: therefore, the nothingness becomes the dark. The nature of this argument is unimportant, but not the consequences. This man was still timid in setting up his method. He intended to prove the story of the creation "ratione et auctoritate", by reason and authority. Reason proceeds by a logical argument, authority by a sacred statement; but what he wanted to do was to prove the conformity of reason with authority. The divine authority says that God created the world out of nothing, which is rationally inconceivable. Reason, however, proves that nothing *is* something. So authority is con-

firmed, authority is reasonable. He was convinced that the statement derives its truth only from the authority of the dogma. Logic
only contributes the formal presentation of this truth which makes
it accessible to human reason.

This was an isolated attempt around 800. From the ninth to
the eleventh century, the great controversies concerning Transubstantiation took shape, that is, the sacramental transformation of
the bread and wine of Holy Communion into the body and blood
of Jesus Christ. The problem was: whether Christ was really,
physically present in the bread and wine or merely symbolically
and spiritually, as the Logos, the word of God, which nourishes and
revives the human soul. The orthodox assumption of the physical
presence of Christ in bread and wine was confronted with the
logical impossibility that the accidental qualities of bread and wine
—color, taste, tangibility—persisted even after the sacramental consecration, which was supposed to effect the transformation of the
substance. Bread and wine were supposed to disappear, as such,
through the consecration—but still they looked and tasted like
bread and wine. The man who revolted against the assumption,
on logical grounds, was another cleric from Tours, the headmaster
of the Cathedral School of St. Martin, Berengar. He had the courage to contend that even God in His omnipotence had not the
power to preserve accidental qualities, to make bread and wine
look and taste like bread and wine after they had ceased to be
these substances, that is, that even God had no power to invalidate
logical conclusions and effects. This was a clear revolt of reason
against authority. And Berengar had to pay for this bold venture
with suffering defamation and anathema, with a broken heart
and a ruined existence.

The consequence was a vehement reaction against any attempt
to reform theology by dialectic methods. Developments, however,
could no longer be arrested, and the role and value of dialectics
began to move into the foreground of the controversies. Logical
speculation could no longer be suppressed or disregarded. Minds
were fully awakened to it. In the eleventh and twelfth centuries,
the antagonism between Realism and Nominalism began to flare

up within dialectic learning. And a crucial dispute on the problem of the Holy Trinity paved the way for the theological reception and assimilation of dialectics, for the incorporation of the logical method in the system of the Christian doctrine. This was the actual start of Scholastic philosophy.

In this dispute on the Holy Trinity, which was carried on by two eminent clerical scholars, Roscellin, from Compiègne in France, and Anselm, from Aosta in Italy—who later became Archbishop of Canterbury and one of the paramount figures of Scholastic philosophy, indeed, the transformer of theology into true philosophy—in this dispute, the Nominalists, Roscellin and his school, contended that universals and general qualities do not exist in reality, but are empty words. Only individual beings and individual attributes are real. If, accordingly, the three personalities of the Holy Trinity formed one entity, then not only the Son, but also God the Father and the Holy Ghost would have been incarnated, would have walked in the flesh and died on the Cross. As this is inconceivable, there is no Holy Trinity, but rather three separate deities. Thus, the implications of logic gradually undermined the basic dogma of the church.

But in this eleventh century, the opposing party, in contesting the argument of its adversaries, did not reject dialectics as such, any longer, it did not decline the application of dialectics to theological problems. On the contrary, it used logical arguments in order to sustain and substantiate its views. In doing so, Anselm of Canterbury not only instituted Realism as a philosophical principle, he inaugurated Scholastic philosophy as such, and laid the foundation of the system that was completed by Thomas Aquinas. Anselm passionately advocated the use of dialectics for a better understanding and a thorough confirmation of the Christian teachings. Man should proceed from faith to understanding, he should believe in order to understand. This formula of Augustine now assumed a new significance, for in the mean time dialectics had expanded and undergone an independent development.

We may realize the new and powerful position of logic when we consider that Anselm not only ventured to prove the existence of God by rational arguments, but to demonstrate the necessity of Jesus' death to the end of a reconciliation of God with men. He argued that God, the Almighty, had no other means to save sinful man and at the same time His own honor, that had been offended by man's sinfulness, than by the spontaneous sacrifice of Jesus Christ. God is subject to a logical necessity. And Anselm explicitly declared his intention of proving this by logical arguments in order to make it apparent to everyone, even to the infidel, and "quasi nihil sciatur de Christo", as if one knew nothing at all about Christ. And it was not the revolutionary Nominalist party, but the leading orthodox party that was now proceeding in this manner.

The spell upon dialectics had been broken and the dispute on the universals became an internal discussion within Scholastic philosophy. It was the time of the crusades and of the growing power and ambition of the church that wanted to conquer the world, not only materially but also spiritually. The church sought to transcend its boundaries with the help of arguments powerful enough to convince the highly cultured infidel. Communications and interrelations had been established between the Christian world and the world of Islam, where a parallel philosophical movement had developed. In all the three great religions, Islam, Judaism and Christianism, a synthesis of their respective religious doctrines with Greek philosophy—and in this period that meant Aristotelian logical speculation—had been accomplished. What was achieved in Christianism by Anselm of Canterbury, and later by Thomas Aquinas, was accomplished in Judaism by Moses Maimonides, and in Arabian Islam most conspicuously by Ibn Rochd, or as he was called in Latin, Averroës. He was born in 1126, in Cordoba, lived as a judge and physician and friend of the Caliph Al-Mansur, and died in 1198 in seclusion, persecuted and confined for his allegedly blasphemous views.

From the eighth century on, the Islamic scholars in the Near East had become acquainted with the whole work of Aristotle through Syrian translations, and from there, this knowledge had been transmitted to the Arabs and the Jews in Spain. Through the mediation of the Spanish Christians, it penetrated into Christian

Europe in the twelfth century, accompanied by the Arabian and Jewish interpretations. This whole literature, the translation of the Aristotelian texts as well as the philosophical treatises of Arabian and Jewish philosophy, found a well-prepared ground among Christian Scholastics, and gave the final impulse toward the emancipation of reason and science.

In his treatise on "The Agreement of Religion and Philosophy", Averroës proves by the Koran that the laws of religion itself "invite man to reflect upon existing things with his reason . . . and to strive zealously to recognize them. Thus," he declares, "according to the law of religion, it may be necessary for man . . . to learn to know things that stand in the same relation to speculation as tools to work. And if another has investigated this matter, it is clearly our duty to inform ourselves of his results, whether or not he be of our faith." This remark of Averroës refers to the Greeks, and what he says of the necessity of cooperation in prosecuting investigation and knowledge is probably the first formulation of the principle of modern science: "It is difficult for anyone to know spontaneously, all that is requisite [for examining the syllogism] . . . If, for example, our age did not have the arts of geometry and astronomy, it would be impossible for one individual—even if he had the leisure—to make a study of the shapes and measurements of heavenly bodies and their distance from one another. This is obviously true not only of the theoretical but also of the practical arts, none of which can be created by a single person. How much more then, is it true of the art of arts, philosophy . . . Thus it is clear that a study of the ancients is necessary, according to the law of religion." And philosophy, therefore, is actually the most perfect form of worshipping God.

But the great mass of men is not capable of philosophical interpretation, that is, rational demonstration of the truth. So "while it is the duty of the elect and the learned to interpret, it is the duty of the masses to keep to the letter of the Law; they must not become familiar with that interpretation." To give an analogy: when a patient seeks a physician, the duty of that physician is not to discuss his knowledge with those who ask his advice—since he cannot make doctors of them all—but to give them simple orders and prescriptions. In the same way, the masses must not learn the interpretation of philosophy. "For the physician is to the health of the body, as the law-giver to the health of souls ... The health of souls is called the fear of God." Religion, therefore, is only a special method of instructing the masses, open to imagination rather than to reason, in philosophic truths, through revealed law which they must obey and through sensuous pictures of rewards and punishments that appeal to the imagination. Such a position comes dangerously near that of a freethinker of the eighteenth century, like Lord Bolingbroke, who wanted to preserve religion merely as a means of keeping the lower, uninstructed classes in check.

Averroës exerted a decisive influence on Scholastic philosophy and gave rise to a powerful school of Christian scholars, called the "Latin Averroists". The new distinction of an esoteric from an exoteric truth, and the implied supremacy of philosophy over theology, began to work in the Christian mind. Equipped with dialectics, the scholars were convinced of holding the destiny of the Christian dogma and the church in their hands. One of them, after having delivered a brilliant lecture, is said to have exclaimed: "O Jesus, how much did I strengthen and enhance Thy doctrine. Indeed, if I were Thy enemy, I would be able to invalidate and refute it by even more striking arguments."

So the whole structure of the Christian doctrine was penetrated and undermined by reasoning. Rational activity flooded dogma. In order to keep up appearances, to be free to argue at will, the Latin Averroists invented a distinction between the necessary and the true—the necessary being the logical and the true being the statements of the dogma and the Revelation. This permitted them freedom in concerning themselves with the necessary, the logical, without questioning the so-called true, which became more and more negligible and neglected. Thomas Aquinas (1227–1274) wanted to stem the dialectic tide, but, as a matter of fact, he systematized the distinction of the Averroists by drawing a definite line between objects of faith and objects of science. He taught that faith expresses the voluntary agreement of the intellect with truths that are inaccessible to rational proof. Hence the act of faith is determined not by reason but by will. And, therefore, one and the same thing cannot be believed and rationally seen, it cannot be an object of faith and of rational understanding at the same time: "Non est possibile quod sit de eodem fides et scientia."

This meant a new and ultimate separation of knowledge and faith, and, consequently, a separation of those concerned with theology and those concerned with knowledge. More and more of the theologians and true believers became suspicious of philosophical arguments and surfeited with dialectic controversies. More and more they increased the number of "objects of faith", which were taboo to reasoning, and diminished the number of "objects of science". And eventually they turned to mysticism, which more completely satisfied their religious wants. This made for the growth of the mystical movement which led to the Reformation. Luther himself condemned and repudiated Scholasticism.

On the other hand, reason and knowledge were set free by this separation. For those concerned with knowledge, the objects of knowledge grew immeasurably. The acquaintance with the physics of Aristotle and with neo-Platonic natural philosophy stimulated empirical studies. New political problems evolved with the rise of the new national and territorial powers. In the second half of the thirteenth century, the Franciscan friar, Roger Bacon, emphasized the importance of two rational methods, far too neglected in the universities of his time: mathematical demonstration and experimental investigation. He set Greek and Roman teachings above all medieval learning and insisted upon a more thorough knowledge of ancient texts. He devoted himself to extensive empirical and experimental studies. He constructed optical instruments which proved his acquaintance with very important facts concerning refraction and magnification. He was close to inventing gun-powder; he even foresaw the use of steam for ships and cars, and predicted automobiles and aeroplanes. The researches of Pierre Duhem have shown that in the fourteenth century some scholars of the University of Paris, stimulated by discussions on Aristotle, started the work of invalidating the Aristotelian concept of the

cosmos and anticipated the mechanics of Galilei and the Copernican system of the universe. Jean Buridan and Albert of
Saxony worked out a law of impetus. Albert of Saxony discovered
that the fall of a heavy object is evenly increased motion. He, as
well as Franciscus de Mayronis and Nicolas Oresme, already assumed that the eighth sphere of the fixed stars was motionless and
that it was the earth that moved. From the static, physics began
to go over to the dynamic. The new evaluation of sensuous, physical
phenomena, the growing sense for the autonomy of the material
world, inspired investigation to grasp nature in extenso, quanti-
tatively, that is mathematically, rather than in intenso, qualita-
tively, i.e. philosophically. Autonomous reason traveled in the same
direction and was now free to pursue her goal of the technical
domination of nature. The connection between all of these trends
becomes clear in the work of Leonardo da Vinci, who is representative of many artists of the time in combining investigation and
invention with art. Mathematics made rapid progress; analytical
geometry, logarithmic calculation, arithmetical progressions, were
developed in close connection with the study of nature. Finally,
the idea of an infinite universe began to dawn. And with these
elements—materiality, dynamics and quantitative explanation of
infinite nature—the premises of modern science were given. The
methodical questioning of nature, the experiment, came into use.
It was the beginning of a great movement of science and technical
invention that has gone on uninterruptedly from then until now.

For a long time, to be sure, science was still involved with magic
and mystic ideas. And the habit of thinking of the universe as a
closed, intrinsically connected whole survived the liberation from
dogma for a long time. Parallel to religious mysticism that shifted
the living God to the soul of man, a cosmic mysticism, that shifted
God to nature, developed. Hence, the advancements of science first
took place within the framework of naturalistic pantheism. Those
Italian investigators who made the first great scientific finds were
all nature-philosophers. They still thought of the universe in terms
of one harmonious cosmos quickened by a single soul, an "Unom-
nia", unity of all beings (Francesco Patrizzi), a "coincidentia

oppositorum", the agreement of contrasts (Nicolas Cusanus). One of the chief works of Kepler has the title "Harmonice Mundi", the harmony of the world. Even such minds as Giordano Bruno and Galilei, who in their special investigations were already pursuing the problem of the infinite, were still enthralled by the concept of the artistic harmony and perfection of the universe. Galilei even deliberately avoids using the word "infinitesimal", which he circumscribes by expressions such as "extremely small" or "very tiny". Not until much later, among the scientists of Northern peoples, was this concept of a closed universe finally done away with, and the modern concept of wholly material, infinite nature substituted.

Thus the progress of thought seems to turn to the same world picture from which it proceeded, the neo-Platonic. But in the mean time, decisive events had taken place. The last temporal remains of an old religious concept were no longer strong enough to halt the progress in experimental science. With the development of Christianity and within Christianity, the physical world had once and for all separated from the spiritual, the religious world and had become valid in its own right. Reason was free. The autonomy of science had been founded.

ART

As a result of the reform movement, religion became more and more shut off from the rest of the human soul. It became a mere segment of psychic existence. As a result of Scholastic speculation, Reason and Science won their complete independence. A parallel process went on in art, which, at the turn of our modern era, also came to constitute an autonomous sphere of man's activity.

This development is one of the most important processes in the great disintegration of the unity of human life that takes place at this time. To gauge its significance, we must study it from different points of view: from the subjects of art which gradually shifted from religious to profane themes, and from the way in which these subjects are treated. In the change of style, the increasing attention paid to texture, structure and composition shows a closer, more careful and detailed perception of nature. Man visualizes and represents nature in order to master her spiritually. Here, in fact, we observe, more clearly than in any other field, the crucial turn in man's relation to nature, which is the fundamental feature of this period. An important change takes place in the creative impulses of the artist as well as in the function and position of art in human life. It is no longer cult and piety that determine the creation of works of art and the demand for them, but the glorification of profane personalities and of worldly events, an adornment of public and private life, and, eventually, the search for a new knowledge, a spiritual illumination of the visual world. And this leads us to the role and position of the artist within society. The artist is more and more appreciated as an individual, and his own desire dictates the subjects and the form of his work, as they seem best suited to carry out a purely artistic task. All these various manifestations of one process purport the same development: the emancipation of art, and its autonomy as a specific sphere of human activity.

In order to understand this, we must go back once more to the very origins of all intellectual activity of the human being. Art, and with it handicraft—originally it was included in handicraft— is the first form of human expression of which we have direct evidence. The origin of language, music and the dance is dark. But in prehistoric caves in Spain, Southern France and Southern Italy, there are well preserved *rock carvings,* done perhaps in the higher paleolithic age. Similar carvings have been discovered in Africa, and some scholars assume that they belong to the same cultural area. Relics of *rock paintings,* which are of a later period and more advanced in technique, have been found only in the Spanish and French region. It is very significant that carvings and paintings like those of the paleolithic age are still made by the otherwise culturally lowest of the African natives of today, the Bushmen, a fact which suggests that in other respects, too, these tribes may be on the same level of civilization as men in a very early stage of mankind.

These earliest documents of art, which have been discovered in increasing numbers since the end of the last century, already show a style that we like to call naturalistic. At first they render only the contours, later a more detailed shape, and still later even colored shadings of the mammoth, bison, reindeer, rhinoceros and other animals, always drawn with great accuracy. There is even a hint as to why these paintings were made, for there are marks that show man shot at them with arrows. So, as we may conclude from analogous proceedings among primitive people of today, this naturalistic rendering is in reality a magic procedure. It is an attempt to seize upon the living animal by conjuring his exact form into an image and then doing away with it by shooting at that image. So, in the earliest known period of mankind we already find a sort of naturalism in art. But it is fundamentally different from all later naturalistic style in its motivation and its pre-individual or typical mode of representation. We may call it magic naturalism.

Another variety of primitive artistic expression is also motivated by magic procedure, and we may even assume that this is the earlier, since the technical perfection of the "naturalistic" rock pictures presupposes a long development. These early art objects show an opposite style, namely a simplification or abstraction of natural forms, resulting in the genesis of the *ornament* which is to be found engraved or painted on arms, tools and other objects of daily use. This over-simplification is not a conscious abstraction, comparable to the procedure of modern decorative art, but rather a simplification such as one finds in the drawings of children. Ornamental art probably began with man's painting and tattooing of his own body, and originally this was not meant as adornment, but as a magical, protective or terrifying measure, or a vesting with magic signs which endow men with demonic forces. Since, among primitive peoples, man's belongings, his clothing and objects of daily use, are considered as part of himself, as an extension of his personality, these objects were covered with the same signs used

for the protection and strengthening of his body. In Greek ornaments we often find the so-called apotropaeic sign, that is, a sign
intended to avert evil influences. It is the abbreviated drawing
of an eye whose purpose it is to catch and divert the effects of the
evil eye. The labyrinth of lines on Persian rugs are also intended
to snare the evil eye of the visitor and to divert its ill effects from
the host. Geometrical figures may have developed from the endless
repetition of these abbreviations. Primitive peoples, like children,
tend to emphasize and intensify every statement, all utterance,
through repetition, in order to seize upon it completely, to drive
it to extremes—it is a sort of fascination, a trance aroused in them
by an expression. The same holds true of primitive music. So all
empty space on objects is covered with such repeated signs, all the
more as the empty space is dreaded as being peopled by uncontrol-
lable demonic powers or giving access to the intrusion of such
powers—a phenomenon which is well-known under the name of
"horror vacui", horror of the void. We may suppose that this procedure of abbreviation and repetition, in assuming a ritual character,
gradually promoted the sense for visual regularity in man, and
eventually led him to enjoy regular forms and to use them as true
ornaments. But such a purely ornamental use may be assumed with
certainty only for a more advanced cultural stage.

   There is probably another origin of the ornament, as suggested
first by the anthropologist Karl von den Steinen, who explored the
customs of the Bakairi Indians in Brazil. He derives the abbreviated
signs from the gestures that primitive man uses to help him describe
some phenomenon or happening. Accordingly, these signs may
have been a prolonging, a perpetuation of speech, as a means of
communication—for instance, for the purpose of marking the
places where certain animals and plants are found or where certain
events occurred. Such abbreviated signs for purposes of communication apparently led to the origin of picture writing. The earliest
known writing—Egyptian hieroglyphics, Accadian cuneiform
writing, Chinese, Tibetan and Indian writing—probably developed
from such naive pictures of a house, man, mountain, tree, fish or
bird. Through further abbreviation and combination, ideograms

evolved: signs for words, syllables and finally sounds, that is, letters. It has recently been discovered that some letters in the Phoenician, Chinese and Sioux Indian alphabets have a "dactylographic" origin, that they originated in a finger language similar to that of the deaf-mutes of today, a language that rendered objects through finger gestures and that was later put down in drawings. Among the Sioux Indians, gesture and picture language both existed simultaneously and corresponded closely to each other. It is known that many primitive groups, like the Sioux Indians, wrote down their gestures. Hence we have a possible clue to the development of part of the alphabet of the Phoenicians, the merchants of the ancient world, who were probably forced to communicate through gestures.

There is, finally, a third kind of primitive artistic expression, namely *primitive sculpture,* which arose with the conjuring of demons into the fixed shape of idols. The earliest idols we know belong to prehistoric periods, and these are by no means naturalistic, as they emphasize special forces and qualities, which are attributed to these demons. The so-called Venuses of Willendorf, in Austria, and Menton and Brassempouy, in France, show an overemphasis of breast and womb as a sign of fertility.

When we reach the stage of developed religion, the first great historic culture, that of the Egyptians, we are at once confronted with a very much advanced standard of artistic achievement in sculpture, painting and, before all, architecture, which, in fact, originated in Egypt.

There are three main types of buildings that gave rise to *architecture:* the tomb, the sanctuary and the palace. In the Egyptian religion, the care of the dead, who were supposed to survive and to preserve their earthly shape in a different sphere, played a predominant part. Thus the residence of the dead, the tomb, was of paramount importance. Monumental architecture begins with the pyramids. The sepulchral buildings (Mastaba) and their perfected form, the pyramids, derive from the burial mound, from the heap of earth and stones that primitive peoples pile up in order to cover the dead. While light and perishable material was used for the huts of the living, stone was used for the first time for the residence of the dead, that had to have permanence. In later periods, the Egyptian tombs were built into rocks in order to protect them even more, and to make them quite safe for eternity. Since, in Egyptian civilization, the divine king, the dead ancestor and the actual deity merge, the palace, originally an expansion and enrichment of the ordinary house, the interior of the tomb that is a faithful reproduction of the habitation of the living, and the temple, corresponding to the residence of the divine king, all derive from the same root. A court and halls connecting with it lead into the most secret, most holy interior. The halls are broken up by a veritable forest of pillars that emphasize the mass of material and prevent the impression of connected space. The pillars support the roof. They originate in the supporting tree-trunk—the palm tree—and the ornamentation of the capitals is suggestive of leaf and flower. In addition to their functional significance, the pillars are also symbols. They express the blossoming of earth and assume the shapes of lotus, papyrus and aloe, among others. The ceiling with its painted birds and stars represents the sky. So the halls come to symbolize world space.

In the empires of the Near East that were far more exposed to the migrations of peoples and to the conquests of all-powerful neighbors than relatively remote Egypt, the palace and the temple assumed the character of a fortified castle. They were built on elevated sites and continued this elevation by their structure, rising in terraces to the height of several stories and topped by a bastioned tower, "the hill of heaven" or the "mountain of God"—"ziggurat". The biblical Tower of Babylon was nothing but the "ziggurat" of Babylon. Here too, the structure of the temple corresponds to that of the palace; the residence of the king, the "tenant farmer" of the deity, is a replica of the house of God.

The transition from the Oriental to the Greek era is provided by a civilization that, in the second millennium, extended from the realm of the Cretan sea kings to the Asia Minor of the Trojan War and the archaic mainland of Greece (Mycenae, Tiryns, Thebes). The palace of King Minos at Knossos on Crete, the remains of which were excavated by Arthur Evans in 1900, this "labyrinth" of Greek mythology, transcends the Oriental form through its size, its complexity and the civilized luxury of its technical appointments, especially its water system. Countless square rooms gave on a wide central court and smaller side courts, so that—so the Greeks believed—no stranger could have found his way out of this maze. The palace had, moreover, several stories. There were no separate temples. The holy of holies was enclosed in the palace.

The temple as an independent architectural form, deviating from that of the palace, first appears in Greek architecture. It, too, originated in the main hall, the "megaron" and the open, pillared and roofed portico of the simple archaic dwelling, but from this point on, house and temple developed along different lines. The "megaron" developed into the elongated "cella", the residence of the god. And the narrow portico widened to the great open halls that surrounded the central temple on all sides. The structure was raised from the earth by steps. This simple, basic form constitutes a complete innovation, since it supersedes the frontal direction and develops in four directions. The temple became plastic. And this was the beginning of the varied and magnificent development of this structure that led to the architecture of the Athenian Acropolis and its central political temple, the Parthenon. The flat roof developed into a ridge roof, the entablature became more complex and the pediment afforded an opportunity for rich adornment with colored friezes done in high relief and fostering the vividness of sculpture. The pillar undergoes a varied development of base, capital and shaft. It is in the Greek temple that, for the first time, the individual portions of a building have a life of their own without disturbing the balance of the whole. Contrasts are combined to overcome the ritual rigidness of the East; they are even used to accentuate the general effect.

The Greek city, the first scene of the public life of a free people, called for a new kind of gathering place, the "agora", the assembly and market-place, the theater where the dramatic spectacles were staged, the "stadion" where the athletic competitions and feasts were held and the gymnasium where young men were trained for physical fitness. The temple, by and large, provided the model for all public buildings. The private house developed into a structure with a character of its own; it grouped around an inner court ("aule," "atrium").

The next impetus to architectural evolution came from the Romans, who combined their new finds in engineering with Greek and Etruscan traditions. The columns were incorporated in the walls, and the new feature is the predominant use of the arch, taken from the Etruscans. As Rome grew into a vast metropolis, the dwelling houses of the masses were raised to three or more stories.

In imperial Rome, in the first centuries of the Christian era, an entirely new architecture arose, baths, palaces and temples, which mark a complete break with Greek tradition and, at the same time, the beginning of a new era. The chief monuments of this architecture are the baths of Titus, Caracalla and Diocletian, the palace of Domitian, the basilica of Maxentius and the Pantheon. The universal political system of the Roman Empire was reflected in the gift of the Roman engineers for organizing and unifying gigantic volumes. Greek architecture was based on the balance of diversified tectonic forms, and it was the harmonized contrast of various formal elements that constituted the idea and the charm of the Greek building. While the Greeks worked with columns and the entablature, the Romans created through the arch and the vault the prevalence of spherical space in a closed building. In the medieval Romanesque, and especially in the Gothic churches, this inner space grew into a covered immensity, into a cosmic blend of living light and shade. The technical prerequisite for this development was the introduction of a new structural element, the pointed arch, the ogive. And this complex space of the Gothic cathedral, with its vast perspective, forms a transition to the spatial sphere of modern painting, which arises at the end of the Middle Ages and plays an important part in the new exploration of nature.

The autonomy of art is connected with an increasing grasp of objective nature. It is, therefore, most clearly reflected in sculpture and painting. The *sculpture and painting of the Egyptians* was bound up with hieratical forms. In the painted scenes of daily life, given to the dead to take with them into their tomb, all the manifold activities of the Egyptian people, such as agriculture, cattle-breeding, hunting, navigation and shipbuilding, were depicted in a stereotyped way. The various performances are only indicated, all the more so since there is no background, no living space in which the figures move. All motion proceeds in a flat, profile position. The statues of gods, divine kings and nobles are rendered in a formal, ceremonial attitude, the arms close to the body, one foot forward. There is the same flatness in the one-way direction and in the purely frontal position of the bodies. They are deliberately shown in a sublime and motionless pose fitted for eternity.

A certain release from this rigidity, however, begins in the picturing of the lower classes of the population, of the attendants, the servants of kings and great officials. On the one hand, these unimportant people, as shown in the pictures, were to make the surroundings of their dead master in his eternal existence adequate and accustomed, so that he might be able to continue his usual life, and, consequently, they had to be represented as realistically as possible. On the other hand, it did not matter so much if the lower classes struck eternal attitudes. So within the limits of this inescapably formal art, a more lively, natural characterization set in. During the short period of that revolutionary king, Amenophis IV (Akhenaton, 1370–1352 B.C.), even the figures of the gods, the divine king and his family, show a more realistic animation and expressiveness. To summarize: Egyptian art for three thousand years—with the exception of Akhenaton's reign—rendered its world in a typical and ritual manner.

An epoch-making innovation begins with *Cretan vase-painting*: free, individual ornamentation, that playfully follows the diverse forms of nature, is created here. If, in the course of generations, it happened in the Orient that some external impetus gave rise to the incorporation of a new form of nature in ornamentation.

it was immediately stereotyped and endlessly repeated, as, for instance, the palmetto, the rosette, the lotus. This ornamentation corresponds to the formal epithets of Oriental and also of Homeric poetry, such as "the rosy-fingered dawn", "swift-footed Achilles", "the wine-dark sea". On the Cretan vases, animal and plant forms, especially the multiform sea fauna, were continually varied with a close observation of nature, and used purely decoratively.

Greek art (sculpture, wall painting and vase painting) represents a decided progress in the observation of nature. In the evolution from archaic beginnings in the seventh and sixth centuries to its climax in the fifth century, we can follow the gradual awakening to life and the shift from early, hieratical stiffness to the growing sense for the animated body, and finally to the three-dimensional figure that can be viewed from all angles. At the same time, the themes of art become greater in scope. They include the whole world in all its rich diversity, though mostly under cover of depicting the innumerable adventures of anthropomorphic gods and divine heroes. This clinging to religious and mythical themes implies one principle characteristic of the Greek approach to nature. As the philosophers were prevented from going too far in empirical science, from devoting themselves utterly to the observation of nature, because they were limited by the concept of a divine cosmic order, so the artists were kept within the secret bounds of harmony, which is but another, more sensual expression, an instinctive, physical conviction of that divine cosmic order. Of course, all high artistic achievement implies some sort of harmony. In one way or another, harmony is the inherent principle of all art creation, since it is the task of art to show us an organic coherence. And so, indeed, art took over the function of religion in our profane modern world. But in order to achieve harmony in a wider and more complex sense, the artist sometimes has to go beyond earlier established limits. He has to explore the extreme, which in itself may seem harmful and ugly. This a Greek artist hardly ever permitted himself, and we may therefore speak of the Greek approach to nature as of a harmonious naturalism.

So there was a very definite restriction imposed on all attempts at a too radical characterization and individualization. The demand for portraits increased as people dedicated their pictures to deities— a residue of primeval offerings. Statues or busts of famous states- men, thinkers, Olympic prize-winners, were erected in halls of honor. We hardly know, however, how Pericles, Plato or Sophocles really looked, for all preserved portraits are more or less types in the manner of divine representations, they are, as we would say, idealized. All youths look a little like Apollo, all men with a beard, a little like Zeus, all women like Hera or Athena. Only Socrates is an exception. His ugliness is faintly indicated, although it, too, is somewhat like that of a Satyr.

As Greek art freed itself from hieratical forms, it also became free from an exclusively hieratical use. It became a means of adorn- ment. Even in Egypt, the house of a noble was embellished by painted walls and marquetry, mosaic on tessellated floors, showing natural scenes, plants and animals, and so drawing the surround- ing scenery into the interior of the house. In the Greek city, the passion for ornamentation in the things of everyday life found a vent in a special kind of painted pottery that became a vast in- dustry. Its products were exported even to Italy and the Crimea of today.

Another epochal feature of Greek art, connected perhaps with its new, far-reaching popularity for decorative uses, is the fact that here, for the first time, the artist stands out as a single, well-known personality. The Greeks were the first to hand down the name of an artist. In the ancient Orient, he was considered an ordinary artisan, and his work was valued no more highly than that of other craftsmen. Among the Greeks, the work of art was esteemed much more than handicraft; not so, in general, the artist. He was, to be sure, known, and won fame in his field, but the sculptor, at least, was still in a lower social class, together with the craftsmen, since he performed manual work which was regarded with contempt. In the dialogue "Paideia" of the Greek author, Lucian, the sculptor is described as an unfortunate person in a dirty smock, looking like a slave, crouching down, bending at his work, kept down in every respect. He thinks of making his statues harmonious and sublime, but not himself. For this reason, he is valued less than his chiselled stone. Painters were in a better social position, as their work was considered more detached from the material and less strenuous physically.

The furthest advance toward nature in antiquity was achieved in *Hellenistic and Roman sculpture and painting*. This was a period of transition in every respect, the great divide of human history. The ancient tribal units dissolved and the World Empire was forming. Amidst the vast intermingling of cultures and stocks, the rootless individual arose, facing the newly established universality. Accordingly, in Hellenistic art we find the first true portraits in history, the first penetrating characterization of an individual. Up to then, no description of age or social condition had been attempted in portraits. The attributes of age were given, but not its physical characteristics. Children looked like adults reduced in size, and old people did not show the natural withering of their bodies. Now all of these features were stressed, and marks of social and professional standing were crudely emphasized. Examples of this are the statue of a fisherman and of an old shepherdess, both in the Palazzo dei Conservatori in Rome, and the statue of a drunken old woman in the Capitoline Museum. To Roman portraits is due the crucial innovation which prepares and provides one of the main elements of medieval presentation. This innovation consists in a new emphasis on the face. In Greek art, no special emphasis was given to the face. Expression emanated equally and harmoniously from the whole body. In Rome, the face becomes the focus of life of the body and the statue looks out upon the world, faces the world in a naturalistic way. Finally, in the first period of Christian painting, a crucial progress in this direction can be observed.

Portraits from Egypt which are painted on wooden coffins of mummies—a residue of the Egyptian custom of preservation of the dead—show a predominance of the eye over the other parts of the face. Here the eye acquires that inward gaze produced by Christianity, a special trait that dominates the art of portraiture from then up to our times.

This is the most advanced stage which the characterization of the individual reached in antiquity. The further development of the portrait centers in the monuments of the deified emperors and it tends to a gradual re-hieratization of the persons rendered, but with new elements and with a new meaning that lead to the Christian art of the Middle Ages. Medieval portraits of certain persons on coins, miniatures and ivory carvings are idealized suggestions of similarity without any effort toward actual likeness.

Under the domination of the Christian ideology and the Christian faith, personality became submerged in a flood of spirit, but the individual persisted and developed secretly and anonymously. The evolution of Christian sculpture in the later Middle Ages reflects this surreptitious development. The hieratical portrait of Constantine, and that of the Vandal Stilicho are among the last true Roman portraits, and portraits do not reappear in the Christian world until centuries later, and then as humble, consciously anonymous figures of donors and artists, who are crowded into corners of pictures that tell the story of saints, or interpolated in a worshipping throng like a shyly hidden signature.

Besides the expressiveness of the human face, the Romans, as we said, transmitted another element of equal importance to medieval art: they rendered space to convey the idea of boundlessness, of infinitude. The immense inner space of the Roman buildings diverted the eye from the walls and pillars that, as such, still preserve antiquity's feeling for the proportions of the human body. This forms a transition to the development of the cathedrals of the Middle Ages, in which space is utilized to convey a spiritual sphere. Before the Greeks developed their own architecture and sculpture, compact forms of structures and bodies were the accepted standard, and space was only a surrounding, an accessory element without any significance of its own. The Greeks used space to bound the architecture of their temples and the sculptured images of bodies harmoniously. But the interpretation of the vastness of the universe, through space, belonged to the Romans, who were dominated by a feeling for immensity. So while the new significance of the human face derives from the increased attention to individuality, the new significance of space reflects the rising counterpart of the individual, universality.

The Roman wall paintings have been called Roman Impressionism, because of the floating and almost illusionary rendering of the atmosphere, because of the spatial element that unites the bodies. These wall paintings of a later period had a manifest influence on early Christian catacomb painting, which is the nucleus of medieval art. To be sure, this influence consists merely in a transmission of formal elements. The meaning of artistic presentation was radically reversed by the Christian concept of life, and soon the Christian spirit transformed the inherited elements. In the early catacomb paintings we still sense the presence of that effective space of the Romans, only that its interpretation has changed completely. Space is no longer an earthly, a sensuous element, it is celestial and spiritual. It lifts the human figure beyond the earthly world. In the mosaics of the churches of the fifth and sixth centuries, space, laid out in blue and gold, symbolizes the heavens, ethereal widths and depths resplendent with light.

Christian medieval art is based, then, on the two elements inherited from the Romans: the power of space, symbolizing the universe, and the predominance of the eye, symbolizing the individual. Both became spiritualized to extremes. After the downfall of the Roman Empire, when the world had divided into a spiritual and a terrestrial sphere, when the body had been degraded and rejected, space became the symbol for the spiritual sphere where bodily appearances vanish and only divine souls exist. The eyes, and the human face dominated by them, became the seat of the soul. The body was entirely neglected. In early Christian sculpture it shrinks into a wretched, almost mummified appendage of the face. And more than this: all corporeal representations or scenes become merely allegorical, they cannot be understood per se, by the senses alone, they are mere clues and suggestions, the significance of which must be known. Man has to raise himself toward the deity by the strength of his spiritual faith, of his knowing devotion.

So—superficially at least—this art seems to have lapsed into hieratical rigidity. Even the old Oriental frontal position of the figures, the unrelated way in which they are placed side by side, has returned. But this rigidity of medieval art is utterly different from the original stiffness. A new spirit, the spirit of faith, floats over all, unites the figures and relates them to one another. On the other hand, as in the case of scholastic theology, this apparently arrested development is fermenting with secret life, to burst out into the open in due time and to pervade the human face through the expression of the eye. The animated and inspired faces of the medieval saints, the Virgin Mary at the Annunciation and at the Visitation, mirror the devotion and the feelings of the anonymous sculptors who imagined and made them. These artists, in their profound fervor, tried to penetrate deeply into the soul of the figures rendered, into the spirit of the lives of the saints, and by the intensity of their search they were led to a new form of characterization, to a new animated realism, which was gradually also extended to pose and gesture and, in this way, again reached and included the body. This deeper realism was enhanced by the spiritual theme, and sprang, in fact, from this theme which did not exist in antiquity. To Greek and Roman art, soul and body were not as yet separate entities, and so it lacked that immense tension which drove the medieval artist into his extraordinary intensification and sometimes exaggeration of expression that began to exceed the limits of harmony. The Northern peoples, indeed, especially the Germans, had never known or felt the need of the classic concept of harmony. According to its origin, this rising Gothic naturalism might be called spiritual naturalism. In Italy, however, the sensuous order of harmony had never been completely forgotten, as, in general, the pagan tradition had never ceased to be effective. The instincts, the ways of life, the conceptions of the Italians, were imbued with this tradition and sense of harmony. And the fusion of the newly gained spiritual depths and intensity of expression with the ancient, ever-valid instinctive rule of harmony—this synthesis was the groundwork for the art of the Renaissance.

In *Italy,* the decisive drive toward realism came from the reform movement of St. Francis of Assisi and his mendicant friars, from this attempt to revive a pure and genuine Christianity which was to become effective on earth in a brotherly community of all earthly creatures. It was the emphasis on this earth that was new and that tended toward a new realism. The evolution of *Renaissance Art*— broadly speaking—was inaugurated by the sculptor, Giovanni Pisano, and the painter, Giotto, in the thirteenth century, and came to a climax in Leonardo, Raphael, Titian and Michelangelo. It was an extremely intricate development, a step-by-step conquest of the problems of perspective, the richness of relation between human beings and their surroundings, the complexity of composition, the vivacity of movement and the profound and detailed characterization of face, body, pose and texture. These artists were "uomini universali"—men who had mastered all the knowledge of their era. They were often simultaneously architects, sculptors, painters, philosophers and inventors; to them, art was a science, science was an art. Artists attained a high social position among the unconventional, unprejudiced citizens of these Italian communities. They were never identified with craftsmen and were considered on a level with scholars, poets and the whole intelligentsia, a ranking that contrasted sharply with the standards of antiquity and the early Middle Ages. Many of the Renaissance artists led the life of grand seigneurs and joined the company of the princes and the rich merchants whose palaces and villas their works adorned.

Renaissance art, as a whole, came closer to nature. It was much more concerned with the empirical object than even the most advanced achievements of antiquity. This was due partly to the spiritual experiences of the Christian era applied to the rediscovered or revived pagan traditions of Italy, which involved a new evaluation of the body. There was, moreover, the general tendency of this epoch: under the influence of the political and economic evolution of the Italian cities, a sharp contrast to, indeed a conflict with, medieval spirituality and religiousness developed. This resulted in the innovation of the Italian Renaissance, the secularization and individualization of human life. The world of physical phenomena, the physical, profane world, grew to be of prime importance. The human body was again shown in its nakedness and studied more intensively and accurately than ever before. For the first time it was stripped of the cloak of divinity and regarded for its own sake, for sheer pleasure, not only in its appearance, but in the laws by which it is governed. This exclusive concentration on the empirical world of bodies indicates a new attitude toward nature.

Restrictions, however, still persisted regarding the subjects of art as well as the manner in which they were treated, and these restrictions still prevented art and artist from being fully autonomous. In the Renaissance art of Italy, the classical rule of harmony and the standard of the human body as the center of the world still remained unshaken. The description of happenings and personalities, stories of the Bible and the saints, Greek and Roman legends, and the fêtes and personalities of Italian rulers furnished the themes of sculpture and painting and were used as a background even when the artist wanted to express a most personal experience. As to the manner in which these themes were treated: the organic form of the human body still constituted the core, the structural scheme of the picture. The scenery had become elaborate as a result of the discovery of perspective, but it was arranged around the human body, it was dependent on the human body, it derived its significance from it and was a foil for the motion and gesture of man. This corresponds to the prevalence of the narrative element, an element essentially foreign to integral art that aims to render appearance per se. One might say that the principle of sculpture, the compact form of the body, extended its rule into painting also. The sculptural principle prevailed in painting. And so even perspective was organized in a closed sphere. If we speak of naturalism in Italian Renaissance art at all, we must keep in mind that it was still a harmonious naturalism.

Italian Baroque is a further advance toward realistic portrayal of thought and emotion as well as of the outer, physical world. In exaggerating content, it elaborates form to the bursting point. This tendency was enhanced by the increasing demand for representative display and pomp on the part of public and private patrons.

Yet the exuberance of Baroque art was, so to speak, evenly distributed over the whole human form; a certain degree of harmony
was preserved. Just as Leonardo is representative of the Renaissance,
the development of Michelangelo's work typifies the transition
from Renaissance to Baroque.

So Renaissance and even Baroque artists, in their new concentration of attention upon nature, were still moved and unconsciously guided by the need of formal harmony, by the need for
beauty, in the old classical sense, deriving from the order of the
symmetrically balanced, organized and animated human body.
They did not want to render nature purely as such, nature at all
costs. They wanted to show this balanced order in nature, and they
still shrank from overstepping the limits of this balanced system
too far. At this period, the study of natural science was, in a like
manner, still hampered by the deep-rooted concept of a fundamental harmony of nature, of a whole and balanced cosmos. This limitation is clearly expressed in Michelangelo's judgment of Flemish
painting, of which he says that "it will please . . . persons who
have no ear for true harmony . . . (It is) of stuffs, bricks and
mortar, the grass of the fields, the shadows of trees, and bridges
and rivers, which they call landscapes, and little figures here and
there; and all this, although it may appear good to some eyes, is in
truth done without reasonableness or art, without symmetry or
proportion, without care in selecting or rejecting . . ." Of Italian
painting, on the other hand, he says, that it strives for "the perfection which unites itself with, and joins God; because good painting is nothing else but a copy of the perfections of God . . ." Harmony was also the main appeal of Italian art that aimed at, and
was expected to provide, adornment and recreation and the representation of public or private glory and power. Art was still incorporated in the actual present community and its political, cultural activity.

In all these respects, the Northern countries of Europe, especially
the Germanic countries, show a very different attitude. And here
the decisive turn occurred that resulted not only in the genesis of

true, complete modern naturalism but also in the perfected autonomy of art.

This process has its roots in the disposition of the *Northern populations* that had not been intrinsically connected and impregnated with classical traditions and consequently had not been hampered in their pursuit of nature by either an innate sense or a preconceived idea of harmony. The evolution of naturalism in Gothic art led to the characterization of the human face which extended to the rendering of the attitude and gestures of the figures. Here the mere physical forms were already pervaded and transfigured by the intensity of expression.

The decisive turn was promoted by two secularizing factors. The courts of the French kings and the great French nobility, especially the Dukes of Berry and Burgundy, developed into pre-eminent cultural centers, and the luxury of their residences and mode of life drew artists from all countries into their orbit. Influences of the new Italian Renaissance mingled with the last development of Gothic style; the Italian approach to nature fused with Gothic expressiveness. The second factor was the rise of the Dutch and German cities, their bourgeoisie and their bourgeois spirit. The new naturalistic movement sprang up in the Flemish region, where the dominion of the dukes of Burgundy adjoined the area of the rich Dutch cities, which, at the beginning of the fifteenth century, became centers of trade and of textile manufacture. While princely residences, the cathedrals and the sepulchers still gave a prominent place to sculpture, the bourgeois use of painted shrines, as well as the manufacture of tapestries, promoted painting. So the shift from princely to bourgeois culture implied the shift from sculpture to painting. This was a fundamental change.

Flemish artists inaugurated the new naturalism at the end of the fourteenth and the beginning of the fifteenth century—the sculptor, Claus Sluter, and his school, who worked for the French princes, and the painters, Hubert and Jan van Eyck. The van Eycks invented oil painting, and thus opened up new and immense possibilities for the development of this art. In their painting we can still trace the after-effects of Gothic spiritual naturalism and the influence of the Italian Renaissance. But besides, there is a completely new facing of nature and a ruthless search for the empirical object without any regard for organic balance and harmony of form. On the famous altar of Ghent, the bodies of Adam and Eve, with their particular ugliness, disclose the new purpose, the new aim of art: the pursuit of nature in itself, of nature purely as such. This is the first manifestation of true naturalism, a naturalism which we may call an investigating naturalism, and which gradually opens up the infinite space of nature. Scholastic Nominalism and the rise of empirical science contributed greatly to this development, in legitimizing and promoting empirical observation and in stressing the particular, the individual, the minute detail.

But there were still other motives that determined this process. They became effective in the craftsman spirit, the petit bourgeois spirit of the German inland cities. The German painters of the late fifteenth century were craftsmen educated by the minute procedure of handicraft. And the fundamental rift between city and flat country in Germany led the citizens to envisage nature as a wild and chaotic sphere, an inhuman, even anti-human sphere—which the German countryside really was. In Italy, the country was humanized, it was a frame for human life, it was influenced, cultivated and formed by man. In Germany, it was an unmastered wilderness, adverse to man. Man did not move within nature as within a familiar, friendly environment. He faced nature as an object of fascination and exploration. Where the Italians investigated Nature as a macrocosm of the human microcosm, these Northerners investigated it as an element alien and inimical to man.

The result of all this was the art of the German painters of the fifteenth and sixteenth centuries: Albrecht Altdorfer, Wolf Huber, Hans Baldung Grien, Lucas Cranach, Mathias Gruenewald, and Albrecht Duerer, who was, in part, subjected to Italian influence. For the first time this art was essentially painting, since the intrinsic and unique quality of painting was the dominating principle in these pictures. Atmospheric space, the deep infinite space of nature, which only painting can explore, is the main component of these pictures. The human figures moving within this elemental sphere are almost accessory, they are merely part of it, indeed, they are outweighed and overwhelmed by it. The chaotic forms of the vegetation are much more powerful. It is only a logical consequence of the whole trend of this art, that here in Germany the first pure landscape was painted by Altdorfer. This first landscape without a human figure marked the complete detachment of the pictorial from the narrative element.

As infinite space, the chaotic wilderness of nature, furnished the subjects for this art, formal harmony, the balanced order deriving from the structure of the human body, was entirely broken up. These paintings are irregular, fragmentary or overcrowded, and without perfect coherence and homogeneousness. From this time on, the "pictorial", the "picturesque", the principle of exploring the phenomena of nature per se, becomes the dominant principle of art.

A corresponding change took place in the motivation and the appeal of this art. These pictures are no longer a part of larger units, like the wall paintings of cathedrals or the miniatures of books. They are created as independent, isolated paintings in their own right. They are made for the collector, the connoisseur who contemplates them for themselves, for their specific interpretation of the visual world. This process of detachment, as well as the habit of collecting pictures, began in Italy, but it assumed its real significance later and in the Northern countries, as a result of the new mode of painting.

And so, finally, the artist is carried away by this more and more thorough and far-reaching exploration of the secrets of space, the display of atmospheric light and its effects on the color and texture of materials—this leads to Rembrandt, who inaugurated modern painting. Thus the role of the modern artist is established. His task is no longer the service of divinity, not adornment and decoration, not narration, not even the interpretation, through the visual, of an order beyond the visual. For him the visual world is no longer a means; it has become an end in itself. The road that led from the human figure to pure landscape narrows now and leads to the still life as at once the most limited and widest field of purely visual exploration. In his searching of the purely visual, the modern artist penetrates, finally, into the abstract structure of physical forms. Reaching the core of the visual, he transcends it. This long process, started by the concentration of the Northern artists on the visual per se, meant the complete autonomy of art.

ECONOMY

THE LAST TWO CHAPTERS dealt with two parallel movements of secularization and emancipation of human activities. We saw how Reason as well as Art flowered in antiquity under the permanent rule of an eternal, divine order. But both had to pass through the narrow channel of Christian doctrine in order to free themselves, and to become autonomous once and for all, through a process of growing friction with the rigid authority of Christian dogma. The result was the rise of the natural sciences and, in art, of the first true naturalism.

Both these movements not only set free science and art respectively; by implication, they created the modern concept of nature and inaugurated the modern relation of man to nature. Other developments were working in the same direction and helping toward the same effect. The most important of these laid the foundations, created the elements of modern economy, and opened up nature as an object and a sphere of human exploitation.

Under the influence of materialistic ideology, modern sociologists and economists trace back all economic activities to the very beginning of human civilization. In seeking to prove that human life at all times and in all epochs was determined by material, economic circumstances, they tried to discover capitalism in Rome, in Greece and even in Babylon. Once more it must be emphasized that we have to be extremely careful in applying modern terms to conditions and events of past epochs and civilizations. No clarity, no exact knowledge can be derived from so indiscriminate a use of well-defined terms. It can only lead to confusion and misconception. When we consider the various human activities as isolated phenomena, separated from the general sphere of life in which they took place, we can indeed trace their origins very far back, to the very beginnings of the history of mankind. But we have to take into account the role they play in a civilization as a whole, and the place, the position they occupy with respect to other activities and trends of that civilization. We have first to establish what the dominant trend of a civilization is, in order to find out the exact position and, accordingly, the exact character of a special activity and a special phenomenon in the different periods of the history of man. When we look at history from this point of view, we find that what the materialistic ideology contends is not true, that human life has not been determined by economic motives and economic circumstances at all times. On the contrary, at different stages of mankind very different motives prevailed. The motive of producing goods and making money, economic classification of people and economic disparities, that is, the disparity of wealth, and the ownership of the means of production were not the decisive factors in society prior to the end of the Middle Ages.

We have already seen that the one great antagonist of technology and economy is religion. Religion sanctifies the natural forces and binds men to rituals, customs and apprehensions, to all the sacred concepts and ways of life that prevent him from an unrestrained and undivided pursuit of worldly purposes. So in all periods in which religion still exerted an effective power upon man, an exclusive or even decisive determination of human life by economic reasons was impossible. The growing influence of economic motives upon human life was linked to the process of secularization, it was a symptom of secularization, of the dwindling of religious power over man.

So it does not mean very much when we say that a number of institutions and procedures of modern economy have their roots in early antiquity. There is, for instance, evidence of a sort of clearing business in ancient *Egypt*. A man could deliver his wheat crops to the granary of the Pharaoh, a fact that is well known from the story of Joseph, and because of his credit in wheat, he could make payments by assignment. This sort of clearing, however, has a fundamentally different significance from ours; it characterizes a premonetary stage. It is a substitute for payment in kind. The Latin root of the word capital is "caput", head, and it indicates that the original measurement of property and barter was the number of heads of cattle. The Latin word for money, "pecunia", comes from "pecus", cattle. In Homer, the value of prizes, booty and slaves is expressed throughout by numbers of cattle. This was because cattle were the noblest sacrificial animals and, in the barter with the gods, became a standard of value, that is, they received the characteristic of money. Gradually, precious metals were introduced, first as a means of evaluation and later of exchange, originally because of their sacramental significance (gold had a magic quality in Egypt, silver in Babylon), but also because of their rarity and their resistance to oxidation. They were, however, intended chiefly for external, intertribal trade, which occurred in the form of an exchange of gifts between rulers, and for this purpose they were used in the shape of jewelry such as rings and chains. In internal trade they appeared only as bullion or as unwrought pieces. Accordingly, they could not be easily carried and they had to be weighed for every purchase. Currency in Egypt remained at this stage of development until Hellenistic times. The first Cretan money consisted in metal bars shaped like cattle hides. The origin of the coin is to be found in the stamp of the minter, certifying where a piece came from, as a guarantee that the weight of the bullion was correct. The Babylonian and Israelitic Shekel was such a stamped metal bar. True coin, such as we know today, was first introduced in Lydia, and perfected by the Greeks. By its very shape, it assumed the character of the first real money, and that does not only mean the quality of a standard of value or a means of payment, but of an actual means of exchange, suited to circulation. So, obviously, clearing and checks in Egypt did not have the same meaning as similar procedures in modern economy. It did not signify an acceleration or increased flexibility of commerce, but a mere mode of payment in kind.

We also have evidence of an inland trade and of credit operations in *Babylon and Assyria* and in other ancient countries of the Near East. In these great realms that included many regions and many populations, a widespread trade, far in excess of the local bazaar trade, developed. But the sacred kings and the priests still controlled this trade, and all dealings with foreign lands were entirely in the hands of the king. The merchants were his privileged agents. Priests and priestesses were the noblest among merchants and minters, and the temple was considered the most reliable mint. The temples, too, were the first places for safe deposit, where fortunes and articles of value could be deposited, and, consequently, they were also the first clearing-houses where transfers could be made and credit could be obtained. But there was no highly developed trade and business in the modern sense. The majority of Babylonian trade documents concern transfer of real estate. Transportation of goods was a difficult and long-winded affair because it required travel through regions perpetually involved in tribal wars. A trading trip usually was the matter of a year. The primitive form of money and the ceremonial clumsiness of business transactions show that, in spite of much desultory trade, there was no well-regulated and steady commerce.

The Phoenicians were the first to make sea trade on a large scale a vital part of human activity. This trade, to be sure, consisted largely in warlike raids, piracy and the exploitation of ignorant tribes. It had, however, a certain influence on the social and political order. For the first time, people acquired wealth and political predominance through trade, and the rich merchant families came to constitute a powerful aristocracy which limited the power of the kings and eventually established oligarchic rule.

The same development, only to a much greater extent, occurred in *Greece*. As a result of overpopulation, of the indebtedness and dispossession of the small farmers, the great movement of Greek

colonization began in the seventh and sixth centuries B.C. The new
colonies developed into bases for a relatively extensive sea trade,
in which painted pottery, arms, metal work and oil were exchanged
for raw materials and Oriental products, and thus promoted manufacture in the cities of the Greek mainland. The technical superiority of their coin materially aided the Greeks in outstripping
Phoenician trade, which was merely barter without money involved. The unfolding of true city life, as well as the subsequent
reforms of the political constitutions of the Greek cities which
eventually led to a perfect democracy—all this reflects the growing
importance of movable, individual wealth gained through commerce.

From the various views of Greek life presented, it is already apparent that economy in itself was far from being the main concern
of this people. Greek life was dominated and animated by religious
concepts and by political problems connected with them, by a
naive, impetuous, inquisitive joy in the newly discovered life on
earth, tragically shadowed by the feeling of Promethean daring
that must continually justify itself before a celestial order of things.
The result was an attitude toward life and a mode of life that included a specific scale of values for the activities and callings of
man. We find this attitude and this evaluation all the way from
Homer to Lucian. Its most sublime expression is in the political
writings of Plato and Aristotle. The latter writes in his "Politics":
"The most slavish of occupations are those in which the body is
used the most . . . Peasants and artisans and all hired workers must
of necessity be at the disposal of the polis. But only those who go
armed and those who sit in council are constituent parts of the
polis . . ." "Thus it becomes clear that in the best-governed polis . . .
the citizens may not lead either the life of craftsmen or of traders,
for such a life is devoid of nobility and hostile to perfection of
character . . . Nor may the citizens be peasants . . . for pensive leisure is a requirement not only for political feats but for the growth
of human perfection . . ."

And in the "Laws", Plato deals with the founding of an ideal
polis: "If this is to be a polis near the coast, possessing a good har-

bor but with insufficient produce and needing many imports, it would require a great genius and lawgivers of divine wisdom to prevent it from developing manifold, divers-colored and evil habits as a result of this situation . . . The nearness of the sea is pleasant in regard to daily life, but it is indeed a salty and a bitter neighborhood, for if it brings with it sea trade and petty bargaining, this produces fickle and faithless souls and thus the city becomes loveless and faithless toward itself and toward strangers . . . But if (in addition to having a good harbor) the city had abundant produce, it would export widely and brim with silver and gold coins, and no greater evil could befall it . . . in regard to the maintenance of good and righteous customs."

These formulations may be somewhat extreme. But they foretell what actually happened, and they contain a profound realization of the meaning of human life that mankind has long since lost. They are, moreover, the perfect expression of the Greek point of view. They are, indeed, an exact analogy to the Greek attitude toward the exploration of nature in science and art.

Greek trade was limited and unimportant in comparison with the commerce of the *Roman Empire*. The unifying and organizing of more and more vast areas under Roman rule, the founding of cities, building of roads, the accumulation of riches and the increasing demand for luxuries in the metropolis—all this was a tremendous incentive to commerce. This commerce, in contrast to Greek trade, was almost exclusively concerned with imports. And since it was no longer barter but was handled on a money basis, it could, for the first time, fully exploit the advantages and profits of trading with populations on a lower level of civilization. It was this kind of colonial, or largely colonial, trade that later became a source of wealth for the British, the French, the Belgian and the Dutch people. The result was a huge increase of wealth in Rome and the development of many and varied economic activities and callings. New opportunities arose for money-changers and dealers who first were called by their Greek name "trapezites", later "mensarii", after the table ("trapeza, mensa") on which these transactions were carried out. This table subsequently became a bench, the "bank"—the origin of our modern bank and bankers. There was a great advance in the credit and deposit business, in transfer of payment, shipping, manufacture and other aspects of commercial affairs. When merchants pooled their capital in order to diminish risks, the first trading and shipping companies were formed. The tax-collectors combined forces and formed societies, the shares of which were traded publicly.

All this increase in economic activities, however, did not fundamentally alter the scale of social values. It did not mitigate the open contempt for any kind of work connected with business. It was, of course, acceptable to make money by these means, and even nobles invested their money in business enterprises. But they did not engage in business themselves. Their administrators, sometimes even their slaves, did all the actual work. Senators were explicitly forbidden to concern themselves with business of any kind. And everybody who made money forthwith became a landed proprietor. He ennobled his position by the acquisition of large estates. It was only then, as a landed proprietor, that he was considered socially acceptable.

The social classification of the Romans is best illustrated by a passage from Cicero's "De Officiis"—"Above all, those callings should be condemned that arouse the hatred of the people, such as tax-collecting and the exacting of usury. The toil of a hired worker, who is paid only for his toil and not for artistic skill, is unworthy of a free man and is sordid in character. For in his case, money is the price of slavery. Sordid too is the calling of those who buy wholesale in order to sell retail, since they would gain no profits without a great deal of lying ... Likewise all the craftsmen are engaged in a sordid profession. For a workshop is ill-suited to a free citizen ... But the professions requiring greater skill and knowledge, and intrinsically greater in usefulness, such as medicine, architecture, education, are honorable for people with whose rank they accord. Trade on a small retail scale is sordid, but if it is on a large wholesale scale including the import of many wares from everywhere and their distribution to many people without

any misrepresentation, it is not to be too greatly censured . . .
It is even deserving of the highest praise, if those who carry on
such trade finally retire to country estates, after being surfeited or
at least satisfied with their gains. But of all callings from which
profit is won, none is better than agriculture, nothing more advantageous, nothing more pleasant and more worthy of a free man."

Thus, in spite of economic progress, the old social standard remained unshaken: the great official, the senator, the landed proprietor, were the only respectable and fully accepted elements of
Roman society.

The downfall of the Roman Empire and the anarchic period of
the barbarian invasions and migrations brought about the disruption and disintegration of the whole status of civilization, and so
also of economic activities. Trade was interrupted and languished.
Only Constantinople, the capital of the Byzantine Empire, persisted
as the center of extensive Eastern trade. But as communications
were poor and perilous, this trade of the Orient rarely reached
Western and Northern Europe. In Germanic lands, the old barter
system and payment in kind were re-established. On the old Roman roads along the Rhine and the Danube, Syrians and Jews
still carried on trade to a certain extent. But it was chiefly local
trade, and it took centuries before commerce on a larger scale was
built up among the barbarian populations. Paradoxically enough,
it was the *church* that promoted and encouraged this new commerce in every possible way, even by settling and patronizing Jews
in the new cities. To the Christian doctrine, trade was the most
reprehensible, wicked and indeed detestable of all human activities. But as it was indispensable to civilization and strengthened
the position of the bishops as lords of the cities, the bishops could
not but foster it. First, they discovered the happy expedient of diverting the ill repute attaching to this necessary pursuit to the
Jews, whom they could privilege and condemn simultaneously and
at will. Later, however, when the Christian population—the
Frisians, who were especially inclined to trade, but also the indigenous landed proprietors and administrators—began to relish the

advantages and easy gains of commerce, the Jews were crowded out of trade in goods, and forced to bear the curse of the credit business which was still more objectionable from the Christian point of view. But when the Christians took over the credit transactions as well, the Jews were left with only petty, local moneylending and its despised usury. The Christian rejection of the banking and credit business originated, again paradoxically, in the old Jewish prohibition of the charging of interest, which is frequently expressed in the Old Testament and in the writings of the Rabbis, which Jesus repeated, according to Luke 6, 34, to which the Church Father, Jerome, referred, and which the Lateran Council of 1179 stringently enjoined anew upon the faithful. Economic developments and the financial exigencies of the princes made money-lending a more and more urgent necessity. And it was the papacy itself that introduced the credit business and the taking of interest among the Christian population, when it used its tax- and indulgence-collectors in Italy, for availing itself of the profit to be derived from this kind of business.

The moral inhibitions caused by the dogmatic prohibition of interest were very hard to overcome in medieval mentality, and it was only under the pressure of inescapable circumstances that banking and the money-lending business became acceptable. The Jews were forced into it when they were shut out from trade in goods. Among the Christians, political exiles from the Lombard cities were the first to engage in this field. They were also employed as agents of the papacy. Therefore, the pawn and loan business was called "Lombarding" and the banker a "Lombard".

It is not mere chance that European banking on a large scale first throve in the inland cities of Italy and Germany. The ports of Venice, Genoa, and Pisa (which in the Middle Ages lay close to the sea), rose to power and wealth through an extensive maritime trade. As a result of the crusades, and the conquest of Constantinople in 1204, close communications developed between the Orient and the European continent. The Italian cities, and Venice in particular, inherited the Byzantine trade, and these maritime cities provided the continent of Europe with imported goods. The inland cities that had no access to the sea could not compete with them in this kind of trade. They were compelled to look for a new and more promising variety of business, and this proved to be manufacture and banking. Money-lending was the source of the wealth and power of Bologna, Siena and particularly of Florence. All the great families of Florence that supplied rulers for this city-republic, the Medici, the Albizzi, the Peruzzi, the Pitti, the Strozzi, among others, began as bankers. In the fourteenth and fifteenth centuries, Florence was the center of the money-lending business of Europe. Somewhat later, a similar development took place in Germany. There, too, the maritime cities, the Hansa cities, were concerned exclusively with trade, and only the inland cities engaged in industry and credit transactions on a large scale.

The great *city-republics of the Renaissance* reached their flowering through commerce, and consequently they had no social prejudice against trading as such. The economic development was one of the decisive factors that fomented the secularized spirit of the Renaissance and gradually weakened the moral restrictions imposed by the Christian doctrine. In Venice, however, in the most aristocratic of these republics, a certain aversion against banking persisted, together with a strong repugnance to manufacture which was still despised as an undignified pursuit. The Venetian noblemen, all of whom were merchants, did not deign to engage in manufacturing, even as entrepreneurs. They considered handicraft as "artes sordidae", as a sordid calling in contrast with the "bonae artes", the fine arts. A clear and sharp distinction was made between the artist and the artisan.

In Florence, on the other hand, the so-called craft guilds, which were, for the most part, associations of manufacturing entrepreneurs, became very powerful in the community and played an important part in the frequent revolts and changes of rulership in this city. Characteristically, the guild of the bankers was one of the most prominent among these associations.

In the sociology and history of economics of today, the opinion prevails that modern economy and capitalism have their roots and first appeared in Renaissance Italy. To be sure, many of the forms and institutions of modern business were created, or at least developed, in these cities, and modern business terminology bears the traces of Italian origins to a considerable extent, as, for example, the terms firm, balance, discount, or bankruptcy, "banco rotto", the overturned bench. Modern banking techniques derive chiefly from the shrewd tricks of Italian money-lenders, who attempted to screen the infamous taking of interest. The exact method of bookkeeping and accounting was inaugurated by the administrations of the Italian cities, and it was organized into a system, for the first time, by the great Italian mathematician, Luca Pacioli.

When we look at the whole picture of Renaissance life, however, we still find a fundamental difference between the state of mind prevalent in these cities and the state of mind of modern economists and business men. Although the Italian merchants and bankers were shrewd, efficient and socially unprejudiced, they were above all politically ambitious. They all wanted to be or to become noblemen, princes, rulers of their cities. They all spent their money lavishly and extravagantly for political intrigues, upheavals, feuds, for gaining political power and for displaying and representing political power by an ostentatious and artistically adorned mode of life. Money-making and economic production were instruments for attaining political power and enjoyment of life, but not goals in themselves, not autonomous forms of power. The Medici, for instance, were of humble origin, simple wool-combers at first, later apothecaries and physicians—hence their name Medici and the five pills in their coat of arms. As their prosperity increased, they became bankers, and they continued as bankers and had their money invested all over Europe long after they had become the rulers of Florence, brilliant princes and patrons of the arts. This dominant position was what they really enjoyed and what they were really living for. Today, when we think of the Medici or of other illustrious Italian families, we do not see them as business men but as nobles in their magnificent, fortified palaces, involved in political conspiracies and surrounded by the greatest scholars and artists of their age. Just as Italian Renaissance art was governed by a sense of beauty and by the desire for beauty, so these

Italian merchants wanted to enjoy life and beauty in life. The real change to an economic mentality, to the capitalistic turn of mind that laid the foundation for economy as an autonomous and gradually predominant sphere of life, took place in Germany.

This is due to the particular conditions of the *German Empire* and the *German cities*. Since, in the fifteenth century, the German Empire had become an anarchic scene of rival territorial rulers in constant need of money for their courts and armies, and the emperor himself always required more and more funds, it is easily understood what immense opportunities the banking business was presented with in that country. Everywhere, in Italy, in France and in England, money, at this time, was already playing a great role, but everywhere it was held in check by political power, whether—as in Italy—the business men themselves had political ambitions, or—as in the more westerly countries—a firmly established kingdom knew how to exploit and to cheat the bankers and money-lenders cleverly for its own purposes. Only in Germany were the business people predominant. Only in Germany, money as such had gained a decisive influence on politics.

The other important premise for the development of a purely and specifically economic sphere and mentality was the unique situation of the German inland and craft guild cities. The German cities evolved from the market-place, and developed along economic lines and according to economic necessities. They had no concern with politics. They constituted economic enclaves, as it were, within the anarchic body of the German Empire. In the craft guild city lay the germs of the two great antagonistic and yet intimately connected movements of the modern social and economic world: industry and labor, capitalism and socialism, individualism and collectivism. In describing the organization of the craft guilds and their city, we stressed the social trend of the guilds in their capacity of the first true collectives in human history. This collective trend prevailed in the first period of the rise of the craft guilds. In the course of subsequent developments, however, it becomes clear that, although the craftsmen were true workmen, their position and social rank was very different from that of the modern worker. The craftsmen did not constitute a proletariat. The communities were small, the scope of their enterprises was limited, and the craftsman was master of his enterprise, however severe the restrictions imposed by the guild regulations might be. The guild, though a collective, was still an association of fairly independent individuals who did not merge in their collectivity, who were not overwhelmed by their collectivity.

Thus, in the craft guild, both tendencies, the individualistic and the collectivistic, balanced each other. The many conflicts between these tendencies had not yet begun. And the deep, intrinsic antinomy within the character of the modern bourgeoisie, the vacillating of the bourgeoisie between these two tendencies—collective standard, collective morality, collective government, and individual freedom, individual initiative, individual enterprise—this inherent ambivalence of the bourgeoisie, which is already foreshadowed in the structure of the craft guild, was not as yet fully disclosed.

The individualistic trend detached itself from the collective bond of the craft guild and became engaged in an endeavor which again led it into collective entanglements of a different, technical order. The development of capitalism and industry shows another blend of individualism and collectivity. Under the influence of the craft guilds a mutual penetration and impregnation of trade and handicraft was developing. Even the merchants, the natural enemies of the craftsmen, were forced either to join craft guilds or to form guilds of their own along the same lines. The specific character of handicraft brought its effect to bear on the merchants, and a new spirit arose, a combination of the trading spirit and the working spirit of the craftsman. The German inland cities began to flower.

This movement had two points of departure. In the fourteenth century, the trade of the Italian city-republics increased, drew the German inland cities, especially Augsburg and Nuernberg, into its orbit, and enriched the merchants of these cities. On the other hand, outstanding and influential master-craftsmen, who enjoyed special prestige either through their influence or through bribery, succeeded in securing special privileges for themselves, as, for instance, priority or a larger share of raw materials than was their due. They were able to expand their workshops and to increase the number of journeymen beyond the limits allowed by the guild. In addition to practising their craft, they began to engage in trade, and thus, by their growing fortune, they surpassed other masters in the same field. So from both sides, from the merchants as well as from the craftsmen, a new group of craft-merchants, industrial merchants arose, who brought the lesser masters into lasting dependence upon their credit and their sales. Gradually they employed these lesser masters to work for them and retained the right of sale for themselves. This procedure is known as "putting-out" enterprise.

In Nuernberg, and especially in Augsburg, which had undergone the craft guild rule, entrepreneurs like these, of the guild of cotton weavers, accumulated such large fortunes that they began to engage in a branch of economic activity which so far had not, or not to any considerable extent, been carried on in Germany, at least by Christians, namely, banking and credit operations. From the fifteenth century on, the German credit business rose rapidly in European scope, and Augsburg became a banking center which exceeded even the Italian cities in importance. "Putting-out" enterprises and bankers, whose business extended over Europe, had existed in Italy. The so-called craft guilds of Florence—the only Italian city where craft guilds rose to an influential position—were, in the main, associations of such entrepreneurs, who carried on trade with the craft products of dependent masters. The German development, however, led to three specific results: first, the unique influence which bankers, or to be more exact, the power of credit reached in Germany—this was caused by the political anarchy of the German Empire—second, the way in which the German bankers utilized the extraordinary opportunity with which they were confronted. Economic-minded as they were, they became the first private entrepreneurs to engage in the mining industry on a large scale, and they developed it into a truly modern industry with all the paraphernalia attaching to it. And together with this development, the proletariat was created, with all the characteristic social conditions of insecurity, lack of proper housing, migrations, the truck system and so on. Labor movements also began in this epoch, the movement of the journeymen who could no longer become masters, and later the revolts and strikes of the industrial workers. The third and the most important result was the rise of a true capitalistic spirit.

The best approach to an understanding of this process and of these results is a survey of the initiator of this whole evolution, a man who had the power to turn the political tide of his era, and on whose private economic interest the destiny of the German Empire hinged. This man was the Augsburg merchant, *Jacob Fugger*.

He was descended from a family of small weavers who, in the typical manner, worked up to a prominent position and to considerable wealth. They gained the respect of their craft guild, held offices, married profitably, rose to the rank of "putting-out" entrepreneurs, made money and began to lend money at interest. The territorial princes concerned with the consolidation and organization of their dominions became the debtors of the Fugger family, and Augsburg, the center of wealth, was frequented by German princes in search of money.

At that time, the securities and mortgages that a money-lender took from princes were properties, revenues and taxes of all kinds, and as the mountainous regions of Germany were especially rich in minerals, these riches played a paramount part in credit transactions. The princes did not handle the actual mining of the ore. They had neither the capital nor the reliable administrative staff for such an undertaking; so they let the license for mining operations to private miners for a tithe of the output or a share of the profits. Moreover, they kept for themselves the right of pre-emption of the output at a price lower than the market price. This right was called monopoly. The word derives from the Greek "monos" and "polein": sole selling. It is an institution that goes back to Hellenistic times when the Egyptian Diadochs reserved for themselves the sale of various particularly profitable goods which yielded them enormous riches. Such revenues and such monopolies were the best securities the German princes could give. And from these princely monopolies the later monopoly, in its broader sense, evolved, when merchants collected monopolies of a particular kind and sought to concentrate in one hand all available monopolies of a special article in order to eliminate competition and to dictate the price.

The Hapsburg princes, whose territories were particularly rich in ore, engaged in business with the early Fuggers. When the Hapsburgs rose to the height of their power, when, at the end of the fifteenth century (1493), Maximilian I became emperor and prepared his shrewd system of marriages which won his family Bohemia, Hungary, Burgundy, the Netherlands and Spain, the greatest of the Fuggers, Jacob, "the Rich", as he was called, took over the management of his family business, and with this, the decisive phase in the connection between these bankers and these emperors began, a connection that lasted for generations. The Hapsburgs were in permanent need of ready funds. Sometimes they were even forced to pawn their table silver and their crown jewels. And the Fuggers wanted the mineral wealth of the Hapsburg territories —Tyrol, Salzburg, Carinthia, Bohemia, Hungary, Spain—wealth that Jacob Fugger gathered into his hands under various titles, as monopolies, licenses, mortgages and purchases, and on which he built up his vast mining industry.

In this relation between the Hapsburgs and the Fuggers, the Hapsburgs were always the petitioners and the Fuggers the conceders. The emperors were always in the hands of Jacob Fugger. Charles V would never have become emperor if Jacob Fugger had opposed him. In the famous election of 1519, all depended on Fugger, as the electoral princes sold their votes extremely high. They even raised their prices from day to day. They wanted to be paid in gold florins and under the guarantee of Jacob Fugger and of nobody else. It was an outright auction between Francis I, King of France, and the Hapsburg prince, Charles, King of Spain. And the reason Fugger decided to give the money to the Hapsburg and not to the king of France was solely the private interest of his mining business. Other great German bankers, Welser, Manlich and Herwarth, often supported the French king instead of their own monarch. And Fugger would have acted likewise, had it not been for his mining industry. Much later he reminded the emperor, in no uncertain terms, that "without my help, Your Imperial Majesty would never have obtained the Roman Crown." The German clerics, especially the princely clerics, carried out the purchases of their prebends through the same Jacob Fugger, who was also banker to the pope, so that Fugger could boast correctly that it was he who appointed the German bishops.

But what did he do with all his tremendous power? He could have become a territorial prince himself, like the great Italian bankers, the Medici, for instance. He could have become an omnipotent minister of the Crown, like Jacques Coeur, the French financier of King Charles VII and of Joan of Arc. But he had no political ambitions. He was not even interested in politics, in the German Empire or in his home community, Augsburg. When one compares what the Medici did for Florence with the meagre donations of Fugger, who was five times as rich, one realizes the striking difference between a merchant prince and a petit bourgeois. Jacob Fugger bought estates and jewels and valuable objects, not for pleasure or for love of splendor, but as an investment and in order to show the power of his credit. And he bought them with the funds of his firm and as the property of his firm. What he actually cared for was his business and nothing else. And here he represented the perfect synthesis of the qualities of a merchant and a craftsman.

He allied himself with a Hungarian, Johann Thurzo, who was a mining expert, a kind of engineer and inventor of special mining procedures. With him he founded a company for the exploitation of copper mines in the Carpathian mountains. Originally, he wanted to protect the copper monopoly he held in various other districts from the powerful Hungarian competition; in fact, he wanted to acquire the copper monopoly for the whole European market. But from this commercial speculation, the company developed into a large industrial enterprise with smelting works and hammer mills, roads and dams which had to be built to facilitate transportation, and an extensive technical apparatus to combine these plants with the vast network of trades and mining industries all over Europe. Not only in the German, Bohemian, Hungarian Hapsburg territories, but also in Sweden, Spain, Silesia, the Fugger company exploited silver, mercury, copper and gold mines. Besides, it carried on a vast trade in goods. In Antwerp, which, largely through the activities of the Fugger company, had become a world market and center of exchange, and also in Venice and Rome, the metals of the Fugger mines and the textiles of the German industrial cities were exchanged for Oriental fabrics, jewels and spices. A large and very profitable branch of the Fugger business was the General Agency of the pope, for collecting the fees for indulgences in Germany, the Northern and Eastern countries.

It was a complex and world-wide system, including banking, trade and industry, and it was all organized and directed by one man, Jacob Fugger. We know a good deal about this system and its organization. We know a good deal about Jacob Fugger's relations with emperors and princes and outstanding personalities of the epoch, but all we know concerns only business. We possess, however, very revealing documents that show his mentality, and the special significance of this mentality, very clearly. We possess the agreements of partnership with his brothers and nephews, and we possess his last will. All these are historical documents of the utmost importance. They are true constitutional charters of the capitalistic system.

The procedure laid down in these documents has been termed family politics. But it is far from being that, it is pure business politics. In these family statutes, the family is an object of solicitude merely to "keep the trade going". From the first agreement, concluded between the brothers in 1494, the first consideration was always the business, the enterprise to which all other aspects were sacrificed. The customary form of a family trading company, according to which all capable members of the family were to direct the business for the rest of the family, was abandoned. Instead, the capital of all family members who take no active part in the business was excluded. Only the three directors of the business remain partners with equal shares in the property. If one of them dies, his heirs must be paid off, with the exception of sons who enter the business, but the paying-off must not take place before three years have elapsed and then only in installments, in order not to disturb the continuity of the business. The heirs must accept the last account without any reclamation. By these regulations, all interference from the outside, all danger of a division of the heritage, is averted.

The second agreement between the brothers is still stricter: "In order to keep our male heirs in the business"—so it begins, all present and future shares in mining industries of the company must be excluded from the general inheritance altogether, and must be retained for the sons who become partners and who, in turn, shall be bound up with their mining property, which they are not allowed to sell or to mortgage. In case one of them wants to retire from business, he loses this mining part of his property and he has no claim to compensation. The same regulation applies to estates, houses, jewels and valuable furniture. Though they may be acquired and used by a single partner, they belong to the common business and may not be sold.

Jacob Fugger, who was the initiator of these agreements, committed himself to them just as strictly as the other partners. And he kept his obligations uncompromisingly. In fact, he curtailed his own wife in the severest way, leaving her only her own dowry and ten thousand florins besides. But his entire huge fortune, including estates and household utensils, was to belong to the business.

This man was no Protestant. He grew up before the Reformation and remained a Catholic all his life, partly because of his business connections with the pope and with the Hapsburg dynasty, but probably also because the Catholic Church was far more tolerant toward the new business procedures than the fanatic Protestant reformers. But oddly enough, his character and mentality were already essentially Protestant, indeed, Puritan. This is due to his origin in the German craft guild city, from which the Protestant Reform issued forth. Jacob Fugger devoted himself entirely to his work, to his business. One of his biographers remarks of him, paraphrasing a saying of the Prussian King Frederick the Great, "He

considered himself as the foremost servant of the Fugger enterprises."

But what was the ultimate significance of this service? When, in
his last years, somebody told him to enjoy his riches, he shook his
head and replied that he was of a different mind, that he wanted to
make money as long as he could. These significant words mark an
epoch, for that "different mind" of Jacob Fugger's is, in fact, the
truly capitalistic mind.

Some modern economists and sociologists have tried to prove
that there were traces of capitalism as far back as in Babylon. But
what they discovered is not capitalism. Capitalism is not identical
with wealth and mobile property, it is not identical with money-
making and money-lending, not even with a mere productive investment of property. All this is no capitalism in itself, for all this
may serve a life principle, alien to economic aims, it may be done
for a human end, a human purpose, for something a human being
can enjoy. But here, for the first time, in this German epoch and in
these German cities, business in itself, money-making in itself,
production of goods and heaping up of comforts, assumed such
power over man that he spent all of his vitality, his heart, all his
present and future, all his *human being,* in the literal sense of the
word, in a restless, a persistently growing and devouring production per se, a production, the final meaning of which he has completely lost and forgotten.

And this is the beginning of capitalism, which is the rule of capital over man, the rule of the economic function over the human
heart. Here begins the autonomy of economy, the restless, boundless progress of exploitation of nature and production of goods
which nobody has the leisure or the capacity to enjoy any longer.
The consequences of this development are today clearly revealed.

POLITICS

IN CORRELATION WITH THE rising autonomy of science, art and economy, a similar process went on in the field of politics. This process

takes us back to the sphere of interhuman relations, to the sphere of the human community. While autonomous art, science and economy established the new relation of man to outward nature as an object of exploration and exploitation, autonomous politics inaugurated a new relation of man to his own human nature, a new method of envisaging, exploring and treating the human soul.

From the thirteenth century on, after the downfall of the Stauffer dynasty, the Holy Roman Empire, the symbol of the terrestrial unity of Christendom, began to crumble and to dissolve into a multitude of rising territorial powers. To be sure, the universality of the Holy Roman Empire had been an idea that never fully materialized. The emperors never had complete command of the European world which they claimed as their dominion. Yet this idea of a universal empire had been very powerful, it had virtually been recognized as legitimate, and it had exerted a great influence on the minds of the people. Now it was shattered. Nations were forming on a secular basis. The Italian city-nations, the French nation were flowering, the Spanish and English nations were slowly developing. All these countries had separated from the empire and had done away with the universal claim of the emperors, who, in turn, became separate powers, not only in relation to the rising states outside the empire, but also in relation to the territories within the empire.

The thirteenth century may be considered as the period of transition from the Middle Ages to the Renaissance. The last Stauffer emperor, Frederick II, represented this transition. He brought to a climax the striving of the emperors for the realization of the Holy Roman Empire and of the universal power it implied, and he pressed to extremes the struggle with the pope, the traditional antagonist of the emperors in this contest for universal power. He was the last emperor to decline an alliance with a European king— the King of England once offered him such an alliance—since, by this act, he would have renounced his imperial claim to universal supremacy. When, after two decades of anarchy, the Hapsburg family took over the imperial rule, the character of the empire had completely changed. Its sacred supremacy had vanished, and

worldly sovereignty was established in all kingdoms and principalities throughout Europe.

This new *concept of sovereignty* is the foundation of modern
politics. Neither the term nor the problem of sovereignty existed in
antiquity. The ancient tribal kingdoms, as well as the polis, were
religious entities. Each was a law unto itself. Each had its own exclusive standard which did not apply to any other community.
There were, of course, relations between these communities. There
was trade, there was an interchange of courtesies between rulers.
But there was no common sphere, no common standard of values
which would have made it necessary or natural to define or outline
one system with regard to the other, to state explicitly the intrinsic
independence of a tribal or political rule. A tribe or polis could be
conquered and freed again. But these changes of the present state
did not affect or cast doubt upon the basic legitimacy, the actual
independence of this unit, which had its roots in a divine order.
The nature of the relation between the ancient units is clearly characterized by the Greek term "barbarian". Barbarian was the entire
non-Greek world, which did not count and was not on the level
at which comparisons can be made. The problem of sovereignty
could not arise until a world religion prevailed, a super-tribal,
super-national religion that established a common spiritual sphere
and a common spiritual standard for the different communities
and principalities.

Christianity established the sacred superiority of a universal order,
from which the particular worldly dominions derived their authorization and legitimacy. This Christian, universal order became
effective in two forms: in the spiritual universal rule of the church,
and in the terrestrial universal rule of the Holy Roman Empire.
And the problem and term of sovereignty came into being when
worldly powers developed in opposition to both church and empire.

Sovereignty was first the maintenance of rulership in the face
of superiors. Later, when external sovereignty had been achieved,
the claim of integral rulership was turned inward and was upheld
against inferiors, the lords and the diets. And this internal sovereignty is identical with what is known as absolutism, the doctrine

and practice of the "ancien régime". The French kingdom of the
Capet family was the first to secede from the Holy Roman Empire.
It refused to recognize the supremacy of the German emperor, who
was unable to enforce his claim. The French kings were also the
first to reject the interference of the papacy in French internal
affairs and the influence of the papacy on the French clergy. The
French kings, finally, were the first to introduce the institution of
the "legists", the prototypes of modern officials and ministers of
state, whose task was to check, and, if possible, to destroy the power
of the feudal lords, and to prepare a restitution of the ancient Roman Law, remnants of which were still alive in the customs of the
country. And this implied the restoration of the imperial Roman
concept of rulership as a centralized absolute monarchy, sustained
by officialdom.

So the three elements of sovereignty, emancipation from the
papacy, emancipation from the empire and emancipation from the
feudal lords, were all active in the Kingdom of France. It is, therefore, no wonder that France not only furnished the pattern for all
rising territorial powers, but that she also developed the theory of
sovereignty, the ideological support of the position of the new
territorial rulers. This theory of sovereignty, the first clear definition of modern, secular rulership, started from the opposition
against the papacy and the interference of the Roman Church in
the internal affairs of the kingdom. It was a direct result of the
conflict between King Philippe le Bel and Pope Boniface VIII,
who was captured by the king in Anagni, 1303, an event which
was the prelude to the captivity of the papacy in Avignon, 1305–
1378. The plain statement of the king's sovereignty is of even earlier
origin; in the "Etablissements de St. Louis", a collection of legal
maxims from the time of King Louis IX (the Saint, 1226–1270), it
was expressed for the first time: "Li rois n'a point de souverain es
choses temporiex"—The King has no sovereign in temporal affairs.

The *theory of sovereignty* is the melting pot in which ancient
ideas were transformed for modern political use by very different
forces and to very different ends. Its effects extend not only to the

establishment and the legitimation of the absolute monarchy in France, England and Germany, but also to the French Revolution and the Bill of Rights. And this theory, and so, by implication, the development of the autonomy of politics, is, on its part, based on a new concept of nature, of the working of nature in human institutions. It centers in the so-called *"natural law"*, as distinguished from historic law laid down in codes, or in arbitrary and changing human speculation. Natural law is conceived as eternal, inalienable law, inherent in nature herself, her creatures and her procedures, and discernible by reason.

This concept again goes back to the Greek theories, to the very same Greek realization of the contrast between divine eternity and human change which was the prime motive of all Greek speculation. In this special case, it was necessary to explain why forms of rulership, constitutions and institutions changed in human society, while, unquestionably, an eternal order reigns in the cosmos. This gave rise to the fundamental distinction between an eternal, natural law, which was identical with law in accordance with the underlying Logos, and human, historical law, which was subject to change and to the defective interpretation of human beings. The great pre-Socratic thinker, Heraclitus (about 500 B.C.) raised this problem for the first time. He, of course, as well as Socrates, Plato and Aristotle, considered the sacred law of the polis the closest approximation to the ideal, natural law, and the actual "walls of the city", while the revolutionary Sophists contended that the Athenian law, which they wanted changed, contradicted the natural law. The natural law, the "agraphoi nomoi", the unwritten laws, according to the Sophists and the still more radical Cynics, implied an equal "natural right" for all human beings. A synthesis of the various versions of the problem is to be found in the Stoic interpretation on which the Christian theory of natural law was based. To the Stoics, all law is rooted in nature. Man has an innate knowledge of right and wrong, and true law does not rest on the arbitrary will of a ruler, or on a popular resolution, but on nature, on the law that is born with us, the "lex nata". According to this sacred law of nature, everybody is born equal, with an equal claim to love and comradeship and an equal understanding of right and wrong. The Roman Stoic, Seneca, was the first to proclaim the maxim: "Homo sacra res homini"—to man the human being is a sacred thing. This natural law, so the Stoics contended, has existed from the beginning of time, but has been corrupted by the historical development of man, which led to the imperfect "positive law" and the institution of despotism and slavery. The Stoic theories contributed greatly to the evolution of Roman Law, they brought about the recognition of the individual in civil law, they promoted the transformation of the old tribal law by the "jus gentium", the peregrine law, and they influenced the great Roman jurists and philosophers, of the time of Justinian, who codified Roman Law.

Thus the most radical views and arguments, which later fomented the European revolutions, had already been advanced by Greek thinkers, only that Greek "nature" was not nature in our sense of the word. It was not secularized, but divine nature, identical with the eternal, divine order of the cosmos, and identical with the divine Logos. Therefore, Stoic natural law became the foundation for Christian natural law in which nature fused with the order of God.

This *theory of natural law* underwent curious treatments and interpretations on the verge of the Middle Ages. It turned somersaults, it served every conceivable purpose, it supported diametrically opposed views.

First, it was used by the Christian advocates of the papacy in its struggle for supremacy over the emperors: natural law was divine law, infinitely superior to human, historic law, and could, of course, be administered only by the church. When the antagonism to the emperor became obsolete, and much more dangerous adversaries arose in the shape of territorial rulers, especially of the French monarchs, the new apologists of the cause of the pope, Dominicans and Jesuits, the so-called Monarchomachs—fighters against monarchs—changed the direction of the theory of natural law according to the new circumstances. They complied with the popular trends, manifested in the rise of the bourgeoisie, and the monastic, mystic and Protestant movements, and they attacked the territorial rulers from within their own territories, from a most vulnerable point— their subjects. To this end they shifted from reference to the imme- diate authority of divine nature to emphasis on the natural sov- ereignty of the people, in which, and through which, divine nature expressed herself. This tended to legalize even revolution and regicide. The argument ran as follows: God created nature, and nature, in the course of events, produced the perfect human com- munity. The consensus of this community is the only source of the authority of the ruler. The ultimate purpose of this theory was to deprive the territorial rulers of all immediate authorization by God, which, in fact, they usurped in calling themselves kings or princes "by the Grace of God" or by divine right. The natural sovereignty of the people was to be only a medium, and to remain subject to immediate divine nature which exerts its control through the church. In this way, however, the church herself introduced and stirred up the most revolutionary impulses.

The kings and princes answered with an argument which again refers to natural law, to the natural evolution of human institu- tions. The advocates of the monarchs contended that natural gre- gariousness is the origin of all human community life. The nucleus is the family, which gradually, by propagation and union, develops into rural communities, into provinces and eventually into states. But, so goes the monarchical theory, even animal communities, the communities of ants, bees and cranes, show born leaders, and, on the part of the followers, natural subordination. Similarly, sov- ereignty and obedience are inherent in all human communities. In a well-behaved family, the father exerts domestic power over the wife, the children and the servants. And this domestic power of the father is the true prototype and model of the power of the sovereign of the state. As the wife, the children and the servants, being weaker by nature, subordinate themselves to the father, so, in the evolution of larger communities, the weaker bow to the stronger and by this subordination, openly or tacitly, transfer their natural rights and liberties to the sovereign, once and for all. Through this procedure, the sovereignty or majesty or absolute power of the ruler is brought into being and authorized. According to its nature, this sovereignty is limitless and indivisible.

This is the monarchical argument, as it was advanced in the sixteenth century by the French scholar, Jean Bodin (1530–1596), the friend and counsellor of King Henry III. But Jean Bodin was a tolerant man, even a liberal man, who compromised with the rising forces of enlightenment and has been suspected of sympathizing with the Huguenots. To him, the French monarchy was a "res publica", a republic, although the natural sovereignty of the people was included in the sovereignty of the republic, which, in turn, was embodied in the monarch. Later, the absolute monarchy did not feel secure with the derivation of its authority from the natural consent of a sovereign people, be this consent ever so mythical and irrevocable. For, after all, it was the same basic assumption from which their most fanatical opponents, the monarchomachs, derived their arguments in favor of revolt. So eventually the monarchs and the integral monarchists dropped the theory of natural law and replaced it by the thesis of the direct authorization of the sovereign by God, a thesis exemplified by the divine appointment and anointing of the kings in the Bible. This thesis was advanced in France by Cardinal Richelieu (1585–1642) and by the bishop and educator of the son of Louis XIV, Jacques Bénigne Bossuet (1627–1704), and in England by the Stuart kings, James I (1603–1625) and Charles I (1625–1649). It was a dead end, though, and did not lead any further.

The future belonged to a fourth theory, which again is based on natural law: the theory of the true sovereignty of the people, as it was started by the Calvinistic republicans. This theory derives from the basic concept that the state originated in a free, deliberate covenant of human individuals asserting their natural rights, and it leads straight to the great European revolutions from which modern democracy was born.

As for the functioning of the sovereignty of the new territorial powers, the crucial innovation in their maintenance and expansion was a new, cold, methodical, entirely rational scrutiny of human nature in order to find an adequate treatment for the many human types and individuals, and to utilize the various human weaknesses for gaining control and rulership over men. It was a new applied psychology which can be classed roughly under the term *diplomacy*. Such a new scrutiny and treatment of others implied a new knowledge and a new treatment and discipline and restraint of oneself, of one's own soul.

Diplomacy as a human attitude was, of course, age-old. There have always been diplomatic characters. Ancient history is full of them. A fully developed political and social life, such as the Roman, its many contacts and forms of intercourse, the friction and adjustments among equal competitors for rank and power and wealth—all this involved the development of diplomacy. But it was a naive, spontaneous, instinctive diplomacy, there was no attempt at a conscious use, a methodical searching and training of this faculty. The first true school of diplomacy in this new sense was again the Catholic Church. The very principle of its existence, the coordination of different tendencies, stocks, intellectual trends, of various grades and types of human faculty and character, required a very refined art of treating people. The Holy See was the center of a system of world-wide relations which had to be balanced and managed to the utmost advantage of the church. The papacy knew how to impress people by ceremonial display, by magnificent spectacles. It knew how to avail itself of the service of secret agents and unofficial mediators without losing face. Every ecclesiastical council was a scene of such official pomp and secret machinations, by which the true issues were reached. The papacy perfected the institution of special delegates and nuncios, whose task was not only to carry a message, or to negotiate, but also to sound a situation and to spy out potential allies and opponents. For a very long time, diplomats were regarded merely as "honorable spies" and met with the utmost suspicion and misgivings on the part of rulers and population.

When we discussed the difference between the medieval emperors and the new dynasties that rose to power after the anarchy of the thirteenth century, the Hapsburgs, the Luxemburgs and other families that achieved territorial rule, we saw that new faculties were needed for the task of consolidating and gaining control· of these territories. It was not the violent, aggressive exuberance of the former lords, and not the power of an immediate, overwhelming intensity of temperament, which was required now; it was patience, economy of forces and means, caution and calculation. All the new families exhibit these features. What a striking contrast between the Stauffers, these brilliant gamblers and adventurers, and the Hapsburgs, unostentatious, guarded and shrewd, who planned and acted for a long future, indeed, for generations. They were the first masters of diplomacy on a European throne, and their teacher was the Roman Church.

As a historian of diplomacy puts it, however, the Roman Church appears only as the high school of diplomacy when we confront it with the Republic of Venice, which may be considered as a university of diplomacy. This powerful republic, which in the fifteenth century gained control of half of Northern Italy, of the whole Adriatic Sea, Istria, Dalmatia, the major part of the Greek archipelago, Candia and Cyprus, which had established a vast system of colonies and fortified ports around the Mediterranean—today we should call them bases—which owned a fleet of 3,500 merchantmen, a navy of forty-five galleys manned by 12,000 sailors—this mighty republic was especially predestined and directed to the mastery of diplomatic technique by the particular structure of its constitution. It was ruled by a class of merchant patricians who were anxious to uphold a stable government and to prevent continuous upheavals and changes in rulership, which had weakened the power of the other Italian city-republics. On the other hand, they knew one another and themselves very well, they knew the temptations of ambition and will-to-power to which they were most susceptible. So they established a strict system of common discipline and complex mutual control. Every one of them was constantly watched and prevented from rising to individual prominence. Whatever one of them achieved on behalf of the community was not considered as a personal accomplishment, but was credited to the republic, or to the ruling class to which he belonged and which was identical with the republic. Achievements as well as honors were shared by all alike. They had to wear black in order to make personal distinction impossible. To move within this atmosphere of utter suspicion, was extremely difficult and dangerous; and on the part of the individual, as well as on the part of the government, this system required and brought about a high perfection of diplomacy. A living reflection of this situation was the mysterious atmosphere of this curious city itself, an atmosphere that can be sensed even today. Under the gay exterior of feasts, carnivals and merriment, lurked an uncanny gloom that made it quite plausible that every now and again a man might disappear suddenly and forever from a laughing group—which was a not unusual occurrence.

This internal diplomacy, which was the very life of the Venetian aristocracy, was only the training field for the vast system of international diplomatic service which was introduced by this republic. First of all, Venice inaugurated the institution of commercial diplomacy, that is, of the modern consular system. At all important centers of trade, the Venetians had their "bailos", representatives and agents, who exercised the functions of the consuls of today. The "bailos" had to supervise the shipment of goods, to negotiate on tariffs, duties and excises. They exerted police authority and even judicial power over Venetian citizens living in the city where they held office. And, like modern diplomats, they also had the right of exterritoriality. These consular officials had to make out reports and to keep "diaries" that show a remarkable capacity for cool and clever observation of the conditions and ways of life of foreign populations. But these diaries are insignificant compared with the famous reports of the Venetian ambassadors, unique documents of the history of diplomacy and a treasure-trove of description and characterization of the outstanding personalities and events of the epoch. These reports show the Venetian diplomats at work, observing the appearance, the temperament, the habits and the surroundings of all the rulers and statesmen of the time. The salient figures of European politics, the Hapsburg emperors and kings, Francis I and Henry IV of France, Henry VIII of

England, the popes, the Turkish sultans—all are described in minute detail: how they worked, loved, enjoyed themselves; whom they favored and who had influence upon them, what sort of men and women had access to them.

A few notes on the Hapsburg king, Philip II of Spain, will illustrate the type of these reports and, at the same time, the new type of ruler. "The king prefers to handle affairs through documents, because he does not like to talk to many people. He is more expedite in writing than any secretary . . . He keeps an eye on all his affairs and knows everything . . . He reads by the light of a candle before sleeping . . . The nuncio of the pope said that he has now been at the court for five years and that the king has never talked to him except on official affairs, and his answers have always contained mere generalities . . . The king is extremely suspicious. His servants say: 'From a smile to the knife there is only finger's breadth' . . . The king is of a kind, that he would not move or betray himself by any movement, even if there were a cat in his trousers." From these few features, we can gauge the character. The method of cumulative observation unfolds the picture of the soul.

Venice had brought the art of diplomacy to rare perfection. But we can find a similar method and procedure in all the city-republics of the Renaissance. The institution of permanent ambassadors was first introduced by Francesco Sforza, the Duke of Milan. The particular contribution of Florence was that it furnished the theoretical foundation of the art of domination, the first theory of power, evolved by Niccolò Machiavelli.

Machiavelli's theory marks an epoch, not so much because its analysis and its conclusions and recommendations convey substantially new experiences. Many rulers and politicians before him had shaped their conduct along his lines. But what is new and epoch-making is his candid and ruthless awareness, his fearless facing and expressing of facts. Very much had had to happen before this was possible.

Machiavelli's theory, however, has been misinterpreted in many respects by superficial representation—especially in our days. It is essential to keep in mind the personal circumstances of the man, which are the premises for his theory. Machiavelli, who lived from 1469 to 1527, came of a noble Florentine family, that had held high offices in the Republic through centuries, but had finally become impoverished. In an interval between the expulsion and the restoration of the Medici family, around 1500, that is to say, in a brief republican interregnum, he held the office of secretary to the republican government, to the so-called "Ten Men for Freedom and Peace". In the fourteen years of this official service, he acted as a correspondent in internal and foreign affairs, he drew up the treaties with foreign powers and successfully carried out many special missions as an envoy of his city. Four times he was sent to the King of France, twice to the emperor, and twice to the pope. He is even credited with an important innovation: he attempted to transform the mercenary army of Florence into a national militia.

When the rule of the Medici was restored, he was imprisoned and dismissed, and from then on he lived in very poor circumstances on his little estate near Florence, prevented from using his political genius in the service of his country. He was a man of action and he suffered from his forced inactivity, all the more since, with pain and sorrow, he watched anarchy spreading among the Italian cities, ruinous party strife, and the perpetual invasion and ravaging of Italy by the Spanish and French armies. It was the time when the Hapsburg Charles V and the French Francis I were engaged in their struggle for Italy. The Italian cities, in their disunion and division and with their small mercenary armies, were unable to stem the tide. They were victims of the intrigues and appetites of the mighty.

So Machiavelli, eliminated from the political scene of action, unable to utilize his knowledge and experience, wrote his famous book, "Il Principe", ("The Prince"), which, as it is to be expected from a thoroughgoing politician, is a mixture of opportunism and true conviction. His motives are revealed in a letter written from his country place, on December 10, 1513, to his friend, Francesco

Vettori, who was the Florentine ambassador to Rome: "When evening comes," he writes, "I go home and step into my study, take off my dirty and dusty peasant garb and put on a robe of state, and so I enter the venerable courts of the ancients where I am kindly received and provided with the fare which is so truly mine and for which I am born. Then I do not feel shy in asking them the reasons for their deeds, and they answer me, and for hours I am free from trouble, I forget my hardships, and I no longer fear poverty and death . . . And so I have put down what I gained from these talks, and I wrote a little paper on the principality . . . what it is . . . how it is won and upheld, and how it may be lost. If you have ever liked any of my whims, this one will please you. And to a prince, especially a new prince, it should be most welcome, I think. For that reason I am addressing it to Giuliano de' Medici . . . I am compelled to do so by the necessity that urges me, as I am eating out my heart and cannot go on like this without being contemptible because of my poverty. Besides, I wish these Medici gentlemen would take me into their service—if only to let me move stones for them. For if I could not succeed in winning them over, I should be sorry for myself! If they read this little book, it will prove to them that I have neither slept nor wasted my time during these fifteen years I have spent on politics. And anybody should be glad to employ a man who has become rich in experience at the cost of others."

From this letter, one motive for writing the book becomes clear: Machiavelli wanted to get back into active life. And so he thought that some hints as to how to handle and retain rulership might serve as an introduction to the prince. But this is not the only and not the main motive of the book. This is the letter of a practical man, but it is not the tone of a simple career-hunter. This becomes even more evident from the book itself, which is not only objectively, but also subjectively, a frank document. The harshness of its statements betrays a profound bitterness and disillusionment concerning human nature, indeed, a "metaphysical despair", as G. A. Borgese, the historian of Fascism, puts it. "The lust for power and property," says Machiavelli, "is a very natural thing. And those who indulge in it, will always be praised and never rebuked if they have the power to satisfy their appetites. Only when they have the appetites without the power, then they are considered guilty and criminal . . . One must remember that men must be either caressed or destroyed, for a slight insult they will avenge, but against a heavy blow, they are powerless . . . Those cruelties are well employed—if it be permissible to use the term well of evil things—that are administered at one blow for self-preservation, and that are pursued no further, but even exploited for the good of one's subjects. Those cruelties that are used sparingly at first and increasingly later on, are ill employed. Therefore, outrages and injuries should be inflicted all at once. In this way, there is less time for them to be felt, they cannot hurt to their full extent. Favors, on the other hand, should be rendered gradually, so as to give them time to be appreciated . . . One should not permit oneself robbery, since the death of a parent is more easily forgotten by men, than the loss of a heritage . . . War cannot be abolished, it can only be delayed. But in this case, it is the enemy who profits . . . How laudable and worthy it is for a prince to be loyal and to live in righteousness and without deceit, is evident. But experience shows that princes who cared nothing for faithfulness and who knew how to turn people's heads by deceit, got the better of those who relied on their righteousness . . . So it is not at all necessary, indeed, it is not even useful for a prince to have good qualities, but it is necessary and useful that he appear to have such qualities . . . He should care only for being victorious and for maintaining his ruler-ship. His means will always be declared honorable . . . for the mob will always be captivated by what appears on the surface, and by the final outcome. And in all the world, there is nothing but mob . . ."

Some of these sentences sound like well-known utterances of Mussolini and Hitler, utterances that can, in fact, often be traced back to Machiavelli. But there is a very important difference. In Machiavelli, a clear knowledge of these things was attained by a man who still knew what is noble and what is dignified, it was attained from a background where all human values were still effective. This background is more clearly apparent in the other books of Machiavelli which he wrote during the same period and which differ essentially from the teachings of "The Prince". And the very bitterness and strain by which this knowledge was acquired, the ruthless striving toward truth, reality and objectivity, this sense of the factual, distinguish Machiavelli from the Fascists of today, who have completely lost the sense for truth, who have been carried away and overwhelmed by their own deceits, who have fused with their own hoax. A clear awareness, a true psychological knowledge like Machiavelli's, can be sustained and maintained only by someone able to hold himself on a plane beyond and above the facts, a plane from which he surveys events and people and even himself. But when the methods of "The Prince" are applied indiscriminately, when man becomes accustomed to a world he has perverted, his very foundation totters and what remains is mere criminality and bestiality.

In the last chapter of "The Prince", the inmost motive of Machiavelli comes to the fore. It is a passionate appeal for a savior of Italy. A new sense of Italian community, of a common Italian nationality, emerged from his grief and anxiety at the anarchy and helplessness which let the Italian cities become objects of the great rivalries of foreign rulers. And just as Dante, two centuries earlier, had appealed to the Emperor Henry VII to re-establish peace and order in the Christian world, and to become the imperial savior of Christendom, so Machiavelli appealed to the Medici to establish order and unity in Italy and to save her from the barbarians. It was a desperate appeal, for there was not even a definite person to whom it could be directed. The book was meant for Giuliano Medici who died before it could reach him. His nephew, Lorenzo, to whom it was ultimately dedicated, was a mediocre substitute. And the man Machiavelli had actually had in mind, in writing his book, was Cesare Borgia, the shrewd and violent Duke of the Romagna, who had perished years before as a fugitive in a skirmish in Spain. The savior did not appear; instead, this dangerous book became the bible of unscrupulous rulers throughout the centuries.

In France the new methods of exploring and mastering human nature developed further. The first pragmatic psychology came into being, the first consideration of the individual human soul— one's own and that of others—with a hitherto unknown freedom from religious and moral premises. Michel de Montaigne (1533– 1592), the descendant of a noble family of Gascony, lived in the Epicurean retirement of his castle and wrote his famous "Essays" with the intention of "studying myself rather than any other subject." His point of departure is doubt of the general validity of the moral laws, which seem to him rather the result of customs, and differently developed among different peoples. With sceptical superiority, he deprecates the fanaticism of conflicting beliefs. He strives toward an "art of living", toward a harmonious form of life that is according to nature and yet not subject to nature, that is characterized by self-control but not by self-suppression. He strives toward an "absolute, as it were, divine perfection in legitimately enjoying one's own existence" and searches for the means to achieve this perfection. The entire body of the extensive "Mémoires" of French statesmen and courtiers, is marked by this half exploratory, half pleasurable form of psychology, by this desire to know men, to deal with them correctly, to exploit them, and at the same time, to form one's own mind to yield the greatest possible power and happiness. Self-control is desirable, not only in order to control others, but to taste the proud delight of the supremacy of one's own rational will over one's own nature. It is a mixture of Stoicism and Epicureanism, but without the religious roots that gave a vital meaning to these trends in antiquity. It is a new and completely profane form of asceticism, aesthetic asceticism, asceticism for the display of a sovereign personality. The chief aim is to lead an exquisite life, a life of elegance in the true meaning of this word—selective, with taste and propriety. And such an attitude toward life excludes formless or unrestrained emotions; for unleashed feelings, unaware of themselves, cannot be savored, tasted, and so they can easily be "in bad taste". In this way, diplomacy became more refined and more spiritual. It began to permeate private life, both private inner life and social life.

The extremes to which this rational Epicureanism was carried can be seen in "Les Liaisons Dangereuses", a novel of the late eighteenth century, by Choderlos de Laclos, in which the author describes the a-moral toying with their own souls that the members of the French aristocracy indulged in: how they did not permit themselves human impulses—love—indeed treated expressly those they loved in the most pitiless manner, out of sheer delight in a brilliant, frivolous power over themselves and others.

As soon as the unrestricted sovereignty of the many territorial and national units had been established, and the competition for power among these sovereign dominions had broken loose, as soon as extreme national individualism had been created, the opposite trend toward *international collectivity* came into being.

As the idea of a universal Christian community, of the Holy Empire, lost its power, a vague anxiety dawned in human minds, a presentiment of the international anarchy to come. All that was left of the old universal order was the attempt to establish the so-called "balance of power". Such attempts were largely the result of fear in a group of nations that one dynasty or nation among them might become too powerful. Accordingly, leagues and alliances were formed, and these gave rise to counter-alliances. A balance could be maintained only through consecutive wars and intrigues and a continuous change in partnership of the groups concerned. The founder of the power of the Medici, Cosimo, was the first to conceive of a system of balance of power among the Italian republics, under the veiled hegemony of Florence. Later, England became the classical representative of the principle of balance of power. Its insular remoteness and the economic character of its sovereignty predestined it for this role. The efforts toward equilibrium in imports and exports led to the attempt to establish political equilibrium also. From Henry VIII on, whose maxim it was, "Cui adhaereo praeest"—He, with whom I am allied, has superiority—England has always taken the part of the weaker in order to maintain this equilibrium. And this policy proved to be very profitable to the country. In an address to parliament, December 31, 1701, this attitude of the government was for the first time proclaimed as a principle, and since that time, this principle has been voiced almost every time an English king addressed parliament.

Another attempt in the direction of international collectivity was the ideological Utopia and the theoretical effort to bring about international agreements, international law and international organization. Such efforts arose in the most various quarters: the Dominican, Francisco Victoria (died 1546) and the Jesuit, Francisco Suarez (1548–1617) emphasized that "humanity, although it is divided into peoples and states, still possesses a certain unity, not only as far as race is concerned, but morally and politically too. This is proven by the natural admonition to mutual love and charity that holds good for all people of all nations. And so, although every state, republic or kingdom is a complete entity in itself . . . they are never self-sufficient to such an extent that they are independent of one another's help and cooperation . . . Because of this, they require laws that guide them to such cooperation and give directions for it." These Spanish clerics even ventured to say that the infidel have a right to own property—a very important point in regard to the colonial conquests—and that religious differences did not constitute a reason for war. Alberico Gentile (1551–1611), whom the Inquisition persecuted as a heretic and who was later a professor at Oxford, wrote a treatise, "De Jure Belli", in which he tried to establish a body of laws that would be valid even in case of war. These laws were based on the unchangeable laws of nature, particularly of human nature, on an "instinctus naturae" identical with the sublime common sense of humanity. In the seventeenth century, the German philosopher, Christian Wolff, even worked out a complicated plan for a league of nations and the means by which individual nations could be forced to fulfill their obligations.

The first reply to Machiavelli, whether or not it was intended as such (which is not certain), was made by the Dutch humanist, Desiderius Erasmus of Rotterdam, who denounced the ambition and vanity of princes and advocated a system of international arbitration and peaceful settlement of all disputes. He claimed that wars were not waged for the good of a people, but only to satisfy the ambition of some prince or other. But, of course, it was "The Prince" of Machiavelli, and not the "Institutio Principis Christiani" of Erasmus, that became the manual of the European rulers. And the history of all projects for lasting peace and international organizations, from Erasmus and Grotius and the Abbé de St. Pierre to Rousseau, Jeremy Bentham and Immanuel Kant, and to the League of Nations, makes rather a depressing record.

All these attempts were necessarily doomed to failure, as all lasting and reliable international agreements between individual nations and states presuppose such agreements within all nations and states. An international peace organization presupposes a national peace organization, that is, a true democracy that works effectively, and up to now there were only a few countries in the world where such an even temporarily true democracy could be maintained. The gravity of the problem is increased by the fact that it would require the establishment of such a democracy in all nations in order to guarantee a solid international peace organization. After all the experiences in our epoch, it must be apparent to everybody that the readiness of a number of great nations to cooperate is of no avail, provided that even a single powerful state is left to defy such cooperation. This fateful problem, that obsesses us today, emerged in the Renaissance with the establishing of many sovereign states, with the principle of sovereignty and the theory of power. It leads to the discussion of the European anarchy that prevailed throughout the modern era.

ANARCHY AND TRANSCENDENCE
OF THE SECULAR WORLD

SECULARIZATION MEANT ABOVE ALL that the earthly realm became autonomous, that man became independent of religion and lived by reason, face to face with objectivated, physical nature. But the autonomy of the earthly realm implied that the various divisions and functions of human life became independent, not only of the power of religion, but of one another. The norm-giving role of religion was gradually taken over by public morality. The Catholic, universal church, which was to comprise the whole of Christianity, disintegrated into various national churches, and, in the Protestant countries, the ruler of the state again became the head of the church. But while, in the pre-Christian era, the union of religious and political rulership had signified the predominance of religion over the state and over the whole of human life, it now represented the predominance of the state and the worldly community over religion, the dependence of religion upon profane purposes and requirements. From this time on, religion, to be sure, became a province of its own, a separate department of human life, but it was the least independent, the least vital activity of all, it was the dilute residue of a once all-comprising force. Religion became a separate province by dint of being more and more restricted in its effectiveness and in its sphere of action.

The very process that ended the autonomy of religion brought about the autonomy of science, of art, of economy, of politics, the development of which we followed in the last chapters. None of these worldly, purely human activities, however, could either claim the entire heritage or take over the comprehensive character of religion. When man was released from this all-comprising power, his manifold special human forces, activities and aims were set free. And as there was no longer an unquestioned superhuman order automatically to restrict and hold together the myriad impulses and inclinations of the human being, these continued unchecked, in a more and more scattered and specialized development. The process of autonomization went on, as all the means, methods and instruments created in the deployment of the new autonomous activities gradually became ends in themselves, and this process eventually brought about the profound anarchy which today prevails in the human world. The emancipated activities and techniques outgrew the mastery of the human being, who became increasingly helpless to hold them together, to coordinate and integrate them. The disparities and discrepancies arising within this crowded system of human life, and the growing incapacity for meeting the situation, aroused the human mind to the secret anxiety and panic which is one of the intrinsic causes of the present world-catastrophe.

As a consequence of the autonomization of human activities, man faced the task of consciously recovering the conformity and consistency of his world on the basis of his new, worldly, empirical experiences. And a recovery of the concept of a consistent order of the world is the prerequisite for man's mastery of his world and his life. The effort necessary to organize the overgrown divisions of human experience and knowledge, to overcome the anarchy of the human world, leads inevitably to the transcendence of the individual and to the progressive collectivization of the human world and of human life. Rationalization and technology are bound to produce a collective form of life, as will become apparent in the following discussion.

NATION

THE RISING AUTONOMY OF POLITICS manifested itself in the establishing of the principle of sovereignty and its theoretical justification, in a new, rational method of exploring and treating human nature to the end of the maintenance and expansion of power, that is to say, diplomacy, and in the theoretical legitimation of these methods, the theory of power. From the aspect of human evolution, modern history, however, consists not only in the struggle between particular powers. Of prime significance is the rise, the friction, the growing antagonism of different *forms of rule.* Up to the first world war, history meant essentially political history: the setting down of wars, revolutions, diplomatic intrigues and treaties, the study of leaders and statesmen, their political designs and attainments. The mere shift of predominance absorbed the main, if not the entire, interest of historians. This kind of history, which has been well called "drum and trumpet history", no longer concerns us greatly. Its value stands and falls with the point of view which considers political power the highest achievement of man. Although we are still in the grip of this mentality and are forced to endure the consequences of its sway, another concept of human life and another state of mind, to which political history is merely boring, have long been forming.

In tracing the struggle between various kinds of sovereignty, we may distinguish four essentially and characteristically different forms of rule, or community, which have been contesting with one another from the sixteenth century to the beginning of the twentieth century: the empire, the nation, the democracy, and the state. Although all of these different forms occur more or less simultaneously during the entire modern age, the weight, the vital significance, the center of gravity shifts from one to the other so that we are justified in considering them as consecutive stages in human evolution. In the course of their own evolution, some peoples pass through several of these types; they develop from one into the other, thus demonstrating them as successive historical stages. In following such changes, we shall recognize a definite trend toward collectivity in this sequence of the forms of rule.

The oldest of these forms is the *empire,* as it traces back directly to the Roman Empire. The basic feature of this prototype of all later empires was the integral monarchy, as the emperor derives from the office of the imperator which implied unrestricted command. According to its Caesarian origin, moreover, it was a purely personal monarchy, which did not develop into a dynasty until later. It was, at any rate, understood as being essentially different from the kingdom, which is a monarchy derived from divine origin or from a sacred or traditional aristocracy. A further basic feature of the Roman Empire was its universality, the inclusion of all the peoples of the inhabited world under one rule and in one community. And a third feature was the centralization of the regime, the convergence of rule in a core, in a dominating model home community from which it took its issue. This convergence later developed into bureaucratic centralization. These three basic features of the Roman Empire set the example, and determined all subsequent empires, though none of these latter combined and realized all of them as completely as the Roman prototype.

The successor of the Roman Empire was the Holy Roman Empire, which, owing to its feudal structure, lacked centralization. The other element of the empire, universality, deteriorated steadily through the ages. Gradually the meaning of the term "empire" was stripped of its universal quality altogether, and reduced to the designation of a monarchical rule, including populations and compact areas of different stocks.

In the modern period, the Holy Roman Empire persisted as a mere shadow, a relic, a retrospective idea. This idea, however, with the glory of its past and of its universal claim and splendor, still exerted a lasting influence, a magic fascination on German minds throughout the centuries, to such an extent, indeed, as to hinder and misdirect German evolution. It was stubbornly upheld by the Hapsburg dynasty, that used it as a shield and a screen for its unfounded claim to super-national rule. The Hapsburgs were not based upon a specific nation, but solely upon their family power and family cohesion. They were instinctively and violently anti-national. They maintained themselves as emperors, as the pre-eminently imperial family, and shrewdly played on the sentimental German allegiance to the outworn but seductive idea of the Empire.

And when, as a result of the Napoleonic wars, even the ghostly husk of the Holy Roman Empire vanished, and the Hapsburg Emperor, Francis II, renounced his German Imperial Crown in 1806 in transferring his crown and title to his private Hapsburg dominion, he founded the empire of Austria, later Austria-Hungary, which lasted another century until it crumbled in the first world war. According to the modern concept of empire, the dynastic Hapsburg monarchy of Austria-Hungary, which comprised populations of different stock, was a model empire. Throughout the modern era, we shall find the Hapsburgs the exponents and supporters of the principle of empire, be it as Holy Roman or as Austrian emperors.

We must still consider later versions of the empire, in order to clarify their character. There were three: the German Reich, as it was founded by Bismarck, the Napoleonic Empire, and the colonial empire, the pattern of which was set by the British Empire. None of these are genuine, pure empires.

The German term Reich derives from the Latin "regnum", kingdom, and, following the evolution of the Frankish regnum into the Holy Roman Empire, the name Reich was transferred to the Empire, and has remained the German designation for empire since that time. The so-called second German Reich, founded by Bismarck—in reality it was the first true German Reich, the first superficial unification of the German people—was no actual empire, as it consisted of an almost exclusively German population, with the exception of small Polish and Danish minorities. It was a federation of territorial states under the leadership of Prussia, whose king, through the constitution, received the title of German Emperor, not Emperor of Germany. It was called Reich because of the sentimental and edifying appeal of this ambitious title, which, moreover, emphasized the competition and, at least, parity with the Austrian and the Russian Empires.

The Napoleonic Empire approximated the original character of the empire most closely, and was, in fact, a conscious emulation of the Roman Empire, as is manifest even in the art and styles of the period. After the first great conquests of foreign countries and populations by the armies of the French Revolution, it was established as an imperatorial, autocratic rule of a revolutionary, personal monarch who wanted to avoid the allusion to the traditional, royal monarchy of the "ancien régime". Napoleon derived his authority from the French Revolution which had been directed against the "ancien régime". The Napoleonic Empire, like the Roman, evolved from and centered in the predominant country of its origin, and finally it renewed the claim of universality, of world domination. It was, however, a mere episode in an essentially national evolution which remains the prevalent, underlying trend of French history throughout its various periods, and so the Napoleonic episode, in spite of its analogies to the Roman Empire, belongs to the development of another form of rule, namely that of the nation.

The British Empire, finally, the colonial empire, has very little in common with the old principle of empire, though the character of the British rule has often been compared to the Roman methods of domination. First of all, the King of England has always remained the traditional, constitutional and national King of England, even after the colonial empire had been established. When Lord Beaconsfield had made Victoria Empress of India, she was still, first and foremost, Queen of England; the imperial title never preceded the royal title, a fact that indicates the inferior role of the colonial title. And in general, modern colonies differ fundamentally from political provinces in that they are intended for economic exploitation alone. The British never interfered with the native populations of their colonies beyond the reach of their economic interest, which, of course, was fairly extensive. But British institutions in the colonies were meant for the British only. The British never wanted to Anglicize foreign populations, as the Romans had wanted to Romanize them. So the colonial empire that evolved from economic enterprise has a predominantly economic character. From the economic expansion of England and the formation of its economic colonial empire, the modern concept of imperialism has derived.

To sum up: The true concept of the empire is represented in the modern era solely by the Hapsburg monarchy, and necessarily forms a reactionary antagonist to the modern kinds of rule and community: the nation, the democracy and the state.

In dealing with the beginnings of France in the early Middle Ages, we saw the *nation* as a folk structure which forms after the creation, and under the prevalence, of a world religion. A nation is a worldly community, based on a special folk character, on a homogeneous mode of life, on the special customs, institutions and cultural forms evolving from the interaction of specific popular stocks and the specific nature of a country. The sum of the profane customs and achievements of such a community gradually develops a stock of instinctive memories which we call tradition. Tradition intrinsically connects every individual of the community with the vital treasure of his ethnic past. The whole complex of customs, habits, achievements, becomes a focus of life for the individuals of the community, a focus which is a profane analogy to the role of the deity among ancient tribes, and thus tradition is the profane religion of a nation.

This definition serves to distinguish the nation from the tribe and the polis, both of which are essentially religious communities. Contrasting the nation, not with earlier forms of communities, but with forms emerging later than the nation, with the modern democracy and the modern state, we must stress the spontaneous, instinctive formation of the nation. The nation does not form deliberately by concerted action, like the democracy, for instance, that is the result of exertions and revolutions, it does not form in accordance with clearly conceived plans and purposes, like the state, it is, in a word, no collective. It comes into being from a vital center, an inner source, not from outward goals. So, as a community, it is upheld by a common origin, a common past, rather than by a common life together and a common activity in the present and for the future. The term nation, "natio", means birth, and it hails from the medieval universities, where it was used to indicate ethnic extraction, the folk origin of the students, who were designated as "natione Gallica, Anglica, Fiorentina", etc. So the nation is inherent and complete in the individual. No common recognition, no actual cooperation is necessary to produce such a community.

This character of the nation makes it possible for the community to be represented by a personality that embodies the tradition in a perfect and symbolic manner. The individual recognizes and enjoys his nationality in the glory and the power of his leader or monarch, in whose feats he participates vicariously. The French Royal Dynasty, termed the "sang de France", the blood of France, represented the nation. It became part of the tradition of the nation, it became its core, as the capital was the core and pattern of the country.

It was only under the strong influence of the *democracy* developing from Germanic peoples and Germanic movements, such as the Reformation, and under the pressure of economic circumstances arising in the course of the eighteenth century, that the terms nation and nationality assumed a democratic meaning, designating the bulk of the people, the concept of the people, in opposition to its dynastic representation. In the period of the French Revolution, and at the beginning of the nineteenth century, the nation was identical with the people. Later, however, when the reactionary forces mobilized the national instincts and aroused an explicitly nationalistic movement in opposition to the progress of democracy and international socialism, the term resumed its old meaning. Though, from 1789 on, France developed an imperfect democracy, it always remained a nation. The Dutch and the British, on the other hand, began as nations and, in a way, have always remained nations. But their life center shifted, advanced toward a more present, visible, active community, that is, toward a democracy. The Germans attained neither a perfect nationality nor a true democracy. They developed the *state,* which is a form of community, more active, more purposeful, more rational and collective than the democracy. To the Germans, the state was an outward substitute for the nation, and prevented the development of the democracy. Germany began as a collection of territorial states, the private dominions of princes whose territories had been accumulated through mere dynastic opportunities and whose populations had no natural cohesion whatsoever, but were held together merely by an authoritative administration. Prussia, that developed from a colony, perfected the concept of the German state on the basis of the craft guild city and the Lutheran doctrine.

The most recent form of modern community, the *socialist state,* the classless state, combines the features of the state with those of the democracy, in order to achieve a perfect collective. It evolved as an ideological design from the socialist movement in the nineteenth century, and a first attempt at its realization was made by the Russian people, that was especially predestined for this development.

The principal partners in the great political game at the beginning of the modern era were the *French monarchy* and the *Hapsburg dynasty*. The struggle for supremacy in Europe between these two powers was the main theme of the sixteenth and seventeenth centuries. It started with the famous election of the German emperor in 1519, in which, as we remember, Jacob Fugger decided the issue when he lent money to the Hapsburg king of Spain, Charles V, and not to the French king, Francis I. This decision raised the Hapsburgs to the zenith of their power. The struggle proceeded with the contest for supremacy in Italy, fought out in the four Italian wars between Francis I and Charles V, from 1521 to 1544. In their feud with the Spaniards who held Southern Italy, the French had invaded Italy before this, in 1494 and 1499. These conflicts had arisen when the pope applied to France for help against the Stauffers. As a result of this appeal, Charles of Anjou, the brother of the French king, Louis IX, had become king of Naples and Sicily. The Sicilians revolted against the French rule in 1282, in the famous Sicilian Vespers, and gave their crown to Peter of Aragon, the husband of the granddaughter of the Stauffer, Frederick II. Peter's descendant, Alfons V, added Naples to his territory. In this way Spain gained control of Southern Italy. The continued struggle made Italy the battlefield of French and Spanish troops that alternately ravaged the country. The rivalry be-

tween France and Hapsburg continued, with intrigues and meddling in the internal affairs of their respective countries, which,
at the time, were in a constant turmoil of religious conflicts, until
at last, in the Thirty Years' War, France dealt the final blows to
the weakened Hapsburg dynasty. The great contest ended with the
victory of the French national monarchy, the triumph of the nation
over the mere dynasty and its outworn family empire.

All the other powers of the epoch, England, Sweden, the Netherlands, the Italian cities, the pope and the German territorial rulers,
were merely secondary partners in the great struggle, and changed
sides frequently according to their interests. There was, of course,
a second important issue, namely, the religious struggle between
the Protestants and the Catholic forces which rallied in the Counter-Reformation. It was the fight for the maintenance and the
political establishment of Protestantism in the world, which, in
the final analysis, meant the preparation and development of the
democracy. The religious motives, however, were sincere only
among certain princes and noblemen and among the lower orders,
and even here they were intermingled with national and democratic trends, as in Bohemia, in Sweden, in the Netherlands and
in France, and with the claims of territorial powers against the
emperor, as in Germany.

France was unsettled for nearly thirty years of the sixteenth
century by the Huguenot wars. The international war of the
seventeenth century in Germany, known as the Thirty Years' War,
from 1618 to 1648, also started from religious incidents, and, in
its first stages, the religious issue prevailed. The cogent motives
and results of all the events, however, were political. First of all,
the leading antagonists of the period, the French monarchs and
the Hapsburgs, were both Catholic. They were Catholic because
the Catholic doctrine was a conservative and authoritative creed,
and the Protestant reform, especially in the Calvinistic version,
turned out to be a democratic and indeed revolutionary movement.
The Hapsburgs, moreover, were kings of Spain, where the fight
for the church against the Arab infidels—who held parts of Spain
from 711 to 1492—had made Catholicism an integral element of

Spanish nationality. And in Germany, where the Lutheran movement had been protected by some prominent territorial princes, the Hapsburg emperors in suppressing the Protestants were making a last and vain effort to subdue the territorial powers. But their Catholic stand did not prevent either the French or the Hapsburg monarchs from scheming and uniting with Protestant powers whenever this seemed expedient in their struggle for supremacy. The very same king, Henry II of France, who cruelly persecuted the Huguenots in his country, made an alliance with the German Protestant princes that sealed the defeat of the Catholic emperor. The French king, Henry IV (1589–1610), changed his religion three times in the course of dynastic quarrels which were intertwined with the religious party strife of the Huguenot wars. He finally became Catholic in order to win Paris and the crown of France. He was credited with saying, "Paris vaut bien une messe", Paris is well worth a Mass. The most bigoted Hapsburg emperor, Ferdinand II, chief of the Counter-Reformation, did not shrink from uniting with the Lutheran Prince-Elector of Saxony in the Thirty Years' War, and he was very firm in rejecting all interference on the part of the pope in the affairs of his dominions. And finally, it was the alliance of Cardinal Richelieu with Protestant Sweden that wrecked the international position of the Catholic Hapsburg emperor.

So the crucial issues, and the crucial effects of all the wars, upheavals, leagues and treaties, were plainly political. The upshot was twofold: the established supremacy of France and the first beginnings of democracy in the Protestant regions. In the Treaty of Westphalia, which concluded the Thirty Years' War, the principle had been laid down that everybody had the right to that form of faith which prevailed in his country or which was the religion of his government: "Cujus regio, ejus religio." This meant the political recognition of Protestant countries.

In general, the sixteenth and seventeenth centuries were the age of the nation, and we can grasp their true purport only in viewing the development and the cultural supremacy of the two successively leading nations of this epoch: Spain and France.

Spain had a short period of predominance about 1500 and in the first part of the sixteenth century, when the trend of the epoch coincided with the disposition of her national character and made her the leading nation of Europe. The unification and the inner establishment of the nation had only just been accomplished. In 1469, Ferdinand, the successor to the throne of Aragon, married Isabella, the heiress of the crown of Castile. They became rulers of their respective countries in 1479 and 1474. In 1479, the focal regions of Spain were united under one rule. In 1492, the rulers conquered Granada from the Arabs and expelled the last remnants of Islam from Spanish soil. In the same year, Christopher Columbus discovered America and inaugurated the colonial conquests of Spain. In 1496, Joan, the daughter of Ferdinand and Isabella, married Philip, the son of the Hapsburg emperor, Maximilian I, who, on his mother's side, had inherited Burgundy and the Netherlands. The result was the succession to the Spanish throne (1516) of the later Hapsburg emperor, Charles V, the son of Philip and Joan, and the incorporation of Spain in the vast dominion of the Hapsburgs. Internal consolidation followed the liberation of the united country and the establishment of its colonial and European power. The position of Christian Spain as a militant outpost against Islam had identified faith with national defense and national aspirations; it had made Catholicism, a most ardent and violent Catholicism, an ingredient of the national character. So the Spanish Inquisition was established, partly as an attempt to integrate Spanish nationality, partly as an instrument of the ruler to subdue the feudal lords and to get rid of any dangerous and politically suspect personality. The Spanish Inquisition was a political, not a religious institution, it was part of the political administration, and all interference of the Roman Church was excluded. Its principle was the identification of pure faith with pure blood. Pure blood, Spanish blood, was supposed to express itself through the purity and zeal of Christian faith. The Spanish procedure has been compared to modern race discrimination, especially as it resulted in the wholesale expulsion or burning of the Jews and the Moors. But this is a misconception, because the profession of Christian faith could protect a man from persecution. Quite a number of Jews who were outwardly Christians but secretly continued to adhere to their own religion and even to perform its rites, the so-called Marranos, could thus escape the fateful consequences of their Judaism. Incidentally, the whole measure was ineffective, as interbreeding had been going on for centuries, and the Spanish lower classes, as well as the Spanish nobility, were thoroughly impregnated with Jewish and Moorish blood.

The first Hapsburg monarchs completed the organizational work of Ferdinand and Isabella. A Spanish nobleman and soldier, Ignatius de Loyola, transferred the struggle for faith to the spiritual field and combined military, religious and court discipline in his methods. He founded the order of the Jesuits, those masters of Christian diplomacy and of the scrutiny of the soul. And all these tendencies —the national character and tradition, the attitude and the interest of the Hapsburg monarchs, and the activity of the Jesuits—brought about the movement of the Counter-Reformation, which, for a brilliant moment, put Spain at the top of the European world. The colonial conquests filled the country with riches. But these remained mere gold, mere riches that were not utilized to any productive ends but spent lavishly for the expansion of political power and for military conquests and adventures. The Spanish army was the model army of the epoch because of its infantry, which, in organization and tactics, surpassed the methods of the Swiss—who had been the teachers—and the German mercenaries. A new order of command was instituted: the general and the admiral are of Spanish origin. Admiral derives from the Arab "amir", "emir", prince. A powerful navy, the famous Armada, was built. It was the great epoch, the only great epoch of Spanish art and literature and this, together with Spanish etiquette, introduced by the Hapsburgs from their court in Burgundy, and transformed into the rigid, haughty and sternly ceremonial pomp which has become proverbial, exerted a strong influence on the mode of the epoch.

This period of Spanish predominance was very short. The power of the nation was exhausted in the fruitless suppression of the Dutch upheavals, in French and English wars. The Spanish branch of the Hapsburg dynasty degenerated rapidly, and the population—the church aiding and abetting—fell prey to idle grandees and landed proprietors. This has not changed very much to this day, in spite of all heroic attempts to liberate the people. The last of these efforts, in our time, was killed by the Fascist forces and by the cowardice, or even tacit consent, of the other European governments.

It was the *French nation* that inherited the leading position in Europe at the end of the sixteenth century and held it until the end of the eighteenth. The French nation, we recall, formed very early in the Middle Ages as the first nation in history. It started with the emergence of the Capet dynasty from the Ile de France and its urban center, Paris. We have already stated the premises of the expansion of the French nation: the Romanization of the country, the continuity of the Capet dynasty in direct succession from father to son. We saw further that in France the feudal system was firmly and generally established, and that the concentration of large main regions in the hands of powerful feudal lords eventually helped the kings to bring the country under their control, by various means. The fact that the popes, absorbed as they were by their struggle against the emperors, allowed the French kings liberties in the appointment of their bishops, a privilege denied the German rulers, was of great help in this first period. As a result, the French clerics were especially devoted to the monarchs and supported them against the lords. At the beginning of the twelfth century, Louis VI, the Fat, the first energetic monarch since the foundation of the dynasty, made his teacher Suger, a humble abbot of St. Denis, the first of his counsellors. This was the beginning of the institution of the "legists". In a war for possessions in Lorraine, waged with the German emperor, the first national movement, the first national support of the king, became manifest. Under the successor of Louis VI, a fateful event took place which determined French history for two centuries to come. King Louis VII had married the heiress of extensive Aquitaine, comprising Poitou, Guyenne and Gascony, in central and south-

western France. The king divorced the Duchess of Aquitaine
because she did not bear him a male heir. She promptly married
Henry Plantagenet, Duke of Normandy and Count of Anjou,
Maine and Touraine, whose mother was a daughter of the King
of England, and who soon afterwards succeeded to the English
throne as Henry II. This meant that the English king owned more
than half of France. To be sure, the major part of these possessions was recovered by the son of Louis VII, the next outstanding
king of France, Philip Augustus. But the thorn in the flesh of
France remained. And in addition to the problem of interior expansion and consolidation, and the extension of the French sphere
of influence in the Mediterranean through the crusades and the
control of the papacy, the expulsion of the British and the fight
against English claims and attacks were the main concern of the
French monarchs until the great rising of the nation under Joan
of Arc in 1429. This long lasting task of driving the English out
of France fomented the national movement. It is usually heroic
defense, deliverance from a powerful intruder, that fosters national
efforts, and adds up to, or at least substantiates, a national tradition.
Of course, the line between defense and expansion soon becomes
fluid and the people comes to enjoy the glory of expansion and
power more and more. So the great war of deliverance which is
connected with the almost legendary story of the maid of Orléans,
has become one of the fundamentals of French tradition, and, at
the time, resulted in a great popular flowering and economic and
political expansion. The marvelous rise of a shepherdess to military leadership, her treacherous extradition by the Duke of Burgundy, and her sacrificial death at the stake after a witches' trial
staged by the English, are not so interesting for our point of view.
What concerns us here is the unique position of the dynasty which
at this moment revealed itself in its symbolic significance. This
dynasty had a decidedly hereditary character that appears in the
strong and the weak rulers alike. Although Charles VII was an
especially weak specimen of the dynasty, he shows all its characteristic features: carefreeness, levity, whimsicality, inconstancy,
disloyalty, but all this combined with a strong sense of royal dig-

nity and, before all, of a glowing enjoyment of life and a refined
taste for life. In short, one may characterize this as a gay despoty,
in sharp contrast to the Hapsburg regime, which was never gay
but stern and rigid, or, at best, in its Austrian form, lax. A cour-
tier of Louis XIV once expressed it very well: "La France est une
monarchie absolue, tempérée par la chanson" (France is an absolute monarchy tempered by song). And there is a word of Louis
XIV himself that says the same thing but turns it into a maxim of
great wisdom: "En augmentant de puissance, il faut redoubler
de grace" (As your power increases, you must redouble your
charm). This character of French rulership became a life principle
with Philippe le Bel, Francis I, Henry IV and other French monarchs. This is how they attracted people, how they lured the lords
into becoming courtiers and forming court society, how they kept
the devotion of their servants and ministers, in spite of their not
infrequent outrageous ingratitude and perfidy. This gay and fes-
tive splendor in their attitude and their mode of living, which
was so much in accordance with the ways and the inclinations of
the French people, made their regime deep-rooted and exemplary,
and softened the effect of the many hardships they imposed on the
people in the most unscrupulous manner.

Under Charles VII, England again held the greater part of
France. The king even had to remove his residence from Paris to
Bourges, and the court was divided by violent party strife. The
country was impoverished by plundering and requisitioning English and French mercenaries, by marauding peasants, bad crops,
famine and pestilence. In the midst of all this, the king with his
mistress led his usual court life of careless spending and parading.
And still the unoccupied regions helped him and supported him to
the utmost. Again and again, their diets raised hundreds of thousands of pounds and encouraged him to maintain his position.
Without his having anything to do with it, the leaders of the national movement arose, Joan of Arc, the other commanders and
the financier of the campaign, Jacques Coeur, who afterwards, in
the position of powerful minister, saved him and satisfied all his
extravagant demands, who later brought the country to great eco-

nomic prosperity and was finally ill-requited for his unflinching devotion. This whole national movement resulted in the expulsion of the English from France, in the lasting religious independence of France, the so-called Gallicanism, in economic recovery, in the beginnings of the French standing army, and laid the ultimate foundation for the rise of France to European supremacy. And it would not have been possible without the firmly established position of the royal dynasty, that remained effective in spite of the personal weakness and almost passivity of Charles VII. This phenomenon is expressed by a French saying: "Henri, Charles, Louis meurent, mais le roi ne meurt pas" (Henry, Charles, Louis may die, but the king never dies).

Against this picture of the dynasty at its ebb, let us hold that of the dynasty at its peak, represented by Louis XIV (1643–1715). Louis XIV is the paragon and symbol of the French national monarch in all the brilliant and evil qualities of his kind. He even became the type of ruler for the whole period. In spite of the skilful preparations of Richelieu, the supremacy of France in Europe would never have been achieved without the embodiment of this supremacy in the living figure of Louis XIV. He completed the task of attaining this supremacy by his politics, but even more by his mere existence.

First of all, he integrated the absolute monarchy. It had been the custom of the monarchs to delegate much of their authority to their devoted counsellors and often to one chief counsellor and minister, so that, while the king ruled, it was the minister who governed. The most famous of these powerful chancellors was Cardinal Richelieu, who exercised authority on behalf, and in the name, of Louis XIII, removed the assembly of the "états généraux", the estates general, and thus created the preliminaries for perfect absolutism. Louis XIV was his own Richelieu. In his youth, he had been profoundly impressed by the frivolous revolt of the nobility against the stern regime of Mazarin. This revolt called "fronde", after a forbidden children's game of throwing stones, had plunged the country into four years of anarchy. Louis XIV assumed personal control of the government, concentrated the entire adminis-

tration in his own hands and initiated the strictly centralized
organization of France, which has persisted up to our time. He defined the various branches and functions of the administration in
different departments and councils, all of which met under the
presidency of the king. Thus the organization of the modern min-
istry was given. Louis XIV also assumed control of the army and
abolished the formerly fairly independent commands of the High
Constables and the Grand Admirals. By all this, he established
important preliminaries for the modern state, but he did not create
a true state. The true state is a collective, a super-individual unit,
and his device: "L'état c'est moi", I am the state, made the state
identical with his personal rule. The ministers were only counsellors of the king in his most secret affairs. Saint-Simon remarks
that they had neither permanent appointments nor written con-
tracts, nor did they have to swear an oath of office; their status
was suspended in mid-air. Their duties began with an invitation
from the king to participate in his private councils and ended
when the invitation ceased to be forthcoming.

Yet more important than the work of Louis XIV was his person, which not only was, but was intended to be symbolic and
representative in every smallest detail. As he himself united the
blood of the Capets, the Hapsburgs and the Medici, so various
traditions merged in his diplomacy and way of life. He was not
only the grandson of the Bourbon, Henry IV, but also of Philip III
of Spain and of Maria de' Medici. And his rule and court combined the magnificence of the Florentine Renaissance courts and
the hierarchical discipline of the Hapsburg ceremonial with the
grace and enjoyment of life of French royalty. He regarded the
business of ruling as his work and his duty, but at the same time,
he relished this work. "Our occupations," he wrote in his memoirs
for his son, "are sometimes less difficult than our amusements . . .
what is most necessary for this work, is also pleasant, my son, for
it consists in keeping one's eyes wide open and fixed upon the
whole of the world . . . in always knowing the secrets of all courts,
the moods and weaknesses of all princes and ministers, in being

informed of the countless things that others believe hidden from us . . . I do not know what entertainments we would not sacrifice for this, if mere curiosity furnished it." Thus the world became a spectacle for rulers, and, on the other hand, the life of the king from morning till night was a spectacle for the nation and for the world. His rising in the morning, the famous "lever", his meals, his functions of state, his amusements, his entire day until he retired to bed, was a public ceremony. Life at court, down to the last detail, was a precise ritual presented to the world in playful lightness that was to express a superior form of living. Enjoyment was intentional and symbolic and the intention itself was a matter of enjoyment. Contemporary commentators emphasize his perfect grace and courtesy of commanding, his natural dignity, his unshaken self-control and the deliberateness of even apparently spontaneous behavior. Louis XIV created an appropriate setting for this courtly spectacle in Versailles, the model of the European royal residence. The spacious splendor of its castles, parks and fountains, that were wrested from the barren and swampy land at a colossal cost, is the architectural expression of a national monarchy. There could be no better reflection of the innermost attitude of this court than the famous hall of mirrors. The royal residence expanded to a city, since all the nobles who wanted to play any role whatsoever, had to live where the king lived. Not only did the king wish to wean these nobles away from a self-sufficient life in their feudal castles, not only did he want to supervise them continually, he actually made them entirely dependent on his bounty for all the material means of life. For the nobles were always in debt. In this period of prosperous economic development, their tradition did not permit them to follow any profession or calling. They could not even farm the land to any appreciable extent. Only court and military positions were deemed worthy of their rank, and to attain these, they had to be near the king. The royal word: "That is someone whom I do not see" was equivalent to ruin. The court population multiplied and served to keep the king remote from the people and, at the same time, united with them. On the one hand, the nobles were the kindred of the royal family, especially of the illegitimate children, on the other, a new money aristocracy and "mésalliances" with rich burghers were coming into vogue.

The result of this elaborate form of representation was a kind of profane hieratization of the king. He and his family were considered as beings of a higher order. Bishop Bossuet writes: "The throne of the king is not the throne of a man, but the very throne of God. Therefore the person of the king is sacred . . . he represents the majesty of God." But he adds the very significant words: "The king is a public person and in him the whole nation is embodied." Even Lorenzo de' Medici, "il Magnifico", had said: "True princes represent the whole of their people." Here we have the principle, the creed of the nation.

It may easily be imagined what far-reaching consequences this exalted representation had on international relations and diplomatic intercourse. Louis XIV introduced an important new element into international relations which is a reflection of his conduct of life. This new element is the *prestige* which has since become an important principle and a most useful, but at the same time, most delicate and dangerous instrument of the politics of the great powers. If employed with the shrewdness and self-possession of Louis XIV, it could produce magical effects. But the slightest wavering or blunder might lead to unwelcome conflicts or irreparable humiliation and defeat.

Louis XIV knew how to avoid conflicts which he did not desire, without losing face. "Ne se brouille pas avec moi qui veut," he said, not everyone who wants to, can quarrel with me. And these proud words in themselves express a maintenance of prestige, the keeping of the initiative. After the death of Mazarin, when Louis XIV came into power, this new principle was put into practice in dealing with Spain, with the pope, Genoa and other powers, and always with complete success. The sensitiveness and challenge with which it was applied founded the tremendous respect of the European powers for the inaccessible majesty of France. The decisive conflict with Spain hinged on a matter of precedence of the French and

Spanish ambassadors at European courts. Superficially it seemed a mere question of etiquette, but great symbolic and even actual significance was involved, since precedence sometimes involved priority in diplomatic negotiations. This war of etiquette had been going on since the days of Charles V. Now it was to be settled once and for all. At a court ceremony in London, in 1661, the French ambassador announced that should the Spanish ambassador dare to drive up first before the palace gates, his servants would sever the reins of the Spanish carriage. The Spanish ambassador reacted to this threat by reinforcing his reins with chains. A struggle accompanied by bloodshed ensued. Louis XIV immediately sent home the Spanish ambassador in Paris, and delivered an ultimatum to Madrid, stating that if, in the future, the French ambassador did not have precedence at all the courts of Europe, the most dire consequences would follow. Philip IV, the Hapsburg king, did not feel strong enough to face a war with France, and did not merely yield to the proffered demands, but even made a formal apology to the King of France, by a special envoy who expressed the regrets of Spain before the assembled French court. A record of this apology was made and sent to all the courts of Europe. This jealous guarding of prestige, as well as all the royal and diplomatic procedures, were imitated by the French nobles in the conducting of their private affairs. The number of duels in Paris increased enormously.

Today, in the era of democracy and state, the art of handling prestige has been lost, and the word itself is in ill repute. It is, of course, an indication of progress that a man or a nation should no longer be inclined to jump at the defense of his honor or to go to war for every slightest incident. But there is also another side to the matter. Whoever wants to exercise authority or to maintain a position has to keep his prestige to a certain degree. A precautionary observance of prestige may often prevent the attack of an arrogant opponent. In the book of Preston Schoyer, "The Foreigners", the story of British prestige in the Orient is told: "There was a battle across the Yangtze not so many years ago, Northern troops against Southern, and along came a British steamer. She tooted her whistle, then some bugles blew and the fighting stopped till she was safely by." Such was the magic power of British prestige in the Orient. This power is gone. But if the British statesmen of the last decade had been aware of the vital importance of prestige in dealing with the Fascist powers, the world would not be where it is today.

DEMOCRACY

THE PRINCIPLE OF THE NATION, exemplified in the development of France, means the establishment of a rule in which a profane and popular community participates for the first time. In contrast to the Empire, which was based on a universal Christian mission, on dynastic interest and on a system of private, individual relations between feudal lords and vassals, in contrast also with the territorial state founded on only dynastic interest, national rule is founded on a popular community, and it would not have become so powerful without this strong support. This popular community of the nation is, however, still a natural community of birth, origin, tradition, common habits, attitudes and ways of life. A community which is established by birth and not by any common act or cooperation is inherent and complete in every individual, and the individual in whom this community is most perfectly embodied is the leader who attains his position as symbol, either by the present intensity and fascination of this representation, or by hereditary, genealogical, traditional authority. The former was true in the case of the Italian city-nations, with their frequently changing tyrannies or principalities, and in the belated Napoleonic rulership after the French Revolution. Even the rise of Mussolini is an anachronistic relapse of typically nationalistic representation; not so the rise of Hitler, whose power has rather the opposite origin, the "Fuehrer" being revered for exactly those qualities with which the average German is not endowed. The latter was developed by the French royal dynasty which grew into a traditional leadership and became part of the tradition.

The center of national activity was the maintenance and expansion of the power of rule which was embodied in the dynastic regime. The actual object of government was the *administration of power,* not the administration of the country or the state as such. All matters not connected with this essential task of maintenance of power did not concern the government. They were left to customary self-regulation, to the intrinsic rule of tradition. No particular effort was made to insure the well-being of the people. This implies, on the other hand, that the administration did not exceed the limits of the task of maintaining power. To be sure, this task involved a greater and greater extension of the administration. The immense costs of the royal court, of armies and navies, called for increasing attention to the raising of funds, to the exploitation of economic resources and the creation of new resources. The religious troubles which arose from the spread of Protestantism required a stricter civil administration and interference in jurisdiction. All this meant an expansion of royal control and promoted the development of officialdom and governmental regulation. But the entire administration centered in the interest of the personal monarch, it was fostered and also limited by the personal interest and personal, indeed arbitrary, will of the monarch. And, according to this personal origin of the administration, personal methods and personal interests prevailed throughout royal officialdom.

This character of the administration becomes especially clear from the conditions prevailing in two important fields: jurisdiction and finance. Jurisdiction was confused and corrupt throughout the "ancien régime". The old judicial prerogatives of the feudal powers persisted, even long after the lords had become courtiers, so that a royal and a non-royal, private jurisdiction, which frequently interfered with each other, existed side by side. Of course, the absolute monarch reserved for himself control and intervention. He had the so-called right of evocation that enabled him to bring any case before his judicial council. Besides, certain persons had the privilege to have their cause pleaded immediately before the Supreme Court of the King. His intervention, however, was exercised mostly for political reasons or as a matter of personal favor. On the other hand, he occasionally intervened without any judicial sentence either by the "lettres patentes"—open letters—which decreed acts of grace, liberally granted to the nobility, or by the much dreaded "lettres de cachet"—sealed letters—which meant imprisonment or banishment, without hearing, of any person in ill favor. Sometimes the king even issued blanks to his ministers which they could use at pleasure as "lettres de cachet". All judicial offices, royal or private, were purchasable or to be let. The sale of offices was one of the most lucrative sources of income of the king. The buyers frequently resold their purchase. The judges, accordingly, were most receptive to bribes, and the influence of powerful persons was practically unlimited. Only by keeping all this in mind, can one realize the importance of the English Petition of Rights and the Writ of Habeas Corpus that afforded legal protection against such measures.

In the administration of finance, also, all offices were sold, with one exception: the administration of indirect taxes was let to lease-holding companies. There was, however, not much difference between the royal administration and the private administration of the companies. For even the royal officials shared in the surplus when the revenues exceeded a certain minimum. It may easily be imagined how unscrupulous the methods of collection were, all the more as there was no protection whatever for the taxpayer. The burden of the personal income tax, the "taille", was carried by the bourgeois and the peasants only. The nobility were exempt from it, because originally this income tax represented a duty for redemption from military service. Since in the time of King Philip Augustus, when this tax was instituted (1215), military service was an exception among bourgeois or peasants but the regular profession of a nobleman, the nobility, as a class, was exempt from this tax once and for all.

Besides the examples cited in the case of jurisdiction and finance, another very important instance in the economic field clearly shows the difference between mere administration of power and true administration of a country or state, between a purely personal regime and a government which takes into account the actual development and future of a country. The French "ancien régime" never overcame the early stage of a careless, unmethodical exploitation of immediate resources without thought of consequences. Two great attempts were made during the "ancien régime" to bring about a lasting prosperity of France. The first was made by Jacques Coeur, the financier of Charles VII, and the second by Colbert, the great minister of Louis XIV.

After the salvation of the country and the dynasty, Jacques Coeur engaged in vast economic activities. He combined the position of private entrepreneur with that of an almighty royal official. French commerce became his monopoly, but as he was vested with royal authority, and was an excellent national minister devoted to the king, this unification and systematization of the economic forces of the country promoted and increased the prosperity of the realm. He had agencies in all the main cities. He recognized the important location of the province of Languedoc, which extended along the Rhone River to the Mediterranean coast, and which, by connecting the Rhone and the Loire, could become a commercial link between the ocean and the rich Northern centers of Burgundy and Flanders, on the one hand, and the Mediterranean, on the other. He strengthened this province in every possible way, by special privileges, fairs, canals, harbors; he built a large new fleet of galleys, purged the sea of pirates, and for a time supplanted the foreign competitors, the Italian, Catalonian, Provençal merchants, in the great Levantine trade. It was, in fact, the first time that the economic expansion and competition of France was felt in the area of the Mediterranean. But it was to remain a brief episode, because this most ingenious, indeed irreplaceable man suddenly fell into disfavor with the king, as a result of an intrigue of his rivals and influential debtors. He was accused of a number of petty offences which he had very probably committed, but on behalf and with the knowledge of the king, and of a crime of which he was guiltless. Posthumously and solemnly he was cleared of the suspicion—a charge brought by a paid witness—of having poisoned the mistress of Charles VII. He was imprisoned and sentenced without hearing and, after an adventurous flight, died as a poor exile on a Greek island. His vast property was confiscated and sold at auction on behalf of the king. Such confiscations of the property of disgraced people were another lucrative resource of French monarchs. But what is more important: from one day to the next, the whole economic structure of Jacques Coeur crumbled, all his establishments and institutions, his whole commercial system. And with it, the vast trading system, the economic position and influence of France were gone. This is a striking instance of the character and the effects of a purely personal regime.

Two hundred years later, the great Colbert, the financier of Louis XIV, who provided the means for the splendid court, the buildings, the armies, the wars of this brilliant and unscrupulously extravagant king, tried desperately to set France to work, to make it economically strong and prosperous, to organize it along economic lines. He wanted to transform France into a place of business and manufacture where everyone worked, into a strong country that produced everything it required and a considerable surplus that would enable it to export goods, to snatch unto itself the trade of competing countries and thus to divert the world's money into its channels. He believed that the amount of money circulating in the world was stabile, since the various populations and their requirements were stabile, and that, therefore, the only way to seize upon money was to deprive others of it, that all commerce was a war for money, a conquest of money. We can see how even this reformer of economics did not think along economic lines but according to concepts of political power prevailing in his epoch and country. In order to carry out the projected reforms, it was important to emphasize both production and parsimony. In his "Lettres, Instructions et Mémoires", he writes to the king: "One should confine all the activities of subjects as far as possible to such as work in with our great plans, that is, agriculture, commerce, war by land and sea ... If Your Majesty is able to concentrate the entire population on these four callings, you will be the supreme ruler of the world." To accomplish this, all forms of work and all classes that serve the common weal were to be "honorable and prosperous", all others were to be discouraged and degraded. He pleaded for fewer nuns and monks, fewer idle officers of justice to plague and hinder the people, for better means of transportation, and obviation of the hundreds of different kinds of local custom-duties, excises, and weights and measures. He pleaded for a king who knew the state of his country's finances, who honored merchants, received them, admitted them to his council; who traveled through his country, supervised manufactures and saw to it personally that law was observed.

This was the great project Colbert presented to Louis XIV and tried to convince him to accept. But if the king really had accepted it, he could not have remained what he was. He would have had to alter the very foundation of his regime. So Colbert worked sixteen hours a day to organize the economy of France. He, like Jacques Coeur, built a new fleet of merchantmen; he created the French navy. He, too, constructed roads and canals. He brought order into the accounts of the royal revenue by instituting the "budget", according to the precepts of the English economist, Thomas Mun, and increased the sources of this revenue by promoting manufactures and protecting them through tariffs, and by furthering trading companies and the development of colonies. He reduced the generous number of holidays, but even so, there were still thirty-eight a year, not counting Sundays.

But how could he bring his plans to fruition in a country with a huge class of idle aristocrats exempt from all taxes and burdens and only concerned with the ceremonies and festivals of the court! How could he succeed at a court which spent money recklessly, with a king who was not in the least interested in economy and economics, who had no regard for those of his subjects who were engaged in industry and commerce, but cherished only his brilliant and gay cortège of noblemen! What could he do under a system of privileges, of antiquated nationalized guilds, and all sorts of inveterate feudal and provincial customs and regulations which prevented a free flow of trade! How could he make headway against a monarchical policy that ruined the bourgeoisie and the peasants by overburdening them with taxes and the abuses of the aristocracy, and that drove the most industrious part of the population, the Protestants, out of the country! Much like Charles VII, Louis XIV ruined some of his most efficient manufacturers, to whom he owed the prosperity of the royal industries. Colbert himself had no illusions about the difficulty of introducing commerce to a kingdom where "neither the people in general, nor the private individuals had ever actually applied themselves to it, where indeed, trade was in a way adverse to the genius of the nation". His efforts remained futile, and after his death in 1683, his achievements and his order gradually fell into decay and the country drifted toward the revolution. The same tragic destiny befell the later French economic reformers, such as John Law, Necker and Napoleon's financier, Ouvrard.

These examples show the natural limits of the purely national regime which is identical with a purely political regime, a regime exclusively concerned with the administration and display of power. Such a regime is most effective and impressive when upheld by personal rulership and symbolical representation, by the monarch, and the personal methods he must use. But, according to its personal principle and methods, its effectiveness is confined to the narrow range of a personal existence and personal vitality. It was doomed to failure when a new form of rule arose which rested on a broader, impersonal basis, on a system of activities, achievements and institutions designed for increasing productivity, for long-range developments. This new form was the democracy, and its principle of life, its raison d'être, was not politics but economy.

Unlike the nation, the *democracy* is not inherent in and represented by the individual, it is a community based on common activity, on common achievements and institutions of coordinated, equal individuals, it is a manifest, active and effective community. Imagine a lonely man stranded on a remote island or living in a deserted place. He is still a representative of his national community, he still retains the quality, language, appearance, traditions and attitudes that are the substratum of his nationality. But he cannot possibly be an actual member of a democracy, as he lacks the supplementary co-existence of other individuals and the institutions that alone make this form of community real.

In considering the development of modern democracy, we

must keep in mind that there were ancient forms of democracy. First of all, human evolution started with a form of community which bears a certain resemblance to democracy. In the early stage of primeval, primitive community, before the predominance of a sacred chieftain had developed, all members were apparently equal, they acted in common and deliberated in common, they shared their life, their property, their guilt. We find traces of this primeval condition in the early stages of all ancient tribes and peoples. And presently we shall see that the beginnings of modern democracy are connected with the remainders of this early condition among the Germanic peoples.

Furthermore, there is the democracy of the Greek, especially of the Athenian, polis, which—if we discount the institution of slavery —represents one of the most perfect forms of democracy that we know of. The very word democracy is of Greek origin. When Pericles, in his famous funeral oration, defines a democracy as a government of the whole people, in contrast with oligarchy which is a government of only part of the people, we are reminded of Lincoln's classical formula: "Government of the people, by the people, for the people."

All these ancient forms of democracy, however, are intrinsically different from modern democracy. They are, in the first place, no integral, autonomous democracies, for democracy does not form their sole, or at least their main, constituent element and founding principle; ancient democracy is not identical with the community itself. In the primeval community, it is the demonic life principle of the tribe that reigns and governs equally in all the members through innumerable ancestral rites and sacred regulations. Here, the independent, self-determined individuals who could form a true democracy have not as yet developed. Here there is no outward regulation of common life and work—communal life is directed from a secret, intangible core, effective in every member of the community. "When studying the warfare of the people of the Western Solomon Islands," Dr. W. H. Rivers relates, "I was unable to discover any evidence of definite leadership. When a boat reached the scene of a headhunting foray, there was no regulation as to who should lead the way. It seemed as if the first man who got out of the boat or chose to lead the way, was followed without question. Again, in the councils of such people there is no voting or other means of taking the opinion of the body. Those who have lived among savage or barbarous peoples in several parts of the world have related how they have attended native councils where matters in which they were interested, were being discussed. When, after a time, the English observer found that the people were discussing some wholly different topic, and inquired when they were going to decide the question in which he was interested, he was told that it had already been decided and that they had passed on to other business . . . The members of the council had become aware, at a certain point, that they were in agreement, and it was not necessary to bring the agreement explicitly to notice."

Even Greek democracy represents only a certain stage of the polis which always remained dominated by religion. The Greek polis is a sacred entity of its own, above its citizens, embodied and working in its citizens. Democracy in the polis meant the unfolding, the amplification and differentiation of the community into a variety of developing individuals. Modern democracy means a striving of perfected individuals toward the formation of a common order which evolves from their cooperation. Here, the individuals are first, and through their collective action the democratic community is achieved. This essential difference between ancient and modern democracy implies and explains a further difference: Modern democracy evolved, not, like the Greek, as an extension of public duties, but as a conquest of individual rights. Modern democracy arose from movements of liberation from or defense against foreign or domestic rulers, from a common fight for freedom and individual, civil liberties: "freedom of speech", "freedom of worship" and, above all, "freedom of economic opportunity". Self-government is preeminently a means of safeguarding and protecting the private individual in his unrestricted economic enterprise. Thus modern democracy came more and more to mean freedom and lack of interference from the government, even from self-government, which was delegated to expert politicians. The life center of modern democracy, then, is not political, as in the ancient democracies, but economic. This is the second fundamental difference.

The chief impetus to modern democracy was economic progress, and this progress, in turn, was largely the result of religious movements, of the secularizing effects of Protestantism.

The first beginnings of modern democracy in Europe are connected with the remainders of the primeval form of the tribal community among the Germanic populations. This becomes evident in the evolution of the *Swiss democracy*. The early constitution of the Germanic tribes was like that of a primeval community in which members shared equally. When the tribal core had been destroyed through Christianization, the old customs of equal distribution of soil and of common administration of the community were retained, except in those cases where intermixture with Roman civilization and the development of the Frankish kingdom and the Holy Roman Empire brought about radical changes. In the remote mountain valleys in the center of Switzerland, certain remnants of that ancient Germanic community remained untouched and were carried over to the present. The influence and significance of the old pagan tribe was removed, and what was left over was only the form of that early community, with its implication of equality of feelings and habits among its members. What remained, therefore, turned out to be true democracy.

Edward A. Freeman gives a good account of the proceedings of these early communities: "Year by year . . . the traveler who is daring enough to wander out of beaten tracks and to make his journey at unusual seasons may look on a sight [in Switzerland] such as no other corner of the earth can any longer set before him . . . He is there in a land where the oldest institutions of our race, institutions which may be traced up to the earliest times of which history or legend gives us any glimmering, still live on in their primaeval freshness . . . There year by year, on some bright morning of the springtide, the Sovereign People, not entrusting its rights to a few of its own number, but discharging them itself in the majesty of its corporate person, meets in the open market-place or in the green meadow at the mountain's foot, to frame the laws to which it yields obedience as its own work, to choose the rulers whom it can afford to greet with reverence as drawing their commission from itself ... [On a Sunday morning in May] from the market-place of Altdorf ... the procession makes its way to the place of meeting at Boezlingen. First marches the little army of the Canton, an army whose weapons never can be used save to drive back the invaders from their land ... Before them all, on the shoulders of men clad in a garb of ages past, are borne the famous horns, the spoils of the wild bull of ancient days ... Then, with their lictors before them, come the magistrates of the commonwealth on horse-back ... The people follow the chiefs whom they have chosen to the place of meeting, a circle in a green meadow, with a pine forest rising above their heads and a mighty spur of mountain range facing them ... The multitude of freemen take their seats around the chief ruler ... whose term of office comes that day to an end. The Assembly opens; a short space is first given to prayer ... Then comes the business of the day. If changes in the law are demanded, they are then laid before the vote of the Assembly, in which each citizen of full age has an equal vote and an equal right of speech ... The chief of the commonwealth, now such no longer, leaves his seat of office and takes his place as a simple citizen ... It rests with the free will of the Assembly to call him back to his chair of office, or to set another there in his stead".

Here the people itself is the legislative body. Today this ancient form of democracy is preserved only in some peasant communities, but traces of it, such as the referendum, have been taken over by the whole Swiss Federation. The peasant communities of the Forest Cantons were the nucleus for the Swiss Federation, its independence and democracy. This evolved in the thirteenth century from the defense and rebellion against the Hapsburg lords, who were of Swiss origin and owned large estates in Switzerland when they rose to their position in Germany. Thus the Swiss democracy is the oldest in the Europe of today. Under the growing influence of the craft guilds, the cities, from the fourteenth century on, joined the confederation of peasant communities. This confederation was at first loosely knit and changed its members frequently. It gradually became stronger through the membership of neighboring communities and cities, through meddling in the political quarrels of the day, as a consequence of the struggle against the three great adversaries, the Hapsburgs in the East and the Dukes of Burgundy and Savoy in the West. The Swiss had developed a new military technique based on the mass effect of infantry, and it was they who invalidated the military power of the knights who still used the old feudal method of equestrian single combat. Because of their striking success, Swiss soldiers were hired by foreign powers and were the most sought-for mercenaries in the Renaissance. They fought the wars of French, Italian and German rulers and, in the course of their victories, sometimes acquired territories which the democratic communities then held in subjection, just as princely rulers would have done. On the other hand, it made the country susceptible to foreign influence since the foreign powers paid regular sums to Swiss officials who acted as their agents in hiring troops. Because of these and other concomitant evils, such as loss of manpower, party strife and so on, opposition against mercenary service for Swiss soldiers sprang up, and the Swiss developed that policy of neutrality that afterwards became a basic principle of their little federation exposed on all sides to the appetites of great powers. This situation also proved an encouragement to pacifism, first advanced by the Zurich reformer, Ulric Zwingli, a movement that is inherent in all democratic evolution. Like America, like Holland, like England, the Swiss Federation had an epoch of conquest and expansion. But in contrast with the policy of the nation, the democracy, based mainly on economic activity and concerned with problems of internal order, is bound to be pacifist in principle. Economic activities call for steadiness, for undisturbed trade and for regular, predictable developments. Only in the early stages of economic development, when colonies are founded, and then again in the stage of over-ripe capitalism, the stage of struggle for waning markets, do economic activities lead to war.

In many Swiss cities the craft guilds became predominant and joined their form of democracy with that of the peasant communities. The peasants of the urban communities, however, and of the city patricians were kept in bondage, and the democracy of the guilds degenerated as it did elsewhere. Throughout the modern period, the internal conditions of Switzerland were affected by the fluctuations of European politics and social tendencies, and a thoroughgoing democracy, a general liberation and suffrage, were achieved only gradually in the course of the European revolutions of the eighteenth and nineteenth centuries. The present Swiss Federation was established in 1848 and the present constitution dates from as late as 1874.

Switzerland is the only country, besides the United States, that evolved from a nucleus of genuine democracy and that preserved this nucleus through the years and through all attempts at distortion or obliteration. Switzerland is also the only country, besides the United States, where democracy has become the very substance of the community, the substratum of nationality. The country consists of four different national stocks, Germanic, French, Italian and Romansh, which it has united in a true community. These people are not German, French or Italian. Despite their different language and their different ways of life, they refuse to be counted among their respective kindred across the border. They are, and want to be, Swiss and nothing else. And when we investigate the nature of this quality of being Swiss, we find that it is the quality of being members of a democracy.

Swiss democracy would have remained an isolated phenomenon, and it could hardly have maintained itself, or developed into what it is now, without the broad trend of European democratization that sprang from other sources. The main drive toward democracy came from the development of the economic view, that is the result of progressive secularization, of the wane of religious power over man, and of the promotion of economic activity by the Protestant movement. We saw how the struggle between pope and emperor, in which the Italian communities played an active part, discredited the authority of the church; how the growing secular spirit and the flowering of trade in Renaissance Italy gradually overcame the ancient feudal and Christian prejudice against economic professions and activities, and, in a certain sense, equalized individuals and classes. The same process was going on in the German maritime cities of the Hansa, and in the Dutch cities, where commercial prosperity had created a rich and powerful bourgeoisie that outweighed the nobility of the country.

The *Reformation,* taking its issue from the craft guild city, was the democratization and secularization of religion itself, and furthered democracy through both of these tendencies. It was a democratic act, as it abolished the authority of the pope and of the aristocratic hierarchy. It established what it called the freedom of Christian man, and based the administration of religious life on the parish, the congregation of the laymen. The devoutness of these early Protestants, their subjection to the guidance of their creed, had the most revolutionary political effects. Their religious self-administration set the example for, or rather, it implied, worldly self-government as well.

The Protestant movement, as a secularization of religion, changed the direction of piety. The pious mind was diverted from a contemplative, spiritual preparation for salvation, from the devotion to holy works alone, to the seeking for salvation in active life and through achievements in the affairs of this world. These profane achievements were either for the benefit of the worldly authorities and of the state, or they involved economic activities which, by their very nature, again promoted the progress of democracy.

The Reformation was started by Luther, but in radiating all over Europe, it split up into different theological as well as national movements and versions. The most important and influential of these was the Swiss, inaugurated by Ulric Zwingli, the French, headed by Jean Calvin, and the Swiss, Rhenish and Dutch movement of the Anabaptists. All these various forms of Protestantism influenced one another. The ultimate effect and scope of the Lutheran movement was confined almost wholly to Germany. There it became one of the most important elements in the formation of the Prussian and German state. The Calvinistic movement created the religious community of Geneva, and then, through its merging with Anabaptist elements, laid the foundation of the English and American democracy.

The Reformation, as inaugurated by Luther, was purely religious. *Luther* never intended to exceed theological limits. He was the great divide of German history and a crucial divide of all European history. Many medieval elements were still housed in his brain. His inclination to authority, his concept of a stable society ordained by God and not to be changed by man, traces back to the social concept of medieval Catholic doctrine.

In the Middle Ages, Christian society was regarded as an analogy to the individual human body, since it was, in the mystical sense, the body of Christ. Every organ, and so every profession and calling, has its special God-given function that must be carried out unerringly in order to maintain the entire organism. All functions are dependent upon one another and receive their justification and their duties from the whole. The model of social organization, the "cosmos of all callings", is the church, and in her image, all of society is formed, as Wyclif describes in a tract: "The Church is divided in these three parts, preachers, and defenders, and . . . laborers . . . As she is our mother, so she is a body, and health of this body stands in this, that one part of her answer to another after the same measure that Jesus Christ has ordained it . . . Kindly man's hand helps his head, and his eye helps his foot, and his foot his body . . . and thus should it be in parts of the Church . . ." And thus, according to Catholic doctrine, it should be in Christian society as a whole. With Luther, this concept still prevailed. He was utterly conservative and radically opposed to economic progress, to the development of trade and banking. In this respect, the Catholic party was much more progressive and indulgent.

But Luther was not only a medieval monk, he was of peasant origin, and the barbarian, chaotic nature, the now heavy and now violent temper of the German peasant, was the basic layer of his character. He dreaded his own chaos and tried to control it, and yet this was the very element that, after difficult conflict, proved the motor that drove him to revolt. He, too, was very much influenced by the moral atmosphere and the viewpoint of the craft guild, by the prevalent morality which was, in part, an achievement of his precursors, the German mystics. So he was not only a monk and a peasant but also a petty bourgeois. It is in passages of his "Table Talks" that one senses, for the first time, the staunch, humdrum and somewhat musty atmosphere of a German middle-class family. The German peasant and the German nobleman were savage, anarchic beings—barely amenable to order. The Reformation was the first meeting place of these three elements, the nobleman, the peasant and the burgher, and that they did meet was the work of Luther's character and doctrine. It was he who created the modern German, the German type of ruler and the German type of subject.

It was only through harrowing struggles that Luther reached his revolutionary decision, and he consumed all his energy and strength in carrying out religious emancipation. Since he dreaded the forces he had unleashed within himself and in the people, he was always intent upon restricting the social effects of his revolutionary act. He upheld authority vehemently, and since he had removed ecclesiastical rule, he turned this authority over to worldly rulers, to the territorial princes, some of whom became his patrons and his protectors. He encouraged them in an almost unlimited use of the prerogatives of rulership, in assuming that God had imposed worldly rulership on sinful man as a means of correction. And man, according to him, must suffer this rule without complaint, without attempting to modify even its worst abuses. Man must remain where God has placed him. He must not strive for promotion or change. These views reflect medieval concepts of Christian society as well as the order of the craft guild city. But the character of the social order alters at once when spiritual, ecclesiastical authority is replaced by the material, disciplinarian authority of worldly rulers, when the rule of the craft guilds, which evolved from a consensus on public welfare, is replaced by the rule of a princely dynasty concerned only with the maintenance and expansion of power. So, in liberating the Christian mind and faith, Luther literally chained the secular personality even while he was

making it secular, in directing it to salvation through the fulfilment of worldly tasks. It was a terrible position into which to put
the human being. Man was rendered an instrument, a drudge, a
hopeless subject of the state. Luther was not a social or political
reformer. He made of religion a locked compartment of human
life that has nothing to do with the rest of human existence. This
is most manifest in Luther's stand in the revolt of the German peasants, who were stirred up by the religious and political troubles of
the time and who, partly under the leadership of starving and virtually proletarian knights, tried to liberate themselves from the
wretched conditions imposed by the great nobility. Luther roused
the princes fanatically and even hysterically against the peasants.
He wrote: "Hearken, dear lords, save and help . . . Let him who
can, stab, strike and strangle . . . These are such strange times that
a prince can go to heaven more easily by spilling blood than others
through prayer." The same man who proclaimed the freedom of
the Christian turns furiously against the peasants' attempts to free
themselves from bondage. "There is to be no bondage, since Christ
has freed us all? What is all this? This only makes Christian freedom fleshly! . . . This is therefore against the Gospels, it is an act of
piracy in that each one robs his master of his body. For a bondsman
can be a Christian and have Christian freedom, just as a prisoner
and a sick man can be Christian, even though they are not free. All
this [talk] is directed toward making men equal and of making
a worldly, external kingdom of the spiritual kingdom of Christ.
And this is impossible. For a worldly kingdom cannot persist unless there is inequality, so that some are free and others captive,
some are lords and others subjects." He even goes so far as to forbid
the Christians, enslaved by the Turks, to strive for their freedom.
"For you are robbing and stealing your body from your master, your
body that he has bought or acquired in some other way, so that it
be no longer yours, but his property, like cattle or other goods".
This monstrous concept, that separates the soul of man completely
from his body and deprives it of any vital activity, explains the
attitude of the German to authority. It made possible the Prussian
state and the Third Reich, in which even devout Protestants ac-

cepted without contradiction whatever was imposed upon them, and began to resist only when their creed was challenged.

With the peasant revolts and peasant wars that spread over Germany and parts of Switzerland the rise of the *Anabaptist movement* was connected, a movement diametrically opposed to Lutheranism. For it made the most radical claims and evolved schemes of social revolution deriving from the Bible and from primeval Christianity. This movement was not an outcome of the Reformation, though its growth was furthered greatly by the Protestant trend; it sprang from much earlier sources, from the mystics, from Wyclif and Hus, and possibly even from the Waldensian movement. Even before the Reformation, in the fifteenth century, pamphlets appeared, written by minor clerics but expressing and reflecting the feelings and desires of the common people, especially of the peasants. The most important of these hailed from the Black Forest, where a great revolt of the peasants started subsequently. It was directed against the lords and princes and against the Roman hierarchy. It refers to a divine natural law, which is contrary to the prevailing historical law, and accordingly does not countenance the corrupt institutions of serfdom and bondage, but grants to all men equal rights to pastures, woods and waters—at this time, in fact, the peasants were forbidden to hunt and to fish. The author of this pamphlet considers common property, communism, the true and genuine order instituted by God and invalidated by sinful man. He advocates the secularization of property and the revenues of the church, the abolition of ecclesiastical and secular rulership, of the monasteries and of donations to the church; the only ruler of the country is to be the emperor, and only he should levy taxes and establish a uniform coinage. He rages against big capital in any form, against bankers and holders of monopolies as well as against the clergy and the princes. But even the emperor is considered subject to law and justice, and if he fails in the exercise of his duties, the people may impeach him. For, it is said, "the people makes the emperor, but the emperor does not make the people."

These are advanced principles, they even anticipate modern

socialist tendencies. And in these pamphlets we may already find the characteristic features of Anabaptist teachings. They derive their authority not only from the Bible, as the Protestant doctrines do, but from personal, individual inspiration and conscience, from a prophetic spirit, from the presence of God in the individual soul. The preachers of the Anabaptist movement were all prophets. They were continually expecting the early advent of a sacred millennium in which all their dreams and claims would be fulfilled. Among them were humble and steadfast men who died as martyrs for their conviction. The princes and the city authorities, even Protestant city authorities, took a hideous revenge on these preachers for the effects of their preaching. They drowned them and burned them wherever they could, for they realized that this was a vast and dangerous revolutionary movement, spreading all over Germany, Switzerland and the Netherlands. It incited the peasants and the poor city folk to Utopian dreams and to the revolt necessary to achieve their fulfilment. It tended to restore and to revive the Evangelical community that "did not elect a worldly authority from among themselves", but was a perfect community without any explicit law and rulership, a community in which peace, love, charity and mutual help reigned supreme. In accordance with these ideals, the Anabaptists rejected the use of arms and other customs not substantiated in the Gospels, particularly infant baptism and the taking of oaths. Once, in Zuerich, in 1525, when they were persecuted and driven from the city, they met secretly for a last time before leaving and read the Bible together for comfort and support. In this hour of deep emotion, one of them rose and asked his "brother" to baptize him. And so they all baptized one another as a solemn pledge of holy community. And this, according to their tradition, was the beginning of the custom of anabaptism, or adult baptism, which later became a principle with them, as they believed that baptism should only take place in full awareness of the sacrament. They subsequently termed themselves Baptists instead of Anabaptists.

When, in the course of persecutions, the élite of their leaders had been killed, more and more vulgar, confused and violent people took their place. In announcing the coming of the Kingdom of God at a certain date, these preachers took upon themselves the role of sacred prophets and savior kings. And when the Kingdom of God failed to materialize and more and more obstacles began to tower in their path, they started riots and mass upheavals. They took the offensive, stormed the churches and destroyed the images of the saints, for as a result of the religious trends that referred to the Scriptures, a new iconoclastic movement had arisen, since in the Bible, of course, there is no allusion to or authorization for the worship of images. They seized the property of the church, dislodged the clergy, killed dissenters; and eventually the Dutch prophet, Jan Matthisson from Haarlem, succeeded in assuming control of the city of Muenster in Westphalia, which, for one year, from May 1534 to June 1535, became the headquarters and the center of propaganda of the movement and the scene of a phantastic Biblical kingdom, a mixture of ecstatic devoutness and dissolute mob rule. The city was presently besieged by the troops of the bishop and of allied princes, but it was also valiantly and shrewdly defended. The prophet was killed in a skirmish, and another Dutchman, the tailor, Jan Bockelson from Leyden, established what he called a new Israel or a new Zion, a theocratic regime headed by "twelve elders of the tribes of Israel", with the Holy Scriptures as civil code and a distribution of common works along the lines of the craft guild city. When Jan van Leyden made himself an Oriental king and introduced polygamy, the whole experiment degenerated in gross orgies. Eventually, the troops of the bishop occupied the city and the leaders were tortured and executed in public.

In many Dutch and Rhenish cities, similar attempts to seize control of the community were made, but they were not successful. The Anabaptist movement had lapsed into a peaceful emulation of primeval Christianity, when it was regenerated in the Netherlands by the preacher Menno Simons (1492–1559) the founder of the Mennonite sect, who refused to take an oath and to perform military service. Yet the Anabaptists were always ready for revolutionary moves, they were an important motor in the liberation of the Netherlands and in the English, as well as in the American Revolution.

The movement in itself, however, would not have been able to safeguard the new spirit of reform, to conquer and to maintain its position amid the turmoil of struggle of the European political forces, and to prepare the way for the development of democracy. While the Lutherans were too conservative, too much absorbed by purely theological problems, and wholly compliant to the rule of princes, the Anabaptists, on their part, were too radical, too Utopian and confused, too out of touch with political realities. They expected a miracle, they wanted to realize the perfect human community, the ultimate ideal of humanity, and they wanted to realize it at once. The Protestant cause would not have been able to withstand the onslaught of the Counter-Reformation without the political ingenuity of the other great reformer of the epoch, Jean Calvin.

Jean Calvin was born in 1509, in Noyon in the Picardy, and was reared in the family of a French nobleman. In 1523 he was sent to Paris to attend the "Collège Montaigu", where, at about the same time, Ignatius de Loyola, the founder of the Jesuit order, pursued his studies. The same Spanish instructor educated both. In considering the doctrine and work of Calvin, these three facts are of special significance: his French nationality, the aristocratic environment of his youth and, above all, his education by the same master who taught Loyola. On the Protestant side, Calvin is the exact counterpart of Loyola who led the Counter-Reformation. He is the only peer of the Jesuits, the only one who was able to match their qualities. Because of this, and because the spirit of the times was on his side, he saved the Protestant cause.

He began with theological studies and later took up jurisprudence. He became acquainted with the writings and teachings of the humanists who, by their criticism, fostered the opposition against the church. In this period, the humanistic intelligentsia played a role similar to that of the literati of the enlightenment in the eighteenth century, before the French Revolution. Without taking a decisive step, they undermined the established system.

And just as in the eighteenth century, French society and nobility, which was always alive to the most advanced intellectual fashions, flirted with the new ideas until they grew serious. The writings of Luther were eagerly read and discussed.

Calvin's first plan was to work for a general purge, for a profound regeneration of the Catholic Church, in the manner of the humanists, especially of Erasmus of Rotterdam. But suddenly, in about 1533, he had a great awakening, an experience akin to the inspirations of prophets, converts and religious reformers before him, from Paul, Augustine, Peter Valdes and Luther who was struck by lightning, to Zwingli who faced death by pestilence. "As by a sudden beam of light," Calvin writes, "I now realized, after my mind had long been prepared for a great test, what an abyss of errors, what a deep filth I had been submerged in up to now. So I did, my Lord, what was my duty, and, alarmed and condemning my former life with tears, I set out on Thy way."

After having proclaimed the evangelical principles in a speech at the Sorbonne on All Saints Day, 1533, he had to flee to Southern France, and soon afterwards went to Basle in Switzerland, in order to resume his theological studies systematically. The result was a book that established the fundamentals of his doctrine, the "Christianae Religionis Institutio", the Institutes of Christian Religion —the first complete system of Protestant theology. Neither Luther nor Zwingli laid down their principles in a coherent, theoretic system. Even Melanchthon, the theorist of Lutheranism, worked out only loose arguments and commentaries. Calvin's "Institutes" appeared in 1536 and were revised several times. His theory assumed its definite shape in 1540.

Calvinism is a Romanized form of Protestantism. It bears the traces of French nationality and of the aristocratic character of its originator. It is a curious blend of the Protestant democratization of religion with an infusion of the national principle and the aristocratic qualification for promoting an élite. It is congenial to Jesuitism in that it makes Protestantism pragmatic and political; it introduces fanatic discipline and methodical organization of the entire individual and communal life of its adherents. Lutheranism reduces religion to the role of a moral police, assisting and sanctioning the much more effective governmental police. Calvinism, on the contrary, is a totalitarian religion, claiming predominance and control over every profane institution and activity. Nothing is excluded from the immediate religious concern. So, as it had to embrace the whole body of individual and communal life, it actually revolutionized individual and communal life, and in doing this, in engaging in the social and political problems of its age, it, too—in the opposite way to Lutheranism—led to a secularized world.

The magnificence and the glory of God is at the core of Calvin's theory. His God resumes the personal shape of Jehovah, the God of the Old Testament. The stress shifts from Jesus to God the Father, and from the New to the Old Testament. And it is the old Jewish concept of God as the personal, omnipotent ruler of the world, and of the world as the scene of the glory of God, that is restored in Calvinism, only in a much more radical and indeed autocratic interpretation. In Judaism, God is not an arbitrary power. He has made a covenant with man and has committed Himself to the observance of the Law. He has revealed Himself and He is in constant contact with every human being. In Calvinism, God is an arbitrary power, inscrutable in his arbitrariness. His will dominates the world and His glorification is the idea of the world. In His omnipotence, He has, from the outset, predestined some to virtue and salvation by "His gratuitous mercy, totally irrespective of human merit", others He has doomed to vice and damnation "by a just and irreprehensible but incomprehensible judgement." The fact that not all men could be converted, is taken as a proof of God's predestination. No one is absolutely certain which group he belongs to, and, in any case, he can do nothing to alter his destiny. Calvin goes much further than Augustine, Wiclif or Luther. He carries the Pauline principle of the grace of God to the extreme. By his theory of integral predestination he dealt the heaviest blow to Catholicism, which appealed to the human will and effort to secure salvation through good works. Augustine had attributed the power of absolution to the church.

Luther had at least admitted the possibility of justification through faith. But if predestination is fixed and irrevocable, if salvation cannot be obtained by human will, the institution of the church is struck at the very root. The reply to Luther was that faith cannot effect salvation, that the order is quite the reverse: there would be no faithful, if there were no elect.

Thus the Calvinistic doctrine bears the traces of its French origin, it has a clearly national and aristocratic character. It is democratic in that it abolishes all differences of worldly, social or hierarchical, rank. But it institutes an absolute monarchy of God. It establishes its own religious aristocracy by birth, a religious élite of saintly and pure people chosen by God. It creates a religious nation and nobility. The term "nation" is justified in this connection because the life of these saints in itself was not religious, not ritual, but profane. It consisted of profane activities under confessional, moral control.

Hence the meaning of personal existence was no longer the gain of personal salvation—the goal of all Christian striving up to this point—for God had already decided as to who was to be saved and who not. Nor is it the realization of a revealed plan of God, as in Judaism, of the establishment or re-establishment of a kingdom of justice and peace and love on earth. Here it is the question only of the "gloire" of God and of the display of His magnificence. For the sake of this glory, the profane world is sanctified, is to be permeated with holiness. Therefore man's inner faith is not enough —there must be active work. It is true that the individual can do nothing about his own salvation, but by the righteousness of his life he can verify his membership in the group of the elect. Provided he carries on his work under the strict observance of due moral and religious obligations, and if, under these conditions, he prospers in his work, this may be accepted as proof of his salvation. Accordingly, wealth and well-being prove hard work and diligence and may be taken as a sign of being in the grace of God. Poverty, on the other hand, that had been respected and even exalted in early and medieval Christianity, becomes contemptible, the proof of idleness and vice. All this made for the stern reserve and solitude of the Puritan, for a profound distrust of one's neighbor, indeed, of one's brother, for nobody could know in what state of grace the other was, and whether evil might not accrue from intercourse with him. This fostered individualism, as everyone had to care for himself. Charity and working for the common weal, were ordained, but not for the sake of the human being or of the human community, but only for the glory of God and to show the excellence of His order. Aside from this, all feelings and impulses of justice, mercy and compassion must be suppressed when the majesty of God is at stake, and neither the elect nor the damned have a right to complain of injustice.

The Calvinistic regulations for social and economic activities were severe and meticulous, but practical. Calvin broke with the Catholic and Lutheran disapproval of trade, banking and the taking of interest. He scorned Catholic hypocrisy that cursed all of these pursuits in theory and encouraged and exploited them in practice. He also recognized that the Lutheran stand against modern economic methods could no longer be upheld. His own preoccupations as the leader of a bourgeois community, in which trade played a considerable part, led him to this conclusion. It was his desire to govern all of human life by his religious rule, and so he openly furthered all economic activities and declared them justifiable, provided they were carried on under his own supervision and with the restrictions he imposed. "Calvin deals with usurie as the apothecarie doth with poyson," wrote an English divine in 1611. Only interest desirable for production is permissible and then only a certain determined maximum. Poor people should be lent money without interest and the question of security should be waived. The debtor must have at least as much advantage of the transaction as the lender. Money-lending should not be a steady calling and the striving for gain must not be deleterious to one's neighbor. On the other hand, Calvin wrote in a letter: "Is there any reason why the profits from business should not be greater than those from landownership? How does the merchant make profits? From work and care and diligence!" The accumulation of riches is not only allowed, it is prescribed. Man must accumulate riches for God, whose administrator he is. He must account for every farthing, he must economize for God. He may change his profession at will, should he be able to serve the glory of God better in another field, and whether this is so will be shown by increased gains. But to enjoy riches in a leisurely manner is sinful. Just as man must work, so earned money must continue working through productive investment. Frivolous pleasures, such as the theater, dancing and singing, were considered a crime and punishable as such in strict Calvinistic communities—as in Geneva and New England. Waste of time was one of the worst sins. Every hour spent on something other than divine service or work meant defrauding and robbing God. Calvinists, moreover, were obliged to refrain from those unscrupulous ways of making money that the Catholics utilized without hesitation, such as privateering, colonial speculations, lease of offices and taxes, credit operations with princes, and monopolies. They were forced to earn their money by intensive methods, by the rational exploitation of market conditions, by manufacture, and in manufacture, by technical improvement and shortening of the work processes. When we consider that these profane saints committed themselves to the utmost economy and increase of property, that they threw all their vitality and religious zeal into business, that the Puritans, indeed, under the hostile regime of France, Holland and England could hold no positions in public life and were entirely dependent upon trading, we may imagine to what extent they were driven to promote industrial, technical and capitalistic developments.

Out of this economic constitution, modern capitalism, the capitalist state of mind, developed and expanded. It was not created by Calvinism, for—so we found—it emerged from the special conditions of the German craft guild city, but the spirit of Calvinism gave it the decisive impetus, so that it spread and intensified until it became dominant in England and America and later all over the world. In the course of rapid economic development, the religious motive gradually receded and deteriorated. For a time it persisted in the form of a moral code of commercial honesty, but eventually, with the increasing rush of competition and opportunities, with the growing anonymity of enterprise, only the mere skeleton of the Puritan way of life remained: the suppression of all subjective human impulses—attachment to one's fellow men or to one's ego and the pleasures of life—professional activity per se and the breathless tempo of work. In the end, the power and the glory of God were replaced by the power and the glory of goods. The result was capitalistic man, who no longer enjoys his existence as an individual, who no longer enjoys the fruits of his labors, but consumes his strength and his energies in impersonal, mammoth enterprises. Enterprise became the ethics of living. The economic transcendence of the individual was complete.

The social structure and order of the Anglican peoples becomes apparent in the Calvinistic religious constitution. Socially, Calvinism, as well as Anglican liberalism, means individualism under collective protection, individual competition safeguarded by a commonwealth government. It means a democratic beginning and an aristocratic result. The Calvinistic divine ruler admits no difference of rank among men, but only a difference of individual quality, of individual predestination manifested through personal efficiency. When, in the place of the divine ruler, we put the democratic government which holds all citizens theoretically equal, competing on equal terms and prevailing through natural fitness and personal efficiency, we have the ideal structure of the English and American democracy. In England, this democracy was somewhat tempered by monarchical and feudal traditions and by an initial development along national lines. In America, the democracy developed in its integral form from the very outset.

There is, however, a sharp distinction between original Calvinism, the Calvinism of the community of *Geneva,* and the later Calvinism of the diaspora which was affected by its unusual political and social conditions, and, moreover, underwent Anabaptist influence. It was this later Calvinism that formed the Anglican democracy. Since Calvin claimed control of religion over all of human life, the reform and indeed revolutionizing of the social order and the political community came as a corollary. He wanted to create a community of pure and saintly men, a community of the elect. The full revolutionary and political significance of his claims could not make itself felt in his parish in Geneva, which had been independent and reformed before his advent. And personally he was inclined to be authoritative and aristocratic. Not until the diaspora, did the control over every aspect of living necessarily lead to political revolution.

For a time Calvin fled to Italy from the Inquisition. After a brief visit to his native town of Noyon, he intended going to Strasbourg and, on his way there, he passed through Geneva (1536). At first he only wanted to spend the night there, but in the end he turned the city into his new Jerusalem. Geneva had just completed her liberation from the Dukes of Savoy—the ancestors of the present Italian dynasty which, as the Hapsburgs, originated in Switzerland. In the course of this struggle for freedom, evangelical reforms had been introduced. There was a great deal of confusion about the new organization of the church and the community, and when the leader of the Protestant movement, William Farel, heard that Calvin, whose book he knew, was in the city, he persuaded him to stay and help him build up the new community. Calvin set to work, and it was a hard task to convert this lively and frivolous Geneva into a community of saints. The city resisted fiercely, but the fanaticism and the political ingenuity of Calvin triumphed. The people of Geneva were eventually stamped with that austere character that is preserved there up to this very day. More than that: Geneva became the headquarters, the international political center of Protestantism; it became a symbol of the expanding movement, as Moscow is for the communists today. In the midst of a damned world, the people of Geneva felt that they were the chosen, and this unique realization of Calvin's concept inspired Puritans everywhere in the world to their revolutionary deeds. The discipline and organization of this community, and the political maintenance and expansion of the Protestant cause, makes Calvin equal to Loyola. Both men were fanatic disciplinarians with inflexible rigor and indeed cruelty toward themselves as well as others.

In Calvin's community, there were no priests. Everyone was to be his own priest. The Bible in its literal interpretation became the civil code of the community. The Geneva parish was not in the least democratic. They were governed by ministers and presbyters. These twelve presbyters, corresponding to the twelve Apostles, were appointed by the aristocratic councils assisted by the ministers. After rigid examinations, the ministers were appointed by their own colleges. The aristocratic community council in which the religious element was the decisive, controlled everything and everyone, not only in public, but also in private life. "The office of the elder," it was said, "consists of watching over the life of everybody". The city was divided into quarters, each headed by one of the elders. Every household, irrespective of rank, had to be open to regular inspection, and every move, opinion, action and word in the home or on the street, in society or in church, was under constant supervision. Control extended even to the number of courses that could be served at a meal, the color and fabric of clothing. Punishments were ruthless. Between 1542 and 1548, when the city had 16,000 inhabitants, there were fifty-eight executions and seventy-six expulsions. Torture was used systematically, and once even a child was beheaded for daring to strike his parents. Spectacles and plays were prohibited and all public houses were closed. Thus the holy community was a city of glass, as R. H. Tawney puts it.

The spread of Calvinism had *revolutionary effects* everywhere in Western Europe, and in the course of these revolutions, modern democracy developed step by step. In the Netherlands, that belonged to the Spanish Hapsburgs, the activity of the Anabaptists challenged and aroused the Inquisition, but Calvinistic forces took the lead in the revolution. Under the direction of Calvin and with the help of the French refugees, Calvinistic communities were organized all over the country. They became powerful centers of resistance, and carried out the war of liberation which freed the Netherlands from Spanish rule, established the Dutch republic and made Calvinism the official religion. In France, the Huguenot communities with their Presbyterian constitution, where the presbyters were elected by the community, secretly formed independent units involving republican tendencies. The Palatinate became Calvinistic and, by implication, the leading Protestant force in the first phase of the Thirty Years' War. In Scotland, the Protestant movement, under the leadership of John Knox, who was in close connection with Calvin, overthrew the rule of Mary Stuart, and here also, Calvinism became the dominant religion.

England, situated between the Protestant Netherlands and Protestant Scotland, was bound to become the scene of the crucial struggle. Here, the destiny of the Protestant cause was decided. This struggle was simultaneously a struggle against the absolute monarchy, and more than that—in it, the English nationality, the English character, as it is today, was born. In the friction between the Romanic and Germanic elements, of which it is composed, it reached its definite shape. English nationality emerged complete only after this stormy period, when all had quieted down under the rule of William and Mary, at the end of the seventeenth century. And it was completed together with the first establishment of democracy. Both are one and the same.

England had had a long and special preparation for this development. Her whole history tends in this direction. There is a widespread belief that English democracy originated in the Magna Charta of 1215. This is a legend created by the interpretation of certain jurists of the English revolution. The Great Charter, though it is an important document, though it is a bill of rights, was mainly concerned with the maintenance of the prerogatives of the feudal aristocracy against the power of the king. The preliminaries for English democracy lie much deeper. They lie in the subterranean persistence of Germanic freedoms as they were preserved in the Swiss democracy, for instance. The kings of England had distorted them for their own selfish purposes, but could never abolish them entirely. The gradual recovery of these old freedoms under new forms is a long and complicated process. It runs through the various transformations of parliaments that here, other than in France, were from the very outset political assemblies, summoned chiefly for voting supply, through the foundation of the House of Commons by Simon of Montfort in the thirteenth century, and the transformation of the feudal law into common law under Edward I, also in the thirteenth century, through the principle that the consent of parliament is essential for legislation, established in the fourteenth century, the evolution of the idea of representation of the people in the Commons and their growing influence at the end of the Middle Ages. The Great Protestation (1621) and the Petition of Rights (1628) were further steps, but these already introduced the great revolution.

A crucial impetus to the development of English democracy, however, came from the English monarchy's breach with the Catholic Church. This breach was initiated by personal and dynastic motives of Henry VIII, who was wholly indifferent to religious matters but wanted to divorce his wife Catherine in order to marry Ann Boleyn, a procedure the pope refused to allow. Henry VIII was supported in this decision by his minister, Thomas Cromwell, a violent and unscrupulous man, who wanted to abolish the monasteries and to enrich himself and his party with the confiscated property of the church. (One of his descendants was Oliver Cromwell.) Henry put himself at the head of the English Church. He did not alter the Roman rites but persecuted Catholics and Protestants alike. Under his son, Edward VI, Protestantism penetrated into England, but the result was the founding of the High Church which combined a Protestant doctrine with a Catholic constitution and service. It was at this time that the Book of Common Prayer was instituted. Protestantism, however, had not as yet taken root in the people. Its adherents were, for the most part, members of the gentry who became "gospellers" merely because they wanted a share in the confiscated estates of the Roman clergy. When Catholic Queen Mary restored the Roman Church and persecuted the Protestants most cruelly, the people were on her side. But under the rule of Elizabeth, who re-established the High Church, and especially under the Stuart kings, who aimed at an absolute monarchy and again favored the Catholics, the power of the Puritans together with Anabaptist influence increased more and more, and the result was the great revolution.

A new, more radical and more democratic branch formed among

the Puritans: the Independents. They rejected the aristocratic religious constitution of the Presbyterians. They rejected the religious guidance of any church authorities and sought God in the inner self, in the soul of the individual. To them the church was complete "wherever two or three faithful people congregate in the name of the Lord." Politically, they were just as radical. They were the Jacobins of the English Revolution, and it was they, who, under their leader, Oliver Cromwell, for the first time executed a king and inaugurated modern democracy. It was, to be sure, a far cry to the completed form of English democracy. The present state, which still does not constitute the entire supremacy of the people, was not attained until the beginning of the twentieth century.

The most advanced form of modern democracy was established in the United States. Again it was the Puritans and Anabaptists who paved the way. Here the Puritans could make a clean start from which to develop their free communities. Here they found a vast field for economic expansion. The impetus that came from Evangelism, the colonial beginning and the economic field of work, all united in the shaping of the modern democracy.

STATE

MODERN DEMOCRACY MEANS individualism under collective protection, free individual competition safeguarded by a commonwealth government. This structure was foreshadowed in the Calvinistic concept of individual striving for prosperity as a proof of personal salvation, under the religious safeguard of the common weal. Later this safeguard was provided by the democratic government, though less effectively because of the dwindling influence of a superhuman authority and the growing importance of the prosperous themselves. Democracy, then, shows a tense ambivalence, a fluctuation between individualistic and collectivistic trends, and its functioning depends on the maintenance of balance between the two.

In the form in which it has been developed in Germany, the *state* is a collective unit in which the individual is completely subject to and dominated by a common goal that institutes and constitutes the state. The common goal of the state does not necessarily derive from a common will of its constituents; it is imposed on the individuals by a ruler or a leader or an abstract ideology, by an authority above and beyond the people, and this is the one fundamental feature that prevents the state from being an integral collective. In a fully developed state, however, the ruler is no longer a merely personal ruler, he includes himself in the subjection of all to the common goal. Though it is he who determines the common goal, he also subjects himself to it. The goal of the state is an abstract idea separated from the personal ruler. This is the difference between the French monarchs who clearly identify the regime with themselves, and the Prussian monarchs who considered themselves as "the first servants" of the regime. And this difference implies an intrinsically different conception of rulership.

Rudimentary beginnings of the state are to be found even in early antiquity. In fact, the first elements of the state are established when the first deliberate organization of a people sets in. In the ancient Oriental kingdoms, in the Greek polis, and especially in the Roman World Empire, the structure of the state is traceable. It is implied in the establishment of an extensive bureaucracy and the various institutions of a more and more complex administration. But the ancient state is no pure state, no autonomous state. It does not coincide with the substance of the community, it does not form the only, or the predominant, substratum and life principle of the community. It is a mere function of a different substance and life principle which really governs and constitutes the community, a function of the essence of the tribe, the deity, the divine king or the sacred city-state and its common cause, the "res publica". Accordingly, our modern meaning of the word does not exist in antiquity. There is no word for state, in our sense, in the ancient language. In ancient Rome the Latin word "status", from which our "state" derives, signifies state only in the meaning of "condition". Our modern term "state" starts on its career in the Renaissance, when we find the term "stato di Firenze", or "stato di Milano", an expression in which the meaning of the condition of a government turns into and fuses with the meaning of the constitution, the order of a government. Machiavelli introduced this term into political theory. His "Principe" begins with the words: "Tutti gli stati, tutti i dominii che hanno avuto ed hanno imperio sopra gli uomini . . ."—"all the states, all the forms of rulership which had and have control over men . . ." From these words, however, it becomes clear that "state" is still identical with rulership. The all-comprising, all-pervading meaning of the word, designating the ideal abstract of the organized community, was perfected together with the phenomenon itself, in Germany, where the term "Staat" assumes an abstract and almost majestic significance.

It is no mere coincidence that the state in its autonomous and abstract form originated in Germany, and especially in the territorial dominions which were in distinct contrast, indeed in opposition, to the "Reich", the vague, mystical and magical supreme unity. The territorial dominions had first been "lands", the private estates of the magnates. But when these magnates began to collect territories scattered all over the country, when they began to organize a common administration of these various estates, this name of "state" was the only term which could express adequately both the interior administration and the administrative unit of these territories. They had no substantial foundation; there was no nation, not even a compact, regional, provincial community of the lands and the populations. The regional communities and populations were cut asunder by the inorganic dominions. The people were only an unimportant appendage of the land. The princes, who were always short of money, often sold them to foreign powers as mercenaries. There was, in fact, nothing to unite these territories except dynastic property, dynastic rule. As organization proceeded and began to outgrow the mere administration of private estates, it was, therefore, quite natural that the state should emerge as a completely autonomous and abstract entity. It reached its perfection only in *Prussia*. We may even say that it was created in Prussia, which had become and, up to now, has remained the model state.

This is due to various constitutional factors that converge to a unique predisposition for this particular development. First, there is the special character of the land and its territorial and cultural evolution. What was to become the Prussian kingdom took issue from two territories which originally were not geographically connected. It was not until 1772, when Frederick II (the Great) conquered the land lying in between, that they formed a compact territorial body, and this was long after the constitution of the Prussian state. These two territories, situated in the extreme North and Northeast of Germany, were the *March of Brandenburg* and the *dominion of Prussia*. "March" originally means borderland, and the outposts at the frontiers of Christian civilization were called marches. The term "landmark", in the meaning of boundary stone, shows a corresponding significance in English.

The Christianization and land cultivation of these two territories, which had separate and different beginnings, were the last, the most difficult and the most methodical undertakings of this kind in Germany. Only in the twelfth century, after Poland, Scandinavia, even Russia, had been Christianized, were these last pagan enclaves incorporated in the Holy Roman Empire. The land was sandy, dismal plain, or swampy forest, a grim, unyielding soil. The population consisted of Slav tribes and Prussians, a stock of uncertain origin. The Christianization and cultivation of these areas was true colonization in the modern sense of the word. It was not conquest by the compact might of tribal rulers, but the undertaking of heterogeneous people intent upon a mission and the acquisition of land.

Knightly settlers moved into Brandenburg under the aegis of the Cistercian monks, the active order which was first to engage in worldly works of common usefulness, especially farming. These monks founded monasteries and farmsteads all over the country, and from these points they directed the settlement and the systematic clearing and cultivation of the land. The native population provided a foundation of serfdom that sustained the manorial German or Slavonic lords. It was in this period that "Junkertum", the rule of rural landed proprietors of noble origin was born and developed. In 1415, after a century of mismanagement, savage feuds of the nobles and internal anarchy of the country, which had nevertheless become an electorate in the meantime, the Emperor Sigismund granted the harassed and impoverished March of Brandenburg to Frederick, a Hohenzollern prince, for his assistance—a solid advance of money—in the matter of acquiring the imperial crown. And thus began the career of the Swabian Hohenzollern family.

The other territory, Prussia, was also partly plain, partly pathless forest and interspersed with swamps and lakes. Its inhabitants were the savage and stubborn Prussians, who had resisted numerous attempts at conversion. But here a very interesting and significant experiment of administration foreshadowed the later work of the Hohenzollern in an astonishing way. This was the rulership of the Teutonic Knights.

The *Teutonic Knights* were one of the three great orders of knighthood that were a creation of the crusades. The other and older orders, Romanic in origin, were the Hospitalers or Maltese Knights, and the Templars. As the name of the first of these orders indicates, its original function was the care of sick or wounded crusaders and pilgrims. The Templars were named for their house in Jerusalem, which was located at a point where Solomon's Temple was supposed to have stood. Hence the buildings that housed this order in European cities, were known as "temples". Another function was gradually added to the care of the sick: the safe conduct of pilgrims through the endangered regions of Asia Minor and Palestine, the protection of holy places and the continuous struggle against unbelievers and the pirates of the Mediterranean who threatened sea-faring pilgrims. The orders became a permanent guard of the church. They were semi-monastic organizations, a combination of monkhood and knighthood. Through the membership of powerful European noblemen, through large donations of non-active members and expeditions in the Mediterranean, they gradually acquired great wealth, capital and property in the countries of Europe, and turned to economic activities among others—the Hospitalers to agriculture, the Templars to banking on a large scale. Thanks to their distribution over all of Europe and the Orient, thanks to their intellectual and knightly prestige, the Templars became the most important financial power of the thirteenth century and engaged in all the financial transactions and credit business of the time. This, however, led to their destruction when the French king, Philip the Fair, seized upon their fortune by the pseudo-legal methods that French monarchs were in the habit of employing against local merchants and Jews. Through the denunciation, imprisonment and torture of its members, the order itself, whose main power and influence lay in France, was destroyed.

The Teutonic Knights, however, embarked on a special trend of development when, in 1226, they had the pope appoint them for a permanent crusade against the remainders of paganism along the Northeastern frontier of the Holy Roman Empire. Their Grand Master, Hermann von Salza, also succeeded in establishing cordial relations with Frederick II, who granted the order the imperial insignia of the Black Eagle. This auspicious beginning was in the manner of a strange prognostication of Prussia's rise to the German Empire. The order followed a call of the Cistercians and the Duke of Massovia for aid in the Christianization of the Prussians. They conquered and established a large territory which, owing to its remote situation, became more and more independent from papal as well as from imperial authority. They made themselves independent of the emperor by transferring all their holdings to the pope and taking them back as fiefs of the church. And the far-away pope had no means of making his influence effective on their activities. Thus the Teutonic Knights, in preserving their semi-monastic constitution, developed into a military and commercial corporation of great power and wealth. They were a very unusual and significant social phenomenon, as they turned a monastic order into a true collective. They used the principles of the monastic community to build up a most active organization that pursued thoroughly worldly aims. Centuries before actual Protestantism, they made Christian asceticism secular and extravert. Their asceticism centered in the community and not in the individual soul, in a state for its own sake and not for the glory of God. They kept the monastic vows of obedience, chastity and poverty; they kept the monastic "hours", the times of the day set for prayer, the "vigils", the nightly services, and strict confession. But while the discipline of the monastic order was intended to separate one from the other, to isolate the individual for concentration and recollection even to the extreme of maintaining complete silence, the Teutonic Knights turned this discipline into collectivity. They lived a communal life; their cells were separated only by uncurtained partitions, they ate from common bowls, they slept in large, lighted halls. All their property, even down to objects of daily use, was held in common. They wore uniform clothes and the same uniformity prevailed in the construction of their castles, down to the most minute detail of the interiors and in the schedule of their day, no matter where they happened to be. The grand master depended on the chapter for all important decisions. He was responsible to the community and could be removed. All offices, including the highest, were continually watched over by a strict system of mutual control.

Long before the general consolidation of territorial dominions, this community of knights organized its landed property with methodical skill. They initiated a special combination of military and economic methods, which was to become the system of the Prussian state. They subdued the Prussian population by force of arms, curbed them to the point of serfdom, wiped out their language and their customs and forced them into the organization of a territorial militia. In order to keep this people down, they summoned German settlers, both noblemen and burghers, into the country. They disciplined and balanced all ranks and classes of the region. They founded cities, granted them municipal and commercial privileges, protected their free peasants against the landed proprietors and let them grow wealthy, and held their clergy in a state of subordination. They inaugurated a rigid administration with unflagging supervision of accounting, a separation of the private management of the order from the management of state property, uniformity of law, measures, weight and tender, all of which was unprecedented at the time, as applied to such a large area. They themselves competed with the towns they had founded, in that they carried on extensive trade by allying themselves with the Hanseatic League, and in the later Protestant manner, they, in contrast to the Romanic orders of knighthood, refrained from irregular or crooked ways of conducting business. In foreign countries and at home, they had agencies and maintained a whole staff of economic aides and administrators. All this was done for the sole purpose of strengthening and increasing the power of their consolidated property, a power which they did not enjoy individually, nor, like the Calvinists, hold as a gift of God and for the glory of God. Nor, in holding this power, did they represent the prestige of a nation, or a patrician élite, as, for instance, the Venetian aristocracy. From this super-individual quality, this abstractness, this unsubstantiality of a collective power, emerges the idea of the state as it was later perfected by the Hohenzollern monarchs.

In extending their dominion, the knights penetrated into Poland and Lithuania, thus arousing a strong reaction in these countries which united for the counterblow. And the long struggle that followed ended in the defeat of the knights in the battle of Tannenberg which marked the beginning of the decay of the order. This took place in 1410, in the very days when the Hohenzollern became electors of Brandenburg. The order also deteriorated internally through its growing commercialism and loss of discipline.

In 1525, the grand master of the order happened to be a Hohenzollern. In order to save the country from Polish pressure, he dissolved the decadent order, became Lutheran himself and Lutheranized and secularized the territory he received as a fief from the Polish king. His relatives in Brandenburg seized the opportunity, and, through marriages, tutelage over an insane heir and bargaining with the Polish king, they gradually gained control of Prussia.

The *Hohenzollern dynasty* belonged to that group of families that rose after the downfall of the Stauffers and the disintegration of the feudal empire. Their slow and steady ascent is in sharp contrast to the brilliant rise, the imperial dignity and human magic of the Hapsburgs who seemed to be admirably adapted for the great period of transition from the Middle Ages to the New Era. The Hohenzollern appeared designed for a much later age. In viewing the first part of their career, one wonders how a succession of sheer mediocrities was steadily able to augment their property and to enhance their position. And they accomplished this by their unpretentiousness, by their petty shrewdness in seizing opportunities, in being useful to the emperors and bargaining with other powers, by what English historians of Prussia (I. A. R. Marriott and C. G. Robertson) call "their fidelity to attainable ends". Their rise through the centuries was like a career of bureaucratic promotion: from burgrave of Nuernberg to vicar and elector of Brandenburg, to duke and king of Prussia, until at last they became German emperors for a few decades. Again and again in this family, fathers warned their impatient sons, as one of the early electors, John George, called "the Economist", did: "To become mighty and terrible—that is not the point! Save yourself and Brandenburg from exaggerated ambition!" And when the sons became rulers, they behaved like their fathers. Two main characteristics of the Hohenzollern, however, are manifest from the first—their military gift and their economic efficiency; but these qualities did not become apparent as the daring of a warrior or a speculator, but rather as the circumspection of an officer and an official. There is a fundamental difference between sheer bellicosity and militarism. Louis XIV was much more bellicose and arbitrarily and provokingly aggressive than the Prussian monarchs. He really enjoyed the challenge, the adventure and the glory of war, as he himself confessed: "J'ai trop aimé la guerre!" The Hohenzollern did not enjoy war, they enjoyed their army—which is quite a different thing—they enjoyed the formidable disciplinarian instrument they had evolved and its precise, machine-like functioning. They liked the petty, routine duty, the daily drill and the manoeuvres, but, though they believed in it, they did not actually like war in itself. The Great Elector, Frederick William, who created the army, worried sincerely about the "blood and tears" of his country, from which he had to wring his army. King Frederick William, who inaugurated and personified militarism, who perfected the army, who made it into the most admired and dreaded, the most efficient weapon of Europe, could never make up his mind to use it, and was deeply disturbed by scruples as to the problem of justifiable war. Of course he wanted a war, so that he might be able to test his marvelous instrument, but at the same time, he shrank from it, and waited all his life for what he might permit himself to consider as "a right and just occasion". In his political testament he wrote to his son: "I beg of you, my dear successor, not to be the aggressor in an unjust war . . . Study history and you will see by the examples of King Louis XIV of France, King Augustus of Poland and the Elector of Bavaria, that unjust wars come to no good end . . ." His son, Prince Henry, was an extraordinary strategist and his military talents were considered by experts as even greater than those of his famous brother, Frederick the Great. And yet he combined with these military qualities, a distinct dislike, indeed a distaste, for war, which he occasionally showed candidly and demonstratively. And his eminent brother, Frederick, who did become an aggressor and started unjust wars, took this upon himself as a terrible burden; he was perfectly aware that he was committing an anarchical act, that he was betraying and invalidating his better self, the humane, enlightened mind he had professed in youth and expressed in his pamphlet against Machiavelli. He was a broken man from the day he assumed rulership. He despised the human beings whom he was supposed to treat in such a way. He despised himself, because he felt subject to this duty enjoined on him by the state. "Soyons donc fourbe," he goaded himself on. "Let's be a scoundrel!" In the midst of the battles of the Seven Years' War, he once exclaimed: "O God, if there is one, save my soul, if I have one!" And when, after this war had been brought to a successful conclusion, he was receiving congratulations on the most glorious day of his life, he replied: "The most glorious day of my life will be the day when I leave it."

This ambivalent attitude of the Prussian monarchs gives an idea of the intricacies and complexities of the German character. There is a deep rift between the concept of an objective lawfulness, which these monarchs connected with the idea of the state and wanted to institute within the boundaries of their state by all possible means, even by autocratic means, and the awareness of the lawlessness and anarchy which prevailed in international relations, and, accordingly, their duty to cope with this lawlessness, a duty to which they considered themselves committed by the task of preservation and aggrandizement of their state. The care for the consolidation, organization and administration of their poor and scattered territories, was a task more difficult than that of any ruler in Europe. In the course of this work, the goal—the state as an institution in itself—developed an existence of its own. It became an abstract entity of its own, separate from personal or dynastic rulership. And even the rulers felt themselves subject and bound to the law of this abstract entity, the state. The well-known words, "I am the first servant of the state" were said not by one but by all outstanding Prussian monarchs. They expressed the true and naive conviction of even the most despotic characters among them.

This attitude does not diminish the fateful significance of the Hohenzollern regime. On the contrary, it shows only more clearly the pernicious implications of this regime which point to the present total state. For the utmost aggression and bellicosity of a personal monarch, the utmost selfishness of a greedy dynasty is less dangerous than this unselfish devotion to an abstract moloch of collective power which, as a supreme, objective being, eventually justifies the most bestial acts as a duty, a service, a self-sacrifice to a super-individual and quasi-idealistic end. Here lie the roots of the current events. There is still an immense difference between Hitler and the Hohenzollern, between the state of mind and the human standard of both. But the prerequisites for Hitler, the state of mind of the German people, and its relation to the state, originated in the Prussian experiment which, to a great extent, was a creation of the Hohenzollern family.

The influence of Lutheranism was also fundamental for the development and concept of the state, and of the Prussian state in particular. The Hohenzollern monarchs were secular-minded and not very much concerned about religion, though many of them were pious men. But their piety was not dogmatic and their religion became more and more identical with general public morality in conformity with the purposes of the state. Hence they changed their creed often and easily. They became Protestants, turned from Lutheranism to Calvinism and back to Lutheranism and then again to Calvinism, in accordance with political interests. They became Calvinist because of the acquisition of the Rhenish dominions of Cleves, Julich and Berg. Brandenburg and Prussia, however, were firmly Lutheran, and the dynasty inclined toward the Lutheran doctrine which did not interfere with their worldly regime, and even favored and supported its principles. King Frederick William I, though formally Calvinist, rejected the fundamental principle of his own creed, the dogma of predestination, and prohibited its discussion in his country, as he considered it disturbing to the minds of the people and against the interest of the state. As army chaplains he chose only Lutherans. The only Hohenzollern who seriously pondered religious problems was the free-thinker, Frederick II.

While Calvinism favored free individual competition and the formation of an economic élite, Lutheranism was predestined to produce a community of hard-working burghers and officials, a compact, unbroken community in which everyone had his fixed and limited professional function and competence, that assumed the character of an office held on behalf of the community. The inevitable consequence was an economy controlled and balanced by the state, an economy which proceeded and progressed not by individual competition, but as a whole collective body competing, in a body, with foreign economies. According to Luther, nobody was permitted to overstep his post, his calling, except in the regular, indeed bureaucratic course of promotion, that was left to God or to his appointed temporal authorities. In addition, Luther had provided these authorities, the kings and princes, with authorization of an unlimited use of their worldly power. He made a very significant and fatal distinction between their official function and their private personality. He severed the function from the man: "A prince can be a Christian, but he is not bound to rule as a Christian . . . His personality is Christian, but his office or principality has no concern with his being a Christian." This attitude illustrates how far secularization of the religious motive had developed in this religious doctrine. Uttered by a religious reformer, these words are far more pernicious than the theory of the layman, Machiavelli. These were the ideas by which generations of Lutheran ministers were trained to support unconditionally whatever their government imposed upon the people. Compare with this Calvin's preface to his "Institutes", addressed to the French king, Francis I: ". . . whoever does not reign to the end of serving God in His glory, is not a ruler, but a brigand. And whoever expects long prosperity in a reign not governed by the sceptre of God, by His sacred word—is under a delusion . . ."

The results become clear in the structure of the Prussian state: a collective where everyone was only a link in the machine-like rotation of functions, a social assembly-line.

The *Prussian state* was created by the three outstanding personalities of the Hohenzollern dynasty: the Great Elector (1640–1688), King Frederick William I (1713–1740) and Frederick II, the Great (1740–1786). After the death of Frederick II, the family lapsed into mediocrity and even gradual degeneration. Of these three personalities, the most important was King Frederick William I, though Frederick II was the only genius of the family. But this genius did not fit into the framework of the state and so he suppressed it in order to accomplish the task the almighty state required of him.

The Great Elector laid the foundations. He established the standing army that he could only maintain with the help of subsidies from foreign allies. He defeated the Poles and the Swedes, however; he made himself independent of the Poles in his capacity of Duke of Prussia, he expanded the dominion of Brandenburg by the acquisition of Pomerania and Magdeburg and he instituted the absolute monarchy by curbing the diet and the Junkers. His son, Frederick I, won the grant of the royal crown by the emperor. King Frederick William I actually shaped the Prussian state. He developed and perfected the army and made it the core of the whole administration. He emancipated it from foreign subsidies and based its support on strictly controlled and efficiently promoted domestic economy. Under his rulership, the state evolved from the administration of mere dynastic property and became an independent entity, to the regulations and taxes of which the king subjected his own possessions. Frederick II completed this work merely in regard to the external position of Prussia, which he raised to the rank of a grand power, an equal of the imperial power of the Hapsburgs. He waged war against the Empress Maria Theresia, defeated her and conquered Western Prussia and Silesia. As a result, Prussia was rounded off and became a mighty European power.

It must be remembered that the point of departure for the evolution of the Prussian state was the miserable Hohenzollern territory, the hard and unproductive soil, the shattered, disconnected lands, which, moreover, had suffered terribly from the devastations of the Thirty Years' War. From the very beginning, this country was a "have-not" and the Hohenzollern, high as they rose, always remained newcomers and upstarts. Wherever they arrived, they encountered mightier rivals who held better positions, the Hapsburgs, the French and the British. And this made for perpetual strain, indeed for over-strain, for a superhuman effort that colored all their achievements with a somewhat artificial character that they impressed on all of Germany when they took the lead into the Second Reich. They could not afford to compete with their rich and dignified rivals, the Austrian, French and English monarchs. They had to be and they were efficient, energetic and economical to the extreme. With the exceptions of the first king, Frederick I, who, like the other provincial princes of that epoch, wanted to emulate Louis XIV, and later, in the nineteenth century, the new Kaiser, William II, who wanted to play the part of a romantic emperor, they all led the life of petty bourgeois, and were eager to utilize every resource they could lay hands on. They had to repopulate their bare lands after the Thirty Years' War, and they had to put severe pressure on this new population in order to obtain money for establishing their military power. This they needed not only to increase their might but to preserve and organize their divers territories into a consistent unit. These circumstances caused the army to assume a unique role which it was not granted anywhere else. It became the main structural factor of the country. The history of the Prussian army is, by implication, the history of the Prussian state. The army begot the new officialdom and the activity and control of this officialdom, together with the Lutheran doctrine, shaped the whole character of the population. The king, Frederick William I, was the prototype of the Prussian officer, as well as of the Prussian official. He was the most striking example of that special Prussian combination of military and economic efficiency. "I am the field-marshal and the finance minister of Prussia," he said of himself.

An army of mere mercenaries was too expensive and not effective enough to perform the task of organization. The concept of organizing a country by means of an army could be realized only by a new system of discipline and drill. This had already been developed among the Dutch and Swedish troops. The scholarly, humanistic princes, Maurice of Orange and William Louis of Nassau, utilized the pattern of the Roman legion for transforming the loose order of the feudal levy into modern units with rank and file, methodical training and drilling practice, with rules and commandos. They also did away with the captains who had been independent military entrepreneurs, who hired themselves out together with the troops they commanded. They created the commissioned position of the modern officer and military instructor. The Dutch troops, however, were still an army of mercenaries who were particularly well paid in compensation for their new training and discipline. The Swedish army of Gustavus Adolphus was the first army raised by draft, and it added the national spirit to the new discipline. But even this army was not permanent; it dissolved after the Thirty Years' War.

The Prussian army was the first to combine the new methods of training and discipline with the establishment of a standing army. It was, in fact, the first standing army in the modern sense of the word. The methods of recruiting were draft and compulsion, both

making use of force and deception, much like the methods practised by the recruiters of the French Foreign Legion. Force was
applied at home toward Prussian subjects, deception toward people
of foreign countries. Peasants were simply arrested by their landed
proprietors, people of "mean extraction" in the cities were seized
and taken to the fortresses. The sons of nobles were not exempt
from this practice though they, of course, served as officers. Gendarmes of the king went to the estates and took them from their
families for the cadet corps. The commitment of soldiers was indefi-
nite. The regulations of 1726 state: "When one takes the oath to
the flag, one renounces oneself and surrenders entirely, even one's
life and all, to the monarch, in order to fulfil the Lord's will; and
through this blind obedience one receives the grace and the confirmation of the title of soldier." The methods of training were
most severe. Corporal punishment was practically unlimited. The
only restriction was that the captains were to pay for a disabled
man. Drilling methods, like the goose-step, were the means of
breaking the individual will and producing uniformity and a collective functioning of the utmost precision, in which no distinction
was made between the essential and the non-essential. Officers were
subject to no less rigid discipline and subordination. They had to
live with their soldiers, unlike French officers who lived at the
royal court. They had to wear uniform all the time. The most
minute details of their life were regulated: their religion, their
social intercourse, their expenditures. Even royal princes underwent
exactly the same treatment. Evidence hereof is the cruel curbing of
the young Frederick the Great. He frequently suffered severe corporal punishments, and after he once had tried to escape with two
friends, he was condemned to look on at the execution of one of
them.

From the army evolved the new officialdom. It carried military
discipline over into civil life and imbued the country with the spirit
of discipline. Superannuated officers and men were transferred to
the civil administration. Corporals and sergeant-majors were the
preferred candidates for the lower offices. The whole body of ad-

ministration, moreover, proceeded from a military office which was in charge of providing the necessary funds for the maintenance of the army, the General War Commissariat. The new civil administration not only managed the royal estates in the most efficient way, it developed a system of economic planning and stimulation that transformed the mercantilistic practices of the epoch into all-comprising, totalitarian control. The entire subsequent development of German political economy has followed the main lines of this policy up to the present day.

Unannounced inspections and spies checked up on the reliability of the officials. An official guilty of false reports, delays or bribery, was publicly struck in the face and imprisoned for life, if not hanged. On the other hand, the king pledged those who would serve him "with unsullied fidelity and untiring diligence" that "they can be firmly confident that I shall support them against the whole world and permit no intrigues except such as purpose to improve the civil service. I shall condemn no one before I have personally examined him in the presence of the informers."

The king also checked up in person on his administration and provinces. He was the kind of ruler Colbert had wanted Louis XIV to be. "He had to see with his own eyes what was taking place. Undeterred by the worst kind of roads and by inclement weather, he made frequent journeys to all his provinces. On these journeys he reviewed his regiments, held meetings with his various local officials, examined the accounts of his estates, inspected the military stores and magazines, and in general learned as much as he could about local conditions . . . It was not without reason that George II of England called him the 'king of the highroads'." One morning, on a walk through Potsdam, he met a group of people who were waiting for the postmaster who had overslept. With his own hands he helped to awaken the man by smashing the windows, with his own hands he thrashed him, and then apologized to the public for the laziness of his servant. On these walks, which were called "tours de bâton" because of the frequent canings that occurred whenever and wherever people did not behave as they should, he supervised and observed everything and everybody. An edict issued by the king in 1723 reads: "The huckstresses and other saleswomen on the streets and in the markets are not to sit with open mouths, but are to spin wool and flax, knit, or sew— under punishment of losing their concessions."

Statistical reports gave a current record of the number and the condition of workshops, farms, tools and workers. Manufacturing was greatly encouraged; consumption was guided and regimented. Economically useful refugees like the Huguenots, and the Protestants from Salzburg, were drawn into the country. Craftsmen, farmers and experts in special fields were transplanted by force from one province to another, according to economic needs. The working tempo was accelerated. Mail couriers had to function within a minimum time-limit. John Toland gives the same reports of Prussia that recent travelers in Fascist countries used enthusiastically to bring home: "I may truly say, that, without asking Questions of any Body, a Traveler may distinguish this Country by most sensible effects, as soon as he enters it. The Highways are here kept in better Order than elsewhere, the Posts are more regular, public Carriages are more expeditious; and wherever the ways divide themselves, there are strong Pillars erected with as many pointing Arms as there are Roads, bearing, in Letters cut or painted, the Names of the next Stage, and telling the number of Miles to that Place . . ." Even the idea of systematic breeding of a new, particularly vigorous race of men was planned by Frederick William I. Especially robust human specimens, grenadiers and Dutch peasant girls, were selected and ordered to marry and to provide many children.

Cultural life was similarly controlled. The sciences were promoted only in so far as they could serve official purposes. Only professors of economics were highly esteemed. But even these had to take their orders from the king who, as a matter of fact, had the greatest contempt for all intellectual activity. It was only with difficulty that he could be prevented from abolishing the Academy of Science that his father had founded on the French pattern. The funds necessary for its maintenance, which he considered entirely superfluous, he entered under the heading, "Expenditures for the King's fools". And he appointed to the presidency a man whom he actually used as a buffoon. He considered philosophers mere windbags and drove distinguished scholars, such as Christian Wolff, out of the country. Theological controversies were prohibited. "Salvation in heaven is God's province; all the rest is mine." This was the strictly Lutheran device of Frederick William I.

Frederick William I, the first representative of the Prussian type, and the variety of mankind he created, demonstrates a new form of the transcendence of the individual. The capitalist entrepreneur sacrifices his personal life for a business enterprise, the industrial nature of which already bears the earmarks of collective organization but which has still a purely private character. Its purpose, its raison d'être, is the accumulation of capital. But the Prussian already transcends Self in favor of a super-individual unit. Recently there has been talk of "Prussian socialism". But actually the purpose of the Prussian state is not the collective itself, that it has created and that works for it, not the good of the community itself, but an abstract aspiration toward political power independent of the real community of the people. The abstract concept of political power per se without reason or content—that is the meaningless meaning of this tremendous and perpetual effort that, in accordance with its inner law, cannot end until the world is conquered. And this concept is entirely in keeping with the restless and roaming character of the German people.

The Prussian state represents a perfect, gapless functioning, in which everybody is tied to his special job within the whole working process. On the one hand, it corresponds to the scheme of a Lutheran community, on the other, it is the archetype of the total state, not only because it claims control over every sphere of public and private life, but also because of its essentially unideological, indeed anti-ideological character. It was devoid of any substantial principle, of any idea of life, of the glory of God or the glory of a nation. Prussia was no nation in her own right, neither did she stand for German nationality and greatness. She was a perfect collective, but a collective that did not derive from the consensus and common will of a people, nor aim at the palpable well-being of a people. Her sole obsession was the dynamic functioning, was the ever-expanding, ever more powerful working process of the collective, the sport of building up power as such, a power that in reality was enjoyed by none, not even by the rulers, that was not meant to be enjoyed but to be followed as a "damn duty", an infinite, chimerical ideal in itself.

This original idea of the state was established and carried out by the Prussian monarchs in its pure-bred, artificial form. It was like an experimental preparation, a social homunculus, constructed of whatever stock of people was available, provided they proved fit for the task. The original form later swallowed and assimilated other intellectual, economic and social elements in the course of its expansion over Germany. It fused with the national movement of the wars of liberation against Napoleon, in which Prussia took the lead, and with the romantic and idealistic philosophy of the epoch—in this period, Hegel furnished the first theoretical formula of the state. It fused with the industrial revolution and incorporated the effects of the broad economic developments of the nineteenth century. The result was the Reich of Bismarck. Even at this time, Heinrich von Treitschke clearly formulated the principle of the total state: "The core of the state is power. The state is not there for the citizens. It is an end in itself. Since the state is power, it obviously can draw into its sphere of influence all human activities in so far as they are apparent in the external lives of men . . . Under certain conditions, the state will control human life as much as it is able to do so." Well, the certain conditions presented themselves. The state absorbed and assimilated the manifold social, economic, technical, intellectual and psychical revolutions, the anarchical witches' Sabbath of the period after the world war. The result was the National Socialist Total State which owes its formidable efficiency to the well-established concept of the Prussian state.

PREDOMINANCE OF ECONOMY AND
TECHNOLOGY: FREE ECONOMY

THE VARIOUS STRUGGLES for power waged between particular powers were only the surface display of an underlying and intrinsic
conflict between three main forms of community: the nation, the
democracy, the state. The different powers were only the exponents
of the different forms and principles of community which they
developed and perfected. And the shift of predominance from
Spain and France, in the first part of the modern era, to Britain
and Germany, in the later part, signified a general progression from
one form of community to the other, from the nation to the democracy and the state. This, at the same time, meant a growing trend
toward collectivity.

We saw that the nation is still a community of origin, birth and
tradition, effective in every separate individual. This makes possible a perfect and comprehensive representation of the community by a model individual, a personal monarch. The democracy
preserves the individual component of the nation, indeed emphasizes it, through expanding and equalizing the actual community and its management among the people, and through instituting the free initiative, the private enterprise of individuals.
But, by implication, it inaugurates the establishment of common
action, of collective action of individuals, and active protection of
individuals: self-government. The state goes still further in this
direction, as its very substance, its exclusive principle, consists in the
common action, in the collective work of individuals for an abstract idea of the community and its ever-expanding power.

The growing trend toward collectivity is confirmed by the transformation of the individual himself. The perfect capitalist, the final
result of the Puritan movement, and the extreme devotee to the
state, the perfect Prussian, have one essential feature in common
—they both transcend their individuality, they both go beyond
their personal existence toward an abstract goal. They both discard
the enjoyment of present, personal life in pursuing this abstract

goal: the capitalist spends all his vitality for the growth of his productive enterprise and the Prussian type sacrifices all his energies and concerns to the growth of power of his abstract state. These two super-personal attitudes, the capitalist and the Prussian, lead to two different forms of collectivity. The capitalist attitude, and the specific activity deriving from it, originates in religious and economic individualism and the very limited political collectivity it implies. The collectivity of democratic self-government is intended as a minimum of collective procedure, as a mere protection of individual competition. In fact, this limited collective activity of democratic self-government proves a means for warding-off collectivity. The government is supposed to be a mere referee appointed to enforce the rules of the game. Thus the capitalistic enterprise proceeds in pursuing individualistic aims steadily and fanatically. And yet, by exploiting all human energies for the relentless endeavor to produce goods and to perfect the process of production, it created the very instruments of a virtual automatic collectivity which evolved in the growth of huge industries and industrial and capital organizations, in the network of capitalistic world economy and in the technical interrelation and interdependence of men and peoples all over the world. By his super-personal, objective activity and by his breathless, individualistic competition, the capitalistic individual became entangled in the anonymous collectivity of his mechanical inventions.

Capitalist economy brought about an unintentional collectivity of an international, world-wide scope, a collectivity it refuses to acknowledge and, therefore, is unable to master. And the discrepancy between the persistently individualistic and competitive human attitude of capitalistic society and the inevitably collective technical situation it developed is one of the main causes of our present anarchy. The Prussian attitude, on the other hand, brought about an intentional, coercive, authoritative collectivity confined to a restricted, particular unit which it plans to exalt and expand to a degree of power that may dominate the whole world. This devouring and chimerical collectivity, and its incompatibility with the technical situation of our world, is another cause of our present anarchy. In opposition to both of these attitudes and their embodiment in the English and American capitalistic democracy and the Prusso-German state, respectively, a third collectivity arose in the socialist movement which aimed at the free and intentional collective deriving from the common will and resulting in the common welfare of the people and the peoples. The conflict between these three attitudes, between these three ways to collectivity, is the great theme of the second part of the modern era. Between these main centers of modern evolutionary currents the struggle for an organized human community, the struggle for a collective order, is taking place. It began with the evolution of the capitalistic economy and society.

This evolution comprises two closely allied developments: the development of free economy and the development of world economy. *Free economy,* in our sense, does not mean international free trade as contrasted with protectionism, for internal free trade is, to a certain degree, quite compatible with external protectionism. It means the liberation of economic forces from feudal privileges, commercial monopolies, guild regulations and restrictions, internal customs and the burden of bondage. This liberation has been the main objective of progressing democracy in England, of the French Revolution and the German Revolution of 1848, and is reflected in the development of a specifically economic theory from the end of the seventeenth century on. The development of the system of world economy began with the great discoveries, at the end of the fifteenth century, and proceeded with the establishment of the various colonial empires, especially with the expansion of England. It was further promoted by the industrial revolution and the progress in technical inventions and in the natural sciences.

In the first period of the new era, when the Romanic nations, the Italian city-nations, Spain and France, took the lead, man was enraptured by his newly discovered rational power which seemed to him unlimited. And accordingly he used this power in an indiscriminate, violent, autocratic way. He aimed at a complete subjugation of nature, that was made to obey his most wanton whims.

The power of rational man, to whom nothing appeared impossible, was the issue of this epoch. All that mattered was human efficiency, human cleverness, human mastery. There was, to be sure, an impersonal power that evaded the will of man. It was termed Fortune. But there was a current conviction that capable and intelligent people could induce Fortune to take their part. Historical developments and changes were, therefore, the work of great men who were able to shape events and conditions according to their aims. This general outlook was fundamentally altered through economy. In the emergence of economic thinking we can observe the crucial turn to another concept of history, to the concept that history is made by conditions, not by persons. From economic theory, the science we call sociology eventually evolved, the study of objective social conditions and connections that cannot be neglected or forced without harmful consequences in the long run. It implies the concept of human society as a distinct phenomenon.

Up to that time, a *concept of economy* as a definite sphere of human activities and conditions did not exist. Economy was interpreted in its literal meaning, as the rules of good individual housekeeping, according to the first economic treatise, the "Logos Oikonomikos" of Xenophon, a disciple of Socrates. Even Francis Bacon still used the word only in this sense. Ancient and medieval authors, Plato, Aristotle, Cicero, the Church Fathers and scholastic thinkers, pondered over the value of economic activities, such as trade, handicraft, agriculture, in general, and they expressed elaborate views on these matters. But they did so only fragmentarily and in connection with their comprehensive theory of the human world and the political structure. A specifically economic speculation began to develop when the new worldly dominions in their competition for power and prestige were urged to raise money wherever they could find it, and to make their countries as productive of money as possible. Economic speculation began as the practical speculation of statesmen and monarchs. The man to whom the first economic doctrine has been attributed was Colbert, the minister of Louis XIV. It was even named Colbertism for him, until Adam Smith dubbed it more scientifically *"mer-cantilism"*. Colbert was not the initiator of the doctrine, he had a predecessor, the French minister, Sully; and, on the whole, it evolved gradually from the competing endeavors of various rulers from the fourteenth and fifteenth century on. After Colbert, the Prussian king, Frederick William I, brought the method to real perfection and gave it a new turn which has influenced German economy ever since.

In accordance with this origin, mercantilism was never a true system, but merely a practical way of reasoning and proceeding that naively applied the practice of a private business to the economy of a whole region. The successful merchant furnished the example which the rulers eagerly followed. And some of these rulers were very successful merchants themselves, as for instance, the English kings, Edward IV (1461–1483), and Henry VII (1485–1509), who carried on trade personally and privately, shamelessly using their position for obtaining personal privileges so that they grew so rich as to become independent of parliament. The absolute monarchy of the Tudors was the result of this private trafficking of kings.

Money made the princes independent of their feudal lords and helped to invalidate the old feudal order. Money made them independent of the diets and parliaments wherever these exercised a certain influence by their right of voting supply, as in England. Money enabled them to establish their absolute monarchy and their external power. This is why they favored the cities and the commercial bourgeoisie, why they emulated the financially proven methods of administration created by the cities. Up to that time, only an economy of private individuals or groups had existed, of business houses, trading companies, or, at most, cities. Now the rulers aimed at the economic unification of their countries by improving communications, building roads and canals, making homogeneous coinage, obviating internal customs, nationalizing guilds and, last but not least, encouraging and protecting trade and manufactures. It was they, in fact, who created national economy, political economy, a term which arose in this period. The pattern

of mercantilistic economy was the private business of the merchant who aims at a surplus of funds, at an active balance at the
end of his year. Accordingly, the main concern and main principle
of the rulers and of their economic administration was to achieve
an active balance of trade. Trade was considered the very foundation of economy. In consequence, this method was called mercantilism.

In pursuing these aims, the mercantilistic rulers at first naively
confounded wealth with money, with a treasure of bullion. Portugal and Spain up to the reign of Philip V, that is, until 1700,
considered the increase of gold and silver as the exclusive goal of
national economy. This clinging to the fascination of precious
metals amid a changing and broadening European economy was
one of the main causes of the ruin of these first colonial powers.
In England, every export trader was bound to bring home part of
his proceeds in specie. Foreign buyers had to pay fifty per cent in
cash. Importers had to use the whole of their proceeds for the
purchase of English goods. Export of money was prohibited altogether. These restrictions became untenable when English trade
began to expand to the remotest parts of Europe and to Asia, when
in the second half of the sixteenth century, the new trading companies were founded, especially, the East India Company, which
was privileged by Queen Elizabeth in 1600. These merchants had
to export bullion as well as specie in order to do their business.
Thomas Mun, an executive of the East India Company, published
"A Discourse of Trade, from England unto the East-Indies" (1621),
in which he proved that Indian goods, purchased for silver, when
re-exported or resold, yield more money in the end than what
was originally exported. This was the first breach in the narrow-
est practice of mercantilism. The traffic restrictions were gradually removed. In 1663, the prohibition of export of money was
abolished. This happened after the restoration of the Stuart regime,
which was closely related to the East India Company. But the general course of mercantilistic methods persisted. The tendencies
toward the accumulation of bullion, toward an active balance of
trade, the use of protective tariffs, continue up to the present time,

even in countries which generally adhered to the principle of free trade.

The absolute rulers attained a concept of national economy in a geographical sense, an economy of the compact area of their country. They were, however, still far from grasping or even paying attention to the idea of national economy in an intrinsic sense, to the infinitely complex system of the consistent economy of a national people. In their greed for power, they handled economy by whatever haphazard regulations seemed appropriate for special purposes and requirements. Manufactures were established without considering in the least whether conditions prerequisite for their prosperity existed. Trade was promoted by privileges and monopolies granted to individual merchants, or to companies, without a qualm for the consumer or the ruin of entire classes of the population. Colbert had held the opinion that the number of people in the world and the amount of money in the world was stable, and that, accordingly, commerce is a war for money. In his time, this point of view even seemed to be supported by facts, since it was only as a result of the technical developments of the eighteenth and nineteenth centuries that the great upward sweep of industry caused the increase in the population of Europe. Technical development is also a prerequisite for the development of markets, for the stimulus of demand through the offer of novelty wares. But Colbert's thoughts were superior to his practice. In his "Lettres, Instructions et Mémoires", ideas like these mingle with strictly mercantilistic maxims: "Our neighbors [the English] who consider commerce the principal element of strength in their states, know from experience that freedom, whether for commodities or merchants, helps to make commerce flourish. . . . To put commerce on its feet, two things are necessary, security and freedom . . ." In this protagonist of mercantilism, the new principles began to germinate. He himself recognized the principles that were destined to overthrow his system.

The great movement against monopolies, privileges and trade restrictions, the great struggle for the *liberation of inland trade* and for a new concept of national economy, began in *England* in the second half of the sixteenth century, in the Elizabethan period. Again and again, in 1571, 1601, 1641, parliament assailed monopolies. Sir William Petty pointed out in his treatise, "Political Arithmetic" (published 1691), that a superfluity of money is just as harmful for the country as a lack of money. He was among the first to call for comparative statistics as a foundation for effective trade regulations. It was he who formulated the principle that "labor is the father and active principle of wealth", thus anticipating the theory of Adam Smith. He even evolved a basic idea that was later expressed by David Ricardo and finally led to the teaching of Karl Marx, that the value of an object is dependent upon the amount of labor necessary for its production. Thus, for the first time, stress is laid on the basic economic importance of labor, that, in addition, came to be sanctified by the Protestant teachings of the epoch. This marks the beginning of the transition from the static to the dynamic system of economy. In the same year, Sir Dudley North pointed to the fact that wealth is not synonymous with the possession of gold and silver and that internal trade is just as important to the country as external trade. He fought against trade restrictions. All trade was to be free. Nicholas Barbon went even further in his "Discourse of Trade" (1690). He condemned the entire theory of the balance of trade and, with it, the fundamental thesis of mercantilism.

In *France,* where the pressure of the absolute regime was much stronger, much more inflexible than in parliamentary England, the opposition grew more violent and led straight to the Revolution. It started from the very court of Louis XIV, from the Marquis de Vauban, Marshal of France, who rose from humble birth to his high position as chief of military engineering, and who is famous as an architect and for his construction of fortifications. But beyond this, he concerned himself with the problems of government and with the welfare of the country. He was a radical opponent of Colbert's, and criticized the abuses of the government until he lost the king's favor. His contemporary, Pierre Boisguillebert resumed the English arguments against mercantilism, but he sounded the first typically French note in the free trade argument by turning against the overemphasis on trade and advocating a return to agriculture as the basis of national economy. "Criminal money" was to be the slave, not the master, of commerce. He stormed against the "un-French, Italianized" Colbert and his regimentation. He already spoke of natural laws in economy that cannot be disregarded with impunity, and even uttered the revolutionary thought that in a free social order the interests of the various classes of society, of individuals and of the community, yes, even of the different peoples in the world, would coincide. With this, the direction of the entire subsequent development in France is given. Always under the influence of English trends, the opposition proceeded in the famous writings of Bishop Fénélon and of Montesquieu. But the man who gave the first impetus to the revolutionary movement was a trade official in the middle of the eighteenth century: Vincent de Gournay. He was deeply influenced by the English free trade pamphlets, some of which he translated into French. He tried to abolish French restrictions and regulations and gave rise to great industrial and commercial activity. To him is attributed the famous saying of economic liberalism: "Laissez faire, laissez passer"—let (trade) work, come and go by itself. His followers, who formed the so-called "commercial school" of economic speculation, later evolved the first true economic theory, the theory of the so-called "économistes", or *physiocrats,* as one of the group, Dupont de Nemours, termed them according to their fundamental assumption, the rule of Nature. Their opposition against mercantilism was twofold. They attacked controlled and regulated economy, and pleaded for individual freedom of economic activity on the ground of the natural law that was beginning to predominate in the political and religious theories of the epoch. And they opposed to the mercantilist overvaluation of trade, the economic precedence of agriculture, the natural source of wealth, and the basic importance of raw materials, the products of nature.

According to them, human society consists of a number of individuals, all of whom possess equal natural rights. Every one of them knows best and takes the best care of his own interest, as Nature teaches him to do. Society rests on an agreement between these individuals, which, of course, limits their natural freedom in so far as it is incompatible with the freedom of others. The government is an indispensable evil that should be limited to a minimum of interference. As to the economic implications, the natural right of the individual includes the right to the natural usufruct of the proceeds of his work. Accordingly, his work must be preserved from any hindrance and restriction and its proceeds must be guaranteed, that is, individual property must be sacrosanct. Every citizen must be allowed to use his working power to the limit and, therefore, freedom of commerce and freedom of competition must be unrestricted. Here we already have the scheme of modern democracy.

This scheme was, however, connected with features deriving from specifically French conditions. Despite all efforts of mercantilistic reformers, France had remained a predominantly agricultural country. But the French peasants were the most oppressed class of the population. So it is quite understandable that economic liberation in France assumed the form of an agricultural theory. It is, moreover, characteristically French that even this revolutionary theory could not conceive that the limited function of the government could be carried out by any but enlightened "legal despotism" that was to combine the power of giving and carrying out the law. In a like sense, the leaders of the French Revolution endeavored to force the people toward true freedom.

To the physiocrats, only those works are really productive that augment the amount of raw materials to be used by human beings. And the true annual addition to the wealth of the community consists in the surplus of agricultural and mineral products over the costs of their production. On the amount of this net profit depends the wealth of the community as well as the progress of its civilization. The craftsman merely transforms the raw materials, and the increase of value they gain by his labor only equals the amount of food and other materials consumed in their fashioning. The achievements of trade, finally, have no substantial value at all, since they merely transfer the existing wealth from one hand to the other, and the profit they yield is a pure liability to the community. Therefore, this profit should be as small as possible. All professions besides agriculture may be useful, but they are unproductive, as they derive their income from the surplus yield of the farmer.

It is easy to realize the revolutionary power of this theory, and, as a matter of fact, this movement already formed part of the *French Revolution*. One of its leaders was Turgot, the minister of Louis XVI, who once more tried to avert the catastrophe by timely reforms, by the complete abolition of inland duties, of the corvée (a compulsory service exacted from the peasants), and the guild regulations, only to be dismissed by the king. Another prominent member of the group was the father of Mirabeau, the leader of the first phase of the revolution. And the influence of the physiocrats made itself strongly felt in the Constituent Assembly of 1789. In this French Revolution, which was the great signal for the political and economic emancipation of the bourgeoisie on the European continent, many developments and trends converged, political, economic and intellectual. In the main, however, the French Revolution is an offspring of the English and American revolutions. What was French in this revolution was the special character of the "ancien régime" which it overthrew, the lax, careless oppression of a monarchy grown senile, the idle, weary playfulness and the coquettish intellectual self-repudiation of aristocracy. French, also, was the special character of the movement itself, the ecstasy of national élan that swept it along. But the actual impetus and the ideological support came from the Protestant, English, American influences and examples. The progress of English parliamentary control of the government, of English economic freedom and expansion, was, in France, a steady incitement to criticism and to theoretical as well as practical reforms. The leaders of French enlightenment—Montesquieu, Voltaire, the physiocrats, the encyclopedists—all of these bear the traces of English influence, methods and thought. Lafayette and his Frenchmen who participated in the American war of liberation brought home American ideas and concepts. And the French Declaration of the Rights of Man was shaped to the pattern of the American Bills of Rights. On the whole, the rule of terror, with its cult of Virtue and Reason, looks like a repetition of the Calvinistic community on a broader, atheistic basis. "Freedom consists not in doing what one wants to do, but in doing what is right. The general will of the republic is right. The Committee of Public Safety knows what that general will is ... When the Committee interferes with a citizen selfishly following his particular and erring will it is, in Rousseau's words, forcing him to be free ... The protection of judicial procedure must be denied the wicked ... for the metaphysical reason that ... the wicked are not really to be considered as legal persons ..." As the excellent historian of the French Revolution, Crane Brinton, states, the emotions of the Jacobins "were centered upon an abstract system of value-judgements ... with a flaming, unreasonable desire of coming to grips with the promises of abstract felicity, with a passionate intention of acquiring virtue as other men acquire wealth." So the French Revolution signifies a convergence of the tendencies of all modern forms of community: the nation, the Protestant community, the democracy, and even, in a way, the state. Even the socialist movement derived some inspiration from this revolution.

The outcome of the French Revolution was, however, predominantly economic liberation. The removal of the old feudal privileges had, in the last period of the "ancien régime", retained a merely economic significance, as the feudal property had been an inalienable entail on which no loan could be taken, and as this property had been free from taxation. This was, after all, an intolerable burden on the really productive part of the population and a hindrance to economic progress. Another effect of the revolution was the removal of the guild regulations, which meant freedom of economic activity and competition. And the final result was the liberation of the peasants, which, under the circumstances prevailing at the end of the "ancien régime", was also a matter of chiefly economic import. The moral and physical burdens of serfdom had gradually vanished or become insignificant. What remained and made itself strongly felt was the economic distress. The personal services, duties and pledges had, for the most part, been converted into disbursements in money and in kind, into taxes like the "taille" and the head tax, into ransoms for the right to move from place to place, into manifold restrictions on inheritance. And what was liberated was no longer the ancient freehold, as it had existed at the time before this period of serfdom, not the self-sufficient and self-supporting residence on a land sanctified by a patrimony of generations, but the unrestricted disposal of the soil and its products, the unrestricted right of producing and selling goods and of acquiring and accumulating capital. The free farmers and tenants were just as overburdened with taxes as the villains. And so the privileges of the nobility had become a mere deprivation of "that energy to work which can be infused only by a feeling of free possession", as an edict of Louis XVI, in 1779, already puts it. Since the French Revolution—and this is its main effect—the predominance of economic interest has become firmly established all over the world.

In *England,* no second revolution was needed to bring this about, though at the time of the French Revolution the situation of the common man was no less distressing than in France. Just at that time, the English gentry, the class of the "country gentleman", had consolidated its reactionary and socially oppressive manorial rule in parliament and in the country. And it is no wonder that the higher classes in England considered the French Revolution, which had, to a great degree, been a product of English developments, with misgivings and resentment.

The progress of democracy in England, from the time of the establishment of the constitutional regime under William and Mary, was much slower, much more gradual, and it was brought about not by a revolutionary event but by an evolutionary process, not so much by deliberate acts of the popular will—though these were not lacking—as by the pressure of circumstances. This was due to the fact that among all classes of the population the predominance of economic interest had become almost a tradition, and the prevalent economic activity had found a special outlet in the vast expansion of English trade, in the development of the colonial empire and in the growth of a powerful industry. This made for a certain elasticity of government that prevented the worst clashes. There was a parliament that governed the country and there was a fairly reliable supreme jurisdiction. The parliament, of course, was far from being democratic. It was controlled by the manorial gentry, that not only formed an Upper House appointed by the king, but also controlled boroughs and towns and, by a system of voting favorable to them, by open and secret influence, and finally through shameless bribery, simply nominated the members of the Lower House. Still, to a certain degree, it registered public opinion, and sometimes the gentry was solicitous of the interests of the manufacturers even when these ran counter to their own agricultural concerns. The promotion of manufacture and trade had become a general, national preoccupation. The reason for this was the economic turn of mind of the gentry, and the special character and specific origin of the new English nobility that was in distinct contrast to all of continental nobility and the French nobility in particular. For this nobility was relatively new; it had emerged from trading, and for centuries had been refilled, revitalized by bourgeois elements. What was accomplished in France in 1789 had been done in England three centuries earlier. In the fifteenth century, in the Wars of the Roses, the old feudal nobility of England had been completely annihilated—it had, in fact, destroyed itself—and was gradually replaced by wealthy wool-traders who, as landed proprietors and sheep-breeders, increased the wool trade, their wealth and thus their landed property. They were knighted and formed a new gentry, and the richest and most powerful of them moved up into the old positions of lords. They were joined by the group of upstarts who had made their fortune by taking possession of the secularized church property under Henry VIII and his successors. Subsequently, also, continuous social intercourse and intermarriages between the gentry and bourgeois merchant families took place. Again and again, rich merchants rose up into the gentry, and frequently the younger sons of nobles became merchants. In addition to this historic relationship of the nobility to the burghers, still another factor furthered the connection of the governing strata with the people: the two-party system. This had developed during the Restoration period, from the conflict between the Catholic-French tendencies of the court faction of Charles II (Tories) and the High Church, anti-French landed nobility (Whigs). The names of both parties were originally derogatory: Tory was an Irish word meaning robber, and Whig a Scotch word for the country nobles who drove into town in their buggies, and urged on their horses with the call of "whiggam". This nickname was then used for the Scotch adversaries of the king and assumed the meaning of rebel. The permanent existence of an opposition implied constant criticism and appeal to public opinion and thus imposed certain restrictions on the government and offered a vent for the discussion and even reform of unfavorable conditions.

At the end of the eighteenth and the beginning of the nineteenth century, a rift developed between the gentry who concentrated on their manorial rule, on agriculture and sheep-breeding, and the increasingly important group of manufacturers produced by the industrial revolution. It has been rightly said that at that time two nations existed side by side in England. Between these two nations, the struggle for an ever-broader democracy, the struggle for free trade went on. And the struggle for internal free trade, that is, for the abolition of privileges and monopolies, mingled with that for external free trade, for the abolition of protectionism and of the remaining mercantilistic practices.

The movement for free trade was led to victory by the ever-rising power of the commercial and industrial developments. Against these mighty trends, no resistance was possible. But along with them and supporting them, the *English economic theory* developed and provided capitalistic economy with its theoretical foundation. After Sir William Petty had stated (in 1691) that "labor is the father and active principle of wealth", David Hume contended, in the eighteenth century, that all actual power and wealth consist in the national working capacity. He regarded an international division of labor as the basic principle of trade, and he proved that the prosperity of one nation furthers rather than hinders that of its neighbor. Here we find an early awareness of the universal interdependence that was to become ever greater by the forthcoming industrial and technical developments. David Hume had a decisive influence on his close friend, the man who is considered the father of modern economic science, on Adam Smith, the author of "An Inquiry into the Nature and Causes of the Wealth of Nations" (1776). His point of departure is a concept similar to that of the physiocrats, according to whom the natural self-interest of the individual is the basic motor of economic life. The objective mechanism of economic life directs the self-interests of individuals toward an automatic agreement, a common social system of harmony. Accordingly, economic life will reach its perfection when it is left to its own direction, to the free competition of individuals who, by this competition, are induced to exert the maximum of energy in pursuing their economic ends, in developing their forces and faculties and in achieving the lowest costs of production. Thus, one is the guardian, the stimulus of the other. And all parts of the population will benefit: the consumer will be provided with the cheapest goods, the entrepreneurs will be unlimited in the use of their capacities and the workers free to choose the job that secures them the highest wages. As with the physiocrats, the task of the government must be strictly confined to safeguarding the right functioning of this competition. Only that the Englishman, in contrast to the French, demands complete self-government of the people. "It is the highest impertinence and presumption . . . in kings and ministers," so he writes, "to pretend to watch over the economy of private people, and to restrain their expense . . . they are themselves, and without any exception, the greatest spendthrifts in the society."

Wealth is attributed by Adam Smith not solely to external or internal trade. In labor he finds the most important source of wealth, and the measure of value. And the increase of productive capacity of labor depends to a large extent on its division, which is more applicable to industry than to agriculture. Therefore, agriculture is bound to lag behind in economic evolution. The origin of division of labor he finds in the disposition of human nature to exchange one thing for another, to convert one thing into another. He demonstrates that a certain accumulation of capital is a prerequisite for this division, and that the degree of its perfection depends on the scope of the market. When division of labor is established, every member of society, in satisfying his needs, is obliged to avail himself of the cooperation of others. A medium of exchange comes into use—money—and so the concept of value is created. Under primitive conditions, the value of goods is determined solely by the amount of labor they represent. And so the measure of the exchange value of goods is labor. Labor is the "natural price" of goods. But this natural price is in contrast to the "market price", which develops later on, which is determined by the conditions of supply and demand and is expressed in terms of money.

Adam Smith laid only the groundwork for the theory of free trade economy, and his concept must not be confused with the orthodox systems of capitalistic economy which were later worked out by David Ricardo, whose "Principles of Political Economy and Taxation" appeared in 1817, and by the so-called Manchester group of Cobden and Bright in the eighteen thirties. On the one hand, Adam Smith still shows a high evaluation of the agricultural class, whose interest he declares to be in close and inseparable connection and conformity with the general interest of the community. On the other hand, he states that the interest of the capitalistic class never completely coincides with the public interest. For the capitalistic profit rate tends to rising and declining, not like the ground rent and labor wages, in conformity with the general prosperity or ruin of a country. On the contrary, it is naturally low in rich, and high in poor countries. And in the "Wealth of Nations", this bible of individualistic national economy, we find the following: "The violence and injustice of the rulers of mankind is an ancient evil, for which, I am afraid, the nature of human affairs can scarce admit of a remedy; but the mean rapacity, the monopolizing spirit, of merchants and manufacturers, who neither are, nor ought to be, the rulers of mankind, though it cannot, perhaps, be corrected, may very easily be prevented from disturbing the tranquility of anybody but themselves."

Not until 1820 did the theory of free trade spread and find support in the public opinion of England, for it was not until then that the technical development and expansion of industry began to make itself felt. It was at this time that public pressure was first exerted on economic legislation. The merchants of London presented parliament with a memorandum that pointed out the destructive effects of certain prohibitive and protectionistic regulations, and demanded freedom of trade. The chamber of commerce of Edinburgh followed with a similar petition, and a committee from the lower house gave a report that was virtually a proclamation of the principle of free trade. In 1823, the action of the London merchants was repeated in more energetic ways, and step by step, legislation had to cede to the growing pressure.

In this period, the advance of a new progressive and liberal social element was emphasized for the first time. While up to this point, the merchants who had grown rich had cherished the sole ambition of becoming country gentlemen, "cotton lords", now the industrialists became conscious of common interests and of their importance for the country, and formed a separate, compact group in opposition to the country gentlemen. The struggle between the old and the new England, between manufacture and manor, had begun, and rapidly involved politics. *Industrial development* became the *pace-maker for democracy*. The first impetus to parliamentary reform had, indeed, come from other, from lower levels of society, primarily from the population of London that in the eighteenth century constituted one-tenth of the entire English population and was the only body of people who had maintained their county of Middlesex and Westminster free from the influence of the gentry. When, in the year 1769, their candidate, John Wilkes, whom they had elected over and over with an ever-increasing majority, was rejected by the lower house again and again, London declared for the first time that the lower house did not represent the people. Wilkes became the leader of the first movement that insisted upon parliamentary reform, that eliminated the secrecy of parliamentary sessions and defended the freedom of the press. In 1780–85, the freeholders of Yorkshire made a new attempt at parliamentary reform that aimed at breaking the influence of the rich landed proprietors. This was the last call for freeholders. Soon after, the free English peasantry was entirely done away with by the so-called "enclosures" and transformed into a labor proletariat. The enclosures were confiscations of land by the great landowners. They had been current since the end of the Middle Ages, and their work was completed toward the end of the eighteenth century. The cause of this procedure lay only partially in the greed of the landowners, "those bloody boars", as a seventeenth century sermon terms them, "with their two damned fangs: money to buy friends and to close the eyes of the law, and a bad conscience that does not hesitate to swim to Hell through a sea of blood." There was also a factual cause. English agriculture was very much behind that of the continent, since wool was the chief article of export of English economy and the landowners, therefore, were most interested in the greatest possible amount of pasture land. The peasants raised only enough grain for their own needs and for those of the nearby towns. When, in the eighteenth century, attention was directed to agriculture and cattle raising, a sudden and ruthless change to new methods was made. The increase of land to be cultivated, promised by the confiscation of private property, appeared an advantage to national economy and thus seemed to justify the robbery of the big landowners. The abolition of the English peasantry, a unique phenomenon in Europe, significantly furthered the industrialization of the country. Home customs and traditions that have persisted among European peasants up to the present, and that have held up technical and economic development, were destroyed at one blow.

The decades after the French Revolution had already been filled with labor unrest that the radical leaders of the period, the scientist, Joseph Priestley, the Quaker, Thomas Paine and the peasant's son, William Cobbett, had directed toward a demand for parliamentary reform. But all efforts had been futile, especially since the English people had been intimidated by the spectacle of the French Revolution and driven, for the most part, into the backwaters of the gentry. The expansion of industry finally set the reform movement going. The manufacturers demanded the political influence that corresponded to their increasing importance for the country. They had the means to enforce these demands and were backed more and more by public opinion. Reforms in parliament helped the freedom of trade. In 1846, the economic privileges of the gentry fell away through the repeal of the corn laws, and in 1853, the fiscal immunities of the gentry were annulled.

The great manufacturers involuntarily became the pioneers for the rights of the lower classes. Organization of factory work had taught the workers to organize for the defense of their own interests. And the two-party system furthered the discussion of social evils, since industry and landed gentry reproached each other with the oppression of workers, through their conservative and liberal parties. Thus a series of alleviations of the most conspicuous social evils took place. In the twenties of the nineteenth century, the right of the working class to form combinations and to strike for higher wages was recognized. In 1867, city workers were given the right of suffrage, in 1884, land workers. Tenant farmers had attained the uninfluenced exercise of this right as early as 1872. But universal suffrage for all men over twenty-one and all women over thirty was not enforced until 1918.

In the course of this whole development, therefore, the industrial revolution gave the main impetus to democracy, and progressing democracy, in turn, freed trade. Purely political problems recede behind economic problems from this time on. More and more, the parties become exponents of economic interests, and politics becomes a mere instrument and vehicle of economy.

PREDOMINANCE OF ECONOMY AND
TECHNOLOGY: WORLD ECONOMY

THE DEVELOPMENT OF free economy is closely connected with other and still more important developments that converged in the for-

mation of *world economy* and released economic endeavors all over
the world. They effected the great social revolution, in which we
are entangled today, in preparing that ever-closer interrelation and
interdependence of people and peoples which amounts to an undis-
closed, automatic collectivity.

Before the great discoveries of the fifteenth and sixteenth centuries, trade on a relatively large scale existed. There were international connections, and, in individual cases, as for instance, in the
case of the Italian, Flemish and Hanseatic cities, one may even say
that a predominant part of the community depended on these international economic connections. These, however, did not form
a coherent system; they were no more than many single, particular
relations between private merchants, trading companies or commercial bodies of cities. And, as a whole, economic activity did not
make itself felt as a powerful or decisive element in international
life.

Three distinct areas of trade had developed on the peripheries of
the European continent: the area of the Mediterranean, the area of
the Dutch and Flemish coast and the area of the Baltic Sea. These
peripheral centers were connected with one another, not only by
sea, but also by equally well-defined, local inland centers. The area
of the Mediterranean was by far the largest and most important.
This state of things began to change, not only because of the mercantilistic rulers' keen interest in making money, but particularly
when the *great discoveries* drew the distant regions of the old continents, Africa and Asia, and the new continent of America into
the European orbit, and gradually made them parts of colonial empires of European powers.

Curiously enough, the evolution of European economy was, from
the outset, connected with religious undertakings. Economy took
over its rule directly from religion. The first economic impetus, the
rise of the Italian cities through trade, had been brought about by
the crusades. The second impulse in this direction was given by the
Reformation. The third and greatest was also linked with religious
aims, with the struggle and competition with the Mohammedan
infidels, and with missionary undertakings. The crusades had still

been a mere opportunity from which economic expansion sprang as a by-product. But in the adventurous explorations of new lands, potential riches were already effective as an initial motive equal to religious aims.

The movement took its issue from the little country of *Portugal*. This country had become an independent kingdom as a result of the fight against the Moors, which was carried on from the base of a narrow strip in the North, the region of Porto, to a gradual conquest of the Southern portions of the country, by crusading French knights under the leadership of Henry of Burgundy, in the eleventh century. The King of Castile granted Henry all the land he would conquer from the Moors as an independent dominion; this dominion started as a county and was later raised to a kingdom. By its geography, Portugal has been singled out as a separate part of the Iberian peninsula, since her great rivers, that spring from the Castilian plateau, are not navigable near their source but down in the plains toward the sea, which thus became the main sphere of activity of the population. The fight against the infidels, and the inclinations to adventurous cruising and sea trade, were the founding features of this little nation. The man who became their national hero, and who has been glorified in the epic of the Portuguese poet, Luis de Camõens, "The Lusiads" (the Lusitanians), was Prince Henry the Navigator, who, as the grand master of the Knightly Order of Christ, utilized the crusading spirit and the rich funds of the order for explorative and, at the same time, commercial enterprises. He wanted to ruin the Mediterranean and Oriental trade of the Arabs, the source of Islamic power, by discovering a new water-way to India, and he wanted his people to inherit this vast trade. He planned something which later, in a different and unexpected way, came true, the diversion and displacement of the Mediterranean trade which, so far, had been the dominant trade of the Western world. Developments of various kinds had paved the way for these enterprises. The great conquests of the Mongols in the thirteenth century, in uniting most of Asia, the Near East and Eastern Europe under one rule, opened direct communications between Europe and the Orient and raised the prospect of an alliance against the Moslems. From the twelfth century on, travelers of all creeds had begun to explore distant parts of the old continents. The Jewish Rabbi Benjamin de Tudela (in Navarre) traveled through Persia and Central Asia to the borders of China. In the thirteenth and fourteenth centuries, the Polo family, Venetian traders on the Black Sea, journeyed to Central Asia, China, Burma and India. In the fourteenth century too, the most eminent of Arab travelers, Ibn Batuta, set out from his home in Morocco and crossed Northern Africa, Egypt, the Near East, Arabia, Eastern Africa to India, Ceylon and China. On the other hand, after the translation of Ptolemy's geography into Latin, in 1410, the idea that the earth is a globe took hold of European minds and tempted the imagination with the prospect of reaching Asia by sailing to the West.

So Henry the Navigator, in order to conquer and displace the Arab trade, hoped to achieve a direct communication with Guinea on the West coast of Africa, by sea, and to find a sea route to Ethiopia and India. From 1418 on, he dispatched several well-equipped expeditions which explored the Island of Madeira and discovered the Azores. In the course of a century, the Portuguese undertook longer and longer voyages. They circumnavigated the great West African capes and the Cape of Good Hope, until Vasco da Gama succeeded in sailing around all of Africa and reached Calcutta in 1498. From 1501 on, a regular Portuguese traffic with India was carried on, and Lisbon soon became the chief European market for Oriental products. Conquests on the East African coast followed. Forts and factories were established in India, treaties with the indigenous rulers were concluded, a Portuguese governor of India was set up. In 1509, the Moslem fleet was defeated and annihilated and the Red Sea route closed. The Mamelukes in Egypt had dominated the great water-ways from the Persian Gulf to the Syrian ports, and from the Red Sea to Alexandria, and from these ports, the Venetians had carried the trade over to Western Europe. The Egyptian Sultan had seen to it that the quantity of goods was limited and prices high, so that when the Portuguese closed the

Red Sea route, they were in a position to undersell and to gain possession of both the Egyptian and the Venetian trade. This reacted on German inland trade. The economic revolution was on.

The second stroke was the discovery of America, which proceeded from *Spain*. The disposition of the Spanish country and the Spanish people was utterly different from Portugal and the Portuguese. Spain was by her nature and national character not a maritime but a continental country, based on agriculture, viticulture, silkworm- and cattle-breeding. Land communications were difficult owing to the many vast plateaus surrounded by mountains. Most of the rivers were not navigable, since they were torrents in the rainy season and dried up in summer. Estuaries and harbors were poor. The country was self-supporting, and there was no need and no stimulus for colonial expansion. So it was, in fact, one man who gave the country this new direction toward a colonial empire which topped the brilliant rise of the nation in the sixteenth century. It was Christopher Columbus, who most probably was a foreigner—his origins are somewhat mysterious and kept so deliberately by the man himself. There is much discussion among scholars as to whether he was an Italian, a Portuguese or a marrano, a converted Jew.

The travels of Columbus were followed by the voyages of the Portuguese, Cabral, and the Florentine, Amerigo Vespucci, to Guiana and Brazil. After his return from his second trip to Brazil, Vespucci wrote a report on his journeys. Apparently, these travel descriptions passed through many hands, and one year after the death of Columbus, a Latin edition, made after a French translation, appeared under the title, "Four Voyages of Amerigo Vespucci", in St. Dié in Lorraine. The editor of this probably much corrupted text was a young professor of St. Dié, Martin Waldseemueller, born in Freiburg im Breisgau. This little German professor dared to suggest giving the name of America to the countries described by Vespucci. In the introduction to his edition he remarks, among other things: "The fourth continent could well be named Ameriga or America, that is to say, the country of Amerigo, since it is he who discovered it." Vespucci himself most likely had nothing to do with all this and claimed no credit whatsoever for his discovery. But he did indeed speak of a "new world". Waldsee-mueller's suggestion was taken up by Swiss and Austrian scholars, and on the oldest known map bearing the name of America, printed in 1522 after the woodcut of a German woodcutter, the name "America Provincia" is used to designate the coast of Brazil south of Cape Augustine. It was in Germany that the name of America was first used, but only for the coastal regions of South America. In Western Europe, the new continent was called India or The New World for a long time to come. It was not until the end of the sixteenth century that the big atlas of Ortelius brought the name America into general use.

At the beginning of the sixteenth century, a number of Spanish expeditions completed the exploration of the new continent, until, in 1521, Fernão de Magalhães, a Portuguese in the service of Spain, found his way through that strait at the Southern end of America that has been named for him, and entered the South Sea which has been called "Mare Pacificum". He traveled along the West coast of South America, then turned North and reached the Philippines, where he was killed in a fight with natives. But one of his vessels continued on its westward course and returned safely to Spain. Thus the circumnavigation of the globe was completed.

During the first part of the sixteenth century, the Spaniards advanced their conquests all over the American continent. They took Peru, Chile, Argentine, Mexico, Central America, Florida, Texas and California. In 1580, Philip II of Spain, in his capacity of son of a Portuguese princess, seized the opportunity of a vacant Portuguese throne to claim the crown of Portugal, to invade the country and to unite it with Spain for half a century. As a result, most of America, as far as it was explored, became a dominion of Spain. But it was at once contested by the English through the raids of Francis Drake. And soon afterwards, in 1588, when the Spanish Armada was destroyed by an English fleet, the Spanish sea power, and, by implication, the Spanish colonial empire, was dealt a blow from which it could not recover.

But there were deeper and more intrinsic causes for the down-fall of this mighty empire and the decline of Spain. The Spanish monarchy and the Spanish nation were inherently inadequate for the task of holding such a colonial empire. The Iberian peninsula was flooded with riches almost too suddenly. Trade flourished but begot only gold and silver and not a lasting prosperity. The minds of Mediterranean people were still dominated by the ancient and naive idea of treasure, of stable and immobile treasure, as the substance of all wealth. The sole aim of the colonial empire was to extract as much, and that as quickly as possible, from these territories and from their population. The wide, fertile regions of the Southeast of the United States are marked on the old maps of the Spanish explorers as "worthless territories" because no precious metals had been found there. But the treasure of the native rulers and of the temples yielded bullion worth hundreds of thousands of pesos. And the output of the famous silver mines of Potosi, in the region of the Bolivia of today, went on increasing from year to year.

This was the beginning of mass emigration to the colonies, where the Spaniards lived sumptuously as grands seigneurs and landed proprietors, at the cost of the natives who were robbed of their property and freedom. According to Canon Law, infidels had no right of property. The Spaniards imposed the system of "encomienda" on the conquered countries. This was shaped along the lines of their domestic feudal landed property. The colonists absorbed more and more domestic products, such as silk and wine, which the colonies were not allowed to grow. So viticulture, silk-spinning and weaving, wool and cloth manufacture developed rapidly in Spain and were another source of wealth. Since at first Spain monopolized the supply of her colonies, prices went higher and higher, and traders made enormous profits. This dizzy prosperity, however, crumbled as fast as it had risen because of the character and the social structure of the Spanish people, which, like that of the French, was essentially national. An idle and haughty aristocracy of grandees and hidalgos (knights) dominated the country and set the example for the whole population—an aristocracy based on landed property, on court and military service. They considered it unworthy of their rank to engage in commercial or industrial activity. Thus the increase in wealth did not enhance but rather diminish economic activity, since it was used only to glorify the position of the individual, to permit him to stop working and to retire to a life of dignified idleness. More and more, foreign goods were bought up for colonial export and Spanish commerce became merely intermediary trade; colonial money was carried away to Holland, France and England. Instead of encouraging trade and industry, the king hindered and suppressed these by exorbitant duties and taxes. The expulsion of the Jews and the Moors deprived the country of expert commercial and agricultural elements. And the many political entanglements and wars of the Hapsburgs exhausted the manpower, the funds and the energies of the nation. Its power vanished before it could actually unfold. Its colonial and economic predominance was inherited by the liberated Netherlands and particularly by England, who was more fitted to the task, and who was the first to break with the old, narrow commercial system dating from early antiquity, resting on the ceaseless drain of resources and foreign populations and aimed solely at hoarding money.

This old trade system, the foundation of which was the stable center of treasure, was closely connected with a monarchical, aristocratic constitution; it was the economic complement corresponding to this constitution. Goods were won through the exercise of power and through exploitation, and were used for the development and enjoyment of power. And the aristocratic, essentially political turn of mind of the Romanic nations was a hindrance to the grasp of new forms of economy. Modern economy, that rests on the dynamic process of productive circulation of goods, necessarily involves expansion of public life, a collective cooperation, and hence implicitly leads to democracy. The objective conditions of the new world situation all tended in the direction of this change. The influx of American silver contributed as much to the great economic revolution that took place at the beginning of the modern era as the displacement of Mediterranean trade. It was, in fact, an important stimulus to the expansion of European industry. This influx of silver made prices go up while wages remained down. This, in itself, meant an accumulation of capital. The silver, moreover, went to the Near and Far East through Dutch and English trade, since Europe purchased more than it sold in the East. Owing to the primitive economy of the Oriental peoples, silver was hoarded there and went out of circulation. Hence prices in the Orient did not rise, and European merchants could buy very cheaply. So again there was an accumulation of capital which was used for colonial expeditions and for the building of factories. The right and productive exploitation of these conditions demanded a new point of view that developed only very gradually among the Northern, Germanic peoples of Europe.

The rise of Dutch colonial power is inversely joined to the crumbling of Spanish power and the narrow, resentful policy of the Hapsburg monarchs. It originated in the liberation of Protestant Holland from the oppressive and fanatic Spanish Catholic regime. *Holland,* like Portugal, was a maritime country, with the difference that her bourgeois population was Protestant. Holland was a sober federation of cities, not a Romanic monarchical and crusading nation. In every respect, politically, economically and socially, the Dutch are a transitional phenomenon between old and new forms, between city-republic and territorial state, between Italian or Hanseatic patrician oligarchy and democratic government, between piratical trade and modern capitalism, between monopolism and free trade, between the colonization technique of the Romanic nations and the English.

Even the Dutch "Great Privilege" bestowed upon the daughter of Charles the Bold, Duke of Burgundy, in 1477, when she assumed the regency of the Netherlands, clearly shows the light and shadow of the Dutch constitution, the characteristics that brought about the rise and the fall of the Netherlands. The "Great Privilege" may well be compared with the Magna Charta. In this document the rights of the regent are strictly defined. Without the consent of the estates, she may neither marry, declare war, coin money nor levy taxes. Offices may only be given to citizens and may not be leased. No one may hold two offices. The "Great Council and Supreme Court of Holland", which was to be appointed, has no jurisdiction in matters subject to provincial and municipal courts. The regent may exercise her power only in so far as it is not in conflict with the privileges of the cities. And the cities are not obliged to pay taxes that their diets have not approved of. This charter expresses not only democratic but, at the same time, regionally particularistic tendencies.

Modern Holland is the result of a democratic fight for freedom against the alien dynasty of the Hapsburgs. The constitution that crystallized from this struggle for liberation resulted in a state only theoretically, actually in a federation of cities and country districts. As long as William of Orange lived, this great statesman reconciled conflicting interests. After his death, the government passed over into the hands of the States General that exercised only an advisory function and depended upon the individual decisions of the fifty-six cities, the corporations of the landed nobility and the peasants. The cities, moreover, were under the rule of an oligarchy of rich merchants. Hugo Grotius compares the Netherlands of 1622 with the Amphictyonic League of the Greeks. They were, he said, an agglomeration of independent republics, each with individual privileges, customs and traditions.

One might regard these Dutch republics as city-nations, after the manner of the Italian city-states, had there not been a certain common feeling sprung from a sense of union, and had not the Dutch already shown certain characteristics beyond the purely national, with all its implications. Above all, they were totally unprejudiced, sober and practical. They had a certain feeling for comfortable living and for power, but they lacked the regal ostentation of the Italians. They were essentially merchants, and the interest in money outweighed everything else. Practical advantages dictated their decisions. To gain independence, they held together fanatically, only to disintegrate in struggles concerning their private interests. Singly and collectively they compromised again and again with their hereditary Spanish foes. Even during the war, they continued trade with Spain, even trade in arms, and deceived their allies un-scrupulously. During the period of the first religious wars, they were ardent Protestants who insisted even stubbornly on partic-ularities of faith, such as Lutheranism, Calvinism, Anabaptism. But when it was a matter of business, they had no trouble in coming to agreements with one another as well as with their Catholic brethren and with Jews. The Calvinistic merchants demonstrate an atrophy of religious influence on the conduct of life. On the whole, the Dutch were the first to carry through a general toler-ance. In the colonies they won over the natives, in opposition to their Spanish and Portuguese competitors, through their refraining from missionary coercion. In the famous Treaty of Hermannszoon with the Banda tribes of India, that laid the foundation for their colonial empire, the natives were assured of peace and freedom of worship. Finally, the Dutch have always propagated free trade without much theoretical deliberation, wherever this seemed prac-tical and useful to them, especially with regard to Cromwell's Navi-gation Acts. But their driving motive was only to obtain trade monopolies. Their methods within their own country were no different. Miriam Beard tells the story of Cornelis Bicker, one of the leading merchants of Amsterdam, a share owner and chief director of the Dutch West India Company: "He rose to immense wealth with the Company, after the memorable year 1628 when the Admiral Piet Heyn captured the Spanish silver fleet, and a fifty per cent dividend was declared, due at least as much to piracy as to busi-ness. However, Cornelis . . . sold out promptly at great advantage. Then he went to work through his elder brother, Burgomaster Andries, who had the government of Amsterdam under his thumb, against the Company . . . The Bicker clan put through a law ending the West India Company's monopoly of trade with America . . . And Bicker, by fitting out his own ships and competing with the Company he formerly directed, made a splendid harvest."

As long as Portugal and Spain could keep foreign traffic from their colonies, the Dutch had to confine themselves to the inter-mediary commerce between Lisbon and Amsterdam. But especially after the liberation, commerce and wealth increased, and Philip II,

and after his death, Philip III still more effectively, barred the
Dutch from the harbor of Lisbon in order to cut them off from
the source of European trade. With this fateful act, the Spanish
kings actually promoted the ruin of their own country. For now
the Dutch decided to abandon the intermediary trade along the
West coast of Europe and to ply direct commerce with the Orient.
This was initiated by the private enterprise of two Amsterdam merchants, and, when their expeditions had proved successful, larger,
well-armed fleets were sent out, and other cities followed suit. Finally, the great commercial cities of the Netherlands united for a
common enterprise and, in 1602, founded the Dutch East India
Company, that started on its career under the protection and with
the participation of the government. The richest and most powerful
of the Dutch cities, Amsterdam, became predominant in this
company and gradually superseded Lisbon as the center of European trade. In 1609, the famous Bank of Amsterdam was founded,
a financial center not only of Holland but of all Europe and the
forerunner of the Bank of England. In violent struggles, the Dutch
ejected the Portuguese from the most important of the Moluccas.
They conquered the Sunda Islands, and Batavia became the center
of their new colonial government and trade. By the middle of the
seventeenth century, all the shores and islands of the Indian Ocean
were in Dutch hands. They also extended their rule in the West
Indies by breaking Spanish commercial predominance through
contraband trade on a large scale, and by capturing the Spanish
fleets with their cargo of silver. After the decline of Flanders and
Brabant that capitulated to Spain, the enterprising Protestant population of these regions emigrated to Holland and with them, industry. The chief interest, however, continued to center in trade.

But even the Dutch did not break radically with the methods
practised by the Mediterranean peoples. The East India Company,
too, excluded foreign vessels from their colonial trade, in order to
be able to monopolize Oriental goods and to fix the prices at will.
They too exhausted the resources of their colonies for the sake of
immediate gain and without care of the future. They too exploited
and robbed the natives to the utmost. The country was, moreover,

too small to support such a vast empire and the economic strain of a sea power and a continental army large and efficient enough to match their greedy neighbors, the French in particular. It lacked the splendid isolation and unassailability of the British Isles. And owing to the particularism and the party strife of the cities, it also lacked an efficient national government. Military defense was neglected, and left, as everything else, to private enterprise. So they were bound to succumb when the English power began to rise.

It was *England* that actually created world economy through the tremendous sweep and sway of her economic evolution which not only assumed universal range, but, since it was the instrument, the main concern of British rulership and British hegemony, made economy the ruling factor of the epoch. The main concern of Spain and France was politics, the struggle for immediate power, that is to say, territorial dominion, military superiority and diplomatic prestige. Economic strength was valued only as a subordinate, subsidiary expedient to furnish the financial means for political power. In England, economy fused with politics, it became an equal, if not a superior of politics. And thus a new method of indirect domination, a new way of exercising power and influence was brought into being; power through wealth, influence through economic superiority, was introduced as the ruling principle of the world. Territorial expansion, as such, lost its prime importance; colonial dominions derive their value from economic resources, from the range of economic development they afford and represent. This is how and why a little country like England could rise to a dominant position.

What predestined England to this new kind of domination, and to the creation of the new methods that helped her to this dominant position, was a special and unique combination of circumstances. The most fundamental of these is her insular location. When the times of primitive warfare were over, it was impossible to invade England. We have seen that even the most refined modern military machinery has not been able to overcome this difficulty. So England was spared the necessity of maintaining a powerful regular army in order to protect the country. And, on the other hand, she naturally held aloof from the contest for territorial expansion and the endless rounding-off of territorial dominions. A second factor was the democratic disposition, the broadening of the basis of rulership, which prevented an unquestioned identification of the people with the political ambitions and the lust for power of a personal monarch. The third factor which contributed to the new English way of domination was the extermination of the old feudal aristocracy in the fifteenth century, and the formation of a new commercial-minded nobility. And the fourth, most important, element was the novel combination of a powerful industry with a vast oversea trade. This combination, which nowhere else was brought to such perfection and nowhere else developed into such a predominant national concern, is indeed the founding element of world economy. This combination, moreover, existed from the beginning; English oversea trade and English industry were born together.

In the Middle Ages, English history as a whole is a merely local history with regard to European evolution. And, at a time when the great Italian merchants, when the Frenchman Jacques Coeur, the Hanseatic League and the bankers and entrepreneurs of the German inland cities displayed an economic activity of European scope, English merchants were hardly making themselves felt on the European market. Economically, England concerned herself with agriculture, sheep-breeding and wool trade, and, in addition to this, to a small extent, with the exploitation of tin mines; and the export of these goods was in foreign—Italian, Flemish, German —hands. This condition began to change only when, under King Edward III, in the first half of the fourteenth century, the English manufacture of cloth got under way, stimulated by Flemish immigrants. In proportion as cloth was now exported instead of wool, the export passed over to English merchants. A company of English export traders was privileged by the kings, the so-called "merchant adventurers", a loose organization similar to that of the Hanseatic merchants. But it took considerable time for this little company to become important. They did not really start upon their career before the beginning of the sixteenth century when the Tudor kings wanted to get rid of the influence of foreign traders. And not before the time of Queen Elizabeth, at the end of the sixteenth century, did they succeed in outstripping and defeating the Hanseatic merchants. An English export trade to any considerable extent was not possible as long as English navigation and shipbuilding were relatively undeveloped. English sea power began only in the second part of the sixteenth century.

It is also noteworthy that banking was unknown in England until the first half of the seventeenth century. Up to then, the merchants used to deposit their bullion and coin in the Tower. Charles I, who was in need of money, simply seized these deposits, and this experience gave rise to the development of banking in England. First, the merchants kept their money at home. But in the disorders of the English Revolution, the merchants, and especially the landed proprietors who were threatened by the sack of their estates, found it convenient and, at the same time, profitable to put their money out at interest to the goldsmiths. So the goldsmiths accumulated a considerable amount of capital and became the first bankers of England. And when eventually in 1694, under William III, the Bank of England was founded, it met with furious opposition on the part of the goldsmiths.

These English goldsmiths are important not only for England but for economic evolution as a whole, in that they originated paper money and the modern check. Continental banks and bankers had, to be sure, already issued promissory notes that were transferable and could be used as payment, but only in the limited circle of such persons as had deposits in the banks in question. The English goldsmiths, however, issued "goldsmith's notes", called "banker's notes" since the middle of the seventeenth century, that were accepted in payment everywhere. Since more of these were in circulation than the banker could cash at once, the procedure already involved permanent credit, without interest, of the public to the signer of the note. The goldsmiths, on their part, used this credit to assist the merchants and even the government with loans. This whole practice was taken over subsequently by the Bank of England. The public banks that served as a pattern for the Bank of

England, the Genoese "banco di San Giorgio" and the Bank of Amsterdam, neither issued generally circulating, publicly recognized banknotes nor widened the circle of their activities beyond their actual depositors. The Bank of England already used money in a productive fashion and made it accessible to trade and industry. Thus it became the first modern, national bank.

In the Elizabethan period, the great movement of colonial and economic expansion began, incited by the discoveries and the Portuguese and Spanish colonial conquests. In order to thwart the threatening power of Spain, Elizabeth had decided to assume the leadership of the Protestant forces, to support the Netherlands in their struggle for independence and the French Huguenots in the religious struggles of their country. This developed into an open war between England and Spain. An English navy was created that destroyed the Spanish Armada in 1588, and at the same time the first oversea enterprises started through the foundation of oversea trading companies, essentially different in their organization from companies like the "merchant adventurers". The old companies had been mere associations of personally participating merchants who traded on their own individual accounts and paid entrance fees and contributions covering the common expenses. The new companies were what was called a "chartered company", that is to say, a joint stock company with collective capital and collective liability, vested with a delegated sovereignty to conquer and secure the bases and territories necessary for carrying on and for protecting the new colonial trade. At that time, colonial trade meant warfare against natives as well as against European competitors. While the Portuguese, Spanish and Dutch expeditions were more or less government expeditions, taking possession of the colonies for the crown and setting up official governors, the position of the English government was rather that of a personally not liable partner of a limited company. It did not run any risks, it accepted only a very limited responsibility, it interfered only once in a while by claiming a share in the profit or exacting duty for the renewal of a privilege, and it supported the company only in so far as this was compatible with the commercial and political interest of the nation. This procedure established flexible relations between official and private interests; the private entrepreneurs became semi-official and the patronage of the government non-committal. A kind of intrinsic partnership of private individual and national community sprang up, and became a characteristic feature of English life; it is an expression of the democratic tendency.

The first of these companies was the Muscovy Company for the trade with Russia and the Near East. It was founded in 1553 and later entitled "The Fellowship of English Merchants for Discovery of New Trades". The next was the African Company, which financed a trade in gold and ivory and especially the slave trade of John Hawkins, who brought home so much money that he was knighted by the queen; he chose a chained Negro as his heraldic emblem. Curiously enough, his ship was called "The Jesus". This was the beginning of English slave trade, that did not end until the nineteenth century.

The companies that financed the adventurous piratical raids of Francis Drake, the nephew of Hawkins, were still more important, not only because they were more profitable, but because they are the direct financial ancestors, so to speak, of the Empire of India. Drake raided the Spanish fleets along the American shores, escaped the battleships sent out to chase him, and disappeared to the West in circumnavigating the globe. He brought home such quantities of plunder that the stockholders, one of whom was the queen, went mad with joy. The queen received more than £250,000, apart from jewels. From her share in the proceeds she paid off the royal debts. With the rest of the capital, the Levantine Company was founded. In this the queen also participated, and it averaged profits of three hundred per cent. After it dissolved, the accumulated capital of this company became the stock of the British East India Company, which was privileged in 1600. It was vested with the rights to acquire and rule territories on condition that the rule was in conformity with English laws. It was headed by a governor and twenty-four directors who were to be elected annually at the meeting of the stockholders. The regulations that the directors of the

Company issued to their subordinates were very puritanical. Blasphemy, gambling, drinking and feasting were strictly forbidden. In a letter of instruction of 1610, we find sentences like these: "And because there is no means more prevalent to strengthen and confirm the ways of the godly in righteousness than the spirit of God, which is the guide into all good motions, and no aim more pregnant to support and uphold the sinner from falling into wickedness than the Grace of God . . . we exhort you in the fear of God to be very careful to assemble together your whole family [that is, all the employees of the trading post] every morning and evening and to join together in all humility with hearty prayer to almighty God for his merciful protection . . . Comport yourselves both in your habit and housekeeping in such comely and convenient manner as neither may disparage our business nor be accounted too excessive in expenses." These founders of the East India Company were apparently of the same stamp as those of Plymouth and Boston.

The Company had to struggle hard with the Portuguese, the Dutch and finally the French. The French had also created a "Compagnie des Indes", which, however, was headed by statesmen and soldiers, and lacked the English independence from governmental control and so from non-commercial motives or whims. After several unprofitable beginnings by Henry IV, Richelieu and Colbert, the French company began to thrive in the eighteenth century, and then, in conjunction with the conflict between England and France, in the War of the Austrian Succession, the struggle between the two India companies was won by the English. In 1784, the political control of India was taken over by the English government, and only the management of trade was left in the hands of the Company.

The origins of the British dominions in America are more complex. The Spaniards did not extend their conquests beyond the Southern part of North America, as they considered the Northern regions waste and worthless land. Stimulated by the new discoveries, the English king, Henry VII, sent out Italian merchants, John and Sebastian Cabot, in 1497 and 1498, to explore the new

Western way to the Orient. He ordered Cabot to seize all lands he might discover, for England, provided that they did not as yet belong to any other Christian power. So England claimed the American East coast from Newfoundland down to the Gulf of Mexico. At the beginning of the seventeenth century, however, the French started explorations and settlements along the St. Lawrence River. In 1627, Richelieu organized the "Company of the Hundred Associates" to colonize New France, and granted it all lands between Florida and the Arctic Circle. So France became a dangerous competitor in the West as well as in the East.

In the mean time, since the end of the sixteenth century, when Sir Walter Raleigh founded Virginia, the English settlements had been launched on their memorable career. As Virginia at first proved a failure, the true start was again made by chartered companies, the London Company and the Plymouth Company, which sent out expeditions in 1606. These were the companies with which the Puritans entered into negotiations when they wanted to escape the cruel persecution of the High Church under Archbishop Whitgift, and still remain British subjects. They took over the privilege of the companies, granting the land and the right to establish a community. An actual charter could not be obtained. And so they set out on their Mayflower Pilgrimage which inaugurated a new epoch of humanity, inasmuch as it instituted the first community on earth founded by a free covenant of equal individuals, as the theorists of natural law had pictured and prescribed.

The constitutional forms of the various *American settlements* reflect in their diversity the fluctuating conditions of England in this most critical and formative period of her history. Residues of feudalism and absolutism, Catholic and High Church features, alternated with Puritan and democratic trends. The proprietary colony, based on the investiture of a lord with the land, is reminiscent of feudal conditions. The Crown colony is a product of the absolute monarchy, and the corporate colony is a true democracy vested with a charter. The aims and constituents of these settlements were also manifold. Despite the ambitions of the English

Crown, that exerted a certain influence, it was, for the most part, spontaneous enterprises that carried and developed colonization— entrepreneurs and adventurers seeking riches and economic prosperity, refugees seeking a haven, missionaries seeking propagation of the faith. But all the various forms of settlement bore the germ of democracy and sooner or later developed democracy. They were characterized by that particularly English, flexible relation between the government and the individual. We have only to compare the methods and results of Latin American colonization, this authoritarian, aristocratic, thoroughly political colonization, which was more the expansion and transplantation of a rule than an immigration and a popular settlement, we have only to compare the methods of the neighboring French with the English way of colonization, to realize fully the fundamental difference, not only between inherent aims of life, but between epochs and ages of humanity. Canada became the pattern of a centralized, absolute monarchy, such as Richelieu and Louis XIV had built up. Count Frontenac, the most distinguished governor of New France, called an Estates General, modeled on French patterns, in Quebec in 1672. In reply to this measure, he received a reproof from Colbert in which the close dependence of the colony upon the mother country was emphasized, and the difference between British and French methods of colonization, becomes unambiguously clear: "The assembling and division of all the inhabitants into three orders or estates, which you have done for the purpose of having them take the oath of fidelity, may have been productive of good just then. But it is well for you to observe that you are always to follow, in the government and management of that country, the forms in force here; and as our kings have considered it for a long time advantageous to their service not to assemble the Estates General of their kingdom, with a view, perhaps, to abolish insensibly that ancient form, you likewise ought rarely, or (to speak more correctly) never, give that form to the corporate body of the inhabitants of that country." Economically, the picture was the same: New France was not greatly concerned with agriculture, but was out for colonial exploitation, especially for the fur trade. Trading

posts and forts were established, and their center for food supplies
and their market was in France. New England began to work the
land and to create a life of its own. The fresh start which made
possible the creation of a perfect democracy in English America
favored the establishment of integral absolutism in the French
dominion. "The administration", says Tocqueville, "interfered
much more than in the metropolis, and—just as at home—wanted
to make Paris out of everything. There were almost as many officials as burghers . . . more informed as to the interests of the rulers
than the rulers themselves . . . always busy and always sterile . . . If
one wants to study the spirit and the vices of the rule of Louis XIV,
one should go to Canada."

Of course, it was that particular English looseness of the relation
between the government and the private individual, it was the
prevalence of the economic interest which eventually gave rise to
American independence. But, on the other hand, for all its elasticity, it proved most effective in building up a colonial empire.
It promoted economic expansion and it brought about world
economy.

America, or, more precisely, the United States of America, did
not only carry out the English system but went beyond it to an
entirely new and indeed unique creation. Her history is not comparable to any history of any people in the world. Thanks to the
remoteness and virginity of the American continent and to its late
appearance on the horizon of the old world, this history shows
lines of classical clearness carved out sharply from the complexity
of world history. It has a distinct beginning in the full light of
historical knowledge, and it proceeds as a similarly distinct development from a group of small colonies toward a mighty, united
people. But the history of the United States is unique in still other
respects. This country shows us the only colonial enterprise that
succeeded in developing not only a great people but a new civilization of its own, and in playing a crucial part in the modern
world. It was a form of colonization that Charles Beard rightly
compares to the colonizing methods of the ancient Greek cities,
when overflowing populations spontaneously moved to the islands

and the shores of the Mediterranean, to become independent communities of their own. Ancient colonies, however, were compact stocks of their home communities, not the association of individuals of different stocks as is the population of the United States. And here we face another essential feature of America. The American people is a community founded and developed by individuals. This is implied in the epoch in which this foundation took place. No other nation has its roots in this period. The European nations were built up by a slow, subconscious, involuntary merging of their original stocks. They were built up in the twilight of complex historical processes rather than by the clear free will and self-determination of men themselves. The American people, on the contrary, as it was founded by individuals of the most different descent, was deliberately established by the free, conscious will of these individuals, by the association and coordination of various reasons. Since there were distinct reasons which induced these individuals to settle in the new world, these settlements show from their beginnings the pre-eminently rational character of planning and building and living according to clearly conceived purposes. This was not a kind of life where the premises were given or handed down for generations. It was a fresh start from a completely new basis. The colonists had to take the orders and rules of their life from the outside not from the inside, from their aims not from their customs and traditions, from the future and not from the past. Hence America's proverbial progressiveness and optimism, hence her living from day to day, the symbol of which appears in the advancing frontier, her footing in the present, in the moment. Hence her contempt for ideologies, her high estimation, almost overestimation of visible facts and experiences. Hence the preponderance of journalism, which, to be sure, has attained a truly classical standard in this country. Traditions, as far as they existed and subsisted in the new nation, were chiefly traditions brought over by the colonists from abroad. And these very traditions, the traditions of the personalities who shaped the new nation in the main, the traditions of the Protestant creeds, bore an element of rationalism in themselves.

The foundation by individual agreement, and the ensuing rational character of this colonization, caused America to start as a democracy, to preserve and maintain democracy throughout her history, up to this very day. America is the first and only country in the world that was founded as a democracy, that was built up step by step, by covenants, compacts, declarations of rights and liberties between free individuals, among whom every one had the same right and the same opportunity. It is the first people to have a written constitution, in fact, the people that created the written constitution. Thus America is an integral democracy, the first community in the world—with the exception of the Swiss—in which democracy is the sole substratum of life, in which all specific forms of life derive from democracy, in which nation and democracy are synonymous. Democracy was further promoted by the natural conditions which the early settlers faced in the American wilderness. It was kept alive by the fact that these early conditions continued to prevail even after the original settlements had become states and confederations and had developed social and economic disparities among their populations. The moving frontier, lasting a whole century, always preserved and restored the first conditions of individual settlers, pioneers, freehold farmers and traders, jealously defending their freedom and equality, and it was the influence of these frontiersmen that corrected the trends of powerful individuals and groups in the Eastern and Southern sections to establish social, political and economic predominance. Thanks to the frontier, democracy could root so deeply in the minds and moods of the people as never to lose ground under the fluctuations and the menace of such special interests. Only today, when a fundamental change of all human civilization is taking place and spreading through the world as a panic, as contagious anarchy, this democracy is in serious danger, and its salvation, synonymous with its renewal, is a vital question not only for this country but for the whole world.

The outcome of the Civil War, which was a victory for the democratic forces, bore the features of destiny, corresponding to the broad trends of American history and world history as a whole.

The North was bound to conquer through all the assets democracy had helped to develop: the large population of free white people, the more efficient organization and the financial, industrial and technical superiority. It was the exact parallel to processes we find in European history. Everywhere in Europe too, the South was left behind, owing to its conservatism; everywhere it was hampered by its residues of patriarchal and aristocratic habits. And, as a whole, the democratic development of the American people was furthered, not only by the positive factors mentioned above, but no less by the absence of a pre-individual past that European history dragged along with it. In America, fixed ranks or castes never existed, as there were no sacred monarchs and long established feudal nobility, no court or hereditary society, no guilds and no villages with their inveterate customs, their folk traditions and communal grounds. There were none of all those weatherworn, overgrown and interwoven institutions, the origins and often the meaning of which nobody knew any longer, but the magic power of which people could never actually overcome. No American-born person may be fully able to realize this European way of life under the perpetual and ever-present burden of immemorial memories. And one of the many dark impulses of the present barbarism which is raging over Europe, is certainly that of doing away with this glorious but oppressive burden, an impulse which has been voiced by intellectuals in all European countries, first of all by Nietzsche.

Thus American history, owing to its lack of those pre-individual, pre-democratic historical layers, has a very uniform character, distinctly different from that of European history. Although it contains violent wars against England, Spain, France, Mexico and the Indians, although one may, at some special turning points, properly speak of an American struggle for power, the main object of this history is not politics, but economy. The American Revolution itself arose from economic quarrels with the motherland. The Civil War was a parallel to the English struggle between manufacture and manor. It was, as Miriam Beard terms it, "the victory of business over Plantocracy". We may further recall that it was the motive of gaining control of the Mississippi River at the end of the eighteenth century, in order to secure a safe way of transportation for American trade, that gave rise to early American expansion. And yet, the most important territorial gains were made by treaties and purchases, the Louisiana Purchase in 1803, the treaty with Spain in 1819, which added Florida, the treaty with Great Britain concerning the Oregon country, the purchase of Alaska in 1867, and so on. Owing to the absence of feudal castes and of the custom of deep-rooted social differentiation, established by these castes in the European countries, America has not known any social revolution, nor any serious class struggles up to the present time. In America the role of the European classes is represented rather by geographical sections with their economic problems. The main object of American history was the economic penetration, cultivation, mobilization and organization of her huge continent, and the development of new industrial and technical methods, on the large scale so huge a continent required and afforded. This eventually gave America the lead in the economic and technical field. By this development even the social problems were largely reduced to economic problems, since, given the economic opportunities, there was always an outlet for the individual to make a typical American career. It is only during recent decades that a change in this respect was slowly preparing.

Since American colonization started from private enterprise and stockholders looking for productive investments, from individual traders and farmers seeking individual wealth, from Puritans who threw all of their religious zeal into business, the very foundations of this country made for an essentially capitalistic order of American life. Even farmers in this country were not the same as that stable, conservative and self-sufficient class of European peasants with their attachment to the soil and to their old-fashioned, ethnic customs. American farmers and pioneers were capitalists, though for a long time primitive capitalists, making as much money as they could out of their labors. They were even, for a long time, the most progressive-minded people in this country. In fact, America is the most essentially capitalistic country in the world. This means that, in contrast with European institutions, every undertaking in this country—public utilities, railways, telegraph, radio, universities, theaters, museums and athletic clubs—originates in a private enterprise, in a foundation of private capital.

It seems a providential coincidence that capitalism as a phase of world history happened to rise at the same time as American exploration, though, of course, these two events are intrinsically connected with each other. Capitalism was the most efficient vehicle for the exploration and mobilization of the American continent, while, on the other hand, no other country of the world could have furnished such miraculous opportunities for the development of capitalism. America and capitalism brought each other to their peak. Nothing but private capitalistic enterprise could have better achieved the exploitation of the huge natural resources of this country, could have created the means of transportation and communication necessary for this exploitation, could have brought about the mass production appropriate to the requirements of such an enormous land and its people. Only private capitalistic initiative and competition was likely to raise such a country to a standard of civilization which matched the European world. We may find the proof in the failure of regimentation in the early Crown colonies and proprietary colonies, in the failure of the so-called communistic beginnings of New Plymouth, and in the inefficient methods of Latin American colonization. Only the limitless possibilities offered to private enterprise by so vast and so rich a continent could stimulate capitalism to the overwhelming technical achievements it reached in America. This, however, does not imply any such consequences for the future, since the condition of the world is changing fundamentally.

According to her beginnings and her development, America is a country of fanatic individualists, politically and economically. It was a hard struggle to effect unity among these independent-minded people and to establish the amount of centralized power and control in a federal government necessary for the defense and the organization of so vast a country. Hence, American democracy drives the defensive character of modern democracy to extremes.

It is always ready to defend the individual against interference on the part of the administration, and suspects intrusion upon individual rights in all government action. Accordingly, every measure is regarded less from the point of view of the community than from that of the individual. This attitude, which up to the beginning of the twentieth century corresponded to the trend of the times and the condition of this great isolated continent, is being questioned more and more by world developments, and will have to be modified if democracy is to be maintained.

On the other hand, the American people harbors the antidote to this attitude more than it seems to realize. However individual-*minded* American people may be, they are, paradoxically, very collective-*natured*. There is as much hidden, unconscious, potential collectivism striving within them, as there is in capitalism itself. The colonial situation of the first American settlers, and the frontier situation which perpetuated the early colonial conditions for over a century, at first developed individualism, but afterwards fostered collectivism. Facing new conditions of life in a blank, overwhelming wilderness put men on their own feet, and left to their own initiative the first steps toward domesticating and cultivating the virgin nature before them. But soon this very offensive against nature, and the defensive against the dangers of the elements and of the Indian population, called for increased cooperation, and so, afterwards, did the tremendous task of technical and industrial organization and exploitation of the country. Thus the circumstances created an individualistic and independent mind, and, at the same time, a collectivistic way of life among the American people. They created the big, overcrowded cities, a concentration of industrial work, a mass production and, consequently, a standardization of life, unheard-of in Europe, and, last but not least, an habitual inclination of American people toward gathering together, toward sociability and social activity, which is all the more striking as it is combined with such vehemently professed individualism.

America is the model for the structure and the functioning of the modern democracy, and American history shows to what high degree modern democracy is economically determined and how it has promoted the power of economic and technical processes over all of public and individual life.

The unheard-of industrial and technical achievements of America were evoked by the task of taming and exploiting Nature, a task set by the vast space and the rich and unexhausted continent, by the frontier which lasted for centuries. But America is only the model example of a process that has become general within the last two hundred years. Everywhere it was the *open frontier* that was responsible for the rise of capitalistic economy. And with the end of frontiers all over the world, corruption and decay of this capitalistic form of economy set in.

England's frontier consisted, in the first place, in her colonies and dominions. Among these, Canada evolved as the remainder of the American possessions when the French were overpowered by the immigration of English loyalists after the declaration of American independence. Australia, discovered partly by the Dutch, partly by James Cook, 1768–1771, developed from a British convict settlement, which was gradually supplemented and transformed into a very progressive commonwealth by the immigration of free settlers, who took up sheep-breeding. Later Adelaide was founded by a new chartered company, the South Australian Association. New Zealand also originated in a chartered company, the New Zealand Association of 1837. The African dominions and colonies developed from the expansion and protection of commercial interests, and from the necessity of securing a communication line to India through the Mediterranean and the Red Sea. Again explorers, merchants and chartered companies paved the way. And it was the struggle against French and German competition and menace that eventually forced Britain to adopt openly imperialistic methods and to resort to warfare and conquests. Aside from her reprehensible treatment of Ireland, England has accumulated no mean store of guilt in the Boer Wars, in India and elsewhere. But in comparison with other colonial powers, and considering the mental temper of the whole epoch, it is relatively slight. And it must be admitted that she usually tried to reach her goals by the peaceful means of negotiation, and that the English government evinced real reluctance to imperialistic methods, as is apparent from the attitude of Gladstone in 1877, when he hesitated for a long time before using force against Egypt. "We cannot enjoy the luxury," he warned, "of taking Egyptian soil by pinches . . . our first site in Egypt, be it by larceny or be it by emption, will be the almost certain egg of a North African Empire that will grow and grow until another Victoria and another Albert, titles of the Lake-sources of the White Nile, come within our borders; and till we finally join hands across the Equator with Natal and Cape Town, to say nothing of the Transvaal and the Orange River on the south, or of Abyssinia or Zanzibar to be swallowed by way of viaticum on our journey. And then, with a great Empire in each of the four quarters of the world, and with the whole new or fifth quarter to ourselves, we may be territorially content, but less than ever at our ease; for if agitators and alarmists can now find at almost every spot 'British interests' to bewilder and disquiet us, their quest will then be all the wider, in proportion as the excepted points will be the fewer." What he foresaw has indeed come true, and it is, at any rate, noteworthy that he did not like the prospect.

By this great process of commercial and colonial expansion over all continents of the globe, by the competition, the filiations, the reactions it aroused, the scene was set for the development of world economy. Into this immense arena, free trade was let loose, free trade that had been carried through in England from 1823 on. When the London merchants called for the abolition of the protective system, they demanded it "even though other nations should be slow to establish reciprocity." They were sure of their superiority. At first the colonies were merely sources of raw material. More and more they were developed into markets. The English colonial empire became the much envied and emulated pattern for the nations of Europe. It created the new, economic style of imperialism, after the old, purely political style had perished with Napoleon. The whole world was searched for colonial and market potentialities. In addition to the actual colonial frontiers, there were the frontiers of nations with a backward economic development, in Eastern and Southern Europe, in the Far East and in South America. They played the same role as the colonies, and like these, they became objects of economic expansion for the great nations. The Balkans, for instance, were a frontier for Austria. And we shall see, later, how the rivalries of colonial and economic imperialisms kindled the First World War and, with it, the world crisis of today.

England had not only a colonial frontier but another in her own country that played the same role as the great American frontier. This was the Northern part of Britain, a waste, pathless region with scarcely any cities or even villages, where miserable dwellers were sparsely scattered and lived in caves or earthen huts—a semi-barbaric rim of Europe. The civilized political and economic life of England was limited to the South, up to the eighteenth century. It was at this frontier that the third great economic movement began, the movement that in conjunction with free economy and world economy has transformed the civilization of man: the *industrial revolution*. In their search for new ways and methods of economy, enterprising Puritan business men discovered this region. Here there were no guild regulations, no monopolies and no officials; here it was easy to escape the supervision of the government; here they could launch their revolutionary activities without hindrance, from the middle of the eighteenth century on. And just as in other branches of economy—in agriculture, banking, even in trade—a certain backwardness in England's development proved to be her best asset, her best opportunity to excel more civilized countries. In comparison with the rest of the European continent, English industry was little advanced. Only Italy, France, Holland and Germany had made important technical inventions up to this point. But the Italian, French and Dutch industries were, for the most part, concerned with luxury articles: silks, tapestries, porcelain, mosaic and glass. Continental inventions had been made in connection with clocks, telescopes and other optical instruments, vehicles, pumps, guns and war machines, games for the parks of great gentlemen and other things of the same sort; the invention of machinery for production was relatively in its beginnings, and its development was retarded by guild regulations and the resistance of craftsmen. Industrial labor on the continent was relatively expensive, since the great masses of people were peasants. In England the new rising class of entrepreneurs did not have to bother about guild regulations. They found cheap labor among the English, Scotch and Irish country folk who had been robbed of their land by the gentry and forced to work on the big estates for starvation wages. They were, therefore, the first to realize the possibilities that lay waiting in mass production. They were the first to quicken with the offensive spirit of modern economy—not only to use inventions but to encourage them systematically through the setting of concrete goals and the offer of prizes. Customers were not only to be satisfied, but to be lured by traveling salesmen, through propaganda and novelties. These tendencies had already prevailed among the Dutch Puritans, but the English industrialists were the first to exploit these possibilities.

The last, in logical sequence, of these four constituent elements of modern industry—mechanization, systematic invention, mass production and soliciting of customers—was labor discipline, which led to the development of the modern factory. Machine and mass production required a new precision of work that could only be attained through rigid drill. The "putting-out" system, the domination of the entrepreneur over the home-worker, is old. The new industrialists took this for their point of departure. A common place to work in, the so-called factory, had also been in existence for a long time, in individual cases. Mining, the first modern industry that is impossible without collective labor, the industry that symbolizes the typical attitude of modern man who is confronted with the superior powers of nature to be exploited, had developed the common place of work, with all of its accompanying phenomena. There is evidence that there were common places of work existing in the English cloth manufacture of the sixteenth century. But it was the machine that begot the modern factory, that coordinated people in time and space in the most exact manner and joined them to form a functional, super-individual unit. All these elements of modern industry now developed simultaneously, each affecting the other; modern labor and the machine created each other.

At first the new English cotton manufacturers suffered from lack of labor, particularly since the agricultural enclosures had not progressed so far at that time. Lancashire and Cheshire, where the climate was moist enough for the spinning of cotton, were sparsely populated. This prompted the entrepreneurs to use machines. Experiments were made, prizes offered. The results were the famous, fundamental inventions that were made in quick succession: the water frame of Arkwright, 1769, the spinning jenny of Hargreaves, 1770, the mule of Crompton, 1776, the self-acting mule of Kelly, 1792. These heavy and massive machines, that could only be used where there was water-power, made home work impossible. The workmen were forced to go to a place of common work and to live near it. Thus new industrial cities came into being. But water-power was not present everywhere, and the same problem arose in regard to pumps in mining. These difficulties brought about the following development: Matthew Boulton, of the metal industry, who had not enough water-power to run his factory, financed the mathematical instrument maker at the University of Glasgow, James Watt, and encouraged him to pursue his experiments with the steam-engine, in which he had been preceded by earlier inventors, and to bring the invention to the stage of applicability. In 1775, the steam-engine was ready to be introduced into industry. Richard Arkwright, originally a barber and wig maker, who had invented the water-frame, also used the steam-engine in his spinning mills in 1785. He and the pottery manufacturer, Josiah Wedgwood, were the begetters of the new labor discipline. Wedgwood, who was the first to tune the ceramic industry to mass production and so to surpass European luxury manufactures, who, in order to save the expense of employing designers, used classical patterns for his wares in his factory "Etruria", was a much-feared employer, who punished severely any deviation from his scheme. Arkwright is the originator of one of the most terrible innovations of modern industry; since the peasant workers of Lancashire had thick and awkward hands that were too slow and unskillful to handle machines successfully, he went to the parish workhouses where the poor were imprisoned at that time, and began to train the children of the poor for mechanical work, "their small fingers being more active." This usage soon became general. Arkwright was also responsible for a new division and chain process of work and arranged for ruthless supervision of labor. With this, the modern factory was launched upon the world. The modern factory is the prototype of an economic collective, just as the Prussian army represents the core of the state collective.

As long as there was a scarcity of labor, wages were high. But soon the many peasants who had been expropriated flooded the new factory towns and lowered wages. The reaction of workers to low wages consisted in marrying early and begetting children as one breeds cattle, in order to send them to the factories as soon as possible and so to increase the family income. But this, of course, only heightened competition and so made their own misery greater. This misery was the worst mankind had experienced up to that time; it surpassed the plight of slavery. Working hours were un-limited—sixteen to eighteen hours were not at all unusual. Man-power was worked without any consideration, and lashed onward to the tempo of the machines. Women and children, even three-year-olds, worked in the factories, often at night, under merciless overseers. There was no legal insurance against accidents, no pro-vision for illness or old age. The factory owners who were them-selves fanatic workers, maintained a clear Puritan conscience through all this. Conditions were not changed until the Tories spurred social reform with the purpose of keeping down the industrial upstarts, and until the labor movement made itself felt.

The successes and the profits of the new industry were tremen-dous. Around 1820, the cotton mills, that were expanding more and more, still required skilled workers. The workers availed them-selves of this opportunity to demand higher wages. But this only drove the manufacturers to further mechanization of labor. In 1825, a new self-acting mule was patented in Manchester, that made skilled labor superfluous and produced smoother yarn. The same thing happened in weaving. Here the newly invented, automatic power loom threw hand weavers out of work. Around the middle of the nineteenth century, two looms could be operated by one man with an assistant. By 1880 one man could already operate six automatic looms. And the same circle was repeated again and again: industry expanded, absorbed more workers, became more mechanized and cast aside workers. Thus the creation of the modern proletariat is closely connected with the invention of machines and of the technical apparatus of our world.

A similar reciprocal increase took place between growing mass production and the growth of the masses who were to consume it. The rise in industry brought with it an increase in population that was new in history. Fluctuation and wide circulation of profits, new and apparently unlimited possibilities of becoming rich, new vital impulses awakened by new goods of world commerce, invention and industry, and, last but not least, more lively social intercourse—all these factors caused an increase in the birth rate, while mortality was decreased by improved hygiene.

On the English frontier, as later on the American, towns sprouted up out of the earth. The old historic cities grew more slowly, but Liverpool increased from 40,000 in the year 1760 to 552,508 in 1881, Manchester from 40,000 in the year 1760 to 95,000 in 1801 and 517,649 in 1881. It was here, in the North of England, that "Americanism" was really born. Tocqueville gives a moving description of Manchester that he saw with his own eyes in 1835: "On a terrain irrigated by art and nature, palaces and huts are scattered about as though by chance. Everything in the appearance of the city attests the individual power of man, nothing the regulated power of society. . . . Thirty or forty factories rise on the summit of the hills. Their six stories mount into the air . . . Around them are sown at random, the miserable habitations of the poor that can be reached by a multitude of twisting paths. Between them are stretches of uncultivated land that have nothing of rural charm, without having acquired the character of towns. The earth is disturbed and torn in a thousand places. . . . The streets that connect the as yet ill-constructed portions of the big city, are, like all the rest, a hasty and incomplete piece of work: the temporary makeshift of a population eager for gain, that seeks to amass gold in order to have everything at one stroke, and that, in the mean time, is careless of the graces of living . . . Piles of filth, débris from buildings, puddles of stagnant water are here and there in front of houses and in public squares, uneven and full of holes. . . .

"In this infected labyrinth, in the midst of this vast and gloomy mass of brick, beautiful stone palaces arise at intervals and amaze the stranger's eye with their fluted columns . . . But who could describe the interior of those out of the way quarters, those receptacles of vice and wretchedness that envelop and enclose in their hideous coils the vast palaces of wealth! . . . the narrow twisted streets . . . are bordered by houses of a single story whose ill joined timbers and broken floors proclaim from afar that these are the last dwelling-places of man between misery and death. Below these wretched homes is a series of caves reached by a semi-subterranean passage. In every one of these damp and repulsive chambers twelve or fifteen human beings are packed pell-mell . . . All around this region of wretchedness, a stream trails its fetid waters that the labors of industry have tinged with black.

"But lift your heads and you will see all around you, the palaces of industry! You will hear the noise of furnaces, the whistle of steam . . . Here is the slave. There is the master. . . . A thick black smoke covers the town. Through it, the sun looks like a rayless disk. And in the midst of this incomplete day, three hundred thousand human creatures toil without cease. A thousand noises drone incessantly in this dank and dark labyrinth . . . The steps of a busy multitude, the crunch of wheels . . . the scream of escaping steam, the regular beat of looms, the roll of cars . . . It is from the midst of this infected cess-pool that human industry rises and is to fertilize the universe. From this horrible sewer runs pure gold. It is here that the human spirit finds its perfection and becomes brutish; here that civilization produces its marvels and that civilized man returns to savagery."

In addition to the three great branches of development outlined here—the liberation, the expansion and the technical unfolding of economy—there is a fourth, very complex process. This is the growing *rationalization and abstraction of the economic procedure*, which is responsible for the fact that the world economy of today, in spite of its material substantial element, has become intricate and impalpable beyond the grasp of the individual. This process is one of the greatest driving forces to an involuntary and unadmitted collectivity effective in the development of world economy.

It is a far call from the concrete and simple business of Mediterranean or Hanseatic trade journeys, from the loaded transports of armed merchants on the dangerous caravan routes of the Orient or through the wooded and mountainous wilderness of medieval Europe, to a modern business transaction. What a far cry from pirates and smugglers in the flesh to the modern trust! The gap is bridged by a series of commercial groupings. The hanse was still a loosely knit group of merchants trading at their own risk and brought together only for securing the safety of transports. The permanent trading company was a group with pooled resources for the lessening of risks and the expansion of enterprise. In Renaissance Italy, we have the firm (from "firmare", to sign). This was a combination of individual merchants in a business that transcended the person and the span of life of the owners. The mining industry of Central Europe, that demanded large investments over a long period of time, developed the system of "kuxe" (from the Czech "kus" piece, share), or mining ventures that separated the share, the interest in the mine, from the person, but that still maintained the connection with ownership and individual capital, since the owner was committed to further investments in case of need. The chartered companies, finally, are the forerunners of the modern joint stock company that render the share a completely independent article of freely circulating trade. This inaugurates the great process of making business anonymous. Business is no longer conducted by owners, but by executives, and personal, moral responsibility merges into the profit and success of the enterprise, which, in turn, is the moral responsibility of the executives. An impersonal complex of industrial and commercial functions comes into being, and expands to the concern and finally to the trust.

Along with business, the individual altered. He became more and more impersonal. He virtually changed into his function, into his objective interest. The example of Jacob Fugger, of the first real capitalist, showed how even the personal entrepreneur could transcend his personal existence, with its joys and satisfactions, in favor of an abstract enterprise. The Puritans developed this attitude still further. The description of the industrialists of Northern England, in Miriam Beard's "History of the Business Man", gives a clear picture of the transformation of the individual merchant, eager for gain and pleased with his wealth, into the gloomy working machine engrossed only in his task, into the mere executive of his undertaking. There is a direct line from Jacob Fugger's confession that he wanted "to make profits as long as he could" to the statement of the North English Puritan who, in reply to the question, what amount of wealth would satisfy him, said, "a little more", and to John D. Rockefeller's motto: "To succeed is to keep getting ahead all the time." Gradually the person disappears entirely in the abstract collective. The mere motives for gain remain impersonally alive in the collective undertaking, as ghostly methods and procedures. The undertaking per se has taken over those motives and those procedures.

The division of labor in the factory corresponds to the division of capital. In the factory, too, man becomes a function, a mere link in an objective working process. Beyond the pale of the industrial collective in which executives and laborers are joined, the social interests of capital and labor separate. New collectives create many communities of interest, associations of entrepeneurs, unions, cooperative societies and other combinations. Here too, the individual represents only a function of his objective interest-group and this omnipotent collective function affects the psychic and intellectual life of man; it absorbs him and wreaks gradual changes in his personality until he becomes stereotype. The average individual of a modern metropolis is no longer a real person. He is a focus, an intersection point of various collective interests, collective activities, collective inclinations and reactions. His personality consists almost wholly of the specific combination of collective interests that meet within him.

The business shares that are in trade circulation, and the trade in these shares, develop the modern stock exchange. This stock exchange, this market of "shares" and interests hails from the "bursa" (purse), which in the Middle Ages signified a community of individuals living from pooled funds (student houses at the universities), and later indicated gatherings and meeting-houses of merchants, "bourses" in the great European trade centers. The stock exchange increases the abstract and impersonal aspect of the economic process, for it spreads trade and "speculation" among people who no longer have the slightest connection with the enterprises in themselves and still, through their demand and supply, through booms and panics, exert a ghostly influence on the course of economy.

In connection with these developments, the method of calculation and management changes. In the scarcely organized economy of antiquity and the early Middle Ages that knew little of competition or friction, systematic bookkeeping was neither necessary nor existent. Italian Renaissance trade developed bookkeeping and regular accounts ("ragioni", "rationes"), and from that time on, economy steadily proceeded to that state of intricate precision, careful organization and planning of enterprises which is implied in our modern "rationalization".

The working together, working against and working upon one another of all these processes resulted in modern world economy, such as it was up to the outbreak of the great crisis. This economy combined the strictest rationalization with a careless waste of strength and goods. It centered neither in individuals nor in commonwealths. It was determined by hundreds of private collectives, by the private interests of impersonal enterprises and their occasional profit expectations, not by the lasting welfare of human beings and peoples. Thus it could occur that rich harvests of grain, potatoes and coffee were destroyed in the face of starving masses, for the sake of keeping up prices. National economy meant that the powerful interest-groups of a nation influenced the politics of their country. That is why this economy staggered along from crisis to crisis down to the great catastrophe of our times.

I need only to mention the intensive technical, industrial and commercial innovations that the nineteenth and twentieth centuries added to the initial achievements of the industrial revolution and the development of world economy, the application of steam-power and electricity—railway, telegraph, telephone—and, later, automobiles, aviation and the radio, not to speak of the innumerable, less conspicuous, technical inventions that were made with ever-increasing speed during the last one and a half centuries. In fact, since the beginning of this century we have been swept along by a flood of perpetual invention.

To summarize the *results* of this technical and economic progress: First, time and space was contracted by dint of rapid communication, especially aviation and radio. This made for an almost simultaneous interrelation of nations and events. Second, the mechanization, the turn to the rational and the technical, of our work and life. Manual labor was replaced increasingly by machine work. Division of labor and subservience to the machine made man himself into an instrument, into a tool. The "running-belt" is a symbol of that inexorable, mechanically rotating, objective working process that despotically determines the manipulation, tempo and attention of the worker and eventually changes his physical and psychical nature. As I pointed out before, this applies not only to a modern plant but also to the management of business. It applies to the whole economic system, to our entire life. The director of a business and industry, as well as the worker in a factory, depends on the whole working process of a complicated national economy that, in turn, is again dependent on world economy and on international relations. They consequently depend on conditions, events and processes that are no longer within their control. Industry means mass production, and so do our more and more mechanized methods of agriculture. Mass production depends not only on home consumption but on consumption all over the world. Industry often means the need of raw materials that must be imported from foreign countries. Export facilities must be exchanged for import concessions to other countries that are under the same compulsion to sell their goods and that are everywhere beginning to be highly industrialized. Soon there will be no more peoples who are mere objects of economy, no frontiers, no virgin markets where economy may advance by exploitation.

The mass production of standardized goods depends on the masses of industrial and agricultural workers, employees, middle-class people who buy these goods and who must hold jobs and receive decent wages in order to be able to buy them, whose purchasing power and prosperity must accordingly be preserved in order to preserve the prosperity of industry and big capital. For capital can only subsist by growing and expanding, by investment.

This leads us to the third and final result of the progress of world economy: the leveling effect, the inevitable equalization and standardization of individuals and groups. This again implies interdependence. Industrialization means a process of mechanization of life. It converts all our ways of life into mechanized ways by using mechanical devices instead of the living forces of the human body and of the domesticated animal. These new products that exist in profusion, and that are constantly being multipled, are of super-individual scope and force. They have subjected man by accustoming him to their unerring "streamlined" functioning, and have created new standards that all individuals and peoples strive toward. They have made man still more dependent by absorbing him increasingly—every single one of these mechanical devices is calculated to be as efficient as possible, to save time and strength. But there are so many of them, that man is submerged by them. He is so intent upon them, that he turns from human beings and from human interests. Thus, in one sense, they estrange man from man, just as they have estranged man from nature. But in another sense, they unite men by making them all dependent upon the same things. They constitute connecting links between men, they are the links of social life. When we become accustomed to using mechanically produced, standardized goods, when we buy factory-made clothes and dairy products instead of having our clothes made by a tailor or milking our cow, when we use the subway, bus or automobile instead of our horse and buggy, we become more and more dependent on the work and the welfare of millions of people who, by their collective production and mass consumption, enable us to use these standardized goods.

So in this contemporary industrial and technical economy everybody depends on everybody else. That means that everybody depends on the whole, on the whole working process of a unit that actually does not exist. Unlike the single enterprise, world economy up to now, though it calls for cooperation and coordination and though it determines the destiny of every individual, was planned by nobody, organized by nobody, controlled by nobody. World economy was running wild.

Today it is more and more self-evident that the system of unlimited competition, of a natural self-regulation of economy through competition, has invalidated itself by the very expansion of its own system and principle. The hey-day of prosperity through unlimited competition is over, and the discrepancy between the anonymous collectivity of capitalistic world economy and the individualistic mentality of the people who carry this economy, is the paramount origin of the present world anarchy.

THE THREE INTELLECTUAL ATTITUDES
OF MODERN MAN

EVERY PRINCIPLE THAT IS carried out to its fullest implications is bound to reverse itself. From a certain point on, it begins to run counter to its original idea. Indeed, the very idea that brought it into being destroys it; it creates the germs of annihilation. And the more uncompromisingly a system clings to its old idea, the more rapidly it will deteriorate. We observed this phenomenon when we traced the disintegration of Rome and the dissolution of city life in the

Roman Empire through the very application of the system of the polis. We have just noted it, in marking how the unlimited freedom of individual enterprise resulted in an inescapable, anonymous collectivity.

The same thing occurs in the intellectual, cultural and social aspects of the economic development, in the gradual evolution of the bourgeois world and the bourgeois ideology. We shall note how this world and this ideology bred the germs of ideas and social strata destined to undermine and disintegrate its structure.

In dealing with the process of scholastic speculation, we followed the victorious struggle of reason with the authority of the revelation, the Christian dogma and the tradition of the Church Fathers. The outcome of this struggle was the autonomy of reason and science. We further observed the secularization of religion itself through the Reformation. In the course of the modern era, this process of secularization culminated either in the complete dissolution of religion, or—in so far as it still persisted—in its elimination from everyday life. Religion, at best, was relegated to one's leisure, to Sundays and holidays, and had no serious influence on public or private life. During this process, the main features of Christianity, spirit, humanity and history, passed over to a general worldly doctrine, and formed the unquestioned basis of the various philosophical theories and ideologies of the sixteenth, seventeenth and eighteenth centuries.

The human mind had again become aware of the genuine Christian ideas through a new reference to the early Evangelical community, as a result of the mystical, Protestant and Anabaptist movements. These ideas had been uncovered and freed from the many dogmatic incrustations of centuries of theological controversies. But at the same time they became secularized: Christian spirit became human reason, Christian humanity became bourgeois, public morality, English tolerance, French "Égalité et Fraternité", German "Humanitaet". Christian history, finally, the story of man's fall and salvation, became the progress of mankind. And this last idea developed into a powerful secular creed, into the first profane substitute for religion—the creed of progress. Religion, be it genuine, primeval religion or world religion, had been a bond connecting man with his origins, with his source of life in eternity and in the past, it had been a celebration, a sanctification of the past, a belief in the ideal past which was to be recovered. The creed of progress was, for the first time, a belief in the future, a glorification of the future, and an invalidation of the past. Religion had been a tie to a pre-individual, pre-human, superhuman source of life. The creed of progress is a human reference to an ideal mankind, to the tasks and aims of perfect humanity. It is based on the emancipation of profane man, of the human individual, on the self-awareness and self-confidence, indeed overconfidence, of man in his own reason and power, in his power by virtue of his reason.

The *complete invalidation of religion* proceeded in two ways: by the dissolution of religion and implicit transfusion of the Christian ideas into mundane ideologies, and by the elimination of religion from all worldly concerns, from a self-centered world of man and nature. Both of these trends are intrinsically connected with each other in the various intellectual movements, and no distinct line can be drawn between the intellectual groups with regard to these tendencies.

The dissolution of religion begins with the pantheistic tendency inherent in the piety of the German mystics, who taught that Christ may arise in every individual soul and thus may work something more important than the true, personal Jesus Christ had achieved by his life and his passion. This idea means an incorporation of the source of Christianity in the individual soul, an ultimate disembodiment and abstraction of Christ himself and a dispersion of the original Christian motive among so many individuals. It was taken up not so much by the Protestant movement as by the Anabaptists and their successors, the Dutch, Bohemian and German Pietists, who divested personal piety of all specific forms of cultic service and church organization, and conceived it as a blissful sentiment of unification with God in the enthusiastic contemplation of the beauty of his creation.

Another form of this pantheistic trend is evident in the meta-

physical speculation and natural philosophy of Renaissance thinkers. We have encountered it as the structural element that the teachings of Nicolaus Cusanus, Kepler, Galilei and others have in
common. As an example, we may recall the theory of Giordano
Bruno, to whom God was identical with the creative principle and
substance of the universe, with all the diversity of natural beings
and, at the same time, harmony of these contrasting beings. God
is the universe, the macrocosm, and he is also present in the smallest
particle, the monad, which is a microcosm, a miniature universe, a
particular, individual version and likeness of the universe. This
again means an incipient dispersion and dissolution of the deity
into nature.

But it was only after the new relation of man to nature had become clear, after the position of human reason as the master of
nature that could be computed and explored, had been firmly established, it was only after the acknowledgement of the achievements and theories of Galilei and Newton, of Bacon and Descartes,
that the decisive assaults upon religion began. Yet these were not
made by atheists, but by men who considered themselves true
believers, who only wanted to reconcile Christianity with the new
principle of reason, and with nature that follows an inherent mechanical order of its own. These men were Englishmen, proceeding
from groups formed in the course of English religious emancipation and revolution. They were Latitudinarians, the "large-
minded", a liberal wing of the High Church, emphasizing only the
essential and practical in Christianity and favoring tolerance and
agreement with the dissenters—John Locke (1632–1704) and John
Toland (1670–1722) belonged to this group—or they were already
Protestants, mostly Unitarians or Independents.

The teachings of John Toland show how Renaissance pantheism turned into the so-called deism of the enlightenment. Toland advocated "free thinking", which he understood as individual
emancipation from any religious authority and as the forming of
an independent, unbiased opinion by virtue of reason, and in conformity with reason. But on the other hand, he devised for his
community of freethinkers a somewhat fantastic cult of the deity,

which he described in a pamphlet called "Pantheisticon", printed in 1710 and indicating as place of publication, "Cosmopolis". And, indeed, this free service consisted in a sort of enthusiastic natural religion with pantheistic features. The pious mind plunges into the deep contemplation of the solemn harmony and consistency of the universe, and salvation is expected from devotion to the infinite power of elementary nature. Thus the deity is on the point of being dissolved into an objective divinity; God coincides with the harmony, beauty and usefulness of the universe. The role of the priest is assigned to science, which derives its knowledge from human reason and from the revelation of nature. In this rather confused concept, mystical and pantheistic trends converge and pass over into a drift toward modern natural science. Religion, that is, man's relation to the deity, becomes identical with man's relation to nature—a relation of man, fluctuating between reason and enthusiasm, to nature, seen in part as an inspiring divinity, in part as a mute and objective element.

The crucial step from pantheism to deism is concerned with precisely this development of man's relation to nature, or rather with the fundamental change of the character and the meaning of nature. It is the change from the mystical, irrational, emotionally conceived and revered order of nature to an order of nature that is according to human reason, and that must be grasped by the exact methods of modern natural science. In pantheism, nature is divine, nature itself is divinity, nature comprises God, who is identical with the harmony and the inspired and inspiring order of the universe. This concept was the last trace of the idea of a unified cosmos, which had still prevailed in medieval Christianity, when the natural world, degraded though it was, remained a part of God's creation, included in and directed by the will and providence of God. The deity of the deists is merely the creator and very restricted ruler of nature that has become subject to a different, and inherent necessity, the mechanical necessity of the "laws of nature". This mechanical necessity is the true crux of the matter. It is the final obstacle that balks religion. For a mathematical God, a God bound to observe immutable, mechanical laws—such a God is an impossibility. The immutable, mechanical order of nature, this was the nucleus, the starting point from which natural science developed and expanded, and this was the focus of resistance which eventually caused the elimination of God. And, after a complex evolution, this mechanical order of nature took the place of God, succeeded God, in the mind of man.

In scholastic philosophy, human reason had already struggled against the impositions of irrational revelation and irrational dogma. Even in the Middle Ages, the idea of divine omnipotence beat against the necessities of logical conclusion. This matter of logical conclusion, however, was then a mere method, not a fixed, incorporated system; it was applied only in individual issues of dogma, since a consistent field of application was still lacking. Logical conclusion existed merely in its subjective form, as a procedure of the human mind, and not as mechanical processes within a blind, soulless nature. The mechanical order of nature, the "laws of nature", are a projection into matter of the logical system of reason such as to make nature an object of human use. And reason now derived its ultimate confirmation and support from this practical evidence of its logical system. This confirmation and this support did not exist in the Middle Ages. The power of dogma had still been strong enough to counterbalance reason, and this is why the medieval rationalists had to invent the distinction between the necessary and the true, the true being the revelation, and the necessary, the logical conclusion. The result was bound to be the severance of religion from science, the liberation, the autonomy of science, but not its supremacy.

Sweeping advances had followed in the wake of the autonomy of science. The first fundamental inventions had been made, changing the aspect of the earth and the conditions of life. Aside from gunpowder and printing, nothing impressed people more than the invention of the mariner's compass, which has enabled man to circumnavigate the globe and to bring about universal commerce, through which, as Jean Bodin remarks as early as 1566, the world was turned, as it were, into a single state. Two fundamental axioms resulted from this progress and initiated and predestined the evolution of modern man: one is Francis Bacon's axiom that the goal of knowledge is utility, the amelioration of human life and the "service to human comforts" (commodis humanis inservire), the "endowment of human life with new inventions and riches" (dotare vitam humanam novis inventis et copiis). The other is René Descartes' axiom that the laws of nature are invariable and immutable. But in one most important respect Francis Bacon went far beyond Descartes, to whom human reason was still the master of the world and so, of nature. Bacon, who as an Englishman belonged to a more modern age, a more advanced order of thinkers, pronounced the maxim: "We must command nature by obeying it" (Naturae imperare parendo).

This was the status quo when the *English deists* began their endeavors to reconcile Christianity and the existence of a deity with the precepts of reason and the laws of nature. They combine the influence of the new axioms and achievements of science with a progressive Protestantism. As a result of the new explorations and colonizations, a number of foreign religions had become known and had been studied by learned people, Buddhism, Confucianism, the cults and rituals of the Southern populations and the American Indians, apart from the studies of the ancient Greek, Roman, Egyptian, Persian and Babylonian myths and cults, which had been rediscovered by the Renaissance. This new knowledge invited a comparison of the various religions and cults with the Jewish and Christian religions. And this not only suggested the principle of tolerance but undermined the absolute character of all religions, especially of Christianity. On the other hand, the problem of the religious evolution of mankind presented itself, and religion was viewed from the psychological angle for the first time, when all the different dogmas, cults, rituals and institutions were traced back to one commonly human religious impulse. Thus people not only learned from comparison that the various religions had much in common, but all religions appeared merely as different versions of one underlying principle, as different forms that were supposed to have originated in one ideal and general archetype of religion, called natural religion—natural, because it was thought to have evolved from the purest, primeval religious impulse of man. Natural religion was a parallel to natural law and natural economy. All human institutions at that time were derived from a quasi-primeval, ideal abstraction, which was called natural, and at the same time believed to be reasonable, pure and perfect in contrast with the later, "formed" distortions of that model, brought about by human arbitrariness and interest. Here again, nature was by implication the divine, manifesting itself in the purest and most perfect impulse of man. And this natural impulse appeared to be the most reasonable and, at the same time, the most moral and the most practical form of human religiosity. All this fuses: nature is reason, nature is the original and the true, nature is morality, and nature is utility. The whole content of Christianity was reduced and pressed into this scheme. Gradually the revelation, the miracles, the prophecies, the mysteries, original sin and the fall and redemption of man, all irrational and specific features of Christianity, were discarded by a new, devastating, rational criticism of the Scriptures, their sources and their tradition. What remained was a belief in God and in immortality, freedom and virtue; what remained was general, public morality, and it was no longer relevant whether one still called it Christianity, or natural, or reasonable religion. Alexander Pope addresses his "Universal Prayer" to

> "Father of all! In every Age
> In every Clime ador'd
> By saint, by savage, and by Sage
> Jehovah, Jove, or Lord."

This god, who

> "... binding Nature fast in Fate
> Left Conscience free, and will"

is the consummate expression of the modern relation of man to nature, and the laws that He has given are, as a matter of fact, no other than Newton's natural laws. To receive the gifts of nature is the most devout expression of piety.

> "For God is pay'd when man receives,
> T' enjoy is to obey."

In Thomas Paine's "Age of Reason", that clear and complete setting-forth of the deistic point of view, God is represented as the "first cause" of all things, and, as sucl., can be inferred by simple, logical induction. "The only idea man can affix to the name of God is that of a first cause, the cause of all things." This transition of faith into natural science finds a social parallel in the sectarian origin of many of the great natural scientists of the time. Priestley was a Unitarian minister, Dalton a Quaker, Faraday an elder in a community of the Scotch sect of Sandeman.

Thus the English deists had gradually argued away or explained away God and religion. Though they retained both, they had removed them from modern scientific, economic and technical life to a solemn and lofty region where they could serve as philosophical figureheads of that modern life. In the realm of thought, God had assumed the position of an English monarch.

The *French thinkers* were more consistent, more radical, in the face of the challenging social and political position of the church in the "ancien régime". All movements which were gradual, propressive and evolutionary in England grew radical and revolutionary in France, in defiance of the absolute monarchy. Voltaire heaps sarcasm and scorn on the priestly superstitions which, by the so-called "artificial religions", obscured the natural religion of reason and morality. This natural religion, moreover, which is, in the words of Voltaire, "a philosophical system rather than a religion", is not put at the beginnings of mankind, but at the end, as a final goal to be reached by enlightenment. Man will unfold his sublime natural impulse in his rise from half-brutal beginnings in the past, through a slowly ascending evolution. The encyclopedists, and the materialistic, or better, mechanistic thinkers—such as Lamettrie (a physician and disciple of the Dutch physician Boerhave), who died as an exile at the Prussian court of Frederick the Great, or as Holbach, who was a German baron—these thinkers proceeded to integral atheism, and discarded religion and morality altogether. To them, nature was a system of material particles, atoms, held together and moved along by the blind and absolute rule of causality. In Holbach's "Système de la nature", which appeared in 1770 in Amsterdam, we already have a complete outline of the basic scheme of the mechanistic natural science of the nineteenth century: the construction and destruction of the cosmic and terrestrial systems by automatically moving forces, the reduction of all organic processes, of all intellectual and spiritual acts, to inorganic, mechanical foundations, the absolute computability of the world. Descartes already considered animals as automata; Lamettrie applied this principle to the human being, in his treatise "L'homme machine" (Leyden, 1748). He intended to draw the ultimate conclusions from the mechanical premises, the laws of nature. In doing so, he was very modern indeed, since he asserted that matter carries the principle of life and movement in itself, a fact which has become apparent in the development of the theory of electricity and atomic structure—although in a different and less mechanistic sense. Lamettrie also investigated the continuance and independence of vital reactions and processes, in amputated limbs, or the mutilated bodies of animals, in order to prove his mechanistic theory. Mechanical causality, the law of nature, bore off the victory. The invalidation of religion by the deists and mechanists was the last theological controversy to arouse broad public interest and to assume general importance. The struggle of reason and science against religion was over.

As religion waned, the new creed of the future, the *creed of progress,* grew steadily. The belief in God was replaced by the belief in mankind. In Voltaire's theory we can see the connection between the regressive and the progressive tendency, and the shifting from one to the other—natural, genuine religion is considered as an ultimate end, an intellectual climax of human evolution. The creed of progress is the intellectual reflection and expression of a human being who no longer lives according to origins but according to aims and consciously conceived purposes.

When we consider our survey of human evolution up to this point, we are not surprised at the fact that the idea of a progress of mankind did not arise before the seventeenth century. To antiquity, the golden age lay in the past, not in the future. The idea of change was hideous and intolerable to the ancients, who regarded Time as the enemy of humanity. In so far as change was admitted at all, it was recurring change, cyclic change, that was equivalent to the principle of circling eternity.

The idea of true history, true evolution was introduced by the Jewish and Christian missionary and Messianic concept of a single and common destiny of mankind, by the projection of the blessed past, the blessed origin, the golden age of paradise into a blessed recovery at the end of time, in a Kingdom of God to come. In the very center of human history, past and future balance each other. Man lives toward a future, strives after a future which is, however, only a restored past. Human existence still appears as eternity unfurled in a unique sequence. In the Renaissance, people looked back, and that means looked up, to the ancients, who were the models, the wiser, the more perfect of the human species. And it was very hard to overcome this attitude of emulation, of discipleship, of dependence on tradition as a whole and on the traditions of the ancients in particular, who had, in fact, by their example educated the new generation and emancipated them from the authority of the Christian dogma.

The detachment of man from the authority of the past was finally accomplished by the new economic, scientific and technical achievements: by the discoveries, the counterweight of new continents, new natural and cultural worlds, and hitherto unknown tasks, by the new scientific attainments, especially the technical inventions that had no precedent in antiquity, and were the only achievements —aside from the discoveries—to show the superiority of modern man over the ancient. All the thinkers who gradually developed the creed of progress dwelt with special emphasis upon these technical innovations. If modern man was able to broaden the range of his world and the outlook for his prosperity to such a degree, if he was able to dominate and exploit nature for the amelioration of human life and the advancement of happiness of mankind, as Bacon put it, then it seemed clear that man was on the upward path. Bacon's formulation of the real goal of the sciences as "the endowment of human life with new inventions and riches" hit the mark, and a wave of infinite confidence, pride and optimism concerning the future of mankind swept the people. The foundation of the English Royal Society in 1660 and of the Académie des Sciences in 1666 brought the physical sciences into the focus of public attention. Macaulay tells how "dreams of perfect forms of government made way for dreams of wings with which men were to fly from the Tower to the Abbey, and of double keeled ships which were never to founder in the fiercest storm. All classes were hurried along by the prevailing sentiment. Cavalier and Roundhead, Churchman and Puritan were for once allied. Divines, jurists, statesmen, nobles, princes, swelled the triumph of the Baconian philosophy."

In France, it was a characteristically different feeling that strengthened the sense of superiority of modern man. In the reign of Louis XIV, as J. B. Bury writes, men were filled with the conviction that it was a great age, as great as the age of Augustus, and few would have wished to live in any other epoch. Corneille, Racine and Molière satisfied literary taste so utterly that they could not but be considered of first rank. Molière expressed a general feeling when he said: "The ancients are the ancients, but we are the people of today."

The new creed continued to grow in strength, and especially after the industrial revolution and the rise and spread of the new bourgeois classes that owed their successes to the wave of new inventions, it expanded its sway over the European and American world of the nineteenth century. The natural sciences followed the lines prescribed by Bacon, and saw their ultimate goal and their true mission in providing industry with new tools and methods to mechanize, to accelerate manufacturing. They wanted to provide mankind with more and ever more new instruments and comforts of life. And these comforts formed and are still forming the popular concept of human happiness. Impartially and indifferently the sciences, on the one hand, assisted in bettering man's life and mitigating his sufferings and, on the other, in suppressing, in torturing and killing human beings. On the whole, the unrestricted efforts to augment comforts per se, without taking into account their final effects upon human beings, produced such a welter of conveniences and devices that man was buried under it, that man became subject and subservient to it. We are coming to realize that "the endowment of human life with unmeasurable inventions and riches" has been very costly. How much increased strain and suffering, how many inner losses have kept pace with increased comforts! And, due to that dizzy, heedless pursuit of the line of technical progress, the proposed progress of mankind has turned into a most dangerous progress of instruments and materials.

The above survey already suggests the two fundamental attitudes of man toward nature which characterize the intelligentsia of this period: *rationalism and materialism*. The transition from a progress of mankind to a progress of material is expressed, or reflected, in man's passing from rationalism in the sixteenth and seventeenth centuries to materialism in the eighteenth and nineteenth centuries.

In the first part of the modern era, man was extremely proud of his newly discovered rational power, by an adequate use of which he believed he could bring forth almost everything. The representative philosophical system of rationalism, the system of Descartes, is an exact analogy to the economic administration of Colbert and to the absolute rule of Louis XIV. Its basic thesis is the famous sentence: "Cogito, ergo sum"—I think, therefore I am. This means that man's existence is derived from his reasoning, is based on his reason. Nobody, not even God, can bring about that I, who am thinking, do not exist. So reason is the basic certitude. The world consists of two essentially different substances, reason and body. The physical world, organic and inorganic, moves according to mechanical causality. Reason, guided by free will, proceeds by logical, indeed mathematical conclusions. All possible error originates in a wrong, inadequate use of man's will. All error is self-deception. That means that human will, working through human reason, is practically sovereign. Man perceives the physical world not through his senses but solely through reason. But, since reason is sovereign, and cannot be affected by matter, so, in perceiving and understanding matter, reason must, in reality, dominate, indeed create matter, or better, the mechanical order of matter. So the theory of Descartes proves that mechanical causality is the materialization of logical thinking. In the concept of mechanical causality, reason projects its finality, its procedure of the domination and exploitation of nature into matter. The clearest manifestation of this utilitarian procedure of reason is the tool, the machine ("mechane") that serves the domination and exploitation of matter. Reason interprets the laws of nature in the way that most corresponds to mechanical treatment, that is, the form of mechanical causality. This train of ideas is diametrically opposed to the essentially religious world picture that was valid up to the end of the Middle Ages and that based all being upon existence and not upon proceeding and purpose. That world picture sees the world as a quiescent, harmonious system corresponding to the closed, organic form of the human body and of the living creature, in general.

Lamettrie, the first true mechanist or materialist, referred directly to Descartes, and started his theory from the Cartesian system. He proposed to carry the axiom of mechanical causality to its utmost implications by including man's soul, man's reason itself, in the system. This, however, implied a reversal of the relation between reason and nature, as reason now became dependent upon the body, and psychological processes were derived from physiological causes. Thus man became subject to nature. With this, Lamettrie blazed the trail that learning took throughout the nineteenth century—not only the natural sciences, where organic processes were derived from inorganic ones, but also the disciplines concerned with human life: psychology, philology, sociology, all of which were seeking their respective "laws of nature". The mechanical causality, the invariability of the laws of nature, this supposedly unshakable foundation for natural science, was the envied and generally aimed-for standard of all sciences. In fact, scientific was identical with mechanistic. Political economy up to our time, under the lasting influence of the founding English systems, had been searching for "laws of nature" effective in the circulation of goods and money, the fluctuation in prices, the business cycle. All spiritual, moral, psychic factors were deliberately eliminated.

The newly discovered principle of progress and evolution and the principle of mechanical causality proceeded to influence each other. The invalidation of religion resulted in the attempt to find a natural cause for every phenomenon. Prior to this, the whole world had been founded on God, had been traced back to God. Then Nature replaced God and represented the stable and ideal base of all existence, a base that human civilization had only concealed and darkened. When the idea of progress shifted the ideal status from the beginning of the world into the future, it cleared the way for an unprejudiced, empirical consideration of the actual past. And now the realistic search for cause, and the principle of mechanical causality, could each make the other fruitful, could fuse. An exchange occurs between the natural sciences and historical investigation; the former becomes dynamic, the latter mechanized.

So in the field of natural science, natural history arose. The progress of biology to the theory of evolution, from Buffon over Geoffroy St. Hilaire and Cuvier to Lamarck and Darwin, and the development of paleontology and geology connected with it, show how the attitude toward nature gradually changed to the historical and evolutionary point of view. Even the stable laws of nature themselves became dynamic and grew into evolutionary laws. In this process, there were strange interactions; from Malthus, the sociologist, the scientist, Darwin, takes over the "natural law" of the pressure of population on food supply, and its corollary, the struggle for existence. From this, Darwin evolves his law of natural selection by the survival of the fittest, as Spencer formulates it. Spencer himself, the leading sociologist of the nineteenth century, regards the law of progress as a manifestation of a universal law of nature, that is similarly effective in physical and biological development, in the formation of the solar systems, of vegetation and animal forms, and that consists in the development of the simple into the compound.

While natural laws, then, were becoming historical, history was becoming mechanized. Historiography felt rather ashamed of being valued as a second-rate discipline, a not quite serious, not quite scientific discipline, somehow related to romance and story telling—since it was not easy to explain historical developments by mere mechanical causality. At any rate, historians also paid their tribute to mechanical causality by splitting the live stream of historical processes into innumerable petty causes and tracing every cause to another cause, into an infinite past, which meant the disintegration and explaining-away of history. This brought about explanation by origins, and origins of origins, a method that is known as Historicism. And everywhere in the humanities the search for a mechanical causality had the same leveling and disintegrating effect. It prevented a distinction between the essential and the non-essential, by rating all phenomena alike and distrusting and excluding any criterion but that of material evidence. Any judging of material was considered speculative, and what a scholar of the present generation has called "the total suspicion of ideology" began to prevail, that is to say, every author and every scientific group was suspected of ideological prejudices. The materialistic attitude is not limited to the explicitly materialistic theories. It began long before Marxism and, from the nineteenth century on, has dominated all learning and the intellectual outlook of all classes of the population.

Another event in the intellectual field contributed to this development: Immanuel Kant's *Critique of Pure Reason,* that, in the final analysis, discredited and dethroned philosophy. In his critique of reason, Kant intended to purge rational cognition of all dogmatic elements, of all the elements of faith that had unnoticeably conditioned and determined this knowledge. The deists and the rational philosophic systems excluded God, in various ways, from a world that could be grasped by reason. They had deprived Him of any real influence in the world. But nominally they had allowed

Him to persist by identifying Him with Nature, or with a rational principle, or the "first cause", and they even proved His existence inductively, as a logical necessity. But now—also initiated by Descartes—a new philosophic movement set in that was no longer concerned with the objective world itself to be grasped by the exercise of the rational faculty, but with the rational perception as such, with the cognitive faculty of man. We saw that Descartes took as his point of departure that thinking is the foundation and the irrefutable proof of our existence. "I think, therefore I am." Thus, for him, the world flows out of thinking, and along the line of thinking. The objective world, formed by reason, and its rational conception, yes, even shaping, through human thought, are identical to him. And even God is only an "innate idea" of man that necessarily results from the ability to think; ". . . a sola facultate cogitandi necessitate quadam naturae ipsius mentis manat." Since, then, according to rationalism, the world proceeds from thinking, it was inevitable that there should be a philosophical trend that directed attention to the formal thinking process per se, as the source of knowledge and of knowing the world. The problem of Socrates and Plato in antiquity, and of medieval scholasticism, comes up again. Again the question as to the principle and the constitution of the world leads to the question of the cognitive faculty of man and the right method of knowing. But the world of Socrates and Plato as well as that of scholasticism had still been determined by religion; God still had had an absolute and unshakable existence, and as He was present in His creation, the world prevailed over man. Hence the grasping of the world was, by implication, an approach to God, an attempt to grasp Him. This prevented a thorough epistemology. In the mean time, however, nature had become secularized, and rational man, autonomous. Man was no longer an idea, an image of God, but God was an innate idea of man. When man now examined his thinking processes, he did so without reference to God. He no longer tried to fathom the divine within himself, he examined his own nature, and he examined it for purposes of self-control and self-exploitation. In this way the investigations of human processes of thinking and knowing were, in reality, psy-

chological investigations. The theory of knowledge of the Englishmen, Locke, Berkeley and Hume, is essentially empirical psychology; it examines empirical man in his activity of perception,
connection and association of impressions and ideas. Kant's investigations went beyond the boundaries of empirical, psychological
man into a "transcendental sphere", but only to establish these
boundaries as boundaries and to demonstrate that, beyond the pale
of human thought, that which cannot be logically proved—and for
him this meant that which cannot be known—has its beginnings.
He no longer measured human knowledge by the psychological
process of knowing, by the activity of the knower, but by the nature
of the contents, in which he separated the "a priori" given conditions, the "categories" of pure reason, from the phenomena to be
perceived, and shifted these categories to a region lying beyond the
knowable. Space, time and causality are the basic forms of human
perception and, at the same time, its a priori conditions, that it can
by no means escape. So these conditions are actually the boundaries of knowledge, for man can perceive the outside world only
in the form they imply. He can never gain a pure cognition of the
outside world as it really is. He cannot learn to know the "thing
in itself". The world man thinks he perceives is actually a version
determined by the order and structure of his reason. Thus man is
forever bound within the confines of his reason. An unbridgeable
abyss separates him from the objective world. Moral values, and
even God, are only postulates, "ideals" of his practical reason that
have no objective validity. This was the last act of a development
that had begun in the Renaissance, yes, even in scholasticism. It was
the complete separation of rational man from material nature.

Through this radical criticism, Kant expanded the term "dogmatic" beyond its merely religious meaning. In his language, dogmatic is the opposite of what is rational, of what can be logically
proved. But, according to the prevailing views of the time, rational
knowledge was synonymous with knowledge as a whole. And so
every form of intuitive or super-rational knowledge, every religious
assumption of an intrinsic connection between man and the world,
of organic unity and harmony of the world, was branded as naive

and dogmatic. This obviated, once and for all, philosophy's claim to an understanding of the objective world, to the creation of a coherent cosmic picture. Natural science was not impeded by Kant's critique; it went its own way. But philosophy and its claims to the guidance and coordination of all knowledge was definitely outlawed. The systems that came after Kant showed a reversion under the influence of Romanticism. But later, philosophy gradually deteriorated to mere methodology, to a futile search for escape from the cage of the transcendental categories, to a Kantian scholasticism. Discouraged from treating the substantial world, fixed in the magic circle drawn by Kant, it lost all interest in the problems of human life and renounced every form of intellectual guidance of the times. And with the collapse of philosophy's sovereign position, all intellectual guidance for man was lost. The sciences were free to pursue their special materialistic aims, and these led to continued division and subdivision, to disintegration and anarchy. Thus, paradoxically, the most rational, "idealistic" philosophy of Kant actually aided and abetted its diametric opposite, radical materialism, just as, in another age, Luther's religious reforms furthered the secularization of the world.

The materialistic or positivistic trend prevailed throughout the nineteenth century. It imbued the sciences with factual reality, and we owe it much knowledge. On the other hand, its rejection of any spiritually selective principle, its leveling and disintegrating activity, brought about an immense overcrowding of the disciplines with unorganized material, so that in the intellectual field, just as in the practical field, the material, the instrumental world of research overpowered reason and man and became his master. Today even the specialist can scarcely master his field; he is rather mastered by it. It is his field that dictates collective questions and a collective method of working. As a result of overcrowding, there is continued specialization to narrower and narrower fields that can no longer maintain connections with neighboring fields, let alone with the whole completely unorganized mass of human knowledge. Scholars and scientists of every subdivision have evolved a special terminology of their own that nobody else understands. Modern learning has become a Tower of Babel.

To summarize the whole development: Reason, in proceeding to exploit nature, had projected itself into nature, and the result was the concept of mechanical causality. This concept of mechanical causality was extended and applied to the immensity of organic, psychic and intellectual nature and brought forth an additional world of instruments and materialized comforts, that is to say, our whole modern machinery of life. Scientific terms are nothing but instruments of research. Mechanical causality retroactively subjected and enslaved reason and man, so that they became subject to their own creations. In the intellectual and cultural field, this is the parallel to the anarchical condition of world economy, and it is another cause of the present anarchy of our world.

Rationalism, by the very expansion and consequent application of its principle, brought about its inversion: materialism. And materialism, though intrinsically connected with rationalism, indeed, a correlate of rationalism, inaugurated the great *counter-movement against rationalism,* the elementary revolt against reason in which we are involved today. The materialistic advance was only the first front of this counter-movement; it was carried and represented most conspicuously by the socialist doctrine. The next move took its issue from an entirely different attitude, from the third modern attitude of man to nature: romanticism.

The *socialist movement* is a social, an economic and an ideological movement, all in one. Like the materialistic ideology on which it rests, it is an offspring of rationalism. The first socialists at the end of the eighteenth and the beginning of the nineteenth century, Hall, Babeuf, Fourier, Owen, have rightly been called rational socialists. Their thoughts are rooted in the same common ground that produced those of the deists, the free trade economists, the political thinkers of the epoch. Natural religion, natural economy, natural democracy, which were all supposed to have prevailed under the idyllic conditions of primeval mankind, found a counterpart in a natural society where man was pure and good and shared everything with his fellow men. Men were considered equal by nature and equal at the beginning, and only arbitrary deviations from their natural condition supposedly created those historical circumstances which are the origins of all differences among human beings. The circumstances, the surroundings, the specific conditions into which men are born are the sole causes of all inequality and diversity of character and talents, and, by implication, they are the sources of all evil. This point, on which special emphasis is laid, is the nucleus of the later socialist theory of Karl Marx. A disciple of Fourier puts it this way: "Believe that God is good, that man is good, but the social constitution is vicious, and that we must improve society and not man's nature." Ignorance of the unalterable principles of social happiness has brought all misery, and it is reason alone that can correct this failure.

Like their fellow rationalists, these rational socialists were gradually gaining a more solid and substantial historical knowledge, and dropped their imaginary concept of primeval perfection. Robert Owen already asserts "that the past ages of the world present the history of human irrationality only, and that we are but now advancing toward the dawn of reason, and to the period when the mind of man shall be born again." Marx himself was a disciple of Hegel, who is the arch-rationalist of German philosophy. Hegel's "Weltgeist" is nothing but objectivated reason, universal reason which is made the ultimate goal of world evolution. The relation of Marx to Hegel is somewhat analogous to Lamettrie's relation to Descartes. The system of Karl Marx bears many traces of that specifically German rationalism. The particular detail, however, that social circumstances are the sole causes of all human inequalities and miseries, started the socialist reversal of rationalism into materialism. The rational socialists believed that these circumstances were brought about by human arbitrariness. But, in the mean time, the idea of progress and evolution had conquered the world in the theories of Condorcet and St. Simon in France, and in the idealistic philosophy of history in Germany. The almost mechanical causality of economic "laws of nature", as advanced by the

English economic systems, added up to the evolutionary scheme. And from the fusion of these elements Karl Marx evolved his materialistic interpretation of history, according to which social and economic conditions, brought about by economic and almost mechanical causality, create their respective ideologies. Ideas, thoughts, human reasoning—be it ever so logical—are merely a "superstructure", a reflection of economic conditions. This thesis, supported by a broad social movement, implied the first powerful attack on the validity and trustworthiness of human reason. Of course, all the premises and goals of rational enlightenment, all the secularized principles of Christianity, are still alive and upheld in the socialist theory, upheld in fact, more vigorously and consistently than in the doctrine of Manchester liberalism.

In our time, psychoanalysis played a similar role, since it proved, with the rational methods of the natural sciences, the power of the irrational in all psychic and intellectual manifestations, and so, on its part, contributed to the discrediting of reason.

The most dangerous and radical assault against the position of reason, however, emanated from romanticism. *Romanticism* is a very complex attitude, originating from various motives and impulses, but aiming at one end: to merge with unfathomed, chaotic nature, to seek nature, not by reasonably complying with material, mechanical causality, but by plunging enthusiastically into an anarchical element. Romanticism is profane mysticism; it is a mystical union with nature itself instead of with deity. And even when God is invoked, this God is merely a substitute for nature. For romanticism is a late, eclectic movement, created by intellectuals who want to escape the strain of civilization, to seek shelter and to be rejuvenated in the chaos of nature and sentiment.

All romanticism is born of protest against civilization, rationalism, bourgeois life, technology and economy, against everything practical and orderly as such. In fact, it arose as a foil for modern technical and economic civilization. It arose from the "romance", from the Spanish, French, German Renaissance novels, glorifying the chivalry of those belated knights who had been outstripped by the civilization of the rising cities. Later, it was advanced and promoted by Jean-Jacques Rousseau's regression from the refined corruption of modern society to the golden age of primeval man, and from reason to boundless, raving sentiment. It flared in the period of exoticism and excursions into wonderlands that mock the conventions of civilized society, in the travels of Gulliver and in Robinson Crusoe's idyllic life in solitude and with complete lack of technical equipment. It flared in the romances of French writers like Bernardin de St. Pierre and Châteaubriand, who staged their tales against a background of the African or American wilderness and good-natured savages. The mythical past was tracked and conjured, and the Middle Ages were glorified by Macpherson and the German Romanticists. The past per se appeared desirable, the past in which adventures, heroic deeds and sentiments created a vivid life in contrast to the increasing drabness, normality and regimentation of the bourgeois present. Walter Scott, Alexandre Dumas, Victor Hugo, Alessandro Manzoni and the German Romanticists introduced the explicitly historical novel, and all this again contributed to the growth of general historicism. Christianity, in the form of colorful, mystical Catholicism, afforded another romantic escape from the mechanized regularity of the laws of nature and the pedantic order of rational morality. Catholicism meant to romantic intellectuals a kind of spiritual exoticism, of wilful anachronism. And above all, feeling, passionate feeling itself was savored greedily wherever it could be aroused.

In the Western and Southern countries, romanticism kept within the bounds of human destiny and of human emotions. But Germany, which had no real society, no inherent standard of life, no supporting tradition, was the true home of the romantic movement. Here, Renaissance paintings and the novels of the Baroque had already produced a chaotic mixture of reality and imagination. Nature passed over directly into the supernatural, into allegory, demonology and cosmic speculation. Phantasy flew abroad untrammelled in reinless dreams. Witches, devils, elfin lakes, pilgrimages and adventures in the tropics that surpass those of Robinson Crusoe —all this whirls topsy-turvy through the robbers' and soldiers' life of the Thirty Years' War, in the story of the "Adventurous Simplicissimus" of Grimmelshausen, the only true poet of the seventeenth century in Germany. In the early nineteenth century, the German Romantic School developed these characteristics to extremes. Here, romanticism became a principle, an intellectual program, a revolt, not only against reason, but against all restrictions of form. The unmethodical method of these poets begot the free flood of ideas, thoughts, feelings, the endless play of connections and of sentimental transcendence into a super-sensual realm. The late-romanticist, E. T. A. Hoffmann, is the best-known representative of this school.

All these romantic ways are, obviously, ways out of, or ways beyond, actual, present life; they lead into the past or into religion or into the depth and breadth of crude, savage nature and unbridled thoughts and passions. All these escapes featured in modern life as opposition to and criticism of the bonds of reason, the flaws of democracy, the economic and technical implications of the bourgeois world.

There was one focal point from which this romantic protest began to widen into a force of fundamental significance. This was the *worship of the hero,* the great man who embodied the elementary power of genius. From the revaluation of the genius, indeed the first explicit evaluation of the genius as such, from the juxtaposition of the lonely genius to the mass standard of modern life, the new front against the rational order expanded far beyond its original romantic range.

The value of the artist and the thinker had been questioned by the collective orders of democracy, technology and science. As a result of these predominant collective orders which imposed their objective standards, the true artist, and the independent thinker had become fatally remote from ordinary people. They were in the vanguard, and the distance between them and the average, went on widening. They gradually assumed the role of profane prophets, of an utterly unwelcome conscience of their epoch. But what was worse, they separated completely from the sphere of contemporary interests and their language was no longer understood. People in modern jobs who were absorbed by their material aims, by the daily struggle for existence, had neither the time nor the energy to try to grasp the import of the questions posed by artists and thinkers. These questions were human questions directed to the individual soul. But the great mass of people were engrossed in factual, economic and technical problems. The words of artists and thinkers seemed to have nothing to do with every-day life. And those who uttered them appeared as eccentrics, as impractical fools or idle dreamers, good enough to wile away leisure hours and holidays with divers-colored images, to glorify eroticism, or to set up ideals of freedom, of progress and of the common weal, that add lustre to the phrases of after-dinner speeches. Only in so far as they satisfied needs of this kind, were they valued and even honored. Thus the bourgeois public itself challenged romanticism and forced the artists and thinkers into a hostile position toward the world of facts. The slighter and weaker talents satisfied the expectations of the public and were willing to produce romantic glamor. But those who were serious and had a sense of responsibility did not avoid reality, but penetrated through its surface, its conventions and its illusions, to deeper levels. They continued to deal with those fundamental problems of life that had been dropped by mechanized learning, by a church grown weary and by discouraged academic philosophizing. They continued in their search for the meaning of life and became the true pastors of humanity. They were the only ones to cherish the human being, the human community, the world picture as a whole, and thus they took over the function of religion. For the art principle, the principle of harmony, of concentric form, of inner coherence, is actually synonymous with the religious principle, and as such, is in sharp contrast with that of centrifugal natural science. The idea of harmony, of the conformity of a whole in itself and with its parts, grew out of the conception of a divine cosmos. It is, however, not confined to the specific harmony of classical beauty; there is harmony of many different kinds, of growing complexity and scope. So, in modern society, art became the legitimate heir of religion. But even in this modern, secular form, the religious principle was in profound opposition to bourgeois tendencies.

The fundamental estrangement between the broad masses of the people and the artists and thinkers who never lose sight of the large connections, and who are themselves in direct connection with the sources of life, is a modern phenomenon which gave rise to the modern conception of genius, of the unique personality. Genius presupposes isolation and lack of adjustment to environment. This complete estrangement developed along two lines: the social line, that is to say, the change that the position of the great man underwent in society, and another, purely artistic line, that is, the growing complexity and transcendence of his vision.

The hero of antiquity, the sacred or traditional legitimate king, represented his tribe or his nation. He was nothing but the perfect pattern of those virtues and values that were accepted by the people as a whole. Here there were only varying degrees of perfection. To be sure, even in early times the rebellious titan, the tyrant and the revolutionary prophet were in opposition to the hero, the king and the priest. They were the progressive spirits avid for new things, who took the step beyond the usual, and thus opposed tradition. But still they belonged to the same world as the rest of the people. They were condemned, stoned and crucified, but they still spoke a language that people understood. Only what they expressed was new, not how they expressed it. Even the philosophers of antiquity and the Christian martyrs were supported by groups, by sects.

The premise of the modern situation is the complete emancipation of individuality. The modern genius represents a hypertrophy of the individual, the exaggeration of individuality to uniqueness. He is, to be sure, a genius only so far as he expresses things of basic concern to all men, and as he claims to shape his environment. Hence his characteristic tension toward society develops. The first traces of this tense relation are noticeable after the perfection of the individual in the Renaissance. We find them in Shakespeare's fool, this secret reflection of the poet himself, which already shows that social eccentricity, that specific position on the brink of society, that stamps the modern artist. With one foot the fool stands within the pale; the other is outside. Are not even the legs of his long hose of different colors? Is he not motley in general? He is the most trusted confidant of the king, and, at the same time, a Pariah. He is questioned as though he were a Delphic oracle and beaten like a dog. He is feared and mocked. From his inner exile, from his fool's loneliness, he draws his fool's freedom and fool's wisdom—the wisdom of the artist and the prophet. And from his fool's lips issues the sad, sovereign voice of Shakespeare, the voice of the artist and actor who lives and creates on the brink of English society. (Today Shakespeare's fool with all his burlesque wisdom is revived in the attitude of George Bernard Shaw, that enfant terrible of British bourgeoisie.)

The next symptom is the "dandy" in his serious aspect, the eccentric individual, the purely aesthetic individual, who braves all conventions, all gradations of rank and all moral laws, with his principle of presenting a perfect appearance. The connection with the fool is apparent in the relation of Prince Hal to Falstaff. Later the dandy himself becomes the court fool of bourgeois society. He who originally was only an elegant foolish fellow ("dandin") comes to personify a challenge to the bourgeoisie, through his vain, exaggerated "beauty", an a-moral, an anti-moral beauty, and through the paradox of his daring mode of life. In the development from Brummell to Oscar Wilde, Barbey d'Aurevilly, Baudelaire, one can see how the attitude of the dandy becomes sublimated to l'art pour l'art, to a radical protest of the utterly individualistic principle of form against the conventional normalcy of collective ways of life. This tide of ideas united with another movement that, at the end of the eighteenth century, proceeded from Germany, where there was no organized society but only secularized, conventionalized, Christian morality. The rigid barriers of this morality were shaken by dreamy and enthusiastic temperaments that had learned to revere nature from Rousseau, the pietists and Macpherson, and wanted to express and confess their natural feelings. From this general atmosphere produced by the "Sturm and Drang" sprang the passionate "Weltschmerz" of Werther, of the lonely, unbridled genius who defends his rights against society. In "Tasso" and in

"Faust", Goethe has presented Werther's conflict on a higher level. The union of the "Weltschmerz" of the genius with the social "ennui" of the dandy is apparent in Lord Byron. And in Stendhal we find the reflection of this conflict in society; his novels combine the romantic enchantment yielded by the spectacle of the political genius of Napoleon, who evoked admiration even in his German foes, with the keen and clear awareness of the untenability of the heroic in modern bourgeois life. "Le Rouge et le Noir" is actually a farewell to the heroic point of view. Julien Sorel is the modern Don Quixote, whose anachronistic attempts at great deeds are necessarily abortive in the shabby hunt for money and jobs. More recently, Thomas Mann has expressed the social eccentricity of the artist, his conflict with the burgher, in "Tonio Kroeger", and, in a more sublimated form, in "Death in Venice".

A dual attitude on the part of intellectuals developed from the antagonism of genius to the bourgeois world—on the one hand, retreat from environment, flight to the ivory tower of aesthetics, a cult of beauty for beauty's sake, of art for art; and, on the other hand, a bitter criticism of current values and ideals. The intellectuals attacked the materializing and rationalizing of life, the rule of mediocrity that had developed along with the influence of the masses in public affairs. They saw life becoming colorless, harried and superficial, a panorama of machines, money-making, police regulations and party quarrels. They gave due warning that the inner life of the individual no longer had time or space to unfold in, that great deeds, thoughts and feelings had lost the right to exist. It was the effect of democracy and economic development, it was the predominance of practical reason and the overrating of reason as a whole, against which they turned. For the first time, a new pessimism as to the future of the human race was allied to their criticism. They began to doubt that humanity was on an upward path. So the issue of progress, the crisis of the idea of progress, was fermenting everywhere in the late nineteenth century. And with this critical issue, the present moral and ideological crisis gradually approached.

Goethe had already spoken ironically of a future age when "every one" would be "a sicknurse to everyone else." The German poet Friedrich Hoelderlin, one of the most moving characters of human history, unrecognized and forgotten during his lifetime and ending his days as a mad prophet, a lodger with a petty craftsman in a small German city, spoke of his nation in this way: "Barbarians from time immemorial, grown more barbarous through industry, science and even religion, profoundly incapable of any divine emotions, spoiled to the marrow for the gifts of the holy graces . . . dull and devoid of harmony like the shards of a cast-away vessel—these were my comforters. You see craftsmen, but no men, thinkers, but no men, priests, but no men, masters and servants, boys and adults, but no men—does this not resemble a field of battle where hands and arms and all the limbs are strewn about in fragments, while the shed blood of life soaks into the sand? . . . It is heart-rending too when one regards your poets, your artists and all who still value genius, who love and cultivate beauty! O Pitiful Ones! They live in the world as strangers in their own house. They are exactly like the sufferer Odysseus when he sat at his door in the guise of a beggar while the insolent suitors noised in the hall and asked: 'who has brought this vagabond to us?'" In England, Carlyle, who was a romanticist, hero-worshipper and socialist in one, wrote in 1850: "The chief end of man being now, in these improved epochs, to make money and spend it, his interests in the Universe have become amazingly simplified of late . . . If the Universe will not carry on its divine bosom any commonwealth of mortals who have no higher aim . . . if the unfathomable Universe has decided to reject Human Beavers pretending to be Men, and will abolish, pretty rapidly perhaps, in hideous mud-deluges their markets and them, unless they think of it? In that case it were better to think of it: and the Democracies and Universal Suffrages, I can observe, will require to modify themselves a good deal!" In France, Flaubert, no romanticist, but a realist, writes at about the same time: "Against the stupidity of my time, I feel floods of hatred that suffocate me . . . I wager, that within no more than fifty years the words . . . moralization of the masses, progress and democracy will have become a sickening refrain and will sound grotesque."

At the end of the nineteenth century, Friedrich Nietzsche proclaimed the coming transvaluation of values, the inevitable collapse of civilization. Very few people knew of him during his lifetime. Through his unparalleled loneliness and madness, he, as Hoelderlin, symbolized the terrible estrangement of genius from environment and the tragedy of being a generation ahead of his time. He stood at the mouth of that great current that leads from the "Weltschmerz" of the eighteenth century to the nihilism of our own day.

And again it was romantic motives that gradually led to the appreciation and glorification of genius: adoration for the extraordinary, for the miracle of man that crashed into every-day life, for the being from another world, who, just because he was of another world, spoke another, scarcely comprehensible, language. Through honest and dishonest, merely snobbish admirers from the bourgeoisie, through groups of an intellectual élite, who flattered themselves that they were among the initiate, the way was paved for the reception of genius that later turned into a veritable cult. When, after the world war, the bourgeoisie, harried by the growing social movement, took refuge in radical individualism, it seized upon this cult of genius and all of the catchwords that the intellectuals of the nineteenth century had used against these very burghers, and used them as weapons to fend off socialism. The result was the frame of mind that brought about fascism.

TRANSCENDENCE OF ART

THE PROFOUND ESTRANGEMENT between the artist and society does not only express itself in the social position of the artist but also in the character of his vision and in his form of expression, that become more and more removed from the world, the concepts and the language of his public. This part of the process must be considered more extensively, since it is complicated, and of particular importance in that it demonstrates the main tendency of modern human development with exemplary clearness.

For such a survey it is necessary to keep in mind the historical and essential foundations of art. It may be recalled that in the first period of human history, religion combined and dominated all the fields of life. Religion, science and art were inseparably united; the magical, the ethical and the aesthetic were one. The world was conceived as a pantheon or a divine cosmos, a harmonious, organic structure, a primary and coherent whole. And from the idea of the cosmos, the art principle of a closed system, of inner coherence, of harmony, is derived. According to the idea of the cosmos, harmony reigns within and among the individual spheres of the universe: the entire world, the macrocosm, is just as much an organic whole as the microcosm, that is, as man, as the atom. And the congruence of all individual structures constitutes the coherence of the whole.

Up to the time of the Renaissance, man saw, thought and lived by this principle which is simultaneously religious and artistic. Thus knowledge had not as yet separated into fundamentally different forms of expression. The Bible, Homer, Hesiod are theology, poetry, natural history and history, all in one. The art forms of the lyric, the epic and the tragedy are all combined in the early epics, in the drama of antiquity—one grows from the other. Greek philosophy unites the knowledge of the divine, of nature and of man in one artistic, poetic mode of expression. Painting and sculpture testify to their more deep and vivid grasp of the human form in the representation of gods and saints. The most significant factor in this is that the essential and the real still coincide, that is to say, what is represented is real or believed to be real. What is of main concern to man is shown life-size. There is not as yet any need for condensation, for symbolic representation, for fiction.

Among the Greeks, however, there is already some evidence of division. They developed profane history, mathematics and science. Medicine was studied as such, and this means that salvation, the salvation of the soul, became separate from physical welfare and the healing of the body. (The Oriental prophets, Zarathustra and Jesus, still healed the soul and the body in one.) At that time, to be sure, there was one basic principle that held together and that dominated all forms. And only the complete secularization of the world since the Renaissance brought about the radical separation of man from nature, and so, of the organic from the inorganic principle, of the intrinsic, plastic, closed coherence, whose archetype is the living organism, from an extensive, measurable, unclosed coherence, that reflects the rational, purposeful exploitation of nature by man. With this, the separation between art and science is given, and it becomes clear why science is mainly natural science even where it involves the humanities. Through the secularization of the world, a purely physical, material, surface form of nature developed, which was deprived of divinity, of its intensive, religious connections and offered an ever-growing, an ever more populous field for man's exploitation. In his effort to grasp this vast reality in its full size and extent, man had to avail himself of measurement and calculation. If he wished to utilize this reality for his goals, he was forced to derive the laws governing phenomena, by way of logical abstraction, laws that would permit him to deduce the same results from the same premises and so, gradually, to create the premises that would yield the desired results. This led to the development of science, which, in accordance with the infiniteness of material nature, cannot be stable, but can only be fragmentary and progressive. Science is not something that is once and for all times; it is always in flux, investigation that is constantly moving on. The material vastness of nature, the demand for generally accessible, exact, reliable evidence—all this involves cooperation and a super-individual grasp. Science is, therefore, collective knowledge. Science develops an objective consciousness that transcends individuals and generations. Art, on the other hand, is intrinsically personal knowledge, knowledge that is confined to the individual, that proceeds from the individual and is intended for individuals. It is knowledge that in the old religious way is concerned with closed coherence, with perfection, that is essentially perfect. This old art knowledge, too, was placed in a new situation through the growing mass of worldly activities and human problems. In the forms of the gods, in myths, in the life of Christ and of the saints, art had found and spontaneously embodied the ultimate truth. But faced with the diversity and fullness of the profane world, art was forced to select her objects, to separate the essential from the non-essential in order to maintain unity, coherence and plasticity. Art was no longer able to render the whole in its reality, the supreme meaning of the world in its full scope, as it was conveyed through the images of the gods. In order to show the coherence embodied in a perceptible form, a representative figure had to be chosen, a being or an event, designed to serve as a symbol by which the individual coincides with the general. To reach the essential, art must abandon complete reality. The essential must be symbolized through something unreal and merely probable, through something fictitious. And this is the origin of artistic fiction.

This result is brought about with the perfection of the individual at the time of the Renaissance. Since the center of gravity shifts from the divine essence of life to the individual, so the shape and the idea of a work of art, in order to be valid for its era, must represent the thousand, incomplete complexities of daily life in an exemplary fashion, just as in political life the national monarch represents and symbolizes the countless members of a nation. The work of art must choose and embody the one essential from a multiform reality.

With the development of democracy, the organization of economic and social collectives, the rise of social problems, the human life-center moves from the individual to the superindividual unit. The sciences bring to light an immense mass of experiences of a collective character. And just as the representation of a people by a personal monarch, just as personal methods of government, are shaken and replaced by a regime of abstract laws and constitutions, so, gradually, the artist's representation of the common life through the symbol of individuals and their fate runs the danger of no longer expressing the essential, the basic meaning of contemporary events. The masses of population that have sprung up invalidate the individual and his personal destiny, and the collective, standardized interests, the concerns of mechanized functions and of social layers—these are the things that affect man above all. This becomes a fateful dilemma for art, with her principle of representing closed, plastic coherence. If art clings to the palpable, individual motif, it loses all symbolic significance and sinks to the level of mere entertainment and diversion. Art becomes intrinsically untrue by emphasizing something that no longer holds the center of the life-stage. Through this descent, "kitsch" comes into being—worthless novelties good for nothing but feeding the hunger for sensation of jaded brains, with the help of romantic banalities. But if art remains true to her task, she becomes more and more remote from the realm of the tangible, from the realm of the individual and his fate, and her effort to fathom a basic truth, the deeper significance of life, leads her into abstract spheres, to a state of transcendence alien to contemporary man.

This fundamental transformation of the theme of art is not only due to the changes in the world that serves her as a model but also to a necessity inherent in the evolution of art herself. Different contents demand and develop different forms and techniques of presentation. And changes in style, in their turn, bring about changes of subject-matter. The result is an inner, autonomous evolution of art that is, nevertheless, in close connection with general human evolution. It is characteristic of true art to precede human development, to shape it in advance and thus to initiate it. But, at the same time, this relationship carries the germ of that fateful break between the artist and his world.

It has often been denied that there was a consistent, consecutive evolution of art corresponding to the evolution of man. Even those who believe in the steady progress of mankind are wont to consider art the only field of human activity exempted from the general law of progress. This point of view has a sound cause. It expresses the feeling of the fundamental difference between the art principle and the science principle—and it is the latter that produced and fed the belief in progress. As a matter of fact, every work of art and every art movement is a closed and perfect whole. The work of art is an end in itself. And the principle of harmony, of intrinsic conformity, of closed coherence is present unchanged in all the art manifestations of all the ages of mankind. It is equally present in an ancient tragedy and in a piece of Greek sculpture, as it is in the "Ulysses" of Joyce and in a picture by Cézanne. But it is wrong to conclude from this that art has not experienced a consistent evolution as have all other human manifestations. Only the evolution of art is not as apparent as that of science, the very principle of which is evolution. The evolution of art is not apparent because of this ruling principle of perfection in every individual piece of work. The development proceeds on a more fundamental level. All true art includes the factor of innovation; all true art means a conquest of new contents, clothed in adequate forms; all true art advances along the foremost front of what can be expressed. And if, today, a personal life is described, or a naturalistic landscape is painted in the style of the nineteenth century, such work, even though it be technically perfect, will no longer be live art. It will not enrich the intrinsic knowledge of the world and of man, a knowledge which it is the specific task of art to gain, and because of the shallowness of repetition, it will not even reach the radiance and perfection of those works that expressed the same thing for the first time.

The development of science is conquest in the dimension of latitude. The development of art is conquest in the dimension of depth. It proceeds by breaking through the bounds of traditional harmony and by integrating new life-strata, new dissonances and disparities that have developed in the mean time, into a deeper and more comprehensive harmony. It is the mission of the artist to master the whole of contemporary life and knowledge, to present it to the mind palpably and clearly and to re-create again and again the organic coherence, the meaning of man and of the world. In the course of the past two centuries, the development of art was turned from the sphere of bodily plasticity to more and more abstract and spiritual regions through the changes in her contents and methods. The art of today is characterized by an increasing loss of sensual substantiality and a corresponding increase in transcendence.

This is true of all forms of art. One example must suffice: literature.

Dante's "Divine Comedy" belongs to a species of poetry characteristic of antiquity. Dante still unites all the branches of the knowledge of his world in a great epic, and what he describes is not fiction but reality, the reality on which the Christian faith is based. The characters in his great poem are historical—heathens, Christians, contemporaries—and they express their relation and attitude to the truth of the Christian dogma. But they do not move on a historical plane, they do not belong to any particular time, they belong to an eternal paradise, purgatory and inferno, to a three-fold world that abolishes the sequence of time and concentrates time in such a way that temporal reality becomes identical with supreme truth. This type of religious poetry had long repercussions and was revived, through Protestant piety, in Milton's "Paradise Lost", for instance, in Bunyan's "Pilgrim's Progress" and Klopstock's "Messias". When, however, we compare these works with the "Divine Comedy", we see that the realities and the knowledge of the contemporary world are no longer included in the religious pale, but that this religious pale now constitutes only a limited part of human existence.

The beginning of the new era is heralded by the Italian love-stories of the Renaissance, and by the Spanish books of chivalry and picaresque novels (social satires centering on the adventures of a rogue). These take place in their contemporary world and unfold the lives of imaginary persons. They are "fiction". The Don Quixote of Cervantes is already a symbol, the representation of a human attitude, characteristic of his epoch, by a carefully chosen character. Cervantes did not as yet, to be sure, conceive his hero as a thoroughly developed, individual personality. Don Quixote is still a class type seen from a satirical point of view, and, therefore, he still has elements of a general reality. It is only the satirical exaggeration of the conflict of this antiquated knight with a new world that gives him both a certain uniqueness and his symbolic significance.

Shakespeare's characters, on the other hand, are complete individuals, unique, pronounced and sharply differentiated personalities. Even where history is pictured, the emphasis is not on historical reality, but on the free rendering of specific persons and their destiny, full of general human significance. History is only the external frame and stimulus for unfolding a free play of characters and happenings. As characters grow in general significance they take on greater particular significance, they become more intensely individual. These persons received their individual character by the fact that they expressed temperaments and feelings, not only of their Elizabethan world, but of the human world in general, and that they were lifted out of their time and their locality, into a general human sphere. The extraordinary fullness and power of Shakespeare's dramas is not due entirely to the genius of the poet, but also to the fortunate moment in which they came into being. Or rather: this fortunate moment is part of Shakespeare's genius, for a genius arises only in response to the need of the hour. In Shakespeare's time, the destiny of peoples coincided with the destinies of their monarchs and nobles. The characters, passions and deeds of representative persons expressed the essential aspects of the age. Human life was synonymous with the flux of human, personal relations. And so, in this essentially political epoch, human relations were still entirely expressed by the action of the moment, by the physical gesture. That is why drama that takes place in the present became the dominant type of writing of that time. The drama is the most condensed, the most concentrated form of the poetic symbol.

This is also the reason for the direct contact of the poet with his audience—they obviously lived in a common sphere, on the same plane of feeling and thinking. The subject matter of the poet was that of daily life. That does not mean that the knowledge and language of the poet did not transcend the current capacity of perception. His inspiration and his insight carried him far beyond, into hitherto unfathomed depths. And in the midst of exciting action performed for the masses, there are shining words that the poet says to himself, to himself alone, secret words for which there can be no audience. And the awareness of this inner solitude creates the first embodiment of the estranged genius, the fool, creates that hidden communication of his personal destiny, that appears in "The Tempest". Here it is of importance to note that not the general theme of Shakespeare's work is remote from the audience, but only the special, human wisdom of genius.

The democratic and economic development of the following centuries brings with it a growing complication in administration and social conditions. The individual comes into conflict with objective, collective claims, with an external, fixed, bourgeois moral convention. Since the decisive factors of life no longer coincide with purely human, personal interactions, they can no longer be grasped in the compressed form of actual feeling and in the action of the moment. Essential events no longer lie in action but in the long drawn-out psychic and mental processes of which action is a mere end-product or by-product. Thus a presentation of sequences of development, the novel, takes the center of the stage. Balzac's "Comédie Humaine", which concludes an evolutionary phase initiated by Shakespeare, still deals with human motives and problems. Individual destinies and passions are symbols of a more broad and general significance. But characters are developed only by relating the whole course of their lives in detail. And the individual is already imbued and conditioned by the effects of a state of affairs which begins to play a part of its own; the vast perspective of social life is visible behind individual human destiny. In Balzac, too, his magnificent understanding not only of the psychic, but also of the social structure, is woven into an exciting tale meant for the masses. But even here there is no essential split between the sphere of individual every-day life and the scene that the poet uses for his background.

Goethe was the first to mirror split worlds. His thoughts and images move in a sphere that no longer belongs to life per se, but to a very much enriched and erudite culture. In his effort to establish a comprehensive connection between the various contents of his world, there is a conscious strain created by the tension he feels between the real and the essential, between the exigencies of in-

dividual life and the vital questions of human existence and of
nature. These questions would only occur to the educated, or rather,
to scholars. They are on another, on a higher plane. Here, for
the first time, the problem of civilization emerges, the conflict of
the individual with his cultural world. Goethe's temperament was
elemental and stormy. His entire life-work can only be understood
as a tremendous effort to master human instincts and passions and
to integrate them in the cultural order of man, to create harmony
not only between the overpowering contents of culture itself but
also between human urges and the demands of a highly developed
society. Goethe was concerned with equilibrium, with human,
artistic and cosmic order. In "Werther", human passion still pre-
dominates in plot and in style. Passion does not yield; it leads
to the hero's suicide. And all this is still presented in a very subjective and lyrical way. In "Tasso", "Iphigenie" and in "The Elective Affinities", elemental urges and relations are subordinated to
the law of form, of measure, of cultural harmony represented by
educated society, by humanity, by sublimated morality. The educated individual of modern times is subject to the law of self-control
and renunciation. "Tasso" and "Iphigenie" are no longer true
drama, because here the tragedy takes place in the psychological
background of the action, in the tender and secret stirrings of the
heart. Actual events are reduced to the role of end-products of
feeling. In the "geometric" structure of "The Elective Affinities",
the sublimation and symbolic lucidity of the plot are carried to the
point of depriving the characters of their rich individuality, their
palpability. The man who strives to harmonize the conflicts, who
represents man's higher responsibility in a cultured society, this
mediator is an almost allegorical figure, as his name "Mittler"
indicates. And the cosmic drama of "Faust"—the first to treat
the theme of man's transcendence, of the daring, modern Prometheus, the secularized human mind that tries to dominate the
universe by knowledge—this great drama takes place on another,
purely spiritual plane; the sphere of wonted everyday life is left
behind. It is not surprising that the essential work of Goethe remained alien to his contemporaries, as he himself often remarked

with bitterness. It was met with shy reverence on the part of the public, who were only attracted by the urbanity of his genius that maintained the contact with his contemporaries through poems for various occasions, through lyrical utterances and experiments in all the more popular forms of writing.

The nineteenth century brought the romantic flight from reality, and this also was a removal to the sphere of erudite culture. The excursions of the romantic imagination frequently utilized the results of the theoretic, historical, geographic and natural sciences, and it is no mere coincidence that it was romanticism that gave a powerful impetus to learning. The reaction to this was decided realism, the first deliberate turning to the purely factual, material contents of modern life. Once more, the individual represents life symbolically. But when, in "Madame Bovary", Gustave Flaubert relates the average life of a middle-class woman in a small provincial town, in great detail, or, in "Un Coeur Simple", the life of a servant, the intended commonplaceness of his story is already accompanied by social overtones. It is not the representative human characters but rather the commonplace itself that is in the focus. The social average has taken the place of the human symbol, and this means that the contoured character is beginning to dissolve. The local color of the individual character is modified by the Pleinair of the social sphere. The realist Flaubert, like no other, strove for perfection of form in the work of art. The problem of his work and of his life was the equilibrium of the Valeurs, the harmony of the parts. He was the first to devote weeks to achieve the absolute rightness of a sentence. But here, for the first time, there is a sharp division between the problems of form and the content it presents. Goethe still applied his sense of harmony to the very substance of his world, he aimed at the molding of his society, at the establishment of an inner coherence of contemporary culture. His was a last struggle for the beauty, the lofty significance of the world. Flaubert, the middle-class foe of the middle class, deliberately turns to the unbeautiful, to the plain, to the minutiae of every-day life in his striving for beauty, and by the choice of such humble themes he emphasizes the perfection of his form.

Thus "l'art pour l'art", deliberate artistry, is kindled by the most materialistic subject-matter, that contributes the minimum of charm and inherent form. Flaubert too made an attempt to unite the disintegrating contents of the bourgeois life of his times. This attempt, the fragment, "Bouvard et Pécuchet", was, however, only meant as a mocking compendium of the accumulated facts of the unwise scholarship of the nineteenth century. The sequence from the comprehensive world harmony of the "Divine Comedy", from the desperate effort of Faust and of Wilhelm Meister to unify all of modern culture, to Flaubert's unsuccessful caricature of bourgeois knowledge, this sequence reflects the progressing disruption of modern culture.

Guy de Maupassant, in exploiting the conquests of his teacher Flaubert, sacrificed the symbolic value of characters and lost the passionate striving for pure form. His stories become graceful routine anecdotes, though they are told in a masterful way. The mass production of this author was responsible for the whole genus of modern light fiction. The inner development of the new realism becomes clear in Zola. Dickens already had described a specific class of the population, the English middle class with its special problems, and interfused his novels with social criticism. In Zola's novels, however, the social conditions in themselves are the protagonists. They constitute the characters and the theme. Individuals are nothing but the products of their social conditions, of their class destiny. Zola considered his art a form of science and pursued it with scientific method and thoroughness. In his "experimental novels", he treats of all the classes and strata—peasants, financiers, workers—and of the economic and social processes—the stock exchange, the small storekeeper's ruin through the department store, the problems of population, drunkenness and prostitution. And when Zola, following Balzac's "Comédie Humaine", writes a cycle of connected stories on French society mirrored in a family history, he does this to show social development and the problems of heredity. In all his works he tries to establish social laws. He is not concerned with the life of the individual, to which he devotes very little attention and the minimum of a thread-bare psychology.

Individuals are no longer symbols but experimental animals. Men no longer develop or reflect social problems, as in the case of Balzac, but social problems find their embodiment in man. Zola was the founder of the whole school of French, English, German, American naturalists, from Gerhart Hauptmann and Galsworthy to Sinclair Lewis and Theodore Dreiser.

In this literary current, the individual merges with the external collective, and fiction with social reality. The Russians and the Scandinavians, however, initiated another, more intrinsic dissolution of the individual. Man is separated into his sub-individual and super-individual elements, and the point of departure is a more and more investigatory psychology. Long before Freud had scientifically established the threefold division of the soul into the id, the layer of the subconscious, the super-ego, the layer of the super-conscious moral controls, and the intervening narrow province of the real, conscious and acting ego, these layers had been discovered by literature. The rebellion of the subconscious begins with Dostoievsky. He is the father of modern psychology. He undermines and blasts the stolid ground of human personality. In Shakespeare, Goethe and Balzac, human passions and urges are still subjective. They are integrated in, and subordinate to, personality; they are parts of a rounded whole. Here the urge is a prefiguration of human will; the individual is completely aware of this urge, he can yield to it or not; at any rate, he expresses it and operates with it. Since Dostoievsky, urges constitute an objective sphere, an underworld, an id that dominates the personality and the authority of which is unchallenged. Even if Dostoievsky still calls this id an illness, a devil, a demon, it is nevertheless the headquarters of crucial events, the source of external and internal developments that are released and clarified through confession. In Tolstoi's work, insignificant impressions frequently reveal the depth of the subconscious and illumine life down to childhood. In the story, "The Death of Ivan Iljitsh", a dish of cooked prunes releases a train of dim memories in the invalid, just as later, in Proust, the taste of a piece of cake dipped in tea is the point of departure for the "Remembrance of Things Past". With all this, the sphere of the subconscious is opened—a weighty discovery! Both Dostoievsky and Tolstoi have given a comprehensive picture of Russia that is their world—one in the "Brothers Karamazov", the other in "War and Peace". Here too, not the characters are the focus of events, but the dark abysses of the anonymous Russian soul.

From the opposite side, but not without a deep, inner relationship to the Russian writers, Ibsen discovered the sphere of the super-ego. His themes are the practically chronic struggles of conscience of the bourgeois that spring from the inhibition and suppression of natural urges through middle-class decency and good manners. With his subtle moral dialectic, Ibsen has woven these struggles of conscience into a ghostly cloud that continually broods over the scene. He has made conscience into an objective, predominant element of life, that no longer resides within man but beyond and between men, and snares the sophisticated sinners and penitents in labyrinthine complications. This conscience sometimes even takes the shape of allegorical demons, of modern Furies that expose man's guilt and drive man on. The wild duck, for instance, that is tended in the garret of the family Ekdal, symbolizes the bourgeois docility of men who are no longer free, and calls forth the sacrifice of the little daughter after she is cast off by her father who has learned that she is not his child. Another example are the white horses of Rosmersholm, that appear only when a misfortune is in the offing. Another, the "rat lady" in "Little Eyolf", who lures the child into the lake, the child that became a cripple because he fell from the table in a moment when his parents were oblivious of him in an orgy of the senses. The ethical problems become so abstract and complex that they can no longer be solved and are lost in the scepticism of the poet. But they create an atmosphere of oppressive significance of every word and every event, and this atmosphere caused the special effect of Ibsen's dramas. This super-ego, this secret tribunal of the human soul is the real hero; the individuals are only the transparent carriers of their problematic guilt that has almost ceased to be personal guilt, but grows out of the subterranean layers of the personality. For in the final analysis, the conscientious scruples of Ibsen's characters are only reflexes, rationalizations of neurotic fears and ghosts of the subconscious. Ibsen has expressed this himself:

> "What is life? a fighting
> In heart and in brain with Trolls.
> Poetry? that means writing
> Doomsday-accounts of our souls."

In the plays of the other great Scandinavian, Strindberg, especially in the Chamber Plays ("After the Fire", "The Pelican", "The Ghost Sonata"), ethical problems have been dissolved in the stagnant mire of a forced life together. Guilt can no longer be fixed, can no longer be attributed to one person or another. It is a permanent state of whole families. Individual relations and characters have lost their individual values and flow apart in a general mist of psychic decay. Even the spook of the abysses is no longer embodied—it has become omnipresent.

Thus in the representative literary production at the end of the nineteenth century, the individual I is no longer the bearer of action but the passive object of impersonal powers and currents, be it for the purpose of experiments in regard to social conditions, be it as the victim of volcanic outbreaks of the soul. From this time on, in the literature of the twentieth century, the loss of substance, the dissolution and the transcendence of individual life is accelerated. More and more, personal destinies and relations become the mere occasion, the mere material for the presentation of social, cultural or metaphysical needs. The path the bourgeois century has taken becomes especially clear when we compare the basic features of the work of Thomas Mann with the fundamental ideas of Goethe, to whom he has an inner relationship. For he too is concerned with affirming and saving human form that is guaranteed by civilization. But while Goethe still attempts to build up the human form from within, from the harmony of human substance and elements, and to force the powers and contents of personality, society and nature into one cosmos, the twentieth-century writer is no longer capable of mastering such a task.

Thomas Mann's fundamental aim is, as it were, the negative of
Goethe's. He stakes off the human form from without, from the
periphery. In his work, he traverses various border-regions, the
spheres of physical and psychic forces that are more powerful than
the individual and that endanger personality: the degeneration of
a family ("Buddenbrooks"), disease ("The Magic Mountain"),
crime ("Felix Krull"), erotic enchantment ("Death in Venice"),
the play with psychic powers ("Mario and the Magician"), the
impersonality of modern government ("Royal Highness"), the
hypertrophy of genius ("The Beloved Returns"), the mythical
chaos and the totemistic and animal dregs in the depth of the
soul ("Joseph and His Brothers"), the disruption of the organism
("The Transposed Heads"). And herein the writer himself is
often deluged and swept along by the power of the forces he has
conjured. The subconscious currents of the ego, with all their
flotsam and jetsam, break forth with greater strength than he is
prepared to admit. They can only be controlled by the flexible
irony characteristic of his style, by the continual motion of going
beyond, leveling down, keeping the all-too-serious threats within
bounds.

If the work of Thomas Mann is permeated with speculative
elements, the writing of André Gide, the leading exponent of
contemporary French literature, is governed throughout by thinking as such. The problems are no longer represented in his characters, which, like marionettes, are directed from above. "I try to
wind the various threads of intrigue and the complexity of my
thoughts around these little living bobbins that all my characters
are." Gide's thinking still circles around moral questions. He fights
for the last outposts of antique and Christian morality: How can
the individual preserve his personality in the face of growing
anarchy, of the scintillating unreliability of his inner life that is
escaping his control? How can personality be formed, how can it
be saved, and where is the soil on which the knowledge and will
of man can still persist? Only one basic demand is left, that of
sincerity. But how can one be sincere if the experience of modern
man shows that the psychic factors are most uncertain, that fact

and imagination interact, and that in this process the fact is changed, even dissolved, through the influence of imagination? "If I turn toward myself, I no longer understand what this word means. I never am what I think I am—and this varies incessantly, so that frequently . . . my morning self would not recognize my evening self. Nothing could be more different than I am from myself. It is only in solitude that I occasionally see the substratum, that I attain a certain steady continuity; but then it appears to me as though my life were slowing, stopping, and that I shall actually cease to be." Sincerity demands that the inner life be expressed in its fullness. But in order to survive as a personality on these dangerous tides, it is constantly necessary to go beyond, to transcend. What Thomas Mann achieves through irony, Gide tries to do by surpassing himself ("se dépasser"),—a residue of his Puritanical origin, but divested of all religious meaning.

André Gide, too, yielded to the legitimate desire of the poet to express his world in a single, comprehensive work. But this work, the novel, "Les Faux Monnayeurs" ("The Counterfeiters"), can no longer give the contents of this world directly through the characters and events in themselves. It shows them by means of their mirror images in spectators, through reflections of reflections, through the concentric play of reflections. The action consists in the mutual impressions that the characters have of one another, of the diary of one contemplative, main character that represents the author. In addition to this, the author accompanies his description with his own occasional observations. And finally, Gide has written a commentary on his own novel in the subsequent "Journal des Faux Monnayeurs". Through all this, the sphere of thought built up around the events attains prime importance, and the forms are dissolved into their speculative reflections.

The forcible harrowing of the psychic soil that was taking place on all sides profoundly changed the character and the form of narrative. The emphasis no longer lies in external action, or in a development manifesting itself in tangible processes. External action shrivels to a mere impetus, to a line of demarcation along which the much more important subterranean currents of the soul are brought to light. Memories, dreams, association-sequences of feeling, imagination and thought, the organic interplay of sensuous impressions—all this emerges in the natural order, in the lightning change from consciousness to subconsciousness uninterruptedly begotten by the newly discovered soul. The external, tangible story is replaced by the "inner story", which is no longer the story of an active and purposeful being but of one who is subject to many varied experiences. Thus it comes about that the excess of experiences of a day, of an hour, often fills many pages and even volumes. The first instance of such an inner story is Richard Beer-Hofmann's "Death of George", published in 1900. Here the Viennese poet develops the imaginary fullness of inner life from the simple experience of death. Marcel Proust brought this technique to its utmost perfection, and his influence has spread it everywhere in all the significant literary products of our days.

French literature, more than any other, has an excellent touchstone with which to gauge the changes in its prose style. Since the "ancien régime", French authors have examined the changing problems of their epochs against the background of French society. For the French writer, French society represents human society, and cycles of novels in which various centers or developmental stages of society are depicted through a group of related persons are a typically French invention. It would be a very instructive literary and sociological investigation to trace the changes in problems, technique and style as applied to the same subject, from Choderlos de Laclos, Stendhal, Balzac and Zola to such different modern authors as Sar Péladan, Romain Rolland, Roger Martin du Gard, Jules Romains, Henri de Montherlant and, above all, Marcel Proust. The peculiar ambivalent character of Marcel Proust's work is due to the fact that, while he is still within the pale of French society, he breaks through the bounds of this pale by his method and manner of seeing. He still takes the traditional forms and institutions of society so seriously that he has been called a snob, but, with all this deep respect, he destroys them through his new psychological insight. At times, this produces a grotesque discrepancy between the unimportance of the subject-matter and the scope of the method. The most petty details of social behavior and ritual give rise to digressions that lead into super-sensual realms. The result is the complete dissolution, not only of social, but also of human continuity. The unity of the personal character is annihilated through the "pointillistic" analysis of psychic conditions, through the projection of the psychic condition of the spectator into what is seen, through an excessive sensitiveness in observation that is exaggerated to metaphysics of sensual perception and that destroys the object. An interrelationship, a single psychic complex is created by the atmosphere of a book that someone begins to read, by the blue color of a curtain that diverts him, by the shining buttons of a passing conductor, by the posture in which all of this is perceived.

During the last decades, this new technique has been applied in various ways by the better-known authors of all countries. We find traces of it in D. H. Lawrence's epics of erotic life, in the social satires of Aldous Huxley, in the dangerously delicate pastels of Virginia Woolf, in which the entire gravity of inner life is driven to the nerve-ends, and in the scurrilous accounts of the Austrian Robert Musil, whose cycle of novels is characteristically called "The Man Without Qualities". In all these authors we find the same scattering of human personality, the same blurring of characters in the play of mirroring between individuals, the same fusion of the I with the sensual, objective outer world, with fragments of landscape, public life, scientific results, transcendental meditations. An unlimited participation of all in all is manifest, the psychic precipitate of that technical and economic interrelationship that modern civilization has brought about. Ernest Hemingway added an important innovation. He dissolves inner events in the continual flux of every-day life. He derives the significant from the most insignificant peripheral particles of the most commonplace human intercourse. In the trilogy of John Dos Passos, the modern metropolis plays the main role. There is no unified story; episodic, unconnected destinies are only synchronized and the description is interrupted by "montage", by unforeshortened, unchanged reality, by newspaper clippings, by camera-eye pictures and by biographies. of real persons in American public life.

The special feeling for life dominating all this modern writing, can be illustrated by a few sentences from Virginia Woolf's "Mrs. Dalloway": "She would not say of any one in the world now that they were this or were that . . . She sliced like a knife through everything; at the same time was outside, looking on. She had a perpetual sense, as she watched the taxicabs, of being out, out, far out to sea and alone; she always had the feeling that it was very, very dangerous to live even one day . . . She knew nothing . . . she scarcely read a book now . . . and yet to her it was absolutely absorbing; all this, the cabs passing . . . what she loved, was this, here, now, in front of her; the fat lady in the cab. Did it matter then, she asked herself, . . . did it matter that she must inevitably cease completely; all this must go on without her; . . . somehow in the streets of London, on the ebb and flow of things, here, there, she survived, Peter survived, lived in each other, she being part, she was positive, of the trees at home . . . part of people she had never met, being laid out like a mist between the people she knew best, who lifted her on their branches as she had seen the trees lift the mist, but it spread ever so far, her life, herself . . . " Here is the complete dissolution of the individual as well as of the I.

All these authors, however, have still not drawn the ultimate conclusions from the modern state of affairs. Although they have deprived the individual of his value as a symbol, although this individual has passed the expression of fundamental life-problems on to super-individual or sub-individual powers and currents, the forms of individual destinies persist, and through them the impersonal forces are manifested. The devaluation of the individual has been carried to a climax by two writers, each of whom, with his own special brand of intransigence, chose one of the two possible ways that lead beyond the individual. They are Franz Kafka and James Joyce. Kafka's way leads to the parable, which is an abstraction of the symbol. The symbol is no longer clothed in flesh and blood, in a single, individual event. The whole scene of action is lifted to a transcendental plane where the inner meaning does not spring from sensual phenomena, but appears as pure abstraction. The individual does not walk the ways of our world; he is anonymous and imaginary. The characters have no names. They are mere skeletons, mere ciphers of personality. The entanglements of plot are purely hypothetical. Kafka's main theme is the helplessness of man before the superior power of the mechanical causality evident in our complicated civilization, for instance, in the technique of bureaucracy, and even in the present development of human nature itself. It is the desperate struggle of innate human feelings and urges that try to maintain themselves in the face of the exigencies of an inhuman world. This irrational human feeling walking in human form plays the role of the victim-hero in these modern fables. In an irrational way, they represent a world rationalized ad absurdum, by an image of pure and ghostly transparency; they reproduce unsensual confusion with minute sensual clarity. And although they are permeated with profound, moral emotion, the form of expression is classically balanced, precise and even dry. Kafka had a number of followers in his use of the modern parable, especially in Germany, where Ernst Juenger chose this form for his last book "Auf den Marmorklippen" ("On the Marble Cliffs") in order to express ideas hostile to the Nazi government. Every symbol implies a hidden meaning, and through its abstractness, the parable heightens the cryptic character of the symbol to such a degree that it becomes a conundrum that must be solved. This art form, used by Kafka only to confront man with his civilization, assisted Juenger both in revealing and disguising his criticism of current politics.

Joyce takes the opposite path. He does not condense the human being to the point of abstractness, putting it in an abstract world remote from time and place. On the contrary, the boundaries of human personality are extended until there is no personality left; the individual is a mere vessel of the wild chaos of contents of the modern world. Once more, in "Ulysses", an artist dares to undertake the fundamental task of all art, to give a comprehensive picture of his whole contemporary world. And this entire world, in all its dimensions, in its historic length, its present breadth and its psychic depth, is forced into a single day, the sixteenth of June, 1905, one day among others in the life of an average person, a Mr. Bloom, in Dublin. The layers of civilization, from the contemporary world over the history of Ireland representing world-history to a mythical paraphrase of Homer's "Odyssey", the phases of which appear in Mr. Bloom's sixteen hours, are all caught in the story of this one day. The characters grouped around the hero, are part of himself, they are only reflections of the various strata of his soul, from the rational to the animal, and what takes place between the characters is only the interplay of the functions of the modern soul in all its disparity. In order to represent this anarchic, incoherent whole, all styles, from the naturalistic to the surrealistic, are employed, all the accumulated knowledge of our time, the elements of ten languages. And all these elements and methods are tuned to one another with the most subtle understanding of art. Joyce runs the gamut from tone harmony to the region of keen, almost scholastic argument. This tremendous effort, which has placed art on a plane of rational exactness, has, however, only produced a picture of total decay, a whirl of disconnected feelings, urges, values and realizations. The inner coherence is unraveled into a net of thousands of complex associations. This is evident even in the language; in his last work, "Finnegan's Wake", Joyce tried to create a symphony of meanings by word and sound associations, and to carry through a work of four-story significance. But this very attempt at ultimate synthesis has only brought about a complete disintegration of language itself. And so only one thing is proved by this last, encyclopedic attempt to comprise the world in one picture: that today's world cannot be conveyed by any hitherto known means of art. The world has reached the point where the whole can no longer be symbolically represented by the single, concrete instance. Modern reality has assumed such enormous breadth that its verities and its synthesis have become abstract and can no longer be expressed through a sensuous picture. In pursuing the essential verities of modern reality further and further, art itself became transcendent and abstract and more and more removed from its own sensuous and pictorial sphere. With all its strenuous effort to adjust to the increasingly transcendent character of those verities, it can no longer establish the true coherence of the modern world by clinging to the principle of fiction, to the symbolic representation of the whole through one concrete instance.

We saw how in the course of the last century, symbolic fiction became more and more permeated by broad inclusions of immediate reality. Science as well as photographic description have broken into art and robbed it of more and more of its substance. Individual human relations were deprived of their value in favor of social, collective problems that can be represented only in their full scope and exact factuality and not through symbols. The interesting experiments in the direction of a symbolic representation of collective life, such as those of Bert Brecht and Karel Čapek ("R.U.R.") led to the dramatic parable, that, in spite of occasional human features, has the abstract character of the Marionette performance. Collective happenings can be represented successfully only in the film, that opens up new dimensions of space and time and makes possible a fusion of the epic and the dramatic as well as mass effects, simultaneousness of presentation and subtle transitions that words alone could not convey. But here, more than ever, fiction passes over into the representation of reality. The great significance of moving pictures lies in the fact that they are able to reproduce modern reality in its own dimension.

The psychic conflicts within the ego have been shifted from the sphere of subjective consciousness into the region of the subconscious, that is to say, from the personal to an impersonal, typical sphere, increasingly claimed by medical psychology. Much of what formerly was considered personal tragedy is now classed as clinical cases; and this is the result of psychoanalysis. Suffering becomes pathology. The tragedy of Ibsen's Hedda Gabler would be impossible, even ridiculous today: it is a known psychiatric phenomenon. Personal experiences, as a whole, have become relatively unimportant in the light of the two great general problems: the obsession and confusion of the I by the mass of unorganized facts of modern reality, and the inhibition of natural urges and impulses through modern civilization. Accordingly, the themes and forms of modern literature are largely determined by the findings of psychoanalysis, in so far as these findings had not already been anticipated; the symbolic character in fiction is only a transparent sheath around psychic strata that are revealed by associative processes, somewhat analogous to Freud's free association. More and more the essential literary works of our time require speculative, even scientific arguments to effect their inner cohesion. The gradual process of intrusion of theoretical reality upon artistic fiction is especially apparent in the trilogy of Hermann Broch, "The Sleepwalkers", that treats the disintegration of values from 1888 to the end of the First World War. Each of the three novels deals with a stage of this process and the method of rendering varies with the subject-matter. While the first novel has still the form of closed narrative, the last is dissolved into a multitude of fragmentary reports and monologues that give an anonymous character to the individual destinies, and is permeated by speculative digressions.

Art is no longer able to exercise its vital function of showing, or rather, of re-establishing, the inner coherence of the world; a symbolic representation of the modern world that goes further than that of Joyce is hardly thinkable. Neither is modern learning capable of carrying out this task; such has never been its goal, even in principle, because of its collective, extensive and always fragmentary character. And yet a grasp of the inner connections of the world is now, as always, a vital necessity for mankind; it is the indispensable premise for any future order. The practical mastering of our world depends upon whether the inner coherence of our world can be re-established. The solution of this problem can only lie in one direction: in the union of artistic form and principle with the content of learning, in the union of the truths of art and learning. And this means the reunion of the essential with the real. Scientific findings, that is to say, reality in its true scope, that has already influenced the themes and the methods of art, will gradually become the subject-matter of art. Art will abandon the principle of symbolic representation, of fiction, and will have to represent the inner coherence of our world by the facts themselves. Learning, on the other hand, will only be able to halt the growing process of specialization into fields that are increasingly losing connection with one another, if it accepts the artistic, philosophical principle of inner coherence and the trend toward a common order. In this way, the efforts of art and learning can converge and may, in the modern secularized world, produce that unity that formerly existed in religion.

The process that we described is also manifest in lyric poetry, which has changed from the expression of personal feeling to that of collective or transcendent connections. At the end of the nineteenth century, the economic and technical developments had changed the language of the day into the idiom of modern civilization that admitted of no natural transition to formal verse. There was an irreconcilable contradiction between the language of daily life and that of poetry. During the last decades the pursuit of true art impelled many authors to develop a personal language remote from conventional forms. But in the field of lyric poetry, even the basis for a common language of the poet and the public no longer existed. There were two possible ways out of this situation. One important group of poets yielded to the pressure of the epoch; it broke through traditional forms and created free rhythms, even poems in prose. It accepted the state of modern reality and went over to the language of this reality. The leading exponent of this school was Walt Whitman, whose powerful impetus has permeated all of American literature since his day. His rhapsodic tone that unites the abundance of nature with the feelings of modern urban civilization has even colored American prose; the novels of Thomas Wolfe are an epic extension of this stormy lyricism. The second, opposite group clung to the idea of pure poetry, traditional poetry, that led to the esoteric sublimation of form as well as of content. Here the transcendence of poetry is inevitably predetermined by the demands of formal compression and rhythm of expression. The development from Victor Hugo to Mallarmé and Valéry, from Goethe to Stefan George, Hofmannsthal and Rilke, from Shelley and Keats to Gerard Manley Hopkins and T. S. Eliot, indicates how far pure poetry has moved from the plane of contemporary society. In its cryptic terseness and concentration, this type of poetry is accessible only to those few who can reproduce the process of poetic creation within themselves.

The same development can be followed in the plastic arts. The growing predominance of painting corresponds exactly to the shifting of the center of gravity to the novel. If we compare portraits by Clouet, Titian or Holbein with those by van Gogh, Kokoschka or Picasso, we see at a glance the process that has been shown in the field of literature. In the works of the sixteenth-century artists, the last attainable truth of physical appearance coincides with actual every-day reality, with the "resemblance" recognizable to all. Here the presentation of one individual is synonymous with the artistic investigation of sensuous appearance as such. In a portrait of Picasso and Kokoschka, however, we are struck by the immense contrast between the every-day appearance of the person painted and the psychic, even psychological depth of the portrait that has been carried to a metaphysical sphere. The individual is condensed as well as heightened to a psychic attitude, a spiritual type, a superindividual form. And we need only remember the great transformation that took place in the nineteenth century, the development from the ideal, social realism of Millet and from the actual naturalism of Courbet to Pleinairism and Impressionism; the gradual disintegration of the concrete object, first through dissolving light, in Monet's painting, through the "divisions" of the neo-Impressionists, through the idea of structural form of Cézanne, van Gogh, and the Cubists, and the emphasis on the balanced picture in Matisse; and, as a final result, modern abstract painting, and the intrusion of bare fact and scientific precision in Surrealistic "montage" and mechanical constructions—we need only bear in mind this great process and we become aware of an exact parallel to the evolution of poetry. In the application of the Surrealistic principle, literature and plastic arts merge. According to André Breton's "Manifesto", the new form is "pure psychic automatism, by which it is intended to express, verbally or by any other means, the real process of thought. It is thought's dictation, all exercise of reason and every aesthetic or moral preoccupation being absent." And the Surrealistic painters, in rendering their visionary life, with all its "paranoiac" flux, explicitly refer to Freud's free association.

The only art that has been able to develop its new style in full accord with the trends of our period, and to follow its own essential character under the influence of these trends, is, understandably enough, architecture, which in its methods and materials is so intimately correlated with technology. Sullivan's dictum, "form must follow function", is not merely the guiding principle of our technological era but in a way that of architecture itself. Thus for the second time in history it happened, just as it had in Rome, that the scope of their material task led engineers to the creation of the monumental style that, besides answering its great material purpose, expresses the feeling of its period.

People on the street, in stores, in factories, are not in the least aware of the profound change in art when they read books or look at pictures, just as little as they are aware of the unapparent, gradual collectivization and standardization of their own lives. Their awareness has not kept pace with the change in their being. They regard themselves subjectively as mere individuals, and so their concepts and preferences have been arrested in the world of fiction, in the world of tangible, personal destinies, of concrete objects. On their subway and train rides, in their rest periods between their working hours, they still feed on fictitious love-stories and adventures—the adventure of life in a great city being represented by crime and the detection of crime, by the "mystery story". When people look at pictures, what they want is the most faithful imitation of persons, objects and events; they are uplifted by the cliché of formal beauty that has lost its substance long since. In accordance with their needs, books and magazines offer them the tales of expert popular writers for facile enjoyment. These writers borrow just as much of the technique of great authors as they need, to heighten the suspense with which they capture the interest of the public.

The effects of great modern painting are conveyed to the average person very indirectly, via the scale of colors in fabrics or the displays in a shop-window, for instance. And if the public does pay attention to the books or paintings of true artists they only absorb the superficial and the sensational that can be effortlessly derived. And so people are unable to discover the ultimate sources of those crises and catastrophes in which they suddenly find themselves ensnared.

THE PRELIMINARIES OF THE GREAT CRISIS

IN THE PRECEDING CHAPTERS we have seen how it happened that the bulk of the population lagged behind the mental and human standard of the intellectuals, to a hitherto unheard-of extent. The result was an epoch without leadership. The intelligentsia continued to follow its cultural goals; the people turned more and more to economic and technical aims, to the production of capital, of goods, of tools and of the comforts of living. And so the split between the two was merely the symptom of a much more fundamental break, of the estrangement of humanity from the true concerns of man, of the retardation of human development and mental achievement in contrast to the mad pace of the external paraphernalia of civilization. This was the first sign of the great crisis that was inevitably approaching.

The protest of the intellectuals was barely noticed by broad public opinion during the whole of the nineteenth century. It was upheld by isolated personalities of very different ideological origins and aims, by intellectual free-lancers, working and striving counter to the current optimism and the belief in progress that animated bourgeois life and also prevailed in science and popular literature. No one would have ventured to predict that the bourgeoisie itself would ever be susceptible to such views. A great deal had to happen before this could become possible. During the nineteenth century, the European bourgeoisie was still fighting the last stands and positions of the "ancien régime"—it was completing its emancipation in the revolutions of 1830 and 1848. Only toward the end of the nineteenth century universal suffrage got under way. So the bourgeoisie was still on the offensive against the feudality of the past, and it was the collective part of their creed and their ideology, the struggle for democratic self-government that was uppermost in their minds.

On the other hand, the prospect of economic progress appeared unlimited. There was plenty of room in the world which could be exploited by national economies and commercial and industrial enterprises, there were the technical innovations that gave rise to new industries, so that, in general, free competition could remain a peaceful and well-regulated procedure, and did not have to degenerate to a struggle for mutual destruction. America still had her domestic frontier, she stood in the midst of the economic opening of her great continent and the seemingly inexhaustible possibilities that it offered. The European peoples had their "frontier" too, in the colonies from which they first drew raw materials and which they gradually built up into markets, and also in the countries overseas and in the East, where populations were growing and economy was backward. It was only in the nineteenth century that England completed and consolidated her colonial empire. The French conquered their Asiatic, West African and Equatorial African possessions. Belgium acquired the Congo. Besides, the European countries gained rich spoils by successively *dividing up the large Ottoman Empire,* that extended from the Balkans to the Near East and over all North Africa to the Atlantic, and lingered on in a corrupt, despot-ridden and yet helpless condition. The "sick man", as Turkey was called in the nineteenth century, would quickly have fallen prey to the European countries, had it not been for the famous "balance of power" which was not to be disturbed, that is to say, had it not been for the jealousy and the watchfulness of every European government over any possible encroachment or preponderance on the part of the other. Like hungry beasts, the European powers circled around this senile colossus, after they had long secretly agreed upon devouring it. It was only a question of how to prevent the dismemberment of Turkey from turning into a European conflict. The French claimed and took, one by one, Algiers, Tunis and Morocco, with their vast hinterlands. Russia claimed the straits between European and Asiatic Turkey, the region around the Black Sea, and exercised a Panslavic influence on the Balkans which was contested by Austria. Russia got Kars and Batum in the Caucasus, and succeeded in remaining a constant menace. Austria at least reaped Bosnia and Hercegovina. Italy, that, like Germany, arrived late on the scene of action, and was comparatively weak as she was at the mercy of Britain's navy and economy, just managed to get Tripoli. This alleged injury was a constant thorn in her side, incited her governments to the Abyssinian adventures and, in general, added to the inferiority complex of this belated and all-too-vulnerable power. England had no immediate claim, except for a general control of the "balance of power" and a particular control of Egypt and the Suez Canal, which she acquired by purchasing shares of the Suez Company. This whole affair of the dismemberment of Turkey, with all its concomitant circumstances and sequels, with all its petty bargaining and diplomatic fake and fuss about a downright robbery, is an appalling spectacle. But it has special significance, not only because it shows the anarchy and brittleness of the international situation, but especially because it is the true prelude of the great world crisis to come. In itself, it led only to a few peripheral wars, such as the Crimean War, 1854–1856, the Russo-Turkish conflict of 1877, the Egyptian and Sudanese campaign, and the first unsuccessful Italian adventure in Abyssinia. But it was the point of departure for developments which led up to the First World War. The Moroccan crises of 1905, 1909 and 1911 increased the tension between Germany and the Western powers— these were, after all, mere symptomatic events. But the resentment resulting from the Turkish deal drove Italy into her Triple Alliance with Germany and Austria, and it was the continuous Balkan troubles, the main field of intrigues of the European powers, from which the Balkan wars of 1912 and 1914, and eventually the World War, evolved.

The nineteenth century as a whole, however, was a comparatively peaceful period, because the European powers and, above all, the European economies had still their frontier, the vast open space for exploitation and competition. This extraversion of the competing forces was the only factor which prevented or delayed a catastrophe which was sure to arise from unlimited competition.

There were *three developments* which eventually brought about this catastrophe. There was, first, the intrusion of newcomers into the established economic and colonial system, as a result of the belated unification of Germany and of Italy and the Europeanization of Russia and Japan. All this happened at about the same time; united Italy was founded in 1870, united Germany in 1871. The Europeanization of Russia set in with the Emancipation Decree, the abolition of serfdom, by Tsar Alexander II, called the Tsar Liberator, in 1861, and proceeded with the beginning of the industrialization of Russia from 1880 on. The modernization and rapid industrialization of Japan started with the Meiji Period in 1868. The most important and by far the most dangerous, the most imminently dangerous, of these four new elements, was the sudden rise of Germany, as it meant not only the appearance of a new power, but of a new and alarmingly efficient kind of power, a new system which, from the outset, challenged the system of the Western World. It was the crucial contest between state and nation, between state and democracy, that loomed in this encounter.

The second development which prepared the great crisis consisted in the fundamental changes in the social structure of the European countries as a result of the industrial revolution. They started with the rapid growth of the European population as a whole, the most rapid we know of in history. France increased her people by twenty per cent between 1820 and 1870, Germany by fifty-five per cent and England by eighty-three per cent. Larger and larger portions of the population were absorbed by the cities and the industries. This led to the dependence of the majority of the population on industrial prosperity, and hence to the end of national self-sufficiency, to the increasing dependence of whole countries on the consumption of industrial goods, that is, on foreign trade and international relations. Here was the beginning of a vicious circle in which capitalistic economy found itself caught. Free economy, free competition meant the displacement of rivals, and this worked very well as long as the world was divided into producers and consumers of industrial goods. But as industrialization grew all over the world, the rivals to be dispossessed turned out to be the very consumers of the goods on the sale of which the existence of the countries depended. And since there was no international division of labor, since industrialization developed not according to large-scale planning but to individual wish and opportunity, enhanced by national ambitions and greeds, capitalistic economy was bound to get into trouble at last. Foreign trade, indeed, called for peace, for stability and security of international conditions, as free trade economists had emphasized again and again. But when the growing and competing economies came into ever-closer friction, mutual interference, and eventually war, was the inevitable result. War, in turn, destroyed currencies, destroyed the purchasing power of entire countries, but induced them to build new domestic industries in order to decrease import and increase export; and so, together with a loss of consumers, a greater number of competitors was created.

The same vicious circle became effective on the domestic front, where the fundamental change in the social structure made itself felt by the rise of a new class of the population, the industrial worker. This new social stratum that lived under new, specific conditions of economic dependency was molded into masses and driven to organization and collective action by the character of their work and the defense of their interests. The growing pressure of this social and inherently socialistic movement brought about a change in the character and the ideology of the bourgeoisie. It provoked a reactionary attitude in the bourgeoisie, which now began to emphasize its individualistic and competitive aspects but nevertheless built up collective solidarity in the face of the advance of the new labor classes and the new labor movement. The inconsistency of this international social solidarity as directed against the international movement of labor, with the principle and the practice of economic rivalry, the discrepancy between international business ties and capital connections on the one hand, and the competition of national economies on the other, the conflict in domestic economy between the fight against the increase of wages, and the necessity of an increase of purchasing power for the consumers—all these inconsistencies and discrepancies brought the bourgeoisie into that present state of utter confusion that fostered panic and made it susceptible everywhere, to fascist ideologies. This confusion was heightened by a final development: all events became more and more international and, indeed, universal, due to the progress of communications and of the increasing economic and technical connection and interdependence of people and peoples all over the world.

The process of the *unification of Italy* shows striking similarities to that of the *unification of Germany,* besides chronological coincidence and the coalition of the revolutionary movements in both countries. First of all, there is a similarity in the premises of both countries. After the downfall of Napoleon in 1815, and the restoration of the old dynastic powers by the Congress of Vienna (1814–1815), both countries consisted of a conglomeration of dominions. In spite of the fact that Napoleon had abolished a great many petty sovereignties, Germany was still composed of thirty-nine sovereign dominions of the most different size and kind: two of them of European rank, Austria and Prussia; three new kingdoms by the grace of Napoleon, Bavaria, Saxony and Wuerttemberg; and two united by dynastic union with foreign countries, Hanover with England, and Schleswig-Holstein with Denmark. Besides these kingdoms and three Hanseatic city-republics, there were numerous principalities, duchies, grand-duchies and the like. Italy consisted of only eight dominions. Chief of these were: the Kingdom of Piedmont belonging to the Savoy dynasty, the ancient rivals of the Hapsburgs in Switzerland, and extending over the western half of Northern Italy down to the Ligurian coast and Sardinia; the Papal States in the center of the peninsula; the Bourbon kingdom of Southern Italy and Sicily, that, with the one short Napoleonic interruption, had been in existence since the Renaissance; and the Austrian dominions, comprising the former Lombard and

Venetian territories. The other parts, in between, Tuscany, Lucca, Parma, Modena, were divided up among minor Hapsburg and Bourbon princes.

This was the situation in both countries. Here and there the old monarchical powers had triumphed and restored their absolute rule. But, as everywhere in Europe, the revolutionary movement did not die down, and was constantly revived and stimulated by the oppression of withered tyranny. In both countries, the revolutionary movement was simultaneously democratic and national. It aimed at doing away with the old dynastic regimes and at a unification of the country, a liberation from autocratic and foreign rulership. The consecutive French uprisings, the revolutions of July 1830 and February 1848, directed against the restored Bourbon regime, kept the movement stirring. In both countries, Germany and Italy, there was one outstanding dominion which represented a modern trend and focussed the hopes of the youth of the land: in Italy, Piedmont, in Germany, Prussia. And it was, in fact, the leading statesmen of these two dominions, who, after the failure of the idealistic radicals, brought about unification; Cavour in Italy, and Bismarck in Germany. In both countries, the long national prostration and frustration, the belated entrance into the circle of the world powers where they were never quite accepted as equals, especially in regard to colonial possessions, created a deep inferiority complex which played a part in their later outbursts of ruthless violence.

These are the similarities. The differences, however, are far more important and fundamental. The origins of Italy and Germany, the significance of nationality in Italy and in Germany, and the character and the aims of Piedmont and Prussia, imply an essential difference which comes into strong relief in the two superficially similar movements of Fascism and National Socialism. The past of Italy counted two glorious epochs, the epoch of the Roman Empire and the epoch of the Renaissance city-nations—not to speak of the medieval Rome of the Papacy! Italy is the mother-country of Europe, and from the Roman Empire to the Renaissance, it has been the center of the world. It has brought forth three successive hegemonies, political, spiritual and cultural. So there seems to be no conceivable reason for an inferiority complex. All these hegemonies, however, did not overcome the ancient standard of the city-dominion, which was set by the metropolis, Rome. So the Renaissance dominions, such as Venice, Genoa, Florence and Milan, remained city-nations, regional nations, and only relatively late in the Renaissance a feeling of Italian political community arose. This city standard, which implied her regionalism, prevented Italy from being a match for the nations of the modern period, for Spain and France, that were compact, centralized, strong territorial powers. And when, after centuries of subjection to foreign rulers, the Italians attained unity, they were too weak and geographically too exposed to assume the full weight of a modern world power. Moreover, this naive people, that loved beauty and enjoyed life, lacked the hardness, the psychic long range indispensable for the maintenance of a dominant position in this modern industrial and technical world. This becomes quite clear in Mussolini's vain attempt to challenge the world with his people. Mussolini was a European power only as long as he was able to balance the scales between the antagonistic groups of European politics. As soon as he tipped them, this power was gone.

So Italian nationality meant the fusion of regional nationalities that had existed long before and that all traced back to Rome. The idea of Rome, the revival of her glory, dominated all the dreams of Italian unity. The great Italian movements were all revivals of a sacred past, of a beloved and revered tradition. The first was called Rinascimento, Renaissance, that is, rebirth; the second, which led to the unification, was named Risorgimento, which means resurrection, re-emergence. Its course led from a first, futile Roman republic, established after a revolt against the pope (1849) by the Italian and, at the same time, world patriot, Giuseppe Mazzini and the impulsive guerilla leader, Giuseppe Garibaldi, to the final conquest of Rome (1870) by the troops of the new kingdom of Italy, which needed this source and core of the country to complete and confirm its establishment. The movement proceeded by conspiracies of intellectuals, local uprisings, bold strokes and romantic guerilla warfare without any decisive effect, until the leadership was assumed by the government of one of the regional dominions, Piedmont, the only truly Italian-minded government, which was also the only one that had granted and retained a liberal constitution. Among the regions of Italy, Piedmont, paradoxically enough, was the least Italian in origin, just as Prussia, the leader to a united Germany, was the least German. The national initiative of Piedmont was connected with the rise to power of Count Camillo Cavour, a shrewd, clear-headed and practical man who combined a sincerely national and liberal disposition with Machiavellian strategy. Piedmont was a small country, far inferior to its Austrian adversary, upon whose expulsion from Italy the destiny of the nation hinged. Superior diplomacy was needed to carry the cause through partly luckless and partly indecisive military action to final success. Cavour used the intrigues of the French Emperor, Napoleon III, against Austria, and with the help of Napoleon lured Austria into war, much as Bismarck later provoked the war he wanted with Napoleon. With the support of France and with the help of perpetual uprisings and guerilla action in the other Italian dominions, carried out by Garibaldi and encouraged by England, the movement progressed and, after the situation had again become grave, owing to Austria's spectacular victories over the Piedmontese, suddenly the tide turned, and the liberation of Italy was decided in a different theater of war, through the defeat of Austria by Prussia in 1866. The two leading dominions, Prussia and Piedmont, had united in an alliance against Austria, and it was, in fact, Prussia that administered the last and decisive blow for the liberation and unification of Italy.

The character as well as the significance of German unification was essentially different. Germany had no hegemonial past, no political glory and political tradition. To be sure, the medieval German emperors had held a position of universal range, and the connection of German territories and German dynasties with the idea of the universal empire was something to be proud of. But this had been a universal empire, a Holy Roman Empire. There was no Germany in the Middle Ages, not even nominally. The Hapsburg

Emperor, Maximilian I, was the first to include the word "German" in the title of Roman Emperor and Roman Empire, at the end of the fifteenth century, when the universal glory of the empire was over, and when it had become a private Hapsburg possession. The medieval empire derived its glory from Roman and Christian authority. In itself, it was an anarchical, amorphous and practically powerless entity, with not even a core of national tradition, no national dynasty, no urban residential center, no national society or standard of life in the entire course of its history. So it is no wonder that the memory of the Middle Ages had completely died down in German minds and was only intellectually revived by romantic poetry at the beginning of the nineteenth century—in distinct contrast to Italy, where the Roman, Christian and Renaissance traditions were always alive among the people. German minds were filled with memories of the oppression and devastation of their country by domestic and foreign rulers throughout the modern era, and, on the other hand, with the pictures of centuries of French power and glory, of France dictating the fashions and setting the example for the whole world, by the splendor of her "ancien régime", by the fervor and impetus of her revolution, by the grandiose sweep of her Napoleonic adventure. And in the course of the nineteenth century, they watched the steady growth of the English colonial and commercial empire. They compared these two great examples, these two idols of their emulation and profound envy, France and England, with their own lack of everything, their lack of political power, of economic wealth, of cultural unity, of nationality. Hence arose that deep and intrinsic inferiority complex, that "have-not" complex of the German people, that inherent feeling of being fooled and cheated through the ages. Because of this, it has always been easy to fool them by exploiting this very feeling, by diverting anger at domestic affairs in the direction of those constantly and secretly admired and emulated foreign idols.

German nationality, then, had no roots in the past. It lay in the future, it was something to be achieved by hard work, by deliberate effort and collective endeavor. Accordingly, the German idea of nationality, which had first struck the people in the wars of liberation from Napoleon, fused with the idea of the state, with the task of a common, unified German state. Nationality was identical with state. This premise must be kept in mind in viewing German unification. For, from the outset, it pointed to the leadership of Prussia in the institution of German unity.

Among the many German principalities there were only two which had the prestige and the power to claim this leadership: Austria and Prussia. Austria, the dominion of Hapsburg, stood for the old idea of the empire, that is, for a pre-national, super-national idea, indeed, an anti-national idea, according to the general instinctive tendency of the Hapsburgs, who hated and dreaded national movements. As for Prussia, originally she had no nationality of her own, no nucleus of a future German nationality, nor any ambition or aspiration whatsoever to represent or further German nationality. Prussia was a pure-bred state, without any popular or ideological substance, a dynamic rotation of collective functions for the sake of building up power and nothing else. But in the course of events this soulless, functional unit was imbued with the national idea.

Frederick II set off the contest for power between Prussia and Austria in the Seven Years' War (1756–1763) and, by defeating Austria, secured for Prussia a position equal to that of the imperial power of the Hapsburgs. When Frederick died, the strength of the Hohenzollern family dwindled and its weakness made itself felt in a slackening of state discipline. An intellectual reaction set in. The country was stirred by the influence of the French Revolution, and by the rise of German literature and philosophy, which only then had reached their independence from foreign influences. It was the high-tide of ideas, movements and forces from the other German countries, and for a brief and brilliant period it appeared as if Prussia were borne along by the great democratic and humanitarian wave which was sweeping Germany. Freedom, humanity, spirit and history were the order of the day. These were the main themes of German literature and philosophy, which was more universal in trend than that of any other contemporary intelligentsia, as there was no common national sphere, no German national tradition from which this German intelligentsia could start. All the thoughts and systems of the German poets and thinkers were universal and abstract ideals which had no actual connection with the masses or with politics. The fundamental rift between intellectual and political leadership in Germany, to which we have already referred, was never overcome, and it had disastrous effects on German development. The periods of rising political power in Germany were always periods of extreme anti-intellectualism, of utter contempt for intellectual movements and the suppression of intellectual activities. Just the opposite was true in France and in England, where the periods of national supremacy marked a flowering of cultural and intellectual life. The struggle against Napoleon in the first decade of the nineteenth century was the only period when the great intellectual movements of Germany fused with the military and administrative ability of Prussia, when the ideals of universal freedom and humanity took shape in a political war of liberation. Great popular reforms were started in those days, and the Prussian minister Hardenberg proclaimed: "In this country we shall make a revolution from above."

After the deliverance from Napoleon, however, the intelligentsia split up into provincial currents and romantic conceptions, and the political leadership of Germany, the leadership into the so-called "second German Reich", was left to the Prussian Junkers, a class of boorish and stubborn landed proprietors, who still held their peasants in anachronistic serfdom, but who were trained in the military and economic spirit of this machine-like state. From this disciplinary training emerged Bismarck, the first brilliant and only successful statesman Germany ever produced. One may say that he was the only German statesman who compared with the great French and English statesmen—Richelieu, Pitt and Beaconsfield.

Characteristically, the first step toward German unity was not a political, but an economic move. It was the founding of the German "Zollverein" (customs union) which was started by Prussia in 1819. And after Bismarck had established Prussian supremacy over Austria once and for all in the war of 1866, after he had shown the superiority of the combined German military strength over the French, in the defeat of Napoleon III, in 1870, a superiority which could not be challenged from that time on, Bismarck in 1871 founded the German Reich, an association of German states— with the one exception of Austria—under the rulership of Prussia.

For the first time, Germany was united. Suddenly she had become a world power. She was ill prepared for the position she had reached so abruptly. For, though she was united, she was far from being a nation; she had no homogeneousness, no way of life of her own. She was only an agglomeration of provincial customs and regimes under the control of Prussian discipline. As a result, the new Germany confounded nationality with the acquisition of material power, with the functioning and aggrandizement of the state. She tried to offset her intrinsic weakness and instability by material power. She immediately began to compensate for her century-long inferiority and for her emulation of France and England. After Bismarck had been dismissed, in 1890, by the new German emperor, William II, who was the prototype of the upstart and thus the true representative of this empire, Germany herself behaved like a typical upstart. She became a rude intruder on every part of the already fragile world system, on the fairly settled and distributed world markets, where she thrust aside old competitors by her dumping methods, on the colonial continents, where she claimed her "place in the sun", and on the seas, where she displayed her ostentatious naval power. She began to build up huge industries as rapidly as possible. In short, this newly established empire threw its accumulated forces and its vehement vitality into varied projects and pursuits which bore the traces of the old Prussian combination of military and economic skill. It was all the more effective as it assimilated with, and incorporated its militaristic system in, the new industrial and technical procedures, which were especially adapted to its collective working spirit, and the new methods of world economy, which had been developed by the English democracies. Technical invention was taken up systematically and was to provide artificial substitutes for the lacking raw materials. "Ersatz"-inventions opened new fields, indeed a new dimension for industrial production. The combination of a disproportionately powerful army, which, as the First

World War revealed, exceeded the strength of all of Germany's neighbors, with a mighty navy and an aggressively expanding industry, this combined challenge of the respective supremacies of various nations, constituted a threat of unlimited scope. So it is no wonder that Germany disturbed the all-too-delicate balance of power and the no less delicate system of world economy, and aroused fear and resentment among the European nations. But what the German Empire inaugurated in this period was still done with a kind of naïveté. The empire as a whole did not achieve complete coordination of its forces before the First World War. The principles of the old Prussian state in conjunction with modern industrial and technical developments, the grafting of one collectivity upon the other, all this was merely foreshadowed in the pre-world-war Reich.

The other elementary force which threatened the system of the bourgeoisie and arrayed itself against the state and the bourgeois democracy was the *labor class* and the *socialist movement*. Since the rise of Christianity, there have been repeated attempts to bring about an equal distribution of property and happiness among men, and the teachings of Jesus, as well as the example of the early Christian community, were a lasting stimulus to such efforts. The heretic movements in the Middle Ages, the German peasants, the Anabaptists, the Levellers of the English Revolution, all these groups aimed at a just and equal distribution of goods. But two reasons prevented these groups from developing into steady and organized social movements. First, there was the matter of religious motivation, which made them seek personal salvation, which made them expect and rely upon an act of God—the advent of the Day of Judgment and the millennium—and, consequently, let them consider their movement in the light of a preparation. It was only when the Christian faith had lost its power, when oppressed men faced a wholly worldly and completely hopeless situation, that they collected their strength to seek help for themselves and for their future generations on earth. Secondly, working conditions in previous ages were still individual. The peasants, the journeymen of the fifteenth century, the poor dependent weavers of the so-called "domestic" or "putting-out" system, were still doing individual work, work that could be performed from start to finish by a single person and without mechanical substitutes for manpower. The mining industry was the first to develop collective work, and in fact, the miners of the fifteenth and sixteenth centuries were the first about whom conditions and reactions similar to those of modern workers are reported—separation of capital and labor, division of labor, migrations and insecurity of existence, sweat system, truck system and, on the other hand, armed uprisings. These miners, however, worked in remote sections of the country, far from cities and from other mining settlements, and such industries, moreover, were not very numerous in those times. So the movements of these workers had a very limited range. Another industry to develop capitalistic conditions, such as "putting-out" system and factory, and to show the beginnings of division of labor, was the textile industry, which was located in cities and thus favored the accumulation and union of workers. But from the technical point of view it was far less developed than the mining industry, and, up to the eighteenth century, the tools with which the work was performed did not require collective cooperation. Only with the beginning of the machine age, when collective work and mechanically combined work was put into effect, and the new labor discipline where "men, women and children were yoked together with iron and steam and the animal machine was chained fast to the iron machine which knows no suffering and no weariness", only then did a steady labor movement get under way. Workers were taught mass existence and mass action, organized action, by their very work.

There are three main stages of this growing movement, which, of course, interlock: the fight against mechanization, the fight against legislation which failed to protect the workers and yet denied them the right to an effective, that is, collective self-protection, and the fight against the social order of bourgeois society as such and as a whole, the true class war. In the first stage, which occurred mainly in England, the machine and the working class, the modern proletariat, created each other. The machine was the rival, the torturer, the ruin of the worker. It exercised constant pressure upon him, it threatened his very existence. So the first reaction of the bewildered and desperate masses was the fight against the machine. The period from the 1770's to the 1830's was filled with riots in which the workers destroyed the machines and burned the factories. In 1811, the destruction of machines was made punishable by death in England, to little or no effect. The second step was the fight for the legal recognition of the rights of labor. This was still a struggle for the position of the workers within the established system of bourgeois society. The movement started with petitions of English workers to restore the former guild regulations, the old Elizabethan labor code, which was, of course, an absurd suggestion under the new industrial conditions and only shows the complete confusion of the working people. Only gradually the proper method of defense became clear: trade unions and cooperative societies developed, and the right of forming combinations, of collective bargaining and strike was conquered. This phase is characterized by the English and American labor movement, which is mainly an economic and trade, not a political or social movement. The entrepreneurs, and the legislation they influenced, made it as difficult as possible for this movement to develop. Again and again, the law courts tried to waylay the legal recognition of the trade unions in England through hairsplitting sophistries, by declaring, for instance, that unions were, to be sure, "not criminal, but illegal", that their agreements had no binding force and that their officers could use the funds of their organizations ad libitum. Although the English unions expanded tremendously, attempts to suppress them through court judgments extended to the year 1913. The resistance that the not yet fully developed union movement is encountering in America is sufficiently well known. But in these countries of liberal and individualistic democracy, where, up to the First World War, economic expansion and the rivalry of the two great parties produced steady alleviation of the conditions of labor, in these countries, the forms and aims of labor organization were, until recently, primarily intended as a safeguard of equal opportunities for worker and entrepreneur.

Intermediary between the second and the third stage, between a mere labor and a socialist movement, was the movement of the English Chartists from 1837 to 1848, the first organized, socialistic and consciously proletarian action. Its aims were a limitation of the working-day and the right of the worker to enjoy the full fruits of his labors, that Marxian surplus value which is unjustly reaped by the entrepreneur. The antagonism of capital and labor was already clear in this movement, and the government, the "ruling class", was identified with the capitalist class. The concrete goal of the Chartists, however, was merely a political charter, which was planned along the lines of bourgeois democracy, and comprised parliamentary reform, universal suffrage, secret vote and equal electoral districts. The fundamental difference between capitalism and socialism as entire social systems, social orders, was not as yet realized. This distinction, with all its implications, is the basic feature of the actual socialist movement in its various national and ideological versions.

The socialist movement aims at the establishment of a completely new and radically different social order, a "classless society" in which the individual has not only a nominally equal start or equal opportunity, as in the capitalistic democracy, but an equal share of the collective produce, a living wage guaranteed to every worker. In the socialist system, this can be effected only through making collective the means and materials for production. The socialistic doctrine removes the last remnant of the old political order of the world. It uncovers the economic character of the modern world, which the bourgeois democracy had concealed under the superstructure of its political constitution. The political freedom and equality that the lower strata had won in desperate struggles proved worthless, since it had already been superseded by worse economic dependencies. Therefore, the socialists tried to prove that the emphasis of modern life lay in the economic conditions, and that political conflicts and forms of government were nothing but a deceptive façade. They believed that the task of government consisted merely in the regulation of economic processes that the bourgeois democracy had left completely to themselves. Government becomes synonymous with economic and social control. But every act of such a government, of such control, must, of necessity, encroach upon the individual's free disposal of goods and of capital and thus, in the final analysis, on the sacred bourgeois concept of personal property. And this property, in all its gradations from the free right to its use down to its very substance and existence, is the main issue of the furious struggle between bourgeoisie and proletariat, between capital and labor, between individualistic and socialistic forces; it is the issue that underlies the present crisis. To the incomplete collectives of the democracy and the state, the socialist movement opposes the idea of a third, integral collective, of an order in the sense of and for the purpose of a common, equally distributed welfare.

Much time had to elapse, and many grave theoretical and practical struggles had to take place, before this idea could evolve in crystal clarity. Modern socialism is an extensive movement of many different layers and branches, and it is very naive to identify it with Marxism, as is frequently the case. For two centuries, men of all nations, generations and classes worked at it, and all of its elements were already in existence when Karl Marx appeared and synthesized them in his system. When one considers the history of this movement, one sees how it necessarily developed from the historical conditions, yes, from the theoretical and practical preparations of the opposite movement, economic liberalism. Socialism was at first an intellectual movement. Very gradually its theories and tenets had to be forced upon a helpless and dull proletariat. Only two of the important socialist leaders really belonged to the proletariat: Babeuf and Weitling. All the others hailed from higher social levels: Saint-Simon was a French count, Robert Owen, an industrialist, Thompson, an Irish landowner, Hodgskin, a naval officer, Hall, a physician, Cabet, a lawyer, Proudhon, a petty bourgeois and Rodbertus, Fourier, Marx and Lassalle came from well-to-do, middle-class families. Only two among these were Jews: Marx and Lassalle. And so one cannot trace this movement back to either social or ethnic backgrounds of its originators.

The early socialists were rationalists, true children of the period of enlightenment. They did, indeed, investigate the reasons for existing economic and social evils, they were, occasionally, well aware of the deep rift between the classes, but just as they believed that the original conditions of mankind had been ideal and only corrupted by civilization, so they expected an ideal end-condition as a result of the education of man, and a change of heart among the ruling classes. They appealed to kings, ministers, industrialists. They planned communistic, Utopian communities like those outlined by their predecessors, Campanella, Harrington and Thomas More, whose ideal state, Utopia, furnished the name for such imagined perfection. These dreamed-of communities would—so they thought—come out of the "social experiment". Robert Owen, the only one who had sufficient funds for the attempt, made such an experiment by establishing a communistic settlement, "New Harmony", in Indiana, but this collapsed because of the social disparity and human insufficiency of its members. The rationalistic, unhistorical way of thinking of the early socialists caused them to see only an unfortunate episode in the development of industry. And so they sought the salvation of humanity in a return to nature, and the communistic settlements they planned had a predominantly agrarian character.

The man who took the decisive step toward modern socialism, was Claude Henry de Saint-Simon (1760–1825). He was the first to combine the basic elements of the socialist doctrine of today: the realistic and historical survey of social processes; the recognition that economy is the most important factor in public life and that politics are a secondary function; the economic or materialistic view of history, and the derivation of all social organization from the law of property; the interpretation of historical processes as a series of class struggles; the realization of the irrevocable significance of the industrial revolution, and the conception of socialism as a world movement conditioned by industrial development. Saint-Simon observed that the political constitution of France had changed ten times in twenty-five years without any resulting

change in the economic conditions that determine human existence. From this he concluded that political processes are futile and
non-essential. The analysis of his epoch led him to the recognition
that political progress is always the result of economic progress.
He even claimed that the metaphysics of the eighteenth century
were dictated by the interests of the new economic order. The
interests of the industrialists, so he says in his "Système Industriel",
were always defended by lawyers and metaphysicians. Accordingly,
he found that the point of departure for all social order was property: "Those laws that determine property are the most important
of all; they serve as the foundation for the social edifice." But property is not stable. It is subject to change and to development, and
so, to protect property in its old form can only be destructive. "Individual property rights can only be based on the common and
general utility of the exercise of these rights, and this utility can
vary according to the times." In modern times, the fundamental
change is the development of industry.

The concept of industry is the key to Saint-Simon's doctrine. It
reflects the transition from early to modern socialism. Saint-Simon
was still under the impression of the first class struggle between
bourgeois and feudal forces that played the leading role in his
epoch and did not end during his lifetime. But looming behind the
first, he already saw the second great class struggle between the
bourgeoisie and the proletariat. In the first class struggle, he took
sides with the bourgeoisie against the nobility, in the second, with
the workers against the employers. That is why his concept of
industry fluctuates between the two meanings of the word industry.
Sometimes he interprets it in the wider sense of all production in
contrast to the parasitic idleness of the nobility, and fills it with all
the enthusiasm of progressive spirits for the new attainments of
the natural sciences and of technology. But sometimes he uses it
in the narrower sense of mechanized industry. In the first sense,
industry signifies the sum of all those activities that further production for the welfare of the community, not only industry, but
agriculture, trade, science and art. This interpretation resulted from
the experience that natural science promoted and served indus-

try. Scholars are "industriels de théorie"—theoretical industrialists —while the material producers are "savants d'application"—experts in the application of science. The intervening links are the engineers. But equal in social value to the employers and intellectuals are the working masses, "les hommes les moins instruits et les plus pauvres"—the least educated and the poorest—who constitute the major part of the makers of the new civilization. In this sense, entire nations are nothing but great industrial units and, as such, they should be organized into industrial associations that could then be fused in a general economic system in which everyone would feel that he was a member of a company of workers. Industry, says Saint-Simon, has taken possession of every field of life, even of war. Industry, not armies, constitute the primary strength of a country, and rivalries are no longer military but industrial in character. Therefore, economic government shall take the place of political government, and the management of projects in the interest of the community shall supersede the domination of men. Political freedom, won through the revolution, is nothing but an abstract manner of speaking; it did not bring true, social freedom; it set, it did not solve, the social problem. It performed a valuable service, just as the bourgeoisie fulfilled a great historic mission by winning this freedom. But it was only a step, a stage in development. Neither the political nor the economic freedom of the individual nor the protection of personal property can be the ultimate goal of the community of mankind, but an association of production and producers that serves the interests of the majority not of a minority, and where, without consideration of birth, rank, or wealth, those who accomplish most for the welfare of all shall come first. In this conception, the community is already based on work and workers. The ideal of a classless society is given. Liberalism is characterized as a system of boundless egoism that must be overcome, and the exploitation of workers by employers is ruthlessly exposed. But even Saint-Simon cannot as yet imagine his social order under any but industrial leadership. And to the industrialists, as the leaders of a new form of society, he directs his appeal to organize for the welfare of humanity: "Industrialists of all countries, unite!" The industrialists of all countries did indeed unite—but for other purposes. And Karl Marx transferred the battle-cry to the proletariat.

Those who came after Saint-Simon soon relinquished the illusion concerning a change of heart in the industrialists and the hope that they would lead men to a new order. Pecqueur considers the class struggle of the proletariat and the bourgeoisie an inevitable fact: "Proletarians must expect their real enfranchisement from themselves alone!" Bazard and Rodbertus firmly believe that the new socialistic organization of society can only take place through the socialization of the means of production. They prove that the concentration of the means of production and of capital in increasingly large enterprises prepares the way for this socialization, and that the carrying out of the capitalistic principle to extremes forces the change to socialism. "This matter of operating on a large scale, with heavy capital and a great number of workers in one and the same place, is a question of to be or not to be, for the machines . . . this new method of production constitutes a revolution that is industrial, moral and political, all in one."

All the ingredients that go to make up Marxism were, therefore, already at hand; from William Petty on, the doctrine of free trade recognized labor as the chief factor in national economy. Thompson, Hodgskin and the Chartists developed this theory in a way to serve the labor movement, by introducing the doctrine of surplus value which the employers withhold from the workers. The criticism of capitalism and of the exploitation of labor had reached a climax even before Karl Marx. The school of Saint-Simon and the followers of other socialist trends had already discovered that economy held a dominant position in modern society, that all fields and functions of public life, even of intellectual life, were dependent on economic interests. They had come to derive social and historical developments from property and the changes in property. They were familiar with the idea of class separation and class struggle, with the law of the concentration and accumulation of capital, with the realization that the capitalistic principle, carried to extremes, begets the germs of socialism, and with the demand for the socialization of the means of production. The idea of social revolution had been preached by Babeuf, Proudhon and the German, Weitling. Thus the work of Karl Marx is, in the main, the analysis and the résumé of all these trends, in a logical system that he developed through controversy with the various doctrines of his predecessors and with Hegel's philosophy, from which he took over as much as he rejected. This system is magnificently formulated in his book, "Capital".

The views of Karl Marx contain many sociological, psychological and historical errors. The materialistic interpretation of history is untenable. His assumption that socialism could only proceed from a fully developed capitalistic economy has proven false. The only country in which it has come into its own, up to now, was capitalistically undeveloped Russia, and it did so precisely because of the retarded development of capitalism and certain national characteristics that cannot be entirely explained from a materialistic point of view. This point of view also prevented Marx from recognizing the tremendous force that irrational elements—traditions, national customs, sentimental values and metaphysical needs—exert on the souls of masses and of peoples. Such residues have determined the attitude and state of mind of the petty bourgeoisie, and in this, not only the middle class is included, but vast strata of workers who are connected with the employer stratum in feeling. The petty bourgeoisie are an important class of their own in social development, and they have influenced this development differently from the way Marx anticipated. Without their power, national socialism would have been impossible. All such errors must be attributed to the period in which Karl Marx grew up. There is no one who can remove himself entirely from the specific intellectual atmosphere of his epoch. But there is enough that Marx predicted correctly.

In his theory there is one inconsistency which became extremely important; it concerns the way in which the socialistic order is to be established. Marx fluctuates between an evolutionary and a revolutionary method, and the two subsequent branches of his movement, the reform branch in Germany and the revolutionary branch in Russia, were both justified in claiming him for their authority. On the one hand, Marx was convinced that the economic process inevitably ends in socialism. This conviction was the basis for German social democracy, that tried to bring about a socialistic order by peaceful and regulated means, that laboriously schooled the mass of workers in the lore of party and union and fought for the gradual improvement of their living conditions. On the other hand, Marx proposed the axiom that no ruling class voluntarily renounces its power, that the proletariat, therefore, must fight to gain and to maintain power. This means revolution and "dictatorship of the proletariat", an idea derived from the Reign of Terror of the French Revolution. And with all his profound historical and sociological insight, he did not shrink from expecting the impetus to the overthrow of the old order, in favor of socialism, to come from the insignificant, isolated proletarian offshoots of the bourgeois revolutions of the nineteenth century. He was fascinated by the economic process, and did not gauge the moral, psychic and intellectual dimensions, the total and generally human scope of the violent change that was preparing. In spite of the deliberately international plan of his movement, he could not, at that time, realize the universal character of the world of today. He did not realize the terrible difficulties implied in the fact that in this world a new social order cannot be limited to an individual country, not so much because such a country is surrounded by other, hostile countries, but because it is dependent upon these other countries to a hitherto unheard-of extent, because isolation is no longer possible in our era.

The character of revolution has changed very much in the course of time. The uprisings of the Renaissance were local conflicts between families and persons. The Dutch and American Revolutions were national struggles for liberation from outside powers. The first universal revolution was the Reformation, for it was founded on an ideology that implied generally valid, political consequences. It affected the actions of peasants, burghers and nobles. But these various social strata exploited it in diverse and particular ways. The peasant wars, the Huguenot struggles, the Dutch and

English Revolutions, are very different from one another, although the religious component is common to them all. The type, the model revolution of modern times, was the French Revolution: it was purely political; it was founded on a profane ideology; it was the first to develop the characteristics of a modern mass movement, demagogy, terror and propaganda. It was the first unambiguously universal revolution, and the series of revolutions that it begot successively in the various countries of Europe are all propelled by the same social forces and have the same aims. The effect upon its opponents bears witness to the power of its ideas and to its ability to make converts. Edmund Burke writes in 1791: "There have been many internal revolutions in the government of countries, both as to persons and to forms, in which the neighboring states have little or no concern. Whatever the government might be with respect to those persons and those forms, the stationary interests of the nation concerned have most commonly influenced the new governments in the same manner in which they influenced the old; and the revolution turning on matters of local grievance, or of local accommodations, did not extend beyond its territory. The present revolution in France seems to me to be quite of another character . . . and to bear little resemblance or analogy to any of those which have been brought about in Europe . . . It is a revolution of doctrine and theoretic dogma . . . This system . . . makes France the natural head of all factions formed on a similar principle wherever they may prevail . . . The seeds are sown almost everywhere, chiefly by newspaper circulations, infinitely more efficacious and extensive than ever they were . . . To what lengths this method of circulating mutinous manifestoes, and of keeping emissaries of sedition in every court under the name of ambassadors, to propagate the same principles and to follow the practices, will go . . . it is hard to say—but go on it will—more or less rapidly, according to events and to the humour of the time."

The French Revolution, however, was purely political and not social. It fought for political protection and for recognition of an economic condition that had developed spontaneously and chaotically and that already had a subterranean kind of existence; it fought for the power of capital. It was, therefore, relatively limited in its aims and in its effects upon humanity. Theoretically, it created opportunities for all, but provided no practical guaranties. It did not touch the roots of living. The social revolution goes much further—it includes man as a whole. It wishes to give him security but also to bring him under its control. It does not favor a development growing freely and at will; it wishes to establish its own, well-planned order.

In the wake of the English and French Revolutions, there had already been social movements, such as the Levellers, the ideas of Marat and Babeuf and the brief proletarian revolt of the silk weavers of Lyon. But social ideas were only weak undercurrents in these primarily bourgeois revolutions with pronounced capitalistic aims. Article 2 of the constitution of 1793 declared that the rights of man were "Égalité, Liberté, Sureté et Propriété"—equality, liberty, security and property. The same is true of the European revolutions of 1830 and 1848, that only completed the movement of 1789 and 1793 and defended it against attempts to restore the feudal regime. In these uprisings, the bourgeoisie, to be sure, already used the working class in its struggles against the monarchy. In 1830, the French industrialists closed their factories and sent their workers to the barricades. Two years later, these same industrialists, in their capacity of national guards, shot these workmen when they attempted a revolt of their own. When the bourgeoisie had become the unchallenged ruling class everywhere, when the labor movement had been organized and permeated with socialistic doctrines, only then, revolutions assumed the character of social upheavals. But this development did not take place until after the First World War, and the Russians were the first to organize a true and total social revolution. This was also the last true revolution, in the sense that it was voluntary mass action, and it could only succeed under the specific conditions of the vast, isolated country of Russia, with its primitive society. But even this Russian Revolution was dependent upon a world revolution that never took place. The confusion and complexity of social conditions and currents after the First World War, the difference in position and feeling between the

workers in victorious and conquered countries prevented a timing
of revolutionary movements. Unemployment robbed the workers
of their strongest weapon, the general strike. The technical development of the modern warfare apparatus has made impossible the
seizure of power through a coup de main. And the sluggish weight
of the petty bourgeoisie who cling to property, to their habits of
thinking and living, was an overwhelming hindrance to so radical
an upheaval as a social revolution. Even national socialism could
come into power only through the fiction of legality and the deliberate deception of the petty burgher.

Instead of the impossible world revolution, something else, that
had been preparing for a long time, developed: the world itself,
its material conditions, its psychic, moral and intellectual foundations had grown into a gigantic revolutionary turmoil, the convulsive movements of which had swelled beyond the mastery of
man. The revolution has passed from the will of man to objective
events. Man is no more the subject, he has become the object of the
revolution. In order to realize and to control this inhuman change,
all people in all countries must return to the awareness of man
himself, to the human being in man from which we have drifted
farther and farther away within the past centuries. There is a
proverb to the effect that when need is greatest, God is nearest.
This is an old, devout version of the profound truth that matters
must be driven to extremes before a reversal can take place.

The driving to extremes began early in the twentieth century.
There was peace. Among the great European powers there was
apparently more real and lasting peace than there had been from
time immemorial, a peace of half a century, in fact, from 1870 to
1912, if we take the Balkan Wars as the match to the great conflagration. A whole generation could neither remember nor imagine
a European war. War came to be considered as a somewhat exotic,
romantic affair, which happened somewhere in colonies, in remote
uncivilized regions, or in a heroic past. Never had war been farther
from imagination, never nearer to the nerves. It was like the atmospheric tension before a thunderstorm. All events had become

international, and consequently the economic system was most fragile and unstable. Business men, employees, workers everywhere were at the mercy of a change of fashion in Paris, the bankruptcy of a firm in Vienna or Amsterdam, troubles in South Africa, too rapid expansion or production of this or that. In the great economic crises of 1857 and 1873, the interdependence of peoples became clear for the first time. Though they were confined to the economic field, they were both world crises. They revealed the extent to which the new situation had grown beyond human control, the discrepancy between a claim to unlimited freedom of action for individuals and for nations and the subterranean interweaving of their destinies. Overproduction and overspeculation, the chief causes of these crises, might have passed as mere errors in tempo and individual calculation; and the crises themselves, although they took a heavy toll, blew over. But they indicated the doom toward which humanity was steering; and the stock market panics of the nineteenth century were heralds of a general world panic to come. Nobody wanted to believe in the possibility of a large-scale war, but everybody felt that the slightest incident would launch a catastrophe of immeasurable dimensions. So it is futile to dwell on any single event which led to this catastrophe. Anything could have served to unleash it, and the political conflict was, indeed, only an introduction. It began as a normal war, a political war between two groups of powers. Both supposed that they could conclude it in the old way, by military decision. Up to the Battle of the Marne, it still appeared as a normal war based on national alliances. But soon it changed its character and developed step by step into that gigantic civil war of humanity in which we are still involved today, into the struggle for a new world order.

UNIVERSAL CIVIL WAR

AT THE END OF THE nineteenth century, the bourgeoisie had attained predominance. Geographically, further advance was impossible. There were no more colonial frontiers. The most productive territories of the earth had been occupied, the raw materials, the markets divided up. The system of world economy, international business, was established. At the very moment, however, that this system was stabilized, it was threatened by two new and vigorous movements: the intrusion of belatedly unified Germany, and the rise of organized labor and international socialism. So, on the one hand, international capitalism began to reach the limits of its expansion and, on the other, to feel the pressure of new, contesting forces. Three different kinds of collectivity began to challenge the principle of free individual competition: the intangible, ghostly collectivity of international interrelations and interdependence that had developed as a corollary of capitalistic expansion itself; the equally impalpable collectivity of the militaristic Prusso-German state, which devoted the disciplined functioning of its forces to an abstract moloch of power; and the integrally collectivistic order of international socialism. All this formed at the start of our century, but it was not fully apparent before the First World War, that tore the veil from the European scene and laid open the intrinsic conflicts of the modern world.

In many respects, the *First World War* showed completely novel phenomena. It was the first universal war, it was the first total war and it was the first revolutionary war—this does not mean that it either originated from or led to a revolution; the war in itself was a revolution.

It was the first universal war: all previous wars, even the greatest cataclysms of former times, had been localized happenings or, at most, agglomerations of local conflicts. There were always whole countries and peoples that were not affected by them. The war of 1914 was the first to draw the great powers of the entire globe into its orbit. No country could escape its direct or indirect impact. It demonstrated the far-reaching political consequences of the economic interweaving of the world, it reflected that special interdependence which was a result of world economy and world technics. And so it assumed the character of an elemental catastrophe which could no longer be controlled by the power of man. It outgrew the capacity of any single, personal or national rulership.

The World War was, moreover, the first total war, as it revealed and increased not only the international interrelation of peoples and events but a still more important interrelation within nations, which penetrated the very body of human society, an entirely new variety of intersocial relation within the state. In former times, even the greatest military conflict could remain a purely political and military matter, by which large portions of the population were only remotely and indirectly affected. The World War projected modern factory work, the functional interlocking of men and machines, into warfare, into the battle as such, and into the conduct of the war as a whole. It was only natural that this procedure was brought to its utmost perfection and precision in Germany, which was especially predestined and prepared for it by the militaristic, bureaucratic and labor discipline of the Prussian state. For the first time, the interconnection of men and machinery, created by modern industrial work and fully developed by capitalistic economy, was put under the despotic command of a government. Total war engendered the total state.

Not until the tremendous apparatus of destruction built up by the armies of modern civilization was set in motion, did it become apparent to what extent the human being had become mechanized and the masses interlocked. Through the system of perpetual invention, that worked behind the front in factories and scientific institutions, the technics of war materials and the techniques of warfare developed more rapidly and changed more radically in this than in any other previous war. The closed fronts of permanent trenches were the basis of the new warfare, and on this basis, through the combination of air, tank, gas, and mine warfare and massed artillery, the gigantic modern battle unfolded in all directions and far into the "hinterland". For this battle the Germans found the characteristic name of "Materialschlacht", that is, a battle of matériel. In this kind of battle, men are chained to machines in punctiliously geared, collective operations of which no single individual can see the whole, operations from which there is no escape and in which men are, in fact, no more than matériel. Machines, indeed, outweighed men, and the masses outweighed the individual. This modern battle of matériel is a living symbol of the social process which the entire political body evolved during and, more especially, after the war. For the first time, war caught up the entire people, of whose civil life and civilization scarcely anything remained. The reserves of military conscription were exhausted to the last, women were drawn into public service as substitutes, the whole economy was directed only toward war. The origin of all present planned economy lies in the organization of the raw material supply in Germany which was the work of the German industrialist, Walther Rathenau, later minister of foreign affairs. A German author, Ernst Juenger, who prophesied the total state of the Nazis, gave a most accurate description of this development: "So the picture of war as a military action merges more and more with the wider picture of a gigantic industrial procedure. Beside the armies that meet on the battlefield, arise the new armies engaged in communications, foodstuffs, armaments—the array of industry as a whole. In the last phase, there is not a motion, not even that of a woman working at home at her sewing machine, in which, at least indirectly, a military application does not inhere . . ."

The war of 1914 was, finally, the first revolutionary war. By virtue of its universality and totality, it involved every sphere of human life, social, moral and psychic, and began to recast the whole of human civilization. And more than that: it touched on the fundamentals of war as such, and, in going to extremes, it carried the whole concept of war in itself to the point of absurdity. By invalidating and discrediting the principle of war, it implied invalidation of the principle of power politics, of politics in the genuine sense of the word. For, when we reject and disclaim war, we have to give up power politics and national rivalries, that is, unlimited, uncontrolled competition for power. We have to give up gambling with a "balance of power" and all the antiquated intrigues and paraphernalia of international relations of the last centuries. We must even give up the principle of unrestricted national sovereignty. For power politics are based on the assumption that war is the last resort, and are ineffectual without this assumption. The Western nations did not want war after 1918. Their peoples were utterly through with war. But their governments continued the same old game within the "League of Nations" and without; they had neither the courage nor the determination to change the whole concept and the whole system. They carried on with the same policy of balance of power as before, but without the firm resolve to go to war if necessary. So they merely invited aggression and, finally, were compelled to take up arms again—too late and utterly unprepared.

This half-heartedness, the intrinsic weariness and bad conscience about war as such, on the part of the Western nations, is one of the revolutionary consequences of the First World War. The likewise revolutionary effect on the aggressors was to make them drop the last pretense, the last faint appearance of lawful, civilized proceedings, and openly profess the criminality which has always loomed in power politics. The aggressor no longer behaved as a respectable partner in a hypocritically implied system of rivalry; he no longer respected any rules of the game. He discarded the last shreds of agreement and system. Besides, not even the aggressors, in spite of their total education and preparation for war, really wanted war. They intended to do successful blackmailing and to carry out a ninety per cent safe conquest of inferior powers, by threat alone. They, too, at last found themselves lured into an apocalyptic struggle.

So, as a result of that revolutionary world conflagration, war has become decidedly illegitimate, once and for all. This implies the ultimate, most important consequence: war changed its fundamental character. It turned from a vertical into a horizontal war, that is to say, from a political, external war, a war between nations, into a social, internal war, a civil war of humanity, a war passing through all peoples, irrespective of borderlines or front lines, a war between the old forces of anarchic self-interest, greed, and will-to-power, and the forces of human solidarity, human unity and fraternity. This is why the fifth column has assumed so prominent a part in present warfare. Every country has its own, natural fifth columnists. They need not be in communication with the enemy; they agree with him by their very nature and tendency. In all occupied countries there were Fascists in all layers of the population, and in the highest positions—as became sufficiently evident—and in all allied. countries there are Fascists; while, on the other hand, there are people of our political beliefs in the Axis countries, only that fifth columnists in Hitler's Germany have a less pleasant time than those in the democracies.

This development began with the First World War. In the contending armies of both sides, a common, almost brotherly feeling had gradually sprung up. There was a silent, embittered conspiracy of men in whom identical experiences of almost unbearable gravity had melted away all the superficial layers of nationality, class and individuality, down to the ultimate core of man's being. There was a common rebellion of these men against the slogans of chauvinism, and a feeling of how futile and how mad all struggle for power had become in the face of the reality of this mechanized extermination. So penetrating a feeling of human solidarity had never before taken hold of mankind. And on both fronts a resolve took shape: that this must not happen again, that a new and better order was at stake, that this was a war to end war, that the peoples themselves must take their fate into their own hands and establish their common rights in a constitution above and beyond the purely national. The young German painter, Franz Marc, who was killed in action in 1916, wrote early in 1915: "We, in the field of battle, feel most deeply that these gruesome months will not mean a mere shifting of political powers, but that the blood that has been shed will represent an offering made in a profound communion of all peoples for the sake of a common goal . . . Boundaries shall not be set anew, but broken down . . . Let us remain soldiers even after the war . . . for this is not a war against an external enemy, as the newspapers and our honored politicians say, nor . . . of one race against another; it is a European civil war, a war against the inner invisible enemy of the European spirit."

This great human solidarity, that then appeared for the first time, could not maintain itself after the war. But in order to understand the events that followed, we must consider the first immediate result of the war: the Russian Revolution.

Up to the nineteenth century, the history of *Russia* was the history of dynasties and governments rather than the history of a people. It was, moreover, a remote, self-centered history, connected with the outer world merely by territorial friction. The princes of the Moscow region had subjected the originally powerful landed nobility as well as the originally free peasantry more oppressively than was the case anywhere else. In a crude and simplified feudal system, the landed proprietors became servants of the Tsar, forced to perform military and administrative duties, and the peasants, in turn, became serfs of the landed proprietors in order to provide manpower for military service and agricultural labor. Thus all classes of the population were to serve. Under the ruthlessly despotic and bureaucratic regime of the Tsars trade and industry could not develop freely, and only in the course of the nineteenth century a clear-cut bourgeoisie took shape between the great classes of the landed, military or bureaucratic nobility and the peasants. Throughout the centuries, there were continuous, ineffectual revolts on the part of the enslaved peasants. The two outstanding Tsars, Ivan the Terrible in the sixteenth, and Peter the Great (founder of Petersburg-Leningrad) in the eighteenth century, made repeated attempts to introduce European institutions and to establish connections with the West, but it was only after the French Revolution and the Russian campaign of Napoleon that European influence became really effective. The young noblemen who went to France with the army brought home the ideas of the French Revolution, and it was the young officers of the Guards who, in December 1825, started the first revolt with a general program of social and political reforms: abolishment of serfdom, constitutional and even republican democracy. This movement of the so-called Dekabrists (from dekabr, December) was crushed, but immediately in its wake followed the first brilliant period of Russian literature and the formation of an intelligentsia who worked underground for radical reforms and prepared a public opinion which, after the Russian defeat in the War of the Crimea (1855) at Sevastopol, was strong enough to enforce the liberation of the peasants. This campaign had demonstrated the backwardness and economic weakness of the country, the lack of industry and of means of transportation. The government realized that something had to be done, but action was slow and hampered by relapses into the old despotic attitude on the part of the Tsars and the nobility. Industrialization, however, was promoted, and, together with the bourgeoisie, the working class, the proletariat, developed. The revolutionary movement that permeates all of Russian history, and now had found a mouthpiece in Russian literature, was represented by various parties. The oldest, which fought the first battles through individual, terroristic acts, was the party of the "liberty of the people" ("narodnaya volya"), later called the Social-Revolutionary Party. This party made a strong plea for the peasants who still formed the bulk of the population, and advanced an agrarian communism similar to that of the German peasants at the end of the Middle Ages and to that of the Anabaptists: socialization of all private and government estates, and collective cultivation and management by the peasants.

This was, of course, a party of intellectuals. The peasants themselves were illiterate and too benumbed by century-old slavery to express themselves. But though this movement was first carried by intellectuals, it had its roots in the mentality and the impulses of the peasantry. It derived from the primitive "communism" of the ancient Slav community, the "Mir", the spirit and the customs of which were still alive among the peasants. But it is also traceable to religious sources, to the specific mystical, "apocalyptic" Christianity of the Russian people, who, apart from the influence of their powerful and corrupt official Byzantine Church, headed by the Tsar, were held in a state of continuous, Messianic expectation through their popular saints and monks. "Russia, Old Russia, is the Russian monk", so writes Th. G. Masaryk, the founder of the Czechoslovak Republic, in his book, "The Spirit of Russia". "Russia has preserved the childhood of Europe; in the overwhelming mass of its peasant population it represents Christian medievalism ..."

In no country but Russia is there so spontaneous and instinctive a relationship between the intelligentsia and the mass of the people.

The inspiration and the power of the Russian poets flows from the people and from the deep love they bear to them. Dostoievsky dates the birth of Russian literature from Pushkin's "return to the people". "We must bow down before the people", he says, "for from them everything will come to us: our thoughts and our images..." The people merges with the earth, but not in the German, reactionary and racial sense of "Blood and Soil". In Russia, the earth means the immensity, the timelessness and the future of the continent and the people, the groundwork of all humanity. The peasants are the Russian people, and this mass of people, held in bondage and suffering through centuries, also represent Christianity. They are the "bearers of the Lord". For Christianity, beyond all dogma and ritual, is fused with their very being, and that penetration of the human soul by Christ, that was taught in Europe by intellectual mysticism—especially by German mysticism—occurred in Russia as an anonymous, natural process. "Christ roams through the country in the guise of a beggar", says Dostoievsky. This means that poor, tormented and sinful man becomes Christ—the more sinful, the sooner. In the "Brothers Karamazov", the monks say of the holy Sossima "that he is more devoted to the sinful, and most of all to the most sinful." From the criminal to the saint, from nihilistic anarchy, from the nothingness through which Russian man must pass, to the harmony of the Kingdom of God is only a very small step. "We have nihilism, because we are all nihilists" (Dostoievsky). It is from this point of view that we must read the great books of Dostoievsky and Tolstoi, which are all built around crime and sin.

This almost anonymous Christianity resulted in a profound feeling and general mood of universal human brotherhood, and in that later concept of Russian literature, the human being fusing, merging with humanity at large, a human being extinguishing all differences of individuality, rank, or nationality in a mystical union with inmost man. This feeling, common to all Russians, whatever their party or intellectual convictions may be, is the source of the great Russian writers from Pushkin and Gogol to Tolstoi and Dostoievsky, and of the Russian thinkers from Tcha-

adaiev, Kireievsky and Chomiakov to Vladimir Soloviev. "Where
is the strength of the Russian spirit," asks Dostoievsky, "if not in
its striving toward universality, toward all-embracing humanity
... To be a true Russian means being a brother to all men ... to
be a true Russian means nothing but to reconcile European con-
tradictions within oneself, to give European longings an outlet in
the all-uniting Russian soul, to receive all into this soul with
brotherly love, and so, perhaps, to say the last word of universal
harmony, and of the understanding and peace among all peoples
according to the Evangelical law of Christ." The Russian poets
and philosophers interpreted the Panslavic movement in this sense,
as a preliminary to the union of all peoples: "What will the union
of the Slavs bring about? ... Here is something universal and
final ... something that implies the beginning of the end of the
entire previous history of Europe." But Dostoievsky's prophecy
goes still further. The following sentences were written in 1877:
"We believers say ... that only Russia contains the elements requisite for a solution of the fatal problem of the fourth estate, a solution
untainted by hatred and hostility, but that Russia will not speak
until Europe is swimming in her own blood, for before this, no
one would understand our word ... In considering the possibility of a conflict with Europe ... what we fear most is that Europe
will misunderstand us and will confront us with arrogance, with
contempt and with the sword ... as though we were barbarians
unworthy of opening our mouths ... For it seems that we still
have too few of those goods that they understand, and for which
they could esteem us. It will be a long time before they are able
to grasp our fundamental, our most important idea, our 'new word'.
What they require are facts that they can understand today, that
they can understand with their mentality of today." But "Europe
is full of unrest ... Is it perhaps only a sudden and passing unrest?
Not at all! There is a feeling abroad that the time has come for
something millennial, for something eternal, something for which
the world has been preparing from the beginning of its civilization."

All this was felt and written before Russia had undergone the impact of the socialist doctrine, which met with the most violent opposition on the part of the great Russian poets. Dostoievsky still believed that his principles of Russian all-embracing humanity were those of ancient Russian orthodoxy. And it was also a genuinely Russian and, simultaneously, an authentically Evangelical trait that prompted Count Leo Tolstoi, a wealthy landowner of the nobility, to rid himself of his fortune as "of an evil". His conviction that "the evil destroying the world is property" and "that man has only to surrender his desire for land and money in order to enter the Kingdom of Heaven", his decision to leave his estates, his home and his children and to divide up his 600,000 rubles "in order to win the right to do good"—all this was accompanied by the feeling of obeying the commands of Christ. He knew very well that this was no final solution of the social problem: "Let the mechanics invent a machine that can lift the load oppressing us— that would be a good work. But until they have made this invention, let us try in the common way, let us try as peasants and as Christians, whether we cannot lift the burden that is weighing on the people."

All this demonstrates that communism in Russia had a special tradition and that this tradition springs from the social, psychological and spiritual sources of the Russian character. Communism in Russia was originally agrarian communism, proceeding from the seething ferment of the peasants. And so Russian communism is an irrational, religious state of mind, before and beyond all rational doctrine and organization. As late as the eighteen hundred nineties, the Russian Socialist Labor Party was founded under the leadership of Plechanov, and during a party congress in 1903, divided into the moderate minority, the "mensheviki", and the radical majority, the "bolsheviki" under the leadership of Lenin. But even this was democratic in principle until 1917.

Thus "the world of Christ merged with universal enlightenment", as Dostoievsky had predicted. The religious communism of the peasants fused with the intellectual Marxian communism of the workers. Russia skipped the revolution of liberal democracy. The liberalistic movement, as it was represented by the so-called

constitutional democrats, the k-d, "cadets", was weak, and fluc-
tuated between progressive and conservative tendencies. From the
very beginning, it was outstripped by the peasant and worker
movement. Russia proceeded immediately to a proletarian revolution. This was due partly to the character of the people and of
the country, partly to the epoch in which the people awoke. For
under twentieth century conditions any revolution was bound to
become a social revolution.

The Russian Revolution of 1905 occurred after the defeat of
Russia by Japan, the decisive Russian Revolution of 1917, after
the Tsarist armies were crushed by the Germans, and the Russian
people refused to fight the senseless wars of their Tsars any longer.
At that time, the German government allowed Lenin to slip
from Switzerland through Germany into Russia in a sealed car,
and thus provided the movement with its leader. Contrary to the
prediction of Karl Marx that socialism would evolve from the most
advanced capitalistic and industrial economy, the most favorable
point of departure for a socialist revolution was Russia, in spite of,
indeed because of, the immaturity of her economic system and her
bourgeoisie. In Russia, socialism could start from scratch. Tsarism
had broken down completely. The bourgeoisie was weak and undeveloped, devoid of authority and tradition. The masses were
hardly touched by cultural and civilizing influences. There were
no deep-rooted traditions and institutions to clear away. "The
Russian is not conservative, because here, there is nothing to con-
serve" (Dostoievsky). The only palpable power of any importance
and, hence, the only focus of resistance, was the orthodox church,
and that is why it bore the brunt of the most violent attacks and
persecutions of the bolshevists. From this time on, Russian religious
emotion was integrated in Russian socialism; this religious element
of the movement was openly acknowledged by Lunacharsky and
Gorki. So bolshevism would not tolerate the old, Orthodox form
of religiosity, grown rigid in its dogma and ritual.

The masses of the Russian people began to experience the
process of a true awakening, of a discovery of the world from
the very first, such as had occurred nowhere else in this way. The

whole world was revealed and explained to them for the first time, by socialist education. Indeed, these people entered history with the feeling that what they were preparing to build up was not only their own life but that of the whole world. Rationalism and materialism, introduced by Marxian theory and practice, did not have the harmful and disintegrating effects here as in over-civilized Europe. It was balanced by the masses, physically robust, un-awakened, by the mystical emotionalism of the Russian people, by that source of amazing devotion and willingness to sacrifice that is sustaining the Soviet regime through the most terrible difficulties and stress, even today. And so, here, Marxism achieved beneficial results: education in clear thinking and effective work, organization of the community and exploitation of the land. The country is immense and remote, remote by its very immensity. It is extremely rich in raw materials, and it could be developed to the point of being self-supporting if only it were allowed the time and the peace to achieve this gigantic task.

These, then, were precious assets. But—this was the reverse of these assets—the very fact that the people were so primitive, which greatly helped the social revolution, also implied that they were too untrained to exploit their resources and to achieve industrial and technical organization unaided. Industry, the transportation system and technical skill were still on a very low level, and there was a lack both of able men and of the apparatus needed for constructive work. Thus the Soviets faced the task of resisting the many assaults of the capitalistic countries, of educating the people, and, at the same time, of building up the economy of the country, with an untrained people. They needed the help of more advanced civiliza-tions, they needed machines, goods, specialists. When they realized the embittered hostility of the bourgeois world, they hoped and worked for a world revolution and launched their tremendous propaganda drive. But the world revolution did not materialize, for reasons already outlined. The Soviets had to accomplish and defend their new order for themselves and by themselves. This created the political necessity of changing tactics toward the out-side world, of compromising with bourgeois countries and their methods—even with the arch-enemy, fascism—of seizing strategic points, in short, of working in opposition to their own ideology. But at the same time, this ideology had to be protected within the country, which was accordingly sealed to alien influences.

The necessity of carrying the social revolution safely through the many dangers of the epoch produced the tenets and methods of communism, its form of propaganda, in the first place. This ideological propaganda resembled that inaugurated by the French Revolution, but, corresponding to the closer relationship between peoples and a more developed technology, it was much more comprehensive and systematic. Its effectiveness, however, was impaired by internecine strife between social democracy and communism, and was finally left far behind by the national socialist propaganda, that owed its superiority to a shifting ideology, to the appeal to the baser impulses and the moral and mental weaknesses of men, and to the borrowed technique of American advertising. Russian communism developed a most severe party discipline comparable to Prussian discipline, although it springs from other roots. Prussian discipline is sober, rational and authoritative. It demands devotion of the whole man to the abstract state that has no ideological substance and is intent only upon increasing its power. This utmost devotion imposed as an outward duty, a "damn duty", is meant to balance the lack of tradition, the lack of inner support, the insecurity of the German individual, who needs a solid, external frame for his existence. He requires stern, outer pressure to restrain "the beast" within him, as the former chancellor von Schleicher, once formulated it. The German has need of objective service to which he can devote himself unthinkingly. And the demands of the Prussian state collective meet this specific urge to transcend his existence. Russian communism organized the revolutionary enthusiasm and the revolutionary terror, that manifested itself as emotional mass hysteria in the French Revolution, into a disciplined system, and enlisted the religious urge of the Russian people, the urge of the Russian individual to fuse with all mankind. The Prussian state as well as the communistic party demand blind, unconditional obedience. The sacrifice of the communist, however, implies his sympathy with the ideological goal, his share in a real community and in its welfare. But he must, indeed, give up the most precious rights of individual life; he must sacrifice his intellect and his free opinion and—if it be necessary—"not only his flesh and blood but his honor." That is how an erstwhile communist explained the confessions of condemned party leaders in notorious court proceedings. Only with the help of this iron discipline could the Soviet government risk those tactical coups and ideological by-paths that made the greatest demands on the confidence and under-standing of its adherents all over the world, and caused confusion and agitation among its believers. To uphold its discipline, Russian communism created its powerful secret service, that fatal instru-ment of total control that has since become an integral part of the social upheavals of our times.

The mistakes, even sins of Russian communism are obvious. They are largely due to the continuous dangers encompassing a great enterprise, but, to a certain extent, also to the imperfections inherent in the Marxian system. From the first moment on, the Soviets were exposed to furious attacks from a hostile world. The armies of the counter-revolution had advanced far into the country, which was in a chaotic state, without sufficient means of transporta-tion, tools and machinery. The people were ignorant and confused. Under these circumstances, true democracy could certainly not have been established. The Soviet constitution is, as a matter of fact, a notable attempt toward a new, more comprehensive form of democracy. It replaces the old parliamentary system of representa-tion, that has since proved inadequate all over the world, by a hierarchy of committees of selectees, intended to bring about and to systematize the permanent cooperation of the people in the govern-ment. But this constitution has remained rudimentary, in the sense that the communistic party and, within it, the executive committee and, ultimately, a single man seized the power. Dictatorship and terror have thus been perpetuated. The difficult position that had to be maintained between upholding an ideological orthodoxy by discipline, on the one hand, and agreeing to the utmost tactical compromises, on the other, produced a form of jesuitism that threatens to submerge the goal by the means. In its confused tactics, Russian communism ruthlessly betrayed comrades, as in Spain, and carelessly risked the destiny of nations, as in Germany, where the sabotage and the senseless intransigence of the communists, their blind rage against the Social Democrats, helped Hindenburg, and with him, Hitler, to power. Communism deliberately furthered the counter-revolution in order to stimulate the revolutionary energy of the workers through bitter suffering. In the final analysis, it followed an incoherent, zig-zag line, out of sheer "Realpolitik", and when the world revolution did not materialize, it became just as narrowly egotistical and limited as the other powers of the epoch. In all these ways, Russian communism contributed to the growing tendency to make man the mere instrument of an objective process, which had fateful consequences even though the final goal of this process was the common weal. The fault lies not only in the necessity for self-preservation in the midst of constant peril, not only in the more intensive, speeded-up production dictated by necessity, but in the Marxian system itself, with its disregard for personality.

Most important, positive achievements must, however, be set against these negative results: the great material and intellectual uplift of the people, indeed, the creation of the Russian people as an active and thinking community. To what extent they have accepted the new order and identify themselves, the people, with it, has been shown by the miraculous resistance of the Russian masses against the most terrible armies of the world. New Russia has given outstanding suggestions and examples in the fields of education, re-education of criminals, and social institutions. Above all—and this is her fundamental contribution—she was the first to break the rule and the prestige of money in a community. Had she achieved nothing else, this alone would entitle her to undying fame.

It is difficult to obtain a clear view of the true tendency of the present regime. There is a long way even to the complete realization of the material order of socialism, that is, to a true social democracy, especially long, after the interruption in development caused by the catastrophe of this war. But aside from this, the Marxian concept does not suffice to master the universal problems of our age, and to serve as a foundation for establishing even a moderately permanent and adequate order for the world of to-morrow. Nevertheless, the work of the Soviets, though it is incomplete and imperfect, as human endeavors are bound to be, is still a great effort toward a great goal that lies on the road that mankind must go. Whoever considers without prejudice the conditions and the behavior of the other powers will scarcely allow them the right to sit in judgment upon the misdeeds of New Russia.

In *Germany* too, there was something like a socialist revolution, but springing from totally different, indeed opposite conditions— an over-industrialized country, highly developed capitalism and a lack of raw materials, a population in which the bourgeois element prevailed, and a mentality which was overwhelmingly petty bourgeois, from the highest to the lowest classes. Not only the so-called middle class, employees, officials, small merchants, but also big capital and workers were essentially petty bourgeois. Within the large framework of this mentality, however, this population was not at all homogeneous, not held together by a common tradition, but split up into a complexity of regional, religious, professional, ideological, and class differences.

After the brusque interruption of the brilliant career of the second Reich, and the sudden collapse of the hegemonial dreams which had been fostered during the First World War, there was, at first, a complete break-down, an unimaginable confusion. The upper class was stunned; the workers, the soldiers, the progressive intelligentsia expected a vast international movement, a fraternization of the peoples and the immediate establishment of a new order based on the fourteen points of President Wilson and the achievements of the Russian Revolution. President Wilson was considered almost a saint in those days. People believed that he would make true his plan for a peace in which there was to be no victor, no vanquished. But he had not the power to make it come true. He only foresaw, as Norman Angell before him, what history later made true. At that time there was a possibility, at least a theoretical possibility, of preventing the present catastrophe. But history does not work that way. The statesmen of the Entente, and those who had remained in the hinterland, had not had the experience of the soldiers at the front. And in the overwhelming joy of their homecoming, even the soldiers quickly forgot that rare, spiritual experience of human solidarity—a forgetting that was perhaps all-too-human.

And so the peace concept of President Wilson was vitiated from all sides; first, by that grand old man Clémenceau, who was the kind of man to carry on war but not to make peace, because he was too old and completely governed by his past. He projected the past into the future—and so the past, a diabolical caricature of the past, came true. He was amazingly aware of the dangers that lie in the German character. He knew of the revolutionary, nihilistic traits that isolate the Germans from the rest of the European world: "There is in the German soul a sort of incomprehension of what life really is, of what makes its charm, its grandeur, and a sort of pathological, Satanic attraction toward death. Those people love death ... They alone look on war with sang-froid, and, as a result, they prepare it; the Frenchman starts thinking about it the day he is mobilized. And as time goes on, war becomes less a matter of courage, of 'panache', and more and more a matter of preparation." But Clémenceau's remedy was the shallow political method of past centuries. The scene of his action and planning was the political stage of the nineteenth century, the stage of the professional politician and cabinet diplomat, the stage of Bismarck who had, at least, succeeded in achieving a superficial peace and a forty years' prosperity. For the twenty years' peace that Clémenceau counted on he did not even achieve the mere security that the French were longing for, but the opposite, an equilibrium so precarious that only his own generation's passionate and watchful hatred, only a state of constant political and military alertness might have maintained it. At any rate, it did not permit of that drifting along in uneasy pleasures which the Western countries indulged in. But this also he anticipated. He felt that nothing further could be done with the disrupted society of his time: "Hope? It is impossible! ... I can no longer hope, I who no longer believe ... I who no longer believe in what I was passionately attached to, Democracy . . . I pity you for having to breathe the air of a stupid bourgeoisie . . . The French are a people who is on the way out. Bolshevism? Not even that! You are too advanced to have the vigor for a revolution. You will have a deliquescence, and it will not last long . . . You will live the gamy peace of decadence . . . It will be filthy and delicious . . . as when the ancients opened their veins in a bath of milk." He had the courage to see truth unvarnished, and this steady, unerring vision of the truth raises him above his contemporaries, even above his opponent, Wilson. And yet his contrast to Wilson symbolizes the great crossroads of humanity, between yesterday and tomorrow, the triumph of yesterday over tomorrow. Clémenceau marks the beginning of the era of "Realpolitik", that is to say, the principle of anti-solidarity, of impromptu action and that means action only in the case of ultimate necessity, action from hour to hour and that means at the last hour, action from selfish interests and that means isolation. And so the boldest and best-prepared extortioner was able to finish off one country after the other in order to gain un-limited power. Such was the result of the "Realpolitik" of which Wilson's peace was the first victim. Wilson's peace was further vitiated by that petty crowd of old-time political bargainers who ruined the League of Nations in the same way. And Wilson's peace was, last but not least, obstructed by the isolationist forces in his own country. The withdrawal of America from European affairs, which, as has become manifest in the mean time, were matters of universal and so, also, of eminently American concern, this with-drawal is America's share in the responsibility of what has hap-pened since.

The German socialists, who had been brought up in the normal, orderly progress of party formation and bureaucracy, were very much afraid of their own revolution. They did not wish to use violence against the old classes, the officers, the Junkers and big capital. Where violent action or sporadic outrages occurred, they were suppressed with the help of the ruling classes. On the other hand, the socialists started a laborious reform, well-intended laws and regulations that implied a betterment of social conditions, but unfortunately lacked the psychological and material power to make them real, to break the stubborn obstruction of the old-time officials. Reconstruction was encumbered by the never definitely fixed reparations, and the shifting from war to peace industry, as well as the import of raw materials, could only be accomplished through further indebtedness. So it looked as if the country would have to work indefinitely for foreign countries before it could embark on its own recovery. From the very outset, the socialist reform was burdened by this hopeless perspective and with the moral liquidation of defeat. In addition to this handicap, the socialists faced the charge of the bourgeoisie, who accused them of having stabbed the army in the back by undermining the morale of the people. The industrialists were true buccaneers, who sabotaged the government as best they could. In their factories and combines they behaved like territorial princes. One of them, Hugo Stinnes, who had created what they called a vertical trust, a huge agglomeration of enterprises of all kinds—iron and coal mines, shipping and shipbuilding, news-papers and various other trades—frankly declared: "I am Germany. Whoever is a true German, may join me." And as he had jobs to distribute, he was joined by many, who went down with him in his spectacular bankruptcy.

In challenging the government, the industrialists were in an underground agreement with their fellow groups in the Western countries, who, on the one hand, certainly wanted their national reparations but, on the other, disliked the regime of social reform in which they suspected communism, who even secretly favored and encouraged the German military. Furthermore, the Western governments took every means to discourage and discredit the democratic government of the Weimar Republic, and reserved their compliances and appeasements for anti-democratic governments, such as Mussolini's and Hitler's. Everywhere the plight and the attitude of the bourgeoisie was the same. The consequences of the war, the devaluation of currencies and the national ambitions of the new successor states had created new domestic industries. Yet the purchasing power of the people was largely ruined. In the face of new competitors and lost consumers, capital was blocked in its expansion and threatened by the social movement. This brought about the fundamental shift in the attitude of the bourgeoisie. They fortified themselves politically, screened their interests with nationalism and patriotism and, in the Western countries characteristically enough, with pacifism. They collected and availed themselves of all resentments and ideologies that could be useful to them. In fact, every genuinely liberal, democratic, progressive personality or movement was denounced as communist. They would have incarcerated their own forefathers if these had shown up in their midst—just as Jesus Christ would have been burned by the Catholic Inquisition, as Dostoievsky has shown in his "Brothers Karamazov". So the bourgeoisie fell out of the frying pan into the fire and united with their very executioner. The social reform was doomed, and under the cover and protection of bourgeois nationalistic slogans, the Nazi power and, eventually, the Nazi state arose.

NIHILISM AND THE RULE OF TECHNICS

THERE IS A VERITABLE TUMULT of discussion concerning the *origin of national socialism*. There is a militaristic thesis that regards national socialism as a creature of the German army and of German militarism. National socialism is interpreted as the revenge and restoration of the German military caste, that had lost its ruling position after the First World War and tried to reinstate itself by this fake popular movement. It is true that the spirit of the shock troops of the old imperial army, trained for extraordinary duties, carried over into the illegal free-corps, that during the Weimar Republic fought against the Soviets, the Poles and the German revolutionaries, and that these free-corps, in turn, engendered the Nazi storm troops and elite guards. The militaristic thesis can also point to the underground cooperation of the official army with those partisan free-corps, and to the fact that Hitler began his career as a spy and agent of that army. Then there is a capitalistic theory that sees in national socialism the counter-revolution of capital. The German industrialists, as well as capitalists the world over, did, in fact, have a considerable share in the rise of this movement, through their besetting fear of bolshevism. They financed it, and actually established it through their middleman, Franz von Papen. They used it to lure the unemployed into a trap with the slogans of a pretended socialism, but, in reality, to thwart the development of true social democracy in the entire world. There is a political thesis that derives national socialism from the effects of the Peace of Versailles. There is a national-psychology thesis that attributes the development of national socialism to certain deeply rooted German or Prussian characteristics, and puts the responsibility on the whole German people and the German people alone. And finally, there is the gangster theory that claims the German people were tricked and overpowered by a clique of unscrupulous criminals.

All these theories are true up to a certain point, and that is why each, taken by itself, is false. National socialism has no single, specific cause. It has all the just-mentioned causes and many others. For national socialism is no isolated phenomenon; it is the last stage of an epoch, the last apocalyptic dissolution of an outlived order of society. It is the final exaggeration of the century-old struggle of dynasties, nations, individuals and private and national economic enterprises. The so-called dynamism really began in the Renaissance, in the rivalries for political power, and it continued in the free competition of capitalism. It is no mere coincidence that the fascists and national socialists emphasize the Darwin-Spencer theory of the survival of the fittest, which is also the basic principle of Manchester-liberalism. National socialism is merely the utmost concentration of forces in the same struggle for power. It is nothing new; it is the agony and apotheosis of the old. But since every end is a transition, the beginning of a reversal, so the dawn of something new is in national socialism also. The historic function of national socialism is to make a clean sweep; its deed is the ruthless, voluntary and involuntary annihilation and unmasking of all the rotting institutions, slogans, pretenses of modern times. With its magnetic appeal, national socialism draws everything that is shabby, base and egotistical into the limelight. With its swollen lies, its open abuse of all ideologies, it will come to expose everything that is false in them, it will discredit even the smallest hoaxes of our civilization. With its horrors upon horrors, it may so thoroughly imbue mankind with a disgust for slaughter, suppression and persecution, that men will perhaps be ready in the end to work in common. It may, finally, have so utterly exhausted human strength that all peoples will perhaps be weary enough to be willing to pay the price for a new, common order.

National socialism cannot, therefore, be ranked with any such ideological movements as socialism and communism—not even with Italian fascism to which it owes its beginnings. It is a link in a universal revolutionary process which it did not inaugurate but only embodied. From its outset, up to the present day, in spite of its ideological slogans of a new order and a new Europe, national socialism has not had the slightest idea of its true function in human history. In itself, it is nothing but a gigantic national and international robbery, a criminal raid. The whole post-war world was peopled with suspicious characters, with economic and political adventurers, with war profiteers and tricksters—such as Kreuger, Stavisky, Stinnes, the American bootleggers—who, in the jungles of anarchy, were out for prey. National socialism endowed this piracy with a universal scope, transferred it to world politics, national economy, education, law—in fact, to all fields of our civilization—and justified it with Machiavelli's theory of power, with Darwin's principle of the struggle for existence and with Nietzsche's "will-to-power". By carrying these theories to their true, ultimate conclusions, it showed that in the final analysis they all lead to crime. National socialism stole what tools it could for its gigantic raid—not only men, countries, peoples, economies, classes, but all cultural goods and values. There is no ideology, no interest, whether of individual, class or profession, that it did not pervert to a mere means, a ruse of war, and did not hesitate to deny or expose when it had served its purpose. It has retained only such principles as the race theory, anti-Christianism and anti-humanitarianism, which have permanent value as weapons to exterminate the moral and intellectual inhibitions of the human soul. National socialism has no intellectual substratum whatever. This must be remembered in order to understand it correctly. Its ideological basis is pure hoax, conscious, sometimes even acknowledged. Its entire principle is nothing but tactics. Thus it has exploited all forms of community and organization of our time and amalgamated them for its own purposes: nationalism, socialism, capitalism, technocracy and the Prussian state. It has combined all these in a sort of negative synthesis, and laid bare their weaknesses through abuse of their underlying ideas.

The great import of national socialism consists in the fact that it is a symptom, that it reveals and dooms the current condition of the world. Its momentousness is in the fact that it could happen, that it could reach such universal and fundamental scope. More significant than the movement itself is what stands behind it, what supported it and spread it over the world. It has become the melting-pot for all those forces, that everywhere oppose a new, common and humane order, for all the marauders or deserters of human community. This countless, overwhelming mass not only made Hitler's rise possible, it made it a historical necessity. The fact that this mass exists, explains Hitler's notorious, much discussed "luck", that came to his rescue again and again, that bore him higher and higher, when his movement and his career was most endangered. He could easily enlist supporters wherever and whenever he needed them.

The sources of national socialism spring from different levels. Its immediate culture medium was *the condition and the atmosphere of Germany after the First World War,* the material, intellectual and moral anarchy of that period. Germany was a "dual" state, in which the ruling strata of the old regime, the military, the officers, the Junkers and big capital maintained their position and paralyzed the intentions of the republican government through their influence on the administration, the press and the universities. They did everything they could to arouse the people with denunciations of "Wilson's deceit", of the republican government's "fulfilment policy", of the "stab in the back" of the army by the socialists, and to revive and stimulate the old national inferiority complex of the Germans. Worst of all, the courts favored every illegal reactionary movement and its most criminal excesses. Exonerating them with the excuse of patriotic motives, they confused the sense for right and wrong, and destroyed all legal security long before the rise of the national socialists.

Besides all this, two revolutionizing and demoralizing factors, inflation and unemployment, shook the economic and psychic foundations of society, particularly of the middle class. Bit by bit they broke down the resistance of the reasoning faculty in people. Although the true cause lay in the anarchy of world economy and the intrigues of big industry, the republican government had to bear the blame.

The inflation came first, inflation to a degree that was experienced nowhere else. People went away with their monthly pay, and two hours later it was worth a single meal; one day later it was worth a loaf of bread, or a cigar! It was, indeed, a symbolic event. It was as if a hurricane were sweeping away all substantial values. In the wake of inflation, all the other, more precious values were destroyed by the Nazis. The second disastrous factor was unemployment, the result of radical deflation. One cannot overestimate the impact of unemployment on a vast scale upon an impoverished country, the psychic distress even worse than the material, the plight of people who for long generations have been educated for work and grown unaccustomed to leisure, grown impervious to the meaning of leisure, and who were now prevented from performing the work that had become their very life.

A desperado state of mind seized upon the population. The republican government was crippled by an incapable parliament, whose too many parties with their various political slogans represented the conflicting interests of economic groups, and whose ineffectual decisions did not meet the real needs of the country but merely concluded an endless "horse-trading" within and between the parties. The government was hindered through the obstinacy of the officials, through the challenging sabotage of powerful and independent capital. It was discredited by the governments of the Western powers, their petty machinations and their tardy and insufficient concessions. This parliament and this uninspired, picayune administration faced with overwhelming and increasing difficulties did not present a spectacle likely to encourage democracy. And so the cry went up for a "Fuehrer", for the savior who would cut the Gordian knot, or rather, for the adoption of the "Fuehrer-principle" that had fascinated people even before the actual Fuehrer appeared and had recommended itself by its seemingly successful realization in Italy. A place was ready for the man who would wish to occupy it.

That this man was *Hitler* was due to the unique conditions of his origin and of his character. In the first place, he was not brought up in the German Reich and was very probably not even of pure German ancestry. He hails from the Slav border, from Austria, where peoples have mixed for centuries and where continual friction with other nationalities kept the German element in a permanent state of inflammable temper and fanaticism. Furthermore, it is of importance that he is a typical petty bourgeois both in origin and character. His father was a provincial shoemaker—an illegitimate child—a man with ambitions who managed to rise to the post of customs official. Finally, Hitler was from the very first not only a petty bourgeois but a freak petty bourgeois, a petty bourgeois thrown out of his proper course. The story of his youth is a tale of failures. He did not finish high school. At the art academy where he wanted to study painting and architecture he was rejected because he could not pass the entrance requirements, and for three years he lived in a Vienna poorhouse in the company of human failures. He felt superior to the labor proletariat, and led a wretched life as a peddler until the war saved him from his miserable condition. Thus he combined national, class and personal resentments; thus he was predestined to be the representative, not of the German character—for never has German history produced anyone like him—but of the strong resentment that had increased among the petty bourgeois and the unemployed, after the war. This resentment had been unleashed by the indescribable confusion and hopelessness of the situation in Germany, and had crashed through the bounds of reason. A well-informed, responsible person who knew the complexities of the current problems would never have won the support of the people, would never have been accepted as their leader. On the other hand, a true German would never have felt competent to assume the burden of this leadership, for he would have been inhibited by complicated thoughts and feelings and by that lack of self-confidence which the Germans acquired in the course of their fateful history. Mr. Rauschning, an educated and intelligent man, recently told a reporter who asked him why he had joined the Nazis: "In the presence of Hitler, man felt the complications cut out of his mind. And", he added, "we are such complicated people, that there is relief in that." And another German once said to the author, with the same air of relief: "They [the Nazis] are tackling all problems in such a brisk way!"

Hitler has indeed cut out the complications and made everything very simple. He told his audiences that the culpable people were such and such: the Jews, the socialists, the bankers, the department stores, the house-owners, the Allies. He told whomever he happened to be addressing in his meetings that their social antagonists bore all the guilt for their troubles. So, gradually, he won them all over. From Austria, Hitler brought with him something that had never existed in Germany, and with which the Germans were utterly unfamiliar, a rabid form of rhetoric and demagogy. The speeches of German politicians were tiresome, memorized accounts. But Austria had produced brilliant speakers and demagogues, such as the Viennese Mayor Lueger before the war, who was more powerful than the emperor himself, and who, like Hitler, chose anti-semitism as the point of departure for his propaganda, with cold deliberateness. Hitler brought with him the emotional world of the petty bourgeois. But he also brought the superiority over this world that he had acquired through his failures, through his pariah's existence, his hatred of society and his thirst for revenge. His entire career shows the fluctuation between the mental state of the petty bourgeois, that he could never quite escape from, and that conscious superiority which he widened step by step in the course of his career. It took him some time to overcome his deep respect for the ruling classes, for the military, for Hindenburg, for big capital, for his originally revered master, Mussolini, for the world power of England. It was only when he came in close contact

with these and discovered their weaknesses and their vulnerability
that he gradually gained that self-confidence which is really identical with an anarchistic contempt of all institutions, elements and
exponents of our civilization. Since he was not strong enough to
sustain the weight of this feeling that he was unable to sublimate,
it grew into a personal greed for power, into criminal urges. Thus
his own development reflects the progressive disintegration of the
bourgeois world. He began with an appeal to the emotions, to
the resentment and impatience of the petty bourgeois. Thanks to
the superiority gained in his insecure youth, he became a veritable
virtuoso in playing the whole gamut of these emotions. He consciously developed this ability. The methods of propaganda, of
catching people, are the only subjects which he has studied and
which he has come to master thoroughly. He learned from the
propaganda of the Allies in the First World War, from the treatment of human beings by the Catholic Church and the Jesuits,
from American advertising. He learned, and he utilized all these
methods that are the very foundation of his politics. Brilliant
passages concerning propaganda are the only original contribution
in his otherwise inferior book; they are a worthy continuation and
supplement to Machiavelli's "The Prince". The tenet, for instance,
that one must tell only big lies, because no one would believe the
little ones, is entirely in keeping with the words of Machiavelli
to which we have referred. And Hitler acted consistently in accordance with his tenets. He not only lied and deceived on a
grandiose scale and speculated on the cowardice, indolence and
forgetfulness of people, he knew that an accumulation of crimes
and atrocities does not sharpen but rather dulls the world's reactions against them. At first, people do not believe that such things
can be, because they are unable and unwilling to imagine them.
When, at last, they are forced to believe, they have become accustomed to accept them as inevitable. If there is anything of
the genius in Hitler, it is this capacity to go through to the end,
the metaphysical degree of his criminality, the deliberate casting-
off of all those last remnants of inhibitions and moral preoccupations that the ordinary criminal still has. His epochal innovation

is not that he committed the greatest crimes—in this he has had countless predecessors in history—but that he embraced crime as others embrace a faith, that he made crime a norm, that he effected unconditional nihilism. Although his boldness in crime is still bound up with the cowardice of the petty bourgeois, with hysterical fears, although it is tainted with the sadistic symptoms of a stifled sex life that was restrained by the police and by the moral conventions of many generations, and is now exploding in unbelievable excesses—still, it is no small thing for a petty bourgeois to venture this last break with the foundations of his society. That this was possible in a man of his mental and social background, that this could alter the character of an entire country, that this was recognized for a considerable period by the world powers and honored by pacts and all sorts of agreements, all this reveals the rottenness of middle-class civilization. In Hitler, the political deed in grand style, the attempt to conquer the world, has become crime pure and simple and stamped with the characteristics of crime. In this sense, the words that Thomas Mann once said of Hitler, are true: that, together with all other values, he has also dishonored the idea of genius.

The rise of Hitler and national socialism is, however, unthinkable without his precursor Mussolini and *Italian fascism*. Fascism set up a model that the whole German bourgeoisie and, indeed, the bourgeoisie of the whole world regarded as salvation. Even today, in spite of all that has happened in the mean time, large sections of the international bourgeoisie, especially big capital, cannot entirely relinquish this pet idea. Fascism not only wakened a longing that Hitler could satisfy, but its proponent, Mussolini, supported and guided the first steps of national socialism both before and after it came into power. At that time, Nazi chiefs were continually pilgrimaging to Rome for advice. Moreover, fascism, which was internationally recognized, was Hitler's first bridge to the outer world; it was not only his teacher, but his intermediary. And it helped national socialism to establish itself as an international power, through the formation of the "axis".

Later on, as is well known, the tables were turned; fascism became the subordinate of its own creation and proved to be a mere forerunner of national socialism.

Fascism is a transitional phenomenon. It is still half bourgeois. Had it not been for Hitler, the European governments might have become reconciled to it in a process of mutual assimilation. Had not European developments served to strengthen the principle of dictatorship, Mussolini would not have dared to embark on his Abyssinian expedition, that marked the beginning of the end of his key position in Europe. This already shows the fundamental difference between fascism and national socialism. Fascism is a purely political movement; it never went beyond a political range. In spite of its proclamation of a new "civiltà", it did not even succeed in fundamentally changing the social order and the state of mind of its own people, let alone that of secular civilization. It had neither the urge nor the means to achieve this.

Fascism did not rise through an elemental, objective process, but through human initiative. It did not rise from an ideology, to be sure, but it did rise from an idea that is deeply rooted in Italian tradition and that carries on this tradition; here the vital element is inseparably connected with the cultural. Originally, fascism was a purely nationalistic movement, intended forcibly to correct the neglect of Italy by her Allies, and to gain possession of territories that had been promised and withheld. For this purpose, a national revival was to be accomplished, a third Renaissance. So fascism turned out to be a synthesis of the Roman Empire, the Renaissance and the Risorgimento, of Caesar, Machiavelli and Garibaldi. Characteristically, it was planned and inaugurated by a poet.

In 1915, Gabriele d'Annunzio laid its foundation in his war-like oration on that rock of Quarto from which Garibaldi once embarked for his war of liberation. Later, he created the movement through his seizure of Fiume, through the constitution he gave Fiume and the important outer forms and concepts he invented: costume, Roman salute, battle-cry, acclamation, corporate state organization. (Another intellectual advance guard of fascism, active even before 1914, was the Futurist movement of the painter and writer, Marinetti. This movement was a revolt against the burden of an all-too-great Italian past that submerged the country. with a flood of cultural relics and allegedly stifled and degraded the living impulses of the youth of the land.) Fascism, therefore, arose from the entirely subjective and very aesthetic motive of a poet in whose spirit the national tradition was again astir. D'Annunzio had neither knowledge of nor interest in universal problems. This "deputy of beauty" had no concern with leftist or rightist tendencies. His sole preoccupation was "life", radiant life. Only later, when the wave of communism turned toward Italy and caused unrest in Italian workers who were, at bottom, anarchistic rather than communistic, did capitalism use the movement of national awakening to suppress socialist tendencies. And it was then that fascism assumed the character of a nationalistic reaction against modern social developments. Dictatorship, the rule of one representative person, is quite in keeping with Italy's national structure, and the people were accustomed to it. Even under a liberal regime, Giolitti had exerted virtually unlimited influence, and the Middle and South Italian regions had always been ruled by local chiefs. Modern, industrial development was confined to the northern half of the peninsula. Thus Italian fascism was an anachronistic revival of old national forms, rather than a break with tradition.

When one compares the development of the fascist and the national socialist movements, it becomes clear how much less ambiguous, how much more determined by human volition, but also how much more limited in scope, fascism was from the very outset. One comes upon the difference between action directed by a subjective will, and an objective process. Fascism rose to power very quickly, and even the reverses were inconsiderable: 1919, Fiume; 1922, the "march on Rome"; end of 1924, the Matteotti crisis that ends with the unconditional rule of fascism. The "march on Rome" was, to be sure, not the heroic deed of the official epic, but it was a coup d'état that succeeded at the first blow. But how much was needed to advance national socialism! And yet its foes were not stronger, but rather weaker than those of fascism, and the condition at the end of the war—social anarchy and the receptiveness of the bourgeoisie—were much more favorable, the attitude of the military, of capital and of officials much more promising. What drudgery was necessary for fourteen long years, before this rule was finally established after an unsuccessful "Putsch"! How much agreement and disagreement of persons, cliques, "Buende", how many intrigues, how much perjury, change of fronts, financing from abroad! What an intricate machinery of Fate! The seizure of power in 1933 was neither a clear conquest nor an uprising of the people. It was a mere slipping into power—with the aid of an intermediary—between a cheated old man and rival interest groups. And even then the Nazis required an ill-concealed crime, the hoax of the "Reichstagsbrand", in order to establish their power. Italian fascism had a single dictator. Mussolini controlled and dominated all fields of government, including the intellectual field. He is a "uomo universale" like his precursors, the condottieri of the Renaissance. National socialism has a hoard of dictatorial powers that frequently overlap, the party, the army, the Gestapo, industry, Goering, Goebbels, Himmler, Ribbentrop, and innumerable changing cliques and favorites hostile to one another. Hitler himself is a dilettante who does not control any one field in its entirety. He is less a leader than an expert in leadership, who is only called upon to produce enthusiasm in the masses and to give the last, "intuitive" directions. But, on the other hand, fascism had a much more limited scope. Mussolini, with all of his disciplinary organizations, his desperate attempts at modernization, militarization, mechanization, has not succeeded in changing the character of his great people that lives for the gifts of the moment and never desists from criticism. This people has retained its flaws and its graces, its human qualities and emotions, its incapacity to perform objective, super-personal, long-range labors. In failing here, it has maintained itself. With this people, and with the limited population and industry of the country, every attempt at a dominant position in the modern world was bound to miscarry. And the ineradicable humanism, the deep-rooted Catholicism of Italian life, necessarily presented insuperable barriers to any fundamental change in civilization.

Mussolini, who has a Latin mind himself, did not attempt anything of the kind, as long as he was his own master. He let loose an army of sbirri over the country, he performed and sanctioned the worst atrocities, he is, no doubt, an a-moral, unscrupulous scoundrel. But that is not enough to destroy a civilization thousands of years old. His wickedness and his lack of morality is of the old, naive kind found in the tyrants of the Renaissance. It is not a matter of principle, it is not revolutionary, it does not probe to the bottom of things, it is not an open avowal in favor of barbarism. Mussolini's movement lacked the great intellectual and social hinterland, it lacked all those processes that in Germany had been preparing for many generations the turn to unveiled barbarism. The mental equipment of the Germans was not bounded by a traditional form of life. On the contrary, it supplied a latent readiness to respond to mad and diabolical demands with utter devotion and the strength of faith. It seems as if no demand could be great and terrible enough to deliver the German individual from his abysmal, threatening ego. The Germans want to apply their rational, technical forces in order to relieve themselves of them. They want to achieve and to believe at all costs, even to the point of absurdity.

The great work and effect of the national socialist Third Reich was achieved through the focussing of innumerable forces that were at hand and that hastened to proffer themselves as soon as there was a dictatorial challenge. Hardly anything that goes under the name of the Third Reich today hails from national socialism itself. Everything that technologists, economists, scientists and theoreticians of all kinds had thought up independently gravitated toward national socialism and was exploited by it in so far as it was usable: the economic planning of Rathenau and Moellendorff, Schacht's finance-technique, Darré's "Erbhof" theory, Carl Schmitt's concept of constitutional law, "Geopolitics", the race theory, eugenics, the "German creed" of Hauer and Bergmann, let alone what was taken over from foreign countries, such as vacation trips ("Kraft durch Freude") and the "dopo lavoro". And similarly, the ideological preparation that won over the intelligentsia and whole strata of the bourgeoisie, was accomplished by persons who had nothing at all to do with the Nazis, who even repudiated any connection with national socialism.

No intellectual inspiration was responsible for the rise of national socialism. Its concrete beginnings lie in barracks and beer joints, in the confused urges, plots and projects of modern mercenaries and idlers, in regions reached only by the last, journalistic dregs of problems and ideas. The autobiography of Hitler testifies to strong impressions in youth, to war experiences, but to no intellectual influence, to no ideas except such as were provided by the nationalistic history classes in provincial schools of the German parts of the Hapsburg monarchy. Mussolini's intellectual background is quite different, for his mental equipment shows traces of the thoughts of Nietzsche, Karl Marx, D'Annunzio, Georges Sorel and Pareto. The great strength of national socialism lay precisely in the fact that it was untheoretical, even anti-theoretical to the limit, that it was flexible enough to hold out promises to many contradictory interests. The national socialists have always evinced the greatest contempt for intellect, although they have taken it into their service. Their leaders cannot heap sufficient abuse on the "gabblers" and "scribblers", the "brain-brutes" and "side-walk litterateurs", who are said to have confused the minds, paralyzed the will and broken down the discipline of the people, thus obstructing Germany's political power. Hitler even goes so far as to want to restore to the people "the blessing of illiteracy".

Here, then, the break between the sphere of ideas and the sphere of living is complete. But this does not decrease the importance due to the preparation of peoples' minds for national socialism. On the contrary, it gives it historic weight; it confirms the fact that the development has been consistent throughout. The ultimate results and effects of national socialism cannot be understood without taking into consideration the *intellectual premises* from which it has arisen.

In earlier chapters we referred to the counter-movement brewing in the nineteenth century against the bourgeois world, its rationalization, mechanization and vulgarization of life. This movement took its issue from individual artists and writers in the various European countries, and developed the grave problem as to whether human values have been preserved or destroyed, enhanced or invalidated, by technical and economic progress. The critical issue thus raised was a prelude to the moral and ideological crisis of our time.

Criticism began to concentrate on bourgeois morality, and it focussed its attention on two main discrepancies: one, the contradiction between social conditions and the prevailing moral principles; the other, the conflict in the psychic life of the individual, who was urged forward, on the one hand, by his natural impulses and the requirements of the modern struggle for existence and, on the other, held back by the moral conventions of the bourgeoisie.

The French novelists, Balzac and Zola, and the German naturalistic dramatists portrayed the decomposition and hypocrisy of bourgeois society and the struggle of the erotic, capitalistic and political passions. The great Russians confronted true Christianity with the sanctimonious canons of church and state, and the Scandinavian writers, Ibsen and Strindberg, shed light on the corruption and decay hidden, under cover of bourgeois respectability, in individual relationships, in marriages and families. All these authors held that modern existence is such that no one can or does live according to the moral principles maintained by the bourgeoisie. They demanded a new truthfulness and honesty, a thorough examination of life's fundamental sources. Either Christianity and humanitarianism should be applied in earnest, or the right of the individual to his natural impulses should be openly recognized. Yet none of these criticisms went so far as to question the basic value of the Christian tenets and the secular principles deduced from them.

In Germany, and only in Germany, did this criticism develop into an explicit assault against these values as such, because there the civilizing Roman and Christian tradition had not become integrated in the human being, had not helped to form a national tradition, so that the pagan and essentially barbarian element could free itself from the obligations imposed by Christianity. The man who started this revolution that threatens the foundations of the world of man, was Friedrich Nietzsche. Here we can trace only those of his ideas that are related to the present state of things as brought about by national socialism, but we must keep in mind that these represent only part of his vision, and that large portions of his writings not only contradict the Nazi ideas completely but utterly discredit the actions of the dictators of today. This man was a seismograph, who registered all the secret vibrations presaging future developments. But he was a person of the utmost integrity and dignity, with a vehement distaste for all baseness.

In the midst of the present "revolution of nihilism", it is staggering to read the following sentences that were written over half a century ago, and that sounded fantastic even to the worst sceptics of the time: "What I am now going to relate is the history of the next two centuries. I shall describe what will happen, what must necessarily happen: the triumph of nihilism. The whole of European culture has long been writhing in an agony of suspense that increases from decade to decade as if heading for a catastrophe ... like a torrent that is seeking its bourn and that no longer stops to consider, that is afraid to consider."

But what does nihilism mean? "That the highest values are losing their value." Nietzsche describes the transition from pessimism to nihilism, which comes, he believes, from the fact that "the most powerful instincts and those that promised most for the future, have hitherto been calumniated. The time is coming," he says, "when we shall have to pay for having been Christians for two thousand years. We are losing the firm footing that enabled us to live ... for a long time we shall be at our wits' end. We are hurling ourselves headlong into the reverse valuations, with such energy as could only have been engendered in man by an overvaluation of himself." And Nietzsche himself is the one who started this reversal.

To him, the development of mankind from the beginning of

Christianity has the opposite meaning from that which has always been accepted; to him, it is not progress, but decline. He regards it as a gradual conquest of the strong by the weak through a morality that grew out of the instincts and requirements of the inferior. Christian morality is the crafty intellectual weapon discovered by the lower species of humanity, the "slaves", the "herd", the "masses", to dominate the higher, noble species; it is "herd morality", and all of Christianity as such is a "slave revolt of morality." The goal of this morality is the "weakening of the desires, of the feelings of pleasure and pain, of the will to power, to property and more property; weakening in the form of humility, weakening in the form of belief, weakening in the form of repugnance and shame in the presence of all that is natural . . . in the form of a denial of life, in the form of illness . . ." Morality, then, is a counter-movement against Nature's struggle to create a higher type.

But this age of Christian morality is on the wane, and a new, a pagan age is dawning that will "restore to man the courage of his natural instincts . . . Paganism affirms all that is natural, it is innocence in being natural . . . Christianity negates all that is natural, it is against Nature." "Belief in the body is more fundamental than belief in the soul." We have overestimated the value of consciousness. "Our valuation of great men and things is . . . natural: we regard passion as a privilege, we find nothing great that does not involve a great crime . . . From a detached view, it is precisely the growing dominance of evil that one desires, the growth of power, so as to make use of the most powerful forces in nature, the emotions." The thing is to "re-establish the hierarchy of rank", to know "that there are higher and lower human beings, and that a single man can justify whole millennia of their existence . . . that is, one complete, rich, great human being in comparison with innumerable incomplete, fragmentary human beings." But "what determines a man's rank is the quantum of power he has . . . Only through war and danger, can a rank maintain itself." "I am delighted," writes Nietzsche, "at the military development of Europe, also at the inner anarchical conditions: the period of quietude and Chinese apathy is over . . . physical values are appreciated once more . . . handsome men are becoming possible again. The time of bloodless sneaks is past . . . the savage in every one of us is accepted, even the wild animal . . . A ruling race can only grow up from terrible and violent beginnings. Where are the barbarians of the twentieth century?" he asks. "They will be those capable of the greatest harshness against themselves, those who can guarantee the greatest duration of will-power." The strong must be strengthened still more, the weak be still more belabored, so that they may be destroyed the sooner—this is nature's procedure, and ought to be followed. For the strong enrich life, the weak consume and impoverish it. Indeed, a type of the strongest and hardest human being should be consciously and artificially bred. What matters is not mankind, but the superman, not intellect, but life. And life is will-to-power.

Nietzsche's work strikes all the themes that later, chiefly as a result of their development by post-war thinkers, exerted such a tremendous and fateful influence on the youth of Europe. Down to the last details, the Nazis have made his prophecy come true. But airy thoughts are very different from their concrete realization. When Nietzsche dreamed of his "blond beast", he did not imagine that such a reaction against the nineteenth century could still raise to power only a type of man bred by the nineteenth century. For the "Herrenmensch", the master-man, who finally appeared, was the same stuffy petty bourgeois that Nietzsche despised from the depth of his soul, only that he was the more vulgar and detestable because he was devoid of all inhibitions.

There was only one great figure who carried the teachings of Nietzsche over from 1900 to the post-war period, the poet, Stefan George. Of Nietzsche's complex theories, there was one theme in particular that this poet took up and developed: the cult of the great man. For George, the great man has not the exaggerated meaning of the barbaric superman, but that of the complete, harmonious human being, in the Greek sense, in contrast to the modern, intellectually or physically hypertrophied, specialized man. He wanted to develop a type, whose mind and body are at one, whose mind expresses itself in a beautiful body, whose beautiful body is sublimated in mind. He patterned himself on the great European heroes and poets, Alexander, Caesar, Napoleon, Dante, Shakespeare and Goethe, and above all, on Greek youth as it appears in the works of Plato. He surrounded himself with a group of young men and gave them a training that almost amounted to the breeding of a new type. So deeply did the influence of this man stamp itself on young people that one could often recognize a disciple of Stefan George's by his bearing, and by a striking facial resemblance to the poet himself. In their appearance, their behavior and their glowing acclaim of their master and his teachings, his followers set themselves in sharp opposition to the bourgeois world that surrounded them.

The great significance of Stefan George for the development that ensued consists in this living embodiment of the new thoughts, this transmuting of theory into daily life, by the strict hieratical form he gave to his own person and his own way of living, as well as by the shaping of his disciples. Nietzsche was an abstract thinker. George was not a thinker, but a poet and a leader. He was a man of action, a ruler according to the intrinsic pattern of the Renaissance princes, and his poetry and his training of youth were preparatory functions of his leadership. It is true that he began simply as a poet, stemming from Baudelaire and Mallarmé, from their "l'art pour l'art" and their defiant hatred of bourgeois society and middle-class morality. In the midst of this world of the masses, of technics, of naturalism, of "laisser faire and laisser passer", he wanted to restore the value of form, not only artistic but human form, by his poetry as well as by his bearing. In his own way, through living example, he wanted to "restore the hierarchy of rank" and to set the poet at its apex, as the intellectual leader of the state. He wanted to create a new élite, ideal both physically and mentally. To this end, he trained several generations of young people and ruthlessly freed them from the pseudo-morality of the bourgeoisie, from its over-estimation of rational thinking, family life and material interests.

The circle around George, at first only a group of poets, became a kind of order, without specific rules, but with a very definite, indeed, an orthodox, belief, and a deep devotion of the disciples to their master. Eventually, after the First World War, when adherents of this movement occupied chairs in nearly all the great universities and held many important positions in public life, it became a secret state within the state, "The Secret Germany" that dedicated the future to itself. George's poetry shows the growth of this claim. It begins with the shaping of a personal life, it ends with sibylline tablets of the law for a new human society. His last books he called "Der Stern des Bundes" (The Star of the Covenant) and "Das Neue Reich" (The Kingdom Come).

In the intellectual excitement and political turmoil of Germany after the war, George himself became a kind of myth, and this is understandable to anyone who has ever met him. For his outward appearance and bearing, unlike that of the actual dictators who rule the world today, was that of a true prince. It was an anachronistic bearing, and that was why it could never gain supremacy, because the world of today can no longer be ruled by real princes. Nietzsche looked like a German professor and carried himself like one. Only his deep-set and penetrating eyes gave evidence that he was something else. But the first thing one noticed about George was his powerful, Dantesque head, with its prominent bony structure and its mane of wavy hair. He had a slender, graceful body, and wore very simple but unusual apparel, somewhat like a clergyman's, and his manner combined imperious severity with the charm of a grand seigneur. It is characteristic of the impression he could not help making that once, as he was passing by, one street urchin said to another: "Look, there goes the Pope."

He never required the luxuries of living, and he never stayed anywhere for any length of time; living here and there, he appeared and, almost mysteriously, disappeared. He avoided all public places, and would receive no one who had not been brought to him for some definite reason and by reliable friends, and when, rarely enough, he was to be seen anywhere, it was only in the company of some of his young disciples, who were the means of communication between him and the outside world and who made it possible for him to lead his life with his own peculiar and intransigent dignity and consistency.

The impression that his movement made on the youth of Germany was of import for the future events, since George's followers offered an example of both orthodox devotion to a leader and manifest opposition to bourgeois society, and, above all, since they spread the idea of hero-worship, which was the kernel of George's teaching. The powerful creative man was considered the crown of creation; his deed as such was valued without regard for its effect. The fatal result was that this hero-worship became the link between Nietzsche's theory of the will-to-power and that base accomplishment of this will, the Nazi Reich. Trained to worship the hero as such, the youth of the country could no longer distinguish between true greatness and only brilliant criminality. Stefan George himself, whom the national socialists would gladly have exalted into a German D'Annunzio, into an ideal honorary president of the movement, left his country as a protest, as early as 1933, and died as a voluntary exile in Switzerland.

Nietzsche had introduced revolutionary anti-Christianism and the doctrine of a new élite. Stefan George tried to make this élite real, and thus he became an intermediary between Nietzsche's theory and the life of the people. Besides these two clear and decisive minds, the influence of a third personality worked in the same direction, but in a more popular, indeed vulgar sphere: Richard Wagner.

This brilliant but unstable spirit, this "tribune of the people", as Nietzsche calls him, is a product of the nineteenth century, both as an individual and a thinker and artist. His bombastic art and ideas mix romantic and naturalistic, socialistic and heroic, Catholic and pagan, intellectual and sensual, even sexual elements, in a seductive demagogy. All this makes him the immediate ancestor of national socialism, and it is only logical that Hitler should interpret him as such. His teaching, which is influenced alternately by personal resentments and opportunism, contains the germ of the whole stock of concepts and slogans with which national socialism began its career. The poisonous, egomaniac, vociferous tone of Wagner's pamphlets is the same as that of Hitler's messages.

He set the "strong and beautiful man" as a goal. He launched violent attacks against Christianity, democracy and bourgeois civilization, which he called "western" with special, malicious emphasis. But, on the other hand, he re-introduced the people as a factor of power in a mystical and mythical concept. "Not from the filthy foundation of our culture of today," he writes, "shall the art work of the future spring . . . it is not you wise men who are the true inventors, but the people . . . All great inventions are the people's, the devisings of the intellect are but the exploitations, the derivatives, the splinterings and disfigurements of the great inventions of the people . . . It is not you, therefore, who should want to teach the people, but you should let it teach you . . . Our great instructors of the people are in great error when they imagine that the people has to *know* what it wants before it has the capacity or the right to want anything at all . . . It will take the blind involuntary course of Nature; with the necessity of elemental force, it will rend the connection with the power, that is the premise for the rule contrary to Nature."

Here begins the authorization of that vague, utterly indeterminable "healthy reaction of the people" ("gesundes Volksempfinden") by means of which the national socialists have cleared away legality, free science, and free art. But, for Richard Wagner, "the people" means the German people, in a mythical, tribal, Teutonic sense. And in the essay, "Die Wibelungen", he interprets the role of the German people in world history in terms of the Germanic saga, an interpretation that was intended to justify, and that certainly prophesied, the domination of the world by the Germans: "The German people stems from a son of God whose own race calls him Siegfried, but whom the other peoples of the earth call Christ. For the salvation and happiness of his race and of the people that sprang from it, he achieved the most glorious deed, and for this deed suffered death . . . The closest heirs of his deed and of the power won by it, are the "Nibelungen", to whom, in the name of, and for the welfare of all peoples, the world belongs." The hoard, the treasure of the "Nibelungen", is the symbol of all earthly goods, and so, of world domination. "The Germans are the most ancient people. Their king, of their own blood, is a Nibelung and it is as their leader that he shall claim world dominion. The treasure that lends power . . . will be desired by the descendants of that divine hero . . . but it can never be won in slack quiescence, by mere compact, but only by a deed similar to that of him who first won it. This deed, which must always be renewed to transmit the heritage, contains the moral significance of blood-vengeance, of the murder of kin . . ." Siegfried's slaying of the dragon, and his death, become synonymous with Christ's salvation of the world and his expiation of man's sins on the cross, but the difference is that Siegfried's deed is not once and for all, but must be repeated ad infinitum, in order to retain its efficacy. "The God became . . . man, and as a departed man, he fills our spirit with new and intensified participation, in that by his blessed sacrificial deed, he arouses in us the moral impulse of revenge, the longing to avenge his death upon his murderer, and so to renew his deed. The ancient struggle is continued by us, and its fluctuations are like the constant alternation of day and night, summer and winter —finally of the human race itself, which forever and ever, moves from life to death, from victory to defeat, from joy to sorrow."

Here too, then, as in the case of Nietzsche, the Christian interpretation of human history, the common destiny and the one and only life of man, is shattered and replaced by the pagan idea of an eternal recurrence—all this in the sense of a specifically Germanic dynamism, an interpretation contrary to Nietzsche's concept. Very significant too, is the motivation of the historical process, of all of life, on blood-vengeance. The profound German resentment was just as active in Richard Wagner as in Hitler. Finally, as part of his doctrine of Germanic world domination, Richard Wagner introduced and popularized the most important feature of all, in the national socialistic stock in trade: the racial theory and anti-semitism. He took the ideas of Gobineau and promulgated them in the "Bayreuther Blaetter". This, as well as his synthesis of Siegfried and Christ, prepared the way for the ideas of his son-in-law, Houston Stewart Chamberlain, who made Christ an Aryan. It is from Bayreuth that racial anti-semitism in its present form was ushered into the world.

It was, therefore, Richard Wagner who contributed to the world revolution of nihilism that specifically Teutonic note that supplied the political urge. The sum of the motives of nihilism is, however, not complete without taking into account another basic factor that ripened the youth of modern Germany for the terrible enterprises they are engaged in. It is an abysmal loneliness, prevailing in all modern youth, and especially in German young people, whether or not they are aware of it. This feeling of the exposure of the I to the universe, this standing on nothingness and in nothingness, has a long history in Germany. We recall the anarchical mood of Frederick the Great, of this desperate freethinker. We recall the revolutionary deed of Kant who established the inescapable loneliness of the I, and so actually initiated metaphysical nihilism. We can realize the appalling effect of the "Critique of Pure Reason" by the fact that the German poet, Heinrich von Kleist, was close to suicide after having read it. Earnest Christian faith had waned with the development of the natural sciences and the belief in progress. And then this belief in progress itself was undermined by the critical attitude toward modern civilization. Men had been deprived not only of every metaphysical support of their lives but also of all hope for a better future of mankind. Nothing mattered any more but this present world, where conditions were obviously growing worse and worse. Nothing mattered but sheer life, life stripped even of intellect. Marxism had discredited even secular ideologies and claimed they were mere "superstructure" of the prevailing economic framework. Man found himself at the very edge of his existence, face to face with nothingness, and the result was a sense of the utter meaninglessness of existence, a sense of forsakenness in the universe, a sense of organic despair and metaphysical anxiety. Very few people were conscious of all this, but even the duller ones were unconsciously affected by it, and even where it did not express itself, it acted as an irrational spur to the desperate audacity and self-destruction that are desolating Europe.

The first to give expression to this feeling was a devout Christian. This man, a modern Job, was the Danish philosopher, Soeren Kierkegaard. A lonely individual, aware of the danger threatening Christianism, he subjected the Christian faith of his generation to so thorough an examination that it practically amounted to radical scepticism. He fought for his faith like a Protestant Augustine, he maintained his faith against his ruthless, tormenting intellect. He bases Christian faith not on a mere moral postulate but on the despair and fear which the I feels, confronted with nothingness. His criticism of Christianity is, in a sense, a companion piece and a continuation of Kant's critique of reason. He showed the modern nihilists the nothingness of human existence without God. His concept, stripped of its Christian implications, is the kernel of the so-called "Existenz-philosophy" of Heidegger and Jaspers, which, in spite of, or perhaps because of, its extremely complicated and abstract terminology, exerted a tremendous influence on German youth after the First World War. For it revealed the fundamental fear of the nihilistic I, the "shelterless person", as Jaspers calls him, in the face of absolute nothingness.

All these ideas and tendencies were present before the First World War, but it took the tremendous catastrophe to put them to proof. Now people could actually see and feel to what straits mankind had come, and the exaggerated optimism of centuries, that had taken thoughts and promises for reality, now changed to a disconsolate pessimism to which all previous human values appeared as a childish fraud. Since life no longer seemed to proceed upward along a straight line, all perfection was a lie, and all striving for it was futile. Evolution, indeed history, lost its meaning.

This was the mood right after the First World War, when Oswald Spengler's book appeared with its provocative title, "The Decline of the West". The enormous success of this slogan spread the nihilistic password even among those who had never been disturbed in their Christian faith or belief in progress. Spengler wrecked the notion of the continuity of history and, with it, the sense that all men have something in common. For him there are only isolated cultures, independent of one another, each of which rises without rhyme or reason out of nothingness, and sinks, after it has completed its life-cycle, just as individuals are born, live and die. All that these cultures have in common are certain inevitable stages of the life-cycle. These differ according to the character of each culture, but repeat themselves with such unerring uniformity that they become the touchstones for determining the age of any culture and for tracing its immediate future.

Our age is the Germanic age of Faustian, dynamic man who strives for the infinite; the other cultures are past or passing. And although the Faustian culture is already at the peak of its maturity, it still has glorious moments ahead. It is entering upon the phase of the great Caesars, the powerful, ruthless rulers whom it will necessarily produce. Spengler takes the idea of progress away from the world, but in return he gives the Germans the gospel of their superiority and their coming world domination through almighty leaders. Needless to say, for him too, democracy and humanity are symptoms of weakness and decline. For him, the highest form of man is nothing but the beast of prey par excellence, the "inventive beast of prey" that has technics for teeth and claws. And the "race feeling" of the beast of prey, its manifestation of racial strength, is hatred.

It is easy to see how these ideas, stemming from Nietzsche and the Italian thinker, Vico, and spread by journalism in popular slogans, prepared the terrain for national socialism. But under the Hitler regime, Spengler himself has criticized national socialism severely, and has called those of his compatriots who greeted this regime with enthusiasm, "lackeys of success". What he rejected most in national socialism was the residue of democratic heritage in this movement, the demagogic use of popular emotions, the courting of favor of the masses, whom he, like Nietzsche, utterly despised. Still, somehow, Spengler had to take into account the great significance of these masses in the modern state. He tried to solve the problem with what he was the first to call "Prussian socialism". To him, this was only a catchword, dedicated to the Junkers and capitalists and designed to discredit pure socialism.

Pure socialism is common work for a common result that benefits all to the same extent. But Prussian socialism was intended as a revival of the old Prussian State on an enlarged and modern scale. It emphasizes common work, but spirits away the common result. In place of the concrete, living body of the people, which might really enjoy the fruits of its labors, it sets up an abstract, imperialistic state that devours labor but does not distribute the fruits, and that, on top of this, is even glorified the more for it. Work for the common good was decried as materialistic, whereas work for the insatiable power of the abstract state was considered idealistic. Though Prussian socialism was never more than a slogan to Spengler, and though it was a reactionary concept in every respect, it marks the turning point, where the trend moves away from the superman and the great individual toward a new aggressive collectivism.

The next step in this direction was taken by Arthur Moeller van den Bruck, who, in a book published in 1923, declared all political parties, all social classes of the Weimar Republic, to be outmoded, the right as well as the left, the reactionaries as well as the Marxists and democrats. By what he called a "conservative revolution", Germany was to get rid of all the existing prejudices, dogmas and interests, it was to be restored as a world power and was to combine national with social aspirations. To this new Germany he gave the name since adopted by the national socialists, "the Third Reich". Moeller van den Bruck did not have a much clearer idea of German socialism than Spengler, but in contrast to the latter, he sincerely wanted it. His ideas became the focus of a whole group of political and economic projects that later furnished national socialism with arguments and material.

Nietzsche and Stefan George despised the masses and ignored them; Wagner and Spengler despised and cheated them; Moeller van den Bruck made an honest effort to include them·in his new scheme. It remained for Ernst Juenger to see with terrible clarity the role they were destined to play in a world born of nihilism and bred by technics.

Ernst Juenger is the only one among the thinkers of the post-war period who went a step beyond Nietzsche, an important, a decisive step. It is he who bears the greatest responsibility for preparing the German youth for the Hitler state, between 1920 and 1933. Even today, his underground influence is very great, especially in the élite guards, and, if there is anyone at all, it is he who must be taken as the intellectual exponent of Nazi youth. In spite of this, he does not profess to be a national socialist. On the contrary, in hidden passages of his earlier books, and particularly in his recently published "Auf den Marmorklippen" (On the Marble Cliffs), he has voiced his scorn for the "hangmen and their helpers", unambiguously.

Juenger describes the state of mind of that generation of young people whom today we regard as the carriers of national socialism in the world. He has experienced in himself the emergence of this youth, for he has so great a heritage of mental education, of critical acumen and of knowledge of the time before the First World War, that he is conscious of what has happened, that he can recognize and formulate it. True Nazi youth no longer has that consciousness. When Juenger became a soldier in 1914, he had completed high school and had read and thought a great deal; but still, he was only eighteen years old. For him, the war was a decisive experience, the core and point of departure for his views. He realized it, however, not so much as a national and historic event, that may be regarded ideologically or emotionally, but as a typical process of modern technology, as a revelation of the new world power which is technology. He was, accordingly, not interested in the abstract idea of war, but in the concrete phenomenon of the modern battle. He was a model officer and led many actions with extraordinary presence of mind. This presence of mind went beyond the moment of action; he developed it to something that he calls "a second and colder consciousness", an ability to regard himself as an object, to place himself beyond the zone of pain, even of sensation. In the midst of battles, he found the time and the repose to survey the process in which he himself was included, to analyze it and to note down his observations. Later, he described modern battle in several volumes with exactness and enthusiasm, on the basis of these notes. He is chiefly concerned with the role of man in this modern battle which he calls the "battle of matériel". As a previously quoted passage from his writing shows, men and machines are on a par in this kind of battle, man is yoked to the machine in a gigantic process that he can neither behold in its entirety nor escape. He becomes assimilated to the machine; he is part of the machine. Juenger regards this as symbolic for the whole of modern existence. Behind the front, and after the war, this process develops into the total state, to the condition of permanent "total mobilization" that subjects all the forces of the people to a single purpose: the increase of state power.

But total mobilization is only the perfecting of a phenomenon that manifests itself everywhere in modern life, even under a democratic constitution, in every factory, in every stadium, and even in modern amusement parks. Everywhere the human being is completely subject to the demands of a mechanized entity in which he, as an individual, is submerged. No matter where a human being is engaged, he is a member of a collective, he marches in a column, he is a worker and, at the same time, a soldier. And in the face of this governing fact, it is immaterial whether this collective is an empire, a classless society, or a football team. The empire is nothing but a world record; a world record is nothing but technical, purposeless will-to-power.

For Nietzsche, for Stefan George, and for Spengler, the will to power was a function of the human being, of the great individual. For Juenger it is embodied in the collective. But even the collective has no specific coloration; it no longer implies any intellectual values, whether national or social. In it, technics are all-powerful, technics as the new, post-Christian world power. It is no longer a question of a new Germany, it is no longer a question of Prussian or Marxian socialism—all these are values of the past; for they are, after all, values. The new collective that is struggling for power is forced onward by the law of technics inherent in it; it no longer requires any justification through values. The imperialistic, military communism that Juenger proclaims is an inescapable technical phenomenon, and it is idle to speculate whether it is justifiable or desirable. The individual can only maintain himself in this over-

whelming procession of things and machines by acknowledging
himself as a victim, by offering himself as a sacrifice and as-
similating himself to the machine as completely as possible. The
human being rules only in so far as he serves this process. To insist on the personal value, on the human dignity of the individual,
is old-fashioned, bourgeois love of pleasure, and to want existence
to have a meaning is a luxury that no one can allow himself any
more.

Ernst Juenger, himself, still knows about such luxuries as the
meaning of existence and the dignity of man. He still knows about
the Christian values, humanity, spirit, history. But he no longer
wastes energy in combatting all that. He simply states that it no
longer exists. He substantiates his claim by the picture of the young
people who grew up after him and who no longer know anything
about these things. These young people no longer belong to the
anti-Christian era; neither can they be called really pagan. They
are not affected by the absurd attempts of certain German professors to revive the old Germanic religion. They live in a "post-
Christian era" in which Christianity no longer plays a part. They
know nothing of a meaning of life and do not suffer consciously
from the lack of this meaning. If they still sense that fear of nothingness that haunted the thinking generation before them, this
fear becomes effective in them only as an anonymous urge to blind
and unthinking adaptation to the collective, to a technical process
that consumes man entirely. Service to the machine has taken the
place of religious services or of service to an idea. These young
people represent, as Juenger says, "a combination of high organizational capacity and complete color-blindness toward values,
faith without content, and discipline without justification." For
them, "technics and ethics become, in a curious way, synonymous."
We see by their deeds in Europe what such a human type means;
only such a human type can perpetrate atrocities of such mathematical exactitude.

And with this we have arrived at the human core of today's
crisis. Juenger's theory, which really is no theory but exact descrip-

tion, reveals the whole depth of the foundation on which national socialism stands, and this foundation is far more important than national socialism itself. The young people's state of mind that Juenger describes was there before national socialism, it exists above and beyond national socialism, and its premises are given in all countries and in all movements. These premises will not be obviated with the fall of national socialism. Hitler has merely exposed the ultimate consequences that spring from such a state of mind, and therein lies his importance.

It is, to be sure, no mere coincidence that these ultimate consequences were reached precisely in Germany. The development of ideologies, as we have described it, reveals the historical structure of the German phenomenon of our time. The mother-cell is the Prussian state, that unique rotation of functions whose only purpose was the increase of abstract collective power. The organization of this Prussian state was on austere, rational lines, and its military and economic discipline already manifests the principle of technics, of precise cooperation of specialized functions, of the "assembly line", of the "stream line". In Prussian discipline, the autonomy of technics was shaped even before the material equipment of technics was created. Man had already become an instrument in the service and at the mercy of a machine—the dominating machine of the Prussian state.

Democracy, with its accompanying phenomena of industrial revolution and capitalism, and finally, socialism, have added the missing material and social ingredients, the mechanical apparatus and the masses of population. With this, new basic conditions were given that the modern authoritarian regimes must take into account, but which, in their turn, supply them with new means for the domination of men. Prussian discipline exerted itself upon men's outer life. The discipline of modern dictatorship exerts itself upon their inner life as well. It applies the principles of fully developed technology to the psychological subjection of the human soul. Democracy and the growth of population has made peoples into functions of politics in an entirely different way. At the time of the Prussian state, politics were the concern of the few, of monarchs and their cabinet ministers. And if, in spite of Christianity and international law, politics has always been a moral No Man's Land, still it was enough for governments, in so far as they required a justification of their procedures, to reconcile the amorality of politics with the still accepted and irreplaceable standards of Christian civilization, by accusing opponents and mouthing patriotic slogans. Today, the masses actively participate in politics, even under dictatorships. Modern dictatorships require not only the material but the psychic forces, not only the labor but also the will and the faith of people. If a marauding expedition of the universal magnitude the Nazis have intended is to be set in action, then the norms of Christian civilization, mercy, generosity and pity for the weak, and the doubts and criticisms of a moral and intellectual conscience take on the character of technical disturbances in the functioning of the state machinery. The logical answer was to do away with these disturbing factors by extending the amorality of international politics to the sphere of standards valid within the state, to the whole of human life that is to belong to the state alone. Inhuman behavior, impulses to robbery, to power, to crime, all these are consciously made the standard. And this decisive break is due to Hitler.

In this he was helped by the spiritual and mental development of recent generations. The doctrine of power and the will-to-power, proven by Nature through the struggle for existence and the survival of the fittest; the glorification of the genius and hero per se, of the leader's will as creator of law, of the master-man and the master-race; romantic irrationalism, the metaphysical despair of dogma as of reason, the horror of nothingness—all these components, combined with old Prussian and modern industrial mechanization and discipline, resulted in that specific combination of mad irrationality and keen rationality that characterizes Hitler's Reich. The irrational elements are the magic leader to whom everything is to be sacrificed, and the colossal raid projected to boundless extremes, the empire above all empires. All criminal and sex urges that can serve this savior and this end are not only released but stimulated and rewarded. They are, at the same time, collectively coordinated and rationally systematized by that carefully developed military, industrial and administrative organization, of which the Germans, educated on Prussian principles, are capable as is no other people. And the rational spirit of modern technics is the absolute ruler of this organization.

There is no field, there is no age, there is no impulse that has not been technically organized by the Nazis down to the last detail, for the purposes of world domination. The concept of "Gleichschaltung", taken over from the field of technics, is the device of this deliberate, superimposed standardization of souls. The process effective after the seizure of power, the process that in an incredibly short time filtered through all mentalities, movements, activities, from learned societies to barbers' associations and rabbit-breeders, this process that regulated everything to the same pace, to the same degree, like clocks or electric tensions, is unique in history.

The law of technics rules the union between the sexes, from which not only love but even choice is excluded. Selection according to Darwin's theory is being artificially organized. Men and women are mated like beasts. On fixed "sex days" soldiers are coupled with selected girls from bourgeois families, and strict care is taken that the same couple never meets a second time. The children are born in state hospitals and belong to the state. Physically, mentally or politically undesirable specimens are sterilized. Entire peoples are prevented from propagating. "Race factors" are calculated by percentages based on a misapplication of Mendel's principles of heredity. Masses of people are transplanted like species of plants and forced to serve like domestic animals or machines.

The law of technics also operates in the forming of minds, in propaganda and education. Propaganda, as we have said before, follows the methods of American advertising. Russian propaganda imposed only a definite, closed system of rational argumentation with a rational goal. But advertising depends on purely physical appeal. It forces a name, a slogan, upon the memory until this name and this slogan become part of the mind and continue to act within it, mechanically and automatically. Advertising saves people the necessity of critical selection, and when, in addition to this, all competition is eliminated, when a chorus of newspapers, radios and speeches drone the same thing from morning till night, then the mind yields and surrenders to suggestion. The same principle is applied in schools, in youth organizations, in the universities, and all fields of knowledge are tuned to the same slogans and distorted to fit military and technical goals. From the instant man leaves the womb, his every hour is ground in the mill of the state; one organization passes him on to another until he emerges, stream-lined and polished, for the use of the state.

Human impulses to mercy and compassion are destroyed in the soul, not only through education and propaganda, but through the command to be cold and ruthless, through deliberate training. Atrocities, torture and persecution, the slaughter of the Jews, had the subsidiary aim of stifling emotion, of preparing men for total war. Schoolchildren were excused from their classes in order to participate in the burning of synagogues, in the robbing of Jewish stores. Atrocities in themselves are not a specific characteristic of national socialism, even though here they exceed any previous standard. At all times there has been slaughter and sadistic torture of every sort, tolerated, authorized and even executed by governments. The special note of the atrocities of national socialism is that they are performed in a rational, systematic, administrative way. They are characterized by that "second and colder consciousness", that collective consciousness that is inherent in technics. That the ashes of a murdered man are mailed to his family by parcel post, that the cross-examination of terrified Jews is broadcast for the amusement of the radio audience, that human beings are used to test the efficacy of new poison gases—these are indeed new attainments that have never existed in all of history. German physicians did not shrink from mass murder by injections of air bubbles into the veins, and the corpses of victims were turned into fats and soap and lubricants. When one considers this, a horrible vision of Ernst Juenger's does not seem so far removed from reality. In one of his books he describes how he enters an elegant delicatessen store in which human flesh is displayed, and discusses with the sales-clerk the best method of preparing it. On leaving the store, he remarks:

"I did not know that civilization had progressed so far in this city . . ."

The spirit of national socialist practices has already spread to other countries. Through bureaucratic scheming and administrative measures, through deportations or merely by closing the borders, unfortunate fugitives are, to be sure, not killed, but deliberately left to a frightful death. It has been reserved for our era to witness such spectacles as steamers crowded with helpless people roaming the ocean because they are not permitted to land anywhere, or the starving of such victims on the No Man's Land of a river island between borders. Hitler's teachings are bearing fruit!

But this is not the end. National socialism is, after all, still out for substantial power, for substantial booty. But the young people whom Ernst Juenger describes, and who perform the deeds of the Third Reich, go beyond this. For them, national socialism has already become an old-fashioned, romantic movement with much too much ballast of slogans, urges, appetites, waste of energy. For them, national socialism is not sufficiently objective, cold and stream-lined. They are no longer concerned with the national to-do, with the bombastic swindle of ideologies. They are concerned exclusively with the maximum of technical achievement. These young people are brought up on modern sport, on collective competition for the maximum achievement—no matter in what field. Only formal technical achievement is objective enough, is real enough to satisfy them. And so in the world empire, they see nothing but a gigantic world record. Just as today sport has become a serious business in which men stake their ultimate strength, their very lives, so here, the most serious things that men are capable of become sport, and there is a complete fusion of both. Through this, technology itself, technology for its own sake, receives limitless power. Here the last residue of significance is destroyed. This means that, on the one hand, the rational becomes irrational, but, on the other, that the irrational becomes altogether rational. The rule over men by things and machines, man's adaptation to the machine, has come to its climax. World anarchy and the transcendence of the individual existence have reached the state of totality.

In all countries of the world the first traces of such a development can be observed. Among the mass of those greedy for money and power, among the passé socialites and hunters for the sensational among that second group that still serve production or a party, with more or less conviction, among that third group driven through the mills of business by the need of their daily bread, among all these crowds in our great cities, there are already young people who live only for technics per se, mechanical, economic, sport and scientific technics, in whom human impulses are already on the wane. These young people are indifferent to the affairs of men, either individual or collective, they are indifferent to questions of principle, to the why and wherefore of things, they are indifferent to the lives of their fellow men because they are indifferent to their own. Their life no longer belongs to them at all, but rather to that ghostly technics that fascinate them like a cross-word puzzle or a sport championship. "Technics and ethics become in a curious way synonymous . . ."

This is the world in which we live.

UNITY OF THE SECULAR WORLD

THE KINGDOM OF MAN

WHEN, AFTER OUR survey of the history of man, we regard the world of today, we see that current conditions are in a way similar to those of the early stages of human development. The great curve of human evolution seems—though on a different level —to be returning to its point of departure, to a state of chaotic participation. Man is helplessly entangled in a net of universal relations and reciprocal reactions, which he neither understands nor controls. He is continually tormented and shaken with fear. His response to the intangible effects of that ghostly universal entanglement comes in a barbaric, bewildered reaction: he personalizes, demonizes objective forces, makes races, classes, persons responsible for his suffering and persecutes them in blind fury. As of old, the struggle of peoples and groups assumes the character of blood-vengeance. The individual is made to answer for his race, the race for the individual; animal urges are unleashed, men regarded and treated like cattle. The individual is drowned in the group. Human life becomes valueless, and the rights and the dignity of the individual are wiped out. More and more, the picture of man's psychic life, and its reflection in the various arts, come to resemble a new primeval landscape in which fragments of a technical civilization, portions of rationalized consciousness and a wild vegetation of unchecked instincts mingle incoherently in the confusion of anarchy. Everything is in flux, everything is open to question, everything is involved in perpetual change and dissolution.

This process of disruption, which went on during the last century in a slow, hidden approach to crisis, was uncovered and rendered acute by national socialism. We have said before that national socialism is not a new order, it is the climax and the agony of the old. But by driving the old to the extreme, indeed ad absurdum, the Nazis have driven it to the verge of the new. The anarchy of the world of the nineteenth and twentieth centuries had long overgrown the founding principle of our civilization, the human principle. What the whole world had only ignored and left to atrophy the Nazis openly denied. Without shame or compunction, they have drawn the ultimate conclusions from the world situation. They were the first deliberately to penetrate to the extreme boundaries of inhumanity, boundaries that lie beyond bestiality, for in what the Nazis do there is none of the innocent ferocity of beasts. And man, when he does not fall from his human plane, but descends from it in full consciousness, reaches not an animal but a sub-animal level. The Nazis have arrived at the utmost boundaries of inhumanity, not through their piling-up of sheer atrocities, not even through their administrative, indeed didactic perpetration of atrocities, but through their applying the methods of technics to the state, to the order of man. In this way they have degraded man in a hitherto unheard-of manner: they have deprived him of his humanity and made him into a thing. Their premeditated descent from the human level is their crucial, revolutionary innovation; in this they have bared the human core of today's world crisis. They have shown that this crisis is neither purely political, economic nor social, but that it is a total crisis, a moral crisis, a crisis of the whole being of man.

The people of the European continent have experienced this in their very flesh—which is not to say they are capable of consciously grasping the meaning of this experience. But in England and America people have not seen the worst of the horrors—for these are not the bombings—they have not seen them happen with their own eyes, nor happen to their own neighbors and kin. They are, for the most part, far from gauging the scope of what has happened. They tackle the situation only from a military, political, economic or social angle. Some see it as just another, bigger, war, others realize the catastrophe, but attribute it only to the megalomania of the dictators, or to the inherent aggressiveness of the German people, or to the political blunders of their own governments. But only the very fewest are aware that we ourselves and the life we lead have anything to do with what is happening in Europe and that we all house the germs of this kind of development. Hitler is only a symptom, and what he represents will not be destroyed by the defeat of his armies. German "aggressiveness" and German militarism are only the immediate factors that exploded the crisis, but certainly not its origin. And the errors of the various governments are nothing but the automatic results of a state of mind that prevails all over the world in our century.

The Nazis—and in this the Russians were ahead of them—drew another conclusion from the world situation, and their predatory abuse of their knowledge must not deter us from recognizing the significance hidden in this abuse. They have grasped and demonstrated that in the life of a people, as in every organic structure, everything is connected with everything else, that the politics of a country are related to its economic methods, that education is not mere handing-on of knowledge, but a decisive shaping of national life from its very origins, and that the arts and sciences are not purely academic or theoretic functions, but have a vital or fatal influence on the community. The Nazis have demonstrated that the various activities of man can no longer be pursued separately or centrifugally, but that their coordination, their subordination to a directive goal, can produce initiative, performance and vitality far greater than exists in the material sum of all these activities. The goal of national socialism is criminal and anachronistic, but the fact that all the forces of the people have been directed to a single purpose and that this purpose is the radical destruction of our civilization—this calls in question the purpose of that civilization, the meaning of our entire way of life; we are forced to grasp our civilization as a whole to the same degree that the foe confronts us with a whole.

We are called upon to defend our civilization. But what is our

civilization? Is it simply the status quo ante? If this is so, it means
the very condition that bred national socialism. The status quo
ante was in itself an unacknowledged denial of the human principle that originally founded our civilization. The Nazis openly acknowledged this denial and turned it into a motive power. If we
want to meet their fundamental challenge we shall have to counter
it with the original principle of our civilization; total negation
must be answered by affirmation just as total.

Defending our civilization, then, means defending its total, fundamental principle, the forgotten human idea that brought about
all that we comprehend under the term civilization. This principle
is not a static thing, it is a living, moving, expanding impulse and
quality of man; our survey of history has shown us that this idea
and the values it includes are the idea and the values of man himself. This idea, brought to full expression by Christianity, tends to
develop further and further; it is not a status, it is a direction. So if
we want to defend the idea of yesterday we have to carry out an idea
of tomorrow. The human principle can be saved only by seeking its
new form: a higher level of realization. And before this new level,
this position of tomorrow, has been grasped and occupied, the actual struggle against the fascist forces has not even begun.

In this present world crisis, then, it is a question of man, not of
any partial issue. It is idle to discuss new political or economic arrangements before the basic question of the meaning and the direction of future civilization has been cleared up. We do not know
what the concrete picture of the world will be when this war is over.
We do not know to what conditions the plans we make today are
to be applied. And though it is useful and even necessary to make
the most thorough preparations for what is to be, the only thing
that can be established in advance with absolute certainty is *the
meaning, the direction of a new order*. The spirit in which the
world is to be reconstructed must be the first consideration, the concrete forms are secondary and in themselves offer no guarantees of
security. There are various paths to one and the same goal, and the
choice does not depend only on our thinking and planning, no mat-

ter how accurate and circumspect this may be, but on a host of concrete circumstances that we cannot gauge as yet. And, on the other
hand, the best schemes, institutions and constitutions can be so interpreted and handled that their spirit imperceptibly changes to the
reverse of what was originally intended. The Nazis have given us
an example of how the most excellent democratic constitution can
be used to destroy democracy. Our means must—indeed they cannot but—be flexible, our ends alone can—indeed they must—be
clear.

If, therefore, at the close of this book, we look toward the future,
it is not in order to offer detailed prognoses or special remedies. We
are concerned, in the first place, with determining the goal and direction of a future order. Only then will concepts and problems
become clear, only then can concrete suggestions for the solution
of individual questions evolve. That is why the matter of basic principles is the most pressing, far more pressing than statistics and
elaborate plans. These principles should be thought out, and they
should be thought out at once. Events are always more rapid than
thought, because preparatory thinking is never done in time. And
so the danger arises that the greatest decisions mankind is to make
will in the end be patched together out of the remnants of old disorders. These basic questions are not only the affair of scholars, intellectuals and preachers; they concern every single individual, for
the spirit that rules the world to come will be felt by each of us in
his very flesh.

What this book was intended to show is that history is not an
accidental conglomerate of events, not a meaningless come-and-go
of forces, not the deliberate accomplishment of individuals, but a
connected whole, the unified, consistent development of an organic
being that is man. History is a unity, it has a meaning, and so it has
a definite direction. This direction is not merely the work of man's
will, nor can he alter it by an act of will any more than the phases
of youth, maturity and age can be altered within an individual.
Man can determine himself, but only in so far as he recognizes the
processes of his nature, as he foresees the tendency of development,
smooths its path and exploits its forces. To a certain extent, he has

the power to change destructive, convulsive struggle into free, ordered formation. But even in his most Promethean achievements
man with all his insight and foresight has done no more than further an evolution whose germs and scope lay beyond his power.
And so the only guide for our plans and action is to recognize the
direction of human development.

We have shown in our survey that since the Renaissance man's
development has moved more and more *in the direction of collectivity.* At the very moment the individual was completed, the attempt to establish a collective order began. As we have seen, the
sheer necessity of limiting the anarchical struggles for power among
individuals and dynasties forced men toward state and international organization. We saw how the human community changed
more and more from species to collective, from an inner community, spontaneously determined by birth and tradition, to an outer,
consciously created community that consists in cooperation and organization. The form of human community that we call nation is
still embodied in and accomplished through the individual. That
is why the nation, in its purest form, could be represented by a symbolic person, the monarch, and ruled by personal methods. The step
from national monarchy to the democracy and to the state involves
a growing expansion and complication of administrative tasks, a
gradual advance to organized cooperation. We observed the same
process in the field of human knowledge, which develops from artistic and philosophic insights, that is, notions completed in the individual personality and its individual work, to the organized collective experiences of science, which go beyond the personal unit
and depend on the collaboration of many individuals and generations. Inner, intuitive understanding of the world changes to a
quantitive, expanding, rational method of world investigation.
Even the artist is less and less able to comprehend the connections
of the modern world in one closed picture. The ultimate truth of
the artist's vision can no longer be expressed by the symbols of individual figures and destinies. Similarly, we saw how the economic
activities of man developed from the management of individual estates, from the journeys of the individual merchant, to the anony-

mous collective colossus of modern enterprise, to national economy and to the more and more closely intermeshed world economy. In the course of this development, too, methods became more and more rational, systematic, technical, and so passed beyond the individual.

This far-reaching process has brought with it a fundamental change in man. The individual is forced beyond his own bounds; he transcends his personal life. His center of gravity shifts more and more from himself to the collective he must work in. And this means that individual life merges increasingly in collective functions, that it is absorbed by and consumed in collective work. We traced this transcendence of the individual in the participant in capitalistic enterprise, owner, executive or working-man, in the servant of the Prussian and totalitarian state, in the communistic revolutionary, in modern youth devoted to technics and sports. All of these, indeed the majority of modern city-dwellers, have this in common: they have become functions of a collective, and their personal life is little more than what the collective leaves them, a remnant that has less and less to do with personality, since human inclinations and reactions are becoming more and more standardized.

The modern development of man, then, shows one thing with indisputable clarity: the growing tendency toward collectivity and the invalidation of the individual. The trend toward collectivity is inevitable. We cannot evade it, unless we set aside technical and rational progress—which is obviously impossible. Technics mean collectivism. So today everything is collective, capitalism no less than socialism, science and sport no less than industry. We must, of course, gauge the development by the modern city, the most advanced front of modern life, not by the relics of former modes of life that still persist in small towns, in the country and in remote regions. If the current trend continues, the metropolitan mode of life will take in ever wider areas. With agriculture increasingly mechanized and small towns and rural districts "modernized", standardization, collectivization of goods and ways of life will presently spread over whole countries and continents. The fact that considerable parts of the world are as yet completely or partially unaffected by the modern mode of life does not disprove our contention.

What distinguishes the modern *"individualist"* from the modern *"collectivist"* or *"socialist"* is, therefore, not a greater or lesser degree of collectivity in his mode of life; it is simply a difference in the form of collective in which each participates and a difference in interpretation or awareness of the facts. The so-called "rugged individualist" is characterized by emotional remnants of an attitude toward life that was formed in another age and under other conditions and that prevents him from recognizing the true state of affairs. Usually he no longer has any idea of what individuality really is and never suspects that the trends he is encouraging are the very ones most likely to destroy it. For, as we shall see in a moment, what he actually represents is not individuality at all, but private collectivity as opposed to public collectivity, the interest of a collective private enterprise or a collectivized private life in contrast to the interests of the people as a whole. He confuses "individual" with "private".

In order to explain, we must first try to establish what true individuality is. The Oxford English Dictionary defines individuality—according to the very origin of the word—as an indivisible, inseparable entity, "one in substance or essence", "distinguished from others by attributes of its own". So individuality does not mean personal interests and their pursuit, but an inner, personal way of thinking and feeling that suffuses the whole of a person's existence and permeates all of its manifestations and forms. In other words: to have individuality is not so much to be a single one as to be a whole one, it is not so much to have a mind of one's own, as to have one's own mind. A person can live utterly for God, for another, for his work. He can forget himself completely in his devotion or preoccupation and still be a shining example of individuality, provided that what he lives for is his personal relation to God, his personal love, his personal work—a work that bears his features, that reflects the meaning and content of his own life. The work of the artist who achieves a creation complete in itself, of the thinker whose vision interprets the world, of the craftsman of earlier times who wrought an object from beginning to end and put into it the experience of years, of the farmer who saw his labor whole within the circle of the seasons, the work of such a person is literally in his own hands, he is literally at home in it and with it; work is a function of his personal life, not the function of an alien, overwhelming enterprise that imposes the rules for working and even for living. Because his work is such that he can put himself into it, he can take from it what he gives to it—meaning, knowledge, purpose—and in this interplay of two wholes each builds and informs the other, each, in fact gives individuality to the other. But the specialized work of today does not concern the whole human being, it requires and develops only partial and peripheral skills. The division of labor has divided man as well as his work, divided him from himself as well as from his work. And as man loses his wholeness, his indivisibility, he loses his individuality.

To have individuality is to be oneself, or rather it is to have a self to be. How many people in our large cities are allowed to be themselves or, if they have the privilege, have the capacity and the inclination? Even those who still have sufficient leisure no longer know how to fill it with personal life; such things are no longer taught. People are confronted with articles manufactured en masse, with mass conveniences, mass amusements, that is: impersonal objects, ready-made pleasures, too much and too many of everything. An article made by hand is a truly concrete article. It is an individual article that cannot be exactly reproduced and it bears the traces of the mind, the moods and even the weaknesses of the individual who made it. A mass-manufactured article is not concrete: it is a pattern in physical form, a materialized concept, without a trace of individuality and intended not for any one person but for collective types. A truly concrete object is not finished when ready for delivery, and once delivered cannot be used and discarded like a paper cup; it becomes a possession only by being taken possession of, it is acquired in a slow process of mutual assimilation that adds to inner experience, to personal life. Individuality in the object fosters individuality in the enjoyer, as it did in the maker. Such a relationship and such an enjoyment requires space and time to develop, they are crowded out by a multiplicity of uniform objects. The slow study of the object, the experiencing of pleasure, the transformation of pleasure into knowledge and life, all this demands leisure and justifies leisure, and it is this that differentiates leisure from idleness, just as it differentiates pleasure from pastime. Leisure is personal time, time for oneself, the most precious time of all, while idleness is alien, empty, impersonal time, time that must be whiled away, the most valueless and senseless time there is. In our modern cities those who still have time pass it in a veritable "horror vacui", with endless tumult and noise. The very people whose main preoccupation is pleasure know least of all what pleasure and happiness really are. What they take for pleasure is an uninterrupted routine of dulling excitement.

True individuality, as we have seen, presupposes meaning in the life of the individual, and today people find meaning neither in their work nor in their so-called leisure, they no longer even look for any. Work for them has only a purpose, and that lies outside of it: earning a living and making money. The same thing holds true of leisure, which contains less and less meaning, that is, pleasure, and is filled more and more with pastime or sheer exhaustion.

As individuality in modern man is being atrophied by his work and by the content of his so-called leisure, what, then, is left of the individual that the individualist so passionately defends? In the first place the private interest of making as much money as possible, of ascending the income scale. The little man still feels the old delight of the gambler and gold prospector of pioneer times, the dream of a sudden magical opportunity that will convert the underdog into an upperdog from one moment to the next. He clings to the idea of freedom of decision and initiative, even though all possibilities are growing more and more circumscribed. It is this that makes him a "rugged individualist".

But what about those who have arrived, the great entrepreneurs and executives, the chiefs of individualism? In their case, individualism is not limited to the private interest of a person or a family, to the maintenance—and this requires the increase—of their capital. Their interest is necessarily more far-reaching: it concerns influence calculated to maintain the condition of their prosperity, the system of capitalism, influence on national and international politics—in a word, power. But even this effort, this "will-to-power", has far outgrown the stage of purely individual interest. Wealth today provides no greater pleasures or greater joy of living than lesser means attain to. A rich and powerful man, to be sure, has more obvious possibilities of enjoying life: a Renaissance prince or a French nobleman of the ancien régime developed a higher form of enjoyment than a poor peasant. But the condition of the modern world prevents the millionaire as well as the average man from developing his sense of the enjoyment of life, for neither is a free individual. Both lead the same restless, exhausting life of work in the service of a collective function. The big executives rush from conference to conference and usually have an even smaller margin of individual life than their employees. They gulp down their life like a hastily eaten meal, until one day they die of a heart attack. They motivate their private interests with collective interests; they support their principles of individualism and capitalism with arguments of public welfare. The private interests vested in their persons have indeed long ago merged with their anonymous enterprise, have fused with the interests of a private collective. All those motives, arguments and methods that could no longer be justified in the case of the private individual have been transferred to the impersonal private collective where they have found a safe haven.

In the final analysis, therefore, the best that can be said of the best-intentioned individualist is that he is quixotic—or perhaps utopian. He defends something that no longer exists or that can exist only within a truer collective than has up to now been achieved. He fails to see that individualism as it is preached today is a confusion of the issue. Today, in reality, it is not the individual who stands in opposition to the collective, it is the *private collective* that stands in opposition to the *public collective*.

And this brings us to the crux of the question. The contrast between the private collective and the public collective is simply the contrast between a collective *governed by things* and one *governed by man*. To understand what is at stake one must consent for a mo-

ment to set aside class and party prejudice and go back to the simple question: What do people live for? And what is really worth
living for? As Ernst Juenger has demonstrated, even to put such a
question has become a luxury no one can afford; and this in itself
is an evidence of the devaluation of the individual. Yet it is perhaps
not a luxury, but a dire necessity, to investigate this question for
man as a whole, in this, our great crisis.

In the course of its development, free capitalistic world economy
has assumed the character and scope of an elemental force that has
got out of man's control. Any uncontrolled and steadily growing
force becomes a catastrophe that can bury man and his civilization.
The critical turn of modern social development originates in a
vicious circle in which man was involved by capitalistic economy.
Money is the exchange value of goods—goods that exist and can
be acquired, and goods that do not exist and must be produced.
Money becomes "capital" when employed reproductively, and reproduction of money involves production of goods. Capitalism,
however, is not characterized by these processes alone; it does not
come into its own until they become self-reproductive. The great
Italian merchants of the Renaissance, though already engaged in
capitalistic enterprises, tended to consider the money that reproduced itself in these enterprises, that is, the profits, as a means to a
human end. They employed it for personal property, for personal
power, for the adornment and enjoyment of life, and so the capitalistic process circled back to man; it was finite and remained in
the control of man. The turning point came with the advent of the
truly capitalistic mind that regards money chiefly as capital, less to
be enjoyed as personal wealth, than to be re-employed in the reproduction of itself and the production of goods. In this way the capitalistic process, instead of circling back to man, became an end in
itself, and so, in reality, became endless. It made of man a means
and passed not only beyond the individual, but beyond man and
man's control. Capital, reproduced through production, demands
expansion of production and of the means of production. The expansion of production, in turn, demands more and more capital. So
the vicious circle spirals to overwhelming proportions; the snow-

ball becomes an avalanche. In the course of this expansion develop the private collectives, the factories, industries, corporations and concerns, modern technics, mass production and the ungovernable number of objects that crowd our world and weigh our minds. The theme of modern history has become the struggle for goods. Among the capitalistic powers, the private collectives, it is a struggle for potential goods, for production and the means of production; this struggle automatically develops into competition for markets, the cause of more and more devastating crises and wars. For the workers and employees, it remains a struggle for actual goods, for the means of livelihood. This whole process means that goods, potential and actual—the means of production and the means of livelihood—determine the life of man. Goods are no longer subordinate to the good of man, but man to the growth of goods. Production is idealized, it becomes mythical, it is the true deity of our times. Because it affords men work, and that means bread, it takes on the aspect of a life-giving power, to be furthered and expanded at all costs.

Endless production is at once the prerequisite and the ideal of capitalism. And yet it destroys capitalism. For off the production line comes a development that, at a certain point, begins to oppose free capitalistic economy and to undermine its foundations. Capitalism has produced technics, and, through the shortening of distances and time, through the standardization and collectivization of goods, technics has brought about that interdependence of individuals and peoples, of each with all, that has made a latent collective of the men of today. In a world of such dependencies every struggle must necessarily become a catastrophe that causes the whole to founder. And thus free capitalistic economy, through the struggle of private collectives for capital and markets (whether domestic or foreign), is falling into a more and more precarious and paradoxical position. On the one hand, it increases the interconnection of the world through the continued expansion of technical methods and achievements to "backward" fields, on the other, its competitive methods run counter to this interconnection. In the expansion of capitalistic economy there have always been moments when the practices of competition, or discrepancies between producing and purchasing power, have led to depression or war; but now the interdependence within and between nations has made depressions and wars so comprehensive in their ravages that populations, threatened with death or starvation before natural readjustment can, if ever, take place, demand or accept more or less violent forms of government control. And what government control means to capitalism any capitalist will tell you.

Production as an end in itself defeats itself; quite apart from whether it is desirable or not, it appears to be no longer possible. But even supposing it were possible as an economic goal, is it possible as a human aim? The present world catastrophe already bears witness to the devastation which the development of world economy has wrought in the soul of man. What we are undergoing today is a direct consequence of the decay of the human and spiritual values of our civilization. These values collapsed in all countries and among all peoples touched by our civilization, because people are no longer vitally concerned with them in a world where the relations of men to things outweigh the relations of men to men. In such an environment, spiritual and moral values have taken on a somewhat absurd, indeed ridiculous aspect. They are typical subjects of sermons and speeches. No one takes them seriously any more, no one shapes the conduct of his life according to them, no one possibly can, because they run counter to the "practical" world. No one is his own master in his struggle for existence and capital. Actions are no longer human decisions; they are dictated by objective requirements. And even for a pious person to apply what he hears in church on Sunday to his week-day activities, demands such a complicated act of translation that he can hardly undertake it. In the modern world the attempt to be a reasonably good person is not simply a matter of natural disposition, but of deep insight and knowledge. It requires the understanding of complex connections, that is, a mental achievement. Goodness has never ruled the world, but never has goodness been made so hard for man, never has he been weaned away from it as methodically as through the tendency of our age. Out of man's obsession with goods, his entanglement in a net of technical functions and relations, his mental and moral confusion—out of the subservience of man to things have come the barbarism, the state of chaotic participation, that characterize the world of today. And the Nazis' total disregard and contempt of man, their degradation of man to the status of a thing, is only the extreme consequence of this situation.

At the beginning of the great industrial development, there was still talk of human welfare. The rationalistic optimists expected that the new inventions, and those still to come, would enrich and develop man's nature. Machines would relieve him of toil for the bare necessities of existence, they would make human labor more and more superfluous and thus leave him time and strength to live his own life, to live for higher knowledge and happiness. But just the opposite of these fair dreams came true. The aids to existence became ends in themselves, and man lives almost exclusively for the increase and the cult of these aids. He is working himself to death to produce the appurtenances of life.

The optimists of today still endow all-powerful production with the mission of blessing an increasing number of people with a higher standard of living. But what does a higher standard of living mean today? Does it still mean a higher standard of life, more leisure for pleasure through deeper understanding? No, it means more air-conditioning, more washing machines, refrigerators and safety razors, automobiles and airplanes. Of course, modern living conditions mean more and more widespread cleanliness, hygiene, security of daily life. But the comforts of cleanliness of the body are outweighed by the growing barbarism of inner life, and the comforts of hygiene and security in the details of life are largely upset by the terrible insecurity of life as whole. To be sure, many of the modern devices are labor-saving. But, as we have seen, the division and specialization of labor split man from his work, and this means, split his work from his life; it has specialized the place and the time for work, it has brought about a sharp division between work and leisure. In pre-industrial times, work was done leisurely and was interspersed with leisure, and, on the other hand, leisure included much personal and personally fruitful work. Since work has today largely lost personal meaning and life is a mere left-over from work, a "dopo lavoro", since the cult of standardized things continues in the leisure hours, the labor-saving devices save time and strength for little besides work and the recovery from work. The higher standard of living is reduced to this: that in the rare hours of private life men are permitted to enjoy those goods, those mere premises of living, to the production of which they give their lives.

Production as a guiding principle at times runs counter even to technical productivity. Needless to say, just as production is the prerequisite of capitalism, so profit is a prerequisite of production, an indispensable link in the endless chain of production. The invention of a new object or process is not uncommonly suppressed because it threatens to curtail the potential profit of an industry and so to upset production. Such evils, indeed most of the evils generally denounced as part of capitalism, are all-too-often attributed to the profit-making of the few at the expense of the many. But since today individual profit-making has chiefly turned into collective "profitability", a link in the chain of production, the profit-maker is dragged along like everybody else by the vast, autonomous process of production. The role of profitability is secondary. The ruling principle of our world is production, and the true problem is not the welfare of the many against the rule of the few, but the *welfare of man* against the *rule of things.*

The new principle, the saving principle, need not be invented. It emerges from that second, subterranean development that accompanies capitalistic development, the inevitability of which capitalists refuse to see. This second development is inherent in the development of technics.

Just as technics have forced the individual, like it or not, into the private collective, they are forcing the private collective, like it or not, into the public collective. No matter for what ends they have been misused, the technics of modern mass production and modern communications tend to establish a greater proximity between men and peoples. They link nations as well as individuals to one another, they bind the destiny of the rich to that of the poor, the destiny of the employer to that of the employee. Under these conditions, self-sufficiency of the individual and a true independence of groups and peoples are no longer possible. Every partial crisis becomes a general crisis, every local war develops into a global war. Technics, for better or worse, point to unity, whether this be recognized and acted upon or not. When not recognized, the unity they lead to is one of destruction. Even though—indeed, just because— they have been used and abused for most inhuman, selfish and detructive purposes, they have shown us to our cost that men if they are not to fall together must stand together. Paradoxically, technics —over the heads of men—are seen to be developing in the sense of human unity, and that is, in a human sense.

So sheer self-preservation leaves us no alternative but to recognize and act according to the direction of human unity, and this means, to make the latent collective of men into an open collective. The *human collective* toward which the technical interconnection of our world has pointed a brutal way implies the sovereignty of man, of the *welfare of man,* over the rule of things and their production. Being one and organic, involved with human unity and governed by the requirements of man, it is diametrically opposed to the many private collectives, which, governed by the laws of production, must follow the mechanical exactions of objects.

Recognizing this new collective means thinking on a new scale. In regard to space, we must think in terms of the people as a whole, indeed of mankind as a whole; and so, in regard to time, we must plan for a much longer future. Private collectives are particular, specialized units intended to produce specific wares. They are set up to create and supply a specific demand, but not to fill a general need. Their interests are world-wide, yet do not coincide with the interest of the whole world. The pursuit of separate goals makes them unable to gauge—far less to represent—the common weal. They are, nationally and internationally, in conflict with other groups and classes, and more often than not their internationality leads them to render a disservice to the welfare of their nations without serving a universal welfare. Recent years are full of examples of how harmful the effect of private collectives has been upon the welfare of their country and of the world. Tied up as they were with the interests of capital they have not considered the vital political needs of their countries. They have even made agreements definitely injurious to their countries. They have helped shatter the democracy that made them great. Thus the technical situation of the world creates the necessity of unified planning from a point of vantage, from the viewpoint of the welfare of an entire people and of all mankind. The technical situation itself demands that the ruling principle be the welfare of man over and against the idol of production. Not before the power of this idol is broken can man become the master of events, can man become his own master.

When one considers the technical situation calmly, it is not difficult to see the logic of these conclusions. But it is extremely difficult to arrive at calm consideration. Everyone wants a permanent peace, wants security against continual crises. But the instant the requirements for such security disturb habitual thinking, or question private and national sovereignty, there arises a strong emotional resistance, a compulsion to ignore or evade these requirements. On the one hand, they cannot be met except by a new state of mind, a new spirit of cooperation all over the world; and, on the other, the general state of mind is still far from prepared, indeed utterly unwilling to relinquish any comforts or prerogatives, whether of person, class or nation, for the sake of collective security. How can, under such conditions, the welfare of man be achieved? We must first ask ourselves: What is the welfare of man, as expressed in concrete and positive terms?

It is neither the unlimited advantage of the individual nor that of the masses. As we have seen, man is no longer wholly comprised in the individual, as he was up to the eighteenth century. And this state of affairs cannot be re-established merely by volition, as the individualists like to think. If one attempts to do so, the exact opposite takes place: fascist despotism. But neither is the welfare of man synonymous with the current well-being of the masses—as the collectivists believe. It is possible to imagine a condition in which the actual mass of the people is materially satisfied and which still neglects or even destroys all that makes them human beings. During the ten years of Nazi rule, there was undoubtedly a period in which the majority of the German people approved of the regime and were satisfied in a material sense. During this period, Hitler could very probably have risked an honest plebiscite. He had obviated unemployment, people had bread and the possibility of acquiring wealth. Capital prospered, brilliant political coups and bloodless conquests followed one another in rapid sequence. There was even a common purpose—no matter how mad—that inspired the people and seemed worth making every effort for. This well-being of the people, however, was bought at the price of vast armaments, squandering everything the people had and speculating on all they might plunder from other peoples. It was bought at the price of the worst crimes and the education to crime, of the abolition of human dignity. This is an extreme case, but it clarifies a situation that obtains, more or less, for other peoples as well. Momentary material prosperity, no matter how unstable, suffices to satisfy the majority of the people; they are little concerned with its foundations and implications, and even less concerned with or aware of the connection between the permanence of material prosperity and the nurture of true human values, of moral and spiritual values. Higher wages, jobs, business opportunities—the material standard of living—that is what people essentially want and demand. Among Western peoples there is also a genuine desire for freedom of opinion and criticism, freedom of decision and of beliefs, and this desire is essential indeed. But even when all these desires are gratified, there remain two factors indispensable for the real welfare of man, and not included in the momentary satisfaction of the people, two so closely connected that they are almost one: security from future dangers and the care of human civilization. Without the continuity of human civilization, neither material prosperity nor a material standard of living can be maintained. The events of the last decade have made it unambiguously clear that human civilization is not identical with the material standard of living. Human civilization is founded on the spiritual and moral values that make man a human being, that lend human life its only dignity and all its savor. Human civilization stands and falls with the fostering of these values, and the material standard of living stands and falls with human civilization. But this interrelation is no longer felt in daily life. It cannot be proven statistically, and to understand it takes more reflection than most people have time and capacity for. Besides, the nurture of these values demands personal effort, material, moral and spiritual effort, and the results are not immediately tangible. So, of course, the desire for these values is slight.

The welfare of man, then, is not identical with the material well-being of the individual nor with the material well-being of the masses. It comprises the *welfare of the idea of man,* of the human element in man, that is more developed in one person than in another and that most people today have forgotten, abused or managed badly. In this book we have defined the human element in man, the essential human quality, as man's capacity to go beyond himself, to transcend his physical being. And we have seen that in Christianity man has reached a point of conceiving this human element as an idea and of making it the guide of his conduct. Spirit, the capacity to transcend, and humanity, human brotherhood and unity—these are the fundamental values of Christian and human civilization. The great Asiatic cultures have arrived at these same concepts by paths of their own; China and India have cultivated and preserved them better than the Christian world. The freedom and dignity of man, the rights of man, are based on the share of all men in the human quality. But there are human rights not only against the enslavement and the exploitation of man by men, but also against the enslavement and exploitation of man by things. Human dignity is offended not only when man is subjugated by man, but also when he is subjugated by things. Modern history has given numerous examples of how men have permitted themselves to be enslaved and exploited by capital and production, by the material power of the state and by technics—and all this is not enslavement and exploitation by men, but by things. The princes and lords of the "ancien régime", the Russian czars, were despots, but they ruled as men over their subjects. The capitalists and the Prussian kings, while controlling other men, were themselves the subjects of things. They themselves transcended their individual lives in the service of things. In them we studied the growth of human transcendence, but theirs was a transcendence gone astray, it was abuse of man's great capacity to go beyond himself. It was modern idolatry, it is still the modern form of paganism. Human dignity and human rights demand that when man is subservient, and when in this service he transcends his personal being, he serves in a human sense and for a human community.

Granted that the welfare of man must be the guiding principle and that it is founded on the values of civilization, what are the practical consequences? We are faced with a vicious circle: The maintenance of spiritual values depends on people having enough to eat and leisure to appreciate the importance of these values. To grant people their living and leisure is a matter of distribution of work and goods. In practical terms, the welfare of man means the primacy of the problem of distribution: the shift from the *rule of things* to the *welfare of man* is identical with the shift from the *supremacy of production* to the *supremacy of distribution*. Here is where the vicious circle comes in; this shift is impossible without a fundamental shift in the state of mind of people.

Distribution as an economic problem is inseparable from democracy as a political problem—in fact, these are but two aspects of one issue. There cannot be an adequate distribution of work and goods without true democracy, and we shall not have a true democracy in the future unless we solve the problem of distribution, nationally and internationally. Short of a solution of these two problems there will be no peace and no security. The best definition of democracy is still Lincoln's: government of the people, by the people, for the people. Taking care of the problem of distribution presupposes government for the people. Since government by the people is the prerequisite of government for the people, true democracy is the prerequisite for an adequate distribution of goods and work.

In the long run the only alternatives to adequate distribution and true democracy are government-sponsored relief and government subsidies, which eventually lead to fascism. It is of no use to close our eyes to a task forced on us not by wicked men, but by the technical development itself: to subordinate production to distribution, to shape production with a view to securing the necessities of life for every human being instead of leaving the distribution of goods and jobs to the hazards of production. If we don't do this today we shall have to do it tomorrow. Today it may still be possible to ignore the fact that the original goal of technical development has been reached in that the living of all human beings could be secured— were it not for national privileges and the profitability of production. But let us envisage an extreme result of the technical development, a result that already lies in the offing. Let us assume that science succeeds in harnessing the limitless energies released by splitting the atom. Whatever new ways of production this may open, two things are certain: that it will make the work of millions of people superfluous and that such power will make its possessors the masters of the world. In the present circumstances such an invention would confront the whole of humanity with an unimaginable crisis, with the climax of that alternative which all recent crises have already bared: the alternative between enslavement and a realistic social order. To fail to prepare for such a moment is to be guilty of a lack of judgment far more terrible in its consequences than the failure to prepare for war against the Axis.

If "Freedom from Want" and "Freedom from Fear" are to be more than mere slogans and if they are not to be deprived of all concrete content, as was the case with Wilson's fourteen points, they can only mean that the bare necessities are to be secured to all men. "Relief", charity, are humiliating forms of fulfilling one's obligation to see to this elementary security that human dignity demands. A time will come when the present insecurity of existence, the necessity to struggle for a bare livelihood, will appear as barbarous as the bondage of the Middle Ages appears to us today. But what is the price of this security and who is to pay it? With the best will in the world the capitalists alone could never pay it, for no matter to what degree machines may relieve man of toil, the distribution of goods remains always dependent on the distribution of work. The question has been raised whether people who today work for mere subsistence would continue to work if this subsistence were guaranteed. To suppose that the lack of insecurity will destroy the urge to work is to have a wretched conception of man and man's work. One respect in which man differs from the animal is that the quest for food, the physical necessities, are not his sole urges to activity; some, indeed the best of his work springs, on the contrary, from a superabundance of vitality that can develop unimpeded by necessity. Man has still other stimuli to work: the urge to better his living conditions, the desire for the respect of his fellow men, the wish to achieve distinction and fame. Competition of this kind will persist, and it is more in keeping with human dignity than the whip of necessity. It is only a question of what goal a society sets itself. When the worth of a human being is no longer determined by the size of his income and the power of his capital, but by the extent to which he serves the community of his people, the welfare of man, the stimulus will not diminish, it will, however, be more beneficent. In every war, the inspiration of a common cause —in so far as the people believe that it is a common cause—have rendered men capable of achievements unthinkable in the normal times of merely private struggle for existence. Why should not this be possible in times of peace? The building of a new world will bring with it vast, common tasks, tasks for whole generations, tasks that, once they are grasped, will have a stimulating effect of unequalled power. In 1911, William James wrote: "Men now are proud of belonging to a conquering nation, and without a murmur lay down their persons and their wealth, if by so doing they may fend off subjection. But who can be sure that other aspects of one's country may not, with time and education and suggestion enough, come to be regarded with similarly effective feelings of pride and shame? . . . Individuals, daily more numerous, now feel this civic passion. It is only a question of blowing on the spark till the whole population gets incandescent, and on the ruins of old morals of military honor, a stable system of morals of civic honor builds itself up. What the whole community comes to believe in grasps the individual as in a vise. The war-function has grasped us so far; but constructive interests may some day seem no less imperative, and impose on the individual a hardly lighter burden."

James speaks in terms of the individual and the nation. But the international aspect of the question is implicit in what he says. Internationally, distribution of goods and work means a fair division of raw materials and labor among the peoples, and, accordingly, world-wide planned economy. The quarrel as to whether there should be a free or a planned economy will be settled once and for all by the economic chaos of the post-war world. If any kind of order at all is to be established, it must be according to plan, and a plan means "planned economy".

The fear of planned economy centers on two dangers: the regimentation of the individual and the seizure of power by the planners.

It may be that the first danger is inescapable. But whatever hope there is of preserving individuality lies in planning for a unified social order. We have seen that the present state of things has brought about the increasing invalidation of the individual, who is already consumed by the private collective. Whether individual freedom is restricted by the uncontrolled demands of production or by the controlled demand of distribution makes only this difference: that, in the one case, it is subject to inhuman chance, in the other, to human fallibility. The impersonal demands of production have no consideration whatever for special needs and dispositions of an individual, they force him into the schematization of their objective purposes. A planned economy guided by the welfare of man and based on distribution of goods and work, by giving the individual more leisure, would free him to develop a higher appreciation of life. And if such an economy were to plan in terms of a human collective, that is to say, in terms of unity of purpose, it could also permit of a more complex and differentiated organization; unhampered by the rigidities of competition and dealing as it would in a whole, it would have larger possibilities of choice, it could have the flexibility to consider individual needs and qualities. And, most important of all, furthering a human community, a human end, makes work meaningful again—production of goods and making money do not constitute a meaning. So both leisure and work may recover meaning, which is the prerequisite of individuality.

Of course, this whole concept depends on whether the second danger can be met, on the guarantee that the new order be administered in the sense of the welfare of man, not in the interest of private groups and arbitrary powers. In other words, the functioning of a fair distribution of goods and work depends on the functioning of democracy.

Democracy itself is a matter of distribution. Just as the distribution of goods depends on the distribution of work, the distribution of rights depends on the distribution of duties. For sometime now democracy has been deteriorating because the emphasis has been on rights. Up to now, freedom of speech, of worship, of opportunity have been kept largely intact. But these freedoms are seriously endangered, and the new freedoms will be quite impossible, unless the corresponding responsibilities are taken up. Democracy can safeguard freedom, old and new, freedom of and freedom from, only through its renewal and through acceptance of responsibilities that require it to expand in three directions: *economic, dynamic* and *universal*.

The foundation of this renewal is the supplementation of political democracy by *economic* democracy. This means the right of labor to participate in management and the corresponding duty of labor to participate in the responsibilities of management. It means too the right and duty of both management and labor, indeed of all economic groups—industry, agriculture, consumer—to participate in the responsibilities of government. Instead of acting behind the scenes as irresponsible pressure groups without consideration for the country at large, these functional groups would have to elect representatives to assume the same responsibilities as those borne by the representatives of regional groups, the members of the legislative bodies, whose duty it is to balance as best they can the interests of their constituents with that of the people as a whole.

Dynamic democracy demands the increasingly active participation of the people. It is inherent in democracy that the system of checks and balances applies, not only to the relations of the various branches of government, but also to the relations of the people to the government. Government by the people can be government for

the people only in so far as it succeeds in balancing the will of the
people and the good of the people. So long as these cannot be
counted on to coincide, the democratic process at best must always
provide that public opinion shall govern not from day to day—as
today the techniques of the Gallup poll and the race-track totaliza-
tor could together easily permit it to do—but only through periodical elections. The representatives of the people are supposed to protect the people from abusing its power, but the people is supposed
through these periodical elections to protect itself from the abuse of
power by its representatives. The traditional vigilance of the legislative over the executive branch does not suffice; the whole democratic
process is predicated on the vigilance of the electorate over both.
Nor does it suffice to go to the polls; vigilance demands that the
people, not the party machines, select the nominees. But, even if
direct nomination by the people could be facilitated, even if the
people had the leisure and willingness to meet this responsibility, is
the people really in a position to judge the men and their records?
Such a judgment involves a thorough understanding of the issues,
an understanding that private, particular interests and immediate
well-being are tied up with the welfare of the country and human
welfare in the long run. The ultimate goal must be an increasing
approach of the will of the people to the good of the people and an
increasing participation of the people in deciding on the issues. All
this requires more than the information about current events provided by magazines, newspapers and commentators. It requires a
considerable amount of education and self-education, a knowledge
of historical backgrounds, of the interrelation of problems, and of
the principles according to which decisions are to be made. It may
be that such education would be furthered by more leisure and
security. It would, in any event, have to be supplemented by practical experience of the conditions in which fellow citizens live. College students should have a year in factories or in the mines, and, in
exchange, miners and factory workers should have their year of
higher learning. Of course, to consider such possibilities demands
a certain optimism. Despite all the perorations on the fight for
democracy and the preservation of democracy, as soon as it comes

to envisaging the true conditions of democracy today and the possibilities of improving them, one encounters a deep scepticism. Yet we are confronted with the alternative of a better democracy or none at all. If we do not believe that the people will ever be willing or able to pay the rising price of democracy, that the will of the people may more nearly approach the good of the people, we shall lose what there is of democracy. "Nothing future is quite secure," says William James, ". . . democracy as a whole may undergo self-poisoning. But, on the other hand, democracy is a kind of religion, and we are bound not to admit its failure. Faiths and utopias are the noblest exercise of human reason, and no one with a spark of reason in him will sit down fatalistically before the croaker's picture. The best of us are filled with the contrary vision of a democracy stumbling through every error till its institutions glow with justice and its customs shine with beauty. Our better men *shall* show the way and we *shall* follow them; so we are brought round again to the mission of the higher education in helping us to know the better kind of man whenever we see him."

If there is no honest endeavor to make democracy *universal,* if fascist regimes are allowed to persist anywhere on earth, then there is nothing in the world to prevent new wars and crises. A world organization of free peoples must start with establishing an international law codifying human rights and duties and must provide not only the courts but the police to enforce it in all countries. Of course, any international organization can become effective only when peoples themselves espouse it as their cause, when they are convinced that the international administration and jurisdiction is carried out in the sense of universal democracy and not as an instrument for promoting the interest of the great. Universal democracy goes hand in hand with the grant of that fundamental freedom which Pearl Buck has called "the freedom to be free", that is to say, the liberation of those peoples who up to now have merely served the colonial and economic purposes of the big powers. Whether this process of liberation, as part of the whole process of establishing a new order, be a matter of two decades or five—for the incompleteness of modern democracies shows how much is needed for the development of actual self-government—the essential thing is to make an honest beginning, to leave the education necessary for such liberation to the progressive leaders of those peoples and to assist them in their work.

But who is to take the first steps toward the new order, in whose hands will it be to initiate the measures necessary to establish it?

The destiny of the world to come will *depend upon governments*. And this entails the great danger that the old politicians, diplomats and business men, that people who follow the routines and interests of yesterday, will again have charge of affairs—people who will appeal to the habits, the sentimentalities, the self-love of nations in order to maintain their position, their methods and their capitalistic interests. The new order ought to be directed by new men, by those who are young at heart, who have honest plans and faith in man. The Soviets, and even the Nazis, knew that new things demand new men, a new sort of man, and they owe their successes to this recognition.

It is easy, temptingly easy, to fool the people. It was particularly easy in the epoch that has just come to a close, for, within the last fifty years, problems became so complex that, burdened with the struggle for their own private existence, people have despaired of understanding and mastering these problems and shifted the responsibility for their destiny to experts, to politicians. And it is likely to become still more easy in the immediate future; human beings, especially those of Europe, are inexpressibly weary and confused. They do not know what it is that has happened to them, they do not know what it is that they are to desire and, at first, they will probably be prepared to accept anything that promises a little temporary peace and security. They will take what is better for what is good, and almost anything will be better than what has been. In so far as the peoples of the European continent survive the fall of the Nazis at all, one cannot look to them for direction. They will have to be directed, and they will be directed by those men to whom the powerful allied governments entrust their destiny from the very beginning. And so the temptations and responsibilities of allied statesmen will be immense, for only their own conscience and knowledge will guide them. In the light of this, it is a good thing to realize that while people can be fooled—"some of the time"—developments cannot.

The change of direction, of mental attitude, which we have indicated, necessarily constitutes a revolutionary act. And in many and wide circles, especially in ruling circles, there is a fear of revolution, amounting to panic. Order is to be established as quickly as possible and at all costs. There are some who would like to continue where they left off before 1939, before 1933, even before 1914; they would like to dispel yesterday with the help of the day before yesterday, fascism with the help of the conservative powers of the Church, of capital, yes, even of pretenders to fallen thrones. There are others who are quite prepared to move with the times, but who are not aware how far the times have moved. But the world situation is in itself revolutionary. Whether we like it or not, we are in the very midst of the greatest revolution in the history of mankind, and it is not in the hands of diplomats to arrest this process. Their position will be that of the man who is recovering from a grave disease and who pretends he has not been ill at all. He resumes his accustomed routine and tries to do everything he did before. And only the alarming symptoms which ensue teach him that this is no longer possible and that there is a decisive change in his whole organism. The events of the decades just past cannot be ignored or undone. The deeds and sufferings remain in the world. They will have long repercussions, and their influence will go on in silence. This time they have penetrated to the roots of man, and so the cure must begin at the roots. As Sir William Beveridge has said, "a revolutionary moment in the world's history is a time for revolutions, not for patching". Human civilization is at stake. To preserve it means to renew it from its very foundations.

One cannot establish order as such. One can only establish an old order or a new order, and which it is to be must be decided upon from the outset. Should one re-establish the old order, it would have no permanence. Reactionaries have never been able to block revolutions, they have only made them more violent. The revolutionary process can be controlled only by taking it in hand oneself, honestly and early, step by step. Then the fundamental change of attitude needful today will not be brought about by bloodshed and anarchy in a single shattering revolution, but by hundreds of revolutionary moves in a gradual and peaceful process. Everything depends upon whether the change of attitude is set in action at once, whether it will be felt in every measure. If its start is delayed, the forces of the old order, the forces of inertia, will preponderate, and the fatal, masterless development will take its course. Suffering, oppression and rootlessness have made people not only weary, but disintegrated, ripe for change. Millions have lost their possessions and, often too, their homes. They have been wrenched out of their habits and their habitual ways of thinking. Everything within them is in a state of psychic flux. This makes them easier to form, to win over. This is the moment when they can be led in the right or the wrong direction. One can point out new ways, gain their confidence and educate them to freedom and a community of peoples, through honest care for them and a new justice in the social and economic order. Or, under cover of high-sounding words, one can give them over to old, discredited leaders, to old abuses and malpractices. This is a unique and decisive moment and it will not last long.

The reactionaries of today should follow the example of their great ancestor, Edmund Burke. He contended passionately against the principles of the French Revolution, yet we know now that he could not hinder either its expansion or its results. But he himself knew the limits of human will in controlling the forces of human development, and this knowledge distinguishes him from those who came after him: "If a great change is to be made in human affairs ... every fear, every hope will forward it; and then they, who persist in opposing the mighty current ... will appear rather to resist the decrees of Providence itself, than the mere design of men. They will not be resolute and firm, but perverse and obstinate."

The many inhibitions against change generally express themselves in a popular antithesis that, upon examination, ceases to be one: *realism versus idealism*. Now that the decisions concerning a future world order are becoming more imminent, the "cool and sober heads", the "realistic" politicians are warning against "unthinking idealism"—just as they did in 1918. By this they do not mean only those who think that the best of possible worlds can be set up from today to tomorrow, but all who believe that it must be set up as a goal. By this, they mean us, who consider a universal and social community possible, indeed inescapable. Today it is not difficult to refute the arguments of the political "realists". One has only to recall the results of their politics within the past twenty years. The signposts of the present catastrophe were maxims such as these: "We are not going to fight a war for the Jews", "We must not go on an ideological crusade", "We cannot be the gendarmes of Europe", "England first, France first, Holland first, Belgium first, America first". While these views were being expressed, the Nazis and the Japanese were making preparations, the extent of which the "realists" found themselves compelled to recognize only after the invasion of Poland, Belgium and Holland, only after Pearl Harbor. It may be said against Stalinist Russia that she, too, has concerned herself with Russia first of all, but it may be said for her that she realized that her interest, like that of every country, coincided with collective security. And it was the "realism" of the Western powers and the ensuing failure of collective security that brought about the counter-realism of Russia's pact with Germany and her invasion of Finland. Czechoslovakia outraged by Hitler, when Russia had been fully prepared to support her, was still to the Western governments "a far-away country of which we know nothing". These governments regarded the most vicious crimes and atrocities as the private affairs of sovereign states that permitted of no intervention. But because a war was not to be waged "for the Jews", because "ideological crusades" were anxiously avoided, because no one wanted to "police Europe", because England, France, Belgium, Holland or America were always to "come first" and the civilization of mankind last—because of all this, millions of people are suffering and dying today: not only Jews, not only Chinese, not only Abyssinians, not only Spaniards, but people of all peoples of the world.

This fact is a truism; it is obvious to everyone. And yet, even now, there are strong currents of opinion that aim toward the resumption of the methods of non-intervention, unrestricted national sovereignty and balance of power. Subordination to a really binding international law and organization is once more declared intolerable for the pride and traditions of great nations. Well, a great deal seemed intolerable before it became indispensable. Only a few decades ago, everyone walked and rode as he pleased through the streets of the cities of the world. Everyone had to look out for himself. But when traffic became mechanized and reached a point of confusion that endangered public safety, the city took over authority, made traffic laws and placed policemen at points of intersection to see to it that automobiles did not run into one another and into the crowd. And from that time on, everyone, without exception, has been limited in his self-determination. Where it is a question of traffic amongst individuals, necessary measures have long been taken. Where it is a question of traffic amongst nations, where the existence of entire peoples is at stake, there is insistence on sovereignty, just as within nations there is insistence on unimpeded private initiative. The most powerful machines are permitted to crash into the helpless crowd and into one another; confusion reaches incalculable proportions—and the "realists" go on saying that human nature makes it impossible to set up a world authority that can maintain international law and order.

The past decades have taught us that the advocates of "Realpolitik" are no longer realistic politicians, but that today it is they who are "unthinking", anachronistic and Utopian. The "idealistic" programs of international solidarity, of the responsibility of every people for all peoples and of all peoples for every people, of the supremacy of human rights and duties over the "sacred egoism" of nations—these programs, much maligned for their idealism, are today the only genuinely realistic form of politics; the antithesis, that is, breaks down.

The same holds true of the conditions within individual nations. Here too, idealism has become a subject for mockery and contempt. The social psychologists of today who realize that man is losing his moral support, that there is danger of social disintegration, know of almost no other remedy than the appeal to the well understood self-interest of the individual. This view is justified in so far as it is directed against the stereotype preaching of moral precepts that all-too-obviously contradict the practical rules of life currently accepted in both politics and economy. But here again the old antithesis creates confusion. Self-interest is understood to be realistic, interest in humanity at large to be idealistic. In lieu of preaching a conduct of life which is impossible in the present circumstances one must teach that it has become unrealistic to go on trying to further self-interest without furthering the interest of the whole people and the welfare of man. The point is not the impracticality of moral precepts but rather the impracticality of the current "practical" rules of life. And the notion of the identity of self-interest and common interest must be taken as a start for changing the constitution of the world itself, so that what is necessary may become possible: to live and to act in accordance with a Christian civilization.

Of course, a merely rational appeal to the self-interest of the individual is not enough. Practical self-interest is not the only motive that activates man. He has his irrational individual passions and urges which drive him on, sublimated or not. But there is a still deeper irrational stratum where an innate anxiety, a shudder of loneliness and forsakenness, a sense of homelessness in the universe, a vital need for super-individual support and comfort, are alive. These anxieties and needs are even more deep-rooted than and at least as real and concrete as rational self-interest and individual passions. They were met in the early periods by religion, the partly physical, partly spiritual bond that connected man with his source of life, they were met later by the purely spiritual bond of faith in a universal God and Savior. In modern man they are mostly left to themselves, they are neglected and half-buried, and many people hardly know any longer that they exist. Yet the more complex modern life becomes, the more difficult to understand, the more this fear amounting to panic, the more this need for super-individual support grows. Left to themselves, these urges find their outlet in the forms of uncontrolled emotion and mass hysteria we have experienced in our time. They seek dulling in sensations, they respond to the prophecies of religious sects, to the voices of demagogues. We have seen that self-interest has not prevented the modern individual from transcending his own being, but for lack of a common human purpose and goal his transcendence has taken him down inhuman paths. All the various senseless goals, all the modern idols that this transcendence of the individual has served, capital and production, technics for their own sake, the power of the state, belief in the superiority of a certain race—all these are substitutes for a bond of human faith that scarcely exists today and that man requires for his inner being in the course of his entire life, not only when he is exposed to the dangers of the battlefield.

Many people, it is true, are still believers in the teachings of the churches, but the demands of their belief and the demands of the world today become daily more incompatible. True Christians have only one way out of the thicket of modern life, and that is the assumption of a double truth: their private life runs counter to their business life. They are kind and helpful in their personal associations and grow hard and inconsiderate the moment their business or calling is involved. The building of a new morality, the transformation of faith necessary today, can no longer be demanded of the churches. This transformation can take place only within modern life itself, it means the transformation of that modern life. And if a new faith can arise, it can only be faith in the idea of man. Such a faith does not mean the deification of man. The Renaissance identified man with the great and powerful individual, Enlightenment interpreted him as mankind, as the sum of concrete individuals. But the idea of man is neither the one nor the other. It does not mean the dominating genius who justifies everything through his vitality and mastery, and it is independent of the naive expectation that mankind will become better and happier solely through the development of its rational capacities and the improvement of material living conditions. The idea of man means the human element in man. From time immemorial, man has been searching for this idea, and in all his concepts of deity he has in reality been groping for an idea of himself. First he clothed this idea in physical or rudimentary forms, since he could not seize upon it in any other way. The concept of man made in the image of God is, inversely, the concept of God as the prefiguration and ideal of man. Those who today have a true faith in God still tread a human path. But in all the others—and there are many—whose faith in God has lost its vitality, the human faculty of transcending will go on turning to inhuman ends and leading to disaster until there grows upon them a faith in the idea of man in a pure and unveiled form, a Religio Humana.

Here the sciences must play an enormous part. In our age, a faith that includes the whole of man cannot but be enlightened, cannot exclude man's immensely developed rational faculties. Man cannot fall back into the irrational, he can only proceed to the superrational. This means that man's belief in the idea of himself can only live if it is substantiated by the body of knowledge created in the course of centuries, it can be comprehensive only in so far as knowledge becomes comprehensive. Man masters his world and his development when he masters his knowledge, commands a picture of his known world. In fact, knowledge becomes knowledge only when scattered single experiences are integrated in a coherent whole.

As we have seen, pre-rational religion had furnished man a comprehensive and comprehensible picture of his world and an orientation in it. Religion was dislodged by rational knowledge, and especially by natural science, which, by its own principle of following outward nature in its various aspects, was bound to disperse into a multitude of autonomous specialized fields of research. More and more, science emancipated itself from the philosophical preconceptions from which it emerged. It refused to be guided by any dominating metaphysical principle and took its directions exclusively from the specific objects it investigated through empirical observation and experiment. Natural science set the pattern for all the other fields, for the social and political sciences and the humanities, which as far as possible adopted the rational and empirical methods of natural science and attempted to discover "laws of nature" in human manifestations as well. All of them aspired to become as scientific as natural science. The result was a centrifugal development, away from a general principle and toward specific generalizations, away from an intuitional center and toward a factual periphery. This involved a twofold process of expansion and dissolution. The realm of man, of man's conscious learning, expanded to unimagined regions, but, simultaneously, man became alarmingly unable to master this realm intellectually. Specialized fields of knowledge grew to be autonomous; they overwhelmed the human mind with a mass of factual material piling up ad infinitum and lost all connection with one another. In the sphere of knowledge, too, man did not control his objects, he was controlled by them.

This development, obviously, implied a shift from theory to practice. Increasingly, the great conquests of the sciences served to further technical progress and material well-being and fell short of furnishing a comprehensive picture of the world. Even the arts— which, as we have shown, had taken over this function originally fulfilled by religion—even the arts came under the sway of that disrupting development.

Within the last few decades, however, a new trend has begun to manifest itself, and the leaders in this new trend are the very sciences, the natural sciences, that had started the process of dissolution. In pursuing its rational and experimental methods, natural science is transcending the sphere of the rational, it has arrived at dissolving concrete matter, at questioning the unrestricted validity of "laws of nature" and of the principle of causality; its grasp is reaching the borders of the super-rational. In modern physics a coherent picture of a sphere of knowledge, a true cosmos, is again in the making: a closed and, at the same time, a dynamic system, in which the whole corresponds to its parts, the greatest to the smallest. Unfortunately, because of the complexity and abstract nature of its concepts, modern physics is only accessible to the initiate and very remote from the layman. In biochemistry, in biology and medicine a sense of the intrinsic interconnections of organic processes, a sense of the organic wholeness of the living body, is redeveloping.

But—with the exception of the modern psychologic knowledge and methods, especially psychoanalysis—those disciplines concerned with human affairs, history, the social sciences and the "humanities", are far behind this new trend. They still insist on letting empirical facts rule indiscriminately and seem completely to ignore that facts in themselves are senseless and worthless until they are interpreted and linked together from a guiding view of the whole, until there is some orientation that makes it possible to distinguish the essential from the non-essential. So the research of these disciplines stagnates in the stage of test, check and file. Understandably, interest in the study of history and the humanities has decreased to such a degree that these subjects are threatened with being abandoned by public support. Yet this in itself is a symptom of the dangerous condition of our civilization. In this gravest of human crises, nothing is more urgent, nothing more vital than the knowledge of man, of his vast historical background and the direction of his evolution, of his distinct nature and position in the universe, in a word, of the idea of man as shown by the totality of his existence.

The sciences have a great responsibility: they alone can furnish the picture of the whole, the teaching of the whole, on which man's mastery of his world depends.

If man succeeds in gaining control of his vastly expanded and enriched world, then all the depths of horror of the past decades may appear to have been a retreat into darkness necessary to a true advance of man. The new order would be an order that, for the first time since the Holy Roman Empire, would comprehend the entire world and bring it into a state of peace and vital equilibrium. For the first time, it would again be an order that has the welfare of man for its all-important focus. In the Holy Roman Empire, this welfare was salvation, a purely spiritual welfare that rested in the hereafter, in the grace of God; soul and body were far apart, precisely as far as heaven and earth. The Kingdom of God and its ideal order floated high above man, and below, in the earthly realm of the emperor, that secular dynamism was in the making, which later rent the world in the struggle for power of dynasties, nations and economies and led it from crisis to crisis. Since that time man has come of age. He has cast off the authority of the church, and his coming

of age is an irrevocable fact, no matter how immature he may be for
the task of directing himself. The directive no longer comes only
from above, it comes from below, not only from a Creator, but from
a creation, from conditions that man has produced, without knowing it or wishing it, in his mad chase for earthly goods. But men disregard the commands of their creation just as they have disregarded
the commandments of their Creator. In today's technological situation is hidden the same human significance that was revealed by
the Word of God, only that today, the idea is no longer separate
from matter. It is deeply and secretly incorporated in matter and so,
for the first time, it may have the prospect of materializing. Pure
ideas tend to become doctrines rather than reality. Nor will the new
order be created by the pure idea, it will be tortured out of men
through cruel and bitter necessity—how bitter, coming generations
alone may know.

The idea of man, the counsel of a new humanism, are certainly
the very last things to move the present world to a fundamental
change. But we may expect this idea to force itself upon men when
the course of events brings them to see that without human community and fraternity they are all lost together, that man needs
goodness as he needs his daily bread.

BIBLIOGRAPHY AND NOTES

Foreign books are referred to in their original versions when an English translation does not exist or is incomplete. Otherwise, only the titles of the English editions are given. I have refrained from indicating editions of the sources, original or translated; they can be obtained from the large encyclopedias of the various nations. Besides these encyclopedias, the *Cambridge History* may be consulted throughout as a general reference book.

INTRODUCTION

p. 8, l. 26 Theodor Haecker, *Was ist der Mensch?* Leipzig, 1933.—Reinhold Niebuhr, *The Nature and Destiny of Man*, Vol. I: *Human Nature*, New York, 1941.

p. 8, l. 31 Alfred North Whitehead, *The Function of Reason*, Princeton, 1929, pp. 23–30.

p. 8, l. 33 John Dewey, *Philosophy and Civilization*, New York, 1931.

p. 9, l. 31 Oswald Spengler, *Man and Technics, a Contribution to a Philosophy of Life*, New York, 1932.

p. 10, l. 11 Wolfgang Koehler, *The Mentality of Apes*, 2nd ed. New York and London, 1927.—S. Zuckerman, *The Social Life of Monkeys and Apes*, New York, 1932; *Functional Affinities of Man, Monkeys and Apes*, New York, 1933.

p. 10, l. 29 Henri Bergson has a special position among the vitalistic thinkers because he combines vitalistic with spiritualistic elements. For him, the vital impulse in the human being is transformed into spiritual intuition *i.e.* "instinct that has become disinterested", and it is this irrational reflective faculty that constitutes an essential difference of man from the animal. Cf. *L'Évolution créatrice*, Ch. II.

p. 11, l. 21 Max Scheler, *Zur Idee des Menschen*, Abhandlungen und

Aufsätze, Leipzig, 1915, Vol. I; *Die Stellung des Menschen im Kosmos,* Darmstadt, 1930.—Reinhold Niebuhr, *op. cit.,* p. 162. As far as we can see, Max Scheler, and not Martin Heidegger, was the first to stress the human quality of transcendence.

p. 22, l. 4 Oswald Spengler, *The Decline of the West,* two vols., New York, 1926–1928.—Arnold J. Toynbee, *A Study of History,* six vols., London, 1934–.

p. 24, l. 3 *Chuang Tzu, Mystic, Moralist and Social Reformer,* transl. from the Chinese by Herbert A. Giles, 2nd ed. Shanghai, 1926, Ch. XII, pp. 147 foll.

p. 24, l. 8 Ku Hung Ming, *Papers from a Viceroy's Yamen* and *Story of a Chinese Oxford Movement.* The term "fox mind" is taken from Thomas Carlyle.

PRIMITIVE MAN

J. G. Frazer, *The Golden Bough, A Study in Magic and Religion,* seven parts in eleven vols., London, 1913–1914.—Émile Durkheim, *The Elementary Forms of Religious Life, a Study in Religious Sociology,* New York, 1915.—Lucien Lévy-Bruhl, *How Natives Think,* London, 1926; *Primitive Mentality,* New York, 1923; *The "Soul" of the Primitive,* London, 1928; *Primitives and the Supernatural,* New York, 1935.— B. Malinowsky, *Crime and Custom in Savage Society,* New York, 1926.

p. 34, l. 3 Knud Rasmussen, *Intellectual Culture of the Iglulik Eskimos,* Copenhagen, 1929 (Report of the Fifth Thule Expedition 1921–1924. Vol. VII, No. 1) p. 56.

p. 35, l. 8 Lévy-Bruhl, *How Natives Think,* first part, Ch. II.

p. 35, l. 27 W. E. Armstrong, "Rossel Island Religion", in *Anthropos,* Vol. XVIII–XIX, 1923–1924, p. 5.

p. 36, l. 2 Elsdon Best, *The Maori,* Wellington, N. Z., 1924 (Memoirs of the Polynesian Society, Vol. V.) Vol. II, p. 452.

p. 36, l. 5 Gunnar Landtman, in *Unexplored New Guinea,* by Wilfred N. Beaver, Philadelphia, 1920, p. 309.

p. 36, l. 9 W. Ahlbrinck, *Carib Life and Nature* (Reports of the Twenty-first Congress of Americanists, 1924) p. 221.

p. 36, l. 14 W. Skeat, *Vestiges of Malay Totemism* (Transactions of the Third International Congress for the History of Religions, I) pp. 98–99.

p. 36, l. 27 Jean Piaget, *The Child's Conception of the World,* New York, 1929, p. 124.

p. 37, l. 24 Elsdon Best, *op. cit.,* Vol. I, pp. 397–398.

p. 37, l. 30 A. Thalheimer, *Beitrag zur Kenntnis der Pronomina personalia und possessiva der Sprachen Mikronesiens,* Stuttgart, 1908, p. 71. For more instances cf. Lévy-Bruhl, *The "Soul" of the Primitive,* first Ch. III.

p. 38, l. 19 Lévy-Bruhl, *op. cit.,* first Ch. IV, passim.

p. 38, l. 26 Lévy-Bruhl, *op. cit.,* second Ch. II.

p. 38, l. 36 J. G. Frazer, *Totemism and Exogamy, a Treatise on Certain Early Forms of Superstition and Society,* London, 1910, Vol. IV, p. 72.

p. 39, l. 8 Lévy-Bruhl, *op. cit.,* pp. 106–107.

p. 39, l. 14 Baldwin Spencer, *Native Tribes of the Northern Territory of Australia,* London, 1914, p. 36.

p. 40, l. 30 J. G. Frazer, *The Scapegoat,* New York, 1935.

p. 43, l. 19 J. G. Frazer, *Totemism and Exogamy,* Vol. IV, pp. 59–60.

p. 44, l. 16 J. G. Frazer, *op. cit.,* Vol. IV, p. 5.

RELIGION

Eduard Meyer, *Geschichte des Altertums,* five vols., 3rd ed., Stuttgart and Berlin, 1902–1933.—G. F. Moore, *History of Religions,* two vols., New York, 1919–1927.—*Kulturgeschichte des Alten Orients* by A. Alt, A. Christensen, A. Götze, A. Grohmann, H. Kees, B. Landsberger, Munich, 1933.

ORIENTAL KINGDOMS

G. Maspero, *Life in Egypt and Assyria,* London, 1892.—Adolf Erman, *Life in Ancient Egypt,* London, 1894; *Handbook of Egyptian Religion,* New York, 1907.—J. H. Breasted, *A History of Egypt from the Earliest Time to the Persian Conquest,* 2nd ed., New York, 1919; *Development of Religion and Thought in Ancient Egypt,* New York, 1912.—Hermann Kees, *Aegypten,* Tübingen, 1928; *Totenglauben und Jenseitsvorstellungen im Alten Aegypten,* Leipzig, 1926.

A. Jeremias, *Handbuch der altorientalischen Geisteskultur,* Leipzig, 1913.—L. W. King, *History of Babylon,* London, 1919; *Babylonian Magic and Sorcery,* London, 1895.—L. J. Delaporte, *Mesopotamia. The Babylonian and Assyrian Civilisation,* New York, 1925.—Morris Jastrow, Jr., *Aspects of Religious Belief and Practice in Babylonia and Assyria,* New York, 1911.—S. Langdon, *Babylonian Wisdom,* London and Paris, 1923.—F. Boll and C. Bezold, *Sternglaube und Sterndeutung,* Leipzig, 1918.

Fr. Spiegel, *Eranische Altertumskunde,* three vols., Leipzig, 1871–1878.—
J. H. Moulton, *Early Zoroastrianism,* London, 1913.

J. Garstang, *The Hittite Empire,* New York, 1931.—Gustave Glotz, *La civilisation égéenne,* Paris, 1923.

J. Wellhausen, *Israelitische und Jüdische Geschichte,* 6th ed. Berlin, 1907.
—Rudolf Kittel, *A History of the Hebrews,* London and New York, 1908–1909.—Simon Dubnow, *Weltgeschichte des jüdischen Volkes,* ten vols., Berlin, 1925–1929, Vol. I.—S. W. Baron, *A Social and Religious History of the Jews,* New York, 1937.—C. L. Woolley, *Antiquities of Ur, an Introduction to the Eighth Temporary Exhibition of the Joint Expedition of the British Museum and of the Museum of the University of Pennsylvania to Mesopotamia,* London, 1930.—Elias Auerbach, *Wüste und Gelobtes Land, Geschichte Israels von den Anfängen bis zum Tode Salomos,* Berlin, 1932.—Oscar Goldberg, *Die Wirklichkeit der Hebräer,* Berlin, 1925.

p. 63, l. 5   E. A. Wallis Budge, *The Literature of the Ancient Egyptians,* London, 1914, pp. 51–52.

p. 68, l. 35   Albrecht Alt, *Die Ursprünge des israelitischen Rechts,* Leipzig, 1934. (Berichte über die Verhandlungen der Sächsischen Akademie der Wissenschaften zu Leipzig, philol. hist. Klasse, 86. Bd. 1934, I. Heft.)

p. 69, l. 12   W. W. Davies, *The Codes of Hammurabi and Moses,* New York and Cincinnati, 1905, Articles 16, 117, 147, 175, 199, 250, 251, 252.

THE GREEK POLIS

Georges Contenau, *La civilisation phénicienne,* Paris, 1926.

J. B. Bury, *A History of Greece to the Death of Alexander the Great,* London, 1914.—Karl Julius Beloch, *Griechische Geschichte,* 2nd ed., four vols., Strassburg, 1912–1927.—J. G. Droysen, *Geschichte Alexanders des Grossen,* new ed., Berlin, 1917; *Geschichte des Hellenismus,* 2nd ed., three vols., Gotha, 1877–1878.

N. D. Fustel de Coulanges, *Ancient City, a Study on the Religion, Laws and Institutions of Greece and Rome,* 11th ed., Boston, 1901.—W. Warde Fowler, *The City-State of the Greeks and Romans,* London, 1907.—A. H. J. Greenidge, *A Handbook of Greek Constitutional History,* London, 1902.

Otto Kern, *Die Religion der Griechen,* three vols., Berlin, 1926–1938.—

Erwin Rohde, *Psyche, The Cult of Souls and Belief in Immortality among the Greeks*, London and New York, 1925.

Jakob Burckhardt, *Griechische Kulturgeschichte*, 3rd ed., four vols., Berlin and Stuttgart, 1898.—*Greek Civilisation and Character. The Self-Revelation of Ancient Greek Society*, Introduction and Translation by Arnold J. Toynbee, London and Toronto, 1924.—Werner W. Jaeger, *Paideia: The Ideals of Greek Culture*, Oxford, 1939.

p. 76, l. 6   Martin Buber, *Das Königtum Gottes*, Berlin, 1932, Ch. 4, p. 63 foll.

p. 81, l. 20   Otto Kern, *Die Religion der Griechen*, I, p. 85.

p. 81, l. 26   Otto Kern, *op. cit.*, I, p. 76 foll.

p. 90, l. 24   William Kelly Prentice, *The Ancient Greeks*, Princeton, 1940, p. 66 foll.

THE EXPANSION OF ROME INTO A WORLD EMPIRE

Theodor Mommsen, *The History of Rome*, (Everyman's Library), four vols., London and New York, 1911; *Römisches Staatsrecht*, 3rd ed., three vols., Leipzig, 1887–1888.—Eugen Taeubler, *Der römische Staat*, Leipzig, 1935.—Gaetano de Sanctis, *Storia dei Romani*, four vols., Torino, 1907–.—William E. Heitland, *The Roman Republic*, Cambridge, 1923.—Eduard Meyer, *Caesars Monarchie und das Prinzipat des Pompejus*, 2nd ed., Stuttgart and Berlin, 1919.—Gibbon, *Decline and Fall of the Roman Empire*, ed. by J. B. Bury, seven vols., London, 1896–1900.

W. R. Halliday, *Lectures on the History of Roman Religion*, Liverpool and London, 1922.—W. Warde Fowler, *The Religious Experience of the Roman People*, London, 1911.

A. H. J. Greenidge, *Roman Public Life, London*, 1901.—W. Warde Fowler, *Social Life at Rome in the Age of Cicero*, New York, 1927.—Ludwig Friedländer, *Roman Life and Manners under the Early Empire*, four vols., New York, 1908–1913.

GREEK PHILOSOPHY

Eduard Zeller, *A History of Greek Philosophy from the Earliest Period to the Time of Socrates*, two vols., London, 1881; *Socrates and the Socratic Schools*, 2nd ed., London, 1877; *Plato and the Old Academy*, London and New York, 1888; *The Stoics, Epicureans and Sceptics*, new ed., London

1880.—Theodor Gomperz, *Greek Thinkers,* four vols., London, 1901–1912. —Paul Shorey, *The Unity of Plato's Thought,* Chicago, 1903.—Werner W. Jaeger, *Aristotle. Fundamentals of the History of his Development,* Oxford, 1934.

E. Caird, *Evolution of Theology in the Greek Philosophers,* Glasgow, 1904.

GENESIS OF CHRISTIANITY FROM JUDAISM

W. F. Albright, *From the Stone Age to Christianity,* Baltimore, 1940.— Johannes Pedersen, *Israel, its Life and Culture,* I–II, London and Copenhagen, 1926.

S. Dubnow, *Weltgeschichte des jüdischen Volkes,* I and II.

James Darmesteter, *Les prophètes d'Israël,* Paris, 1895.—Ernst Sellin, *Der alttestamentliche Prophetismus,* Leipzig, 1912.—Hermann Gunkel, *Die Propheten,* Göttingen, 1917.

E. Schürer, *A History of the Jewish People in the Time of Jesus Christ,* 2nd ed., five vols., Edinburgh, 1890–1894.—A. C. McGiffert, *A History of Christianity in the Apostolic Age,* New York, 1897.—B. J. Robinson, *The Sayings of Jesus, their Background and Interpretation,* New York and London, 1930.—R. Travers Herford, *Pharisaism, its Aim and its Method,* New York, 1912; *The Pharisees,* London, 1924.—George F. Moore, *Judaism in the First Centuries of the Christian Era,* Cambridge (Mass.), 1927.

p. 141, l. 31   see J. H. Breasted, *The Dawn of Conscience,* New York, 1933.

DOGMA AND CHURCH

A. C. McGiffert, *A History of Christianity in the Apostolic Age.*—S. Dubnow, *Weltgeschichte des jüdischen Volkes,* Vols. II and III.

Benjamin W. Bacon, *Jesus and Paul,* New York, 1921.—Joseph Klausner, *From Jesus to Paul,* New York, 1943.—C. H. Dodd, *The Mind of Paul,* Bulletin of the John Rylands Library, Vol. 17, No. 1, Manchester, January 1933.

Franz Cumont, *The Oriental Religions in Roman Paganism,* Chicago, 1911; *The Mysteries of Mithra,* 3rd ed., London, 1910.—R. Reitzenstein,

Die Hellenistischen Mysterienreligionen, 2nd ed., Leipzig and Berlin, 1920.
—Edwin Hatch, *Influence of Greek Ideas and Usages upon the Christian Church,* 3rd ed., London and Edinburgh, 1891.—H. Leisegang, *Die Gnosis,* Leipzig, 1924.—Preserved Smith, *A Short History of Christian Theophagy,* Chicago and London, 1922.

A. C. McGiffert, *A History of Christian Thought,* two vols., New York and London, 1932–1933.—Adolf von Harnack, *History of Dogma,* transl. from the 3rd German ed., seven vols., London, 1896–1905; *The Mission and Expansion of Christianity in the First Three Centuries,* two vols., London, 1908.—L. M. O. Duchesne, *Early History of the Christian Church,* three vols., New York, 1909–1924.

UNIVERSALITY AND INDIVIDUALITY

Christopher H. Dawson, *The Making of Europe,* New York, 1939.

Mikhail I. Rostovtsev, *The Social and Economic History of the Roman Empire,* three vols., Oxford, 1941.—S. Dill, *Roman Society in the Last Century of the Western Empire,* new ed., London, 1906.—F. F. Abbot and A. C. Johnson, *Municipal Administration in the Roman Empire,* Princeton, 1926.—Fustel de Coulanges, *Histoire des institutions politiques de l'ancienne France,* Vol. V, *Les origines du système féodal,* Paris, 1914.

Jakob Burckhardt, *Die Zeit Konstantins des Grossen,* 5th ed., Leipzig, 1924. —Alexander Vasiliev, *History of the Byzantine Empire,* two vols., Madison, 1928–1929.

Camille Jullian, *Histoire de la Gaule,* six vols., Paris, 1908–1926.

Carl Schuchhardt, *Vorgeschichte von Deutschland,* Munich and Berlin, 1928.—*Das alte Germanien, Die Nachrichten der griechischen und römischen Schriftsteller,* ed. by Wilhelm Capelle, Jena, 1929.—Martin Ninck, *Wodan und germanischer Schicksalsglaube,* Jena, 1935.—F. W. Schaafhausen, *Der Eingang des Christentums in das deutsche Wesen,* Vol. I, Jena, 1929.

James Bryce, *The Holy Roman Empire,* new ed., London, 1923.—Percy Ernst Schramm, *Kaiser, Rom und Renovatio* (Studien der Bibliothek Warburg), Leipzig, 1929.

p. 170, l. 25   Marcus Aurelius, *Meditations,* I, 14.

p. 182, l. 11   Migne, *Patrol,* Vol. LIX col. 285 (S. Aviti Viennensis cp. LXXXIII).

p. 182, l. 22   Migne, *Patrol,* Vol. XXXI col. 1172 (Pauli Orosii Hist. liber VII cap. XLIII).

RISE OF THE HOLY ROMAN EMPIRE

James Bryce, *The Holy Roman Empire.*—Henri Pirenne, *A History of Europe from the Invasions to the XVIth Century,* New York, 1939; *Economic and Social History of Medieval Europe,* London, 1936.—Lynn Thorndike, *The History of Medieval Europe,* rev. ed., Boston, 1928.—Charles Seignobos, *The Feudal Régime,* New York, 1912.

Fustel de Coulanges, *Histoire des institutions politiques de l'ancienne France,* six vols., Paris, 1891–1931.—Augustin Thierry, *Récits des temps mérovingiens,* new ed., two vols., Paris, 1858.—Jules Michelet, *Histoire de France,* nineteen vols., Paris, 1898–1899, Vols. 1–9.—Michelet, *History of France* in two vols., New York, 1845–1851.—Ernest Lavisse and others, *Histoire de France depuis les origines jusqu'à la révolution,* nine vols., Paris, 1900–1911, Vols. 1–5.—Jacques Bainville, *History of France,* New York, 1926.

W. Giesebrecht, *Geschichte der deutschen Kaiserzeit,* 5th ed., six vols., Leipzig, 1881–1895.—Karl Hampe, *Deutsche Kaisergeschichte in der Zeit der Salier und Staufer,* 3rd ed., Leipzig, 1916.—Bruno Gebhardt, *Handbuch der deutschen Geschichte,* 7th ed., two vols., Stuttgart, 1930–1931.

Andreas Heusler, *Deutsche Verfassungsgeschichte,* Leipzig, 1905.

Ferdinand Gregorovius, *History of the City of Rome in the Middle Ages,* eight vols., 1895–1909.—William Barry, *The Papal Monarchy,* New York and London, 1902.—Marshall W. Baldwin, *The Medieval Papacy in Action,* New York, 1940.—T. F. Tout, *The Empire and the Papacy,* London, 1903.

DISINTEGRATION OF THE HOLY ROMAN EMPIRE

James Bryce, *The Holy Roman Empire.*—Andreas Heusler, *Deutsche Verfassungsgeschichte.*

Charles H. Haskins, *The Renaissance of the Twelfth Century,* Cambridge (Mass.), 1939.—E. P. Cheyney, *The Dawn of a New Era 1250–1453,* New

York, 1936.—J. Huizinga, *The Waning of the Middle Ages*, London, 1924.

F. v. Raumer, *Geschichte der Hohenstaufen und ihrer Zeit*, five vols., Leipzig, 1878.—I. Jastrow and G. Winter, *Deutsche Geschichte im Zeitalter der Hohenstaufen*, two vols., Stuttgart, 1897–1901.—Ernst Kantorowicz, *Frederick the Second 1194–1250*, New York, 1931.—Erich von Kahler, *Das Geschlecht Habsburg*, Munich, 1919.

Léon Gautier, *Chivalry*, London, 1891.—Otto Frhr. v. Dungern, *Adelsherrschaft im Mittelalter*, Munich, 1927.

Jakob Burckhardt, *The Civilization of the Renaissance in Italy*, transl. from the 15th German ed., New York, 1935.—John Addington Symonds, *Renaissance in Italy*, (The Modern Library), two vols., New York, 1935.

Ludwig von Pastor, *The History of the Popes from the Close of the Middle Ages*, thirty-four vols., London, 1891–1941, Vols. 1–12.—Leopold von Ranke, *The History of the Popes during the Last Four Centuries*, three vols., London, 1913; *History of the Reformation in Germany*, three vols., London, 1845–1847.

Robert Davidsohn, *Geschichte von Florenz*, four vols., Berlin, 1896–1925. —M. Poëte, *Une vie de cité, Paris de sa naissance à nos jours*, Paris, 1924.

Henri Pirenne, *Medieval Cities, their Origins and the Revival of Trade*, Princeton, 1939.—Carl Stephenson, *Borough and Town*, Cambridge, 1933. —S. Rietschel, *Die Civitas auf deutschem Boden*, Leipzig, 1894; *Markt und Stadt in ihrem rechtlichen Verhältnis*, Leipzig, 1897.—Paul Sander, *Feudalstaat und bürgerliche Verfassung*, Berlin, 1906; *Geschichte des deutschen Städtewesens*, Bonn and Leipzig, 1922.—G. F. Renard, *Gilds in the Middle Ages*, New York, 1919.

H. Rashdall, *The Universities of Europe in the Middle Ages*, Oxford, 1895. —Charles H. Haskins, *The Rise of Universities*, New York, 1923.

REFORMATION

Adolf von Harnack, *History of Dogma*.—Otto Bardenhewer, *Patrologie*, Freiburg i.B., 1910.—Ernst Troeltsch, *The Social Teaching of the Christian Churches*, two vols., London, 1931.

Ignaz von Döllinger, *Geschichte der gnostisch-manichäischen Sekten im früheren Mittelalter*, Munich, 1890.—Edvard Lehmann, *Mystik in Heidentum und Christentum*, 2nd ed., Leipzig, 1918.—*Die Viktoriner, Mystische Schriften*, ed. and transl. by Paul Wolff, Vienna, 1936.—Ch. G. A. Schmidt, *Histoire et doctrine des sectes des Cathares ou Albigeois*, Paris, 1849.—H. J. Warner, *The Albigensian Heresy*, two vols., London, 1922–1928.—James Gibson, *The Waldenses*, 3rd ed., Edinburgh and London, 1909.

Max Heimbucher, *Orden und Kongegrationen*, 3rd ed., two vols., Paderborn, 1933–1934.—E. C. Butler, *Benedictine Monasticism*, 2nd ed., New York, 1924.—Luigi Salvatorelli, *Life of St. Francis of Assisi*, New York, 1928.—Patrick Cowley, *Franciscan Rise and Fall*, London, 1933.—Pierre Mandonnet, O.P., *Saint Dominique*, Paris, 1937.—John Herkless, *Francis and Dominic and the Mendicant Orders*, New York, 1901.

Herbert H. Workman, *John Wyclif*, Oxford, 1926.—Reginald L. Poole, *Wycliffe and Movements for Reform*, London and New York, 1911.—Johann Loserth, *Huss und Wiclif*, 2nd ed., Munich and Berlin, 1925.

Leopold von Ranke, *History of the Reformation in Germany.*—F. von Bezold, *Geschichte der deutschen Reformation*, Berlin, 1890.—J. Köstlin, *Martin Luther, sein Leben und seine Schriften*, 5th ed., two vols., Berlin, 1903.—Heinrich Boehmer, *Luther im Lichte der neueren Forschung*, 4th ed., Leipzig, 1917.—R. Seeberg, *Die Lehre Luthers*, two vols., Leipzig, 1917–1920.—Lucien Febvre, *Un destin: Martin Luther*, Paris, 1928.

p. 243, l. 36   Dionysius Areopagita, *Peri theiōn onomatōn*, VII, 3.

p. 248, l. 26   Johannes Tauler's *Predigten*, ed. Arndt and Spener, new ed., Berlin, 1841, I, p. 65, similar passages pp. 159, 186, 188 foll., and others.

REASON AND SCIENCE

A. C. McGiffert, *A History of Christian Thought.*

I. L. Heiberg, *Mathematics and Physical Science in Classical Antiquity*, London, 1922.—Charles Singer, *A Short History of Science to the Nineteenth Century*, Oxford, 1941.

Henry Osborn Taylor, *The Mediaeval Mind*, 4th ed., two vols., London, 1927.—Maurice de Wulf, *Philosophy and Civilization in the Middle Ages*, Princeton, 1922.—Etienne Gilson, *The Spirit of Medieval Philosophy*, London, 1936; *Reason and Revelation in the Middle Ages*, New York, 1938.—

Martin Grabmann, *Die Philosophie des Mittelalters*, Berlin, 1921; *Die Geschichte der scholastischen Methode*, two vols., Freiburg i.B., 1909–1911.—Franz Overbeck, *Vorgeschichte und Jugend der mittelalterlichen Scholastik*, Basel, 1917.—E. Crewdson Thomas, *History of the Schoolmen*, London, 1941.—E. Vacandard, *The Inquisition*, New York, 1915.

Ernest Renan, *Averroës et l'Averroisme*, 4th ed., Paris, 1882.—Antonin G. Sertillanges, *S. Thomas d'Aquin*, 4th ed., Paris, 1925.—Jacques Maritain, *St. Thomas Aquinas*, London, 1931.

Charles H. Haskins, *Studies in the History of Mediaeval Science*, 2nd ed., Cambridge (Mass.), 1927.—Pierre Duhem, *Le systéme du monde, histoire des doctrines cosmologiques de Platon à Copernic*, five vols., Paris, 1913–1917; *Études sur Leonard da Vinci*, two vols., Paris, 1906-1913.—Lynn Thorndike, *A History of Magic and Experimental Science*, six vols., New York, 1923; *The Place of Magic in the Intellectual History of Europe* (Studies in History, Economics and Public Law; ed. by the Fac. of Pol. Sc. of Col. Un., vol. XXIV, no. 1), New York, 1905.—Leonardo Olschki, *Geschichte der neusprachlichen wissenschaftlichen Literatur*, Vol. I: *Die Literatur der Technik und der angewandten Wissenschaften vom Mittelalter bis zur Renaissance*, Heidelberg, 1918, Vol. II: *Bildung und Wissenschaft im Zeitalter der Renaissance in Italien*, Leipzig-Florence-Geneva, 1922; *Galilei und seine Zeit*, Halle (Saale), 1927.

p. 258, l. 10 Tertullian, *De praescriptionibus adversus haereticos*, Cap. 7.
p. 258, l. 13 Tertullian, *De carne Christi*, Cap. 5.
p. 269, l. 28 Averroës: *Philosophie und Theologie*, transl. from the Arabic into German by M. J. Müller, Munich, 1875, pp. 3 foll.
p. 270, l. 5 *ibid.*, p. 22.
p. 271, l. 5 S. Thomas Aquinas, *Quaestiones Disputatae De Veritate*, Quaestio XIV, Art. IX. (S. Thomae Aquinatis Quaest. Disp. Vol. IV, Ed. Quinta, Taurini-Romae MCMXXVII p. 24.)

ART

C. F. C. Hawkes, *The Prehistoric Foundations of Europe*, London, 1940.—M. Hoernes, *Urgeschichte der bildenden Kunst in Europa*, Vienna, 1915.—Ernst Grosse, *Die Anfänge der Kunst*, Freiburg i.B. and Leipzig, 1894.—Eckhardt von Sydow, *Die Kunst der Naturvölker und der Vorzeit*, Berlin, 1923.—Hugo Obermaier, *Fossil Man in Spain*, New Haven, 1924.—Hugo Obermaier and Herbert Kühn, *Bushman Art, Rock Paintings of South-West Africa*, London and New York, 1930.—Leo Frobenius and Douglas

C. Fox, *Prehistoric Rock Pictures in Europe and Africa*, New York, 1937. —F. Adama van Scheltema, *Die altnordische Kunst, Grundprobleme vorhistorischer Kunstentwicklung*, Berlin, 1923.—Edward Clodd, *The Story of the Alphabet*, New York, 1907.—Karl von den Steinen, *Unter den Naturvölkern Zentralbrasiliens*, Berlin, 1894.—J. E. Harrison, *Ancient Art and Ritual*, New York, 1913.—Leo Frobenius, *Das unbekannte Afrika*, Munich, 1923.

Sheldon Cheney, *World History of Art*, New York, 1937.—Karl Woermann, *Geschichte der Kunst I. Urzeit und Altertum*, 2nd ed., Leipzig and Vienna, 1924.—F. M. Simpson, *A History of Architectural Development*, three vols., London and New York, 1921–1929.

Ludwig Curtius, *Die antike Kunst: Aegypten und Vorderasien*, Berlin, 1923.—Baldwin Smith, *Egyptian Architecture as Cultural Expression*, New York, 1938.—Hedwig Fechheimer, *Die Plastik der Aegypter*, Berlin, 1914. —Wilhelm Worringer, *Egyptian Art*, London, 1928.—C. L. Woolley, *Antiquities of Ur*.—Bruno Meissner, *Grundzüge der babylonisch-assyrischen Plastik*, Leipzig, 1915.

M. Burrows, *The Discoveries in Crete*, New York, 1907.—A. R. Burn, *Minoans, Philistines and Greeks*, New York, 1930.—H. Th. Bossert, *The Art of Ancient Crete*, London, 1937.

A. von Salis, *Die Kunst der Griechen*, Leipzig, 1922.—W. J. Anderson and R. Phené Spiers, *The Architecture of Greece and Rome*, 2nd ed., London, 1907.—Emanuel Loewy, *Die Griechische Plastik*, 3rd ed., two vols., Leipzig, 1920.—Ernst Pfuhl, *Malerei und Zeichnung der Griechen*, three vols., Munich, 1923.—*L'Art en Grèce des temps préhistoriques au début du XVIIIe siècle*, by Christian Zervos (Editions "Cahiers d'Art") 2nd ed., Paris, 1935.

P. Omati, *L'arte in Roma dalle origine al secolo VIII*, Bologna, 1938.— Franz Wickhoff, *Roman Art*, London, 1900.—Herbert Koch, *Römische Kunst*, Breslau, 1925.—J. J. Bernoulli, *Römische Ikonographie*, 4 vols., Stuttgart, 1882–1894.

Ch. Diehl, *L'art chrétien primitif et l'art byzantin*, Paris, 1928.—C. R. Morey, *Early Christian Art*, Princeton, 1942; *Mediaeval Art*, New York, 1942.—Josef Strzygowski, *Ursprung der christlichen Kirchenkunst*, Leipzig, 1920.

Max Dvořak, *Kunstgeschichte als Geistesgeschichte,* Munich, 1924.—Wilhelm Worringer, *Form in Gothic,* London, 1927; *Griechentum und Gotik,* Munich, 1928.—Erwin Panofsky, *Die deutsche Plastik des 11. bis 13. Jahrhunderts,* Munich, 1924.—Wilhelm Pinder, *Die deutsche Plastik im ausgehenden Mittelalter bis zum Ende der Renaissance,* Potsdam, 1924.

Adolfo Venturi, *A Short History of Italian Art,* New York, 1926.—Max Dvořak, *Geschichte der italienischen Kunst,* two vols., Munich, 1927.—F. J. Mather, Jr., *A History of Italian Painting,* New York, 1913.—Erwin Rosenthal, *Giotto in der mittelalterlichen Geistesentwicklung,* Augsburg, 1924.—Heinrich Wölfflin, *Die klassische Kunst,* Munich, 1912; *Die Kunst der Renaissance. Italien und das deutsche Formgefühl,* Munich, 1931.—Georg Sobotka, *Die Bildhauerei der Barockzeit,* Vienna, 1927.

Max Dvořak, *Das Rätsel der Kunst der Brüder van Eyck,* Munich, 1925.—Wilhelm Worringer, *Die Anfänge der Tafelmalerei,* Leipzig, 1924.—Curt Glaser, *Zwei Jahrhunderte deutscher Malerei,* Munich, 1916.—Ernst Heidrich, *Die altdeutsche Malerei,* Jena, 1909.—Max Friedländer, *Van Eyck bis Breugel,* Berlin, 1921.—*The Paintings of Rembrandt,* ed. by A. Bredius, Vienna, 1937.

p. 290, l. 27 Charles Holroyd, *Michelangelo Buonarrotti,* with translations of three dialogues from the Portuguese of Francisco d'Ollanda, London, 1903, p. 240.

ECONOMY

Herbert Heaton, *Economic History of Europe,* New York and London, 1936.—S. B. Clough and C. W. Cole, *Economic History of Europe,* Boston, 1941.—Max Weber, *General Economic History,* New York, 1927; *Gesammelte Aufsätze zur Sozial-und Wirtschaftsgeschichte,* Tübingen, 1924.

Lujo Brentano, *Das Wirtschaftsleben der antiken Welt,* Jena, 1929.—Fritz Heichelheim, *Wirtschaftsgeschichte des Altertums vom Palaeolithikum bis zur Völkerwanderung,* Leiden, 1938.—Bernhard Laum, *Heiliges Geld,* Tübingen, 1924.

Werner Sombart, *Der moderne Kapitalismus. Historisch-systematische Darstellung des gesamteuropäischen Wirtschaftslebens von seinen Anfängen bis zur Gegenwart,* 4th ed., three vols. in six, Munich and Leipzig, 1921–1928, Vols. I and II.—Henri Eugène Sée, *Modern Capitalism, its Origin and Evolution,* New York, 1928.—Lujo Brentano, *Die Anfänge des modernen Kapitalismus,* Munich, 1916.—James Parkes, *The Jew in the Medieval Community,* London, 1938.—Robert Davidsohn, *Geschichte von Florenz.*—K. Th. von Inama Sternegg, *Deutsche Wirtschaftsgeschichte,* three vols., Leipzig, 1879–1901.

Ernst Troeltsch, *The Social Teaching of the Christian Churches.*—Richard Ehrenberg, *Capital and Finance in the Age of the Renaissance,* New York, 1928.—Jakob Strieder, *Zur Genesis des modernen Kapitalismus,* Leipzig, 1904; *Studien zur Geschichte kapitalistischer Organisationsformen,* 2nd ed., Munich and Leipzig, 1925; *Jacob Fugger the Rich, Merchant and Banker of Augsburg,* New York, 1931.—Miriam Beard, *A History of the Business Man,* New York, 1938.

　　p. 298, l. 29　Aristotle, *Politics,* 1329a Bekker (Rackham, in Loeb Classical Library, 1932, p. 579).

　　p. 298, l. 34　*ibid.,* 1328b–1329a Bekker (Loeb., p. 575).

　　p. 299, l. 12　Plato, *Laws,* IV 704d, 705a (Platonis opera rec. Burnet, Oxford 1906, Vol. V, 1).

　　p. 301, l. 6　Cicero, *De Officiis,* I, 42.

　　p. 313, l. 2　Jakob Strieder, in *Jacob Fugger the Rich,* Ch. 4, p. 66.

POLITICS

Thomas I. Cook, *History of Political Philosophy from Plato to Burke,* New York, 1936.—R. W. and A. J. Carlyle, *A History of Mediaeval Political Theory in the West,* London, 1903.—Heinrich Rommen, *Die ewige Wiederkehr des Naturrechts,* Leipzig, 1936.—Otto von Gierke, *Natural Law and the Theory of Society 1500–1800,* Cambridge, 1934; *The Development of Political Theory,* New York, 1939; *Political Theories of the Middle Ages,* Cambridge, 1922.—Adolf Dock, *Der Suveränitätsbegriff von Bodin bis zu Friedrich dem Grossen,* Strassburg i.E., 1897.

Otto Krauske, *Die Entwicklung der ständigen Diplomatie,* Leipzig, 1885. —B. L. Freiherr von Mackay, *Die moderne Diplomatie, ihre Entwicklungsgeschichte und ihre Reformmöglichkeiten,* Frankfurt a.M., 1915.—R. B. Mowat, *A History of European Diplomacy 1451–1789,* New York, 1928.— Harold Nicolson, *Diplomacy,* London, 1928.—*Le relazioni degli ambasciatori veneti al senato durante il secolo decimosesto,* racc. ed ill. da Eugenio Alberi, three series, fifteen vols., Florence, 1839–1863.—Willi Andreas, *Die venezianischen Relazionen und ihr Verhältnis zur Kultur der Renaissance,* Leipzig, 1908.—Charles Diehl, *Une république patricienne: Venise,* Paris, 1921.

Charles Dupuis, *Le principe d'équilibre et le concert européen de la paix de Westphalie à l'acte d'Algesiras,* Paris, 1909.—Christian L. Lange, *Histoire de l'internationalisme,* Christiania, 1919.—Jacob ter Meulen, *Der Gedanke der internationalen Organisation in seiner Entwicklung 1300–1800,* The Hague, 1917.—S. J. Hemleben, *Plans for World Peace through Six Centuries,* Chicago, 1942.—J. Huizinga, *Erasmus,* Basle, 1928.—Veit Valentin, *Geschichte des Völkerbundgedankens in Deutschland,* Berlin, 1920.—R. B. Mowat, *Diplomacy and Peace,* London, 1935.

D. E. Muir, *Machiavelli and His Times,* London, 1936.—Friedrich Meinecke, *Die Idee der Staatsraison,* Munich and Berlin, 1924.—Alfred Cobban, *Dictatorship, its History and Theory,* New York, 1939.

p. 324, l. 18 *Notes* taken by Leonardo Donato (1573) ed. Bernhard Erdmannsdörffer (Berichte über die Verhandlungen der sächsischen Gesellschaft der Wissenschaften 1857, Vol. 9, pp. 38 foll.) cf. Alberi I 6, 27.

p. 326, l. 25 Niccolò Machiavelli, *Tutte le opere storiche e letterarie,* Florence, 1929, pp. 884 foll.

p. 327, l. 30 Niccolò Machiavelli, *Il principe,* Chs. 3, 8, 17, 18.

p. 331, l. 19 Francisco Suarez, *Tract. de leg.* Lib. II, Cap. XIX, n. 9.

NATION

Walter Platzhoff, *Geschichte des europäischen Staatensystems 1559–1660,* Munich and Berlin, 1928.—R. B. Mowat, *The European States System,* London, 1923.

Otto Cartellieri, *The Court of Burgundy,* New York, 1929.—Rafael Altamira y Crevea, *Historia de España y de la civilización española,* five vols., Barcelona, 1900–1914; *Manual de historia de España,* Madrid, 1933.—C. E. Chapman, *A History of Spain,* New York, 1922.—Henri Hauser, *La preponderance espagnole (1559–1660),* Paris, 1933.—Waldo Frank, *Virgin Spain. The Drama of a Great People,* new ed., New York, 1942.—Eberhard Gothein, *Ignatius von Loyola,* Halle, 1895; *Staat und Gesellschaft des Zeitalters der Gegenreformation,* Berlin and Leipzig, 1908.—A. H. Verrill, *The Inquisition,* New York, 1931.

J. Ch. L. Simonde de Sismondi, *A History of the Italian Republics,* (Everyman's Library), New York, 1917.—Carlo Cattaneo, *La città considerata come principio ideale delle istorie italiane,* Florence, 1931.—Luigi Salvatorelli, *A Concise History of Italy from Prehistoric Times to Our Own Days,* New York, 1940.

Charles Seignobos, *The Evolution of the French People*, New York, 1932.
—Jacques Bainville, *Histoire de France.*—Ernest Lavisse, *Histoire de France*, esp. Vols. 4 and 7.—Comte Georges d'Avenel, *Richelieu et la monarchie absolue*, 2nd ed., four vols., Paris, 1895.—Louis Batifoll, *Richelieu et le roi Louis XIII*, Paris, 1934.—Carl J. Burckhardt, *Richelieu, His Rise to Power*, New York, 1940.—*The Memoirs of the Duke of Saint-Simon on the Reign of Louis XIV and the Regency*, two vols., New York, 1936.—Saint-Simon, *Mémoires; scènes et portraits; anecdotes etc.*, 7th ed., (Mercure de France), Paris, 1922.—Chamfort, Collections des plus belles pages, (Mercure de France), Paris, 1905.—Hippolyte Taine, *The Ancient Régime*, new ed., New York, 1876.

Carlton J. Hayes, *Essays on Nationalism*, New York, 1926; *The Historical Evolution of Modern Nationalism*, New York, 1931.—Harold Nicolson, *The Meaning of Prestige*, Cambridge, 1937.

p. 351, l. 3 *Mémoires historiques et instructions de Louis XIV pour le dauphin, son fils*, Part I, Book I (1661), *"Amour du travail"*, Oeuvres de Louis XIV, Paris, 1806, Vol. I.

p. 352, l. 9 Bossuet, *Politique tirée de l'écriture*, Book III, Art. II. Cf. also Book IV, Art. I. On the other hand, Bossuet gives the stringent advice that "the prince should begin with himself in ruling with firmness, and make himself master of his passions . . . He should resist his proper will and be severe foremost toward himself." *op. cit.*, Book IV, Art. II.

p. 352, l. 12 *Opere* di Lorenzo de' Medici, il Magnifico, Bari, 1914, II, p. 111.

p. 354, l. 2 Preston Schoyer, *The Foreigners*, New York, 1942, p. 27.

DEMOCRACY

François Guizot, *History of the Origin of Representative Government in Europe*, London, 1861.—James Bryce, *Modern Democracies*, two vols., New York, 1921.—A. F. Hattersley, *A Short History of Democracy*, Cambridge, 1930.—Irwin Edman, *Fountainheads of Freedom. The Growth of the Democratic Idea*, New York, 1941.

A. Gasquet, *Précis des institutions politiques et sociales de l'ancienne France*, two vols., Paris, 1885.—Pierre Clément, *Jacques Coeur et Charles VII*, Paris, 1886.—A. B. Kerr, *Jacques Coeur, Merchant Prince of the Middle Ages*, New York, 1929.—C. W. Cole, *Colbert and a Century of French Mercantilism*, two vols., New York, 1939.

C. F. Cameron, *Switzerland*, London and Edinburgh.—Wilhelm Oechsli, *History of Switzerland 1499–1914*, Cambridge, 1922.—William Martin, *Histoire de la Suisse, essai sur la formation d'une confédération d'états*, Paris, 1926.

Preserved Smith, *The Age of the Reformation*, New York, 1921.—J. S. Schapiro, *Social Reform and the Reformation*, New York, 1909.—Ernst Bloch, *Thomas Münzer als Theologe der Revolution*, Munich, 1921.— Georg Tumbült, *Die Wiedertäufer*, Bielefeld and Leipzig, 1899.

R. N. Carew Hunt, *Calvin*, London, 1933.—M. E. Chenevière, *La pensée politique de Calvin*, Geneva, 1937.—F. W. Kampschulte, *Johann Calvin, seine Kirche und sein Staat in Genf*, two vols., 1869–1899.—E. Choisy, *La théocratie à Genève au temps de Calvin*, Geneva, 1898.

Max Weber, *The Protestant Ethic and the Spirit of Capitalism*, New York, 1930.—Ernst Troeltsch, *The Social Teaching of the Christian Churches*. —R. H. Tawney, *Religion and the Rise of Capitalism*, new ed., London, 1929.—J. B. Kraus, *Scholastik, Puritanismus, Kapitalismus*, Munich, 1930.

F. W. Maitland, *The Constitutional History of England*, Cambridge, 1931. —Edward A. Freeman, *The Growth of the English Constitution*, London, 1887.—Emile Boutmy, *The English Constitution*, London and New York, 1891.—St. B. Liljegren, *The Fall of the Monasteries and the Social Changes in England leading up to the Great Revolution*, Lund, 1924.—Samuel R. Gardiner, *The First Two Stuarts and the Puritan Revolution 1603–1660*, new ed., New York, 1904; *History of the Commonwealth and Protectorate*, four vols., London and New York, 1903.—François Guizot, *History of Oliver Cromwell and the English Commonwealth*, two vols., Philadelphia, 1854.

p. 360, l. 5   Quoted by Ernest Lavisse, *Histoire de France*, Vol. VIII, Book 2, Ch. IV, p. 174.

p. 362, l. 14   W. H. Rivers, *Instinct and the Unconscious*, Cambridge, 1920, pp. 95 foll.

p. 364, l. 25   Edward A. Freeman, *The Growth of the English Constitution*, pp. 1 foll.

p. 368, l. 25   John Wyclif, *Select English Works*, ed. by Thomas Arnold, Vol. VIII, *Miscellaneous Works*, Oxford, 1871, pp. 130, 131, 134; quoted by R. H. Tawney, *op. cit.*, p. 25.

p. 370, l. 16   Martin Luther, *Wider die räuberischen und mörderischen Rotten der Bauern*, 1525, Weimar ed., Vol. 18, p. 361.

p. 370, l. 28   Martin Luther, *Ermahnung zum Frieden auf die zwölf Artikel der Bauerschaft in Schwaben*, 1525, Weimar ed., Vol. 18, pp. 326 foll.

p. 370, l. 32   Martin Luther, BA, IV, 1, p. 479, quoted by Troeltsch, *Social Teaching*.

p. 378, l. 26   quoted by R. H. Tawney, *op. cit.*, p. 106.

p. 378, l. 26   Calvin, *Letter "De Usuris"*, Opera X, I (Corpus Ref. Vol. 38), p. 247.

STATE

Georg Jellinek, *Allgemeine Staatslehre,* 3rd ed., Berlin, 1914.—Heinrich von Treitschke, *Politics,* two vols., New York, 1926.

Hans Delbrück, *Geschichte der Kriegskunst im Rahmen der politischen Geschichte,* seven vols., Berlin, 1908–1936.—Alfred Vagts, *History of Militarism,* New York, 1937.

George A. Campbell, *The Knights Templars, their Rise and Fall,* London, 1937.—Heinrich von Treitschke, *Origins of Prussianism (The Teutonic Knights),* London, 1942 [Prussian point of view].—Stanislaw Zajaczkowsky, *Rise and Fall of the Teutonic Order in Prussia,* London, 1935. [Polish nationalist point of view.]

J. A. R. Marriott and C. G. Robinson, *The Evolution of Prussia,* Oxford, 1915.—Johann Gustav Droysen, *Geschichte der preussischen Politik,* five vols., Leipzig, 1868–1886.—Reinhold Schneider, *Die Hohenzollern,* Leipzig, 1933.—Robert Ergang, *The Potsdam Führer. Frederick William I., Father of Prussian Militarism,* New York, 1941.—Pierre Gaxotte, *Frederick the Great,* London, 1941.—Friedrich Meinecke, *Die Idee der Staatsraison,* Book II, Ch. 5: *Friedrich der Grosse.*—Herbert Blank, *Preussische Offiziere,* Oldenburg, 1932.

p. 393, l. 17   Herbert Eulenberg, *Die Hohenzollern,* Berlin, 1928, p. 87.

p. 393, l. 27   Ernest Lavisse, *Histoire de France,* Vol. VII, p. 135.

p. 394, l. 11   Georg Küntzel and Martin Hass, *Die Politischen Testamente der Hohenzollern,* Leipzig and Berlin, 1911, Vol. I, p. 89.

p. 394, l. 27   *Letter to Podewils of May 12, 1741,* Politische Korrespondenz Friedrichs des Grossen I, 245.

p. 394, l. 29   Reinhold Schneider, *Die Hohenzollern,* p. 236.

p. 394, l. 32—*Der König. Friedrich der Grosse in seinen Briefen und Erlassen, sowie in zeitgenössischen Briefen, Berichten und Anekdoten,* Munich-Ebenhausen, 1912, p. 400.

p. 397, l. 1 Martin Luther, *Wochenpredigten über Matth. 5–7* (1530–1532) Weimar ed., Vol. XXXII, p. 440.

p. 400, l. 14 Frederick William I., *Erlasse und Briefe*, Leipzig, 1931, p. 24.

p. 401, l. 18 Acta Borussica, Berlin, 1901, Vol. III, 651, quoted by R. Ergang, *op. cit.*, p. 112.

p. 401, l. 28 Robert Ergang, *op. cit.*, p. 49.

p. 401, l. 33 Fritz Winter, *Abriss der Geschichte des Beamtentums*, 2nd ed., Mannheim, 1929.

p. 402, l. 5 Corpus Constitutionum Marchicarum, Berlin and Halle, Vol. V (1740), Part II, Col. 355–358 (No. LXXXI).

p. 402, l. 24 John Toland, *An Account of the Courts of Prussia and Hanover*, 2nd ed., London, 1706, pp. 6–7.

p. 403, l. 8 Acta Borussica, Vol. II, 1898, pp. 128–129.

p. 404, l. 31 Heinrich von Treitschke, *Politik*, 4th ed., Leipzig, 1918, Vol. I, Book 1, Ch. 2, p. 69.

FREE ECONOMY

J. K. Ingram, *A History of Political Economy*, new ed., London, 1923.—Eric Roll, *History of Economic Thoughts*, New York, 1942.

L. P. Packard, *The Commercial Revolution 1400–1763*, New York, 1927.—E. F. Heckscher, *Mercantilism*, two vols., London, 1935.—J. W. Horrocks, *Short History of Mercantilism*, New York, 1925.—C. W. Cole, *Colbert and a Century of French Mercantilism.*—B. Suviranta, *The Theory of the Balance of Trade in England*, Helsingfors, 1923.

Alexis de Tocqueville, *On the State of Society in France before the Revolution*, 3rd ed., two vols., London, 1888.—Daniel Mornet, *Les origines intellectuelles de la révolution française, 1715–1787*, Paris, 1933.—Hippolyte Taine, *The Origins of Contemporary France*, three vols., New York, 1878–1885.—Albert Mathiez, *The French Revolution*, New York, 1928; *After Robespierre*, New York, 1931.—Crane Brinton, *A Decade of Revolution (1789–1799)*, New York and London, 1934.—E. L. Higgins, *The French Revolution as told by Contemporaries*, New York, 1929.—Albert Sorel, *L'Europe et la Révolution Française*, eight vols., Paris, 1885–1904, Vols. 1–4. —Georg Jellinek, *The Declaration of the Rights of Man and of Citizens*, New York, 1901.

G. M. Trevelyan, *English Social History, a Survey of Six Centuries*, London and New York, 1942; *History of England*, New York and London,

1934.—Lujo Brentano, *Eine Geschichte der wirtschaftlichen Entwicklung Englands,* three vols. in four, Jena, 1927–1929.—J. M. Kulischer, *Allgemeine Wirtschaftsgeschichte,* two vols., Munich and Berlin, 1922, Vol. II.— R. B. Mowat, *The Wars of the Roses 1377–1471,* London, 1914.—St. B. Liljegren, *The Fall of the Monasteries and the Social Changes in England.* —R. B. Mowat, *England in the Eighteenth Century,* New York, 1932; *Europe 1718–1815,* New York, 1929.—Geoffrey G. Butler, *The Tory Tradition,* London, 1914.—Sidney Webb, *Studies on the Local Government in England.*—E. S. Furniss, *The Position of the Laborer in a System of Nationalism, a Study in the Labor Theories of the Later Mercantilists,* Boston and New York, 1920.—G. D. H. Cole and Raymond Postgate, *The Common People 1746–1938,* London, 1938.—Simon Haxey, *England's Money Lords,* New York, 1939.

p. 416, l. 3   Georg Jellinek, *The Declaration of the Rights of Man.*
p. 416, l. 13   Crane Brinton, *A Decade of Revolution,* p. 160.
p. 416, l. 19   Crane Brinton, *op. cit.,* p. 161.
p. 420, l. 31   Adam Smith, *Wealth of Nations,* Book II, Ch. 3.
p. 422, l. 3   Adam Smith, *op. cit.,* Book IV, Ch. 3, Part 2.

WORLD ECONOMY

Ramsay Muir, *The Expansion of Europe,* 3rd ed., New York, 1928.—J. E. Gillespie, *A History of Geographical Discovery 1400–1800,* New York, 1933.—Percy M. Sykes, *A History of Exploration from the Earliest Times to the Present Day,* London, 1935.—Henry C. Morris, *The History of Colonization,* two vols., New York, 1900.—Salvador de Madariaga, *Christopher Columbus,* New York, 1940.—William H. Prescott, *The Conquest of Mexico and the Conquest of Peru,* two vols., The Modern Library, New York.—L. D. Baldwin, *The Story of the Americas,* New York, 1943.— Clive Day, *History of Commerce,* rev. ed., New York, 1925.—Miriam Beard, *A History of the Business Man.*

R. A. Newhall, *The Crusades,* New York, 1927.—George Young, *Portugal Old and Young, a Historical Study,* Oxford, 1917.—Théodoric Legrand, *Histoire du Portugal,* Paris, 1928.—Edgar Prestage, *The Portuguese Pioneers,* London, 1933.—Kurt Häbler, *Die wirtschaftliche Blüte Spaniens und ihr Verfall,* Berlin, 1888.—F. A. Kirkpatrick, *Spanish Conquistadores,* London, 1934.—E. J. Hamilton, *American Treasure and the Price Revolution in Spain 1501–1650,* Cambridge (Mass.), 1934.

J. E. Barker, *Rise and Decline of the Netherlands,* New York and London, 1906.—George Edmundsson, *History of Holland,* Cambridge, 1922.

Ramsay Muir, *A Short History of the British Commonwealth,* two vols., London, 1920–1924.—H. B. Richmond, *The Invasion of Britain. An Account of Plans, Attempts and Countermeasures 1586–1918,* London, 1941. —Howard Robinson, *The Development of the British Empire,* New York, 1922.—John A. R. Marriott, *The Evolution of the British Empire,* London, 1939.—James Truslow Adams, *Building the British Empire,* New York and London, 1938; *Empire on the Seven Seas,* New York, 1940.—David Hannay, *The Great Chartered Companies,* London, 1926.

E. P. Cheyney, *European Background of American History, 1300–1600,* New York and London, 1922.—Alexis de Tocqueville, *Democracy in America,* two vols., New York, 1904; *Notes de Voyages (Voyage aux États-Unis, Voyage en Angleterre),* Oeuvres complètes, Paris, 1877, Vol. VIII.—James Bryce, *The American Commonwealth,* new ed., two vols., New York, 1920; *Modern Democracies.*—F. J. Turner, *The Frontier in American History,* New York, 1920.—Charles A. and Mary R. Beard, *The Rise of American Civilization,* new ed., New York, 1937.—S. E. Morison and H. S. Commager, *The Growth of the American Republic,* two vols., New York, 1942. —L. M. Hacker, *The Triumph of American Capitalism,* New York, 1940. —Gustavus Myers, *History of the Great American Fortunes,* The Modern Library, New York.—A. M. Schlesinger, *The Rise of the City 1878–1898,* New York, 1933.—Thurman W. Arnold, *The Folklore of Capitalism,* New Haven, 1937.

J. H. Clapham, *An Economic History of Modern Britain,* three vols., Cambridge, 1926–1938.—Lujo Brentano, *Geschichte der wirtschaftlichen Entwicklung Englands.*—W. Cunningham, *The Growth of English Industry and Commerce,* 5th ed., two vols., Cambridge, 1910–1912.—C. R. Fay, *Great Britain from Adam Smith to the Present Day,* New York, 1928.

A. Toynbee, *Lectures on the Industrial Revolution of the Eighteenth Century,* London, 1927.—P. Mantoux, *The Industrial Revolution in the Eighteenth Century,* New York, 1929.—H. L. Beales, *The Industrial Revolution 1750–1850,* New York, 1928.—F. C. Dietz, *The Industrial Revolution,* New York, 1927.—A. P. Usher, *A History of Mechanical Inventions,* New York and London, 1929; *The Industrial History of England,* Boston and New York, 1920.—E. Cressy, *Discoveries and Inventions of the Twentieth Century,* 2nd ed., London, 1923.—M. and C. H. B. Quennell, *The Rise of Industrialism 1733–1851,* New York, 1932.—G. W. Daniels, *The Early English Cotton Industry,* Manchester, 1920.—J. L. and Barbara Hammond, *The Town Labourer 1760–1832,* New York and London, 1925; *The Age of the Chartists 1832–1854,* New York, 1930.—Friedrich Engels, *The Con-*

dition of the Working Class in England in 1844, New York, 1892.—Karl Marx, *Capital,* Vol. I.—B. L. Hutchins and A. Harrison, *History of Factory Legislation,* London, 1911.—Allen Clarke, *The Effects of the Factory System,* New York, 1899.—M. C. Buer, *Health, Wealth and Population in the Early Days of the Industrial Revolution,* London, 1926.—W. J. Warner, *The Wesleyan Movement in the Industrial Revolution,* London, 1930.— W. J. Wilkinson, *Tory Democracy,* London and New York, 1925.—Max Beer, *Social Struggles and Thought (1750–1860),* London, 1925.—Alice Hamilton, *Exploring the Dangerous Trades,* Boston, 1943.

F. L. Nussbaum, *History of the Economic Institutions of Modern Europe,* New York, 1933.—Werner Sombart, *Der moderne Kapitalismus* and *The Quintessence of Capitalism,* New York, 1915.—The "Modern Business" Series of the Alexander Hamilton Institute, New York.—W. Z. Ripley, *Trusts, Pools and Corporations,* new ed., Boston and New York, 1916.— Émile James, *Les formes d'entreprises,* Paris, 1935.—Robert Liefmann, *Cartels, Concerns and Trusts,* London, 1932; *Die Unternehmungsformen,* 4th ed., 1928.—Walther Rathenau, *Zur Kritik der Zeit,* Berlin, 1912; *Vom Aktienwesen,* Berlin, 1917.

p. 434, l. 32   Miriam Beard, *A History of the Business Man,* pp. 302 foll.

p. 441, l. 15   quoted by C. F. Lavell and C. E. Payne, *Imperial England,* New York, 1918, p. 52.

p. 443, l. 34   Lavell and Payne, *op. cit.,* p. 76.

p. 444, l. 12   Tocqueville, *L'ancien régime et la révolution,* Oeuvres compl., 7th ed., Vol. IV, Ch. IV, p. 373, note.

p. 452, l. 19   Gladstone, *Gleanings of Past Years 1851–1877,* New York, 1879, IV, 357.

p. 458, l. 35   Tocqueville, *Notes de voyage. Voyage en Angleterre,* Oeuvres compl., VIII, 365 foll.

THE THREE INTELLECTUAL ATTITUDES OF MODERN MAN

W. C. D. Dampier Wetham, *A History of Science,* London and New York, 1930.—A. Wolf, *A History of Science, Technology and Philosophy in the Sixteenth and Seventeenth Centuries,* New York, 1935.—A. P. Usher, *A History of Mechanical Inventions.*—Charles Williams, *Bacon,* New York, 1934.—L. T. More, *Isaac Newton,* New York, 1934.

G. J. Holyoake, *The Origin and Nature of Secularism,* London, 1896.— A. C. McGiffert, *Protestant Thought before Kant,* New York, 1911.

J. B. Bury, *The Idea of Progress,* London and New York, 1932; *History of the Freedom of Thought,* New York, 1913.—Christopher H. Dawson, *Progress and Religion,* New York, 1938.

W. E. H. Lecky, *History of the Rise and Influence of the Spirit of Rationalism in Europe,* new ed., two vols., London, 1877–1878.—Lucien Lévy-Bruhl, *History of Modern Philosophy in France,* Chicago, 1899.

F. A. Lange, *The History of Materialism,* 3rd ed., London, 1925.

Friedrich Meinecke, *Die Entstehung des Historismus,* two vols., Munich and Berlin, 1936.—Ernst Troeltsch, *Der Historismus und seine Probleme,* Vol. I, Tübingen, 1922.

Georg Simmel, *Kant,* 4th ed., Munich, 1918.

Karl Marx, *Der historische Materialismus,* ed. by S. Landshut and J. P. Mayer, two vols., Leipzig, 1932.—Georg Lukacs, *Geschichte und Klassenbewusstsein,* Berlin, 1923.—Karl Mannheim, *Ideology and Utopia,* New York, 1936.

C. E. Vaughan, *The Romantic Revolt,* New York, 1907.—R. B. Mowat, *The Romantic Age,* London, 1937; *The Victorian Age,* London, 1939.—Rudolf Haym, *Die romantische Schule,* 3rd ed., Berlin, 1914.—Friedrich Gundolf, *Romantiker,* two vols., Berlin, 1930–1931.—Benjamin E. Lippincott, *Victorian Critics of Democracy,* London and Minneapolis, 1938.

Jules Barbey d'Aurevilly, *Du Dandysme et de George Brummell,* Paris, 1887.—Otto Mann, *Der moderne Dandy,* Berlin, 1925.

p. 475, l. 26   J. B. Bury, *The Idea of Progress,* p. 82.

p. 492, l. 20   Hoelderlin, *Hyperion, Book II,* transl. by Carol North Valhope, "Twice a Year", Nos. 3–4, 1939–40.

p. 492, l. 31   Thomas Carlyle, *Latter-Day Pamphlets, The Present Time,* 1850.

p. 492, l. 36   Gustave Flaubert, *Correspondance,* troisième série, *lettre à Louis Bouilhet,* 1855; *à Mlle. Leroyer de Chantepie,* 1857.

TRANSCENDENCE OF ART

p. 507, l. 6   Henrik Ibsen, *Lyrics and Poems,* transl. by Fydell Edmund Garrett, London and New York, 1912.

p. 508, l. 28   André Gide, *Journal des faux-monnayeurs*, Paris, 1927, p. 26.

p. 509, l. 10   André Gide, *Les faux-monnayeurs*, Paris, 1925, p. 93.

p. 519, l. 1   Alfred H. Barr Jr., *Fantastic Art, Dada, Surrealism*, New York (Museum of Modern Art), 1936.

THE PRELIMINARIES OF THE GREAT CRISIS

Benedetto Croce, *History of Europe in the Nineteenth Century*, New York, 1940.—G. Lowes Dickinson, *The European Anarchy*, New York, 1916; *The International Anarchy 1904–1914*, New York and London, 1926.—R. B. Mowat, *The Concert of Europe*, London, 1930.—Erich Kahler, *Der deutsche Character in der Geschichte Europas*, Zurich, 1937.

Michele Rosi, *Il popolo italiano negli ultimi due secoli (1700–1923)*, Rome, 1924; *L'unità italiana (1849–1881)*, Rome, 1931.—Benedetto Croce, *A History of Italy 1871–1915*, Oxford, 1929.—A. Solmi, *L'unità fondamentale della storia italiana*, Bologna, 1927; *L'idea dell'unità italiana nell'età napoleonica*, Modena, 1934.—Gaetano Salvemini, *Mazzini*, 4th ed., Florence, 1927.—G. M. Trevelyan, *Garibaldi and the Making of Italy*, London, 1911.—Alfredo Oriani, *La lotta politica in Italia*, 4th ed., Florence, 1921.

Ignaz Jastrow, *Geschichte des deutschen Einheitstraumes und seiner Erfüllung*, 3rd ed., Berlin, 1890.—Friedrich Meinecke, *Weltbürgertum und Nationalstaat*, 5th ed., Munich and Berlin, 1919; *Das Zeitalter der deutschen Erhebung (1795–1815)*, Bielefeld and Leipzig, 1906.—Guy Stanton Ford, *Stein and the Era of Reform in Prussia*, Princeton, 1922.—Hans Blum, *Die deutsche Revolution 1848–1849*, Florence and Leipzig, 1897.—Heinrich Friedjung, *The Struggle for Supremacy in Germany 1859–1866*, London, 1935; *Das Zeitalter des Imperialismus 1884–1914*, three vols., Berlin, 1919–1922.—Moritz Busch, *Our Chancellor; Sketches for a Historical Picture*, two vols., London, 1884.—Bismarck, *Gedanken und Erinnerungen*, three vols., Stuttgart, 1898–1921.—Otto Hammann, *Der neue Kurs*, Berlin, 1918; *Zur Vorgeschichte des Weltkrieges*, Berlin, 1918.—*Zwölf Jahre am deutschen Kaiserhof*, Aufzeichnungen des Grafen Robert Zedlitz-Trützschler, ehemaligen Hofmarschalls Wilhelms II., Stuttgart, 1924.

J. H. Clapham, *The Economic Development of France and Germany 1815–1914*. Cambridge, 1921.—Bernadotte E. Schmitt, *England and Germany 1740–1914*, Princeton, 1916.—A. Sartorius von Waltershausen, *Deutsche Wirtschaftsgeschichte 1815–1914*, 2nd ed., Jena, 1923.—Thorstein Veblen, *Imperial Germany and the Industrial Revolution*, New York, 1915.—G. M.

Trevelyan, *British History in the Nineteenth Century 1782-1919*, new ed., London, 1937.—P. H. Emden, *Money Powers of Europe in the Nineteenth and Twentieth Centuries*, New York, 1938.

Max Beer, *Allgemeine Geschichte des Sozialismus und der sozialen Kämpfe*, five vols., Berlin, 1922-1923.—G. D. H. Cole, *A Short History of the British Working-Class Movement*, three vols., London, 1925-1927.— H. W. Laidler, *A History of Socialist Thought*, New York, 1927.—Karl Diehl, *Über Sozialismus, Kommunismus und Anarchismus*, 2nd ed., Jena, 1911.—Karl Kautsky, *Vorläufer des neueren Sozialismus*, two vols., 2nd ed., Stuttgart, 1909.—William B. Guthrie, *Socialism before the French Revolution*, New York and London, 1907.—Lewis Mumford, *The Story of Utopias*, New York, 1922.—Eduard Bernstein, *Cromwell and Communism; Socialism and Democracy in the Great English Revolution*, London, 1930.—T. C. Pease, *The Leveller Movement*, Washington, 1916.— Harold J. Laski, *The Socialist Tradition in the French Revolution*, London, 1930.—H. de B. Gibbins, *The English Social Reformers*, New York, 1902.—S. C. G. Charléty, *Histoire du saint-simonisme (1825-1864)*, Paris, 1931.—G. D. H. Cole, *Guild Socialism*, New York, 1921.—Franz Mehring, *Karl Marx*, Leipzig, 1933.—Sidney and Beatrice Webb, *The History of Trade Unionism*, rev. ed., London, 1920.—Lorenz von Stein, *Geschichte der sozialen Bewegung in Frankreich von 1789 bis 1850*, ed. by Gottfried Salomon, three vols., Munich, 1921.

Brooks Adams, *The Theory of Social Revolutions*, New York, 1913.— Crane Brinton, *The Anatomy of Revolution*, New York, 1938.—L. P. Edwards, *The Natural History of Revolution*, Chicago, 1927.—H. M. Hyndman, *The Evolution of Revolution*, New York, 1921.—Henri Sée, *Évolution et Révolutions*, Paris, 1929.—Karl Kautsky, *Terrorism and Communism. A Contribution to the Natural History of Revolution*, London, 1920.—Nicolai Lenin, *State and Revolution*, New York, 1932.—Leon Trotzky, *Terrorismus und Kommunismus, Anti-Kautsky*, Hamburg, 1921. —Georges Sorel, *Réflexions sur la violence*, 7th ed., Paris, 1930.—Paul Schrecker, *Le problème de la révolution dans la philosophie de l'histoire*, "Renaissance," Vol. I fasc. 1 and 2, New York, 1943.—Curzio Malaparte, *Coup d'État. The Technique of Revolution*, New York, 1932.

Max Wirth, *Geschichte der Handelskrisen*, 2nd ed., Frankfurt a.M., 1874. —Felix Pinner, *Die grossen Weltkrisen im Lichte des Strukturwandels der kapitalistischen Wirtschaft*, Zurich, 1937.

p. 522, l. 33 The outbreak of the great crisis was already very near in the 1880's. Then, as later in 1914, its focus was the imperial heir of the

Austro-Hungarian monarchy—Crown Prince Rudolf, who claimed a cultural mission for his Hapsburg Empire in the Balkans and the Near East and burned to start the contest with Russia while she was still backward and unorganized. His whole short life was dominated by his sense of what was ahead and by his attempts to bring about a premature outbreak of the brewing events. While he dreamed of becoming the enlightened leader for a future age of democratic welfare, he actually became entangled and consumed by a desperate struggle for Hapsburg predominance. The crisis was not ripe, however, and his hegemonial advances into the Orient only paved the way for the rival he hated most, the clumsy Prussian Wilhelm. Rudolf's "Orient railway" was the vanguard of Wilhelm's famous Bagdad project. An excellent picture of this first stunted crisis is given in the book by Werner Richter, *Kronprinz Rudolf von Oesterreich*, Zurich, 1941.

p. 541, l. 19   Constantin Pecqueur, *Des intérêts du commerce*, I, 63.

p. 544, l. 32   Edmund Burke, *Thoughts on French Affairs*, 1791.

UNIVERSAL CIVIL WAR

Walther Rathenau, *Deutschlands Rohstoffversorgung*, Berlin, 1916; *Der neue Staat*, Berlin, 1919.

Albrecht Mendelssohn Bartholdy, *The War and German Society*, New Haven, 1937.—Wm. K. Pfeiler, *War and the German Mind*, New York, 1941.—*Krieg und Krieger*, ed. by Ernst Jünger, Berlin, 1930.—Ernst Jünger, *Storm of Steel*, Garden City (N. Y.), 1929; *Feuer und Blut*, Hamburg, 1926.

German Students War Letters, New York, 1929.—Franz Marc, *Briefe, Aufzeichnungen und Aphorismen*, two vols., Berlin, 1920.—Ludwig Renn, *War*, New York, 1929.—E. M. Remarque, *All Quiet on the Western Front*, New York, 1929.—*Lettres d'un soldat 1914–1915*, 18th ed., Paris, 1917.—Paul Raynal, *Le tombeau sous l'arc de triomphe*, 14th ed., Paris, 1924.—Henri Barbusse, *Le feu*, Paris, 1916.—R. C. Sherriff and Vernon Bartlett, *Journey's End*, London, 1931.—John Dos Passos, *Three Soldiers*, New York, 1921.

F. Nowak, *Medieval Slavdom and the Rise of Russia*, New York, 1930.—Pavel N. Miliukov, *Histoire de Russie*, three vols., Paris, 1932–1933 [liberalistic view].—D. P. Mirski, *Russia, a Social History*, London, 1931 [Marxist, but fairly broadminded].—Georges Plékhanow, *Introduction à l'histoire sociale de la Russie*, Paris, 1926 [Menshevik view].—Mikhail N. Pokrov-

ski, *Brief History of Russia*, two vols., New York, 1933 [Bolshevik view].
—Bernard Pares, *A History of Russia*, New York, 1928 [independent].—
S. R. Tompkins, *Russia through the Ages from the Scythians to the
Soviets*, New York, 1940 [independent].—Thomas G. Masaryk, *The
Spirit of Russia*, two vols., London and New York, 1919.—Leon Trotzky,
History of the Russian Revolution, three vols., New York, 1932.—Boris
Souvarine, *Stalin*, New York, 1939.—Sidney Webb, *The Truth about
Soviet Russia*, New York, 1942.—Hewlett Johnson, Dean of Canterbury,
The Soviet Power, New York, 1941.

Harold Nicolson, *Peacemaking 1919*, Boston and New York, 1933.—James
T. Shotwell, *At the Paris Peace Conference*, New York, 1937.—John May-
nard Keynes, *The Economic Consequences of the Peace*, New York, 1920.
—Edward Hallett Carr, *International Relations since the Peace Treaties,*
London, 1937; *The Twenty Years Crisis 1919–1939*, London, 1939.—Rajani
Palme Dutt, *World Politics 1918–1936*, London, 1936.

Arthur Rosenberg, *A History of the German Republic*, London, 1936.—
Max Weber, *Gesammelte politische Schriften*, Munich, 1921.—Herbert
Kraus, *The Crisis of German Democracy*, Princeton, 1932.—Ernst Fraenkel, *The Dual State*, New York, 1941.—Frederick L. Schumann, *Germany
since 1918*, New York, 1937.

p. 550, l. 19 Ernst Jünger, *Die totale Mobilmachung*, Berlin, 1930.
p. 552, l. 32 Franz Marc, *Das geheime Europa*, Das Forum I, 12, Munich,
1915.
p. 554, l. 33 Thomas G. Masaryk, *The Spirit of Russia*, I, pp. 3, 5.
p. 556, l. 10 Dostoievsky, *On Pushkin*, 1880.
p. 556, l. 15 Dostoievsky, *Three Ideas*, 1877.
p. 556, l. 30 Dostoievsky, *On Tolstoi's Anna Karenina*, 1877.
p. 556, l. 35 Dostoievsky, *On Tolstoi's Anna Karenina*.
p. 557, l. 19 Tolstoi, *What is to be done? Appendix: On the Census in
Moscow 1882*.
p. 561, l. 7 Charles Plisnier, *Faux Passeports*, Paris, 1937, pp. 257 foll.
p. 564, l. 22 Jean Martet, *Le tigre*, Paris, 1930, pp. 74 foll.
p. 565, l. 7 René Benjamin, *Clémenceau dans la retraite*, Paris, 1930, pp.
230, 239, 244, 249.

NIHILISM AND THE RULE OF TECHNICS

Ernst Fraenkel, *The Dual State*.—Ernst Posse, *Die politischen Kampf-
bünde Deutschlands*, Berlin, 1931.—Friedrich Wilhelm von Oertzen, *Die*

deutschen Freikorps 1918-1923, 6th ed., Munich, 1939.—Ernst Röhm, *Geschichte eines Hochverräters*, Munich, 1931.—Emil Gumbel, *Verschwörer*, Vienna, 1924.—Ernst von Salomon, *The Outlaws*, London, 1930; *Die Kadetten*, Berlin, 1933; *Nahe Geschichte*, Berlin, 1936.—Edwin Erich Dwinger, *Prisoner of War*, New York, 1930; *Between White and Red*, New York, 1932.

Konrad Heiden, *A History of National Socialism*, London, 1934; *Hitler*, London, 1936; *One Man against Europe*, Penguin Books, 1939.—Adolf Hitler, *Mein Kampf*, New York (Reynal and Hitchcock), 1941.—Hermann Rauschning, *The Revolution of Nihilism*, New York, 1939; *The Voice of Destruction*, New York, 1940.—Ulrich von Hasselbach, *Die Entstehung der NSDAP 1919-1923*, Leipzig, 1931.—E. A. Mowrer, *Germany Puts the Clock Back*, London, 1913.—Frederick L. Schuman, *The Nazi Dictatorship*, New York, 1935; *Europe on the Eve, the Crisis of Diplomacy*, New York, 1939; *Night over Europe, the Diplomacy of Nemesis 1939-1940*, New York, 1941.

Daniel Guérin, *Fascism and Big Business*, New York, 1939.—Fritz Thyssen, *I Paid Hitler*, New York, 1941.—Joseph Borkin and Charles A. Welsh, *Germany's Master Plan, the Story of Industrial Offensive*, New York, 1943.—Franz L. Neumann, *Behemoth, The Structure and Practice of National Socialism*, Toronto and New York, 1942.—Gregor Ziemer, *Education for Death, the Making of the Nazi*, London and New York, 1941.—Sigmund Neumann, *Permanent Revolution. The Total State in a World at War*, New York, 1942. Robert A. Brady, *Business as a System of Power*, New York, 1943.

Gabriele d'Annunzio, *Regenza italiana del Carnaro, Disegno di un nuovo ordinamento dello stato libero di Fiume*, Fiume, 1920.—A. Marpicati, *Fiume*, Florence, 1931.—G. A. Borgese, *Goliath, The March of Fascism*, New York, 1937.—Gaetano Salvemini, *The Fascist Dictatorship in Italy*, New York, 1927; *Mussolini diplomate*, Paris, 1932.—Domenico Saudino, *La genesi del fascismo*, Chicago, 1933.—Louis Rosenstock-Franck, *L'économie corporative fasciste en doctrine et en fait*, Paris, 1934.—Ignazio Silone, *Fontamara*, New York, 1934; *Bread and Wine*, London and New York, 1936.—Vilfredo Pareto, *The Mind and Society*, four vols., New York, 1935.—Georges Sorel, *Réflexions sur la violence*.

Karl Schmitt, *Der Begriff des Politischen*, Hamburg, 1933.—Donoso Cortés, Marqués de Valdegamas, *Essays on Catholicism, Liberalism and Socialism*, Dublin, 1874.—Andreas Dorpalen, *The World of General Haus-*

hofer, New York, 1942.—Hans W. Weigert, *Generals and Geographers, the Twilight of Geopolitics,* New York, 1942.—Ferdinand Fried, *Das Ende des Kapitalismus,* Tat-Schriften, Jena, 1931; *Autarkie,* Tat-Schriften, Jena, 1932.—Hjalmar Schacht, *Grundsätze deutscher Wirtschaftspolitik,* Oldenburg, 1932.—Hans F. K. Günther, *Der nordische Gedanke unter den Deutschen,* Munich, 1925; *Rassenkunde des deutschen Volkes,* Munich, 1926.—Wilhelm Stapel, *Der christliche Staatsmann, Eine Theologie des Nationalismus,* Hamburg, 1930; *Die Kirche Christi und der Staat Hitlers,* Hamburg, 1933.—Erich Ludendorff, *The Nation at War,* London, 1936.

Rohan d'Olier Butler, *The Roots of National Socialism 1783–1933,* London, 1941.—E. G. Gruendel, *Die Sendung der jungen Generation: Versuch einer umfassenden revolutionären Sinndeutung der Krise,* Munich, 1932. —Karl Loewith, *Von Hegel zu Nietzsche,* Zurich, 1941.

Friedrich Nietzsche, *The Complete Works,* eighteen vols., Edinburgh, 1910–1927; *Der Wille zur Macht,* Leipzig, 1917.—Stefan George, *Poems,* English-German ed., transl. by Carol North Valhope and Ernst Morwitz, New York, 1943.—Friedrich Gundolf, *George,* Berlin, 1920; *Stefan George in unserer Zeit,* Heidelberg, 1913.—Friedrich Wolters, *Stefan George und die Blätter für die Kunst,* Berlin, 1930.—Richard Wagner, *Prose Works,* eight vols., London, 1894–1900.—Houston Stewart Chamberlain, *Foundations of the Nineteenth Century,* two vols., New York, 1913.—Soeren Kierkegaard, *Fear and Trembling,* Princeton, 1941; *The Sickness unto Death,* Princeton, 1941; Selections from the Writings of Kierkegaard, Austin (Tex.), 1923.—Lev Shestov, *Kierkegaard et la philosophie existentielle,* Paris, 1936.—Martin Heidegger, *Sein und Zeit* (Jahrb. f. Phil. und phänomenologische Forschung, Vol. VIII); *Was ist Metaphysik?* Bonn, 1931.—Karl Jaspers, *Die geistige Situation der Zeit,* Berlin and Leipzig, 1931.—Oswald Spengler, *The Decline of the West,* New York, 1932.— A. Moeller van den Bruck, *Germany's Third Empire,* London, 1934.— Ernst Jünger, *Der Arbeiter, Herrschaft und Gestalt,* Hamburg, 1932; *Blätter und Steine,* Hamburg, 1934; *Das abenteuerliche Herz,* Hamburg, 1938; *Auf den Marmorklippen,* Hamburg, 1939.—Otto Petras, *Post Christum,* Berlin, 1935.

p. 567, l. 22   Hans Ernest Fried, *The Guilt of the German Army,* New York, 1942.
p. 567, l. 31   Franz L. Neumann, *Behemoth.*
p. 568, l. 11   Friedrich Wilhelm Foerster, *Europe and the German Question,* New York, 1940; F. J. C. Hearnshaw, *Germany the Aggressor throughout the Ages,* New York, 1941; Leopold Schwarzschild, *World*

in Trance, New York, 1942; R. M. Brickner, *Is Germany Incurable?*
Philadelphia, 1943; and others.

p. 584, l. 15   Nietzsche, *Der Wille zur Macht,* passim.

p. 588, l. 20   Richard Wagner, *Das Kunstwerk der Zukunft.*

p. 589, l. 22   Richard Wagner, *Die Wibelungen.*

p. 594, l. 32   Ernst Jünger, *Ueber den Schmerz, Blätter und Steine,* p. 200.

p. 596, l. 30   Ernst Jünger, *op. cit.,* p. 212.

p. 601, l. 2   Ernst Jünger, *Das abenteuerliche Herz,* p. 12.

THE KINGDOM OF MAN

Ralph Waldo Emerson, *Man the Reformer.*—Henry Adams, *The Education of Henry Adams.*—William James, *Memories and Studies.*—Edward Bellamy, *Looking Backward 2000–1887; Equality.*

Charles Péguy, *Basic Verities,* French-English ed., transl. by Ann and Julian Green, New York, 1943.—Paul Valéry, *Regards sur le monde actuel,* Paris, 1931.—José Ortega y Gasset, *The Modern Theme,* London, 1931.—Georges Bernanos, *Les grands cimetières sous la lune,* Paris, 1938; *Scandale de la vérité,* Paris, 1939; *Lettre aux Anglais,* Rio de Janeiro, 1942.—Julien Benda, *The Treason of the Intellectuals,* New York, 1928; *Discours à la nation européenne,* 3rd ed., Paris, 1933; *La grande épreuve des démocraties,* New York, 1942.—Émile Giraud, *La crise de la démocratie,* Paris, 1925.— Robert Aron et Arnaud Dandieu, *La révolution nécessaire,* Paris, 1933; *Dictature de la liberté,* Paris, 1934.

Walther Rathenau, *Zur Kritik der Zeit.*—Karl Wolfskehl, *Bild und Gesetz,* Berlin, 1931.—Rudolf Pannwitz, *Die Krisis der europäischen Kultur,* Nürnberg, 1917; *Deutschland und Europa,* Nürnberg, 1918.—Thomas Mann, *Order of the Day,* New York, 1942.—Josef Popper-Lynkeus, *Das Recht zu leben und die Pflicht zu sterben,* Dresden, 1878; *Das Individuum und die Bewertung menschlicher Existenzen,* Dresden, 1910; *Die allgemeine Nährpflicht als Lösung der sozialen Frage,* Dresden, 1912.—Karl Mannheim, *Man and Society in an Age of Reconstruction,* New York, 1940.—Hans Ernest Fried, *The Frontiers of the Future,* "Free World", August 1943.

Sir Arthur Salter, *The Framework of an Ordered Society,* New York, 1933. —Alfred Zimmern, *The Prospects of Democracy,* London, 1929.—Julian Huxley, *Democracy Marches,* London, 1941; *If I Were Dictator,* New York and London, 1934.—*Social Insurance and Allied Services.* Report by Sir William Beveridge, New York, 1942.—G. D. H. Cole, *Social Theory,*

London, 1920; *Europe, Russia and the Future,* London, 1941.—Harold J. Laski, *Where Do We Go from Here?* New York, 1940; *Reflections on the Revolution of Our Time,* New York, 1943.

Thorstein Veblen, *The Theory of the Leisure Class,* new ed., New York, 1931.—Christian Gauss, *A Primer for Tomorrow,* New York, 1934.— Henry A. Wallace, *The Century of the Common Man,* New York, 1943. —Ernest S. Griffith, *The Impasse of Democracy,* New York, 1939.—Charles E. Merriam, *The New Democracy and the New Despotism,* New York and London, 1939.—*The Constitution Reconsidered,* ed. by Conyers Read, New York, 1938.—*The City of Man. A Declaration on World Democracy,* New York, 1940.—Emery Reves, *A Democratic Manifesto,* New York, 1942. —Alfred A. Bingham, *The Techniques of Democracy,* New York, 1942. —Garet Garrett, *Ouroboros or the Mechanical Extension of Mankind,* New York, 1926.—Lewis Mumford, *Technics and Civilization,* New York, 1934.—Harold Loeb, *Life in a Technocracy,* New York, 1933.— John U. Nef, *The United States and Civilization,* Chicago, 1942.—Robert M. Hutchins, *Education for Freedom,* Baton Rouge (La.), 1943.—Robert S. Lynd, *Knowledge for What?* Princeton, 1939.—C. D. Burns, *Leisure in the Modern World,* New York, 1932.—A. N. Pack, *The Challenge of Leisure,* New York, 1934.—*Security, Work, and Relief Policies,* Report of the Committee on Long-Range Work and Relief Policies to the National Resources Planning Board, Washington, D. C., 1942.—Carl Dreher, *The Coming Showdown,* Boston, 1942.—Max Lerner, *It Is Later Than You Think,* New York, 1938.—Stuart Chase, *The Road We Are Traveling, 1914–1942,* New York, 1942.—Herbert Agar, *A Time for Greatness,* Boston, 1942.—Carl J. Friedrich, *The New Belief in the Common Man,* Boston, 1942.—Hans Kohn, *Not by Arms Alone,* Cambridge (Mass.), 1940. —James Marshall, *The Freedom to Be Free,* New York, 1943.—Pearl Buck, *What America Means to Me,* New York, 1943.

p. 625, l. 35   William James, *Memories and Studies, The Moral Equivalent for War.*

p. 629, l. 18   William James, *Memories and Studies, The Social Value of the College-Bred.*

p. 632, l. 32   Edmund Burke, *Thoughts on French Affairs.*

INDEX